FOURTH EDITION

HUMAN RELATIONS
A Job Oriented Approach

ANDREW J. DuBRIN

Professor of Behavioral Sciences
College of Business
Rochester Institute of Technology

Prentice Hall, Englewood Cliffs, New Jersey 07632

DuBrin, Andrew J.
   Human relations : a job oriented approach.

   Includes bibliographies and indexes.
   1. Industrial sociology.   2. Personnel management.
3. Organizational behavior.   I. Title.
HD6955.D82   1988   658.3   87–32684
ISBN 0–13–445503–7

Once again to my daughter
Melanie

Editorial/production supervision
and interior design: **Eleanor Ode Walter, Allison DeFren**
Cover design: **Ben Santora**
Manufacturing buyer: **Ed O'Dougherty**

 © 1988 by Prentice-Hall, Inc.
A Division of Simon & Schuster
Englewood Cliffs, New Jersey 07632

Printed in the United States of America

10 9 8 7 6 5 4 3 2 1

ISBN   0-13-445503-7

Prentice-Hall International (UK) Limited, *London*
Prentice-Hall of Australia Pty. Limited, *Sydney*
Prentice-Hall Canada Inc., *Toronto*
Prentice-Hall Hispanoamericana, S.A., *Mexico*
Prentice-Hall of India Private Limited, *New Delhi*
Prentice-Hall of Japan, Inc., *Tokyo*
Simon & Schuster Asia Pte. Ltd., *Singapore*
Editora Prentice-Hall do Brasil, Ltda., *Rio de Janeiro*

Contents

3   Job Satisfaction and Morale   65

Are you satisfied, motivated, or both? 66;   Consequences of job satisfaction and dissatisfaction, 67;   The measurement of job satisfaction and morale, 70; Causes of job satisfaction and dissatisfaction, 73;   General strategies for improving satisfaction and morale, 76;   Boosting satisfaction and morale through modified work schedules, 78;   Summary of key points, 84;   Questions and activities, 85;   A human relations case: The disgruntled checkout clerks, 85; A human relations incident: The laid-back financial consultants, 87; Notes, 88;   Suggested reading, 89.

4   Creativity and Decision Making   91

The stages of creative thought, 93;   Misperceptions about creativity, 94; Creativity, problem solving, and decision making, 95;   What is your creative potential? 100;   Characteristics of the creative worker, 104;   Characteristics of the creative organization, 106;   Entrepreneurs, intrapreneurs, and creativity, 107;   Improving your creativity through self-help, 109;   Summary of key points, 112;   Questions and activities, 113;   A human relations case: The food company skunk works, 114;   A human relations incident: The traditional thinkers, 115;   A human relations exercise: Creative problem solving for ailing hospitals, 117;   Notes, 117;   Suggested reading, 118.

5   Job Stress and Burnout   121

The meaning of stress and burnout, 122;   The symptoms and consequences of stress, 123;   Stress and job performance, 127;   Individual sources of stress, 129;   Organizational sources of stress, 132;   Job burnout: One consequence of long-term job stress, 136;   Individual methods of stress management, 139;   Organizational methods of stress management, 144; Employee assistance programs (EAPs), 147;   Summary of key points, 149; Questions and activities, 150;   A human relations case: The stress epidemic, 151;   A human relations incident: How to combat lethargy, 152; A human relations exercise: Are you dealing with stress properly? 153; Notes, 154;   Suggested reading, 156.

6   Job Conflict   157

The meaning of job conflict, 158;   A summary model of job conflict, 159; Sources of conflict, 159;   Sexual harassment and job conflict, 165;   Line versus staff conflict, 167;   The constructive and destructive sides of conflict, 169;   Individual methods of conflict resolution, 171;   Organizational methods of resolving conflict, 176;   Summary of key points, 179;   Questions and activities, 180;   A human relations case: The dethroned president, 181;   A human relations incident: Who has the right to tell whom what to do? 182;   A

Preface

Does the world need another book about human behavior in organizations? One answer is "Yes, because few of the major problems have yet been solved. Perhaps this book will be the one to reduce the low productivity, dissatisfaction, and strife present in so many places of work." From a less grandiose standpoint, it is important to note seven features of the fourth edition of the book that the author believes justifies its writing.

First, human relations and organizational behavior is a continuously expanding body of knowledge. Current books become dated quickly. This book is a concise yet comprehensive analysis of understanding and dealing effectively with human problems in organizations. The text includes traditional topics plus a range of contemporary topics. Among the latter are coping with procrastination, organizational culture, getting along in a bureaucracy, sexual harassment, personal productivity, computer-generated stress, intuition in decision making, and recognizing self-destructive behavior.

Second, the emphasis in this text is upon the reader and what he or she can do to handle situations. In contrast, most human relations and organizational behavior texts emphasize how managers should handle employees.

Third, the approach to writing this book resembles that used in communicating with a general audience without sacrificing scholarship. We also avoid being patronizing, condescending, overly conversational, or "cutesy." An attempt has been made to retain reader interest by writing in a style suited to both students without work experience and experienced workers.

Fourth, classical topics that have suffered from overexposure, such as the Hawthorne studies, Maslow's need hierarchy, and Theory X and Y, receive summary mention. In their place, this book emphasizes modern developments stemming from these keystone ideas, such as the expectancy theory of motivation and participative decision making.

Fifth, every major concept presented in the text is illustrated with an example—a feature that received the enthusiasm of many readers of the previous three editions. My experience has been that people best comprehend concepts that are translated into a concrete "for instance."

Sixth, an attempt is made to explain how many of the concepts in this book can be used to enhance individual and organizational effectiveness, including the improvement of productivity and satisfaction. Such application of knowledge is woven into the body of the text rather than placed in a separate, implications-for-practice section.

Seventh, more attention is devoted to how knowledge in human relations and organizational behavior is gathered, including research methods. A separate learning module about research methods is presented in the appendix.

CHANGES IN THE FOURTH EDITION

Several important new features are included in this fourth edition of *Human Relations*. More extensive use is made of graphics, and key words are printed in **bold** upon first mention. Two new chapters are added: Job Satisfaction and Morale, and The Effective Organization (back upon popular demand from the first two editions). The chapter on power and politics has been transferred to part three, dealing with interpersonal influence. The overall summary chapter is deleted, and several more complex cases are added. Many new topics have been added, many old ones have been deleted, and more than half of the cases and exercises from the third edition have been replaced. Similarly, more than half of the examples and vignettes are new to this edition.

The Instructor's Manual has been substantially enlarged. Each chapter now contains at least 50 objective test questions. In addition, an accompanying video is available, as well as a student activity guide.

The target audiences for this book are students of human relations, organizational behavior, and industrial sociology in colleges, and participants in supervisory and management-training courses. This text is also suited for courses in applied psychology and organizational psychology that emphasize practice more than research and theory.

ACKNOWLEDGEMENTS

A book of this nature requires the cooperation of many people to write and publish. My primary thanks go to my editorial team, Susan Jacob, Catherine Rossbach, and Julianne Eriksen. I also thank the production and marketing staffs of Prentice Hall for their contribution to this project. The instructors who adopted the first three editions of this book receive my enthusiastic appreciation. Many of them have contributed constructive suggestions that have been incorporated into this edition.

I thank the following people for their comments and suggestions that have helped shape the current edition of this text: John M. Cozean, Central Piedmont Community College; Ruth V. Kellar, Indiana Vocational Technical College; Burl Worley, Allan Hancock Community College; F. A. Zaccaro, Hofstra University;

Dorothy E. Harrison, Temple Junior College; Jo Ann P. Reaves, Florence-Darlington Technical College; Gerald D. Slusser, Germanna Community College; N. B. Winstanley, the Rochester Institute of Technology. In addition, three published reviews of previous editions of this text provided excellent suggestions that have been incorporated into this fourth edition. The reviewers were Kenneth J. Miller, Lockwood, Andrews & Newman, Inc.; M. Peter Scontrino, private practice; and Melissa Levi, Data General Corporation. A number of my students have also contributed suggestions for improvement from the standpoint of the learner.

Thanks also to four key people in my life for their interest in my work and their encouragement—Maria Bizo, Melanie DuBrin, Douglas DuBrin, and Drew DuBrin.

Andrew J. DuBrin
Rochester, New York

A Framework For Human Relations

THE MEANING OF HUMAN RELATIONS

At the peak of the season for mailing out promotional letters for mail-order purchases of vinyl shoes, a word processing technician named Jennifer walked into the office of her boss, Shirley. With a disgruntled and distressed look on her face, she exclaimed:

> "Shirley, I'm leaving this job the end of the week. I can't take another day of sitting behind my word processor. As a word processing technician, I don't even feel like a human being. Nobody talks to me; they just fill my in-basket with bundles of letters to process. By mid-morning everyday I get a headache from staring at the display screen. That constant whirring of the disk drive stays in my ears hours after I leave the job at night. I didn't go to school to become an extension of a computer."
>
> "But Jennifer, you can't quit this week. Most of our profits for the year are dependent upon our completing our mailings within the next fifteen days. Quit us now, and nobody else will ever hire you as a word processing technician. Can't you take hard work?"
>
> "Insult me all you want, but my health is more important than my job as a word processing technician for sending out junk mail."

The supervisor involved in this exchange was encountering a human relations problem. So was her employee. Shirley was insensitive to the problems Jennifer faced; thus she was doing a poor job of managing job stress as experienced by an employee. If Shirley had been more adept at detecting signs of computer-generated stress, she might have dealt with Jennifer's problem before it caused Jennifer to leave.

Whenever anybody confronts a problem at work dealing with people, either individually or in groups, he or she is *potentially* making use of human relations. We emphasize the word *potentially* because not everything done to cope with the human element in work organizations can be considered human relations. If human relations were conceived in this manner, it would be a field of knowledge and practice without bounds.

What then is human relations? As defined here, **human relations** is the art and practice of using systematic knowledge about human behavior to achieve organizational and personal objectives. Since human relations borrows ideas from several fields, it is also a body of knowledge in addition to being a practice or an art. An effective executive is a practitioner of human relations. So is an effective member of a task force to improve the quality of service within a hospital.

Both managers and nonmanagers practice human relations in their work. **Managers** are employees who accomplish work through others and have the authority to use resources such as company money to get things done. Nonmanagers are also called **specialists** or **individual contributors,** employees who accomplish work primarily by themselves rather than through others. Specialists and individual contributors have much less authority to use organizational resources.

Human relations overlaps considerably with **organizational behavior,** the study of individual and group behavior in organizations. Human relations is essentially a less technical and more applied version of organizational behavior.

A BEHAVIORAL MODEL OF HUMAN BEINGS

Many readers of this book will have had some exposure to psychology or a closely related field that provided a model of the basic nature of human behavior. It is therefore unnecessary to provide a full conception of what people are like here, yet a few anchor points are necessary. To deal effectively with individuals or small groups in a work environment, you need a basic framework for understanding human beings. Even if the framework you choose is not the most sophisticated available, it is better than no framework at all. A framework gives you a starting point for arriving at conclusions about people, but it should not be an intellectual straitjacket that prevents you from making spontaneous observations.

To use a sports analogy, in developing tennis strategy you might use the general assumption that the best way to beat (deal effectively with) an opponent is to keep him or her running. According to your basic framework about human behavior on the tennis court, a person kept on the move hits more erratically than a person who has the opportunity to hit from one position. You might find this the best strategy to use against most people, but now and then you might have to reformulate your strategy. You might encounter a player who returns the ball best when he or she is kept running about the court. When forced to hit many balls from the same position, that particular opponent feels too constricted and therefore becomes more erratic.

Basic Nature of the Model

Figure 1–1 is a basic model of behavior that reflects current thinking about how people respond to external forces.[1] There are four key elements: (A) the stimulus or outside force, (B) the person, (C) internal or external behavior, and (D) results. We will describe and illustrate the model. It incorporates two basic viewpoints about how people learn and are motivated: the cognitive and noncognitive.

The **cognitive viewpoint** emphasizes the internal mental processes that take place whenever a person is subject to an external force. People behave according to how they react to the stimulus. If people are in control of their senses, they make rational choices—they seek to maximize gain and pleasure and minimize

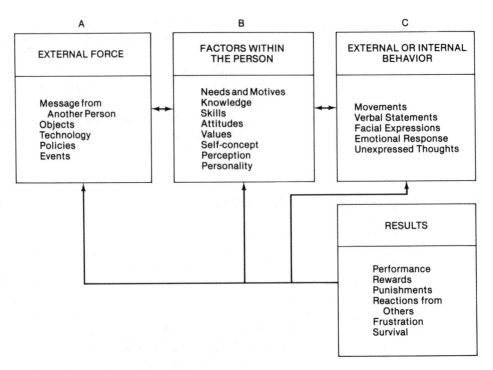

Figure 1–1 A behavioral model of human beings.

SOURCE: Adapted with permission from Henry L. Tosi, John R. Rizzo, and Stephen J. Carroll, *Managing Organizational Behavior* (Marshfield, MA: Pitman Publishing, 1986), p. 114.

loss and pain. To make these rational choices, the person attempts to evaluate the merits of external stimuli (any force that produces an effect).

The **noncognitive viewpoint** emphasizes that behavior is determined by the rewards and punishments an individual receives from the environment. Instead of behavior being influenced by an evaluation of the environment, the consequences of one's past behavior influence future behavior. A noncognitive model of behavior is also called a **reinforcement model** because rewards and punishments reinforce or strengthen responses.

External Force

The behavioral model of human behavior begins when an external force acts upon a person. These forces can take many forms, including messages from others, objects, technology, company policies, or some event. To illustrate the model, visualize this scenario. You receive an unexpected telephone message from Jack, an old friend. After a few moments of small talk, he says to you: "I've got an exciting proposition to offer you. I am a branch manager for one of the world's largest financial services firm. Our latest marketing thrust is to sell Individual Retirement Accounts (IRAs) to people who are just launching their careers. Since you are enrolled in college, you must have loads of contacts with career beginners.

"Just think what a bundle you will make for the rest of your life. Since very few people cancel their IRA policies, you'll be collecting commissions for 30 to 40 years from practically all the people you sign up. And just think, you can work for us full-time or part-time. It all depends on how quickly you want to become rich."

Another way of looking at the factors in (A) is that they are the causes or antecedents of behavior. The message from Jack will cause you to do something, even if you just politely hang up.

Factors within the Person

The external forces (A) act upon factors within the person (B), which are primarily intellectual, emotional, physiological, and physical attributes. Among them are needs and motives, knowledge, skills, attitudes, values, personality, self-concept, and perceptions. These attributes explain and regulate human behavior. All of the attributes are intangible, but they are nevertheless very important aspects of human behavior. They help explain and regulate human behavior.

A given external force will interact with the factors within the person that are most relevant at the time. These factors will influence how a person will respond to the external force. An important point about these factors is that they are all based partly upon past experience. For instance, your attitude toward selling a financial service would be influenced by past experience with life insurance sales representatives. Here is a brief rundown of how the factors listed in (B) could influence your response to Jack's proposition:

Needs and motives. A **need** is a deficit within the individual, such as a need for recognition or accomplishment. If you have a strong need for accomplishment, you may respond positively to Jack's message. A strong motive for wanting to learn more about the deal would be a desire to increase your income. If you needed more money to continue your formal education, you might be very interested in Jack's proposition.

Knowledge. Your knowledge of IRAs, selling, and the spending preferences of career beginners will also influence your response to Jack's offer. Your knowledge could be valid, invalid, or some combination of the two. If you have limited knowledge of IRAs and selling, you might pay little attention to the message. If you believe that students would be eager to start retirement accounts, you would respond positively. If your knowledge tells you that students have no interest in opening retirement accounts, you might not think much of Jack's offer.

Skills. A person's perceived skills influence how he or she will respond to a stimulus. If you perceive yourself to have good sales, communication, or analytical skills, you may be positively inclined toward Jack's proposal. If you do not perceive yourself to have the relevant skills, you will be more hesitant to get involved.

Attitudes. Our **attitudes,** or predispositions to respond, directly influence our receptiveness to an external force. You would be more inclined to respond positively to selling IRAs if you had favorable attitudes toward sales work, retirement planning, and working while attending school. Negative attitudes toward these activities would lead you away from exploring the job further.

Values. A **value** is a strongly held belief that guides your actions. People judge the merits of external stimuli in terms of their values. You would be more likely to explore the IRA venture if you valued money, challenge, and uncertainty. If your values lay in the opposite direction, you would be less inclined to pursue the venture.

Self-concept. Your **self-concept** is simply what you think of yourself or who you think you are. If your self-concept includes the idea that you are a go-getter and a winner, you might be inclined toward exploring Jack's idea further. If your self-concept includes the idea that you succeed only in low-risk situations, you might not want to proceed.

Perception. How people interpret things in the external world is referred to as **perception.** Your perception of Jack, IRAs, insurance companies, and sales work will profoundly influence your decision to explore the idea further. For instance, if you perceive Jack to be honest and sincere, you will be interested. If you perceive him to be devious and slick, you might respond: "Thanks anyway, but I'm very busy these days."

Personality. **Personality** is the persistent and enduring behavior patterns of the individual that are expressed in a wide variety of situations. Personality is a comprehensive concept that includes many of the other factors within the person listed in (B) of Figure 1–1. An example of a relevant personality factor influencing whether you decide to get involved with selling IRAs is your degree of extroversion. An extroverted person is more likely than an introverted person to engage in this type of difficult selling. Another relevant personality trait would be one's level of optimism. Only an optimist would try to sell retirement funds to newcomers to the full-time work force, and to part-time workers.

External or Internal Behavior

Characteristics of the person influence behavior. In response to the external force, the person behaves in some way (C). These behaviors include movements, verbal statements, facial expressions, emotional responses, and unexpressed thoughts. If Jack's proposition interested you, the consequent behaviors would include positive statements to him, a happy facial expression, and an increase in your heart rate.

Characteristics of the person and behavior are closely connected because behavior stems from these characteristics. Furthermore, some characteristics of a person cannot be separated from behavior. For example, skills exist only when they are manifested in behavior, and attitudes usually exist only as thoughts.

Results

Behavior (C) leads to some result or impact on the outside world. Some of the results are intended and some are not. For instance, the intended result of offering assistance to a co-worker is to help him or her and perhaps receive appreciation in return. If you are rebuffed, the result will be frustration. If you decide to follow up on Jack's offer, the results (D) you achieve could include: performing as expected, receiving financial rewards, getting recognition from others, and financial survival.

The arrows in Figure 1–1 indicate that behavior and its results serve as feedback to a person. People learn from their behavior and from its effects.[2] If you jumped at the opportunity to work with Jack and you succeeded, the feedback might include: a strengthening of your self-concept, the development of your sales skills, and an increased readiness to respond to similar offers in the future.

Implications and Uses of the Behavioral Model

The model just presented has some important implications for understanding and dealing with others. We will mention a few of them now. Of course, many of the topics in this text provide more information for understanding and dealing with others. To repeat, the model is intended only as a starting point in explaining human behavior on the job.

The person and the environment contribute to behavior. The standard formula to represent how a person behaves is:

$$B = f(P \times E)$$

The verbal expression is "Behavior is a function of the person interacting with the environment." What we do in a given situation results from the combined influence of our internal characteristics and external forces. Thus a person with strong work values will express these values strongly when a company policy rewards initiative. A person's analytical skills may not be of much help if they are working with the wrong technology.

One direct application of the $B = f(P \times E)$ formula is that you have to understand both the person and the external forces faced by that person in order to understand his or her behavior. If you wanted to help the person perform well, you might need to change the external force (such as the choice of co-workers) to a more favorable one.

Behavior has multiple causes. Both on and off the job, a person's behavior is determined by a number of environmental stimuli and internal characteristics. These stimuli and characteristics may produce a number of different behaviors. An application of this idea is that you should not be personally hurt if your well-intended actions are rejected. Suppose you have good reason to believe that your weekly results are outstanding. You review these results with your boss, and she says: "Not good enough; why can't you work harder?" Your boss may not be responding simply to your results, but to a recent chastisement she received from her boss about producing more.

Self-explanations for behavior may be inaccurate. An important message from this model is that people may not be aware of the forces and motives that are causing their behavior. You therefore cannot always assume that their explanations for their actions are correct. Suppose that you are a supervisor and an employee says to you: "No thanks, I don't want to volunteer to be the first to use that new computer application. I'm so overloaded now that I don't want to fall behind schedule." Further conversation may reveal that the employee really wants to try the new computer application. His problem is he is not confident he has enough computer knowledge to perform well. You may need to encourage him or arrange for additional training.

Individual differences are important. In dealing with others it is essential to recognize that people differ in many significant ways. The sources of these differences are shown in the list of factors within the person (B) in Figure 1–1. An implication of these individual differences is that you may have to understand the uniqueness of a person in order to deal effectively with him or her. If a person is strongly motivated by money, talking about financial rewards will help you motivate that person. Another factor is that if you think somebody has a weak self-concept, avoid insulting that person. To do so will make that person very defensive and ineffective.

Does the concept of individual differences mean that human relations and organizational behavior can provide no firm guidelines for dealing with others? Decidedly not; there are many valid generalizations that give you guidelines for dealing with others. These generalizations can be used as starting points in dealing with others; they may then need to be modified to adapt to individual differences. Here are three general principles of human relations:

- People perform better when they set goals.
- Criticizing people in public makes then defensive.
- When faced with a crisis, employees prefer that the leader take forceful charge of the situation.

We will be discussing generalizations about job-oriented behavior throughout the text. We will also make frequent references to how individual differences influence behavior. Understanding and dealing effectively with others always involves finding the right balance between general principles of human behavior and individual differences.

HUMAN RELATIONS AND ITS RELATED FIELDS

Human relations (HR) is a field that gathers much of its systematic knowledge from the social and behavioral sciences, as well as from organizational behavior, which emerged in the 1960s. Classification schemes differ, but the social sciences are now generally considered to be economics, political science, and history. The three primary behavioral sciences are usually considered to be psychology, sociology, and anthropology. Today, organizational behavior could rightfully be added as a behavioral science. If a diligent scholar were to trace the sources of most scientific studies undergirding human relations principles, he or she would discover that psychologists and sociologists are the largest contributors, with organizational behaviorists gaining ground. More specifically, the body of knowledge now called human relations stems from the findings and observations of organizational psychologists and organizational behaviorists.

The disciplines, fields, and professions dealing with human behavior in work settings overlap considerably, making rigid distinctions among them difficult to draw. These distinctions are not particularly vital when you deal with the application of knowledge. For instance, about twelve different disciplines are now concerned with job stress and burnout. It is much more important to help distressed employees than to assign credit to the right discipline for having developed a particular concept about stress management.

Organizational Behavior (OB)

Organizational behavior is the study of individuals and groups in organizations. As such, OB and HR are quite similar in terms of the topics they study and the fields of knowledge upon which they are based. The big difference between them lies in the dimensions of technical depth, research sophistication, and amount of theory. Human relations today is essentially a less technical and more applied version of organizational behavior. Textbooks in HR and OB contain many identical topics, but organizational behavior texts examine the topics more from a theoretical and research-oriented perspective. Note, however, that we are not reinforcing the overdrawn stereotype that because OB is more theoretical, it is impractical. Good theories, such as the law of gravity in physics and the law of effect in psychology, are very practical. If you believed in neither you would not fear jumping off buildings; nor would you bother to praise your new kitten for having properly used a litter pan. (The *law of effect* states that behavior that is rewarded tends to be repeated.)

Human Resource Management (HRM)

This field, also referred to as *personnel*, is a hybrid, similar in scope to human relations. HRM differs from human relations primarily because it is concerned with the application of a wide variety of personnel techniques and the administration of laws relating to employer-employee relationships. A personnel specialist must use human relations knowledge and techniques, but must also be conversant with personnel testing, employee training, compensation programs, and employee attitude surveys, among numerous other techniques. Not every HRM practitioner, however, is expected to be knowledgeable about all aspects of the field. The field has its own subspecialties. A knowledge of current legislation such as the Occupational Safety and Health Act and the Pregnancy Discrimination Act is also essential.

HOW SCIENTIFIC RESEARCH CONTRIBUTES TO HUMAN RELATIONS

We mentioned above that much of the knowledge of HR and OB is based on research. An example of the contribution of scientific research to human relations is found in a study about the impact of flexible working hours on productivity.[3] Conducted by a team of researchers, this study is considered relevant to practitioners of human relations because so much attention is being paid these days to improving productivity. Reliable information about the effects of flexible working hours on productivity would help both managers and human relation specialists make sound policy.

It is generally accepted that giving employees a say in setting a portion of their working hours improves job satisfaction. The study reviewed here examines the topic of **productivity,** the ratio of output to input taking quality of work into account.

Purpose of the Study

The purpose of the study was to examine the effect of flextime (flexible working hours) on productivity due to improved coordination of physical resources in the work unit. A previous study suggested that when workers have to share resources, such as equipment, they waste some time waiting to use the equipment.[4] With flexible working hours, fewer people are at work simultaneously. This results in less waiting time, therefore increasing the potential for increased productivity.

One hypothesis (educated guess) is that the flextime group with limited physical resources will show a significantly higher level of productivity than its comparable control group. A **control group** is a comparison group that is similar to the group being studied except that it is not exposed to the variable being studied. The second hypothesis is that a flextime group without limited resources will not show a significantly higher level of productivity than its control group.

The researchers were also interested in investigating whether any changes observed would take place immediately, over a long period of time, or both. The time dimension is important because many changes brought about with human relations techniques prove to be short-lived.

Methods and Procedures

The study was conducted in two government agencies. The agency from which the experimental groups were selected had implemented an agency-wide flextime program. The agency from which the control groups were selected did not have a flextime program. Both agencies place employees on an 8-hour day, 40-hour week. The range of working hours for the experimental agency is from 7:00 A.M. to 6:00 P.M. Employees have to work their full 8 hours within this *bandwidth*. The core hours of required on-the-job presence are from 9:00 A.M. to 3:30 P.M. The lunch period can be from one-half hour to one hour in length. The control agency works from 8:30 A.M. to 5:00 P.M. with a 30-minute scheduled lunch.

The experimental and control groups selected from the agencies were the programmers and data entry operators. One reason these groups were selected was because they had quantifiable, direct measures of productivity. The productivity measure for the programmers was the mean amount of central processing unit time used per month (how much time the programmers were actually using the computer). The productivity measure for the data entry clerks was the mean number of accurate entries per person per month.

These groups were also selected because the programming group shared a limited physical resource, the computer. Equally important, the data entry group did not share a resource; each operator had his or her own machine. Over the 2-year period of the study, the number of experimental group programmers ranged from 57 to 63; the control group ranged in size from 59 to 69. For the data entry operators, the experimental groups ranged from 16 to 20, and the control group from 33 to 42. Productivity measures were expressed as per person/ per month averages.

Results of the Study

The major finding from this study was that the shared use of physical resources influenced the relationship between flextime and productivity. Programmers— who shared resources—were more productive when working a flexible than a fixed schedule. Data entry operators—who did not share resources—were about equally productive when working under flexible and fixed hours. Table 1–1 presents these findings.

Table 1–1 Productivity measures for programmer and data
entry groups for the three testing periods

	TIME		
GROUP	Pretest	Posttest	Long Posttest*
Data Entry Operator†			
Experimental			
Mean	32,498	32,900	31,932
Standard			
deviation	2,685	3,017	2,966
Control			
Mean	37,550	36,982	38,178
Standard			
deviation	4,372	2,590	2,102
Programmers‡			
Experimental			
Mean	26.66	35.49	37.71
Standard			
deviation	2.41	3.69	1.48
Control	27.12	28.72	28.49
Standard			
deviation	1.98	2.92	2.73

* The long posttest periods began after one year.

† The productivity measure for data entry operators is the mean number
of cards accurately punched per month.

‡ The productivity measure for programmers is the mean number of
hours of central processing unit time used per person per month.

SOURCE: David A. Ralston, William P. Anthony, and David J. Gustafson, "Employees May
Love Flextime, But What Does It Do to the Organization's Productivity?" *Journal of Applied
Psychology*, May 1985, p. 277. Adapted with permission.

Compare the improvement scores of the experimental groups with the control groups for both data entry operators and programmers in the table. Notice, for example, that the productivity for the experimental group did not improve after flexible working hours were introduced. In fact, the control groups seemed to show a slight improvement even though they remained on fixed working hours. None of the improvement scores for the data entry groups is significant. In contrast, the experimental group of programmers showed a big improvement in productivity scores after it was assigned flexible working hours.

The study also found no significant productivity difference between the flextime data entry operators and the control group. Conversely, the programmers had significantly higher levels of productivity during the posttest periods than did the nonflextime comparison group. These differences held for the entire study.

Implications for Human Relations

If these findings hold in similar studies, management will be able to identify groups within its organization from whom productivity improvements may be expected from flextime. The researchers note that in addition to a high-demand, shared physical resource, one other group characteristic is important: The groups assigned to flextime should have a consistently high workload so that productivity increases are possible. Based on this study, the practitioner of human relations can now be optimistic about the contribution of flexible working hours to increased productivity—when the workers share equipment.

One criticism of this study is that the productivity measure for programmers reflected a very limited definition of productivity. The measure simply noted how much use was made of the computer, and not the quality of the work produced. What criticism can you make of the scientific value of this experiment?

HUMAN RELATIONS AND COMMON SENSE

A computer scientist complained angrily, "Why did my company send me to this workshop on human relations? Anybody with half a mind knows how to be nice to people. Don't they know that human relations is just common sense?"

This computer scientist's first charge can be dismissed quite readily. Human relations sometimes involves "being nice to people," but more important, it involves dealing with people in such a manner that individual and organizational goals are fostered. For instance, in some situations it might be helpful to fire a drug abuser if she refuses to undergo treatment for her problem. Firing in this instance might have a therapeutic value in that it dramatically demonstrates the idea that people are responsible for the implications of their behavior. This woman's drug-abuse problem had impaired her ability to perform satisfactorily as a sales representative.

Common sense is uncommon. A minority of people are highly effective in dealing with other people on the job or in personal life. Aside from those rare individuals who intuitively know how to cope with a variety of people in an effective manner, most people are plagued with interpersonal problems. Virtually all organizations have problems involving people. Thus, if common sense (meaning natural wisdom, not requiring formal knowledge) were widely held, there would be fewer problems involving people.

Since few people have such common sense in matters dealing with other people, human relations training is necessary. Human relations training for personal life might help reduce the number of people chronically dissatisfied with their spouses, children, and themselves. Our present concern, however, is job-oriented behavior.

Common sense requires experience. Louis, an accounting supervisor with 3 months of experience, reported to his boss, Barney, that he was having problems with two accountants in his office: "They spend so much time in my office complaining about each other that it is difficult for me to take care of my other work. Besides, they are wasting precious time. I've about given up on the problem. Do you have any suggestions?"

Barney instructed Louis to bring the two combatants together in his office (Louis's) and hold a three-way discussion about the problem. Barney also urged Louis to make sure that each accountant clearly spelled out the nature of his complaint to the other one.

Louis reported to Barney's office a week later with this comment: "Your approach worked like a charm. They shook hands after the conference, and I haven't had a complaint from either of them in days. How did you figure that one out?"

Barney replied, "It's just a matter of common sense."

True, Barney has learned how to resolve conflict through trial and error and now has common sense about such problems. By chance, he passed on some of his wisdom to Louis. If Louis had supervised people long enough, he too would probably learn good techniques of resolving office conflicts. A more efficient approach would be to read a reliable source about conflict resolution before the problem occurred. Reading about human relations or OB is an economical way of gaining experience. Study an applied subject and you will capitalize upon the experience—and common sense—of others who have been there first. Before skiing down a mountain, why not read a book about skiing or take lessons from a professional?

Human relations sharpens and refines common sense. People with the most common sense often derive the most personal benefit from human relations training. They build upon strengths, which in general has a bigger payoff than overcoming weaknesses. Through common sense, the interpersonally competent individual may be able to handle many situations involving people. With a few refinements, his or her handling of people may be even more effective.

Anne, a sales manager, prided herself on her sales conference techniques. She felt that more was accomplished in her meetings than in most. Yet Anne was still not satisfied. As she told her human relations consultant, "I figure we can still get more out of our meetings. I detect that people are not really talking to each other about the problems facing them. I want communication to flow even better than it does now."

The human relations consultant asked about the physical arrangements in the conferences. Anne explained how people sat around a table with their notebooks, ashtrays, and water pitchers placed in front of them. "Now I see what you are doing wrong," said the consultant. "You are setting up a few structural barriers to communication. Get the people out in the middle of the room, seated in a circle. Let them put their notebooks aside. Get them physically closer to each other."

Anne tried this technique in her next conference and it worked. Communication barriers broke down as people no longer psychologically hid behind tables, notebooks, ashtrays, and name placards. Anne was already effective with people, but by introducing the concept of *overcoming physical barriers to communication* to her repertoire, her effectiveness multiplied.

Human relations sometimes disproves common sense. A final major reason that having common sense does not make the study of human relations superfluous is that common sense can be wrong. Instances exist in which the common sense explanation to a problem is inferior to the explanation provided by systematic knowledge about human behavior. A situation involving a school superintendent in the Midwest serves as a case in point.

Laird, a school superintendent, surprised many of his friends and professional co-workers by his decision to leave school administration. He informed people that effective this September he would be teaching at a school for developmentally disabled children in the South. Several of his co-workers commented, "Laird must be flipping his lid. Why would anybody leave a job as good as his for a lesser job?"

In commonsense terms, Laird's colleagues were correct. Commonsense knowledge tells us that a *good* job is a high-paying job. True, Laird was making in excess of $70,000 as a school superintendent, but to him it was a *bad* job. Therefore, he left to take what for him constituted a *good* job.

From a human relations point of view, what Laird did made sense. Job satisfaction stems from contentment with the nature of the work we are doing. Laird regarded his administrative job as interfering with his helping people. Working in one-to-one relationships with developmentally disabled children, even if the job paid only half as much as his present job, was therefore a rational decision. In this instance, common sense provided the wrong analysis of a person's job behavior, whereas systematic knowledge about human behavior provided the right explanation.

THE HUMAN RELATIONS MOVEMENT

The historical development of human relations knowledge applied to job settings warrants some attention in any book about human relations or OB. Any history of the application of systematic knowledge about human behavior to the job must use some arbitrary milestones. For instance, the crew chiefs concerned with constructing the Egyptian pyramids must have had useful informal concepts of leadership.

The Hawthorne Studies

The human relations or behavioral school of management began in 1927 with a group of studies conducted at the Hawthorne plant of Western Electric, an AT&T subsidiary.[5] These studies were prompted by an experiment carried out by the company's engineers between 1924 and 1927. Following the scientific management tradition, these engineers were applying research methods to solve job-related problems.

Two groups were studied to determine the effects of different levels of illumination on worker performance. One group received increased illumination, while the other did not. A preliminary finding was that, when illumination was increased, the level of performance also increased. Surprisingly to the engineers, productivity also increased when the level of illumination was decreased almost to moonlight levels. One interpretation of these results was that the workers involved in the experiment enjoyed being the center of attention; they reacted positively because management cared about them.

The phenomenon is referred to as the **Hawthorne effect,** the tendency for people to behave differently when they receive attention because they respond to the expectations of the situation. In a research setting, this could mean that the people in the experimental group perform better simply because they are participating in an experiment. In a work setting, this could mean that employees perform better when they are part of any program—whether or not that program is really valuable. The experiment with flextime and data processing workers attempted to get around the Hawthorne effect by taking measures over a 2-year period, since a Hawthorne effect is usually short-lived.

As a result of these preliminary investigations, a team of researchers headed by Elton Mayo and Fritz J. Roethlisberger from Harvard conducted a lengthy series of experiments extending over a 6-year period. The conclusions they reached served as the bedrock of later developments in the human relations approach to management. Among their key findings were the following:

- Economic incentives are less potent than generally believed in influencing workers to achieve high levels of output.
- Leadership practices and work group pressures profoundly influence employee satisfaction and performance.
- Any factor influencing employee behavior is embedded in a social system. For instance, to understand the impact of pay on performance, you also have to understand the climate in the work group and the leadership style of the superior.

The Social Person

A major implication of the studies conducted by Mayo and his associates was that the old concept of an economic person motivated mainly by money had to be replaced by a more valid concept. (Remember Laird, the well-paid school superintendent who switched careers in pursuit of increased job satisfaction?)

The replacement concept was a social person, motivated by social needs, desiring rewarding on-the-job relationships, and more responsive to work group pressures than to managerial control.[6]

Leadership Styles and Practices

As a consequence of the Hawthorne studies, worker attitudes, morale, and group influences became a concern of researchers. A notable development of this nature occurred shortly after World War II at the University of Michigan. A group of social scientists formed an organization, later to be called the Institute for Social Research, to study those principles of leadership associated with highest productivity.

Based upon work with clerical production workers, an important conclusion was that supervisors of high-producing units behaved differently from those of low-producing units. Among the differences in style noted were that supervisors of productive groups in comparison to their lower producing counterparts were:

- More emotionally supportive of subordinates.
- More likely to play a *differentiated role*—plan, regulate, and coordinate the activities of subordinates, but not become directly involved in work tasks.
- More likely to exercise general rather than close or "tight" supervision.

Similar studies were conducted at Ohio State University. Among the key findings also was that people-oriented leadership was generally more effective than production-oriented leadership. Today it is recognized that the requirements of the situation dictate the best (or optimal) leadership style.[7] However, the historical significance of the studies cannot be dismissed. From these researchers emanated leadership-training programs designed to make first-line supervisors more aware of the feelings, attitudes, and opinions of subordinates. Unfortunately, many of the earlier programs overemphasized people awareness and paid insufficient attention to the other aspects of a supervisor's job.

Organization Development

Another major development in the human relations movement is the proliferation of programs and techniques designed to move organizations toward more honest and authentic ways of dealing with work problems and each other. Today many private and public organizations participate in some form of organization development (OD) with the hope of improving organization effectiveness.

Sensitivity training, the first widespread formal OD technique, owes its historical roots to the work of Kurt Lewin.[8] In the mid-1940s, Lewin formalized the technique of bringing a group of people together and helping them examine how their attitudes were received by other members of the group. Additionally, group members were given information about group dynamics. This activity was undertaken as part of a project to make local leaders from several communities understand and implement the new Fair Employment Practices Act.

The group discussion and feedback to members involved in this project became formalized as the T-group, a central aspect of sensitivity training. In 1947, the National Training Laboratory was established at Bethel, Maine, by a group of social scientists from the Massachusetts Institute of Technology and the National Education Association.

Today, an intriguing array of OD techniques are used to improve human relations effectiveness, including the widely known managerial grid, team building, and conflict-resolution exercises. Management by objectives (MBO), a system of management that holds people accountable for their results, is sometimes considered to be part of the OD movement. Some organization development specialists today consider OD to include *all* methods of improving individual and organizational effectiveness. More will be said about OD in Chapter 16.

Job Stress and Wellness

During the last two decades, employers have accepted the idea too much negative stress can harm both individuals and their work performance. Almost all large and medium-sized firms today engage in some type of positive program to help employees deal with stress. Leading the list are **employee assistance programs (EAPs),** formal facilities to help employees whose performance has declined because of distracting personal problems. EAPs take the form of referral to an outside agency, an on-site counseling service, or a combination of the two. The most frequent problems experienced by visitors to the EAP are alcoholism, financial problems, family problems, and drug abuse.

A closely related, but newer, thrust of the human relations movement is a concern for employee **wellness,** a focus on good health rather than simply the absence of disorders. Wellness programs include such activities as exercise facilities on company premises, lectures about stress management and diet, and financial bonuses for not filing medical claims.[9]

THE HUMAN POTENTIAL MOVEMENT

Concurrent with the growth of human relations in work organizations has been the burgeoning of techniques and programs to foster human growth away from the job. These activities are part of the **human potential movement,** the growth of interest in the importance of developing one's potential. This movement reached its apex in California during the late 1960s and early 1970s. The basic message of the human potential movement is that each person is unique, and everybody's primary task is to unfold his or her true self.[10] Millions of people seeking personal growth have participated in programs such as encounter groups, marriage enrichment groups, relationship groups, transactional analysis, and assertiveness training.

During the 1970s the human potential movement began to appear in work settings. A primary example is the frequent use of **career development programs,** a planned approach to helping employees enhance their careers while at the same time integrating individual and organizational goals. The tie-in with human potential is that career enhancement is an important part of reaching one's potential. Career development programs help workers make career decisions that will move them closer to self-fulfillment.

An indirect manifestation of the human potential movement is **outplacement,** a formal method of helping surplus employees find new employment and plan their careers.[11] The growth of outplacement programs has skyrocketed because of the number of firms that have trimmed their workforces in order to reduce costs and increase productivity. Outplacement programs are related to human potential because they help many people rejoin the workforce who would otherwise suffer from long-term unemployment. Being unemployed underutilizes one's potential and leads to discouragement, despair, disillusion, and uncomfortable negative stress.

HOW THIS BOOK WILL HELP YOU

A person who carefully studies the information in this book and incorporates many of its suggestions into his or her mode of doing things should derive the two benefits listed below. People vary so widely in learning ability, personality, and life circumstances that some will be able to attain some objectives and not others. For instance, you might be so shy at this stage of your development that you will not want to try some of the conflict resolution techniques. Or you may be locked into a family business and therefore uninterested in career planning techniques.

Awareness of relevant information. Part of feeling comfortable and making a positive impression in any work organization is being familiar with relevant general knowledge about the world of work. By reading this book you will become conversant with many of the buzz words at work, such as *participative decision making, quality of work life,* and *job burnout.*

Development of human relations skills. Anybody who aspires toward higher-level jobs needs to develop proficiency in such human relations skills as how to motivate people, how to communicate, and how to counsel subordinates with substandard performance. Studying information about such topics in this book, coupled with trying them out now or when your job situation permits, should help you develop such skills.

Summary of Key Points

☐   Human relations is the art and practice of using systematic knowledge about human behavior to achieve organizational and personal objectives. Anytime you confront a work problem dealing with people, the potential exists for making use of human relations.

☐   A behavioral model of human beings presented here is based on both a cognitive and a noncognitive viewpoint. The model contains these key elements: (A) an external force acts upon (B) factors within the person to result in (C) external or internal behavior, which leads to (D) results such as performance and rewards. The behavior and its results serve as feedback to the person.

☐   Implications of this model include these points: The person and the environment contribute to behavior; behavior has multiple causes; self-explanations for behavior may be inaccurate; individual differences are important. The primary application of the model is to help you understand and deal effectively with other workers.

☐   Human relations receives most of its knowledge from the social and behavioral sciences, including organizational behavior. Human relations and organizational behavior cover essentially the same topics, but OB places more emphasis on research and theory, while HR is more applied in nature. The field of personnel or human resource management (HRM) is also related to human relations, although HRM is more concerned with applying personnel techniques and the administration of laws relating to employer-employee relationships.

☐   Much of the knowledge of both HR and OB is based on experimental, or scientific, research. Such research is characterized by using experimental groups, control groups, and statistical analysis. The experiment about the impact of flextime on productivity reported in this chapter illustrates the scientific method in HR and OB. Since HR is based upon research findings and other systematic methods of observation, it is not simply common sense.

☐   The human relations movement began with the Hawthorne studies. Among their major implications was that social as well as economic factors motivate workers. As a consequence of the Hawthorne studies, employee attitudes, morale, and group influences became a concern of social science researchers. Much of their research was conducted about leadership styles and practices. Another thrust in the human relations movement has been organization development—a way of improving organizational effectiveness by emphasizing openness and honesty among people. OD today comprises a wide variety of techniques, including transactional analysis and management by objectives. A current manifestation of the human relations movement is concern about job stress and employee wellness.

☐   The human potential movement is another important component of the human relations movement. Its basic message is that each person is unique, and everybody's primary job in life is to unfold the true self. Many employee programs today, such as career development, fit the theme of developing one's potential.

☐   A formal study of human relations should increase your effectiveness in dealing with yourself and other people. For instance, learning more about how bureaucracies operate will lessen some of your frustrations in dealing with a large, complex organization.

Questions and Activities _____

1. Almost all organizations now make some direct use of human relations ideas or techniques (such as goal setting or participative management). Why do you think HR has "caught on"?

2. Based on what you have read so far, does it appear that human relations could be used to improve social and family life? Explain your answer.

3. Describe how a present or former boss practiced *good* human relations.

4. Describe how a present or former boss practiced *poor* human relations.

5. Do human relations and organizational behavior seem to be sciences? Explain your answer.

6. The study about flexible work hours was based on data processing personnel in a government agency. How confident would you be in generalizing its conclusion about the contribution of flextime to productivity in other settings?

7. How do you think most managers arrive at conclusions about human behavior in work settings? For example, do they rely on common sense, on the collection of case histories, or on the scientific method?

8. A student scored 29 percent on the multiple-choice portion of a test based on the first six chapters of an earlier edition of this book. He was the same student who said in class: "This course is easy. The book is all common sense." How do you explain what probably happened?

9. To what extent do you think the practice of human relations applies equally well to large and small organizations?

10. How valuable do you think human relations knowledge is in an era of high technology?

A Human Relations Case

"WE CAN'T AFFORD HUMAN RELATIONS AROUND HERE."

Tammy was happy to be hired by Bradbury Foods as a supervisor in the main processing plant. It was apparent to her that being a supervisor so soon after graduation would be a real boost to her career. After about a month on the job, Tammy began to make some critical observations about the company and its style of management.

To clarify things in her own mind, Tammy requested a meeting with Adam Green, plant superintendent. The meeting between Tammy and Adam included a conversation of this nature:

Adam: Have a seat, Tammy. It's nice to visit with one of our new supervisors. Particularly so when you didn't say you were facing an emergency that you and your boss couldn't handle.

Tammy: (*Nervously*) Mr. Green, I want to express my appreciation for your willingness to meet with me. You're right, I'm not facing an emergency. But I do wonder about something. That's what I came here to talk to you about.

Adam: That's what I like to see. A young woman who takes the initiative to ask questions about things that are bothering her.

Tammy: To be truthful, I am happy here and I'm glad I joined Bradbury Foods. But I'm curious about one thing. As you may know, I'm a graduate of a business college. A few of the courses I took emphasized using human relations knowledge to manage people. You know, kind of psychology on the job. It seems like the way to go if you want to keep employees productive and happy.

Here at Bradbury it seems that nobody uses human relations knowledge. I know that you're a successful company. But some of the management practices seem out of keeping with the times. The managers make all the decisions. Everybody else listens and carries out orders. Even professionals on the payroll have to punch time clocks. I've been here for almost two months and I haven't even heard the term human relations used once.

Adam: Oh, I get your point. You're talking about using human relations around here. I know all about that. The point your missing, Tammy, is that human relations is for the big, profitable companies. That stuff works great when business is good and profit margins are high. But around here business is so-so, and profit margins in the food business are thinner than a potato chip. Maybe someday when we get fat and profitable we can start using human relations. In the meantime, we've all got a job to do.

Tammy: I appreciate your candid answer, Mr. Green. But when I was in college, I certainly heard a different version of why companies use human relations.

1. What is your evaluation of Adam's contention that HR knowledge is useful primarily when a firm is profitable?
2. To what extent should Tammy be discouraged?
3. What should Tammy do?
4. Based on your experiences, how representative of most managers is Adam Green's thinking?

A Human Relations Incident

THE ROCKY MOUNTAIN ACCOUNTANT

Bart Belladonna had worked very hard to create a good life for himself. His lifestyle has been one of working hard and playing hard. He grew up in Utah, not far from a major ski area, where he also attended high school and college. Bart became a good enough skier to make his high school ski team. He majored in accounting and business administration at college. His first professional employment was as a junior accountant for an insurance firm located in a suburb of Denver, Colorado. Bart considered himself very fortunate to have landed a good job near some of the best ski areas in North America.

Bart approached his job with his characteristic high level of enthusiasm. His first three performance appraisals, given at six-month intervals, were outstanding. One day Bart's boss approached him with this offer:

"Bart, we love you around here. But the good of the firm as a whole comes before local considerations. Company headquarters in Chicago has offered you a position as an internal auditor. The job begins in 30 days. The position is a great stepping stone to bigger and better things with the firm. You'll receive an immediate $4,000 per year salary increase."

Bart was stunned. He asked his boss for one day to think about the offer. The next day he told his boss, "I'm very grateful for the promotion you have offered me. It would really be exciting to work as an auditor. And I agree it would be a big boost in my career. But I don't want to leave Colorado. This is God's country, especially when you're a skier. I'm not willing to trade the beauty of the Rocky Mountains for life in the big city."

His boss retorted, "Bart, grab hold of yourself. With a $4,000 a year raise, you can fly out to Colorado for a ski trip at least twice a year. Are you a ski bum or an ambitious accountant? I just don't understand you."

"I'm sorry you put it that way," said Bart. "But my decision is final. I want to stay put here in Colorado."

1. Explain what happened here using the behavioral model presented in Figure 1–1.

2. Do you think Bart is lazy?

3. How would you evaluate the human relations effectiveness of Bart's boss?

Notes

1. This section of the chapter is based upon Henry L. Tosi, John R. Rizzo, and Stephen J. Carroll, *Managing Organizational Behavior* (Marshfield, MA: Pitman Publishing, 1986), pp. 113–116.

2. Ibid., p. 114.

3. David A. Ralston, William P. Anthony, and David J. Gustafson, "Employees May Love Flextime, but What Does It Do to the Organization's Productivity?" *Journal of Applied Psychology*, May 1985, pp. 272–279.

4. J. C. Swart, *A Flexible Approach to Working Hours* (New York: AMACOM, 1978), cited in Ralston, Anthony, and Gustafson.

5. An original source of information about the Hawthorne studies is Elton Mayo, *The Human Problems of an Industrial Civilization* (New York: Viking Press, 1960). A summary and synthesis of these classic studies is found in Phillip L. Hunsaker and Curtis W. Cook, *Managing Organizational Behavior* (Reading, MA: Addison-Wesley, 1986), pp. 19–20, A19–A21.

6. Interpretation made by James A. F. Stoner, *Management*, 2nd ed. (Englewood Cliffs, NJ: Prentice-Hall, 1982), p. 46.

7. Arnold S. Tannenbaum, *Social Psychology of the Work Organization* (Belmont, CA: Wadsworth, 1966), p. 74.

8. Robert J. House, "T-group Education and Leadership Effectiveness: A Review of the Empiric Literature and a Critical Evaluation," *Personnel Psychology*, Spring 1967, p. 2.

9. Barbara Anne Solomon, "Wellness Programs," *Personnel*, November 1985, pp. 67–72.

10. John Leo, "The Warm Success of Dr. Hug," *Time*, November 15, 1982, p. 84.

11. Hermine Zagat Levine, "Outplacement and Severance Pay Practices," *Personnel*, September 1985, pp. 13–21.

Suggested Reading

BROWN, ABBY. "Career Development 1986." *Personnel Administrator*, March 1986, pp. 45–48, 109.

CUMMINGS, LARRY L. "Towards Organizational Behavior." *Academy of Management Review*, January 1978, pp. 90–98.

LORSCH, JAY W. "Making Behavorial Science More Useful." *Harvard Business Review*, March–April 1979, pp. 171–180.

ORGAN, DENNIS W. "Organizational Behavior as an Area of Study: Some Questions and Answers," in Dennis W. Organ, eds., *The Applied Psychology of Work Behavior: A Book of Readings*. Plano, TX: Business Publications, 1978, pp. 2–7.

RAND, JAMES F. "HR Management: An Integrative Perspective," *Personnel*, June 1986, pp. 50–53.

ROETHLISBERGER, FRITZ J., and DICKSON, W. J. *Management and the Worker*. Cambridge, MA: Harvard University Press, 1939.

STONE, EUGENE F. *Research Methods in Organizational Behavior*. Santa Monica, CA: Goodyear, 1978.

TAYLOR, FREDERICK W. *Scientific Management*. New York: Harper & Row, 1911.

VARELA, JACOBO A. "Solving Human Problems with Human Science." *Human Nature*, October 1978, pp. 84–90.

WREN, DANIEL A. *The Evolution of Management Thought*. New York: Ronald Press, 1972.

Work Motivation and Productivity

LEARNING OBJECTIVES
After studying this chapter and doing the exercises, you should be able to

1. Explain the meaning of work motivation and productivity.
2. Explain how goals contribute to motivation.
3. Pinpoint how human needs are tied in with work motivation.
4. Know how to apply expectancy theory to motivate people.
5. Sketch a program of using positive reinforcement in a work setting.
6. Develop a strategy for increasing your own motivation.

THE MEANING OF WORK MOTIVATION
AND PRODUCTIVITY

At least 50,000 books and articles have been written about work motivation and its closely related topic, job satisfaction. Recognizing that all this literature still left unanswered questions, two leading organizational behavioral consultants published an article entitled "The Key to Motivation" in a journal for human resource specialists.[1] We chose to reprint their article in its entirety, rather than risk any possible misinterpretation stemming from an abridgment. It reads as follows:

> The results of a 20-year-study are in. The answer to the question "What really motivates people?" is: "Go ask your people."

The general thrust of this chapter is to elaborate upon the idea that people are motivated by inner states, or their perception of what is worth pursuing. Before proceeding, we need to pinpoint two meanings of a frequently used term, **motivation.** One meaning is an internal state that leads to effort expended toward objectives. **Work motivation** is therefore effort expended toward organizational objectives. Another meaning of the term is an activity performed by managers or any other person to get others to accomplish work.

The term *productivity* also requires definition because it is used so frequently in conjunction with motivation. A major reason for motivating workers is to make them more productive. Generally speaking, productivity refers to how much a person accomplishes in a given period of time. A productive person accomplishes a lot (achieves output) without consuming too many resources (input). **Productivity** is thus the ratio of output to input, taking into account both quantity and quality. The productivity formula is shown in Figure 2–1.

Quality is an important part of productivity. If quality is not included in the productivity formula, a worker who generated a large amount of unacceptable work in a short period of time would be considered productive. The concept of

Figure 2–1 The meaning of productivity.

$$\text{Productivity} = \frac{\text{Output (quantity and quality of goods and services produced)}}{\text{Input (amount of human, material, and financial resources consumed)}}$$

quality also allows for the fact that a worker could produce a small amount of high-quality work in a long period of time and still be considered productive. If it took you all week to produce one successful five-word advertising slogan, you could consider yourself productive.

Productivity is tied in with motivation because motivation is an important contributor to productivity. However, the concept of productivity relates to every topic in this book. Productivity is built into the definition of human relations, since HR deals with improving effectiveness—a major component of productivity. It can be argued that no human relations technique is valuable if it does not enhance productivity or satisfaction.

WHY MOTIVATION IS A CONCERN TODAY

As organizations of all types strive to become more productive, motivation has gained in importance. At the same time, many forces in society constrain worker motivation. Anybody concerned about motivating others therefore has to be aware of forces dampening the motivation of many workers. If you are a manager, it is obviously important to motivate others. It is also important to motivate co-workers and retail store clerks if you want cooperation and good service. Here is an analysis of why worker motivation has declined today.[2]

Greater instability and diversity of values. People of all ages show relatively rapid shifts in what they believe is really worthwhile in life. Career goals, interpersonal relationships, and even hobbies change at a rapid pace. Diversification of goals decreases job motivation by causing people's efforts to be drawn away from the job. Most people need sharply focused goals to sustain high motivation.

More guaranteed rewards. Today more firms are offering more guaranteed rewards than ever before. They include high salaries and employee benefits that are independent of good performance. Philip C. Grant believes that guaranteed rewards depress employee motivation, because hard work leads to about the same rewards as loafing.

Inability of rewards to satisfy emerging needs. Many workers today seek self-fulfillment on the job, yet not that many jobs offer the opportunity for self-fulfillment. This discrepancy between desire and reality contributes to lowered motivation.

A declining work ethic. Many observers believe that the Protestant work ethic has weakened. Fewer people today believe that hard work is important for its own sake or is the mark of a righteous person. Furthermore, Grant contends that taking pride in one's work is fast becoming obsolete. Determined effort and high-quality individual output are no longer seen by most people as synonymous with personal success.

Reduced costs of failure. Among the mechanisms in society reducing the cost of failure are bankruptcy laws, unemployment insurance, welfare, anti-firing policies of many firms, and even alternative schooling for those who cannot make it in the traditional educational system. Mechanisms of this nature are contrary to requirements for high job motivation, since people are less likely to incur penalties for low effort and performance.

More group production and problem solving. Group effort can dampen motivation in at least two ways. First, people working within a group often have problems perceiving the link between their efforts and group performance. Individual effort thus may not seem to make a difference. Second, group members may not perceive a strong link between group performance and individual rewards. Motivation may suffer when increased effort does not appear to lead to increased rewards. (Expectancy theory, to be described later in this chapter, has much to say about the link between individual performance and rewards.)

Decreased employee loyalty. Large numbers of employees have shifted their allegiance away from their employer and toward labor unions, employee associations, professional associations, and various community organizations. Decreased loyalty typically reduces motivation because it diminishes commitment to organizational goals.

Less supervisory power. First-level managers (supervisors) have less power to control rewards and punishments than they did in the past. Technical experts within the firm and labor unions have taken away much power from the supervisor. Without such control over subordinates, supervisors have difficulty in raising the motivational level of subordinates.

Shorter time perspectives. People today seem to want quick gratification of their desires and are too impatient to develop a long-range perspective. Since so many people have a short-range perspective, they are unwilling to apply extended effort to achieve such goals as advancement and high-level recognition.

The quest for job satisfaction as a primary motive. Consultant Oliver L. Niehouse contends: "In the good old days, money was the prime motivator. What has replaced it, what has become the new prime motivator, is job satisfaction."[3] This shift in the value of importance of rewards means that workers are motivated by such factors as the opportunity to have more time for leisure, a sense of involvement in work, and a desire to be included in important company information. This emphasis on job satisfaction makes many workers appear not strongly work motivated. An employee who says to the boss "I'd rather have a job with flextime than a supervisory position" may appear to have low motivation.

COGNITIVE VERSUS NONCOGNITIVE EXPLANATIONS OF MOTIVATION

Current explanations of human motivation can be divided into cognitive and noncognitive, or reinforcement, theories.[4] Cognitive models emphasize that people make conscious decisions about their behavior, such as "Yes, I'll push for extra sales because my company is known to reward good performance." A cognitive explanation of motivation also emphasizes the fact that people are driven by internal forces that guide their behavior. Among such forces are the quest to satisfy needs for achievement, power, self-fulfillment, and affiliation with others. The cognitive explanations of motivation described here are goal theory, Maslow's need hierarchy, the two-factor theory, other key motives, and expectancy theory. The last is a comprehensive explanation of motivation that integrates the other theories.

Differences between the Cognitive and Noncognitive Models

Noncognitive explanations of motivation are based upon reinforcement theory. They are also referred to as behavior modification, or OB mod. A reinforcement model looks to external factors rather than the inner person for an explanation of why people behave as they do. The external factors emphasized are the rewards and punishments that condition behavior. Noncognitive explanations contend that workers engage in motivated behavior when their behavior leads to a reward or an escape from punishment. The noncognitive motivational approaches described in this chapter are motivation through positive reinforcement and through fear and punishment.

Overlap between the approaches. Although the cognitive and noncognitive models differ, they overlap and can be used simultaneously to understand and control behavior. Inner strivings cause initial behavior, but external forces are major factors in future behavior. In other words, inner motives may trigger behavior, but satisfaction or other rewards derived from performance will cause it to be repeated and even improved. Dissatisfaction, of lack of appropriate reward, causes reduction or elimination of the behavior.[5]

A return to the behavioral model presented in Figure 1-1 will illustrate this important point further. The model contains both cognitive and reinforcement explanations of why people behave as they do. For instance, one aspect of the model contends that people's motives at the time determine whether or not they will spring into action (cognitive explanation). And whether or nor they repeat that behavior depends upon the rewards or punishment they receive from the environment (reinforcement explanation).

Cognitive and reinforcement models of motivation are also used jointly in company programs designed to boost productivity. For example, need theory (cognitive explanation) is referred to to help determine which rewards would be useful in a program of positive reinforcement to control absenteeism (a noncognitive explanation of behavior).

GOAL THEORY AND MOTIVATION

Setting goals is basic to all motivational programs in organizations and to boosting your own level of motivation. Almost every modern work organization has some form of goal-setting program to improve performance and productivity. Goal-setting theory helps explain both the importance of goal setting and the characteristics of goals that lead to improved performance.

Basic Facts

The best established facts of goal theory are shown in Figure 2–2. Underlying goal theory is the basic premise that behavior is regulated by values and conscious intentions or goals.[6] A **goal** is defined simply as what the person is trying to accomplish. Our values create within us a desire to do things consistent with them. Goal-setting theory also contends that hard (difficult) goals lead to a higher level of performance than easy goals. It is also important to make goals specific rather than general such as "do your best."

The goals people work toward tend to lead to improved performance whether these goals are set by them or the organization—providing the individual accepts the goal. Another important consideration is that the goals set by the individual should not be so unrealistically high that they result in frustration due to failure. If you want to earn $300,000 per year, it would be best to begin by setting realistic goals such as finding a good job in a good company or starting a small business. A final important fact about goal setting is that people perform better when they think their performance against goals will be evaluated.[7]

Figure 2–2 The basics of goal theory.

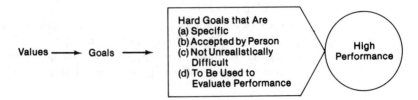

Research Evidence

A substantial amount of research has been carried out in organizations to test the basic propositions of goal theory. The findings are clear on some issues.[8] There is consistent evidence that difficult goals lead to better performance than easy goals. A recent study investigated whether this basic premise of goal-setting theory applied to other cultures. Ninety-two women in a small eastern Caribbean island served as subjects. They made children's clothing at home and were paid on a piece-rate basis. Workers were free to complete any quantity: no quotas were set.

Subjects were randomly assigned to one of three groups. Goals were assigned to members of one experimental group based on previous production. The new goal was 20 percent above the individual's previous high production. Members of another experimental group were asked to "do their best." The control group received no change in instructions. The group with specific and difficult goals clearly outperformed the other two groups. Women who were assigned the goal of a 20 percent increase in performance earned twice as much as members of the control group and 47 percent more than the "do your best" group.[9]

Another well-researched point about goal theory is that difficult but accepted specific goals combined with (a) feedback on results and (b) rewards for reaching goals improve motivation. The results of the study on the garment makers supports this point.

Much research has been conducted on the contribution of employee participation to goal setting. The consensus of these studies is that participation makes an indirect contribution to goal setting.[10] Participation in goal setting can improve performance under these conditions:

1. Participation leads to the setting of a specific goal.
2. The specific goal is more difficult than the one set by the supervisor.
3. Participation improves acceptance of the goal by the employee.

MOTIVATION THROUGH NEED SATISFACTION

The most basic explanation of work motivation is that employees work to satisfy needs or motives. A **need** is a craving or deficit of a physiological (such as hunger) or psychological (such as acceptance) nature. A **motive** is a socially learned force that requires satisfaction, such as the desire to gain power. In practice, the terms are used interchangeably. To motivate people, you give them an opportunity to satisfy important needs or motives.[11]

You find out what these needs are by asking people what they want, or by observing what interests them. For instance, the way to motivate a recognition-hungry subordinate is to tell that person: "If you perform 10 percent above quota for six consecutive months, we will get you a plaque signifying your achievement to hang on your wall."

All need theories of motivation stem from this simple but true premise: People strive to satisfy needs. Here we describe two historically important need theories of motivation, Maslow's hierarchy and Herzberg's two-factor theory. Although both theories are now considered oversimplified, they have alerted managers to the importance of human needs. These theories have also set the stage for contemporary developments in motivation such as expectancy theory. We will outline other important human needs and motives for seeking satisfaction on the job.

Maslow's Need Hierarchy

Abraham Maslow's famous need hierarchy is sometimes referred to as a self-actualizing model of people. Maslow reasoned that human beings have an internal need pushing them on toward self-actualization (fulfillment) and personal superiority. However, before these higher-level needs are activated, certain lower-level needs must be satisfied.[12] A poor person thinks of finding a job as a way of obtaining the necessities of life. Once these are obtained, that person may think of achieving recognition and self-fulfillment on the job. When a person is generally satisfied at one level, he or she looks for satisfaction at a higher level.

A major misinterpretation of Malsow's theory is that people behave as they do because of their quest to satisfy one particular need. In reality, many different motives are dominant at any one time. A drafting technician may satisfy a number of needs (for instance, recognition, esteem, and self-satisfaction) by developing a design that works in practice.

Maslow arranged human needs into a five-level hierarchy. Each level refers to a group of needs—not to one need for each level. These need levels are described in ascending order:

1. *Physiological needs* refer to bodily needs, such as the requirement for food, water, shelter, and sleep. In general, most jobs provide opportunity to satisfy physiological needs. Nevertheless, some people go to work hungry or in need of sleep. Until that person gets a satisfying meal or takes a nap, he or she will not be concerned about finding an outlet on the job for creative impulses.

2. *Safety needs* include actual physical safety as a feeling of being safe from physical and emotional injury. Many jobs frustrate a person's need for safety, such as those of police officers or taxi drivers. Therefore, many people would be motivated by the prospect of a safe environment. People who do very unsafe things for a living, such as racing-car drivers, find thrills and recognition more important than safety. Many people are an exception to Maslow's need hierarchy.

3. *Social needs* are essentially love or belonging needs. Unlike the two previous levels of needs, they center around a person's interactions with others. Many people have a strong urge to be part of a group and to be accepted by that group. Peer acceptance is important in school and on the job. Many people are unhappy with their jobs unless they have the opportunity to work in close contact with others.

4. *Esteem needs* represent an individual's demands to be seen as a person of worth by others—and to himself or herself. Esteem needs are also called *ego* needs, pointing to the fact that people want to be seen as competent and capable. A job that is seen by yourself and others as being worthwhile provides a good opportunity to satisfy esteem needs.

5. *Self-actualizing needs* are the highest levels of needs, including the need for self-fulfillment and personal development. True self-actualization is an ideal to strive for, rather than something that automatically stems from occupying a challenging position. A self-actualized person is somebody who has become what he or she is capable of becoming. Few of us reach all our potential, even when we are so motivated.

Evaluation. The need hierarchy is a convenient way of classifying human needs, but it has limited utility in explaining work behavior. The idea of an individual climbing the ladder of need fulfillment and being motivated by the next highest rung is intuitively appealing. Very little evidence exists, however, to support this notion of progression up a ladder.[13] Another criticism of Maslow's theory is that career advancement may be the true factor underlying changes in need deficiencies. Researchers found in one study that as managers advance in the organization, their needs for safety decreases. Simultaneously, they experience an increase in their needs for affiliation with other people, achievement, and self-actualization.[14]

The major contribution of Maslow's theory has been that it highlights the importance of human needs in a work setting. It is now accepted by managers that when they want to motivate another individual, they must offer that person a reward that will satisfy an important need. At least this represents a good beginning in attempting to motivate others.

Herzberg's Two-Factor Theory

Over two decades ago, Frederick Herzberg reported research suggesting that some elements of a job contribute to satisfaction and motivation.[15] Such job elements are called *satisfiers* or *motivators*. Although individuals and groups vary somewhat in the particular elements they find satisfying or motivating, they generally refer to the *content* (guts) of the job: achievement, recognition, challenging work, responsibility, and the opportunity for advancement. When satisfiers or motivators are not present on the job, the impact tends to be neutral rather than negative. Following this theory, one way to motivate most people is to provide them with the opportunity to do interesting work or to receive a promotion.

In contrast, some job elements appeal more to lower-level needs. Called *hygiene factors* or *dissatisfiers*, they tend to be noticed primarily by their absence. The purpose of dissatisfiers is to prevent dissatisfaction. For instance, you may grumble about having to work in a hot, cramped office with no windows. Because of it you may experience job dissatisfaction or even be demotivated. But a cool, uncrowded office with a view of the ocean will probably not increase your level of job satisfaction or motivation (at least according to Herzberg).

Herzberg and his associates also noted that dissatisfiers relate mostly to the *context* (the job setting or external elements): company policy and administration, supervision, physical working conditions, relations with others on the job, status, job security, salary, and personal life.

Evaluation. The two-factor theory has had a considerable impact on managers. Job enrichment, to be discussed in Chapter 16, owes its origins to the thinking of Herzberg. Nevertheless, research evidence indicates that the premises of the two-factor theory are not so accurate. For one, Herzberg and his associates erred by assuming that virtually all workers are trying to satisfy higher-level needs on the job. A complex, challenging, variable, and autonomous job is motivating for all people who are *operating at higher-level needs.* This generalization is more valid for the majority of higher-level than lower-level workers. But even within a given occupational group, such as professionals or clerical workers, not everybody has the same motivational pattern.

Salary is a prime example of a job element that acts as a motivator for some people and a dissatisfier (used to prevent dissatisfaction) for others. When you currently are worried about money you will work hard, given the chance to earn the amount of money you want. Another confounding factor is that money satisfies so many different needs. Given enough money, you can buy status, recognition, and even accomplishment. To illustrate, money can lead to accomplishment because it can buy education or a small business venture.

Another major reservation about the two-factor theory is the contention that hygiene factors can prevent dissatisfaction, but cannot satisfy or motivate workers. The research evidence tends to refute this contention.[16] It seems logical to any experienced person that hygiene factors such as working conditions or quality of supervision could influence an employee's level of motivation or satisfaction. Would your level of satisfaction or motivation increase if you were assigned a beautiful office, overlooking a bay, with a competent, warm, and friendly assistant seated outside?

Comparison of the Two Theories

The theories of Maslow and Herzberg support each other. As shown in Figure 2–3, satisfiers and motivators relate to the higher-level needs. Similarly, dissatisfiers and hygiene factors relate to lower-level needs. One major difference between the Maslow and Herzberg theories is that, according to the former, an appeal to any level of need can be a motivator. Herzberg contends that only appeals to higher-level needs can be motivational. Figure 2–3 also suggests how to apply these two theories to a job situation.

Achievement, Power, and Affiliation Needs

People seek to satisfy many higher-level needs on the job in addition to those mentioned in Maslow's hierarchy. Among these specific needs or motives are competence, control over one's environment, achievement, power, and affiliation.

Figure 2–3 Comparison of the need hierarchy and two-factor theory.

Maslow's Need Hierarchy	Herzberg's Two-Factor Theory	Managerial Action
	Satisfiers or Motivators	
Self-actualization Self-esteem	Achievement Recognition Work itself Responsibility Advancement Growth	Allow these factors to be present to increase satisfaction and motivation
	Dissatisfiers or Hygiene Factors	
Social (love, belonging) Safety and security Physiological	Company policy and administration Supervision Working conditions Salary Relationship with coworkers Personal life Status Job security	Keep these factors at adequate level to prevent dissatisfaction and demotivation

The last three have been studied extensively by psychologist David McClelland and many others.[17] Much human behavior on the job can be explained by strong motives to achieve important things, acquire power, and affiliate with others.

Achievement need. Many managers and other ambitious people have a strong **achievement need,** the desire to set and accomplish goals for their own sake. People with strong motives for achievement are self-motivated; they persist in their efforts without prodding and prompting from others. Money, status, and power are secondary considerations to these individuals. People with a strong achievement need show three consistent behaviors and attitudes:

- Personal responsibility for solving problems
- A preference for establishing and reaching moderate or realistic goals, but not taking foolish risks
- A preference for situations that provide frequent feedback on results[18]

A strong achievement need is important for managerial work, particularly for **entrepreneurs,** people who establish and operate innovative business enterprises. The achievement need, as well as the needs for power and affiliation, was originally studied by the Thematic Apperception Test (TAT). Subjects were asked to write a story giving their interpretation of a drawing. For instance, the following interpretation of a picture of a man seated at a desk would indicate a need for achievement:

The man sitting there is doing some short-range planning. He's trying to figure out how to take advantage of a downturn in business so he can make the best use of time. I'll bet he's thinking of a new service his company can offer that will really help people.

Like other needs and motives, the achievement need can be measured by a personality test. The person taking the test is asked to indicate the strength of his or her preference for a job with certain characteristics, such as:[19]

The probability is very high that you will influence a large number of people. The probability is very low that you will have a chance to start a new activity from scratch.

Power need. Another important motive of people in organizations is the **need for power,** the desire to control other people and resources. People who climb to the top of organizations often have a strong drive for both achievement and power. The two needs complement each other: Achievement motivation directs people to accomplish worthwhile things; power motivation directs people to take control and draw attention to their own effect on the world.[20]

The need for power can drive us to serve our self-interest or the welfare of others. David McClelland draws the distinction between *personalized* and *socialized* power.[21] A person with a personalized power motive wants to control and manipulate others mostly for personal gain. A person with a socialized power motive desires power in order to serve the good of the organization or society. An executive who organizes a fundraising campaign for a new hospital probably has a socialized power need. Nevertheless, it is not always clear which power motive is dominant. The executive may look forward to having the hospital named in his or her honor, which may be an expression of a personalized power need.

Affiliation. The **need for affiliation** is a desire to seek close relationships with others and to be a loyal employee or friend. Affiliation is a social need, while achievement and power are self-actualizing needs. A person with a strong need for affiliation finds compatible working relationships more important than high-level accomplishment and exercising power. Successful executives therefore have stronger needs for achievement and power than for affiliation.

Figure 2–4 summarizes the discussion of the needs for achievement, power, and affiliation. Then we examine a psychological need that is beginning to receive the attention it deserves.

Thrill Seeking

Our discussion of needs so far still does not explain why some people crave constant excitement on the job, and are even willing to risk their lives to achieve thrills. The answer may lie in the **Type T personality,** an individual driven to a life of constant stimulation and risk taking.[22] A strong craving for thrill seeking

Figure 2–4 Work implications of the needs for achievement, power, and affiliation.

Need or Motive	Typical Behavior of Person with a Strong Need
Achievement	Takes individual responsibility for projects; enjoys organizing activities; not afraid to make waves and take sensible risks; will often choose self-employment.
Power	Looks for the opportunity to control other people, budgets, and equipment; has hunger for more responsibility and will try to climb the organizational ladder.
Affiliation	Befriends co-workers; shows loyalty to the work group and the organization; may turn down promotion if it means breaking old ties and being appointed as the boss over friends.

can have some positive consequences for the organization, including a willingness to perform such dangerous feats as setting explosives, capping an oil well, fighting a fire, controlling a radiation leak, and introducing a product in a highly competitive environment.

The Type T personality also creates problems for employers. These individuals may be involved in a disproportionate number of accidents, drive while intoxicated just for the added excitement and risk, and take risks with company property. For example, Brett, an information systems specialist, was a known sensation seeker. Off the job he participated in hang-gliding, ski jumping, and motorcycle racing. On the job he once wiped out an important file stored on a computer disk. Asked how the incident happened, Brett told his irate boss:

> I admit it, I'm guilty. I was looking to pull a stunt on the computer that no one had pulled before. I tried to make a copy of the file by taking the file out of the B drive and saving it on another disk I put back into the B drive. If I had taken the time to read the manual, this mistake wouldn't have happened. But I like the thrill of trying out my little tricks with the computer.

A person who uses thrill seeking for constructive purposes is a *T-plus*. His or her counterpart who gets into trouble with thrill seeking is a *T-minus*. T-plus people can be quite productive because they are often creative. The famous business promoter and sailing enthusiast Ted Turner appears to be a T-plus person. Can you think of another T-plus person?

MOTIVATION THROUGH EXPECTANCY THEORY

The **expectancy theory (ET)** of work motivation is based on the premise that how much effort people expend depends upon how much reward they expect to receive in return. Expectancy theory is really a group of theories based on a rational-economic view of human nature.[23] The theory assumes that people choose among alternatives by selecting the one that appears to have the biggest personal payoff at the time. Given a choice, most people will opt for a work assignment that will benefit them the most. The self-interest aspect of motivation underlying ET is also found in other theories of motivation—people try to satisfy their own needs and will strive for rewards they think are worthwhile.

ET is currently receiving considerable attention in the human relations and organizational behavior field. Part of its popularity is due to the theory integrating much valid knowledge about work motivation.

Basic Components

All versions of expectancy theory have four major components: expectancy, instrumentality, valence, and the calculation of motivation. A glimpse at ET is presented in Figure 2–5.

1. **Expectancy** is the probability assigned by the individual that effort will lead to performing the task correctly. An important question rational people ask themselves before putting forth effort to accomplish a task is this: "If I put in all this work, will I really get the job done properly?" Each behavior is associated in the individual's mind with a certain expectancy or subjective hunch of the probability of success. Expectancies range from 0 to 1.0. The expectancy would be zero if the person thought there were no chance of performing the task correctly. An expectancy of 1.0 would signify absolute faith in being able to perform the task properly.

   Expectancies thus influence whether you will even strive to earn a reward. Self-confident people have higher expectancies than do less self-confident people. Being well trained will also increase your subjective hunch that you can perform the task.

2. **Instrumentality** is the probability assigned by the individual that performance will lead to certain outcomes or rewards. When people engage in a particular behavior, they do so with the intention of achieving a desired outcome or reward. In the version of ET presented here, instrumentalities also range from 0 to 1.0.

   If you believe there is no chance of receiving the desired reward, the assigned probability is zero. If you believe the reward is certain to follow from performing correctly, the assigned probability is 1.0. For example: "I know for sure that if I show up for work every day this month, I will receive my paycheck."

   The performance mentioned in relation to expectancy is a first-level outcome, and is rooted in the job itself. If you work hard you expect to do such things as produce goods, supply a service, or achieve quality. Instrumentalities

Figure 2–5 A basic version of expectancy theory.

Person will be motivated under these conditions	A. Expectancy is high: Person believes he or she can perform the task. B. Instrumentality is high: Person believes that performance will lead to certain outcomes. C. Valence is high: Person highly values the outcomes.

deal with second-level outcomes—the rewards associated with performing. An instrumentality can also be regarded as the hunch that a first-level outcome will lead to a second-level outcome. For instance, you might have a strong belief that if you produce high-quality work, you will receive recognition from the organization.

3. **Valence** is the value, worth, or attractiveness of an outcome. In each work situation there are multiple outcomes, each with a valence of its own. For instance, if you make a substantial cost-saving suggestion for your employer, potential second-level outcomes include: cash award, good performance evaluation, promotion, recognition, and status. Valences range from −1 to +1. A valence of plus one means that you strongly desire an outcome. A valence of minus one means that you are strongly motivated to avoid an outcome, such as being fired from a job or convicted of income tax evasion. A valence of zero means that you are indifferent toward an outcome. An outcome with a zero valence is therefore of no use as a motivator.

The Calculation of Motivation

Motivation is calculated by multiplying expectancies, instrumentalities, and valences. This relationship is expressed by the formula:

$$\text{Motivation} = \text{Expectancy} \times \text{Instrumentality} \times \text{Valence}$$

An example from career planning will help explain how this process works. Margot believes strongly that she will be able to complete a program of study in engineering technology. She thus has a high expectancy, perhaps .90. She believes a little less strongly that an engineering technology program will lead to a high-paying, interesting job. Her instrumentality is .85. Yet Margot strongly values a potential career in engineering technology. Her valence is .95. When these three components are multiplied (.90 × .85 × .95 = .73), it appears that Margot's motivation will be strong. To develop a valid analysis of her motivation, it would be necessary to calculate her motivation for several different outcomes, such as income, status, and career satisfaction. Motivation could also be calculated for several different expectancies. In addition to her expectancy about graduation, Margot would have expectancies for hurdles such as getting through a certain course.

One important implication of the formula is that a zero value for expectancy, instrumentality, or valence would result in zero motivation, because any number multiplied by zero is zero. Another implication of the formula is that it helps explain why some people engage in behaviors with low expectancies, such as trying to invent a successful new product, write a best-selling novel, or win a lottery. The compensating factor is the large valences attached to the second-level outcomes associated with these accomplishments. Although ET attaches a maximum value of +1 to valences, we think that a range of −100 to +100 would better suit extraordinary outcomes.

How Ability and Motivation Are Linked to Performance

Figure 2–6 depicts how ability and motivation are linked to performance. In order to achieve performance and productivity, both motivation and ability must be present.[24] Ability in this context includes organizational support because people need help to make good use of their abilities. Support includes the right equipment, tools, and help from co-workers. If either motivation or ability is absent, no performance will be possible. If one is absent, no performance will be possible. It is important to recognize the contribution of ability in bringing about performance because our culture tends to overdramatize the contribution of motivation. Too many people uncritically accept the statement, "You can achieve anything you want if you try hard enough." In reality, a person also needs the proper education, ability, tools, and technology.

Motivation is often the key to attaining good results, but at other times nonmotivational factors come into play. For example, a group member might want to achieve high output, but group pressures keep him or her from producing much more than the group standard.

Evaluation and Implications of ET

ET has been well researched, and many studies provide encouraging evidence about the theory. One problem, however, is that ET is so complex that only portions of it can be tested at one time. ET does well as a predictor of occupational choice and job satisfaction. It does less well in predicting how much effort a person will invest in a particular task.[25] Unlike the motivational theory to be described next, expectancy theory has not been translated into a specific program of worker motivation. Expectancy theory, however, has some important implications for enhancing the motivation of workers:

1. *Training and encouragement are important.* Managers should give employees the necessary training and encouragement to be confident they can perform the required task. Some employees who appear to be poorly motivated simply lack the right skills and self-confidence.
2. *The link between rewards and performance should be explicit.* Employees should be reassured that if they perform the job up to standard, they will receive the promised reward. It is sometimes helpful for employees to speak to co-workers about whether they received promised rewards.
3. *The meaning and implications of second-level outcomes should be explained.* It is helpful for employees to understand the value of certain outcomes, such as receiving a favorable performance appraisal. (For example, it could lead to a salary increase and promotion.) People strive harder to achieve outcomes they know to be valuable.
4. *Individual differences in valences must be understood.* To motivate employees effectively, managers must discover individual differences in preferences for rewards. An attempt should be made to offer rewards to a worker to which he or

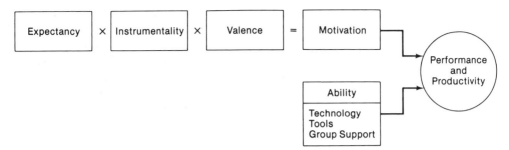

Figure 2–6 How motivation and ability influence performance and productivity.

she attaches a high valence. For instance, one employee might value a high-adventure assignment; another might attach a high valence to a routine, tranquil assignment.

MOTIVATION THROUGH BEHAVIOR MODIFICATION

The most widely used formal method of motivating employees is **behavior modification,** an attempt to change behavior by manipulating rewards and punishments. Behavior modification is based upon two key concepts: the law of effect and environmental determinism. According to the **law of effect,** behavior that leads to a positive consequence for the individual tends to be repeated, while behavior that leads to a negative consequence tends not to be repeated.

The law of effect is a basic principle of psychology. Environmental determinism is a philosophy that stems from this principle. According to **environmental determinism,** our past history of reinforcement determines, or causes, our current behavior. The rewards and punishments we have received make up much of this history.

As mentioned earlier in the chapter, behavioral modification makes no reference to internal cognitions such as needs or motives that influence behavior. Instead, reinforcers shape our lives. If smiling at people brought you the approval you wanted in the past, you will smile again when you want approval. The environmental event that determined your behavior was approval.

The balance of our discussion of behavior modification will consist of a summary of behavior modification strategies, a list of rules for its application, a case history of its application, and a comment about its controversial nature.

Behavior Modification Strategies

Behavior modification is an entire field of study itself. Nevertheless, the techniques of behavior modification can be divided into four strategies:

Positive reinforcement (PR) means increasing the probability that behavior will be repeated by rewarding people for making the desired response. The phrase *increase the probability* means that PR improves learning and motivation, but is not 100 percent effective. The phrase *making the desired response* is also noteworthy. To use PR properly, a reward is contingent upon the person doing something right. Simply paying somebody a compliment or giving them something of value is not positive reinforcement. Behavior modification always implies linking consequences to what the person has or has not accomplished.

PR is used much more frequently in behavior mod programs in organizations for two primary reasons: (1) It is more effective than punishment, and (2) it creates less negative publicity than a systematic use of employee punishments.

Negative reinforcement is rewarding people by taking away an uncomfortable consequence of their behavior. It is the withdrawal or termination of a disliked consequence. You are subject to negative reinforcement when you are told, "Your insurance rate will go down if you receive no traffic violations for twelve months." The uncomfortable consequence removed is a high insurance premium. Removing the undesirable consequence is contingent upon your making the right response—driving within the law.

Be careful not to confuse negative reinforcement with punishment. Negative reinforcement is the opposite of punishment. It involves rewarding someone by removing a punishment or uncomfortable situation.

Punishment is the presentation of an undesirable consequence, or the removal of a desirable consequence, because of unacceptable behavior. A supervisor can punish an employee by suspending the employee for violating an important safety rule. Or the employee can be punished by taking away his or her chance to earn overtime because of violating the rule. The use of punishment as a motivator will be mentioned at several places in the rest of this chapter.

Extinction is decreasing the frequency of undesirable behavior by removing the desirable consequence of such behavior. (It does *not* refer to getting rid of an employee forcibly.) A company might use extinction by ceasing to pay employees for making frivolous cost-saving suggestions. Extinction is sometimes used to extinguish annoying behavior. Assume that an employee persists in telling ethnic jokes. The joke telling can often be extinguished by the group agreeing not to laugh at the jokes.

Rules for the Use of Behavior Modification

To use behavior modification effectively on the job, certain rules and procedures must be followed. Although using rewards and punishments to motivate people seems straightforward, behavior modification requires a systematic approach. The following rules emphasize positive rewards, but they also incorporate the judicious use of punishment. The rules are specified from the standpoint of the person trying to motivate another individual.[26]

***Rule 1**: Choose an appropriate reward or punishment.* An appropriate reward or punishment is one that is (a) effective in motivating a given employee, and (b) feasible from the company standpoint. If one reward does not motivate the person, try another. When positive motivators do not work, it may be necessary to use negative motivators (punishment).

It is generally best to use the mildest form of punishment that will motivate the person. For example, if an employee writes personal letters during the day, the person might simply be told to put away the letters. Motivation enters the picture because the time not spent on letters can now be invested in company work. If the mildest form of punishment does not work, a more severe negative motivator is selected.

A list of potential rewards and forms of punishment to use on the job is presented in Tables 2–1 and 2–2. These can be kept in mind in the quest for appropriate rewards and punishments.

***Rule 2**: Supply ample feedback.* Behavior modification cannot work without frequent feedback to individuals. Feedback can take the form of simply telling people when they have done something right or wrong. Brief memos or messages sent via the person's computer are another form of feedback. Be aware, however, that many employees resent seeing a message with negative feedback flashed across their video display terminal.

***Rule 3**: Do not give everyone the same size reward.* Average performance is encouraged when all forms of accomplishment receive the same reward. Assume one employee made substantial progress in reducing the production of defective parts. He or she should receive more recognition (or other reward) than an employee who made only a minor contribution to the problem.

***Rule 4**: Find some constructive behavior to reinforce.* This rule stems from the principle of behavior shaping. **Behavior shaping** is the rewarding of any response in the right direction, and then rewarding only the closest approximation. Using this approach, the desired behavior is finally attained. Behavior shaping is useful to the manager because the technique recognizes that you have to begin somewhere in teaching an employee a new skill, or motivating the employee to make a big change. It works in this manner:

> Assume that your desk is so messy that you lose important files. Using the principle of behavior shaping, your boss would reward you whenever you make progress in keeping your desk in order. For instance, if your boss notices that you no longer keep old coffee containers on your desk, he or she might comment: "I can see improvement in your work area. Keep up the progress."

***Rule 5**: Schedule rewards intermittently.* Rewards should not be given on every occasion for good performance. **Intermittent rewards** sustain desired behav-

Table 2–1 Rewards of potential use in a job setting

Monetary

Money in form of salary increases, bonuses, profit sharing; company stock; discount coupons; movie, theater, or dinner passes

Durable Gifts

Pen-and-pencil sets; watches and clocks; recognition pins and rings; trophies; small appliances such as toasters, hair dryers

Food and Dining

Company picnics; department parties; coffee, tea, or soft drinks, and pastry; holiday turkeys and fruit baskets; cocktail party; banquet for top performers

Job and Career-related

Challenging new assignment; do more of preferred task; filling in for the boss; good performance appraisal; promotion; freedom to choose own work activity; tuition refund; assignment of new machine such as personal computer or video camera

Social and Pride-related

Recognition and praise; expression of appreciation; privy to gossip and confidential information; asking employee for advice and suggestions; pat on the back; written note of appreciation

Status Symbols

Office with window, private office, bigger office; bigger or fancier desk; plaque indicating accomplishment; freedom to personalize work area (such as painting mural on wall); exclusive use of machine or telephone

---

ior longer and also slow down the process of behavior fading away when it is not rewarded. If each correct performance results in a reward, the behavior will stop shortly after a situation in which no reward is received.

Another problem is that a reward which is given continuously may lose its impact. A practical value of intermittent reinforcement is that it saves time. Few managers have enough time to dispense rewards for every correct response forthcoming from subordinates.

Rule 6: Rewards and punishments should follow the observed behavior closely in time. For maximum effectiveness, people should be rewarded shortly after doing something right, and punished shortly after doing something wrong. A built-in feedback system, such as a computer program working or not working, capitalizes upon this principle. If as a supervisor you are dispensing the rewards and punishments, try to administer them the same day they are earned.

Rule 7: Ignoring certain types of behavior may extinguish them. When people are not rewarded for repeating a desired behavior, they will often discontinue that behavior. For example, if exceptionally good performance goes unno-

Table 2–2 Punishments of potential use in job setting

Feedback on undesired behavior
Documentation of poor performance
Criticism
Withdrawal of privileges
Undesirable assignment, including being assigned the worst equipment owned by the
    company
Threat of sanctions
Fining
Probation
Suspension
Firing
Threat of poor reference if fired
Withholding of any valued reward

ticed, an employee may lose enthusiasm for being exceptional. As one disgruntled secretary said, "Nobody cares if I get out the department reports on time, so why should I?"

Rule 8: *Tell people what they must do to be rewarded.* The employee who has a standard against which to measure job performance will have a built-in feedback system. One of the many reasons a sport like basketball is so motivating is that the path to a reward is so clear-cut. A player can readily see that by putting the ball through the hoop, a reward will be forthcoming (one, two, or three points in some leagues).

Rule 9: *Do not punish in front of others.* The form of punishment chosen should be enough to eliminate the undesired behavior. Being punished in front of co-workers is humiliating. In response, the person may become defensive and angry, and lose respect for the manager.

Rule 10: *Make the reward or punishment fit the behavior.* People inexperienced in applying PR often overdo the intensity of spoken rewards. When an employee does something of an ordinary nature correctly, a simple word of praise, such as "Good job," is preferable to something like "Fantastic performance."

Rule 11: *Change the reward periodically.* Rewards do not retain their effectiveness indefinitely. Employees lose interest in striving for a reward they have received many times in the past. This is particularly true of a repetitive statement, such as "Nice job," or "Congratulations." It is helpful for the person dispensing rewards to study the list of potential rewards and try different ones from time to time.

Rule 12: *Avoid "jelly bean" motivation.* Closely related to rule 10 is the admonition against **jelly bean motivation,** the heaping of undeserved rewards upon another person.[27] It is an acknowledgment of performance that has never materialized. A typical example is a manager saying "Keep up the good work" to an employee who has accomplished virtually nothing all day.

Using OB Mod to Increase Hospital Productivity

In recent years an impressive amount of evidence has been collected showing that the systematic use of PR can improve motivation and productivity. Two major factors seem to underlie its success. First, PR programs can be implemented after a modest amount of supervisory training. Second, these programs are based on both common sense and proved psychological principles. A case history of OB mod (meaning organizational behavior modification) in a hospital setting is presented next to illustrate the methodology and potential benefits of PR in organizations.

Two consultants applied OB mod in order to increase the productivity of workers in one particular hospital.[28] Figure 2–7 summarizes the steps in the OB mod approach that had already been used in many business and industrial settings. Supervisors from representative units of the hospital were trained in the program. One medical staff unit and all the major administrative divisions, with the exception of nursing, were represented.

The supervisors participated in eight training sessions over a two-month period. The training methods and techniques are based on the model shown in Figure 2–7. In step one, the supervisors identified problem behaviors and then measured, analyzed, and provided assistance (intervened) using principles and techniques learned during the training sessions. An important aspect of this program was that the supervisors selected actual problem behaviors they were experiencing with subordinates.

The training sessions were held in a hospital conference room. To encourage interaction among supervisors, they were seated around a large table. The coordinators served primarily as stimulators and moderators once the basic concepts and principles had been presented in the early sessions.

Impact on productivity. The effectiveness of the OB mod program is revealed by the changes in productivity measures of each department, as summarized in Table 2–3. The percent change column presents consistent, often dramatic, evidence of the effectiveness of OB mod in this situation. On the basis of these results, the researchers concluded that the results are so overwhelming that they deserve attention.[29]

A specific example of how the OB mod program was applied will help add life to the statistical analysis presented in Table 2–3. To paraphrase from the research report described here:

> As part of the admitting-office supervisor's strategy for managing the unit, short meetings of all employees were instituted to provide performance feedback.

Figure 2–7 OB mod problem-solving model.

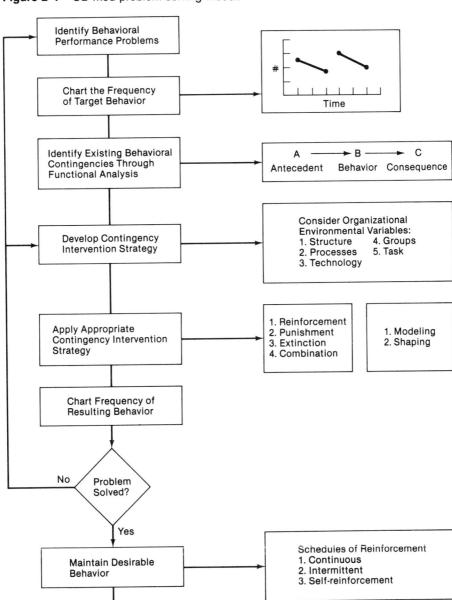

SOURCE: Reprinted, by permission of the publisher, from "The Management of Behavioral Contingencies" by Fred Luthans and Robert Kreitner, p. 13, *Personnel*, July–August 1974 © 1974 by AMACOM, a division of American Management Associations, New York. All rights reserved.

Table 2–3 Productivity changes in a large hospital after the OB mod training program

Unit	Measure(s)	Pre-Intervention	Post-Intervention	Percent Change
Emergency room clerks	Registration errors (per day)	19.16	4.580	76.10%
Hardware engineer group, HIS	Average time to repair (minutes)	92.53	33.250	61.40
Medical records file clerks	Errors in filing (per person per audit)	2.87	.078	97.30
Medical records	Complaints	8.00	1.000	875.00
Transcriptionists	Average errors	2.07	1.400	33.00
	Average output	2,258.00	2,303.330	2.00
Heart station	EKG procedures accomplished (Ave.)	1,263.00	1,398.970	11.00
	Overdue procedures	7.00*	4.000	42.80
Eye clinic	Daily patient throughput	19.00	23.000	21.00
	Daily patient teaching documentation	1.00	2.800	180.00
	Protocols produced	0.00	2.000	200.00
Pharmacy technicians	Drug output (doses)	348.80	422.100	21.00
	Posting errors	3.67	1.480	59.70
	Product waste (percent)	5.80	4.350	25.00
Radiology technicians	Average patient throughput (procedural)	3,849.50	4,049.000	5.00
	Retake rate (percent)	11.20	9.950	11.20
Patient accounting	Average monthly billings	2,561.00	3,424.500	33.70
Admitting office	Time to admit (minutes)	43.73	13.570	68.97
	Average cost	$ 15.05	$ 11.730	22.00
Data center operations	Systems log-on (time)	1:54	1:43	13.40

* *Estimate: All averages are arithmetic means.*

SOURCE: Charles A. Snyder and Fred Luthans, "Using OB Mod to Increase Hospital Productivity." Reprinted from the August 1982 issue of *Personnel Administrator*, p. 72. Copyright 1982, The American Society for Personnel Administration, 30 Park Drive, Berea OH 44017.

His management style was changed to emphasize positive reinforcement for improved performance. Some time after the program was completed, he described his unit as working at top effectiveness. He believed he had achieved an excellent level of teamwork and cited the great improvement in performance as evidence that the entire unit benefited from his application of OB Mod.

Table 2–3 shows the overall productivity improvement of the admitting department. The available data on time to admit patients revealed that an average of 43.73 minutes was required before the OB mod intervention. After the intervention the average time dropped to 13.57 minutes. At the bottom line, the cost per admission, which averaged $15.05 before intervention, dropped to an average of $11.73 after the OB mod program.

The Behavior Modification Controversy

Controversy has surrounded the use of behavior modification by employers. However, the many good results have lessened the criticism in recent years.[30] We will examine the major arguments against OB mod, and the counterarguments.

Arguments against behavior mod. The criticisms raised of behavior modification by employers have been on both technical and ethical issues. Cognitive theorists are concerned that OB mod practitioners neglect the higher thought processes of people. Another issue is that PR addicts people to external rewards, thus depriving them of the joy of good work itself. Critics have also contended that behavior modification manipulates people against their will, thus stripping them of their dignity.

Even when impressive results are forthcoming from PR programs, the research has been criticized for offering the wrong explanation of why the positive outcomes were achieved. It is often argued that goal setting, or some other cognitive process, led to improved results. For example, the admissions supervisor reported on above might have achieved improvements because he finally realized (a cognitive process) that it was time to change his inappropriate management style. Other critics dislike the idea that PR programs break down jobs into small, measurable units—the opposite of a challenging assignment.

Counterarguments. The arguments just mentioned are not strong enough to discount the contribution of a sensible application of reinforcement theory to improving motivation and productivity. Also, many critics of PR programs have a narrow view of how the programs operate. An especially naive criticism is that PR applies only to simplified jobs. Even executives and professionals respond well to contingent rewards. See what happens the next time you compliment your boss or instructor for a job well done.

Another counterargument is that participants in a PR program can use cognitive processes, including attaching valences to rewards. Employees will continue to display high motivation only if the rewards from hard work continue to be true rewards. Should increased productivity lead to ever-increasing work quotas and layoffs, the behavior that led to these negative consequences will soon change. Employees thus have a built-in control against being manipulated toward undesirable ends.

A final counterargument is that an important goal of positive reinforcement is to make good work its own reward. B. F. Skinner, one of the founders of behavior modification, has suggested that feedback and incentive systems be designed in such a way that work gets accomplished and is enjoyable.[31] This critical point requires illustration. Assume that early in her career a tax auditor dislikes (and even tries to avoid) listening to counterarguments from small business owners. After the auditor listens to the first of several angry business owners, she receives systematic encouragement and support from her boss. Gradually the auditor comes to welcome the challenge of resolving disputes with angry taxpayers. It took coaxing (PR), but the auditor eventually became hooked on the intrinsic merits of the job.

MOTIVATION THROUGH FEAR AND PUNISHMENT

Fear and punishment are still widely used in an attempt to motivate employees and maintain discipline. Fear and punishment are closely related. **Fear** is worry and anxiety about a punishment that might be forthcoming. **Punishment,** as defined earlier, is an actual undesirable consequence evoked by unacceptable behavior. Since fear and punishment are used separately as strategies by employers, it is worthwhile to describe them separately here.

Fear

A manager attended a talk about the use of PR to increase productivity. After the talk, the manager commented to the speaker, "Maybe what you say about encouraging people is true in some companies, but not in mine. Our company is a leader in its field. Yet fear is the only technique we use to motivate our management team. Every manager is told by the president that if he makes a major mistake or doesn't give his all to the company, he will be canned. No excuses, no second chances. Every manager in our company is afraid of losing his or her job. Where does positive reinforcement fit in here?"

As this example illustrates, there are some instances in which motivating people through fear will work. But it is a far less effective strategy in the long run than appealing to dignity and self-worth. If you are motivated by fear, you may very well search for revenge. Production workers sometimes use sabotage in retaliation for being motivated through fear. Executives sometimes retaliate against fear by joining another company and taking trade secrets with them.

One reason fear is sometimes effective as a motivator is that most individuals have some need to avoid pain or achieve financial or job security. The strength of such needs depends upon individual and situational differences, but they are usually lower-level needs.

Based on his surveys, Daniel Yankelovich concludes that fear is rapidly losing its clout as a job motivator. One economic reason is that people today are worried less about unemployment than in the past. Factors such as unemployment insurance, welfare payment, and working marital partners ease the sting of layoff. According to Yankelovich:

> The fear of unemployment, of not being able to make a living, of not being able to keep one's family together, is neither as much a part of people's experience nor as devastating a prospect as it once was. Further, the fear of unemployment generally tends to be confined to people who have actually lost their jobs.[32]

Punishment

Punishment and the threat of punishment are widely used in an attempt to motivate employees. Punishment can be used in behavior modification programs, although this is rarely done in work organizations. Punishment is more frequently used by managers. Improperly used, punishment has some serious limitations in motivating people or helping them learn. Properly used, punishment can be beneficial.

Problems associated with punishment. Many people respond poorly to punishment; instead of becoming better motivated, their motivation level decreases.[33] One problem associated with punishment is that the results are not as predictable as those of reward. People respond erratically to punishment. Another disadvantage of punishment is that its effects are less permanent than those of reward. Shortly after the punishment is administered, the person reverts to the unacceptable behavior. Punishment also falls short because it is frequently accompanied by negative attitudes toward the punisher and the activity itself. If you punish another person, expect some anger in retaliation. Many cases of sabotage can be traced to an employee angered by a recent punishment.

Punishment can also lead to **psychological sabotage,** any deliberate behavior that interferes with the achievement of company goals. Common types of psychological sabotage are: "Complaining, criticizing, spreading gossip, absenteeism, tardiness, wasting time, forgetting important details, communicating false information to superiors, failure to report problems, carelessness, laziness, rudeness to customers and clients, and taking the path of least resistance."[34]

A general problem with punishment and threats of punishment is that, like fear, they are tied in with lower-level rather than higher-level needs. As such, they are weak motivators.

Proper use of punishment. Despite the problems we have mentioned, punishment can play a useful role in maintaining discipline in an organization. Employees should recognize that negative sanctions will follow counterproductive behavior such as substandard performance and excessive absenteeism. An effective punishment has these characteristics:

1. It is clearly impersonal and corrective; all rule violators receive the same punishment and are shown what to do right.
2. It focuses on the specific act; the employee is punished for exactly what he or she did wrong, rather than for his or her general behavior.
3. It is relatively intense and quick; the punishment hurts mentally but is over quickly, such as a one-day suspension for smoking in a no-smoking area.[35]

Mel E. Schnake conducted an experiment that demonstrated the contribution of punishment in a work setting. He hired 60 college students to work two successive Saturday afternoons on a task involving recording stock prices. Student workers were exposed to either a co-worker receiving a reduction in pay, a co-worker receiving a threat of reduction in pay, or no punishment.

The experiment indicated that observing a co-worker receiving punishment has a positive effect on observers' productivity without damaging job satisfaction. The workers who observed the reduction in pay achieved more output than those who observed only a threat of reduction in pay. The experimental group also outperformed a control group who witnessed no punishment.[36]

Note that this experiment did not compare the relative effectiveness of punishments and rewards. Do you think temporary workers who received bonuses for good performance would have outperformed those who observed co-workers being punished?

MOTIVATION THROUGH THE RIGHT ORGANIZATION CULTURE

The motivational methods and OB mod program described so far are aimed at motivating people individually or in small groups. A macro (overall or strategic) way of enhancing motivation is to establish an environment or organizational culture that encourages hard work. **Organizational culture** is a system of shared values and beliefs that actively influence the behavior of organization members. Simply put, the organizational, or corporate, culture is its norms.[37]

The concept of corporate culture was popularized by the bestseller, *In Search of Excellence: Lessons from America's Best Run Companies*.[38] The management consultants who wrote the book believed that the right corporate culture can inspire employees to be productive. Similarly, the wrong culture can lead to low productivity.

A new organizational culture cannot be implemented as readily as a behavior modification program. It takes a long time to develop a culture that fosters strong motivation and productivity. It is difficult to reach firm conclusions about organizational culture because the concept is so abstract. Nevertheless, an organizational culture that fosters strong motivation would have several of these characteristics:[39]

1. *An atmosphere that rewards excellence by giving big rewards to top performers.* This characteristic is double-edged: outstanding performers get big raises and promotions while poor performers do not get promoted, get few raises, and may even be terminated.

2. *An atmosphere that rewards creative thought by giving tangible rewards to innovators.* At the same time, few penalties are imposed on people whose creative ideas lead to failure. Penalties for failed ideas discourage innovation.

3. *A pervasive belief that the organization is a winner.* If employees perceive that they belong to a winning team, they will tend to be highly motivated. Proud organizations like IBM, Domino's Pizza, and the Boston Celtics capitalize on this aspect of culture.

4. *A spirit of helpfulness that encourages employees to believe they can overcome setbacks.* Employees believe that when they face job hurdles, the company will provide assistance.

HOW DO YOU MOTIVATE YOURSELF?

People often interpret theories about work motivation as a way to motivate others to accomplish their jobs. Of equal importance, a study of motivation should help you energize yourself. In general, applying the theories discussed in this chapter to yourself should help you understand the conditions under which you are likely to work hard. Following are several specific suggestions and strategies for self-motivation.

Set goals for yourself. Goals are fundamental to human motivation. Set yearly, monthly, weekly, daily, and sometimes even morning or afternoon goals for yourself. For example, "By noontime I will have emptied my in-basket and made one suggestion to improve safety practices in our shop." Longer-range, or life, goals can also be helpful in gathering momentum in spurring yourself on toward higher levels of achievement. However, these have to buttressed by a series of short-range goals. You might have the long-range goal of becoming a prominent architect, but first it would be helpful to earn an A in a drafting course.

Identify and seek out your motivators. Having read this chapter and done some serious introspection, you should be able to identify a few of your personal motivators. Next find a job that offers you them in ample supply. You might have good evidence from your past experience that the opportunity for close contact with people (comradeship or good interpersonal relationships) is a personal motivator. Find a job that involves working in a small, friendly department.

Owing to circumstances, you may have to take whatever job you can find, or you may not be in a position to change jobs. In that situation try to arrange your work so you have more opportunity to experience the reward(s) you are seeking. Assume that solving difficult problems excites you, but your job is 85 percent routine. Develop better work habits so that you can more quickly take care of the routine aspects of your job. This will give you more time to enjoy the creative aspects of your work.

Get feedback on performance. Few people can sustain a high level of drive without getting an objective or subjective opinion on how well they are doing. Even if you find your work exciting, you still need feedback. Photographers may be enamored of the intrinsic aspects of their work. Yet photographers, more than most people, want their work displayed. A display delivers the message, "Your work is good enough to show to other people."

If your boss or company does not recognize the importance of feedback or simply forgets to tell people how they are doing, don't be hesitant to ask an occasional question such as: "Is my work satisfactory so far?" "How well am I doing in meeting the expectations of my job?" "I haven't heard anything good or bad about my performance. Should I be worried?"

Apply behavior modification to yourself. The information presented earlier in this chapter about motivating others through behavior mod can also be applied to yourself. To boost your own motivation through behavior mod, you have to (1) decide whether you should be rewarded or punished for your acts, and (2) administer these rewards or punishments. If the idea of self-punishment is distasteful to you, try using a system which relies solely on positive reinforcers. In any event, you become both jury and judge!

One helpful way to use behavior modification by yourself is to determine which of the twelve rules described earlier would make the most sense in your particular situation. Much depends on which particular motivational problem you are facing.

Increase your expectancies. A practical way of using expectancy theory to increase your own motivational level is to increase your subjective probability that your effort will lead to good performance on a given task. One way to increase your expectancy is to increase your level of skill with respect to a task for which you want to be highly motivated. If a person has the necessary skills to perform a particular task, that person will usually raise his or her subjective hunch that he or she can get the task accomplished.

A strategy for increasing your expectancies in a wide variety of situations is to raise your general level of self-confidence. Self-confident people tend to have high subjective hunches that they can achieve performance in many situations. Raising your self-confidence is a long and gradual process. Its key ingredient is to begin with a small success and build up to bigger successes in an increasing number of situations.

    Raise your level of self-expectation. In Greek mythology, Pygmalion was a sculptor who carved an ivory statue of a maiden and fell in love with it (her?). The statue was brought to life in response to his prayer. According to the Pygmalion effect in motivation, if your boss or teacher has high expectations of you, it will raise your level of performance—even if these high expectations are not communicated to you directly.[40] Although less evidence exists about the possibility of turning the Pygmalion effect inward, it is conceivable that if you raise your self-expectations you can raise your own performance. The net effect is the same as if you had increased your level of motivation. Raising your self-expectation means about the same thing as having a **positive mental attitude,** a conviction that you will succeed.

Summary of Key Points

☐   Work motivation refers to effort expended toward organizational objectives. It also refers to an activity performed by managers or other people who try to get others to expend effort. Productivity refers to how much a person accomplishes in a given period of time. It is the ratio of output to input, taking into account both quality and quantity.

☐   Among the reasons that motivation is a concern today are: changes in values; many guaranteed rewards to workers; difficult-to-satisfy needs; a declining work ethic; reduced costs of failure; group problem solving; decreased loyalty; less supervisory power; shorter time perspectives; and the quest for job satisfaction.

☐   Explanations of motivation can be divided broadly into cognitive and noncognitive, or reinforcement, theories. Cognitive theories emphasize that people make conscious decisions about their behavior and that they are driven by inner strivings. Reinforcement theories emphasize the role of the environment, especially rewards and punishments, in molding behavior. Cognitive and noncognitive explanations can be mutually supportive.

☐   According to goal theory, behavior is regulated by values and conscious intentions or goals. Hard goals lead to high performance when they are specific, accepted by the person, not unrealistically difficult, and used as a basis for performance evaluation. Participation in goal setting improves performance indirectly because it may increase goal difficulty and acceptance.

☐   A popular cognitive conception of motivation is that people work to satisfy needs that are not currently being met. The famous need hierarchy of Maslow contends that people have an internal need pushing them on toward self-actualization. However, needs are arranged into a five-step hierarchy. Before higher-level needs are activated, certain

    * Note carefully that we are referring here to expectations in a general sense, not in reference to ET. The confusion is unavoidable.

lower-level needs must be satisfied. In ascending order, the groups of needs are: physiological, safety, love (or belonging), esteem, and self-actualizing (such as self-fulfillment).

☐ Herzberg's two-factor theory states that some elements of a job, called *satisfiers* or *motivators*, give us a chance to satisfy higher-level needs. These elements or factors include achievement, recognition, and challenging work. In contrast, some job elements appeal more to lower-level needs and are called *dissatisfiers* or *hygiene* factors. They refer to the job setting and include company policy, supervision, physical working conditions, and status. Satisfiers are noted primarily by their presence, while dissatisfiers are noted primarily by their absence.

☐ Much human behavior on the job can be explained by people's strong motives to achieve important things, acquire power, and affiliate with others. The achievement need is the desire to set and accomplish goals for their own sake. Entrepreneurs have strong achievement needs. The need for power is the desire to control other people and resources. Power motives can be directed to personal gain or to social good. The need for affiliation is a desire to seek close relationships with others and to be a loyal employee or friend.

☐ Some job behavior can be explained by the need for thrill seeking found in Type T personalities. Thrill seeking can be channeled into constructive or destructive purposes.

☐ Expectancy theory (ET) assumes that people are decision makers who choose among alternatives by selecting the one that appears to have the biggest personal payoff at the time. ET has three major components: expectancy about the ability to perform, instrumentality (the hunch that performance will lead to a reward), and valence (the value attached to the reward). Motivation is calculated by multiplying the numerical values for all three. ET has several important implications for managing people including linking rewards to performance and understanding individual differences in preferences.

☐ Behavior modification is an attempt to change behavior by manipulating rewards and punishments. Its key principle is the law of effect—behavior that leads to a positive effect tends to be repeated, while the opposite is also true. The basic behavior modification strategies are positive reinforcement, negative reinforcement, punishment, and extinction.

☐ Rules for the effective use of behavior modification include: choose an appropriate reward or punishment; supply ample feedback; do not give everyone the same reward; schedule rewards intermittently; give rewards and punishments soon after the observed behavior; give equitable rewards and punishments; change rewards periodically; avoid "jelly bean" motivation (undeserved rewards). Behavior modification has met with considerable opposition, but has also achieved much productivity improvement in organizations.

☐ Fear is a frequently used but not highly recommended motivational strategy. It works best in the short range and with people who are truly concerned about the consequences of losing a job. Punishment is sometimes necessary in organizations, but it too has weaknesses as a motivational strategy, including retaliation such as psychological sabotage. Properly used, punishment can be an effective motivator. An effective form of punishment is impersonal and corrective, focuses on the specific act, and is relatively quick and intense.

☐ An overall strategy of motivation is to establish an organizational culture that encourages hard work. This includes giving big rewards to top performers, encouraging innovation, and a pervasive belief that the organization is a winner.

☐ Suggestions and strategies for self-motivation include: set goals; identify and seek out your motivators; get feedback on performance; apply behavior modification to yourself; increase your expectancies that you can perform; and raise your level of self-expectation.

Questions and Activities _____

1. What evidence would you need to conclude that a person is well motivated?

2. Is level of motivation a characteristic of an individual that generalizes from one situation to another? For example, do people who work hard seem to also play hard?

3. How can you tell which psychological need a person is trying to satisfy?

4. Maslow's need hierarchy is still widely quoted and discussed thirty years after it first appeared in a book. What do you think accounts for its continued appeal?

5. How might an instructor use PR to raise the level of class performance?

6. How might an individual gather the necessary information to formulate an accurate instrumentality in a given situation?

7. Valences are an important part of ET, yet not much has been written about measuring valence. Suggest a method for measuring a person's valence toward a particular reward.

8. Some people seem to be "go-getters" and "self-starters" from childhood. What have you learned in this chapter that would explain such behavior?

9. What are some of the potential disadvantages of having a strong power need?

10. Identify several rewards listed in Table 2–2 that you think would be particularly effective in motivating higher-level managers and professionals. Explain your reasoning.

11. Answer question 10 for clerical workers and production workers.

12. Why do you think so many managers believe in motivation through fear?

A Human Relations Case

THE PRODUCTIVITY SQUEEZE

Bill Whillock, vice president of purchasing for Farm Equipment Corporation, was invited by the company president to make the first presentation at Monday morning's administrative staff meeting. Whillock announced a plan whereby Farm Equipment will sign a long-term contract with suppliers if they promise to work on improving labor productivity at a 7 percent annual rate. Every supplier to the mammoth farm equipment maker has been offered the same deal. Whillock explained some details of the plan:

"This plan could form the basis for long-term relationships with all our suppliers. We hope it will be a new way of doing business. We will continue to pay for increases in material costs, but we expect labor costs to remain about the same.

"We've got to be competitive with the Japanese. But we cannot do the job alone at Farm Equipment. Our vendors have got to play ball with us. I recognize this is a big shift in policy. Usually we sign yearly contracts with suppliers. Now we are asking for long-term commitments. We are inviting suppliers to talk the offer over with our purchasing agents. In this way we can develop a feel for whether or not the firms can implement the right kind of productivity-improvement programs."

"Stop right there," said Sharon Porter, vice president of human resources. "Some of our suppliers know very little about the concept of productivity improvement. The term *productivity improvement* could mean almost anything from buying a new machine to decreasing absenteeism. What specifically do you have in mind?"

"Sharon, you know very well what I have in mind. Farm Equipment Corporation can't expect our vendors to invest in new machinery on our behalf. We expect them to hold their labor costs stable through increases in motivation. If you can light a fire under some of their employees and managers, the result will be gains in productivity."

"Bill, I think we are going to have to offer our vendors something more specific than exhortations to boost employee motivation. We are going to have to lead the way with tangible programs of employee motivation."

"Sharon, I think you're missing the point. In this economic climate, hunger is the big motivator. A firm that is not willing to go along with productivity increases will starve as far as we are concerned. If our suppliers are hungry enough for our business, they'll find a way to motivate their employees."

1. What is your reaction to Bill Whillock's contention that "hunger is the big motivator"?
2. If you side with Sharon Porter's viewpoint, suggest a feasible approach to improving productivity through increased employee motivation.
3. Based on your knowledge of expectancy theory, evaluate the probable success of Farm Equipment Corporation's plan to obtain the productivity increases from vendors.

A Human Relations Incident

THE POLICE MISSPELLERS

Sergeant Maureen O'Brien grabbed a crime investigation report from her desk and placed it in front of her boss, Lieutenant José Lugo. Pointing to the report, she said to Lieutenant Lugo: "See all these circled words. They indicate spelling errors. Officer Gaudion made twenty-eight spelling errors in one investigation report. I wish I could say that Gaudion is an exception. The truth is that he is far from the worst speller in our platoon. I wish I could get the officers in my platoon to make fewer spelling errors on their daily reports."

With a concerned expression on his face, Lugo commented: "What steps have you taken so far to improve the spelling of your officers?"

"I've done about what I think is feasible. As you know, there is no money in the budget for purchasing word-processing equipment. The electronic spell checkers on those rigs would sure be a big help. I've made sure that our department has given each officer a pocket dictionary. I've also given them clear instructions to use the dictionary when needed. Another step I've taken is to schedule a training program in report writing for all platoon members. The sessions will be held this spring. I'm hoping that will cure the problem of so many misspellings."

"Maureen, I'm not so sure the report writing workshop will do the trick. Your officers are adults. If they haven't learned to be good spellers yet, I doubt a one-day workshop will cure their problems. Your real problem might be that your officers have no desire to be better spellers. Have you thought about that?"

"I have given some thought to the matter. In fact, I've told each officer with a spelling problem that I want very much for him or her to commit fewer spelling errors on police reports."

"Maureen, between now and the next time we talk, I want you to develop a better plan for motivating your officers to make fewer spelling mistakes," concluded José.

1. To what extent do you think the frequent spelling errors made by the officers reflect a motivational problem?
2. What approach would you recommend Sergeant O'Brien take to motivate her platoon to become better spellers?

A Human Relations Self-examination Exercise

HOW STRONG IS YOUR WORK ORIENTATION?

Self-examination can be helpful in understanding the concept of work motivation. Toward this end, we have developed an exploratory questionnaire for self-administration and interpretation. This questionnaire is not scientifically validated. It is primarily a teaching device to help the reader apply motivational concepts to himself or herself. Answer each question "mostly agree" or "mostly disagree" as it applies to you. Candor on your part might provide you with some clues about the intensity of your orientation toward work.

Work Orientation Questionnaire

	Mostly Agree	Mostly Disagree
1. I find it difficult getting started on Monday morning.	___	___
2. Vacations make me tense because they take me away from my work.	___	___
3. When engaging in sports I have trouble concentrating because my mind is usually on work.	___	___
4. The main reason I engage in physical activity is to keep me in shape for work.	___	___
5. Given the chance, I would leave work early to play with my children (or nephews or nieces).	___	___
6. I would cancel a luncheon date with my spouse if that morning my boss asked to have lunch with me.	___	___
7. The biggest thrills I get in life are from my work.	___	___
8. I work primarily so I can pay my bills and enjoy a few luxuries.	___	___
9. When waiting in line in a bank, I get very tense because precious work time is being wasted.	___	___
10. Even when at home, I feel guilty just relaxing.	___	___

11. An underlying fear I have is that a family emergency will take me away from my work for a period of time. _____ _____
12. I would enjoy walking leisurely in the park at 10 o'clock on a workday morning. _____ _____
13. Thoughts of work rarely enter my mind while I'm on vacation. _____ _____
14. I would like to retire as soon as I could afford it. _____ _____
15. Having a spouse and children is pleasant, but it can prevent you from getting the most out of your career. _____ _____
16. I work about fifteen more hours per week than do most people in my occupation. _____ _____
17. Work is meaningless unless it is performed to provide for people close to you. _____ _____
18. During social activities I often think of unfinished business at the office or school. _____ _____
19. (Answer 19A or 19B)
   A. While (or if) my wife was (were) in the delivery room, I brought (would bring) some work into the waiting room _____ _____
   B. If (or when) I gave birth to a child, I would bring (brought) some work to the maternity ward. _____ _____
20. I keep a notebook (or tape recorder) next to me in my car so I can make use of time that might be lost in stalled traffic. _____ _____

Scoring the Questionnaire. The answers in the "work is central to life" direction for each question are as follows:

1. Mostly disagree	11. Mostly agree
2. Mostly agree	12. Mostly disagree
3. Mostly agree	13. Mostly disagree
4. Mostly agree	14. Mostly disagree
5. Mostly disagree	15. Mostly agree
6. Mostly agree	16. Mostly agree
7. Mostly agree	17. Mostly disagree
8. Mostly disagree	18. Mostly agree
9. Mostly agree	19. A or B. Mostly agree
10. Mostly agree	20. Mostly agree

Interpreting Your Score. Extremely high or low scores are the most meaningful. A score of 16 or more suggests dominant "work is central to life" orientation. Work addicts or "workaholics" tend to fall into this category. If your biggest thrills (rewards) in life stem from work and vacations make you tense, you display dominant symptoms of a work addict. You may be losing the capacity to stand back from your work long enough to get recharged and take a fresh look at what you are doing.

A score of 6 to 15 suggests that you have a moderate tendency toward an intense work orientation. Under extreme circumstances (such as income tax season for a tax accountant), you may become a temporary or seasonal work addict. Such behavior is usually functional for the organization.

A score of 5 or less suggests that you have a weak work orientation. It may be necessary for you to prompt yourself with external motivators (such as the prospects of a vacation) to keep yourself involved in your work. It is easy for a person of such a weak work orientation to become lethargic and undermotivated.

Source: Andrew J. DuBrin, *Foundations of Organizational Behavior: An Applied Perspective* (Englewood Cliffs, NJ: Prentice Hall, 1984), pp. 135–137. Reprinted with permission.

Notes

1. Vincent S. Flowers and Charles L. Hughes, "The Key to Motivation," *Personnel Administrator*, February 1981, p. 70.

2. The first nine items on the list are from Philip C. Grant, "Why Employee Motivation Has Declined in America," *Personnel Journal*, December 1982, pp. 905–908.

3. Oliver L. Niehouse, "Job Satisfaction: How to Motivate Today's Workers," *Supervisory Management*, February 1986, p. 8.

4. Donald B. Fedor and Gerald R. Ferris, "Integrating OB Mod with Cognitive Approaches to Motivation," *Academy of Management Review*, January 1981, pp. 115–125.

5. Observation by Henry F. Houser, in book review, *Personnel Psychology*, Autumn 1985, p. 626.

6. Gary P. Latham and Edwin A. Locke, "Goal Setting—A Motivational Technique That Works," *Organizational Dynamics*, Autumn 1979, pp. 72–75.

7. Christina E. Shalley and Greg R. Oldham, "Effects of Goal Difficulty and Expected External Evaluation on Intrinsic Motivation: A Laboratory Study," *Academy of Management Journal*, September 1985, p. 628.

8. Terence R. Mitchell, "Motivational Strategies," in Kendrith M. Rowland and Gerald R. Ferris, eds., *Personnel Management* (Boston: Allyn and Bacon, 1982), p. 286.

9. Jane Punnett, "Goal Setting: An Extension of the Research," *Journal of Applied Psychology*, February 1986, pp. 171–172.

10. Miriam Erez, P. Christopher Earley, and Charles L. Hulin, "The Impact of Participation on Goal Acceptance and Performance: A Two-Step Model," *Academy of Management Journal*, March 1985, pp. 63–64.

11. Vincent W. Kafka, "A New Look at Motivation—for Productivity Improvement," *Supervisory Management*, April 1986, p. 19.

12. An original source of the need hierarchy is Abraham Maslow, "A Theory of Human Motivation," *Psychological Review*, 50 (1943), pp. 370–396.

13. David E. Terpstra, "Theories of Motivation—Borrowing the Best," *Personnel Journal*, June 1979, p. 376.

14. Douglas T. Hall and K. E. Nougaim, "An Examination of Maslow's Need Hierarchy in an Organizational Setting," *Organizational Behavior and Human Performance*, February 1968, pp. 12–35.

15. An Original source of the two-factor theory is Frederick Herzberg, *Work and the Nature of Man* (Cleveland: World, 1966).

16. Terpstra, "Theories of Motivation," p. 377.

17. Michael J. Stahl, "Achievement, Power, and Managerial Motivation: Selecting Managerial Talent with the Job Choice Exercise," *Personnel Psychology*, Winter 1983, pp.

775–789; David C. McClelland, *Power: The Inner Experience* (New York: Irvington, 1975).

18. David C. McClelland, *The Achieving Society* (New York: Van Nostrand, 1961).

19. Stahl, "Achievement, Power, and Managerial Motivation," p. 776.

20. Ibid.

21. McClelland, *Power: The Inner Experience*.

22. Research cited in John Leo, "Looking for a Life of Thrills," *Time*, April 15, 1985, pp. 92–93; Marvin Zuckerman, "The Search for High Sensation," *Psychology Today*, February 1978, pp. 38–40, 43, 46, 96–99.

23. An original version of expectancy theory is Victor H. Vroom, *Work and Motivation* (New York: Wiley, 1964). A later synthesis similar to the version presented in this text is Henry L. Tosi, John R. Rizzo, and Stephen J. Carroll, *Managing Organizational Behavior* (Marshfield, MA: Pitman, 1986), pp. 240–246.

24. Tosi, Rizzo, and Carroll, *Managing Organizational Behavior*, p. 242.

25. Mitchell, "Motivational Strategies,' p. 284.

26. An authoritative source on the use of behavior modification in organizations is Fred Luthans and Robert Kreitner, *Organizational Behavior Modification and Beyond: An Operant and Social Learning Approach* (Glenview, IL: Scott, Foresman, 1984).

27. Kenneth Blanchard, "Jelly Bean Motivation: Know When to Applaud Your Workers and When to Leave Them Alone," *Success!* February 1986, p. 8.

28. Charles A. Synder and Fred Luthans, "Using OB Mod to Increase Hospital Productivity," *Personnel Administrator*, August 1982, pp. 67–73.

29. Ibid., p. 70.

30. Kirk O'Hara, C. Merle Johnson, and Terry A. Beehr, "Organizational Behavior Management in the Private Sector: A Review of Empirical Research and Recommendations for Further Investigation," *Academy of Management Review*, October 1985, pp. 848–864.

31. "Conversations with B. F. Skinner," *Organizational Dynamics*, Winter 1973, p. 39.

32. Daniel Yankelovich, "Yankelovich on Today's Workers: We Need New Motivational Tools," *Industry Week*, August 6, 1979, p. 61.

33. James L. Gibson, John M. Ivancevich, and James H. Donnelly, Jr., *Organizations: Behavior, Structure, Processes*, 5th ed. (Plano, TX: Business Publications, 1985), p. 205.

34. Michael E. Cavanagh, "In Search of Motivation," *Personnel Journal*, March 1984, p. 77.

35. Richard D. Arvey and John M. Ivancevich, "Punishment in Organizations: A Review, Propositions, and Research Suggestions," *Academy of Management Review*, January 1980, pp. 123–132.

36. Mel E. Schnake, "Vicarious Punishment in a Work Setting," *Journal of Applied Psychology*, May 1986, pp. 343–345.

37. Richard Hamermesh, *Making Strategy Work: How Senior Managers Produce Results* (New York: Wiley, 1986).

38. Thomas J. Peters and Robert H. Waterman, Jr., *In Search of Excellence: Lessons from America's Best Run Companies* (New York: Harper & Row, 1982).

39. Cavanagh, "In Search of Motivation," p. 81.

40. Dov Eden, "Self-Fulfilling Prophecy as a Management Tool," *Academy of Management Review*, January 1984, pp. 64–73.

Suggested Reading

ACKERMAN, LEONARD, and GRUNEWALD, JOSEPH. "Help Employees Motivate Themselves." *Personnel Journal*, July 1984, pp. 54–62.

FEENEY, EDWARD J. "Modifying Employee Behavior: Making Rewards Pay Off." *Supervisory Management*, December 1985, pp. 25–27.

GUZZO, RICHARD A., JETTE, RICHARD D., and KATZELL, RAYMOND, A. "The Effects of Psychologically Based Intervention Programs on Worker Productivity: A Meta-Analysis." *Personnel Psychology*, Summer 1985, pp. 275–292.

HELMREICH, ROBERT L., SAWIN, LINDA L., and CARSRUD, ALAN L. "The Honeymoon Effect in Job Performance: Temporal Increases in the Predictive Power of Achievement Motivation." *Journal of Applied Psychology*, May 1986, pp. 185–188.

KILMANN, RALPH H. "Corporate Culture." *Psychology Today*, April 1985, pp. 62–68.

MITCHELL, TERENCE R. "Motivation: New Directions for Theory, Research and Practice." *Academy of Management Review*, January 1982, pp. 80–88.

"Money Isn't the Best Tool for Motivating Technical Professionals." *Personnel Administrator*, June 1985, pp. 63–76.

PINDER, CRAIG. *Work Motivation: Theory, Issues, and Applications.* Glenview, IL: Scott, Foresman, 1984.

"Roger Smith's Campaign to Change the GM Culture." *Business Week*, April 7, 1986, pp. 84–85.

SCOTT, W. E., JR., and PODSAKOFF, P. M. *Behavioral Principles in the Practice of Management.* New York: Wiley, 1985.

Job
Satisfaction
and Morale

LEARNING OBJECTIVES
*After studying this chapter and doing the
exercises, you should be able to*

1. Illustrate the difference between job satisfaction and motivation.
2. Pinpoint important consequences of job satisfaction and dissatisfaction.
3. Explain how job satisfaction is measured.
4. Identify major causes or contributors to job satisfaction.
5. Describe how modified work schedules and telecommuting contribute to job satisfaction and morale.

"Every day is a new challenge. I never know what tough problem is going to hit my desk. If I didn't have a job like this to look forward to, my life would be empty." (A truck fleet supervisor at a soft-drink bottling company)

"My job is a constant hassle. I'm tired of doing other people's dirty work. If I won a lottery tomorrow, I would kiss this job goodbye." (An expediter in a tire-manufacturing company)

The sentiments just expressed illustrate the range of attitudes people have toward their jobs. Some people find their jobs a major contributor to the quality of their lives, while others are intensely dissatisfied. The statements are also an indicator of job satisfaction and morale. **Job satisfaction** is the amount of pleasure or contentment associated with a job. **Morale** is a mixture of feelings, attitudes, and sentiments that contribute to a general feeling of satisfaction. These two meanings are so close that the terms can be used interchangeably. Both morale and satisfaction refer to contentment with one's job and one's employer.

Repeated studies have demonstrated that about three-fourths of workers, all categories combined, are reasonably satisfied with their jobs.[1] As you might suspect, people in high-level, well-paying, and prestigious jobs have the highest satisfaction. Job satisfaction is of current interest because of both humanitarian and economic reasons. High job satisfaction can lead to positive ends, such as loyalty to the company and good mental health. Low job satisfaction can lead to negative ends, such as high turnover and poor mental health. Our discussion of job satisfaction will include causes, consequences, measurement, and improvement.

ARE YOU SATISFIED, MOTIVATED, OR BOTH?

Job satisfaction and motivation are not identical. Satisfaction refers to satisfaction of a need often resulting in a state of contentment; motivation refers to expending effort toward a goal. One way to visualize the relationship between satisfaction and motivation is to use a four-way diagram indicating the extremes—highs and lows—with the middle conditions omitted. These four different possibilities are shown in Figure 3–1.

Contented, relaxed worker. Many people who have worked into a comfortable rut in a bureaucratic organization fall into this category. Some people derive job satisfaction from working in a relaxed, nonpressured atmosphere. If they

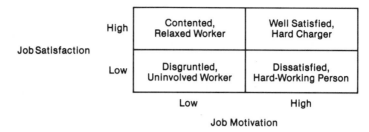

Figure 3–1 Four relationships between job satisfaction and motivation.

had to work too hard, they would experience job dissatisfaction. Family businesses too have their share of contented individuals who expend very little effort toward achieving company goals.

Disgruntled, uninvolved worker. People who fit into this category are often under stress. They dislike their jobs, yet work just hard enough to prevent being fired or receiving serious reprimands. Involuntary enlisted men often fall into this category. However, there are occasional people in managerial positions who dislike their jobs and are not particularly interested in working. Economic necessity (such as the need to pay bills) forces them to work.

Dissatisfied, hard-working person. Many people with a professional orientation work hard even if they are currently dissatisfied with their company, management, or working conditions. Often people with technical training find themselves in jobs that do not properly challenge their capacities. They nevertheless persevere, believing that conditions will improve or they can change jobs later. A professionally oriented person would not want to damage his or her reputation by performing poorly, even if a particular job were unsatisfying.

Well satisfied, hard charger. A person in this category is usually on the path toward self-fulfillment. A quarterback on a winning professional football team fits into this category. Many branch managers and successful small-business persons are also satisfied and hard-working. A young man with a small but busy and profitable landscaping business said of his work: "I happily work ten hours a day because landscaping is my thing."

CONSEQUENCES OF JOB SATISFACTION AND DISSATISFACTION

Extremes in satisfaction and morale are of major significance to individuals and the organization. Here we focus on the following consequences of job satisfaction and dissatisfaction: productivity, cooperative behavior and good citizenship, absenteeism and turnover, job stress, safety, quality of work life, and life satisfaction.

Productivity

One long-standing debate is whether high job satisfaction and morale improve productivity. The most accurate answer is that in the long-run, there are many instances in which job satisfaction does increase productivity. However, this is not always the case. For instance, "dissatisfied hard-chargers" are productive because they hope that hard work will lead them to a better job. Another exception is that a satisfied employee might have faulty equipment that lowers his or her productivity.

High job satisfaction is particularly important for the productivity of employees whose work involves extensive contact with people. One study showed that managers with high job satisfaction were more likely to:[2]

- Listen to others
- Show awareness and concern for the feelings of others
- Be tactful
- Have good emotional control
- Accept criticism

These behaviors are more likely to improve the productivity of workers whose jobs involve extensive contact with people. For instance, it is important for human resource specialists and sales representatives to listen to others and be tactful. Neither of these workers can be effective without listening to others and being tactful.

Cooperative Behavior and Good Citizenship

Although high satisfaction may not always lead to high productivity, it often leads to good results in other aspects of job performance. These helpful aspects of performance center around cooperative behavior and good citizenship. Specifically, employees with high job satisfaction are likely to:[3]

- Help co-workers with a job-related problem
- Accept orders without a fuss
- Tolerate temporary impositions without a complaint
- Help to keep the work area clean and uncluttered
- Make timely and constructive statements about the department or its manager to outsiders
- Promote a work climate that is tolerable and minimizes the distractions caused by conflict between workers
- Protect and conserve company resources such as parts, supplies, and money

Supervisors appreciate these behaviors because they make their job easier. If you exhibit the behaviors characteristic of a satisfied employee, it will strengthen your relationship with your boss.

Absenteeism and Turnover

Employees who dislike their jobs are absent more frequently and are also more likely to quit. This is one of the best-documented facts about the negative consequences of low job satisfaction. A recent synthesis of twenty-one studies has pinpointed which aspects of dissatisfaction contribute the most to absenteeism: (1) Absence frequency and duration (length of absence) is most closely associated with dissatisfaction with the work itself. (2) Absence frequently is related to dissatisfaction with co-workers and to overall satisfaction.[4]

Evidence also exists that if the cause of discontent is modified, job satisfaction will increase and turnover will decrease.[5] A supermarket manager describes an incident supporting this idea:

> Our turnover rate for checkout clerks was pushing 40 percent. That's too high even for this business. Our interviews with checkout clerks who quit showed that most of them objected to getting approval on checks for customers who had checking privileges. Waiting for a supervisor to approve the checks created delays in handling other customers. The checkout clerks hated the growling and angry stares from the impatient customers. We removed the check-approval requirement and our turnover decreased to 25 percent.

Job Stress and Burnout

Job stress is the body's response to any job-related factor that threatens to disturb the person's equilibrium. If stress is prolonged and intense, the employee may suffer a variety of ailments, including heart disease, blurred vision, ringing in the ears, backaches, and gastrointestinal disorders. **Job burnout** is a state of emotional, mental, and physical exhaustion in response to prolonged job stress. Full coverage of job stress and burnout appears in Chapter 5.

Chronic job dissatisfaction is a powerful source of stress and burnout. The employee may not see a satisfactory short-term solution to escaping this type of stress. An employee who feels trapped in a dissatisfying job may withdraw by such means as high absenteeism or tardiness; or the employee may quit.

Employees under prolonged job stress stemming from job dissatisfaction often consume too much alcohol, tobacco, prescription drugs, and illegal drugs. These employees are costly to the company in terms of time lost from the job and payments for medical expenses, including increased medical insurance premiums.

Safety

Poor safety practices are another negative consequence of low satisfaction and morale. Some of the lost time just mentioned can be attributed to job accidents. When people are discouraged about their jobs, they are more liable to have accidents. An underlying reason behind such accidents is that discouragement may take attention away from the task at hand, and inattention leads directly to accidents. Many hand injuries from power tools can be attributed to the operator not paying careful attention.

Quality of Work Life

Quality of work life (QWL) is the extent to which workers are able to satisfy important needs through their job and other experiences with the organization. Modern organizations devote considerable resources to helping employees achieve a high QWL. (Details about QWL programs will be presented in Chapter 15.) All these programs offer employees increased decision-making authority about important matters. The increased responsibility leads to increased job satisfaction for those employees who value more responsibility.

A high quality of work life can also be a consequence of job satisfaction stemming from other managerial action and programs. QWL can be regarded as an organizationwide state of high job satisfaction and morale. Employees who are satisfied with many elements of their job and the company will therefore experience a high quality of work life.

Life Satisfaction

Satisfaction with your job and career has a spillover effect on satisfaction with life. Research conducted with 1,100 workers over a four-year period found support for this consequence of job satisfaction. Specifically, the study found that increases in satisfaction with supervision, pay, and promotion are likely to increase life satisfaction. Conversely, decreases in these factors tend to decrease life satisfaction.[6]

The contribution of the study just mentioned is that it supports a long-standing belief of many human relations specialists: One of the best ways to lead a good life is to find a job and career to your liking.

THE MEASUREMENT OF JOB SATISFACTION AND MORALE

Organizations periodically measure job satisfaction for two reasons. First, they believe that job satisfaction is important in its own right. Second, they believe that measuring job satisfaction provides an index of organizational effectiveness (see Chapter 16). The three primary methods of measuring job satisfaction and morale are attitude surveys, observing actual behavior, and conducting executive rap sessions.

Employee Attitude Surveys

Attitude surveys are the standard method of measuring job satisfaction and morale. These surveys always involve written questionnaires but may also include interviews with employees. Interviews are helpful in explaining the meaning of survey findings. For instance, in one survey 75 percent of the employees said the company's salary system was unfair. Follow-up interviews helped uncover the reason for this perception. New employees were often hired at wages higher than current employees in comparable jobs.

Employee attitude surveys cover a wide range of topics related to job satisfaction and organizational effectiveness. Almost every survey asks questions about standard topics, such as attitudes toward the company and supervision, pay, and working conditions. The survey may also investigate attitudes toward topics of current concern, such as a takeover by another firm, or subcontracting of work to another country. Figure 3–2 lists topics frequently measured in attitude surveys.

Figure 3–2   Topics addressed in most employee attitude surveys.

Leadership, supervision, and management
Job itself
Co-workers
Physical working conditions
Pay, benefits, and other rewards
Career advancement and job security
Commitment to and identification with the organization
Job stress
Training and development
Physical environment
Disciplinary procedures
Management of the firm
Company culture (general working atmosphere)

SOURCE: Based on information in Maryellen Lo Bosco, "Employee Attitude Surveys," *Personnel*, April 1986, p. 65; David R. York, "Attitude Surveying," *Personnel Journal*, May 1985, p. 71.

Written questionnaires. Questionnaires based on rating scales are the most frequently used formal method of measuring job satisfaction and morale. An example of a widely used scale to measure job satisfaction is the Job Descriptive Index. The JDI measures attitudes in five areas: work, supervision, people, pay, and promotions. Respondents are asked to mark each one as yes (Y), no (N), or cannot decide (?) as it relates to their job. A sampling of these questions is given in Figure 3–3.

Figure 3–3   Sample items from the 72-item job descriptive index with "satisfied" responses
indicated.

___

Work

N	Routine
Y	Creative
N	Tiresome
Y	Gives a sense of accomplishment

People

Y	Stimulating
Y	Ambitious
N	Talk too much
N	Hard to meet

Promotions

Y	Good opportunity for advancement
Y	Promotion on ability
N	Dead-end job
N	Unfair promotion policy

Supervision

Y	Asks my advice
Y	Praises good work
N	Doesn't supervise enough
Y	Tells me where I stand

Pay

Y	Income adequate for normal expenses
N	Bad
N	Less than I deserve
N	Highly paid

___

SOURCE: The Job Descriptive Index is copyrighted by Bowling Green State University. The complete forms, scoring, key, instruction and norms can be obtained from Dr. Patricia Cain Smith, Department of Psychology, Bowling Green State University, Bowling Green OH 43404. Reprinted with permission.

Individual and group interviews. Interviews have three key purposes in an employee attitude survey. First, they can be used with a small sample of employees to identify topics worth exploring. Second, they can be used with small samples to learn directly about employee attitudes. Third, after the results are in, they can be used to explore some of the findings in depth.

Interviews offer the advantages of gaining in-depth information and exploring the causes of certain attitudes. Potential disadvantages of interviews are that they are time-consuming, cannot be conducted anonymously, and are subject to interview bias. Bias would occur, for example, if the interviewer had a preconceived idea of where employees stood on an issue. The interviewer might then look for statements to confirm his or her position.

Observing Actual Behavior

Employee attitudes can often be gauged by directly observing their behavior. Among the behaviors that suggest low satisfaction and morale are high absenteeism, turnover, tardiness, high scrap rates, low quality, time wasting, and reading the newspaper during working hours. In general, any form of psychological sabotage could be an indicator of job dissatisfaction.

Despite the obvious validity of linking satisfaction and behavior, the two may not be directly related in the short run. Some employees whose behavior is constructive may be harboring resentment. Their professional pride keeps their behavior on track, yet their dissatisfaction makes them turnover candidates.

Executive Rap Sessions

Another approach to measuring satisfaction and morale is for managers to meet with groups of employees and encourage them to express what is on their minds. **Executive rap sessions** are semi-structured meetings in which a top-level managers meets with a cross section of employees to discuss their concerns. These rap sessions are also referred to as *confrontation meetings* or *gripe sessions*. In a typical setup, a high-ranking manager would meet with a group of about fifty employees at their work site or in a company cafeteria. By encouraging employees to talk freely about their likes and dislikes, the executive hopes to measure the pulse of the organization.

Executive rap sessions do provide many insights about areas of satisfaction and dissatisfaction within the firm. An important limitation of this method is that many employees believe it is unwise to be observed making negative statements about the company. A human resource professional made this comment about the rap session:

> It would take a naive employee to "let it all hang out" at one of these sessions. Top management does have a sincere interest in learning about how employees see things. But if you are too negative in your statements, you can be branded as a troublemaker. Besides, many problems in the firm can be traced to the mistakes of top management. You don't hear many employees directly confronting top management.

Up to this point in the chapter we have examined the nature of satisfaction, along with its consequences, and how it is measured. We now focus on the reasons people experience job satisfaction and dissatisfaction.

CAUSES OF JOB SATISFACTION AND DISSATISFACTION

The two-factor theory of job motivation described in Chapter 2 is also an explanation of job satisfaction. The same elements that contribute to motivation also lead to satisfaction. For example, achieving recognition for one's ideas will both motivate and satisfy most people. Although the two-factor theory has merit in understanding the causes of job satisfaction, it is not the only plausible explanation. Here we present a list of external and internal causes of job satisfaction. External causes relate to the job and the company; internal causes relate to personality factors and personal attitudes.

Again, we caution that the general factors to be presented can be superseded by individual differences. For instance, "mentally challenging work" is a satisfier for most people. However, some people are dissatisfied with mentally challenging work because they prefer to daydream about personal life while at work.

External Causes of Job Satisfaction

The presence of the factors described below will cause or contribute to the job satisfaction of most employees with at least an average work ethic.[7] As you study these factors, evaluate whether they would enhance your job satisfaction.

Mentally challenging work. Most employees crave some intellectual challenge on the job. This need can be met by such means as a troubleshooting assignment, training another employee, or making suggestions for productivity improvement. For instance, an assistant restaurant manager might be asked how the restaurant can decrease the amount of food wasted in the kitchen.

Reasonable physical demands. Work that pushes an employee's physical limits usually becomes unsatisfying. Taxing physical work carried out for long periods of times becomes a source of physical and mental fatigue. A manager of an international company put it this way: "I've been flying back and forth between this country and far-flung locations for ten years. The wear and tear is getting to me. The flights themselves are bad enough. Being hung up in airports for hours and even days is worse. I want a different job where I can put most of my energy into the job rather than to surviving travel."

Contact with end user. The opportunity to interact with the person who ultimately uses your goods and services enhances job satisfaction.[8] Most jobs call for employees to submit their work to their boss or a co-worker, such as an assistant preparing a letter for the department manager. Contact with an end user of client includes these examples: a systems analyst talking to an office supervisor about the backlog of paperwork in the supervisor's department; a production worker visiting a customer to help install a piece of equipment.

Meaningful rewards. Job satisfaction increases directly when employees receive meaningful rewards for performance. A meaningful reward is fair, informative, and in line with a person's needs or goals. A *fair* reward is in line with the size of a worker's contribution. An example would be a note of congratulation from an executive for having performed well on a task force assignment.

An **informative** reward is one that tells you how well you have performed, such as a blinking computer message stating "You are 20 percent ahead of quota right now." A reward in line with one's needs or goals is a reward that has a high valence for the person. An example would be an employee who is heavily in debt receiving a large salary increase or bonus.

Rewards are so closely linked with job satisfaction that another explanation of the link is worthy of attention. According to the **performance-reward-satisfac-**

tion model, if you perform well and receive an equitable reward, your satisfaction will increase.[9] Your perception is important: Job satisfaction occurs only when you think the reward is fair and you perceive it to be valuable. A key implication of this model is that workers are satisfied when they perform well. The common-sense version of this relationship is that we perform well on those tasks we find satisfying.

Helpful co-workers and superiors. Helpful in this sense means giving the employee an opportunity to achieve important job values such as interesting work, pay, and promotions. Job satisfaction is also enhanced when co-workers and superiors have basic values that mesh with others of the employees. For example, an employee with a strong work ethic will experience job satisfaction if he or she works with others who value hard work. Furthermore, the co-workers and superiors should minimize conflict and confusion.

Internal Causes of Job Satisfaction

The causes of job satisfaction described in this section stem primarily from personality characteristics and personal values. However, internal factors also influence whether external factors cause satisfaction. A good example would be the performance-reward-satisfaction model described above: Satisfaction occurs when the person perceives the reward to be fair and valuable.

Interest in the work itself. Job satisfaction stems directly from being interested in what you are doing. Terms to describe this inherent interest in work include *craft instinct, pride in work,* and *self-rewarding work.* Whichever term is used, the message is the same: People who love their work experience high job satisfaction.

Work fitting one's job values. Major job values include autonomy (independence), creativity, helping others, security, and performing technical work.[10] To the extent that employees' jobs allow them to perform work that satisfies these values, their satisfaction will increase. For example, many supervisors have high job satisfaction because they can both help people and stay close to technical work at the same time. (This cause of job satisfaction illustrates the relationship between external and internal states. The job giving you an opportunity to satisfy your values is external, yet your values are internal.)

A feeling of self-esteem. Work that satisfies a person's need for self-esteem contributes directly to job satisfaction. High-status occupations contribute more to self-esteem than do those of low status. The individual in search of self-esteem on the job is thus dependent upon society's perceptions of the status of specific occupations. Feelings of self-esteem also stem from doing work the individual sees as worthwhile. This perception is less influenced by external standards than is the status associated with a particular job or occupation.

Optimism and flexibility. An optimistic and flexible person is predisposed to be a satisfied employee. A pessimistic and rigid person will most likely be a dissatisfied employee. Every company has its share of "pills" who always find something to complain about. No matter what the company does to satisfy such a person, he or she finds another source of dissatisfaction.

Positive self-image. As Robert A. Baron observes, people possessing a positive self-image are generally more satisfied with their jobs than those possessing a negative self-image.[11] A possible explanation is that the people who view themselves negatively tend to view most things negatively. This is similar to the adage: "You have to like yourself first before you can like other people." In this case, you have to like yourself first before you can like your job.

Positive expectations about the job. People with positive expectations about their jobs are frequently more satisfied than those with low expectations. These expectations illustrate a self-fulfilling prophecy: if you expect to like your job, you will behave in such a way that those expectations will be met. Similarly, if you expect your job not to satisfy your needs, you will do things to make your expectations come true. Assume that a person expects to earn low commissions in a sales job. The person's negativism may come through to customers and prospective customers, thus ensuring low commissions.

Good personal adjustment. People who report good personal adjustment away from work tend to have above-average job satisfaction. One reason is that an enjoyable personal life makes job frustrations more tolerable. A more fundamental reason offered by Robert A. Baron is that the skills that help you do well in personal life are also helpful on the job. Among these skills are the ability to get along with others, and to face situations confidently.[12]

GENERAL STRATEGIES FOR IMPROVING SATISFACTION AND MORALE

Since job satisfaction and morale have such important consequences, many managerial activities are directed toward improving satisfaction and morale. It can be argued that almost any constructive action taken by a manager will have some positive impact on satisfaction and morale. A discussion of strategies for improving satisfaction and morale therefore encompasses all of what is known about being an effective manager. Here we will sample several general strategies. In the next two sections of the chapter, we describe the use of modified work schedules to improve satisfaction.

Design Jobs with Satisfying Elements

The entire discussion of external causes of job satisfaction could be converted into a strategy for designing jobs that would be satisfying to most people. Specifically, a job that had these characteristics would result in high job satisfaction and morale for most workers:

1. Mentally challenging work
2. Reasonable physical demands
3. Contact with end user
4. Meaningful rewards (fair, informative, and matched to needs and goals)
5. Helpful co-workers and superiors

Jobs that have such characteristics are said to be enriched. More will be said about job enrichment in Chapter 16.

Remedy Substandard Conditions

The commonsense solution to job satisfaction and morale problems is to remove substandard conditions. In a nursing home, job satisfaction was elevated to tolerable levels only after attendants and food-preparation workers were given a substantial pay increase. In this situation, pay was a substandard condition.

The strategy of remedying substandard conditions assumes that the true underlying problem has been recognized. Employees may complain about something in the work environment, such as poor air conditioning. If their underlying dissatisfaction is really with the quality of supervision—but they are afraid to say so—changing the air conditioning will not improve satisfaction.

Display Concern for Employees

Managers who openly show concern for the feelings, attitudes, and opinions of employees contribute to high morale. People feel better and often work better when they receive reassurance and support from the boss. Concern for employees can also be expressed by such means as asking for suggestions, expressing sympathy about employee problems, and asking questions about an employee's family.

Another important way of being considerate is to pay attention to employees. A standard managerial technique for paying attention to employees is to visit them at their work areas periodically. During the visit, the manager can chat with the employee about work-related topics and solicit ideas for improvement. These periodic incidents of *management by wandering around* should not be overdone; the purpose of management by wandering around is for the manager to keep in touch with people and problems, not to interrupt the flow of work.

Change the Perceptions of Dissatisfied Employees

Job dissatisfaction stems from an employee's perceptions of a particular situation or event. If the perception is clearly inaccurate, the manager can improve satisfaction by helping the employee see the situation more accurately. Often the misperception is based on incorrect information. Assuming the supervisor and other managers are trusted, the dissatisfaction can be remedied by providing employees with new information.

> A group of construction workers expressed dissatisfaction about wages to their supervisor. Their point of contention was that, "Out of state, construction workers get triple-time for work on Sundays and holidays. We only get double-time." The construction supervisor in charge gathered salary data from two out-of-state construction sites. In both sites, the construction workers were receiving double-time for Sundays and holidays. Sharing this information with the construction workers mollified the dissatisfaction over wages.

BOOSTING SATISFACTION AND MORALE THROUGH MODIFIED WORK SCHEDULES

A widely used specific method of boosting job satisfaction and morale is to give employees more say about their hours of work. As noted in Chapter 1, flexible working hours can also increase productivity. For many employees in private and public firms, the standard 8-hour day with fixed starting and stopping times has ended. A variety of modified work schedules have replaced the standard week.

A **modified work schedule** is any formal departure from the traditional hours of work, excluding shift work and staggered work hours. Shift work refers to working evenings or nights instead of days; staggered work hours refer to employees in the same firm working different eight-hour blocks, such as 10 to 6 instead of 9 to 5. The two most widely used modified work schedules are flextime and the compressed work week. Telecommuting and job sharing are also gaining acceptance.

Flextime

Flextime is a method of organizing the hours of work so that employees have flexibility in choosing their own hours. Flextime is also called *flexitime* and *flexible working hours*. More frequent use is made of flextime in offices than in factories, mills, foundries, construction sites, or stores. The major reason is that the system works best when employees do not depend on each other for accomplishing work. Office employees can often do their work by themselves. In contrast, in a lumber mill, certain work would have to stop if the crane operator were not on the job.

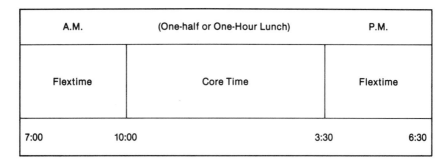

A.M.	(One-half or One-Hour Lunch)	P.M.
Flextime	Core Time	Flextime
7:00 10:00	3:30	6:30

Figure 3–4 Typical flextime working hours schedule.

The basic format of flextime is straightforward. As shown in Figure 3–4, a core is typically from 10 A.M. to 3:30 P.M. Employees would then be free to choose which hours from 7 A.M. to 10 A.M., and from 3:30 P.M. to 6:30 P.M. they wanted to work. Time-recording machines are often used to monitor whether employees have put in their fair share of work for the week. For the vast majority of organizations today, this means 37 ½ or 40 hours.

A variation of this basic format is to divide the core into two time blocks and the flextime into three blocks. This arrangement is shown in Figure 3–5. Under the two-core/three flextime schedule, employees have a greater opportunity to take care of personal business during the day.

Flextime's Contribution to Satisfaction

Numerous reports and studies have shown that flextime enhances job satisfaction. It will be sufficient here to summarize the results of one large study and one report.

Flextime in three service industries. A study of company experience with clerical workers on flextime was conducted among 400 companies in the banking,

A.M.	(One-half or One-Hour Lunch)			P.M.
Flextime	Core Time	Flextime	Core Time	Flextime
7:00 10:00	11:30	1:30	3:30	6:30

Figure 3–5 Flextime schedule with two core periods.

insurance, and utility industries.[13] The results were based on the reports of company officials, not experimental results. In all three industries, an overwhelming majority of company officials noted greater levels of job satisfaction with flextime. Flextime was noted as making a contribution to job satisfaction by 94 percent of banks, 93 percent of insurance companies, and 100 percent of gas and electric companies. Job satisfaction levels did not change for 5 percent of the banks studied, and for 7 percent of the insurance companies.

Flextime was also found to boost productivity (as measured by quantity and quality of work), decrease lateness and absenteeism, and reduce the amount of overtime used. The results of this survey could therefore be interpreted as indirect evidence that job satisfaction can lead to productivity improvement.

Modified work schedule in a government agency. A program of modified work schedules was implemented in the New York City Human Resources Administration. The program included staggered hours, flexible hours, and compressed time. A union official observed that the program has been advantageous to the parents of small children attending day care centers or school. It has helped ease commuting difficulties, and has relieved worker anxiety about being late for work. Finally, modified work schedules have facilitated employees advancing their education.[14]

Compressed Workweek

A **compressed work week** is a full-time work schedule that allows 40 hours to be accomplished in less than 5 days. The usual arrangement is 4-40 (working four 10-hour days). The 4-40 schedule is the second most frequent modified work schedule. Many employees enjoy the 4-40 schedule because it enables them to have three consecutive days off from work. A 4-40 schedule usually allows most employees to take off Saturdays and Sundays. Important exceptions include police workers, hospital employees, and computer operators.

A relatively infrequent compressed work week, the 3-38 work schedule, was implemented for 84 information systems personnel.[15] Under a 3-38 schedule, the employee crams a full week's work into three work days of approximately $12\frac{1}{2}$ hours. One reason for trying the 3-38 schedule was that information systems workers were regularly assigned to overtime. The resulting 6- and 7-day weeks became a source of frustration and fatigue for many workers. Management reasoned that 3-38 would enable 6-day coverage, using two $12\frac{1}{2}$ hour shifts per day. At the same time, there would be no overtime and no reduction in pay from that earned under the 5-40 schedule.

In addition to modifying the regular work schedule, the information systems workers also had their jobs upgraded. Prior to going on 3-38, there were three different jobs, each performed by different employees. The job titles were Burster/Decollator, Input/Output Operators, and Console Operators. To implement the new schedule, all employees had to do all jobs. The effect was to enlarge the variety of tasks and increase responsibility.

SKI PLANT ON PERMANENT THREE-DAY WEEKENDS

Middletown, Conn.—Sometimes when William Riviere mentions his company's four-day work week to outsiders, they think business must be bad. But that's not the case at Olin Ski Co., Inc., a leading maker of high-quality, premium-priced skis. Olin put most of its employees on a Monday-Thursday work schedule in 1972 to compete for labor and to accommodate a younger work force, says Riviere, vice president of manufacturing and engineering.

"It's a job satisfier. It makes it attractive to work at Olin Ski. It's been a good recruiting tool," he says. "Probably one of the first things out of their mouths when they come in for an interview is: "What's your four-day work schedule like?"

A company survey five years ago found that about 98 percent of its workers preferred their four 10-hour days to the traditional five 8-hour days, Riviere says. And today, opinion among the 220 employees in a work force that remains nonunion seems to be just as strong.

"I love it. That was the reason I came to work here. I like my three-day weekends," said a 27-year-old production employee who has worked in the ski factory for nine years.

"I think it's great," agreed a production employee who joined the company shortly before the change. "Everybody likes the four-day week. If they went to five days, a lot would leave."

When Olin decided to try a four-day 40-hour week, the concept was just beginning to get attention from North American businesses. Later in the 1970s when the energy crisis forced awareness of fuel consumption, the four-day week interested more companies, as well as state and local governments, as a way to cut energy costs. Some tried it, while others never got beyond the study stage.

From Olin's point of view, it has gotten what it sought from its schedule. "It's well liked by employees," Riviere says. "Employees tend to be a little more enthusiastic when they come to work, knowing they have only four days to work. It helps draw people to the company."

Anne Peabody, personnel administrator, said that two years after the new schedule was instituted, absenteeism had improved by about 1 percent, but it has not been measured since then. Productivity dropped for several months after the switch, but later exceeded the five-day levels, said a former personnel director at the company.

Source: Excerpted with permission from Deborah Mesce, "Ski Plant on Permanent 3-Day Weekends," Associated Press, July 28, 1984.

The new work schedule deviated substantially from a traditional one. The day shift was from 6:00 A.M. to 6:30 P.M. Monday through Saturday; the night shift was 6:00 P.M. to 6:30 A.M. Sunday through Saturday. Overtime pay was granted for hours beyond $12\frac{1}{2}$; on Saturdays and Sundays employees earned time-and-a-half, assuming they had already worked $37\frac{1}{2}$ hours. (Before reading of the effect of this schedule on job satisfaction, imagine your attitude toward such a schedule.)

Job satisfaction was measured with several questionnaires, including the Job Descriptive Index. Eighteen months after implementation, employees assigned to a 3-38 schedule still preferred it over their previous work arrangement with the company. The employees most likely to favor the new schedule (1) participated in the decision to implement the new schedule; (2) received an upgraded job with the schedule; and (3) had strong higher-order needs (as measured by a separate questionnaire).

Several results of the study tied in with productivity. Fatigue did not appear to be a problem. Payoffs to the organization included reductions in sick time, overtime, and personal leave time.

Telecommuting

Another deviation from the traditional work schedule is **telecommuting,** an arrangement in which employees perform their regular work duties from home or at another location. Usually the employees use computers tied into the company's main office. Yet you can be a telecommuter, or teleworker, without a computer. For instance, you might work at home as an advertising copywriter, a garment maker, or a drafting technician. In addition to communicating by computer, telecommuters also attend meetings on company premises, and stay in telephone contact. It has been predicted that by 1990 the number of telecommuters could reach 10 million.[16]

Advantages of telecommuting. Telecommuting can work well with self-reliant, self-starting, and self-disciplined employees. Telecommuters are usually people who request such an arrangement, and therefore they are likely to experience high morale and satisfaction when given the chance to work at home. Telecommuting offers these potential advantages to the employer:[17]

> *Increased productivity.* Where direct measurements have been possible, productivity increases have averaged about 20 percent.
>
> *Lower overhead.* Since the employees are providing some of their own office space, the company can operate with smaller offices.
>
> *Reduced absenteeism and turnover.* It takes a serious illness for an employee not to be able to work at home. Turnover is decreased because telecommuting jobs are not yet in ample supply.
>
> *Availability of employees in emergency situations.* It is easier to get an employee out of bed to rush to his or her den than to the office. (Critics contend that employees whose computers are hooked to the company mainframe are being exploited because of their constant availability for work.)
>
> *Access to a wider range of employee talent.* This wider talent bank includes parents with young children, employees who find commuting uncomfortable, and others who live far away from the firm.

Telecommuting at a computer consulting firm. One of the most extensive uses of telecommuting is at F International, a computer consulting firm founded by Steve Shirley. Her firm (Shirley is a woman) specializes in designing integrated office information systems, evaluating hardware and software, and helping managers use micro and personal computers. F International employs more than a thousand freelancers in the United Kingdom, the Netherlands, and Denmark. All the freelancers work from their homes, including Shirley. About 84 percent of the employees are women.

The consultants spend about 40 percent of their time working at home; the balance of their work is spent on client premises. Most of the communication among employees takes place by phone and at periodic company meetings. Asked how she organizes and oversees the work of more than a thousand employees working from home, Shirley replied:[18]

> Quality control, which is what you're talking about, is no different in a service industry than on a production line. You take samples so that every now and again you actually have a look.

Job Sharing

Job sharing is a modified work schedule in which two people share the same job, both usually working half-time. The people sharing the job might be two friends, a husband and wife, or two employees who did not know each other before sharing a job. An example of job sharing would be for one person to work mornings, and the other to work afternoons. If the job were complex, the two sharers would have to spend some overlap time discussing the job.

Job sharing has its greatest appeal to people whose family responsibilities are incompatible with a full-time job. A typical situation of job sharing comes about when two friends decide they both want a responsible job, but can only work part-time. Employers benefit from job sharing because employees are likely to be more productive in 4 hours than in 8 hours of work. Also, if one employee is sick, the other will still be available to handle the job for the half day.

Job sharing has several disadvantages to the employees and the employer. You are unlikely to be recommended for promotion if you can only make a half-time commitment to the firm. The firm may have difficulty evaluating, supervising, and rewarding job sharers. For example, should both receive identical raises? How does the company know which should receive credit or blame when something goes right or wrong?

Why Modified Work Schedules Improve Job Satisfaction

Modified work schedules, particularly flextime, boost job satisfaction for two important reasons. One underlying reason is that employees appreciate exerting control over their work schedules. Flextime is a form of participative decision making: Employees help decide which hours of the day they will work. Control and participation of this kind gives employees the feeling that they are being treated as responsible adults.

Another important reason is that modified work schedules make life easier for many employees. Since employees are not confined to the conventional work day, they can accomplish such personally important things as:

- Sleep late on work days
- Avoid rush-hour commuting
- Attend conferences with children's teachers
- Take care of personal errands such as visits to physicians, dentists, psychotherapists, banks, car dealers, and realtors during normal working hours. (This is an advantage because not all these matters can be handled at nights and on Saturdays.)
- Avoid the routine of fixed working hours
- Schedule vacations at times when recreation facilities are not overly crowded

Summary of Key Points

☐ Job satisfaction is the amount of pleasure or contentment associated with a job. Morale is a mixture of feelings, attitudes, and sentiments that contribute to a general feeling of satisfaction. About three-fourths of workers, all categories combined, are reasonably satisfied with their jobs.

☐ Job satisfaction and motivation are not identical. People can experience different or similar levels of satisfaction and motivation at the same time. One example is the well-motivated person who works hard despite dissatisfaction with the present job.

☐ Job satisfaction and dissatisfaction have many important consequences to the individual and the organization. Job satisfaction sometimes leads to increased productivity, particularly for jobs dealing with people. Other consequences of satisfaction and dissatisfaction are related to (1) cooperative behavior and good citizenship, (2) absenteeism and turnover, (3) job stress and burnout, (3) safety, (4) quality of work life, and (5) life satisfaction.

☐ Job satisfaction and morale are frequently measured because they are important themselves and are related to organizational effectiveness. The three primary methods of measuring job satisfaction and morale are employee attitude surveys, observing actual behavior, and conducting executive rap sessions. Attitude surveys use both written questionnaires and interviews.

☐ Job satisfaction is caused by both external and internal factors; however, a person's perception influences whether an external factor leads to satisfaction. External causes of job satisfaction include: mentally challenging work, reasonable physical demands, contact with end user, meaningful rewards, and helpful co-workers and superiors. Internal causes of job satisfaction include: interest in the work itself, work fitting one's job values, a feeling of self-esteem, optimism and flexibility, a positive self-image, positive expectations about the job, and good personal adjustment.

☐ Many managerial activities are geared toward improving satisfaction and morale. A sampling of general strategies toward this end are: design jobs with satisfying elements, remedy substandard conditions, display concern for employees, and change the perceptions of dissatisfied employees.

☐ Modified work schedules are formal departures from the traditional hours of work, excluding shift work and staggered work hours. Flextime is a method of organizing the hours of work so that employees have flexibility in choosing their own hours. Employees are required to work one or two core periods, but can vary their starting and stopping times. Flextime is known to have a positive impact on satisfaction, and may also improve productivity.

☐ A compressed work week is a full-time work schedule that allows 40 hours to be accomplished in less than 5 days, such as 40 hours of work in 3 days. Telecommuting is an arrangement in which employees perform regular work duties from home or another location. Most telecommuting jobs involve communication over a computer. Job sharing is a modified work schedule in which two people share the same job, both usually working half-time.

☐ Modified work schedules contribute to job satisfaction for two general reasons. First, employees enjoy exerting control over their own schedules. Second, these schedules make it easier for employees to manage both their careers and personal life.

Questions and Activities

1. Some management experts think that too much attention is being paid to job satisfaction by organizations. In your opinion, should organizations pay so much attention to job satisfaction?

2. What would it take to satisfy you on the job?

3. Ask an experienced manager or business owner what it takes to satisfy employees these days. Be ready to discuss your findings in class.

4. Give two examples of low-paying jobs that probably provide high satisfaction.

5. Give two examples of high-paying jobs that probably provide low job satisfaction.

6. How do cooperative behavior and good citizenship contribute to productivity?

7. What improvements in personal life do you think are the most likely to lead to improvements in job satisfaction?

8. What would be a "meaningful reward" for you?

9. Do managers need flextime? Why or why not?

10. Assume that you are responsible for hiring three telecommuters. What information about a candidate would you want to convince yourself that he or she would work effectively as a telecommuter?

A Human Relations Case
THE DISGRUNTLED CHECKOUT CLERKS

Rite-Buy is a chain of twenty-one supermarkets, spread out over a two-hundred-mile geographic radius. The company has been in business for thirty-five years and is generally profitable. Despite the presence of larger supermarket firms in their areas, Rite-Buy has been able to hold a satisfactory share of the market. The firm caters to the middle-class and lower-middle-class buyer wants to avoid both high prices and poor quality food.

Rite-Buy's biggest business problem is high employee turnover, particularly among checkout clerks. Melody Parker, vice-president of personnel, was asked by the president to investigate the problem and make some recommendations. Three months later she was asked to present her preliminary findings. She told the president: "I see no strong pattern yet. The best I can come up with is that most of our checkout clerks dislike their jobs. I have conducted exit interviews with a dozen or so clerks who have resigned in the last few months. I have also interviewed employees who have stayed on the payroll more than four months.

"Maybe we need a more systematic study. But I don't notice anything in particular Rite-Buy can do other than double the wages of checkout clerks, and decrease the number of customers they have to serve. If we carried out either action, Rite-Buy would go belly up. To reach the financial goals you have established for the firm, the store managers cannot offer higher wages."

The president said to Parker: "Let me see some of the interview reports. I'd like to review a handful myself, to see if I can find a trend."

"Okay," said Parker, "I'll be back in a few moments with some of my interview notes. I'll get the file for the checkout clerks. Our turnover rates for workers in other areas are about right for the industry."

Twenty minutes later, Parker brought her file to the president. He glanced through the file, and then began to read them in order. Excerpts of these interviews follow.

Bill Kingsley, 18-year-old high school graduate: I'm leaving Rite-Buy because this job is the pits. You work harder than on an assembly line and the pay is much lower. I could take the job part-time when I was in high school. Now I need to make a better buck. I know I can do better than $5 per hour someplace else.

Nellie Baxter, 59-year-old full-time employee: I'm sorry I'm leaving the job because the hours were good. I liked the way my schedule would change from week to week. But my feet, legs, and arms can't take it anymore. I'm so sore after a day's work that I usually have to soak in a tub of hot water for an hour when I come home. Then I hardly have energy for anything else but watching a little TV and going to sleep.

Sue Godwin, 33-year-old part-time employee: I'm not leaving because of Rite-Buy management. You guys are great. It's the customers that are driving me away. You managers should work a checkout counter every once and awhile. The worst people are the coupon clippers. They have no mercy. The line can be twenty customers long and they drag out a month's supply of coupons for you to redeem. You can feel the pressure building up as the person in back of the coupon clipper gets impatient.

The coupon clippers aren't nearly as bad as the weirdos who challenge you on every price. They have the nerve to say things like, "I thought the diet soda was on special today. You gave me the regular price." Even worse they tell you when you have overcharged them one cent on a twenty-five-pound bag of dog food.

Manuel Garcia, 22-year-old full-time worker: I'm leaving out of respect for my friends and personal life. How can a single guy develop a good social life when he has to work most nights and Sundays? I miss being out with my friends. You tell me that if I keep up the good work, I might become a store manager. The problem is that the store manager has an even worse schedule than a checkout clerk. I hope to find an office job.

Sandra Yang, 28-year-old full-time worker: I found the job too physically confining. I always felt boxed in this little work area. The register is in front of me, and the shelf for bagging is right in back of me. You have about as much room to move around in as a bus driver. I'm the physical type who likes some space. Besides that, work like this can give you varicose veins. I'm looking for a job that's better for me physically.

With a sigh of exasperation, the president said to Melody: "I see what you mean that there's no consistent pattern. The checkout clerks who have left have different opinions about what's wrong with the job. If you hear of any fully automated checkout counters, let me know. In the meantime, keep working on the problem. I'll also give it some thought."

1. What recommendations would you make for reducing the turnover of the checkout clerks?
2. Should Melody Parker also be interviewing the clerks who were so satisfied with their jobs that they did not quit?
3. Evaluate Melody's position that store managers cannot afford to pay higher wages for checkout clerks.

A Human Relations Incident

THE LAID-BACK FINANCIAL CONSULTANTS

Boston Securities, Inc., a stockbroker and financial services firm, recently plowed back much of its profits into improving physical working conditions. Improvements in the home office included: free coffee, soft drinks, and tea for all employees; membership in a health club for all professional and managerial employees; personal computers for all financial consultants (formerly referred to as stockbrokers); comfortable new furniture in all offices; and occasional seminars on topics such as health and fitness, conducted during working hours.

Six months after initiating these morale builders, the executive group at Boston Securities decided to evaluate their effectiveness. Maureen DuVal, vice-president of financial planning services, made an analysis that was readily accepted by the other executives. Her words were: "I'm afraid we've gone overboard on building morale. We've developed a bunch of contented cows. Our consultants just aren't hustling for business as much as they did in the past. We've created a resort atmosphere at Boston Securities. We may not have planned to lower productivity, but our generosity accomplished just that.

"If we reverse gears we may have an even bigger problem. It's an old human relations adage that you cannot take away something you have given to employees. The adage holds up even with professionals. I hope we haven't brought upon ourselves a monster problem."

1. How plausible is DuVal's analysis that the morale boosters implemented by the firm have lowered productivity?
2. If DuVal's analysis is correct, what can be done about the problem?

3. What do you think of the adage that management cannot take back anything given to employees?

Notes

1. "Our Love of Labor Not Lost," *USA Weekend*, August 29–31, 1986, p. 14. A synthesis of less recent information on this topic is found in Dennis W. Organ and W. Clay Hamner, *Organizational Behavior: An Applied Psychological Approach*, rev. ed. (Plano, TX: Business Publications, 1982), p. 224.

2. Stephen J. Motowidlo, "Does Job Satisfaction Lead to Consideration and Personal Sensitivity?" *Academy of Management Journal*, December 1984, p. 914.

3. Thomas S. Bateman and Dennis W. Organ, "Job Satisfaction and the Good Soldier: The Relationship between Affect and Employee 'Citizenship'," *Academy of Management Journal*, December 1983, p. 588.

4. K. Scott Dow and G. Stephen Taylor, "An Examination of Conflicting Findings on the Relationship Between Job Satisfaction and Absenteeism: A Meta-Analysis," *Academy of Management Journal*, September 1985, p. 608.

5. Charles L. Hulin, "Effects of Changes in Job Satisfaction Levels on Employee Turnover," *Journal of Applied Psychology*, April 1968, pp. 122–126.

6. Thomas I. Chacko, "Job and Life Satisfactions: A Causal Analysis of their Relationships," *Academy of Management Journal*, March 1983, p. 167.

7. The general list is based on Edwin A. Locke, "The Nature and Causes of Job Satisfaction," in *Handbook of Industrial and Organizational Psychology*, ed. Marvin D. Dunnette (New York: Wiley, 1986), p. 1328. This book is a reprint of the 1976 edition published by Rand McNally.

8. Frederick Herzberg, "The Wise Old Turk," *Harvard Business Review*, September–October 1974, pp. 70–80.

9. Edward E. Lawler III and Lyman W. Porter, "The Effects of Performance on Satisfaction," *Industrial Relations*, October 1967, pp. 20–28.

10. Thomas J. DeLong, "Reexamining the Career Anchor Model," *Personnel*, May–June 1982, p. 53.

11. This and the next two factors are credited to Robert A. Baron, *Understanding Human Relations: A Practical Guide to People at Work* (Newton, MA: Allyn & Bacon, 1985), pp. 315–316.

12. Ibid.

13. J. Carroll Swart, "Clerical Workers on Flexitime: A Survey of Three Industries," *Personnel*, April 1985, pp. 40–44.

14. "Human Resources Update," *Research Institute Personal Report for the Executive*, May 14, 1985, p. 8.

15. Janina C. Latack and Lawrence W. Foster, "Implementation of Compressed Work Schedules: Participation and Job Redesign As Critical Factors for Employee Acceptance," *Personnel Psychology*, Spring 1985, pp. 75–92.

16. "Telecommuting: Is Your Operation Ready?" *Research Institute Personal Report for the Executive*, July 15, 1986, pp. 4–5.

17. Marcia M. Kelly, "The Next Workplace Revolution: Telecommuting," *Supervisory Management*, October 1985, pp. 2–4; "Telecommuting," *Research Institute*, p. 5.
18. Eliza G. C. Collins, "A Company Without Offices," *Harvard Business Review*, January–February 1986, p. 127.

Suggested Reading

BULLOCK, R. J. *Improving Job Satisfaction* (Work in America Studies in Productivity No. 35). Elmsford, NY: Pergamon Press, 1984.

DUNHAM, RANDALL B., and PIERCE, JON L. "Attitude Toward Work Schedules: Construct Definition, Instrument Development, and Validation." *Personnel Psychology*, March 1986, pp. 170–182.

HOLLOWAY, WILLIAM W. "Coping with Employee Turnover in the Age of High Technology." *Personnel Administrator*, May 1985, pp. 108–115.

IVANCEVICH, JOHN M. "Predicting Absenteeism from Prior Absence and Work Attitudes." *Academy of Management Journal*, March 1985, pp. 219–227.

LOHER, BRIAN T., and others. "A Meta-Analysis of the Relation of Job Characteristics to Job Satisfaction." *Journal of Applied Psychology*, May 1985, pp. 280–289.

MARTINSON, OSCAR B., and WILKENING, E. A. "Rural-Urban Differences in Job Satisfaction: Further Evidence." *Academy of Management Journal*, March 1984, pp. 199–206.

NIEHOUSE, OLIVER L. "Job Satisfaction: How to Motivate Today's Workers." *Supervisory Management*, February 1986, pp. 8–11.

NORRIS, DWIGHT R., and NIEBUHR, ROBERT E. "Attributional Influences on the Job Performance–Job Satisfaction Relationship." *Academy of Management Journal*, June 1984, pp. 424–431.

PASCARELLA, PERRY. *The New Achievers*. New York: Free Press, 1984.

RONEN, SIMCHA. *Alternative Work Schedules: Selecting, Implementing, and Evaluating.* Homewood, IL: Dow-Jones Irwin, 1984.

Creativity and Decision Making

LEARNING OBJECTIVES
After reading and studying this chapter and doing the exercises, you should be able to

1. Explain the meaning of creativity and how it fits into decision making.
2. Identify the stages of creative thought.
3. Recognize the contribution of intuition to decision making.
4. Acquire preliminary insight into your own creative potential.
5. Become a more creative problem solver.
6. Describe how the organizational climate and culture influence creativity.
7. Understand how entrepreneurship and intrapreneurship are related to creativity.

Insurance broker James W. Barrett formed a company to specialize in space flight insurance. As he tells the story, the idea of space flight insurance began over 25 years ago. He had just started his own business—in itself unique—insuring overseas Americans in the State Department and the Peace Corps. "But initially I didn't have enough work to keep me busy. So I would drift in once or twice a week."

It was during that time that the pioneering Communications Satellite Corporation, which had only just been formed, was very much in the press. "I found the idea fascinating and had been keeping up with it. Suddenly it dawned on me. These people are going to have to insure. I scratched my head on the subject for a time."

"One day I took the opportunity to call Comsat. Here I was, a 30-year-old. I screwed up my courage and picked up the phone and called. Up to then Comsat had never even thought about insuring satellites. They were so busy trying to get themselves started up. Nevertheless, they talked to me. A number of meetings followed these initial phone calls. A concept of insurance began to emerge. But, good Lord, it was really tough going. It involved a great deal of explaining the complexities of space flight.

"I was an insurance broker, and no insurance company had heard of anything like this. To line up underwriters who would share the risk of an expensive launch, I telephoned at least 50 companies. Those I got to see were few and far between. Aetna was the first one to look at me as if I wasn't crazy."[1]

This case illustrates how creative thinking can have a big impact on a career. At least twice in his career, Barrett observed something that others in the same field had overlooked: Space flights might need to be insured. Creativity can help you in a wide variety of jobs, including those that are basically routine. For example, a clerk in the circulation department of a newspaper noticed that although the cost of first-class mail kept increasing, the number of complaints about service also kept increasing. His conclusion was not to figure out a way of revamping the postal system, but to have his newspaper take over part of the postal system's job. Subsequently, the newspaper he worked for was the first to insert advertising flyers previously sent by mail inside their newspapers. This simple combination of ideas helped that individual eventually to become circulation director.

As implied from these examples, **creativity** is the ability to develop good ideas that can be put into action. The definition presented here was developed by advertising executive Edward H. Meyer, whose business requires a constant outpouring of creativity.[2] **Creative problem solving** stems from creativity. It is ability to overcome obstacles by approaching them in novel ways.[3] The potential contribution of creativity to organizational effectiveness has been explained in these terms:[4]

> Creative decision making and problem solving are two of the most important talents that employees can possess, talents that are necessary for the financial health and prosperity of any firm. Unless a firm can respond with unique products/services, innovative marketing strategies, and creative responses to complex problems, it may find itself losing sales, shares of the market, and profits.

To study creativity, we will first explore its nature, and then explain how creativity fits into decision making. Then we focus on such topics as measuring and developing creativity, the organization's role in fostering creativity, and the creative aspects of entrepreneurs and intrapreneurs.

THE STAGES OF CREATIVE THOUGHT

Since the importance of creativity has long been recognized, much effort has been devoted to understanding the process by which creative ideas surface. Here we are concerned with the five stages in a person's thinking and behavior that produce a creative result.[5]

1. *Problem finding.* The individual discovers that something is worth working on or becomes aware that a problem or disturbance exists. A housing developer might say, "People are getting more and more concerned about the cost of heating and cooling their homes. We've come a long way in offering more efficient cooling and heating systems. What else can we do?"
2. *Immersion.* The individual concentrates on the problem and becomes immersed in it. He or she will recall and collect information that seems relevant, dreaming up alternatives without refining or evaluating them. The housing developer might say, "It seems to me that other industries have been faced with the problem of consumer resistance to the energy costs of using their products."
3. *Incubation.* After assembling the information, the individual keeps it in the back of his or her mind for a while. It has been hypothesized that the subconscious mind begins to take over. Although the individual is not actively working on the problem, it is simmering in the mind. It is therefore justifiable to go for a walk during working hours to engage in creative problem solving. While the problem is simmering, the subconscious may be trying to arrange the facts into a meaningful pattern.
4. *Insight.* If you have ever experienced a sudden insight about a vexing problem, you will understand this step in the creative process. The problem-conquering solution flashes into the mind at an unexpected time, such as while about to go to sleep, showering, or jogging. Creative people often carry notebooks to record these flashes of insight. The housing developer achieved her flash of insight while in a shopping mall: "Why not build compact homes to save energy, just like compact cars?"

5. *Verification and application.* The individual sets out to prove that the creative solution has merit. Verication procedures include gathering supporting evidence, logical persuasion, and experimenting with the new idea. The builder might conduct some market research about the market acceptance of compact houses sold in other locations. Or the builder might take the plunge and build a few houses for speculation.

Tenacity is usually required at the application stage of creative thought, since most novel ideas are rejected as being impractical. Most experienced idea generators recognize that rejection is part of the game. For example, many inventions and developments that later proved to be huge successes were at first rejected by several companies. Xerography and the personal computer are two historically significant cases in point.

MISPERCEPTIONS ABOUT CREATIVITY

Before proceeding, it is important to dispel four misperceptions or myths about creativity. One is that people can be classified accurately as creative or noncreative. In reality, creativity is like height, intelligence, or strength. People vary considerably in these dimensions, but everyone has *some* height, *some* intelligence, and *some* strength.

A second misperception about creativity is that it can be exercised only in a limited number of fields, such as physical science, the arts, and advertising. This type of creativity could be labeled artistic or scientific creativity. Yet creative problem solving can be exercised in almost any field. You can engage in creative problem solving in such diverse settings as manufacturing, office work, administrative work, and home repairs.

A third misperception is that all creative ideas are complex and technical. In reality, most useful ideas are magnificently simple. A classic example is that a whole new industry was formed when two young men decided that computers could be used in homes and small businesses as well as in large organizations. The two creative problem solvers were Steve Jobs and Steve Wozniak, founders of Apple Computer. Here is a less dramatic example of creative problem solving that could nevertheless result in millions of dollars earned or saved:

In the mid-1980s the Internal Revenue Service began sending about 10 million taxpayers postcards instead of tax forms. The postcards are sent to individuals as well as small businesses who used professional tax preparers in the past. People who receive the postcard can mail it back to the IRS if they want an income tax form and an instruction package. Or they can take the postcard to their tax preparer, who will attach the label to the form used in filling out the tax return. The government hopes to save about $1 million in postage and printing costs by using the postcards instead of sending out forms that are discarded. IRS forms are discarded because tax preparers usually have their own computerized forms.

A final myth is that creativity cannot be controlled, managed, or rushed. In reality, in some situations a deadline can be imposed for reaching a creative solution to a problem. A specialist at the Center for Creative Leadership has found that managers can aim at specific, controlled results. One such approach to forcing creativity is the *excursion technique*. This technique was used when NASA was trying to design some sort of buttonlike, zipperlike material that astronauts could manipulate while wearing bulky gloves in space.

After working unsuccessfully on the project for a while, the excursion technique was utilized. The group was asked to construct fantasies based on the words "rain forest." One group member described an image he had in his mind of running through the forest and having the thorns and stickers tear at his clothes. This image led to the development of velcro.[6]

CREATIVITY, PROBLEM SOLVING, AND DECISION MAKING

Creativity is not an end in itself, but an important part of any responsible job—solving problems and making decisions. Although problem solving and decision making are part of the same general process, an important distinction can be drawn between them. **Problem solving** is a method of closing the gap between the actual situation and the desired situation. **Decision making** is the process of choosing among the alternatives that exist to solve the problem. NASA faced the problem of astronauts not being able to readily open and close clothing in space. A decision was finally made to use a new substance called velcro.

The type of decision faced by a person determines how much creativity will be required. A **programmed,** or routine, **decision** is one where the alternative solutions are determined by rules, procedures, or policies. For instance, deciding what to do when a printer ribbon is used up is a programmed decision. A **nonprogrammed,** or unique, **decision** is where a new solution is required because alternatives have not been prescribed in advance. For instance, deciding what kind of insurance business can be offered to the world is a nonprogrammed decision.

Creativity is required to make effective programmed decisions. In many situations, creativity is discouraged when you are faced with a programmed decision. What would happen if a bank teller deviated from standard procedure in cashing a check from a stranger without proper identification?

Here we are concerned primarily with the creative aspects of solving problems and making decisions. However, we must note that creativity is exercised within the context of decision making.

Decision-Making Steps

According to the rational view of decision making, the process consists of seven steps: find the problem, diagnose the problem, generate creative alternatives, weigh alternatives, choose an alternative, implement the alternative, and evaluate

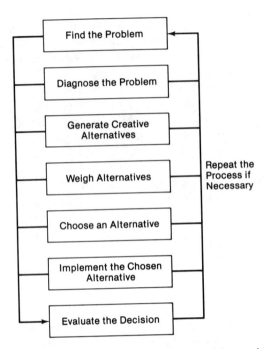

Figure 4–1   The steps in problem solving and
decision making.

the decision. Figure 4–1 outlines the decision-making steps. In some situations
the steps overlap, and the decision maker may skip a step or jump back and
forth between steps.

Find the problem. Problem solving and decision making involve either having a problem assigned to you or finding one. Creative people are usually good
problem finders—they recognize a problem when others are unaware of it. For
instance, several companies today are involved in *remanufacturing*, rebuilding
worn-out equipment and selling it to the public. The rebuilt product, such as
an auto or bus, can be sold much less expensively than a new product. The
man who found the problem of people wanting new cars and used car prices
thought of the idea while working his way through college as a junkyard attendant.[7]

Diagnose the problem. Assume that instead of looking for a problem, you
are faced with the problem of needing money for furthering your education,
purchasing a home, or getting married. The second step in problem solving
and decision making is to diagnose, or clarify, the problem and its causes. It is
essential to have some idea of both the actual and the desired situation.

In the example, you may decide you need an additional $7,000 to make
the intended purchase. Conceivably, it is true that you need to find a satisfactory

way to earn an additional $7,000. Or the real problem could be that you must discover a way to pare down your expenses by $7,000 within the next year.

According to George P. Huber, problem exploration often suffers because of the tendency to define the problem in terms of a proposed solution.[8] For example, you may think you need $7,000 to have a proper wedding. Yet many people get married for under $200! And many managers find that instead of needing a bigger budget next year, they can achieve the same result by introducing more efficient work methods.

Generate creative alternatives. The essence of creativity is found in this step: generating a number of sensible alternatives to the problem at hand. A sound decision is more likely when the decision maker chooses among a number of alternatives. Conversely, many people make poor decisions simply because they did not search long enough for a good alternative. The effectiveness-reducing behavior frequently exhibited at this point is to evaluate each alternative that presents itself, rather than to concentrate on generating many alternatives. If you need an additional $7,000, it's worth your time to dig for many alternatives.

One precaution to take in generating alternative solutions is not to rely exclusively upon your own ideas. People who love their own ideas simply because they have produced them are said to suffer from *ideonarcissism.*[9] Instead of relying on your own thinking exclusively, solicit suggestions from superiors, co-workers, and friends.

Weigh the alternatives. In order to make an intelligent choice, the advantages and disadvantages of each alternative should be specified. To illustrate, one approach to raising $7,000 after taxes would be to work 20 hours per week, at $8 per hour, for 50 weeks. This alternative might have the advantage of raising the proper amount of money. Yet it might have the disadvantage of playing havoc with your regular job, schooling, or personal life. A recommended method of weighing alternatives is to list the advantages and disadvantages of each on a separate sheet of paper.

Choose an alternative. It is important to weigh each alternative; yet the process cannot go on too long. At some point you have to take a stand in order to solve an individual or organizational problem. You have to trust your intuition and take a chance with a plausible alternative. Intuition and hunches are now considered a key aspect of managerial decision making. Most breakthrough decisions are made by business leaders who trust their hunches and seize an alternative without endless analysis.

Roy Rowan refers to the use of intuition in decision making as the **Eureka factor,** the sudden illuminating flash of judgment that guides many executives.[10] The Eureka factor is identical to the insight phase of the creative process. More will be said about intuitive decision making later in our discussion.

Implement the chosen alternative. This step centers around planning and following through on the activities that must take place for the chosen alternative to solve the problem. It can also be regarded as converting the decision. So often people make a decision but fail to implement that decision. Under these circumstances, no decision has been made at all. Let us assume that the money-making alternative you choose is to become a distributor for a milk substitute. Your earnings will come from sales you make yourself and from commissions paid you based on lining up other distributors. (This alternative does run the risk of losing some friends.)

Evaluate the decision. The final stage of the problem-solving and decision-making process involves evaluating the quality of the decision made. Answering the deceptively simple question, "How effective is the decision I made?" is a complex activity. If the decision maker has a clear perception of what the decision was supposed to accomplish, evaluating the decision is somewhat easier. In the situation here, the decision maker has focused upon earning $7,000 within a year without badly disturbing other facets of life. If selling the milk substitute meets these criteria, the decision has been a good one. If this course of action proves to be unprofitable and overly time-consuming, the decision can be considered a poor one. In this case the problem has not been solved, and the decision maker returns to step 1.

Evaluating the outcome of a decision is important for another basic reason. Feedback of this type can improve decision-making skills. One might say, for example, "This time around I chose an alternative without giving careful thought to how difficult it would be to implement."

To evaluate decisions accurately, the decision maker needs to develop and use a strong feedback system. Many managers have difficulty finding the consequences of their actions because they lack reliable information. Subordinates are often reluctant to bring bad news to the attention of superiors. According to a research report on managerial decision making, the higher a manager's position, the more limited are the feedback channels from below.[11]

Limitations to Rational Decision Making

The decision-making steps just outlined generally assume that decision making is an orderly and rational process. (The important exception is that intuition plays a key role in generating alternatives and then choosing one.) Current thinking is that the rational model has been overemphasized. Several researchers have noted that decision making is seldom the logical, systematic process suggested by a literal interpretation of Figure 4–1.[12]

Decision making is often confused because there are so many problems needing attention, and so many emotional factors that enter in. The explosion of the *Challenger* spacecraft is a tragic example. Decision makers at Morton Thiokol, Inc., manufacturers of the booster rocket, knew that their engineers were concerned about the safety of their seals. It had long been known that problems with the seals could be aggravated by low temperatures. However, when the Thiokol officials knew that NASA was impatient to launch on time, officials suppressed the negative evidence.

Observe carefully that both Thiokol and NASA officials were swayed by subtle political forces to neglect information about safety. A *political force* in this context is a pressure to take a course of action in order to please somebody. Thiokol officials wanted to please NASA officials, and NASA officials wanted to please Congress and the public by launching on time.

Another problem with carrying rational decision making too far is that it leads to *analysis paralysis*. The decision maker deals with so many facts that he or she becomes confused, overwhelmed, and unable to make a decision.

The alternative to the rational model of decision making is not to discard facts and figures in making a decision. Instead, the decision maker should attempt to accumulate an ample amount of reliable facts, and then trust his or her intuition. Trusting hunches may mean making some decisions on the basis of incomplete data, but it does allow you to become a creative problem solver. An important part of obtaining reliable facts is to trust the source of those facts.

Computer-Assisted Decision Making

Acceptance of the role of intuition in decision making has led to computer programs that help one make better use of hunches and intuition when attempting to solve problems. Two forms of computer-assisted decision making are decision-making software and artificial intelligence.

Decision-making software is any computer program that helps the decision maker work through the problem-solving and decision-making steps. These programs guide you through the actual steps outlined in Figure 4–1. In addition, they ask questions about such things as your values, priorities, and the importance you attach to such factors as price and durability.

Three representative decision-making programs are Trigger, Lightyear, and Expert Choice. Each is designed for use with personal computers. The decision-making process used in these programs is referred to as intuitive because the programs rely more on human judgment than heavy quantitative analysis.[13] The purpose of these programs is to improve the quality of decisions, rather than make computations or generate data. A decision-making program could help a manager decide whether to market a new product through sales representatives, by telephone, or by direct mail.

Artificial intelligence (AI) is the capability of a computer to perform functions usually considered part of human intelligence, such as learning, reasoning, and listening. Through the use of AI, a computer can be made to think much like a person. One approach to artificial intelligence is to program a computer to ask a series of "if-then" questions, simulating human logic. A second approach is to build enormous databases to incorporate as many facts as possible to fit a particular situation. Another approach is to build a system that links facts the way they might be linked in the human brain.[14] As you might suspect, the technology for AI is complex and esoteric.

AI programs are now available for personal computers. The more advanced use natural language commands rather than traditional computer commands. One of these programs, called Sales Activity Manager, helps track information such as how fast products are selling or how well particular sales representatives are performing. Using a voice command, the sales manager might ask: "How's business in Indianapolis?"

AI programs are promising because they approximate the way people really think. A really effective AI program would function much like a knowledgeable personal assistant who would listen to questions and respond with accurate answers. Skeptics are concerned, however, that AI is still too complex to function well on small computers.[15]

WHAT IS YOUR CREATIVE POTENTIAL?

A logical starting point in studying creativity is to gain a tentative awareness of your creative potential. Psychologists have developed standardized tests (not for use by the general public) to measure creativity. Here we confine our measurement of creative potential to several illustrative exercises. Do not be overly encouraged or dejected by any results you achieve on these tests; they are designed to give only preliminary insights into whether or not your thought processes are similar to those of creative individuals.

UNUSUAL USES TEST

Write down 10 uses for each of the following objects, allowing yourself five minutes per object.

    Red brick
    Pencil eraser
    Household spoon

A glance at several answers given by other people might be helpful to you in examining your own creative potential. A guidance counselor thought of these uses for a red brick: "Doorstop, bookend, paperweight, grind up and make stones for an aquarium, use to settle marital disputes, put behind rear wheel of car when fixing flat, step for reaching on top of refrigerator, insulator for putting pizza on table, newspaper weight when reading at beach or lake."

A purchasing agent thought of these uses for an eraser: "Something to play with

---

while tense, ear plug, toy for kitten, small wire insulator, pellet for harmless gun, poker chip, goldfish bowl decorative float, something to have a catch with, low-calorie chewing gum, place in mouth instead of smoking."

A shoe salesman thought of these uses for a spoon: "Screwdriver, plant and gardening tool, child spanker, shoehorn, sharpen and use for weapon, infant toy, discharge electricity before shaking hands with another person on thick carpet, drumstick, use as a catapult for small objects by pressing quickly at large end, postal carrier signal for rural mailbox."

Interpret your scores in this manner: If you were able to arrive at close to 10 uses for each object (other than repeating the obvious, such as using a red brick for a paper weight), you show good creative potential. If the entire task left you stymied, you need work in loosening up yourself intellectually. Keep on trying exercises of this nature (and study the rest of this chapter).

RHYME AND REASON TEST

Creativity expert Eugene Raudsepp observes that exercises in rhyming release creative energy; they stir imagination into action. While doing the following exercises remember that rhyme is frequently a matter of sound and does not have to involve similar or identical spelling. This exercise deals with light and frivolous emotions.[16]

After each "definition," write two rhyming words to which it refers.

Examples

1.	Large hog	Big	pig
2.	Television	Boob	tube
3.	Cooperative female	Game	dame

Now try these:

1. Happy father   _____ _____
2. False pain   _____ _____
3. Formed like a simian   _____ _____
4. Highest-ranking police worker   _____ _____
5. Voyage by a large boat   _____ _____
6. Corpulent feline   _____ _____
7. Melancholy fellow   _____ _____
8. Clever beginning   _____ _____
9. Heavy and unbroken slumber   _____ _____
10. Crazy custom   _____ _____
11. Lengthy melody   _____ _____
12. Weak man   _____ _____

13. Instruction at the seashore   ____ ____
14. Criticism lacking in effectiveness   ____ ____
15. A person who murders for pleasurable excitement   ____ ____
16. Musical stringed instrument with full, rich sounds   ____ ____
17. Courageous person who is owned as property by another   ____ ____
18. Mature complaint   ____ ____
19. Strange hair growing on the lower part of a man's face   ____ ____
20. Drooping marine crustacean   ____ ____
21. A man, short in height, accompanying a woman.   ____ ____

Answers and Interpretation

Obviously, the more of these rhymes you were able to come up with, the higher your creative potential. You would also need an advanced vocabulary to score very high (for instance, what is a "simian" or a "crustacean"?). Ten or more correct rhymes would tend to show outstanding creative potential, at least in the verbal area.

Here are the answers:

1. Glad dad	**12.** Frail male
2. Fake ache	**13.** Beach teach
3. Ape shape	**14.** Weak critique
4. Top cop	**15.** Thriller killer
5. Ship trip	**16.** Mellow cello
6. Fat cat	**17.** Brave slave
7. Sad lad	**18.** Ripe gripe
8. Smart start	**19.** Weird beard
9. Deep sleep	**20.** Limp shrimp
10. Mad fad	**21.** Short escort
11. Long song	

If you can think of a sensible substitute for any of these answers, give yourself a bonus point. For example, for number 9, how about a booze snooze?

CREATIVE PERSONALITY TEST

The following test will help you determine if certain aspects of your personality are similar to those of a creative individual. Since our test is for illustrative and research purposes, proceed with caution. Again, this is not a standardized psychological instrument. Such tests are not reprinted in general books.

Directions: Answer each of the following statements as "mostly true" or "mostly false." We are looking for general trends; therefore, do not be concerned if you answer true if they are mostly true and false if they are mostly false.

	Mostly True	Mostly False
1. Novels are a waste of time. If you want to read, read nonfiction books.	_____	_____
2. You have to admit, some crooks are very clever.	_____	_____
3. People consider me to be a fastidious dresser. I despise looking shaggy.	_____	_____
4. I am a person of very strong convictions. What's right is right; what's wrong is wrong.	_____	_____
5. It doesn't bother me when my boss hands me vague instructions.	_____	_____
6. Business before pleasure is a hard and fast rule in my life.	_____	_____
7. Taking a different route to work is fun, even if it takes longer.	_____	_____
8. Rules and regulations should not be taken too seriously. Most rules can be broken under unusual circumstances.	_____	_____
9. Playing with a new idea is fun even if it doesn't benefit me in the end.	_____	_____
10. So long as people are nice to me, I don't care why they are being nice.	_____	_____
11. Writing should try to avoid the use of unusual words and word combinations.	_____	_____
12. Detective work would have some appeal to me.	_____	_____
13. Crazy people have no good ideas.	_____	_____
14. Why write letters to friends when there are so many clever greeting cards available in the stores today?	_____	_____
15. Pleasing myself means more to me than pleasing others.	_____	_____
16. If you dig long enough, you will find the true answer to most questions.	_____	_____

Scoring the Test

The answer in the *creative direction* for each question is as follows:

1. Mostly False	7. Mostly True	13. Mostly False
2. Mostly True	8. Mostly True	14. Mostly False
3. Mostly False	9. Mostly True	15. Mostly True
4. Mostly False	10. Mostly True	16. Mostly False
5. Mostly True	11. Mostly False	
6. Mostly False	12. Mostly True	

Give yourself a plus one for each answer you gave in agreement with the keyed answers.

How Do You Interpret Your Score?

As cautioned earlier, this is an exploratory test. Extremely high or low scores are probably the most meaningful. A score of 12 or more suggests that your personality and attitudes are similar to those of a creative person. A score of 5 or less suggests that your personality is dissimilar to that of a creative person. You are probably more of a conformist (and somewhat categorical) in your thinking, at least at this point in your life. Don't be discouraged. Most people can develop in the direction of becoming a more creative individual.

CHARACTERISTICS OF THE CREATIVE WORKER

Before attempting to improve your own creativity, it is helpful to know the characteristics of creative workers. The Creative Education Foundation defines a **creative worker** as someone who approaches problems in a new or unique way.[17] Studies point toward one distinguishing overall characteristic: Creative people are more emotionally loose and open than less creative people.

The emotional looseness of creative people is often manifested in practical jokes and other forms of playfulness. For example, a packaging design engineer roomed with another woman who collected stuffed animals. While the stuffed-animal collector was away for the weekend, the design engineer dressed all the animals in the latter's clothing. She even put high heels on a stuffed giraffe. The joke worked. The animal collector was distressed about a delayed flight home. However, she laughed so hysterically upon seeing her dressed-up animals that her distress was relieved.

Research and Opinion about the Creative Personality

Robert R. Godfrey has grouped the characteristics of creative workers into three broad areas: knowledge, intellectual abilities, and personality. The following list incorporates his thinking with that of other writers and researchers.[18]

Knowledge. Creative thinking requires a broad background of information, including facts and observations. Knowledge is the storehouse of building blocks for generating and combining ideas.

Intellectual abilities. Included here are cognitive abilities such as intelligence and abstract reasoning. Specific observations here include:

- Creative people tend to be *bright rather than brilliant*. Extraordinarily high intelligence is not required to be creative, but creative people are good at generating alternative solutions to problems in a short period of time.
- Creative people have a *youthful curiosity* throughout their lives. Their curiosity is not centered just on their own field of expertise. Instead, their range of interests encompasses many areas of knowledge, and they generate enthusiasm toward almost any puzzling problems.
- Creative people are *open and responsive* to feelings and emotions and the world around them.

Personality. Included here are the emotional and nonintellectual aspects of an individual that facilitate being creative.

- Creative people tend to have a *positive self-image*. They feel good about themselves but are not blindly self-confident. Because they are reasonably self-confident, creative people are able to cope with criticism of their ideas.
- Creative people have the *ability to tolerate isolation*. Isolation is useful because it helps put a person into a receptive mood for ideas. Working alone also helps creative people avoid the distractions of talking to others. (Creativity, however, is sometimes facilitated by interaction with others.)
- Creative people are frequently *nonconformists*. They value their independence and do not have strong needs to gain approval from the group.
- Creative people often have a *Type T personality*. Their thrill-seeking tendencies often lead to outstanding creativity because finding imaginative solutions to problems is thrilling.[19]
- Creative people are *persistent*. Persistence is important, because finding creative solutions to problems is hard work and requires intense concentration.

Synthesizing these lists leads to a general picture of the creative person. He or she is more loose than tight, open than closed, flexible than rigid, playful than always serious, adventuresome than safety-seeking. Several of these characteristics support the popular stereotype of the creative person as somewhat of a maverick, both intellectually and socially.

What Triggers Creativity?

A person with many of the above characteristics will not inevitably bring forth creative solutions to problems. Triggering or eliciting creative behavior from an individual requires the right interaction between person and environment. Support for this generalization comes from the work of a psychologist who has conducted several studies on creativity in organizations. He concludes that the optimal condition for creativity has five ingredients, and when they are all present creative behavior is almost a certainty:

First, you need a person of sound intelligence: someone who has a high capacity for learning, for abstracting, for solving problems, and for making discriminations. Second, the potentially creative person must have a strong ego and be confident that he or she can overcome problems. Third, the person must be faced with a need (environmental condition) that stimulates the formulation of a goal. As the old adage states, "Necessity is the mother of invention." Fourth, a barrier must exist to reaching this goal, and a standard solution to overcoming the barrier (programmed decision) should not be available. Fifth, the person must have **insight,** a broad awareness of the self and environment.[20]

Even when environmental conditions are favorable for triggering creativity, you still need the appropriate personal characteristics and behaviors. Having read these attributes of creative people, think about how well they fit your personality. If it does not appear that you have as many of these characteristics as you would like, pessimism is not in order. Techniques are available that can help an individual develop his or her creative potential, assuming you want to become more creative.

CHARACTERISTICS OF THE CREATIVE ORGANIZATION

To achieve creative solutions to problems and to think of new opportunities, an organization needs more than creative people. Creativity is the combined influence of people with creative potential working in an environment that encourages creativity. An example of an organizational climate that fosters creativity is Bell Labs, the research and development arm of the Bell System. Also referred to as a giant "think tank," Bell Labs employs about 22,500 people. Since it was founded in 1922, the laboratory has been issued 19,000 patents. It has been estimated that Bell Labs has been directly or indirectly responsible for most of the innovations in voice communication in the twentieth century.

The success of Bell Labs has been attributed, in large part, to its special atmosphere or climate. Arno Penzias, a co-winner of a Nobel Prize in radio astronomy, made this analysis: "Unless it can be demonstrated that you're really wasting your time and our money, people leave you alone. The place demands that you work. But it also demands that you think."[21]

Organizations that are able to capitalize upon much of the creative potential of their members have certain characteristics in common. One underlying characteristic is that organizational members are given encouragement and emotional support for attempts at creativity. As you read the following list of more specific characteristics, notice that many of the characteristics of creative organizations are similar to those of creative people.[22]

- Group norms, or an organizational culture, that encourages and expects creativity from group members. This is perhaps the single most important characteristic of a creative organization.
- Rewards, including recognition and money, are given to employees whose innovative ideas have tangible payoffs. (At Eastman Kodak, for example, three workers in one year received $50,000 each for their money-saving ideas.)

- Managers at the top of the organization who support innovation and imagination.
- An organizational structure flexible enough to bend with whatever pressures innovation may bring.
- A process already established for developing new ideas into products or services.
- A trustful management that does not overcontrol people.
- Open channels of communication among members of the organization; a minimum of secrecy.
- Considerable contact and communication with outsiders to the organization.
- Large variety of personality types.
- Willing to accept change, but not enamored with change for its own sake.
- Enjoyment in experimenting with new ideas.
- Encourages people of various education levels and generalists (not only specialists) to contribute new ideas.
- Attempts to retain creative people even during time of financial difficulty.
- Little fear of the consequences of making a mistake.
- Selects people and promotes them primarily on the basis of merit.
- Uses techniques for encouraging ideas, such as suggestion systems, special recognition for patent awards, and brainstorming.
- Sufficient financial, managerial, human, and time resources to accomplish its goals.

ENTREPRENEURS, INTRAPRENEURS, AND CREATIVITY

The focus of creativity in many organizations is on individuals who develop and implement new ideas for products and services. Ordinarily one associates new products and services with business organizations. However, many nonprofit firms, such as government agencies, educational institutions, and hospitals, are also concerned about offering innovative services to the public. Here we describe the nature of entrepreneurship and intrapreneurship, and what organizations are doing to foster this type of creativity.

The Nature of Entrepreneurship and Intrapreneurship

An **entrepreneur** is a person who establishes and manages a business in an innovative manner. Note the distinction between anybody who operates a small business and a true entrepreneur—an entrepreneur offers an innovative product or service. A **small business owner** is an individual who establishes and manages a business for the primary purpose of furthering personal goals.[23] If you establish a company that manufactures and sells laser guns for home repairs, you are an entrepreneur (and a small business owner). If you open a newsstand in a hotel lobby, you are a small business owner but not an entrepreneur. Approximately 650,000 people open small businesses each year in the United States and Canada. Very few of these people are true entrepreneurs.

An **intrapreneur** is a company employee who engages in entrepreneurial thinking and behavior for the good of the firm. Intrapreneurs work somewhat independently inside the firm, with the mission of developing a new product or service.[24] The intrapreneur benefits from the company's backing, and the company benefits from the intrapreneur's productivity. Like an entrepreneur, the intrapreneur begins small. If the new product becomes successful, the intrapreneur commands more resources.

Intrapreneurship has burgeoned in recent years because it is generally recognized that most innovation comes from small organizations. Ideally, the intrapreneur pursues his or her product idea with the intensity of an entrepreneur. Don Estridge, the IBM executive whose business unit developed the IBM PC, made this comment about the importance of smallness: "If you're competing against people who started in a garage, you have to start in a garage."[25]

The entrepreneurial and intrapreneurial personalities have already been described in two places in this text. First, we described the achievement-motivated person in Chapter 2. Entrepreneurs and intrapreneurs are strongly achievement-motivated. Second, the description of the creative personality in this chapter also fits entrepreneurs and intrapreneurs. We will return to the entrepreneurial personality again in a discussion about the entrepreneurial leaders (see Chapter 8). To further your insight into the entrepreneurial personality, here is a description of an entrepreneur provided by one of her employees:

> Jane is an absolute madwoman. She is always on the go, always thinking, and always wanting to get something done. She often handles two phone calls at once. We all love Jane, and we worry about her having a heart attack. A normal workweek for her is 80 hours. If it wasn't for a cellular phone, she would never take a vacation. Jane has made her million dollars, but rumor has it that she's developing a robot that can be programmed to mow lawns.

What Organizations Are Doing to Foster Intrapreneurship

Organizations are taking many steps to foster entrepreneurship within a bureaucracy. The general thrust of these actions is to exempt intrapreneurs from many of the restrictions and controls usually imposed in a large firm. At the same time, intrapreneurs are given extra resources and special privileges.[26]

The establishment of skunk works. Several large firms, including Xerox and IBM, allow selected employees to operate out of **skunk works,** a secret place to conceive new products. The term derives from the fact that something secret and unpleasant is thought to be going on in these off-site locations. Skunk works employees are given latitude in pursuing new products. Major products conceived in skunk works include jet fighter technology, and the original IBM PCs.

   Identification and recognition of intrapreneurs. Intrapreneurs are risk takers—they will pursue ideas and get volunteer help before they receive permission from the firm. Companies are now making an effort officially to recognize employees with ideas for breakthrough products. Once the potential intrapreneur is identified, he or she is officially encouraged by a top executive.

   Allocation of more resources. Many intrapreneurs who have become corporate superstars have used unauthorized resources from their companies to develop their product. Much of the work they have done on new products was originally on their own time. Although not every new idea can be funded, many high-tech companies are now providing money, material, and human resources for intrapreneurs. Another way of giving the intrapreneur resources is to form special project teams to help develop a promising new product.

IMPROVING YOUR CREATIVITY THROUGH SELF-HELP

Creativity can sometimes be improved through formal training programs. At other times, do-it-yourself techniques can be equally beneficial. Here we describe seven strategies and techniques many people have used outside of formal training programs to improve their own creative behavior. In Chapter 8, we will describe group brainstorming and several other methods of creativity improvement.

Overcome Traditional Mental Sets

Most techniques of creativity improvement are based on the same principle: To think creatively, you must overcome a traditional mental set. A **traditional mental set** is a conventional way of looking at things and placing them in familiar categories. Overcoming traditional mental sets is necessary to loosen up emotionally and intellectually. As long as you remain a "tight" person, your creativity will be inhibited.

   Alcohol and other drugs sometimes provide the user with a temporary state of emotional and intellectual looseness that can stimulate the creative process. However, the loss of intellectual alertness from extensive use of these substances usually more than offsets the advantage of temporary looseness.

   Overcoming traditional ways of looking at things is a mechanism by which a person can become emotionally and intellectually looser. A traditional, or rigid, way of looking at something is referred to as a **perceptual block.** People frequently cannot solve problems in a creative manner because they are bound by preconceived ideas. Until a person can look beyond the normal ways of doing things, he or she will probably not find a solution.

One pharmaceutical company owes its surge of success to the ability of two people to overcome the traditional way of thinking about how to ingest medicine. As described by *The New York Times*.[27]

> The conventional path to success in the ethical drug business is to invent a product—preferably a new cure that can generate its own market—then produce and market it. However, the process can be extraordinarily time-consuming and expensive. The many steps can take more than ten years and cost more than $50 million.

Over twenty years ago, when Michael Jaharis and Dr. Philip Frost took over Key Pharmaceuticals, the Miami-based concern had just lost $700,000 on revenues of $1.5 million and was in no position to bring out a new product. So the two partners engaged in some creative thought. They took an existing, familiar drug and found a new way to deliver, or administer it into the body. Jaharis and Frost decided to revitalize a 50-year-old asthma medicine. The drug was rarely used at the time because it was ineffective in small doses and could be toxic in large doses. But the two partners, and other researchers on the project, found a way to cope with the temperamental drug by devising a time-released pill that works for twelve hours. (The drug is now called Theo-Dur.)

The result of their ingenuity has been strong growth ever since. Currently their annual sales exceed $100 million, and their profits are approximately $6 million.

Use the Private Brainstorming Method

Brainstorming, in its usual format, is a technique that involves group members thinking of multiple solutions to a problem. **Private brainstorming** is arriving at creative ideas by jotting down ideas by yourself. The technique is also called "brainwriting." The two creativity improvement techniques already described will help you to develop the mental flexibility necessary for both types of brainstorming.

An important requirement of private brainstorming is that you set aside a regular time (and perhaps place) for generating ideas. The ideas discovered in the process of routine activities can be counted as bonus time. Even five minutes a day is much more time than most people are accustomed to use in thinking creatively about job problems. Give yourself a quota with a time deadline.

Develop a Synergy between Both Sides of the Brain

Neurological and psychological studies of the brain have shed light on creativity. Researchers have been able to demonstrate that the left side of the brain is the source of most analytical, logical, and rational thought. It performs the tasks necessary for well-reasoned arguments. The right side of the brain grasps the work in a more intuitive, overall manner. It is the source of impressionistic, creative thought. People with dominant right brains thrive on disorder and ambiguity—both characteristics of a creative person.

The argument that the left side of the brain controls logic and the right side of the·brain controls intuition has been disputed by biopsychologist Jerre Levy, among others. Her studies show that any mental activity is carried out by both sides of the brain simultaneously. Joined by the corpus callosum, the two hemispheres work together in harmony.[28]

Whether you believe that both sides of the brain work independently or interdependently, the message for creativity improvement is the same. Both logical and intuitive thinking are required. The creative person needs a fund of accessible facts in order to combine them to solve problems. He or she also needs to rely on hunches and intuition to achieve flashes of insight.

The highly creative person achieves a synergy between the two sides of the brain. **Synergy** is a combination of things with an output greater than the sum of the parts. The unique capabilities of both sides of the brain are required. Robert Gundlach, a physicist who has amassed 133 patents in over 30 years of work, explains it this way:[29]

> Being creative means developing a synergy between the left half of the brain— the analytical half—and the right half of the brain—the creative half. I learned that at home during my childhood. My mother was an artist, a painter of landscapes. My father was a chemist, and inventor of Wildroot hair oil. Both my parents influenced me equally well.

Maintain and Use an Idea Notebook

Good ideas are hard to come by, yet they are readily forgotten in the press of normal activities. A standard creativity improvement device of people who are dependent upon novel ideas for their livelihood is to keep an idea notebook with them at all times—including one at bedside. When an idea of any possible merit flashes across your mind, it should be entered in a notebook reserved for that purpose. It is also essential that the idea notebook be referred to frequently to see which ideas are now ready for refinement and implementation.

Borrow Creative Ideas

Copying the successful ideas of others is a legitimate form of creativity. Knowing when and which ideas to borrow can help you behave as if you were an imaginative person yourself. One source of good ideas is conversations with people from other departments and specialties. If you maintain contact with managers and specialists from your own firm or other firms, you will have a pipeline to potentially useful ideas. Reading also serves as a useful source of creative ideas. Newspapers, general magazines, trade magazines, and nonfiction books frequently contain novel ideas about improving your job effectiveness.

A delicate issue is whether you should tell others the source of your novel suggestions. Do you think it is proper to take full credit for ideas you have borrowed from people or printed sources?

Don't Be Afraid to Try and Fail

If you try a large number of ideas, projects, or things, a large number of them will probably fail. Relatively few ideas ever become accepted and implemented. Yet your number of "hits" will be much higher than if you tried only a few creative ideas and all of them were successful. It is the absolute number of successes that counts the most, not the percentage of successes.

Discipline Yourself to Think Creatively

Self-discipline is required for developing your creativity. An important strategy to becoming more creative is to develop the attitude that creativity is both important and desirable. Faced with a job problem or a personal problem requiring a creative solution, one effective starting point is to sit quietly with a pencil and pad and begin to generate alternative solutions. For example, "How can I raise my productivity 15 percent without increasing the number of hours I work?"

The exercises designed to measure your creativity described earlier in this chapter can also develop effective approaches for improving creativity. By disciplining yourself to perform such exercises as "Think of ten uses for a household spoon," you should be able to tackle job problems requiring creativity more readily. One example would be, "What are four different things my company might do with wooden shipping crates after we have removed their contents?"

Summary of Key Points _____

☐ Creativity is the ability to develop good ideas that can be put into action. Creative problem solving stems from creativity, and is the ability to overcome obstacles by approaching them in novel ways. The five stages of creative thought are: problem finding, immersion, incubation, insight, and verification and application.

☐ Misperceptions about creativity include: People can be accurately classified as creative or noncreative; creativity can be exercised only in artistic and scientific fields; all creative ideas are complex and technical; and creativity cannot be controlled, managed, or rushed.

☐ Creativity takes place within the context of solving problems and making nonprogrammed (unique) decisions. Decision making can be divided into seven steps: find the problem; diagnose the problem; generate creative alternatives; weigh the alternatives; choose an alternative; implement the chosen alternative; evaluate the decision.

☐ Current thinking is that the rational model of decision making has been overemphasized. In reality, decision making is often confused because there are so many problems requiring attention, and so many emotional factors involved. Another limitation to rational decision making is that it may lead to "analysis paralysis." Big decisions should be based on both facts and hunches.

☐ Computer-assisted decision making can be helpful in improving intuition. One form is decision-making software that helps one work through the steps in problem solving and decision making, yet emphasizes the qualitative factors. Another form of computer-assisted decision making is artificial intelligence, a computer program that simulates human thinking.

☐ Creative potential can be measured with some degree of accuracy by taking tests designed for that purpose. The tests sampled here include those requiring you to behave creatively and to compare certain aspects of your personality with those of creative people.

☐ Characteristics of the creative worker can be subdivided into knowledge, intellectual abilities, and personality. A synthesis of this information is that the creative personality is more loose than tight, open than closed, flexible than rigid, playful than always serious, and adventuresome than safety-seeking. Triggering creative behavior from an individual requires the right interaction between person and environment.

☐ Organizations that foster creativity give emotional support and encouragement to members and have group norms favoring creativity. Creative organizations also show characteristics similar to those of creative people, including an enjoyment in experimenting with new ideas.

☐ The focus of creativity in many organizations is on entrepreneurs and intrapreneurs, people who develop and implement new ideas for products and services. An entrepreneur is a person who establishes and manages a business in an innovative manner. An intrapreneur is a company employee who engages in entrepreneurial thinking and behavior for the good of the firm. Steps organizations are taking to foster intrapreneurship are (1) the establishment of skunk works, (2) identification and recognition of intrapreneurs, and (3) allocation of more resources for intrapreneurs.

Creativity can often be improved by self-help techniques. Among them are (1) overcome traditional mental sets, (2) use private brainstorming, (3) develop a synergy between both sides of the brain, (4) maintain and use an idea notebook, (5) borrow creative ideas, (6) don't be afraid to try and fail, (7) discipline yourself to think creatively.

Questions and Activities _____

1. Illustrate how the problem-solving and decision-making steps outlined in this chapter could be applied to the situation of obtaining a VCR.

2. A former physicist invented and merchandised a product called *Shoe Goo* that is used to repair holes in athletic shoes. His business was an instant success and continues to thrive. Discuss whether or not "Mr. Shoe Goo" is a true entrepreneur.

3. Give an example of a high-level position that you think does not require creative behavior from the incumbent. Explain your reasoning.

4. Do you know anybody who is highly creative yet unsuccessful by conventional standards? What accounts for his or her lack of success?

5. Does your present program of study at school encourage or discourage creativity? On what basis did you reach your conclusion?

6. Is it important for creative employees to be managed by creative bosses? Why or why not?

7. To what extent would a very strict boss be effective in encouraging creativity from subordinates?

8. Some people believe that being a creative problem solver did them more harm than good on the job. How do you explain the comment?

9. How can a government employee display an "entrepreneurial spirit" on the job?

10. Speak to a creative problem solver you know. Ask that individual how he or she became creative. Be prepared to discuss your findings in class.

A Human Relations Case

THE FOOD COMPANY SKUNK WORKS

Melrose Foods is a large food manufacturer and processor consisting of twenty-one divisions. Many of these divisions are smaller companies purchased in recent years. The executive office, headed by Gardner Appleby, recently decided to establish a research and development group whose responsibility it would be to develop new food products. Appleby explained it in these words to the corporate staff and division heads:

"The time has arrived for Melrose to copy the high tech approach to R&D (research and development). Effective July 1 of this year, we are building our own skunk works. The executive office has chosen Manuel Seda for this key assignment. As you recall, Manuel was a dynamically successful entrepreneur who established Tangy Tacos. Starting in his mother's kitchen, he built up a national distribution for his product in three years. We bought Tangy Tacos for its growth and profitability. But even more important, we bought the talent of Manuel Seda.

"Tangy Tacos will be headed by Wanda Morales while Manuel is on indefinite assignment as manager of our skunk works. Manuel will begin with six competent employees. He and his group can have all the budget they need, so long as it looks like they are on the path to developing successful products."

At this point in Appleby's presentation, Garth Laidlaw, division head of Tiger Pet Foods, waves his hand. "We need clarification, Gardner. You mention that the skunk works will be funded as long as it looks like they are about to develop successful products. Developing a successful new food product is a risky business. About 90 percent of new product ideas never make it to the marketplace. And about half of the 10 percent that do arrive on the market fail within one year."

"I'm aware of those dismal statistics," said Appleby. "But without a push on new product development, Melrose Foods is doomed for stagnation and mediocrity."

"Members of the management team, let us all move forward toward a successful skunk works. And let us all wish Manuel the best of luck."

Three months after the skunk works was established, Seda received a visit from Abbleby. After a brief tour of the facility, Appleby said to Seda: "Manuel, I do get the impression that there is a lot of activity going on here, but it does not seem to be focused activity. Could you give me an update?"

"Gardner, it's premature to expect results. We have been set aside so we can think at our own pace. This is not a crash program. Don't forget, I had been working in the food business for three years before I thought of the idea for Tangy Tacos."

"It's true, we are not expecting immediate results from the skunk works, but you are a pretty well funded group. Could you please give me a hint of any new product idea you have developed so far?"

Seda answered: "Actually we are pretty excited about one new idea. It's a form of instant fish called "Sudden Seafood.' Today's busy and health-conscious professional will love it. You add boiling water to pulverized sea food, and you get a mash-potato-like substance that is actually tasty seafood. We would certainly be the first on the market."

"Revolting," responded Appleby. "I would definitely turn thumbs down on Melrose investing money to market instant fish. Maybe you should interest our Tiger Pet Foods division in that idea. It could be used when traveling with cats."

Three months later, Appleby revisited Seda at the skunk works. The president said, "I'm just doing an informal check again. What new product idea is the skunk works toying with these days?"

"I think we have a real winner on the drawing board," said Manuel. "The country is sick of wimpy soft drinks that have no real flavor, no gusto, and give no boost to the psyche. We have been experimenting with a raspberry-flavored soft drink that has four times the caffeine and three times the sugar of anything on the market. Its tentative name is 'Razzle Razzberry.' It's destined to be a winner."

"Hold on Manuel. You're getting carried away. You're running counter culture. The country is moving away from heavy soft drinks and you're suggesting a product that's practically a narcotic. It sounds like our skunk works might be getting carried away."

"Gardner, it's too bad you don't like this promising idea. Maybe I could meet with you and other members of the executive office to discuss the mission of the company skunk works. I don't feel things are going right."

"It sounds to me like you're getting a little touchy," said Appleby."

1. How would you evaluate Appleby's approach to evaluating the output of the skunk works?
2. Do you think Seda is getting a little touchy?
3. Are Gardner's review sessions justified?
4. What do you think of Seda's request to review the mission of the skunk works with the executive office?
5. What is your hunch about the potential success of Sudden Seafood and Razzle Razzberry?

A Human Relations Incident

THE TRADITIONAL THINKERS

Laura Madison, president of Elgin's Department Store, met with her team of managers at a Sunday brunch. After the meal was served, Madison began her formal presentation with these words:

"I've called this special meeting only because I have to deal with a topic that is better handled in person than by memo. Elgin's has reached a crossroads, and its fate is in your hands. Our share of the market in all five locations has shown a steady decline over the past five years. We have got to do something about this problem, or we will be closing our doors within several years.

"As you know, we've conducted consumer surveys to find out what our customers like about us and what they don't like. The message I get from this survey is that Elgin's lacks imagination. Some customers think we are a bland store that has become blander. If we are to survive, we have to freshen our thinking. We have become too set in our ways."

After Madison continued on for ten minutes about the importance of Elgin's becoming a more imaginative store, she asked the group for questions. Don Battles, the advertising director, was the first to raise his hand:

"Laura, we have heard your charges about Elgin's being bland and lacking imagination. Could you please give us a few specifics?"

"I don't want to offend anybody in particular, but I guess I will have to be more specific," said Madison. "Above all, we don't do anything unusual as a store. Take this Christmas season as a good example. The motif our store chose was to decorate the store with Santa Claus, reindeers, and elves. How traditional can you be?

"Another example is that our special sales are just like everybody else's. We run ads announcing that everything in the store is marked down by a certain percent. How mundane can you be? Furthermore, our stores are not distinctive. They remind me of an average main street department store.

"I'm afraid we have become dull, dull, dull! If I don't get some fresh ideas from you people soon, I'm going to have to hire some creative talent from outside.

"Next question please," said Laura Madison as her management group looked stunned.

After two minutes of silence, Mary Jo Fenton, a merchandising coordinator, asked: "Laura, you set the tone for new ideas in this store. We expect you to take the lead in pointing us in new directions."

"Maybe you have a point, Mary Jo. You now know that I want Elgin's to move forward with more innovation."

1. What do you think of Madison's conclusion that her managers are traditional thinkers?
2. If her diagnosis of the problem is correct, what steps could be taken to help the managers become less traditional in their thinking?
3. What do you think of Madison's approach to solving the problem of limited imagination?
4. What do you think of Madison's idea of threatening to hire some creative talent from the outside?
5. Is Mary Jo Fenton justified in assuming the president should be setting the tone for the store?

A Human Relations Exercise

CREATIVE PROBLEM SOLVING FOR AILING HOSPITALS

B. Lee Karns was brought in as president of Comprehensive Care Corporation, a Newport Beach, California, company that specializes in the management of health-care facilities. The purpose in hiring Karns was to rescue a company in deep trouble. CompCare owned and operated several psychiatric hospitals. Heavy start-up costs for expansion and heavy earthquake damage to one of the hospitals had brought it close to bankruptcy. Karns, who had previously run his own hospital consulting firm, recognized there were many regularly idle beds in community hospitals throughout the country. He also recognized that his firm would be in solid financial shape if two conditions could be met: (a) a substantial number of these beds could be filled with paying patients and (b) CompCare could receive a portion of that additional revenue.[30]

Your job is to suggest one or more solutions to the problem that faced CompCare. Your solution(s) must fit the two conditions specified above. For example, it is unacceptable for you to suggest that CompCare convert two of its hospitals into aluminum-can recycling centers.

Notes

1. Adapted and excerpted from James T. Yenckel, "Outer Space Insurance," *Washington Post* story, January 1, 1982.
2. Edward H. Meyer, "Creativity in Business," *Business Week's Guide to Careers*, September 1985, p. 27.
3. "Creativity: A Special Report," *Success!* March 1985, p. 54.
4. David R. Wheeler, "Creative Decision Making and the Organization," *Personnel Journal*, June 1979, p. 394.
5. Based on Robert R. Godfrey, "Tapping Employees' Creativity," *Supervisory Management*, February 1986, pp. 16–17; synthesis prepared in James A. F. Stoner and Charles Wankel, *Management*, 3rd ed. (Englewood Cliffs, NJ: Prentice Hall, 1986), p. 398.
6. S. S. Gryskiewciz and J. T. Shields, "Targeted Innovation," *Issues and Observations*, November 1983, p. 4.
7. "A Growing Love Affair with the Scrap Heap," *Business Week*, April 29, 1985, p. 69.
8. George P. Huber, *Managerial Decision Making* (Glenview, IL: Scott Foresman, 1980), p. 13.
9. Darrell W. Ray and Barbara L. Wiley, "How to Generate New Ideas," *Supervisory Management*, November 1985, p. 9.
10. Roy Rowan, *The Intuitive Manager* (Boston: Little, Brown, 1986).
11. Morgan W. McCall, Jr., and Robert E. Kaplan, *Whatever It Takes: Decision Makers at Work* (Englewood Cliffs, NJ: Prentice Hall, 1985).
12. McCall and Kaplan; Neil McK. Agnew, and John L. Brown, "Executive Judgment: The Intuitive/Rational Ratio," *Personnel*, December 1985, p. 48.

13. "Programs That Make Managers Face the Facts," *Business Week*, April 8, 1985, p. 74.

14. Gary G. Bitter, *Computers in Today's World* (New York: Wiley, 1984), p. 216.

15. "Artificial Intelligence Finally Hits the Desktop," *Business Week*, June 9, 1986, p. 68.

16. Eugene Raudsepp with George P. Hough, Jr., *Creative Growth Games* (New York: Harcourt Brace Jovanovich, 1977). Reprinted with permission.

17. "Finding Creative Workers," *Research Institute Personal Report for the Executive*, October 1, 1985, p. 4.

18. Godfrey, "Tapping Employees' Creativity," *Supervisory Management*, pp. 17–18; "Finding Creative Workers," p. 4; Eugene Raudsepp, "Are You a Creative Executive?" *Management Review*, February 1978, p. 15.

19. Frank Farley, "The Big T in Personality," *Psychology Today*, May 1986, p. 48.

20. Daniel G. Tear as quoted in *Issues & Observations*, February 1981, p. 5.

21. Quote and other information about Bell Labs is from "Bell Labs: Imagination, Inc." *Time*, January 25, 1982, pp. 56–57.

22. Robert R. Blake and Jane Srygley Mouton, "Don't Let Group Norms Stifle Creativity," *Personnel*, August 1985, pp. 28–33; Maurice I. Zeldman, "How Management Can Develop and Sustain a Creative Environment," *Advanced Management Journal*, Winter 1980, pp. 23–27.

23. James W. Carland, "Differentiating Entrepreneurs from Small Business Owners," *Academy of Management Review*, April 1984, p. 358.

24. Gifford Pinchot 3d, *Intrapreneuring* (New York: Harper & Row, 1985); Keith Atkinson, "Intrapreneurs: Fostering Innovation Inside the Corporation," *Personnel Administrator*, January 1986, p. 43.

25. Quoted in Atkinson, "Intrapreneurs," p. 46.

26. Franck A. deChambeau and Fredericka Mackenzie, "Intrapreneurship," *Personnel Journal*, July 1986, pp. 40–45.

27. Adapted from "Key Pharmaceuticals Owes Its Growth to Timed Drugs," *The New York Times*, July 5, 1982, p. 33 © 1982 by The New York Times Company. Reprinted by permission.

28. Jerre Levy, "Right Brain, Left Brain: Fact and Fiction," *Psychology Today*, May 1985, p. 44.

29. John J. Byczkowski, "Invention's a Necessity at Xerox," *Rochester Democrat and Chronicle*, January 1983, p. 1F. Source of updated information is David Dorsey, "The Curious Cowboy," *Upstate*, April 20, 1986, pp. 6–7.

30. "CompCare: The Business of Treating Alcoholism," *Dun's Review*, August 1980, p. 20.

Suggested Reading

SIMONTON, DEAN KEITH. *Genius, Creativity, and Leadership: Historiometric Inquiries.* Cambridge, MA: Harvard University Press, 1984.

CONRATH, JERRY. "The Imagination Harvest: Training People to Solve Problems Creatively." *Supervisory Management*, September 1985, pp. 6–10.

DRUCKER, PETER F. "The Discipline of Innovation." *Harvard Business Review*, May–June 1985, pp. 67–84.

GOLDSTEIN, MARILYN, SCHOLTHAUER, DAVID, and KLEINER, BRIAN H. "Management on the Right Side of the Brain." *Personnel Journal*, November 1985, pp. 40–45.

KINDLER, HERBERT S. "Decision, Decisions: Which Approach to Take?" *Personnel*, January 1985, pp. 47–51.

MEEHAN, ROBERT H. "Programs That Foster Creativity and Innovation." *Personnel*, February 1986, pp. 31–35.

NEIMARK, JILL. "Mind Mapping." *Success!* June 1986, pp. 52–57.

SMITH, AUGUST. "Choosing the Best Decision Style for Your Game." *Supervisory Management*, May 1985, pp. 27–33.

TJOSVOLD, DEAN. "Effects of Crisis Orientation on Managers' Approach to Controversy in Decision Making." *Academy of Management Journal*, March 1984, pp. 130–138.

Job Stress
and Burnout

"One more day of worrying about whether my job is going to be around tomorrow, and I'll explode," said Alan to a friend. "Last month the company let go of twenty-six managers and professionals. The way I hear it, our division will be next. I've already lost 9 pounds from worrying about losing my job. The pressure is also beginning to affect my work. Last week I was so nervous that I bombed out on a presentation to management."

The same day in the same company, Sherry said to a friend: "I hate to see the company let go of so many good people. Yet, the trimming down of the company has helped me reach new heights. The challenge of trying to outperform others in order to keep my job was the jolt I needed. I think I was getting too complacent when the company never laid off anybody."

The statements by Alan and Sherry highlight the importance of job or work stress. The same statements also suggest that stress can have positive as well as negative consequences. Alan had so much stress that both he and his performance were suffering. Sherry had the right amount of stress—job insecurity was helping her achieve peak performance.

To perform well and advance your career, it is important to identify sources of stress and learn how to keep stress under control. Fortunately, a wide array of techniques and programs are available to help people manage stress. A discussion of a number of them will follow a discussion of the nature, symptoms, and consequences of stress and its related condition, burnout.

THE MEANING OF STRESS AND BURNOUT

Although the terms stress and burnout are part of everyday language, they have several meanings. Here we are concerned with the technical rather than popular meanings of these terms. **Stress** is the mental and physical condition that results from a perceived threat or demand that cannot be dealt with readily.[1] If you perceive something to be dangerous or challenging, you will experience the bodily response known as stress. Alan's sizeup of the potential layoffs brought him negative stress. In contrast, Sherry's sizeup brought her positive stress. When faced with stress on the job, you are usually forced to deviate from normal functioning.

Stress is often associated with strain, yet the two terms differ in an important way. Stress is your response to a force that upsets your equilibrium. **Strain** is the adverse effects of stress on an individual's mind, body, and actions.[2] Alan and Sherry both experienced stress, but only Alan experienced strain.

To add just one more complexity, stress is also tied in with **burnout,** a state of exhaustion stemming from long-term stress. Burnout is a set of behaviors that result from strain. Later in this chapter we will give separate attention to burnout. Keep this relationship in mind to sort out the key terms mentioned so far:

$$\text{Stressors} \rightarrow \text{Stress} \rightarrow \text{Strain} \rightarrow \text{Burnout}$$

THE SYMPTOMS AND CONSEQUENCES OF STRESS

If you experience stress, you display certain signs or symptoms indicating that you are trying to cope with a **stressor,** the force bringing about the stress. These symptoms can also be considered the consequence of stress. With few exceptions, you experience these symptoms only if you perceive the force to be threatening or challenging. An important exception is the stress associated with physical factors such as disease. For example, an overdose of radiation will trigger a stress response in your body even if you are not aware of the presence of radiation.

Physiological Symptoms

The body's physiological and chemical battle against the stressor is the **fight-or-flight response.** The person tries to cope with the adversity in a head-on battle or tries to flee the scene. The physiological changes within the body are virtually identical for different stressors. All types of stressors produce a chemical response within the body, which in turn produces short-term physiological changes.

Among the most familiar reactions are an increase in heart rate, blood pressure, blood glucose, and blood clotting. To help recognize these symptoms, try to recall your internal bodily sensations the last time you were almost in an automobile accident or heard some wonderful news.

If stress is continuous and accompanied by these short-term physiological changes, certain annoying or life-threatening conditions can occur. Among them are heart attacks, strokes, hypertension (high blood pressure), increased cholesterol level, migraine headaches, skin rashes, ulcers, allergies, and colitis.

Unfortunately, prolonged stress also leads to a weakening of the body's immune system, which makes recuperation from illness difficult.[3] People experiencing emotional stress may have difficulty shaking a common cold, or recovering from pneumonia. Evidence is also beginning to accumulate that some forms of cancer, including leukemia and lymphomas, are related to prolonged stress reactions.[4] In general, any disorder classified as *psychosomatic* is precipitated by emotional stress.

Although most of the physiological consequences of stress described here are negative, the right amount of stress prepares us for meeting difficult challenges and spurs us toward peak performance. This issue is explored in the section on stress and job performance.

Psychological Symptoms and Consequences

The psychological or emotional symptoms of stress cover a wide range and show substantial individual differences. Assume two people are faced with the same stressor: The company decides to fire both in order to reduce costs. Person A may be triggered into a depressed mood, mixed with feelings of anger and self-blame. Person B may be triggered into a surge of enthusiasm, mixed with feelings of independence and relief. He or she races home and announces, "Hooray, I've finally found the right excuse to start my own business."

Among the more frequent psychological consequences of stress are tension, anxiety, discouragement, boredom, complaints about bodily problems, prolonged fatigue, feelings of hopelessness, and various kinds of defensive thinking and behavior. People may also experience disturbed inner states as a result of intense or prolonged stress. Here we will describe three of the major psychological consequences of stress, recognizing that psychological and behavioral responses to stress overlap.

Emotion. When faced with stress, people typically react with some form of emotional response. Among the most significant emotional patterns for job-related behavior are anger, fear, and anxiety. The expression of these emotions can be both direct or indiret. A manager who has been demoted may express his anger directly by telling other people in the company how thoughtless the company has become. He may express his anger indirectly by taking an inordinately long time to learn his new job and make frequent errors in the process.

Fear is displayed in response to several job-related stresses. In times of recession many people fear losing their jobs. Their fear reaction typically is to become more and more hesitant to take risks that involve innovative solutions to problems. People fear making mistakes because they fear the penalty associated with having made them. When threats of job loss are high, people fear being fired as a consequence of having made a mistake.

Anxiety is a feeling of apprehension and fearfulness in the absence of specific danger. People experience anxiety when the source of stress is felt, but its implications are not exactly known. A middle manager in a bank talked about his anxiety this way:

> I'm not sure what all these changes mean to me personally, but they have made me so tense that my stomach is churning. I know the bank is trying to promote

more women into officer positions. That must mean that fewer men will be promoted but nobody has said that for sure. Also, a good number of New York City banks have moved into our area. That could have some bad implications for us, but I have seen no problems yet.

Emotional disorder. The vast majority of people have the resilience to handle work pressures without becoming so distressed or disturbed that they succumb to emotional illness. A minority of people, perhaps one in ten, react to severe job pressures by experiencing an emotional disorder. Many of these people were in fragile emotional shape before they experienced the severe job stress. Unfortunately, the job pressure became the "last straw" that brought about emotional disorder. On balance, it should be kept in mind that some jobs—such as air traffic controller or emergency medic—are bad for your mental health.

Defensive attitudes and behavior. People use defense mechanisms to help them lessen anxiety and preserve self-respect. Stress stemming from work as well as personal life can result in this broad group of symptoms. Among the coping attitudes and behavior more frequently found in response to job stress are denial, fantasy, rationalization, and projection.

Denial is an extreme form of defensive behavior in which the person exposed to severe stress denies that a problem exists. An executive was forced into early retirement at age 60 by his firm. He reacted to the forced retirement by taking regular trips to the office for two months. During the day he would busy himself with activities such as reading in the company library and taking plant tours open to the public. In addition, he would confer with his stockbroker and banker. Coaxing by his wife and former boss finally convinced him to accept the fact that he had now entered a different stage of life—that early retirement was no disgrace.

Fantasy represents a type of behavior in which the individual achieves his or her goals and needs through imagination. Denied many times by his company an opportunity to work as an executive, Jeff decided to establish his own "marketing research firm," which he operated during nonworking hours. By judicious use of industrial directories he was able to build up a correspondence file with a number of marketing professors in the United States, Canada, and Europe. His transactions with these people amounted to an occasional exchange of informational letters. Despite the objective facts of the situation, Jeff represented himself to people as the executive director of Market Research International. Close friends tolerated Jeff's fantasy behavior because it amounted to no more than a harmless prank.

Rationalization is the use of socially approved reasons to explain one's behavior. The purpose of rationalization is to defend ourselves against the anxiety associated with the real reason for our behavior. Rationalization is found frequently on the job, as illustrated by the behavior of a sales representative who was accused by his boss of not following up on inquiries. The excuse he offered was:

"I purposely didn't follow-up on on those inquiries. I figured if a prospective customer called back a second time, we would know that the customer is serious."

Projection is a way of protecting oneself from awareness of uncomfortable feelings by attributing them to others. As with other defense mechanisms, projection may surface in response to work stress. Ned, a production control clerk, might aspire to become a manufacturing superintendent. Underneath, he would like to block the progress of better-qualified competitors for such a position. Instead of admitting these feelings to himself, Ned projects them on to others. He contends that the reason he is not being promoted is that others are out to "get him." Projection can lead to paranoid thinking.

Behavioral Symptoms and Consequences

Psychological or emotional symptoms of job stress indicate how people think and feel when placed under job pressures. These symptoms often lead to actual behavior that is of particular concern to the student of human relations in organizations. Among the more frequently observed behavioral consequences of job stress are the following:

- Agitation, restlessness, and other overt signs of tension, including moving your legs back and forth toward each other while seated at a meeting.
- Sudden decreases in job performance due to forgetting to carry out routine activities such as answering mail or returning telephone calls.
- Accident proneness exhibited by an employee who has a good safety record in the past. Or an increased accident frequency experienced by an employee who is already known to be accident prone.
- Drastic changes in eating habits, including decreased or increased food consumption. Under heavy stress, some people become junk food addicts.
- Increased cigarette smoking, coffee drinking, alcohol consumption, and use of illegal drugs.
- Increased use of prescription drugs such as tranquilizers and amphetamines, including diet pills.
- Panic-type behavior, such as making impulsive decisions.
- Errors in concentration and judgment.

This list is a sampling of the behavioral consequences of job stress. Hundreds of symptoms are possible. When workers are placed under too much stress, it tends to exaggerate their weakest tendencies. For instance, a person with a strong temper who usually keeps cool under pressure may throw a tantrum under pressure. The stress symptom of errors in concentration and judgment usually lowers job performance.

Sex Differences in Stress Symptoms

For most of the topics studied in human relations, gender is not an important factor. Stress is an exception. About a dozen scientific studies have investigated whether men and women tend to have different stress symptoms. The most pronounced difference is that women tend to exhibit symptoms of low emotional well-being to a greater extent than men. For instance, women are more likely to get depressed and also report higher rates of emotional discomfort.

In response to stress, men are more likely to suffer from coronary heart disease, cirrhosis of the liver, suicide, and alcoholism. Yet minor physical ailments such as headaches, dizziness, and stomach upsets are reported to be more prevalent in women than men. The overall evidence suggest that men are more prone to serious and incapacitating illness in response to stress. Women more often tend to suffer from less severe psychological problems, yet they have a greater incidence of acute symptoms.[5]

STRESS AND JOB PERFORMANCE

Few people can escape work stress, which is fortunate, because escaping all forms of stress would be undesirable for most of us. An optimum amount of stress exists for most people and most tasks. The inverted J-shaped relationship shown in Figure 5–1 depicts this relationship. In most situations, job performance tends to be best under low to moderate amounts of ordinary stress. Too much stress, and people become temporarily ineffective because they may become distracted or choke. Too little stress, and people tend to become lethargic and inattentive.

Previously it was believed that performance improves steadily as stress is increased, until the stress becomes too intense. It is now believed that performance decreases more rapidly as stress increases.[6] The wrong type of stressor can also

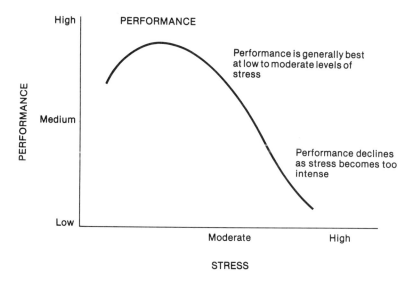

Figure 5–1 The short-term relationship between stress and job performance.

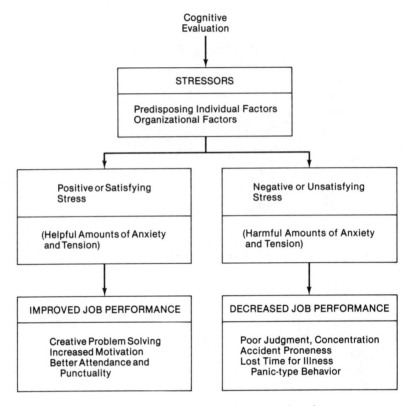

Figure 5–2   How stress influences job behavior and performance.

produce stress that rarely improves job performance, even in small doses. Support for this point was obtained from research conducted with 200 employees in four firms.

The study indicated that negative stress was generally associated with lowered productivity. Also, an optimal level of negative stress was not found.[7] Another study also found that negative stress, such as time urgency, interfered with solving complex problems.[8]

A conclusion to consider is that for most people, challenge and excitement improve job performance. Irritation and threatening events, such as an intimidating boss, generally lower performance.

A Summary Model of Stress and Job Performance

The model shown in Figure 5–2 ties together information about how negative and positive stresses each influence job performance. As described earlier, the individual makes a cognitive evaluation of whether a given event or situation is a stressor. If you perceive an event to be threatening or highly challenging, it becomes a stressor. The stressor can stem from factors within the individual or from the organization. For instance, if the individual has low self-confidence, he or she will experience frequent stress. If the organization expects professional and managerial employees to work 70 hours a week, many organization members will experience stress.

Positive stress. The optimal amount and type of stress is called **eustress**— a positive force in our lives that is the equivalent of finding excitement and challenge.[9] As shown in Figure 5–2, when people experience eustress the result is positive outcomes for themselves and the organization. Problem-solving ability and creativity might be enhanced as the right amount of adrenalin and other hormones flow in our blood and guide us toward peak performance. Attendance and punctuality may also improve because the individual looks forward to the excitement of work.

Nevertheless, even positive stress experienced over a long period of time can impair job performance and harm the individual. Workers who have to gear themselves up for maximum performance on a regular basis, such as entertainers, are frequent victims of stress disorders.

Negative stress. The wrong amount and type of stress is referred to as **distress.** It often results in negative outcomes for the individual and the organization. (Observe that when people use the term "stress," they are generally referring to "distress." The terms stress and distress are therefore used interchangeably.) Several key consequences of distress are shown in Figure 5–2. Above all, people under severe stress make frequent errors in concentration or judgment. For example, many arsonists are business owners who, under the stress of heavy financial losses, arranged for their businesses to be "torched." This criminal act might also be classified as panic behavior.

Errors of concentration and judgment also manifest themselves in less serious matters. Have you ever locked yourself out of your home or lost your keys when under heavy stress? Accident proneness and lost time for illness are other major work consequences of stress.

INDIVIDUAL SOURCES OF STRESS

People often experience job stress based primarily upon their perceptions of the situation, values, and goals, or their personalities. Here we will describe the following individual sources of job distress: Type A behavior, external locus of control, frustrated ambitions, heavy family and personal demands, dislike for rules and regulations, limited tolerance for ambiguity, and negative lifestyle factors.

Type A Behavior

A person who exhibits **Type A behavior** is demanding, impatient, and overstriving, and therefore prone to distress. Type A behavior has two main components. One is a tendency to try to accomplish too many things in too little time. This leads the Type A individual to be impatient and demanding. The other component is free-floating hostility. Because of this sense of urgency and hostility, these people are irritated by trivial things. On the job, people with Type A behavior are aggressive and hard-working. Off the job, they keep themselves preoccupied with all kinds of errands to run and things to do.[10]

Type A personalities frequently have cardiac diseases (such as heart attacks and strokes) at an early age. But not every hard-working and impatient individual is prone toward severe stress disorder. Hard chargers who like what they are doing—including many top executives—are remarkably healthy and outlive less competitive people. New evidence also indicates that people who exhibit Type A behavior recover as quickly from heart attacks as do those with Type B behavior.[11] The latter group is relaxed, patient, and usually nonhostile.

Belief in External Locus of Control

If you believe that your fate is controlled more by external than internal forces, you are probably more susceptible to stress. People with an **external locus of control** believe that external forces control their fate. Conversely, people with an **internal locus of control** believe that fate is pretty much under their control.

The link between locus of control and stress works in this manner: If people believe they can control adverse forces, they are less prone to the stressor of worry about them. For example, if you believe that you can always find a job, you will worry less about unemployment. At the same time, the person who believes in an internal locus of control usually experiences a higher level of job satisfaction.[12] Work is less stressful and more satisfying when you perceive it to be under your control.

What about your locus of control? Do you believe it to be internal? Or is it external?

Frustrated Ambitions

Most organizations need large numbers of employees who are content to work diligently at their jobs without being overly concerned about climbing the organizational ladder. Approximately 1 percent of jobs in any firm are truly executive (policymaking) positions. Thus only a small minority of people who aspire to become executives can be satisfied. The result is a large number of frustrated, dissatisfied people who suffer from the stress of disappointed expectations. Another problem is that many organizations today are reducing the number of managerial positions, making it even more difficult to be promoted.

The stress created by not becoming wealthy and powerful is virtually a pure case of culturally induced stress. With the current trend of people seeking self-fulfillment through work and a high quality of life in general, it is possible that this type of job stress may be on the decline. The leveling off of boom times throughout the world has also had a dampening effect on the career expectations of many young people. Frustrated ambitions are less likely when career expectations are modest.

Heavy Family and Personal Demands

People who place a high premium on leading a full family and personal life often find themselves in conflict between work and personal life. In order to prosper in one's career, some sacrifices are often necessary in terms of personal life. Only the truly well-organized individual can juggle things sufficiently well to perform well in work and in personal life. The constant tugging between the two creates stress for many people. The stronger the value the person places on both areas of life, the greater the potential conflict and stress.

Dislike for Rules and Regulations

Another way of creating stress for yourself in a large organization is to develop an intense dislike for rules and regulations. The pattern of rebelling against rules and regulations within a bureaucracy has been labeled **bureautic** (not bureaucratic) behavior. Such people come to be seen as malcontents by others in the firm.[13] The reason bureautic personalities face so much stress is that they are continually fighting rules and regulations.

Limited Tolerance for Ambiguity

A **limited tolerance for ambiguity** is a tendency to be readily frustrated when situations and tasks are poorly defined. People with a limited tolerance for ambiguity are prone to frustration and stress because job responsibilities are often ambiguous. For instance, a staff specialist might be told by the boss: "Take care of things while I'm out of town." A command of this type can be interpreted in many ways. (More will be said about ambiguous instructions in our discussion of role ambiguity later in the chapter.)

The combination of a Type A personality and limited tolerance for ambiguity increases the chances of distress. A recent study demonstrated that for Type A individuals, an increase in ambiguity is related to an increase in systolic blood pressure, diastolic blood pressure, and triglyceride levels.[14] (Triglyceride is tied in with fatty acids in the arteries that can contribute to heart disease.)

Negative Lifestyle Factors

A **negative lifestyle factor** is any behavior that predisposes one to stress, such as poor eating habits, exercise habits, and heavy ingestion of caffeine, alcohol, and other drugs. People who accumulate these negative lifestyle factors are predisposed to work stress.[15] The reason is that they are in a weakened physical and mental condition. An employee who said he was "freaking out from his job" was referred to the company physician. The physician made these observations about the employee:

> Little wonder that Mr. Watkins displays stress symptoms. He is forty pounds overweight, smokes one pack of cigarettes per day, ingests five diet soft drinks during the day, and backs that up with a six pack of beer each night. His favorite foods all contain a high percentage of animal fat. If he doesn't change his lifestyle, any unusual job pressures may lead him to a heart attack.

ORGANIZATIONAL SOURCES OF STRESS

In many instances, the employer must take the primary blame for creating job stress. We use the word *primary* because neither the individual or the organizational is fully to blame when the person experiences distress. A worker under stress usually has the option to speak up and deal with the problem in a constructive manner. Here we describe nine frequently observed organizational sources of stress, as noted in Figure 5–3.

Figure 5–3   Frequently observed organizational sources of stress

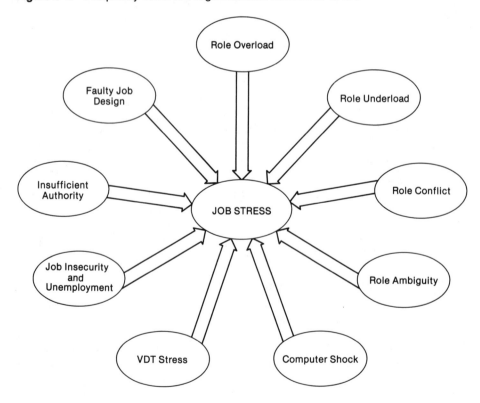

Role Overload

Role overload is a burdensome workload. It can create stress for an individual in two ways. First, the person may accumulate fatigue and thus be less able to tolerate annoyances and irritations. Think of how much easier it is to become provoked over a minor incident when you lack proper rest. Second, a person subject to exorbitant work demands may feel perpetually behind schedule, which in itself creates an uncomfortable, stressful feeling.

Heavy work demands are considered part of an executive's life. However, many people of lesser rank and income are also asked to give up much of their personal freedom and work under continuous pressure during working hours.

Role Underload

A major stressor facing people early in their careers is **role underload,** having too little work to perform. The most general form of underutilization takes place when an employee is given tasks to perform that he or she thinks could be performed by somebody of less education and training. Many employees in professional and technical jobs lament, "Why did they hire a business graduate to do this job? Any clerk could do it equally well."

Role underload creates stress because it frustrates one's desire to make a contribution to the organization. Also, role underload is a stressor because it creates ambiguity. The underutilized person may wonder, "What am I doing here? Why was I hired? Doesn't the company think I can make a contribution?"

Role Conflict

A major organizational stressor is **role conflict,** having to choose between competing demands or expectations. If you comply with one aspect of a role, compliance with the other is more difficult. A basic example would be receiving contradictory orders from two people above you in the organization. Daniel Katz and Robert L. Kahn have identified four types of role conflict:[16]

> *Intrasender* conflict occurs when one person asks you to accomplish two objectives that are in apparent conflict. If your boss asked you to hurry up and finish your work but also decrease your mistakes, you would experience this type of conflict (plus perhaps a headache!).
>
> *Intersender* conflict occurs when two or more senders give you incompatible directions. Your immediate superior may want you to complete a crash project on time, but company policy temporarily prohibits authorizing overtime payments to clerical help.
>
> *Interrole* conflict results when two different roles that you play are in conflict. Your company may expect you to travel 50 percent of the time, while your spouse threatens a divorce if you travel over 25 percent of the time.

Person-role conflict occurs when the role(s) your organization expects you to occupy are in conflict with your basic values. Your company may ask you to fire substandard performers, but this could be in conflict with your humanistic values.

Role Ambiguity

Role ambiguity is a condition in which the job holder receives confusing or poorly defined expectations. Workers in all kinds and sizes of organizations are often placed in a situation where job responsibilities are sloppily defined. As we mentioned in the discussion about individual sources of stress, many people become anxious when faced with role ambiguity. One reason is that being out of control is a stressor. If you lack a clear picture of what you should be doing, it is difficult to get your job under control. Here is a representative example of role ambiguity:

> A man was hired into a management-training program and given the elegant title of "assistant to the general manager." After three days of reading company manuals and taking plant tours, he pressed for an explanation of what he was supposed to be doing in the assignment. His boss told him: "Just try to make yourself useful. I'll be going out of town for two weeks. If you have any questions, ask my secretary for help."

Computer Shock

Despite their contribution to productivity, computers also create stress for many workers. **Computer shock,** as defined here, is a strong negative reaction to being forced to spend many more hours working at a computer than one expected or desires. Among its symptoms are a glassy-eyed, detached look, aching neck muscles, and a growing dislike for high technology. An extreme form of computer shock took place in a bank. Unable to get the information he needed because of the third computer failure in one week, an employee shot the computer terminal with a gun. Computer shock can also be viewed as an acute form of job dissatisfaction, stemming from disappointed expectations about the world of work. As told by Mindy, a manufacturing specialist:

> The reason I majored in business was so I could get a job working with people. I never minded doing my share of writing reports and crunching numbers. I put up with it so I could spend most of my time relating to people. After graduation I took an interesting sounding job as an inventory-control specialist. Little did I know I would be sitting behind a computer almost all day, every day. I hardly talk to anybody. I'm even supposed to communicate with my boss by sending messages on the computer. Now the company is telling me to get more advanced computer training. I'm looking for another job. Especially one that involves working with people.

VDT Stress

Computer shock is a general form of stress associated with computer work that is largely emotional. A more physical form of stress associated with computer work is tied specifically to video display terminals (VDTs). **VDT stress** is an adverse physical and psychological reaction to prolonged work at a video display terminal. One study showed that VDT users were absent from work three or more times a year than were other employees.[17] The symptoms most often reported by VDT workers are:[18]

- Irritability
- Shaking inside the body
- Headaches
- Extreme fatigue
- Pressure in the neck
- Nervousness and high levels of tension
- Stress in general
- Severe eyestrain
- Numbness and tingling in arms, legs, and feet
- Loss of strength in arms and legs

Another source of stress associated with VDT usage is worry about pregnancy disorders. Several cases of women from the same department suffering from miscarriages and birth defects have been reported in the United States and Canada.[19] The working women's organization, 9to5, maintains a "VDT hotline" to answer questions about pregnancy concerns of VDT workers (and the fathers of their fetuses).

Many people believe that these pregnancy concerns are unwarranted and based upon false rumors. The president of a business equipment manufacturer's association contends that there is no causal relationship between damage to the fetus and VDT usage. Similarly, the position of the American College of Obstetricians and Gynecologists is that "There is no scientific evidence to link VDTs with any sort of birth defect or adverse affect to pregnancy, that is, from the display terminals themselves."[20]

Job Insecurity and Unemployment

People have traditionally worried about losing their jobs because of budget cuts and automation. Two current sources of job insecurity are layoffs caused by mergers and acquisitions, and the quest for "lean" organizations. Layoffs often occur after one firm acquires or merges with another for two primary reasons. (1) The merged organization will have duplicate positions, such as two vice-presidents of finance. (2) The organization may have to trim the payroll in order to save money. Major expenses involved in purchasing another firm include stock purchases and legal fees.

A **lean organization** is one in which there is a minimum of nonessential functions and employees. Figuratively, the "fat" has been trimmed from the firm. In order to achieve leanness, many large firms have laid off as much as 20 percent of their workforce.[21] Worrying about whether they will become one of the next to be laid off or asked to retire early becomes a stressor for many workers.

Unemployment itself generates more stress than the threat of job insecurity. Unemployed people, in comparison to employed people, have much higher rates of depression, suicide, homicide, child abuse, and spouse abuse. One study of joblessness showed that people unable to find jobs express low self-esteem, personal powerlessness, and many forms of psychosomatic distress.[22] Part of the problem is that the identity of many people is related to their occupation. Being unemployed is thus a blow to their self-identity.

Insufficient Authority

An axiom of management is that people need the right kind and amount of authority to accomplish their jobs. If people do not have enough authority to carry out their assigned tasks, the situation can be stressful. Imagine yourself as a supervisor given a job to accomplish in a short period of time. You will be held responsible if you fail, but you are not given sufficient authority to work your subordinates overtime or hire additional help. If you are conscientious, or worried about your job, the situation will act as a stressor.

Faulty Job Design

Another important source of job stress centers around flaws within the design of jobs. The job of air traffic controller, for example, is widely recognized as a stress inducer. To illustrate, each air traffic controller at O'Hare airport in Chicago is responsible for landing a plane every two minutes. Simultaneously, the controller must monitor a half dozen others on the screen. Since the pressures are so great, controllers are allowed to work only 90 consecutive minutes during peak hours. Despite these precautions, turnover is high, tenure is short, and psychosomatic disorders such as ulcers and high blood pressure are epidemic.[23]

JOB BURNOUT: ONE CONSEQUENCE OF LONG-TERM STRESS

Job burnout is a condition of emotional, mental, and physical exhaustion, along with cynicism toward work, in response to long-term stressors. Psychoanalyst Herbert Freudenberger observes that burnout is the final stage of an adverse reaction to stress. Even though burnout is not a recognized personality disturbance, its sufferers experience symptoms in common. Physical signs of burnout include lingering colds, headaches, backaches, sleep problems, complexion problems, and stomach distress. Mental and emotional symptoms of burnout include cynicism, irritation, frustration, procrastination, and difficulties in concentration.[24]

Burnout was originally observed primarily among people helpers such as nurses, social workers, and police workers. It then became apparent that people in almost any occupation could develop burnout. Conscientiousness and perfectionism contribute to burnout. If you strive for perfection, you stand a good chance of being disappointed about not achieving everything. Organizations also play a role in contributing to burnout. If your efforts go unappreciated and you are given very little emotional support, your chances for burnout increase.

Before reading about burnout, answer the burnout checklist shown in Figure 5–4. The remainder of our discussion about burnout concerns the behavior of burnout victims, and tactics for managing burnout.

Behaviors Associated with Burnout

Several burnout symptoms have already been mentioned above. Three major behavioral patterns indicate that burnout is present.[25]

1. *Emotional, mental, and physical exhaustion.* Burnout victims are exhausted. When asked how they feel, these people typically answer that they feel drained or used up, at the end of their rope, physically fatigued. Often the burnout victim dreads going to work even though he or she was once idealistic about what could be accomplished.
2. *Withdrawing from people.* Burnout victims try to cope with emotional exhaustion by becoming less personally involved with co-workers. The burned-out employee develops a detached air, becomes cynical of relationships with others, and feels callous toward others and the organization.
3. *Low personal accomplishment.* The final aspect of burnout is a feeling of low personal accomplishment. The once idealistic employee begins to realize there are too many barriers to accomplishing what needs to be done. Often he or she lacks the energy to perform satisfactorily. Managers suffering from burnout hurt the organization because they create a ripple effect, spreading burnout to subordinates.

Treating and Preventing Burnout

Dealing with burnout follows many of the same procedures as dealing with stress. The major reason is that burnout is the end product of stress. If you are burned out, you will have many stress symptoms. Surprisingly, the physical symptoms of burnout are generally less severe than those associated with other major stress problems. Despite the similarities between dealing with stress and burnout, five specific approaches can be noted.

1. To overcome and prevent burnout, develop realistic expectations. One of the reasons employees develop burnout is that they try to be "miracle workers." If you develop realistic expectations, you are less likely to feel crushed when you achieve modest goals. For instance, a safety and health specialist might say: "If I can convince three managers a month to combat safety and health hazards in the workplace, I'll consider it a victory."
2. Reward yourself, just as in self-motivation. Burnout often comes about because we feel that our efforts are unappreciated. A useful antidote is therefore to reward yourself, such as purchasing a new T-shirt, when you accomplish something worthwhile. The message is to take care of yourself, rather than wait for others to give you the reward you deserve.

Figure 5–4   The burnout checklist.

Directions: Check each one of the following statements that generally or usually applies to you.

1. I feel tired much more frequently than I used to. _____
2. I get very irritated at people lately. _____
3. I suffer from a number of annoying physical problems such as neckaches and backaches. _____
4. I often feel that I am losing control of my life. _____
5. I'm feeling pretty depressed these days. _____
6. I get down on myself too often. _____
7. My life seems to be at a dead end. _____
8. My enthusiasm for life has gone way down. _____
9. I'm tired of dealing with the same old problems. _____
10. I've pretty much withdrawn from friends and family. _____
11. Not much seems humorous to me anymore. _____
12. There's really nothing for me to look forward to at work or at school. _____
13. It's difficult for me to care about what's going on in the world outside. _____
14. My spark is gone. _____
15. I know that I have a problem but I just don't have the energy to do anything about it. _____
16. I usually dread going to work or school. _____
17. My friends say that my temper is getting pretty short. _____
18. I don't get nearly enough appreciation from my boss. _____
19. I've begun to feel sorry for myself. _____
20. I find it difficult to get out of bed in the morning. _____

Interpretation: The more of these statements that accurately apply to you, the more likely it is that you are experiencing burnout. If you checked 15 or more of these statements, it would be helpful to discuss your feelings with a mental health professional.

3. Build a network of social support.[26] Burnout victims often feel isolated from others. If you develop a group of friends who will give you emotional support and reassurance, you can soften the feelings of isolation. And as with any personal problem, just talking it over with a friend helps.

4. Attempt to get a job transfer. The fresh perspective that comes from job rotation can help reduce the staleness that may have caused the burnout. For example, to combat burnout in her travel agency, Marles Casto tries to "cross-utilize" employees. She does this by transferring them to different locations to work at the same level. Casto is also planning to offer sabbaticals for employees who have been at the agency for at least four years.[27]

5. Allow for a *decompression period* between work and home life. The interval of time allows the person to shift gears mentally. The originator of this idea, Sharin Levin, suggests: "Listen to the radio, window shop, or stop at a health spa. Rather than be frustrated by commuting, use the time to relax. The key is that you view the time as your own."[28]

INDIVIDUAL METHODS OF STRESS MANAGEMENT

Because stress is such a widespread problem, many techniques have been used to help reduce or prevent stress. The distinction between methods of reducing and preventing stress is not clear-cut. For example, proponents of physical exercise as a way of managing stress and its concomitant tension say that physical conditioning not only reduces stress, it gives you a way of life that helps you prevent stress. Methods of stress management in the control of the individual vary from highly specific techniques (such as the relaxation response) to more global methods that reflect a lifestyle. Among the latter would be maintaining a diet that is free of caffeine, alcohol, excessive sugar, and junk food.

In this section we examine methods of stress management basically in control of the individual. In the following section our attention turns to the organization's role in stress management.

Identify Your Own Stress Signals

An effective program of stress management begins with self-awareness. Midge Wilson, a clinical psychologist, urges that you learn to identify your own particular reactions to stress. Take note of their intensity as well as the time of the day when the symptoms occur. Often the mere act of keeping a record of stress symptoms lessens their incidence and severity. More than likely this phenomenon is related to the realization that you are starting to take charge of your health.

Once you have learned to pick up warning signs, the next step is to identify *what* and *how* you were thinking and feeling prior to the onset of the symptoms. For example, if your boss tells you that your report is needed in a hurry you may begin to fret. What usually triggers stress reactions is your own stream of negative thoughts, such as "I will be criticized if this report isn't finished on time," or "If this report isn't perfect, I'll be fired."

It is crucial to learn how to terminate unproductive, worrisome thoughts. A recommended technique is that of thought-stopping, or canceling. It works this way: Choose either the term "stop" or "cancel" and quietly but emphatically repeat it whenever you catch yourself engaging in anxiety-provoking thought. At first, this may be as many as 50 to 100 times per day.[29]

Eliminate or Modify the Stressor

Underlying any approach to reducing stress is this key principle.[30] Until you take constructive action about reducing stress itself or removing the causes of stress, you will continue to suffer. One value of tranquilizing medication is that it calms down a person enough that he or she can deal constructively with the source of stress.

At times, the first step taken to overcome a source of stress or to reduce the discomfort of stress may seem modest. However, the fact that you are now working toward a solution to your problem may make you feel better about the problem. To illustrate, if you find that working Saturday mornings is creating problems between you and your spouse, it behooves you to deal constructively with that problem. Discuss the problem with your boss and/or your spouse. One man facing this problem spoke to his supervisor and was pleased to learn that he could substitute working late on Thursday nights for his Saturday assignment.

Improve Your Work Habits

People typically experience job stress when they feel they are losing, or have lost, control of their work assignments. Perhaps you are familiar with the distress associated with the feeling that you are hopelessly behind schedule on several important tasks. Conscientious people, in particular, experience distress when they cannot get their work under control. Improving your work habits and time management will help you relieve this source of stress. Chapter 18 is devoted entirely to work habit improvement and time management.

Get Physical Exercise

Physical exercise has become the most widely used method of stress management. The major reason is that physical exercise is widely acknowledged as a tension reducer. Another important reason is that being in good physical condition helps you cope with stress. A person with a cardiac system beautifully toned by an appropriate amount of exercise is less likely to experience a heart attack when overworked than a person whose heart is weak from insufficient exercise. Physical exercise is also beneficial because it helps prepare your mind for tough mental tasks. Finally, being in good physical condition makes you more resistant to fatigue. You can therefore handle a bigger physical or mental workload.

Everyday Methods of Relaxation

The simple expedient of learning to relax is an important method of reducing the tensions brought about by both positive and negative stress. A sample of everyday suggestions for relaxing is presented in Table 5–1. If you can accomplish these, you may not need formal methods of tension reduction such as tranquilizing medication or biofeedback training.

The Relaxation Response

The **relaxation response (RR)** is a bodily reaction in which you experience a slower respiration rate and heart rate, lowered blood pressure, and lowered metabolism. The response can be brought about in several ways, including meditation, exercise, or prayer. By practicing the RR, you can counteract the fight or flight response associated with stress.[31]

According to cardiologist Herbert Benson, four things are necessary to practice the RR: a quiet environment, an object to focus on, a passive attitude, and a comfortable position. The RR is to be practiced 10 to 20 minutes, twice a day. To evoke the relaxation response, Benson advises: "Close your eyes. Relax. Concentrate on one word or prayer. If other thoughts come to mind, be passive, and return to the repetition."[32]

Table 5–1 Everyday suggestions for relaxation

1. Plan to have at least one idle period every day.
2. Talk over problems with a friend.
3. Have a good laugh; laughter is a potent tension reducer.
4. Read books and articles that demand concentration rather than trying to speed read everything.
5. Avoid becoming stressed about things over which you have no control.
6. Breathe deeply, and tell yourself you can cope with the situation between inhaling and exhaling.
7. Have a quiet place or retreat at home.
8. Take a leisurely vacation during which virtually every moment is not programmed.
9. Live by the calendar, not by the stop watch.
10. Concentrate on one task at a time, rather than thinking of what assignment you will be tackling next.
11. Finish something you have started, however small. Accomplishing almost anything reduces some stress.
12. Hug somebody you like, including a pet.

SOURCE: Meyer Friedman and Ray H. Rosenman, *Type A Behavior and Your Heart* (Greenwich, CT: Fawcett Crest, 1975), pp. 207–271; Philip Morgan and H. Kent Baker, "Dealing with Job Stress," *Supervisory Management,* pp. 26–28; "Instant Stress Relievers," *Practical Supervision,* 1986 sample edition, p. 7.

The Quieting Response

Another similar method of stress management is the learning of a quieting response. According to this method you identify a stressor situation which includes minor annoyances such as being stuck in traffic. You then take two deliberate deep breaths, paying attention to relaxing the jaw, the shoulders, and tongue. You tell yourself, "I will not permit my body to get involved in this." This breaks the sequence of the stress response. To manage stress with the quieting response, it will be necessary to repeat the procedure about 20 to 40 times a day.[33]

Muscle Monitoring

An important part of many stress reduction programs is to learn to relax your muscles. You learn to literally loosen up and be less uptight. Muscle monitoring involves becoming aware that your muscles have tightened and then consciously relaxing them. If your jaw muscles are tightening up in a tense situation, you learn to relax your jaw enough to overcome the stress effects.

It is helpful to determine whether muscle tautness occurs in association with some recurring event. If it does, pay attention to the tautness of your muscles on those occasions.[34] For example, you might experience a tightening of your neck muscles whenever you are about to engage in a confrontation. Take a few moments to be aware of that muscle tension. After a while you will learn to relax when you are about to express disagreement with another person over an important issue.

Rehearsal of the Stressful Situation

Imagine yourself having the unpleasant task of having to resign from one job in order to take a better one. You are tense, and your tension level increases as the day progresses. (You have already tried muscle monitoring and the relaxation response, but you still have butterflies!) One approach to relaxing enough to handle this situation is to rehearse this scenario mentally. Most important, rehearse your opening line, which might be something like, "Scott, I've asked to see you to discuss something very important," or "Scott, the company has been very nice to me, but I've decided to make an important change in my life."

It is also helpful to anticipate other aspects of the scenario, such as what you would do if Scott told you that he would not accept your resignation. Or worse, what you would say if Scott turned on you and began to call you ungrateful and unappreciative?

Biofeedback Training

Biofeedback training is a relaxation technique involving an electronic machine that helps you develop an awareness of muscle sensations, pulse rate, breathing rate, and other physiological stress symptoms. After awareness comes the ability to control bodily activities that are ordinarily considered involuntary. For instance, through biofeedback you might be able to slow down your breathing rate. The learning would take place in a laboratory, but you would presumably be able to transfer this learning to a job situation. By slowing down your breathing rate you may be able to regain your composure and increase your effectiveness in the potentially stressful job situation (such as making a presentation to top management).

In a typical biofeedback setup, a person is attached to an instrument that continuously measures muscle tension with an electromyograph (EMG). Feedback of this type is designed to take continuous measurements of the tension level of particular muscles and to communicate this information to the person attached to the machine. As described by two biofeedback specialists:

> The humlike tone emitted by the EMG will change as it senses changes in the level of muscle tension. When the person tenses, the pitch of the tone rises proportionately. Conversely, when the person relaxes, the pitch falls. By hearing the pitch of the EMG tone, the person is able to learn how to control the tension level of his or her body. The continuous monitoring can allow the person to learn to relax muscle tension by continuously rewarding the desired behavior of relaxing with a lower pitch tone.[35]

Biofeedback training does not eliminate stress, but helps the distressed person relieve the physical symptoms of distress and become capable of concentrating on the problem situation. Tension headaches are a case in point. Headaches of this type are usually caused by contractions in the scalp and neck muscles. Using EMG biofeedback, a person can learn to relax these muscles even though the tension-producing stress is still present.

Concentration on Work or Hobby

For those individuals who do not wish to bother or feel uncomfortable going through formal exercises to relieve or prevent stress, a solid alternative exists. Learning to concentrate on a meaningful activity for 30-minute periods can be stress reducing. For example, you might concentrate so hard on what you are studying that the book in front of you (and its contents) is your only touch with reality. Should you prefer tennis as a way of practicing concentration, stare so hard at the ball that it appears to be grapefruit sized. Furthermore, you should be able to read the trademark with clarity—even while playing.

The principle underlying concentration as a method of tension reduction is probably similar to the underlying principle behind other relaxation approaches. Your muscles and brain seem to be energized by carefully focusing them on something quite specific. Even if tension is not reduced, performance in the task at hand is improved!

Choosing the Best Stress Management Technique

A logical question at this point is whether different stress management techniques are particularly helpful for different people or different stressors. A general answer to this question is not yet available. Nevertheless, we do know that not all techniques work equally well for everybody. For instance, many impatient individuals would find it tension-provoking to disrupt their work by practicing the relaxation response. Of perhaps greater significance, relaxation techniques in general may be harmful for some people. Several reports indicate that some people become more anxious or tense when they try to relax. Among their symptoms are restlessness, profuse perspiration, trembling, and rapid breathing.[36]

The best general rule is to try different stress management techniques until you find one that is effective. For instance, you might find attacking the stressor much more useful than the quieting response. If one technique decreases your symptoms to your satisfaction, use it again. Since most stress techniques take time to learn, give each one a fair trial. If it does not work for you, move on to another.

ORGANIZATIONAL METHODS OF STRESS MANAGEMENT

Employers have an important responsibility for reducing and preventing job stress and burnout. It is also part of management's responsibility to create enough stress in the job environment to keep employees challenged and stimulated. Bored employees are often both unhappy and unproductive. In keeping with the major emphasis of this chapter, we will describe several general and specific strategies for reducing and preventing distress.

Practice Good Human Resource Management

What constitutes good human resource (or personnel) management is a book-length subject in itself. Human resource programs include those for employee selection, training, compensation, motivation, and assistance with personal problems (described below). Any one of these programs, properly administered, will help prevent and sometimes reduce stress. For instance, if the right employee is selected for a job, the employee will perform well. Good performance, in turn, helps prevent the stress stemming from job dissatisfaction and feelings of self-doubt.

A compensation program that rewards people for good performance might reduce stress in this manner. Many employees are anxious and tense about not having enough money to cover expenses. If such an employee received extra money for exceptional performance, he or she could reduce some anxiety and tension.

Create Meaningful Jobs

Work has become a central source for the satisfaction of higher-level needs among many managerial, professional, and technical employees. Part of the new emphasis on quality of work life includes the belief that good job satisfaction is part of good life satisfaction. Given such high expectations of work, frustration and stress result for many employees when their work fails to satisfy growth needs. Careful attention to enriching jobs can thus pay dividends in stress reduction and prevention.

Meaningful jobs are stress reducing in another significant way. Resistance to the effects of some forms of job stress is higher when individuals are committed to their work. The product manager who has lived with her product from the idea stage to actual marketing may be able to withstand a heavy workload because of her commitment. In contrast, the computer operations manager may find irregular work hours stressful because he is continually working on "other peoples' problems"—those to which he is not committed.

Clarify Responsibilities

Many forms of job stress are created by ambiguity about what employees are supposed to be doing. It follows that clarifying job duties and responsibilities could reduce and prevent many stressful situations. Sometimes clarification of an employee's responsibilities can eliminate the confusion about his or her role. A case in point is the person assigned to a special task force. That individual receives orders from his or her regular boss and the head of the task force. The result may be role conflict and its accompanying stress because the employee does not know whose orders should receive top priority. The task force leader, the employee's regular boss, and the employee could gather in a three-way huddle to resolve this conflict. In short, a general strategy for reducing stress generated by role conflict is to let employees know what is expected of them, by whom, and when.

Modifying the Organizational Structure

Rearranging or modifying the organizational structure can sometimes reduce and prevent stress. The object is to redesign the structure so that the stressful elements in a job are reduced to a healthy level. One basic example would be to reduce the span of control (number of direct subordinates) of a manager who was overwhelmed with dealing with so many subordinates. The establishment of a complaint department also helps reduce stress for employees who previously had to deal directly with irate customers. Now all complaints are channeled through one tough-skinned employee.

Participative Decision Making

Some employees find it stressful to be left out of important decisions that directly affect their welfare. Therefore another managerial action capable of reducing stress reactions in some employees is the use of participative decision making (PDM). A caution is that participation in routine and trivial decisions is transparent to employees and might tend to increase, not decrease, job stress.[37] The underlying psychology to PDM as a stress reducer is perhaps that many people feel better when they believe they are in control of their jobs. Participating in decision making is one way of gaining more control.

Establish a Supportive Organizational Climate

Organizational climate is the general atmosphere or personality of an organization. Climate can influence employee stress levels in several ways. A firm that has genuine concern for the welfare of people will trigger less stress than a firm that disregards the feelings of people. A supportive climate tends to increase job satisfaction and productivity. Simultaneously, such a climate decreases job stress.

An extensive study conducted in Japanese industry gives credence to the idea that a supportive climate can decrease employee stress. After administering a 596-item questionnaire to 130,000 employees, psychologist Hiroto Kobuta noted that the organization climate influences employee stress. Employees with the most stress worked for *tight companies*, those with rigid and inflexible policies. In contrast, employees who experienced less stress worked for *loose companies*, those with flexible policies.

The tie-in with a supportive climate is that the loose companies were more supportive of employees. The corporation's policy on loans to employees illustrates the difference. A rigid company would set a maximum loan and hold to it, regardless of the reason for the loan. A loose company would allow the personnel department to take into account unusual circumstances, and bend the rule if warranted.[38]

Wellness Programs and Physical Fitness Programs

To help combat negative work stress, many employers offer programs that encourage employees to stay in physical and mental shape. Sometimes these programs are called stress management programs or physical fitness programs. Currently, the emphasis is on **wellness programs**—formal programs to help employees stay well and avoid illness. The types of stress management techniques mentioned in this chapter are included in most wellness programs. Workshops and seminars offered in wellness programs include:[39]

- Stress management
- Weight control (for both overweight and underweight people)

- Smoking control
- Alcohol control
- Nutrition
- Physical fitness
- Preventive health care
- Safety on the job and at home
- Hypertension (high blood pressure) control

All these topics relate to stress management. For instance, proper diet (such as decreasing caffeine and fatty foods) makes one less susceptible to stress. If your physical health is good, you can tolerate more job frustrations.

EMPLOYEE ASSISTANCE PROGRAMS (EAPs)

The personal problems of some employees create so much stress for them that job performance suffers. In response to this problem, over 6,000 employee assistance programs (EAPs) have been created. An **employee assistance program (EAP)** is a formal organization unit designed to help employees deal with personal problems that adversely affect job performance. Some of these personal problems, however, are closely related to the job. For instance, an employee might increase his or her use of alcohol because of work stress. Most large- and medium-size organizations have EAPs of their own, or belong to an EAP that serves many firms. EAPs are found in both private and public organizations.

General Format of an EAP

EAPs take a variety of forms, from simple referral services to fully staffed in-house programs.[40] The referral service means that employees who visit the EAP coordinator are in turn referred to an outside agency for help. Employees come to the attention of the EAP in three primary ways: urging by supervisors, self-referral, and through co-workers calling someone's attention to the problem. In other instances, family and friends urge an employee to visit the company EAP. The accompanying box provides a representative summary of the operations of an employee assistance program. This particular program is used by a number of companies.

Professional specialists employed by the EAP include physicians, clinical psychologists, social workers, nurses, alcohol counselors, drug counselors, career counselors, financial counselors, and lawyers. These specialists hint at the most frequent type of problems referred to an EAP. Among them are alcohol dependency, drug dependency, financial problems, marital problems, personality clashes on the job, and legal problems.

Although supervisors may recommend that employees seek help, the EAP program is designed to be voluntary. Employees therefore make the ultimate decision to seek help themselves. In many organizations, however, supervisors place subtle pressure on problem employees to obtain help from the EAP.

Confidentiality

An essential feature of EAPS is that they are confidential. Publicity about the program emphasizes its confidentiality. Brochures, notices, and articles in company newspapers all state that the program is confidential and that records remain in EAP files only. Neither the personnel department nor an employee's manager has access to EAP records. However, if the EAP specialist thinks the employee is homicidal, suicidal, or a potential saboteur, these confidences will be broken. Despite the confidential of EAPs, the company is aware of which people they refer to the EAP. Yet most EAPs do not reveal the names of self-referrals.

On balance, EAPS have proved to be cost-effective. The cost of these programs is returned many times in terms of the improved job performance of employees who are treated successfully. For example, approximately 75 percent of alcoholics referred to EAPs later return to satisfactory job performance. EAPs are much less successful in treating drug abusers.[41] Another concern about EAPs is that many managerial and professional employees fear attending them. Although the program is confidential, some workers believe they will be labeled "problem people" if they request assistance.

We know that the people who walk in our doors each day are more than just employees. They're one of a kind individuals with complex lives and complex problems. And when a personal problem is making life difficult, it's also making work difficult. The care and attention an EAP provides will help an employee accurately assess the problem and find a way to resolve it.

We're offering this service because we're concerned about each employee's personal well-being and also because it makes good financial sense.

WHAT IS IT? It's a service that provides confidential counseling to help resolve personal problems of an employee.

Your employer has retained the services of PERSONAL PERFORMANCE CONSULTANTS to help employees when a personal problem is getting out of hand, and also to help supervisors when employees are having trouble at work because of problems at home. Since no one is immune to personal problems, it's reasonable to expect that every employee at one time or another could benefit from talking with an EAP counselor. **THE SERVICES OF PERSONAL PERFORMANCE CONSULTANTS HAVE BEEN PRE-PAID BY YOUR EMPLOYER AND THERE IS NO COST TO EMPLOYEES.**

WHO IS PERSONAL PERFORMANCE CONSULTANTS, INC.? Personal Performance Consultants (PPC) is a private consulting firm headquartered in St. Louis. They do

the counseling. They also provide ongoing education and communications about the program.

PPC is comprised of professionals from the fields of psychology, law, social work, and business. Descriptions of the backgrounds of PPC staff members are available upon request.

WHAT TYPES OF PROBLEMS CAN THE EAP HELP SOLVE? The program is set up to help people with all types of personal problems—marital conflict, alcoholism, financial jams, emotional problems, family conflict, etc.

Sometimes people can solve these problems on their own but often outside help makes the difference between stopping a problem cold or going through a long period of struggle and coping, a period when people are unable to be themselves at home or at work.

HOW LONG DO COUNSELING SESSIONS LAST AND HOW MANY ARE NECESSARY? Individual sessions usually last an hour. Sessions for couples and families may last 30 to 45 minutes longer.

Most problems can be handled in three to four sessions—with hard work by both the counselor and you. At the end of these sessions you will have either resolved the problem or developed a detailed plan of action to resolve it, a plan that makes sense to you because you create it along with the counselor. Sometimes this plan may involve referral to a resource other than PPC. This only occurs when long term assistance, specialized care or hospitalization is needed.

ARE THERE ANY COSTS TO ME FOR PPC SERVICES? PPC services have been prepaid by your employer. If you and the PPC counselor decide additional resources outside of PPC are necessary, you will be responsible for any charges associated with the use of these outside resources. Sometimes your group health plan will cover these costs. The decision to use any outside resources is always left up to the client. Most clients (70 to 75%) are served solely through PPC and do not require outside referrals.

IS COUNSELING REALLY CONFIDENTIAL? *YES. EVERYTHING DISCUSSED IN COUNSELING SESSIONS IS COMPLETELY CONFIDENTIAL.* Most employees make their own appointments and can rest assured that their employer won't even know their names. PPC simply does not reveal names of self-referred employees. In some instances, employees are referred to the EAP by their supervisor because of a performance problem. When this is the case the supervisor is given only the following details:

Whether or not the employee kept the appointment.

Whether or not the employee has decided on and is following a plan to solve the personal problem.

All discussion between the counselor and the employee is strictly confidential.

IF MY SUPERVISOR REFERS ME TO THE EAP AND I USE IT, WILL MY FUTURE WITH MY EMPLOYER BE JEOPARDIZED? *ABSOLUTELY NOT.* As always, your job performance determines your future. The decision to use the program is yours and whatever you decide will be respected. On-the-job performance is what counts, not your participation in the EAP.

HOW DO I MAKE AN APPOINTMENT WITH A COUNSELOR? You can arrange an appointment by calling PPC directly between 8:30 A.M. and 5:15 P.M., Monday through Friday. An assistant will answer the phone (if you would rather speak directly with a counselor, just ask). The assistant will ask the name of your employer, your name, and when you would like an appointment.

WHAT HAPPENS WHAN I GO TO THE PPC OFFICE? You'll be met by an assistant who will either take you immediately into a counselor's office or show you to a private waiting room where you can sit, have some coffee, and relax until your counselor is free to see you.

The counselor will begin by reviewing a "Statement of Understanding" describing PPC services and pointing out the confidentiality of the service. The counselor will answer any general questions you have and then ask why you are seeking assistance. This begins the session.

The counselor will not tell you what to do about your problem, but will discuss your situation and help you make up your own mind about what you think, feel and want. If the counselor asks questions, it will be to help you get a better perspective on your situation.

WHERE DOES COUNSELING TAKE PLACE? PPC provides offices at various locations for your convenience. When you call, ask the assistant for locations in your area.

Summary of Key Points

☐ To manage your career or manage others, it is important to identify sources of stress and to learn how to reduce and prevent stress. Stress is the mental and physical condition that results from a perceived threat or demand that cannot be dealt with readily. Burnout is a state of mental, emotional, and physical exhaustion stemming from long-term stress.

☐ Stress has a variety of physiological, psychological, and behavioral symptoms or consequences. The physiological symptoms are tied in with the fight-or-flight response when faced with a stressor. Psychological symptoms include fear, anxiety, emotional disorder, and defensive attitudes and behavior. A major job-related behavior symptom of stress is errors in concentration and judgment. Men tend to have more severe stress symptoms than women, but women have a greater incidence of minor symptoms.

☐ Job stress is almost inevitable. The right amount and type of stress (eustress) enhances performance and personal welfare. Too much stress, or any stress from the wrong type of stressor, leads to distress, which lowers satisfaction and performance.

☐ People often experience job stress based on their perception of the situation, values and goals, or their personality characteristics. These major individual sources of stress include: Type A behavior, external locus of control, frustrated ambitions, heavy family and personal demands, dislike for rules and regulations, limited tolerance for ambiguity, and negative lifestyle factors (poor diet and health practices).

☐ Organizational sources of stress include the following: role overload, role underload, role conflict, role ambiguity, computer shock, VDT stress, job insecurity and unemployment, insufficient authority, and faulty job design.

☐ Job burnout is the final stage of an adverse reaction to stress that includes both physical, mental, and emotional symptoms. Cynicism is pronounced in burnout. The major behaviors associated with burnout are as follows: emotional, mental, and physical exhaustion; withdrawing from people; and low sense of personal accomplishment. Relief from burnout requires treatment of the stress aspects. Other relief tactics include developing realistic expectations, self-rewards, social support, job transfer, and decompression time.

☐ Methods the individual can use in reducing and preventing job stress include the following: identify your own stress signals; eliminate or modify the stressor; improve your work habits; get physical exercise; methods of relaxation: the relaxation response; the quieting response; or muscle monitoring; rehearse the stressful situation; use biofeedback training; and concentrate on work or hobby. It is important to select a technique that suits your style and circumstances.

☐ Organizational methods of reducing and preventing stress include: practice good human resource management; create meaningful jobs; clarify responsibilities; modify the organizational structure; use participative decision making; establish a supportive organizational climate; have wellness and physical fitness programs. Employee assistance programs (EAPs) help employees deal with personal or work problems that are stressful enough to lower job performance. The supervisor refers the stressed employee to the EAP, where he or she is then assigned to the right treatment facility.

Questions and Activities

1. A student once told this author, "You have to give me a deadline for my paper. Otherwise I can't handle it." What does her statement tell you about (a) the stressor she was facing, and (b) how pressure influences her work performance?

2. Why do so many people brag about being burned out?

3. What ambitions or personal characteristics of yours do you think currently, or will in the future, create stress for you?

4. Identify the stressors created by your program of study. What could be done to modify them?

5. How does a person know when he or she is experiencing distress?

6. To what extent do you think the current concern about job stress and burnout is just a fad? Explain.

7. The head of a neighborhood center who was attending a workshop on burnout said to the workshop leader, "So far you haven't convinced me that burnout is anything more than an old-fashioned case of the blahs." How would you respond to this person's comments?

8. Identify two jobs that you think create negative stress for most incumbents, and pinpoint the stressors.

9. Suppose you had financial problems serious enough to impair your concentration on the job. Would you volunteer to seek help through the firm's EAP? Why or why not?

10. Interview a person in a high-pressure job in any field. Find out if the person experiences stress, and how he or she copes with the stress.

A Human Relations Case

THE STRESS EPIDEMIC

Wendy Fernandez, human resources manager at Great Western Insurance Company, sifted through her mail and telephone messages on Tuesday morning. She found about thirty-five requests from supervisors to speak to her about employee health problems. Perplexed about this accumulation of problems, Fernandez conferred with Pete Martin, her assistant.

"What's happening around here that could conceivably be creating so many health problems?" asked Wendy. "Are toxins floating through the air conditioner? Is the LA smog seeping through the building? Are our supervisors putting too much pressure on the workforce?"

"Most likely none of the above," responded Pete. "I think we have a classic case of job stress induced by an outside agent. Let me show you this ad that appeared in the Sunday newspapers. I think the ad is putting ideas into the heads of our employees."

JOB PROBLEMS

If You Suffer From

Nervousness

Low Energy, Irritability, Insomnia, Depression

Headaches, or Other Disabling Psychological Symptoms

That Are a Result of

EMOTIONAL STRESS, HARASSMENT, PHYSICAL INJURY, OVERWORK

While on the Job

Telephone

(213) 655-9999

(818) 999-8888

No Cost To You

You May Be Entitled to Substantial Benefits

COMPENSATION PAYMENTS

EVALUATION

TREATMENTS

CALL ANYTIME FOR FREE APPOINTMENT

Se Habla Espanol

PSYCH SERVICES CENTER

MD's and PhD's

Wendy looked intently at the ad, and then said: "What a weekend for me to be out of town on vacation. I didn't catch the paper this weekend. We certainly can't stop this clinic from advertising. Yet we should alert our managers that this ad could be influencing how employees feel about their health. I suspect it could lead employees to exaggerate their symptoms."

Pete reflected, "That's the business these clinics are in. They prey upon the suggestible and the greedy. For instance, who doesn't feel under emotional stress and overworked these days?"

"I agree with your opinion," said Wendy. "Yet we cannot interfere with any employee's right to complain about health problems or contact this clinic.

"What I intend to do is to discuss this problem with top management as soon as possible. My tentative plan is to send out a bulletin to all managers giving them tips on how to handle complaints about stress and health," said Wendy.

"Have you thought of the possibility that all these complaints will subside once the novelty of the ad has worn off? Besides that, a few employees will go to the clinic and find out that a few symptoms of discomfort will not lead to a settlement in their favor. Word will then get back that unless you have a real problem, going through one of these clinics will get you nowhere."

"That could be," said Wendy. "But I still think this problem needs careful consideration by top management."

1. What action, if any, do you think top management should take about the increase in employee complaints?
2. Should this problem even be brought to the attention of top management?
3. Which of the problems mentioned in the ad might be attributed to work stress?
4. Do you think the ad placed by the clinic is an ethical business practice? Explain your reasoning.
5. Do you think that these ads "prey upon the suggestible and the greedy?"

A Human Relations Incident

HOW TO COMBAT LETHARGY

Administrative assistant Susie Chan was concluding a meeting with her boss, Tricia Golden, the director of marketing research for a major cosmetics company. In through the door entered Bill, a manager on Tricia's staff. With a harassed look on his face, he said to his boss: "Here's the report you needed by 4 P.M. today. I had to work on it until 3 this morning, but at least I made it. I must say it was close to impossible to put together this report in such a short time frame."

"Thank you," said Tricia coolly, "I will be needing this information immediately."

As Bill left, Tricia stuffed the report into a closet full of old reports. Susie asked her boss quizzically, "I hope I'm not stepping out of bounds, but it doesn't look to me like you really wanted that report today. Why did you give Bill such a tight deadline?"

Tricia answered with a smile, "Susie, you're learning how to be a manager in this business. I may read that report next week, or I may never read it. That isn't the point. If you don't give people impossible deadlines they become lethargic. It's much like a lion tamer cracking the whip every once and awhile just to get respect from the lions. An effective manager keeps constant pressure on people."

1. Now that you've studied job stress and burnout, what do you think of Tricia Golden's strategy?
2. Can you offer her any suggestions on managing people more effectively?

A Human Relations Exercise

ARE YOU DEALING WITH STRESS PROPERLY?

How well do you cope with stress in your life? Gauge your ability with the following quiz developed by George S. Everly, Jr., for the U.S. Department of Health and Human Services.

1. Do you believe that you have a supportive family? If so, score 10 points.
2. Give yourself 10 points if you actively pursue a hobby.
3. Do you belong to some social activity group that meets at least once a month (other than your family)? If so, score 10 points.
4. Are you within five pounds of your "ideal" body weight, considering your health, age, and bone structure? If so, give yourself 15 points.
5. Do you practice some form of "deep relaxation" at least three times a week? These include meditation, imagery, yoga, etc. If so, score 15 points.
6. Give yourself 5 points for each time you exercise 30 minutes or longer during the course of an average week.
7. Give yourself 5 points for each nutritionally balanced and wholesome meal you consume during an average day.
8. If during the week you do something that you really enjoy and is "just for you," give yourself 5 points.
9. Do you have some place in your home that you can go to relax or be by yourself? If so, score 10 points.
10. Give yourself 10 points if you practice time management techniques in your daily life.
11. Subtract 10 points for each pack of cigarettes you smoke in an average day.
12. Do you use any drugs or alcohol to help you sleep? If so, subtract 5 points for each evening during an average week that you do this to help get to sleep.

13. During the day, do you take any drugs or alcohol to reduce anxiety or calm you down? If so, subtract 10 points for each time you do this during the course of an average week.
14. Do you ever bring home work in the evening? Subtract 5 points for each evening during an average week that you bring office work home.

Scoring and Interpretation

Calculate your total score. A "perfect" score would be 115 points. The higher the score, the greater the ability to cope with stress. A score of 50 to 60 points indicates an adequate ability to cope with most common stressors. Experts advise against using drugs or alcohol to deal with stress, and instead advocate exercising, eating a balanced diet, and using relaxation techniques to minimize the effects of stress.

Source: U.S. Department of Health and Human Services, 1986.

Notes

1. Genevieve LaGreca, "The Stress You Make," *Personnel Journal*, September 1985, p. 43.
2. James C. Quick, Lawrence S. Schkade, and Mark E. Eakin, "Thinking Styles and Job Stress," *Personnel*, May 1986, p. 44.
3. Steven F. Maier and Mark Laudenslager, "Stress and Health: Exploring the Links," *Psychology Today*, August 1986, p. 44.
4. Ibid.
5. Todd D. Jick and Linda F. Mitz, "Sex Differences in Work Stress," *Academy of Management Review*, July 1985, pp. 410–412.
6. Robert A. Baron, *Understanding Human Relations: A Practical Guide to People at Work* (Newton, MA: Allyn & Bacon, 1985), p. 286.
7. R. Douglas Allen, Michael A. Hitt, and Charles R. Greer, "Occupational Stress and Perceived Organizational Effectiveness: An Examination of Stress Level and Stress Type," *Personnel Psychology*, Summer 1982, pp. 359–370.
8. Kenneth E. Friend, "Stress and Performance: Effects of Subjective Work Load and Time Urgency," *Personnel Psychology*, Autumn 1982, pp. 623–633.
9. Hans Selye (interviewed by Laurence Cherry), "On the Real Benefits of Eustress," *Psychology Today*, March 1978, pp. 60–63.
10. Clive Wood, "The Hostile Heart" *Psychology Today*, September 1986, p. 10. Meyer Friedman and Ray H. Rosenman, *Type A Behavior and Your Heart* (New York: Fawcett, 1975), pp. 100–103.
11. Study from the *New England Journal of Medicine*, reported in Erik Gunn, "Type A Life Isn't Harder on Heart, Study Concludes," *Democrat and Chronicle*, Rochester, NY, March 21, 1985, pp. 1A.
12. Carl R. Anderson, Don Hellriegel, and John W. Slocum, Jr., "Managerial Response to Environmentally Induced Stress," *Academy of Management Journal*, June 1977, p. 260.

13. Victor Thompson, "Bureaucracy and Innovation," *Administrative Science Quarterly*, June 1975, pp. 1–20.

14. John H. Howard, David Cunningham, and Peter A. Rechnitzer, "Role Ambiguity, Type A Behavior, and Job Satisfaction: Moderating Effects on Cardiovascular and Biochemical Responses Associated with Coronary Risk," *Journal of Applied Psychology*, February 1986, p. 99.

15. William H. Hendrix, Nestor K. Ovalle, 2d, and R. George Toxler, "Behavioral and Physiological Consequences of Stress and Its Antecedent Factors," *Journal of Applied Psychology*, February 1985, p. 188.

16. Daniel Katz and Robert L. Kahn, *The Social Psychology of Organizations* (New York: Wiley, 1966), p. 184.

17. "HRM Update," *Personnel Administrator*, January 1984, p. 16.

18. Gail E. Brooks, "VDTs and Health Risks: What Unions Are Doing," *Personnel*, July 1986, pp. 59–60; Robert C. Miljus and Brian Sholly, "How Safe Are Video Display Terminals?" *Personnel Journal*, March 1985, p. 36.

19. Miljus and Sholly, "How Safe Are Video Display Terminals," p. 36.

20. "VDT Hotline Informs Fearful Mothers-to-be," Associated Press story, March 9, 1986; Marilyn Elias, "VDT Danger 'Unlikely,'" *USA Today*, September 30, 1986, p. 1.

21. "The End of Corporate Loyalty?" *Business Week*, August 4, 1986, p. 45.

22. Joan Wolinsky, "Black Jobless Suffer Despair, Self-Blame," *Monitor*, October 1982, p. 21.

23. This problem still exists today, although originally reported in 1978 edition of Katz and Kahn, *Social Psychology*, p. 599.

24. Carol Turkinton, "Freudenberger Views Stress," *Monitor*, October 1983, p. 24.

25. Susan E. Jackson and Randall S. Schuler, "Preventing Employee Burnout," *Personnel*, March–April 1983, p. 59.

26. Baron, *Understanding Human Relations*, p. 294.

27. Katy Koontz, "Beating Burnout," *Success!* May 1986, p. 32.

28. "Beating Burnout," *Success!* January 1985, p. 11.

29. Midge Wilson, "First Aid for Stress," *Success!* September 1982, p. 13.

30. Philip Morgan and H. Kent Baker, "Dealing with Job Stress," *Supervisory Management*, September 1985, p. 27.

31. Herbert Benson, *The Relaxation Response* (New York: Morrow, 1975).

32. Herbert Benson (with William Proctor), *Beyond the Relaxation Response* (New York: Berkley Books, 1985), pp. 96–97.

33. James S. Manuso, "Executive Stress Management," *Personnel Administrator*, November 1979, p. 24.

34. John M. Ivancevich and Michael T. Matteson, *Stress and Work: A Managerial Perspective* (Glenview, IL: Scott Foresman, 1980), p. 222.

35. Robert C. Ford and Jack Hartje, "Biofeedback and Management Stress," *Human Resource Management*, Fall 1978, p. 12.

36. Frederick J. Heide, "Relaxation: The Storm before the Calm," *Psychology Today*, April 1985, p. 18.

37. John M. Ivancevich and Michael T. Matteson, "Organizations and Coronary Heart Disease: The Stress Connection," *Management Review*, October 1978, p. 122.

38. David Cohen, "Japanese Face Up to Stress on the Job," *Monitor*, December 1985, p. 8.

39. Barbara Anne Solomon, "Wellness Programs," *Personnel*, November 1985, p. 68.

40. The overview of EAPS presented here is based on Hermine Zagat Levine, "Employee Assistance Programs," *Personnel*, April 1985, pp. 14–19.

41. Roger K. Good, "A Critique of Three Corporate Drug Abuse Policies," *Personnel Journal*, February 1986, pp. 96–101.

Suggested Reading

BATTEN, JULIE. "10 Jobs That Cause Burnout." *Business Week's Guide to Careers*, December 1985, pp. 41–43.

BEEHR, TERRY A., and BHAGAT, RABI S., eds. *Human Stress and Cognition in Organizations: An Integrated Perspective*. New York: Wiley, 1985.

BENNER, PATRICIA E. *Stress and Satisfaction on the Job: Work Meanings and Coping of Mid-Career Men*. New York: Praeger Publishers, CBS Educational and Professional Publishing, 1984.

DAVIDSON, MARILYN, and COOPER, CARY. *Stress and the Woman Manager*. New York: St. Martin's Press, 1983.

FREUDENBERGER, HERBERT J., and NORTH, GAIL. *Women's Burnout: How to Spot It, How to Reverse It, and How to Prevent It*. Garden City, NY: Doubleday, 1985.

GLICKEN, MORLEY D., and JANKA, KATHERINE. "Beyond Burnout: The Cop-Out Syndrome." *Personnel*, November–December 1984, pp. 65–70.

HELLAN, RICHARD T. "An EAP Update: A Perspective for the 1980s." *Personnel Journal*, June 1986, pp. 51–54.

JACKSON, SUSAN E., SCHWAB, RICHARD L., and SCHULER, RANDALL S. "Toward an Understanding of the Burnout Phenomenon," *Journal of Applied Psychology*, November 1986, pp. 630–640.

MOTOWIDLO, STEPHAN J., PACKARD, JOHN S., and MANNING, MICHAEL R. "Occupational Stress: Its Causes and Consequences for Job Performance," *Journal of Applied Psychology*, November 1986, pp. 618–629.

QUICK, JAMES C., and QUICK, JONATHAN D. *Organizational Stress and Preventive Management*. New York: McGraw-Hill, 1984.

SCHUMACHER, LIND A. "Employee Assistance: How to Help Victims of Domestic Violence." *Personnel Journal*, August 1985, pp. 102–105.

Job Conflict

LEARNING OBJECTIVES
After reading and studying this chapter
and doing the exercises, you should be
able to

1. Specify the major reasons so much job conflict exists.

2. Explain how job discrimination, including sexual harassment, creates job conflict.

3. Understand why line versus staff conflict occurs so frequently.

4. Be aware of both the constructive and destructive sides of conflict.

5. Develop insight into ways of resolving conflict on your own.

6. Summarize several measures organizations can take to reduce and prevent conflict.

THE MEANING OF JOB CONFLICT

As Chuck, a transportation specialist, walked into his office, he noticed that another desk had been moved in. Upset about the new desk, Chuck grabbed the phone and called the maintenance department. The maintenance worker who answered informed Chuck that he was told to move the desk in because the office was now to be shared by two employees. Chuck slammed down the receiver, picked up the other desk, and hurled it into the hallway. Hearing the commotion, Chuck's boss came running to the spot where the desk landed. Chuck's boss suspended him for three days without pay.

The unfortunate incident with Chuck and his boss illustrates two related meanings of conflict. A **conflict** is a situation in which two or more goals, values, or events are incompatible or mutually exclusive. The major incompatibility here is that Chuck wants a private office, while the organization wants his office to be shared. A **conflict** is also a strife, quarrel, or battle. Chuck and his boss quarreled, since Chuck's behavior was incompatible with organizational rules—no throwing company property around!

How Conflict Is Related to Stress, Frustration, and Anger

Conflict is a stressor, as described in the discussion of role conflict in Chapter 5. One reason Chuck acted so irrationally is that he experienced stress when his private office was taken away without warning. Conflict is also tied in with frustration and anger.

Conflict typically leads to **frustration**, a blocking of need or motive satisfaction. Chuck was frustrated because the new desk blocked his motive to maintain the status of having a private office. Frustration, in turn, leads to **anger**, a feeling of extreme hostility, indignation, or exasperation. Throwing a desk into the halls is obviously an act of anger. Anger alters the body's physiology and chemistry. These changes are part of the body's fight or flight response when faced with a stressor.

Levels of Conflict

Conflict encompasses many kinds of behavior in the workplace. A major reason is that conflict occurs at four levels. *Conflict within the individual* occurs when two or more motives clash, such as wanting more pay and less responsibility.

Interpersonal conflict occurs when two people clash, such as two office workers both wanting to gain control of the department's personal computer.

Intergroup conflict takes place when two groups have incompatible desires, goals, or motives. For example, two departments might both want a bigger share of the budget. *Interorganizational conflict* takes place when two firms have incompatible goals, such as one company attempting a hostile takeover of another. Here we emphasize interpersonal conflict, although other levels of conflict will also be mentioned.

The underlying theme to this chapter is that every organization has some conflict between individuals and groups, and some organizations are rampant with conflict.[1] One implication is that if you cannot tolerate conflict and are unwilling to learn methods of resolving it, avoid jobs that involve interaction with people.

A SUMMARY MODEL OF JOB CONFLICT

Appropriate doses of conflict, like stress, can benefit individuals and the organization. Too much conflict, however, can be detrimental or *dysfunctional*. It is also recognized that conflict can arise from many different sources, related to both individual and organizational factors. All these sources of conflict occur at one or more levels. Whether or not the conflict leads to positive or negative outcomes for the individual or the organization depends to a large extent upon how well it is resolved or managed. For instance, properly managed, conflict can become a creative force.[2]

The aspects of conflict just mentioned are depicted in Figure 6–1. Much of the balance of this chapter is an elaboration of the elements contained in this model. Observe that this model of conflict is similar to the model of stress shown in Figure 5–1.

SOURCES OF CONFLICT

Job conflict has many causes. In this and the following two sections we discuss leading sources, or causes, of job conflict. A list such as this needs continuous updating. New sources of conflict emerge from time to time, such as the conflict being created currently by hostile takeovers of one company by another. Although specific sources of conflict can be identified, all conflict arises from the underlying theme of incompatibility among goals, values, or events.

Competition for Limited Resources

An underlying source of job conflict is that few people can get all the resources they want. These resources include money, material, and personnel. Conflicts arise when individuals and organizational units squabble over the available re-

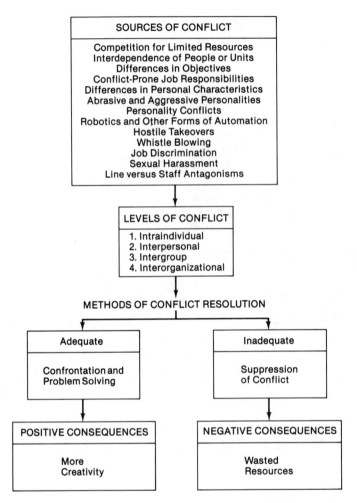

Figure 6–1   Sources and consequences of job conflict.

sources. Even in a prosperous organization, resources have to be divided in such a manner that not everybody gets what he or she wants, as the following example shows:

> A special staff meeting was called to discuss an emergency situation as perceived by Pete, the corporate treasurer of a prefabricated housing company. He made this plea to the rest of the staff: "I don't think you gentlemen realize the gravity of the situation. We are in danger of not meeting our next payroll. We owe the banks $17 million and our receivables aren't coming in fast enough to pay off our notes. I told you people several months back that we need to begin cutting back on a few of the luxuries. We may be a glamour company to the world outside, but we need some restraint internally."

The marketing vice president interrupted with his notes: "But, Pete, we have cut back in many areas at your suggestion. We decided to postpone the construction of our southern plant for the time being. We've cut down on overtime except for emergency situations. We've even discontinued the practice of paying for spouses on company trips."

Replied Pete, "What irritates me, Harold, is the gluttony of marketing. You're as aware of our need for restraint as anybody on the management team. I've been denied the right to hire an additional cost accountant who would have probably paid for himself anyway. I learned yesterday that the president has authorized the purchase of another corporate jet without even consulting me. Why can't the marketing department impress our potential customers with the two jets we already have?"

"There you go again, Pete, taking an accountant's view of the world," retorted Harold.

Interdependence of People or Organizational Units

People who are dependent upon each other almost inevitably come into conflict. Similar to marital partners or roommates, departments requiring the cooperation of another tend to find reasons for conflict. The operations and maintenance units of an airline are thus frequently in conflict with each other because they are interdependent. Without an airplane to service, the maintenance department is out of business. Without a properly serviced airplane, the operations department can quickly go out of business.[3]

Differences in Objectives

When two groups have major differences in objectives or goals, the potential for conflict is high. Although one might argue that everybody working for the same organization should have the same ultimate objective (the success of the organization), this does not always happen in practice. Frequently, smaller units within the organization have different aspirations and desires than does management, propelling the smaller units to act out of self-interest. For example, professionals such as computer scientists who work within large firms believe they should have considerable control over their own working conditions. Often they want the right to choose what problems they will and will not tackle. In contrast, the administration wants to maintain control over such matters. To resolve this conflict, some kind of workable compromise usually has to be developed.

Conflict-Prone Job Responsibilities

A **role** is a set of behaviors or attitudes appropriate to a particular position, regardless of who occupies that position. Roles thus determine what people ought to do as a function of their position. Certain jobs are conflict-prone because of the role occupied by the job holder. Auditors, quality-control specialists, safety specialists, and industrial engineers are among the conflict-prone occupations.

When your job involves criticizing or improving upon the work of others, a high potential for conflict exists. One student expressed the very nature of conflict-prone job responsibilities in her comments about campus security officers:

> It's nothing personal. Those people are paid to be mean. Most students can't afford the types of car that you can count on to start when you want them to. The result is that during a cold spell we often have to abandon our cars for a couple of days. Often you get a ten-dollar ticket that you can't afford. Worse is when you get the car towed away.

Differences in Personal Characteristics

A variety of personality and cultural differences among people contributes to job conflict. One contributor to conflict is the differences in values that stem from differences in age. The *generation gap* can lead to conflict because members of the different generations may not accept the other group's values. Cooperation is sometimes difficult to achieve between older and younger members of a department because older workers question the seriousness of purpose of the younger workers. Simultaneously, the younger workers believe that the older workers are resistant to change and are blindly loyal to the company.

Abrasive and Aggressive Personalities

Some people are predisposed toward job conflict because they are abrasive. An **abrasive personality** is one who is self-centered, isolated from others, perfectionistic, contemptuous, and prone to attack.[4] The abrasive personality literally rubs other people the wrong way.

Closely related to abrasive personalities are **aggressive personalities,** people who frequently physically or verbally attack others. Accurate figures about the incidence of violence on the job are difficult to obtain. Nevertheless, assault (both verbal and physical) is the second most important issue addressed by arbitrators.[5] (An *arbitrator* is an outside party who acts in the role of a judge in settling disputes.) Physical assault is often preceded by verbal assault, because an argument triggers a physical attack. Both verbal and physical attacks are classified as job conflict.

Personality Conflicts

Workplace conflict can sometimes be attributed to **personality conflicts,** situations in which people clash because they basically dislike each other. The two parties usually have a difference in viewpoint that strains their relationship. When a supervisor and employee have a personality conflict, the employee may question the supervisor at every turn. Marcia Ann Pulich describes the predicament of the supervisor caught in this situation:[6]

The employee may not be insubordinate but may approach insubordination. He or she may be sullen or unpleasant in speaking to the supervisor, ignore the supervisor as much as possible, even look through the supervisor as if he or she were not there. Supervisors in this type of situation have a very unpleasant time trying, in turn, to be civil and polite to these employees.

Rather than surrender to a personality conflict with another employee, you are advised to try one or two of the methods for resolving conflict described later in the chapter.

Robotics and Other Forms of Automation

The introduction of new electronic machinery that takes over some of the functions ordinarily performed by humans can be a source of job conflict. The conflict can arise between management and labor over how much automation is necessary. Labor unions and employee associations are particularly concerned about industrial robots taking jobs away from manufacturing employees. Management, in contrast, is concerned that without extensive use of robotics and other computerized equipment, it will remain at a competitive disadvantage. The disadvantage stems from the fact that some foreign manufacturers have high productivity and low costs because they rely so heavily on industrial robots.

Hostile Takeovers of Corporations

A trend in modern business is for firms to expand by purchasing other firms, usually through buying stocks. In many instances, the second firm does not want to be acquired by the first, resulting in a **hostile takeover**.[7] Interorganizational conflict occurs in a hostile takeover because the owners of the firms in question are at odds. Since many of the managers in the acquired firm think they will be dismissed, they enter into frequent conflict with managers of the acquiring firm. The chairman of an energy company makes this comment about hostile takeovers:[8]

> We see companies which took decades to build, companies which have enhanced the welfare of communities, states, and the nation, raided and dismembered for the benefit of a select few.

Although some people defend hostile takeovers as an appropriate expression of free enterprise,[9] they undeniably are a source of job conflict. Even when the takeover is friendly, some conflict is likely to be generated among the members of the two firms.

Whistle Blowing

Whistle blowing is the disclosure of organizational wrongdoing to parties who can take action. Wrongful deeds brought to outsiders' attention include safety defects in automobiles, toxic substances in the work environment, overcharging the government, and cost overruns by the government. A person who blows the whistle on an employer typically enters into conflict with the employer. Although many forms of retaliation by the employer are illegal, the whistle blower usually fares poorly in the firm. For instance, a whistle blower may be passed over for promotion, receive below-average salary increases, and be given undesirable assignments.[10]

Job Discrimination

Job discrimination is an unfavorable action brought against a person because of a characteristic of that person unrelated to job performance. All forms of job (or employment) discrimination are likely to be declared illegal if brought to court. According to the Equal Employment Opportunity Commission (EEOC), there are six major areas where discrimination may occur: age, handicaps (disabilities), national origin, race or color, religion, and sex.[11] Discrimination on the basis of marital status or sexual orientation is usually included under sex discrimination.

Less publicized forms of job discrimination include unfavorable employment decisions against people who are overweight, bald, below-average in height, or physically unattractive. Discrimination can also take the form of sexist language, such as referring to a woman as a "girl," or a nurse as a "male nurse." (More will be said about discrimination in language in Chapter 9.)

A form of job discrimination that receives considerable attention is associated with paying people unequally for equally valuable work. According to the doctrine of **comparable worth,** people performing jobs with different titles, but of comparable value to the firm, should receive equal pay. For example, if an administrative assistant and a manager were performing equally valuable work, they should receive identical wages. The alternative to comparable worth is to let market factors, such as supply and demand, determine wages.[12]

The idea of comparable worth has gained in popularity because many people believe women are paid less than men for work of equal value. Women's groups contend that administrative assistants earn less than custodial workers because the assistants are usually female. Many large business firms are attempting to implement comparable worth without waiting for charges of wage discrimination. They evaluate jobs with respect to factors such as responsibility, skills, and physical requirements.[13]

Job discrimination becomes a source of conflict to the extent that the individual feels blocked because of a characteristic not under his or her control. The person who wishes to remedy the discrimination is forced into conflict. The harassed person must now confront his or her supervisor or lodge a formal complaint. And the conflict does not end there. A person who wins a job discrimination ruling may become perceived as a troublemaker and therefore lose stature in the firm. One woman who won a discrimination claim against her employer said in retrospect: "I should have just found another job and quit. It's no fun being treated like an ingrate."

Our attention turns next to a form of job discrimination that has been known to cause considerable job conflict.

SEXUAL HARASSMENT AND JOB CONFLICT

Much job conflict takes place because women and men are sexually harassed. In one year alone, the Equal Employment Opportunity Commission reached a verdict of harassment in 6300 cases.[14] The general meaning of **sexual harassment** is any unwanted advance toward another individual, including spoken comments, touching, or demands for sexual favors. The EEOC says that sexual harassment is an unwelcome sexual advance, either verbal or physical, where:

1. Submission to the advance is a term of condition of employment.
2. Submission to or rejection of the advance is used as the basis for making employment decisions.
3. Such conduct interferes with an individual's work performance or creates an intimidating, hostile, or offensive working environment.

A current interpretation of sexual harassment adds a fourth point: "Whenever a male is in a position to control or influence a woman's career and uses his power to seek sexual favors from her or to punish her refusal, he and his employer may be in violation of the law."[15] As in this interpretation, sexual harassment usually takes the form of an unwanted action by a male toward a female. Harassment may also include female against male, male against male, and female against female.

Since the advances in sexual harassment are unwanted, a conflict results. The victim faces this uncomfortable choice: "If I submit to my boss's desires, I will be compromising my sense of morality and dignity. But if I do not submit, I may face a serious setback on my job." Many women experience stress symptoms as a consequence of this form of job conflict. Many have been known to get sick, become so tense that they lose interest in their work, stay away from the job, or quit before they find new employment.

Sexual harassment is considered a form of employment discrimination because the harasser treats people unequally based upon their sex. The subordinate who does submit receives preferential treatment, while the employee who does not submit receives negative treatment. Title VII of the Civil Rights Act of 1964 is still the key piece of legislation in the United States that makes sexual harassment illegal. Canadian law is also quite explicit about the illegality of forcing people to trade sex for job favors, or harassing them sexually in other ways.

Actions to Take against Harassment

According to the EEOC, prevention is the best method for the elimination of sexual harassment in organizations. They also suggest that the employer:

1. Bring up the subject of sexual harassment. (In response to this suggestion, many firms now have formal policies prohibiting sexual harassment. If you harass another employee, you are therefore in violation of company policy.)
2. Express strong disapproval.
3. Develop an appropriate punishment for the offense.
4. Inform employees of their right to file a complaint about harassment under Title VII.
5. Develop methods to sensitize all concerned. (Training programs about the prevention and control of sexual harassment have been developed in response to this point.)

The accompanying box presents some suggestions the individual can use to deal with the problem of sexual harassment.

HOW TO HANDLE OR PREVENT SEXUAL HARASSMENT

The potential or actual victim of sexual harassment is advised to use the methods and tactics described below to deal with the problem.

FORMAL COMPLAINT PROCEDURE

Whenever an employee believes that he or she has encountered sexual harassment or if an employee is suspected to be the perpetrator of sexual harassment, the complainant should report the incident to his or her immediate superior (if that person is not the harasser) or to the next higher level of management if the supervisor *is* the harasser. The supervisor contacted is responsible for contacting the Affirmative Action officer immediately regarding each complaint. The officer will explain the investigative procedures to the complainant and any supervisor involved. All matters will be kept strictly confidential including private conversations with all parties.

DEALING WITH THE PROBLEM ON YOUR OWN

The easiest way to deal with sexual harassment is to nip it in the bud. The first time it happens, respond with a statement such as: "I won't tolerate this kind of talk." "I dislike sexually oriented jokes." "Keep your hands off me."
Write the harasser a stern letter shortly after the first incident. Being confronted in writing dramatizes your seriousness of purpose in not wanting to be sexually harassed.
Tell the actual or potential harasser: "You're practicing sexual harassment. If you don't stop, I'm going to exercise my right to report you to management." Or: "I think I heard you right. Would you like to accompany me to the boss's office and repeat what you said to me?"

Source: The formal complaint procedure is based on information in Rochester Institute of Technology, *News & Events*, March 22, 1984, p. 4.

LINE VERSUS STAFF CONFLICT

A comprehensive form of conflict in most large organizations is that between line and staff authority. **Line authority** deals with the primary purposes of the firm, such as the authority of a sales manager in a business. Line managers therefore have direct authority to make decisions about using company resources. **Staff authority** deals with the secondary purposes of the firm, such as the authority of a safety and health specialist in a manufacturing firm. Staff managers therefore have indirect authority because they advise line personnel and provide support services, such as a photocopying center in a bank.

Line and staff workers experience conflict for most of the reasons described earlier in the chapter. There are also five other subtypes of conflict these two groups experience.[16]

Territorial Encroachment

In general, the staff person advises the line person. The latter may accept or reject this advice as he or she sees fit in getting things accomplished. In some instances a staff person has considerable power. For example, if the company lawyer says a particular sales contract is absolutely illegal, management will probably draw up a more acceptable contract. At other times a staff person may be ignored. A personnel research specialist might inform management that its methods of selecting employees are unscientific and unsound. Management may ignore the advice.

Staff specialists and line generalists often enter into conflict when the line worker perceives the staff worker to be encroaching on his or her territory. In the personnel research example just cited, the plant manager and the personnel manager may say to each other: "Who does this character from the home office think he is, telling us how to select people? Our plant is running well. Why is he bothering us?"

Line people see staff people as encroaching on their territory in another important way. Whenever a staff specialist makes a suggestion for improvement to a manager, it automatically implies that present conditions need improvement. If the industrial engineer says, "My methods will improve your efficiency," it implies that the manager is not efficient in his or her current mode of operation.

Conflicting Loyalties

Many staff specialists come into conflict with line personnel over the issue of loyalty to their discipline versus their organization. The staff person feels this role conflict because he or she may want to adhere to a professional code that conflicts with tasks assigned by the firm. An accountant in an electronics firm faced this dilemma when he disapproved of the company's earnings statement.

He felt that the company was using almost fraudulent accounting practices, yet his company pressured him to approve the statement. He finally approved the financial manipulations asked for by the president, but simultaneously wrote a letter of protest. His guilt about violating accounting ethics finally led him to resign from the company. Four months after he resigned, the company declared bankruptcy.

Separation of Knowledge and Authority

In large organizations few executives have sufficient knowledge to carry out their responsibilities. They are dependent upon lower-ranking staff advisors to furnish the appropriate information. For instance, an executive may have to choose a course of action based upon technical advice that he does not fully understand. His dependence on the staff specialist may become a source of conflict.

Another source of conflict arises when the specialist resents being evaluated by a generalist whom he or she feels lacks the appropriate background to evaluate his or her work fairly. A performance appraisal of an engineering technician by a construction superintendent led to a confrontation. The superintendent told the technician he was performing "barely adequately" in his job. In response, the technician replied: "What makes you think you are qualified to evaluate my technical work? You have no specialized background in engineering."

Formal versus Informal Authority

When a line manager wants something accomplished, he or she often has the formal authority to influence the behavior of others.[17] When the department manager requests that the maintenance department repair a venetian blind, the maintenance department usually recognizes this as a legitimate request. Should the same request be made by an engineer in the department, the maintenance department might feel that the request is unauthorized. Staff specialists, and sometimes staff managers, must often go beyond their formal authority in getting things accomplished. Staff and line may thus come into conflict over one or more basic aspects of organizational life.

To compensate for their limited formal authority, staff personnel frequently resort to informal authority to get things accomplished. When a staff person is perceived as misusing informal authority, the result can be intensified conflict. One personnel manager attempted to enhance his informal authority by intimating to line managers that he worked closely with the president, and therefore indirectly held much power. One of his frequently used phrases was "Today when I was talking to Mr. Walker (the president). . . ." One day the head of manufacturing asked Mr. Walker if he had seen the personnel manager recently. Walker replied, "I hardly ever see him. He reports two levels below me." From that point on few people listened to the requests of the personnel manager in question.

Differences in Personal Style

In the past, more so than today, line and staff were distinctly different in personal style. Staff people tended to be better educated, more "modern," more style conscious, and more professionally oriented.[18] Such differences tended to breed conflict. Although many of these differences are probably less pronounced today than when they were originally noted by researchers, many differences still exist. Specialists with advanced formal education are often described by line management as being "ivory towerish." In response, staff personnel contend that line management is "resistant to change" or "old-fashioned."

THE CONSTRUCTIVE AND DESTRUCTIVE SIDES
OF CONFLICT

Job conflict has both constructive and destructive consequences, as do other stressors. The right amount of conflict may enhance productivity, while too much conflict decreases productivity. Figure 6–2 depicts this general relationship between conflict and productivity. Here we summarize what happens when conflict is moderate, and when it is too high.

Constructive Consequences of Conflict

You can probably recall an incident in your life when conflict proved to be beneficial in the long run. Perhaps you and your boss hammered out a compromise

Figure 6–2 The relationship between job conflict and productivity.

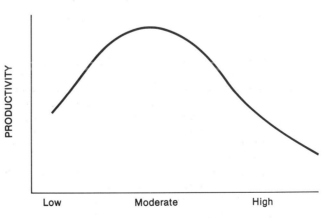

to a problem troubling you only after you complained about working conditions. Properly managed, moderate doses of conflict can produce such benefits as these:

Talents and abilities may emerge in response to conflict. When faced with conflict, people often become more innovative than they would be in a tranquil situation. For instance, when an organizational unit is fighting with management to justify its existence, it will usually provide a creative explanation of how it contributes to organizational effectiveness.

Conflict can lead to innovation and change. When the EEOC first demanded that companies develop affirmative action programs for integrating women and minorities into management, minor instances of conflict emerged. The net effect was to create many good opportunities for groups that had previously been under-represented in key jobs. Conflict about these matters has also diminished.

As an aftermath to conflict, organizations often learn useful methods of resolving and preventing conflict. A case in point are **executive rap sessions,** informal discussions between top management and lower-ranking employees. These sessions emerged because employees wanted more of a voice in company matters. Now rap sessions have become institutionalized in many places. Top management consequently learns of problems before they fester into major crises.

Conflict can provide diagnostic information about problem areas in the organization. If the quality assurance and production departments are in constant conflict, it might indicate that production is using inferior methods or quality assurance is being unrealistic. Either condition requires an adjustment.

Conflict can channel otherwise destructive impulses. One such destructive impulse is the need to attack others physically. Instead of entering into physical combat, an aggressive person may be satisfied to argue about work procedures.

As an aftermath to conflict, unity may be reestablished. For instance, two warring departments may become more cooperative toward each other as an aftermath of confrontation.

Destructive Consequences of Conflict

As you would suspect, conflict can have destructive consequences to both individuals and the organization. Among the more frequently observed are these:

Conflict consumes considerable managerial time. Managers report that they spend as much as 20 percent of their time at work dealing with conflict and its consequences.[19] The net result may be lowered managerial productivity, since less time is spent on problems that can increase profits or save money.

Conflict often results in extreme demonstrations of self-interest at the expense of the larger organization. Units of an organization or individual people will place their personal welfare over that of the rest of the firm. For instance, a labor union may call a strike or a company may engage in a lockout primarily to demonstrate power.

Prolonged conflict between individuals can harm emotional and physical well-being. Stress disorders are a frequent consequence of organizational conflict, because conflict can be a potent stressor.

Time and energy can be diverted from reaching organizational goals when workers are in conflict. In addition, money and material can be wasted. One such example is a meeting called more for the purpose of settling interdepartmental disputes than for discussing how to improve productivity.

The aftermath of conflict may have high financial and emotional costs. Both physical and psychological sabotage lead to adverse financial consequences. At the same time, management may develop a permanent distrust of its workforce, even if only a few people were in fact saboteurs.

Conflict may result in a "me versus them" attitude. Divisiveness of this type can ruin team spirit and the desire to work toward common goals. Each side in the dispute becomes concerned with gaining personal advantage and devalues the ideas of the other. Stalemates may result as members refuse to modify their positions.[20]

Conflict may result in the falsification of information and the distortion of reality. When in conflict, some individuals may be led to lie in order to defend a position. A common manifestation of this problem is falsely accusing the other side when mistakes happen. In one government agency, a budget officer falsely accused a planning group of giving her inaccurate forecasts that resulted in a budget overrun.

So far our discussion of conflict has focused on meaning, sources, and consequences. This information helps us understand conflict and therefore can contribute to managing or resolving conflict. It is also useful to be familiar with some specific strategies and tactics for resolving conflict.

INDIVIDUAL METHODS OF CONFLICT RESOLUTION

Because of the inevitability of job conflict, a career-minded person must learn effective ways of resolving conflict. In this section we concentrate on methods of conflict resolution you can use on your own. All are based somewhat on the underlying philosophy of **win-win,** the belief that after conflict has been resolved both sides should gain something of value. Similarly, the organizational methods of resolving conflict described in the next section are based on a win-win philosophy. A situation in which nobody wins is referred to as **lose-lose.** The individual methods of conflict resolution discussed here are these:

1. Negotiating and bargaining tactics
2. Confrontation and problem solving
3. Appeal to a third party
4. Disarming the opposition
5. Image exchanging
6. Not overemphasizing winning

Negotiating and Bargaining Tactics

Conflicts can be considered situations calling for **negotiating or bargaining,** conferring with another person in order to resolve a problem. When you are trying to negotiate a fair salary for yourself, you are simultaneously trying to resolve a conflict. At first the demands of both parties may seem incompatible, but through negotiation a salary figure may emerge that satisfies both. Managers and staff people must negotiate both internally (for example, with subordinates and bosses) and externally (for example, with suppliers and government agencies).[21] Five negotiating and bargaining tactics will be sufficient to illustrate the nature of the process.[22]

Compromise. The most widely used negotiating tact is **compromise,** settlement of differences by mutual concessions. One party agrees to do something if the other party agrees to do something else. Compromise is a realistic approach to resolving conflict. Most labor-management disputes are settled by compromise. For instance, labor may agree to accept a smaller salary increase if management will subcontract less work overseas.

Some people argue that compromise is not a win-win tactic. The problem is that the two parties may wind up with a solution that pacifies both but does not solve the problem. One example would be purchasing for two department heads half the new equipment each one needs. As a result, neither department really shows a productivity gain. Nevertheless, compromise is both inevitable and useful.

Begin with a plausible demand or offer. The commonsense approach to negotiation suggests that you begin with an extreme, almost fanciful demand or offer. The final compromise will therefore be closer to your true demand or offer than if you opened the negotiations more realistically. A plausible demand is useful because it shows you are bargaining in good faith. Also, if a third party has to resolve a conflict, a plausible demand or offer will receive more sympathy than an implausible one.

> A judge listened to the cases of two people who claimed they were the victims of age discrimination by the same employer. The lawyer for the first alleged victim asked for $10,000,000 in damages; the lawyer for the second victim asked for $200,000. The first person was awarded $50,000 in damages, and the second person $150,000. An inside source reported that the judge was so incensed by the first lawyer's demands that she decided to teach him a lesson.

Allow room for negotiation. Although it is advisable to begin with a plausible demand, one must allow room for negotiation. A basic strategy of negotiation is to begin with a demand that allows room for compromise and concession. If you think you need $5,000 in new software for your department, you might begin negotiations by asking for a $7,000 package. Your boss offers you $4,000 as a starting point. After negotiation, you may wind up with the $5,000 you need.

Make small concessions gradually. Making steady concessions leads to more mutually satisfactory agreements in most situations.[23] Gradually you concede little things to the other side. The hard-line approach to bargaining is to make your concession early in the negotiation and then grant no further concession. The tactic of making small concessions is well suited to purchasing a new car. In order to reach a price you consider acceptable, you might grant concessions such as agreeing to finance the car through the dealer or purchasing a service contract.

Additional suggestions for effective negotiation are presented in the accompanying box. Effective negotiation, as with any other form of conflict resolution, requires extensive practice and knowledge of basic principles and techniques.

Confrontation and Problem Solving

The ideal approach to resolving any conflict is to confront the real issue, and then solve the problem. Blake and Mouton note that confrontation means taking a problem-solving approach to differences and identifying the underlying facts, logic, or emotions that account for them. When conflicts are resolved through confronting and understanding their causes, people feel responsible for finding the soundest answer.[24]

Confrontation can proceed gently in a way that preserves a good working relationship, as shown by this example. Assume that Mary, the person working at the desk next to you, loudly cracks chewing gum while she works. You find the gum chewing both distracting and nauseating. If you don't bring the problem to Mary's attention, it will probably grow in proportion with time. Yet you are hesitant to enter into an argument about something that a person might regard as a civil liberty (the right to chew gum in public places).

A psychologically sound alternative is for you to approach her directly in this manner:

SUGGESTIONS FOR EFFECTIVE NEGOTIATION

1. *Find out how much authority the other side has before negotiating.* For instance, why waste time trying to sell something to someone who lacks the authority to close the deal?

2. *Keep a best alternative to a negotiated agreement (BATNA) before you begin negotiating.* If you know what you can obtain for yourself without negotiating, you are less likely to accept a bad deal.

3. *Legitimize your demand.* A printed demand or offer helps convince the other side of the legitimacy of your demand or offer. An example would be a letter from your company stating the maximum that can be paid for an electronic typewriter.

4. *Ask for something in return for any concession you make.* By asking for mutual concessions, you will not feel you have been taken advantage of.

5. *Negotiate on your own turf.* Negotiators tend to do better when the other side comes to their office. This tactic is also referred to as the "home court advantage."

6. *Nibble.* Ask for a small concession after the other side thinks the deal is closed, such as asking for a can of spot remover after purchasing a couch. ("Nibble," however, is more manipulative than win-win in nature.)

You: Mary, there is something bothering me that I would like to discuss with you.

She: Go ahead, I don't mind listening to other people's problems.

You: My problem concerns something you are doing that makes it difficult for me to concentrate on my work. When you chew gum you make loud cracking noises that grate on my nerves. It may be my hangup, but the noise does bother me.

She: I guess I could stop chewing gum when you're working next to me. It's probably just a nervous habit.

An important advantage of confrontation and problem solving is that you deal directly with a sensitive problem without placing yourself in a position that will jeopardize the chances of forming a constructive working relationship in the future. One of the many reasons confrontation works so effectively is that the focus is on the problem at hand, and not upon the individual's personality.

Appeal to a Third Party

At times, confrontation and problem solving do not work. The party with whom you are in dispute may be unwilling to compromise. Or the person may use his or her formal power to settle the conflict. In those instances, an appeals procedure may be needed. An **appeals procedure** is a formal method of resolving conflict by bringing the issue to a higher level of authority. For instance, union members have a clearly defined grievance procedure for settling disputes with supervisors and the company. Appeals procedures will be described under organizational methods of resolving conflict.

Disarming the Opposition

In many instances of interpersonal conflict the other individual has a legitimate complaint about specific aspects of your behavior. If you deny the reality of that person's complaint, he or she will continue to harp on that point and the issue will remain unresolved. By agreeing with that criticism of you, the stage may be set for true resolution of the problem.

Agreeing with criticism made of you by a superior is effective, because by doing so you are then in a position to ask for his or her help in improving the situation. Most rational managers realize that it is their responsibility to help subordinates overcome problems, not merely to criticize them. Imagine that you have been chronically late with reports during the last six months. It is time for a performance review and you know you will be reprimanded for your tardiness. You also hope that your boss will not downgrade all other aspects of your performance because of your tardy reports. Here is how disarming the opposition would work in this situation:

Your Boss: Have a seat. It's time for your performance review, and we have a lot to talk about. I'm concerned about some things.

You: So am I. It appears that I'm having a difficult time getting my reports in on time. I wonder if I'm being a perfectionist. Do you have any suggestions?

Your Boss: Well, I like your attitude. I think you can improve in getting your reports in on time. Maybe you are trying to make your reports too perfect before you turn them in. Try not to figure everything out to five decimal places. We need thoroughness around here, but we can't overdo it.

Image Exchanging

The essential point of **image exchanging** is that you and your antagonist make it clear you understand the other person's point of view. Empathy of this kind may then lead to a useful and productive compromise. A convenient application of this method is for you to list on a sheet of paper (1) your side of the argument, and (2) what you think is his or her side of the argument. Next, he or she does the same for you. Table 6–1 is an example of how images might be exchanged. Each person makes up his or her image sheet without consulting the other person. After the images are exchanged, discussion (and sometimes fireworks) begins.

Not Overemphasizing Winning

Many people overvalue winning when facing conflict. A public relations executive, Henry Rogers, observes: "You may lose more when you win than you lose when you lose." If keeping a good working relationship with another person is important, it may be necessary to sacrifice a few arguments. To take this approach of winning the war, not just the battle, Rogers advises keeping these points in mind:[25]

How important is my relationship with this person?

How truly important is the issue we are discussing? Is it one of my priorities?

Table 6–1   An image-exchanging list between you and your boss based on a conflict about punctuality

You: My Side of the Story	*What I Think Is Your Side of the Story*
a. I'm usually on time for work.	a. I'm not very dependable.
b. I live on the other side of town.	b. I live too far from the office.
c. Public transportation is unreliable in this city.	c. I take the last possible bus.

Your Boss: My Side of the Story	*What I Think Is Your Side of the Story*
a. You are late too often.	a. I'm as punctual as most people in the office.
b. If you cared more about your job, you would consider moving closer to the office.	b. I think you don't take my transportation problems seriously.
c. If you got out of bed earlier, you could take an earlier bus.	c. I try hard to get here on time. It's not my fault that I'm late sometimes.

How much am I going to gain and what am I going to get out of it if I "win" this battle?

How much am I going to "lose" if I lose this battle?

When you consider these four points, you will probably decide not to escalate conflict in most instances. Do you agree with Rogers that winning isn't everything?

ORGANIZATIONAL METHODS OF RESOLVING CONFLICT

Organizations have developed many formal approaches for resolving conflict because of the recurring nature of conflict in the workplace. Since employees are demanding more rights than in the past,[26] these organizational methods are more important than ever. Some organizational methods of conflict resolution focus on problem solving, while others involve making physical changes in the organization. The techniques to be described here are these:

1. Appeals procedures
2. Superordinate goals
3. The ombudsman
4. Exchange of members
5. Changing the organization structure

Appeals Procedures

Appeals procedures are the most conventional method of resolving job conflict. When you cannot resolve your conflict or gripe at one level, you appeal to a higher authority. The higher authority is ordinarily the common boss of the people in dispute or a member of the human resources department. However, top management in some organizations maintains an **open-door policy,** in which any employee can bring a gripe to its attention without checking with his or her immediate manager.

Sample appeals procedures. Appeals procedures exist in both union and nonunion firms. An appeals procedure used in virtually every union firm is the **grievance procedure**, a formal mechanism for filing employee complaints. The grievance procedure is outlined in a written agreement between the union and the company. The procedure generally follows this format: If a union member thinks he or she has been treated unfairly by the supervisor, that employee can ask the union steward to get involved in the dispute. If the dispute is not resolved at that level, it is moved to a next higher level. Both company and union management are represented at each higher level. If all else fails, an outside arbitrator acts as a judge to solve the dispute.

An example of a grievance procedure in a nonunion firm is an appeal to a hearing officer. A **hearing officer** is a staff specialist who is employed by the firm to arbitrate disputes between employees and management. Even though hearing officers are organization members, they are supposed to be impartial. Before a grievance gets to a hearing officer, it has been heard at lower levels. Hearing officers are more likely to be found in government agencies than in business firms.

The hearing officer grievance procedure produces winners and losers. Compromise settlements take place at lower levels. A hearing officer's decision cannot be appealed within the firm. Nevertheless, any citizen can hire legal counsel to attempt to overrule an employee's decision.

A key advantage of the hearing officer system is that the officer is an expert in labor relations. A disadvantage is that some employees believe a hearing officer cannot be neutral, since he or she is paid by the employer.[27]

Problems associated with appeals procedures. One valid criticism of the appeals procedures is that when the higher-ranked third party settles the dispute, the person or group that has lost may not be psychologically committed to the decision. However, since so many people are culturally conditioned to accept third-party rulings, the approach often works.

Appeals procedures in organizations also have a hidden danger for the individual. You may win your appeal, but you may fall into disfavor with the person with whom you had the conflict. It is therefore best to try to work out your problem through gentle confrontation. A man who brought a dispute with his boss to higher management and won, tells what ultimately happened to him:

> I can't prove that my boss tried to get even. But he sure didn't make life easy for me after higher management ruled in my favor. I never seemed to get a choice assignment, nor did I ever receive a compliment. My performance ratings also went down even though I was working harder than ever. My solution was to keep bugging the personnel department until I got a transfer.

Superordinate Goals

Organizational conflict can sometimes be resolved by helping the people in dispute recognize they are striving for common goals requiring cooperative effort. These **superordinate goals** are common ends that might be pursued by two or more groups, yet cannot be achieved through the independent efforts of each group separately.[28] The superordinate goals do not replace or eliminate the goals of each group. Instead, they represent a higher purpose toward which everybody can strive. An illustration of the establishment of superordinate goals to resolve conflict took place in a health maintenance organization (HMO).

> The pediatric and administrative services departments were in frequent conflict over such issues as scheduling of workloads, referrals to outside psychiatric ser-

vices, and working conditions. Several meetings were called to attempt to resolve conflicts between the two departments. Despite these efforts, the squabbles continued. Annoyed and outraged by what he perceived as immature behavior, the health director told the two departments: "Forget about your petty differences. I'll help you work them out. If you both can't get your acts together, our HMO will be losing more patients than we can afford and still stay in business. Your cutting your own throats, and I want you to stop."

Shortly thereafter, the pediatric and administrative services departments began to work more cooperatively together. Being confronted with the importance of pursuing superordinate goals helped them gain insight into their counterproductive behavior.

The Ombudsman

A number of organizations have created a new position to help resolve employee conflicts. The **ombudsman** is a neutral person designated by the firm to help employees process complaints.[29] *Ombudsman* is the Scandinavian term for a person who helps citizens process complaints against government and cut through red tape. The ombudsman must be skilled in resolving conflict and knowledgeable about organizational procedures.

An ombudsman is granted the right to speak to anybody at any level in the company. He or she is sometimes seen as a lay therapist or a priest. Unlike an arbitrator, the ombudsman does not have the power to make a decision, but he or she can bring a problem to the attention of higher management

What kind of conflict can an ombudsman help resolve? In one company an employee and his supervisor had a heated discussion about whether or not the supervisor was discriminating against the employee because he was black. Claimed the supervisor, "It's your attitude, not your race, that is holding you back from good assignments in my department." The employee brought the problem to the attention of the ombudsman (himself a black man). After the ombudsman brought the problem to higher management, the plant superintendent, ombudsman, and supervisor conferred about the problem. The employee was given a trial favorable assignment (night supervisor on a rotating basis). His attitude improved because of his favorable treatment, and the problem of perceived discrimination seemed to disappear.

Exchange of Members

Empathy helps reduce conflict. One way to acquire empathy for the other side is to work in their department. Exchanging members between groups in conflict (or groups having the potential for conflict) is thus another helpful approach to conflict resolution. Reassigning people in this way can achieve the benefit of introducing different viewpoints in the affected groups. As the group members get to know each other better, they tend to reduce some of their distorted perceptions of each other.

Exchanging members as a method of conflict resolution or prevention works best when the personnel exchanged have the technical competence to perform well in the new job setting. A member of one manufacturing department was transferred to a marketing department in one such exchange of members. He had limited knowledge of marketing and very little interest in learning about it. The apathy and bitterness he displayed on the job tended to intensify rather than lessen intergroup conflict.

Changing the Organization Structure

A widely used approach to conflict resolution is to change the structure or shape of an organization in such a way that the sources of conflict are minimized. The underlying assumption in reducing or preventing conflict by modifying the structure is that personality clashes are not at the root of certain conflicts.

Modifying the organizational structure is a useful way of reducing or eliminating many forms of role-based conflict. Manufacturing and marketing are so frequently in conflict that resources are wasted in settling their disputes. Manufacturing accuses marketing of being willing to sell anything to a customer even if the product cannot be manufactured at a profit. Furthermore, manufacturing contends that marketing wants everything accomplished on an unrealistically short schedule. Marketing, in turn, accuses manufacturing of being inflexible and unresponsive to the demands of customers.

A common solution to this problem has been the creation of a buffer position between manufacturing and marketing. Called something like "marketing liaison specialist" or "demand specialist," this individual becomes the communications bridge between the two groups. He or she interprets the demands of both groups to each other. The plan works except when the interface person feels that he or she has a superfluous job.

Summary of Key Points

☐ Conflicts are inevitable within organizations. A conflict is a situation in which two or more goals, values, or events are incompatible or mutually exclusive. A conflict is also a strife, quarrel, or battle. Conflict is a stressor, and typically leads to frustration and anger. Conflict can occur within the person, or among people, groups, and organizations. Appropriate amounts of conflict can be beneficial to the organization. The manner in which it is resolved helps determine whether its consequences will be positive or negative.

☐ Job conflicts exist for many reasons, including the following: competition for limited resources, interdependence of people or organizational units, differences in objectives, conflict-prone job responsibilities, differences in personal characteristics, abrasive and aggressive personalities, personality conflicts, robotics and other forms of automation, hostile takeovers, whistle blowing, and job discrimination.

☐ Sexual harassment is receiving attention as a significant source of conflict in organizations. It involves any unwanted advance toward another individual, including spoken comments, touching, or demands for sexual favors. Harassment is said to take place when submission to the advances is a condition of employment, or when the conduct interferes with work or creates an offensive working environment. Sexual harassment is considered to be a form of job discrimination and is therefore illegal and forbidden by many company policies.

☐ An almost inevitable form of conflict in modern organizations is that between line and staff personnel. Contributing reasons to this conflict include concerns over territorial encroachment, staff's partial loyalty to its discipline, line personnel's dependence on the expertise of staff people, staff's quest for more authority, and differences in personal style between line and staff personnel.

☐ Job conflict has both constructive and destructive consequences. Positive consequences of conflict include the emergence of talents and abilities, innovation and change, and learning new methods of resolving conflict. Destructive consequences include wasted time, extreme self-interest, emotional and physical harm, and high financial and emotional costs.

☐ Individual methods of conflict resolution include negotiation and bargaining tactics, confrontation and problem solving, appeal to a third party, disarming the opposition, image exchanging, and a deemphasis on winning. Negotiating and bargaining include making compromises, and making small concessions gradually.

☐ Organizational methods of resolving conflict include appeals procedures, the establishment of superordinate goals, using an ombudsman, exchange of members among organizational units, and changing the organization structure.

Questions and Activities

1. Is a basketball game a conflict? Why or why not?

2. Is mountain climbing a conflict? Why or why not?

3. Suppose a manager believes not enough conflict exists in the group he or she manages. What steps can the manager take to increase the level of conflict?

4. Diagnose the source or sources of conflict when nations enter into trade disputes.

5. Identify two techniques described in this chapter that you think are suited to resolving conflict between people in personal life.

6. Almost no top executive in a major corporation is under 35 years of age. To what extent does this fact indicate the presence of age discrimination?

7. Assume you purchase a new car and the dealer refuses to perform a transmission repair without cost covered by the warranty. Which technique described in this chapter might you use to resolve this problem?

8. Do you think more job conflict exists in profit or in nonprofit firms? Explain your reasoning, perhaps backing it up with an incident familiar to you.

9. Identify three occupations where skill in resolving conflict is essential. Explain why.

10. Based on the opinion of students, the study of job conflict is one of the most useful topics in human relations and organizational behavior. How do you account for its applied value?

11. Ask two managers what percentage of their time they spend on dealing with conflict. Be prepared to discuss your findings in class.

A Human Relations Case

THE DETHRONED PRESIDENT

When President Frank Marant gained control of Great Southern Foods from his uncle five years ago, one of his primary goals was to impose a system of financial controls over the $500 million processed foods conglomerate. The 38-year-old Marant was able to accomplish his initial objective. His controls were of some value in salvaging the company when it lost $26 million four years ago. Paradoxically, Marant's tight controls led to his recent downfall.

Insiders say controls were an obsession with Marant. He centralized his management to the point of frustrating leading executives in the company. His insistence upon checking and rechecking caused many a delay in decision making. Operations were virtually strangled in paperwork. One good example: Great Southern's most recent annual report claimed the company would spend $5 million this year to open twenty-five more processing operations. Six months into the fiscal year, insiders report that little work has been done on the projects; because of Marant's insistence upon such a thorough analysis for each project, decisions have been postponed.

Such delayed decision making can be particularly harmful to the fast-moving field of processed foods. The continuous parade of new products in the processed food field makes quick reaction time a necessity. An anonymous personnel director said that "Marant's situation is a textbook example of how a bungling president can mess up a company and bring about his own demise." The same personnel executive was among the fifteen people participating in a palace revolt last month when Marant was stripped of his authority.

The end for Marant came when two inside directors, Joe Palaggi and Dean Wilson, had become upset about the company's lethargy in the fall. During the same time span, a number of key managers in Great Southern had complained to Palaggi and Wilson that Marant's managerial style had been demoralizing. When it seemed that Marant was about to fire two key general managers, Palaggi and Wilson blew the whistle. They went to an outside director to explain how the company was headed toward a rapid decline. Palaggi and Wilson headed a drive to build a dossier of Marant's shortcomings as a company president.

The end for Marant came when Palaggi, Wilson, and three outside directors met in Atlanta. A special board meeting was called. Three dozen operating executives threatened to quit unless Marant was deposed from his chief executive position. The board moved swiftly, stripping Marant of his president and chief operating executive titles. He was reassigned as vice-president of special projects at a $100,000 cut in pay.

Marant informed a business reporter that the whole affair was a conspiracy to remove him because he wanted to run a sophisticated, finely tuned business. A confidant of Marant said that what Marant's antagonists really objected to was his plan to bring in two new marketing-oriented executives from the outside. A countercharge issued by one of the inside directors active in Marant's dethroning was, "Frank just wasn't willing to accept the fact that you can't run a business by reading computer printouts and writing memos. If you don't get out and visit the troops, they'll eventually get rid of you."

1. What do you think of Palaggi and Wilson's method of resolving conflict between themselves and Marant?
2. What should Frank Marant do now?
3. What could have been done to resolve this conflict before it reached such drastic proportions?
4. What label (type of conflict) best fits the method of conflict resolution used by the executives who ousted Marant.
5. Do you think appointing Frank Marant as vice-president of special projects will prove to be an effective compromise? Why or why not?

A Human Relations Incident

WHO HAS THE RIGHT TO TELL WHOM WHAT TO DO?

Midge Baxter, the quality control manager at her company, was sorting through her morning mail. She came across a bulletin from the human resources department announcing a new training film, "How to Spot the Employee Drug Abuser." Under the announcement was a form to be filled out by managers indicating when they would be available for a screening of the film.

As Baxter threw the announcement into a wastepaper basket, she thought to herself: "If I did everything the personnel department wanted me to, I would have very little time to supervise the department."

One week later, Baxter received another bulletin from the human resources department. It was labeled "Second Notice." This time Baxter wrote across the bulletin, "Sorry, no time to attend your film."

Two days later Baxter was visited by her boss, Vince Gomez. He explained to Baxter, "We've been getting some complaints from the human resources department about you. They say that you won't cooperate with them, and they want me to do something about it."

"I resent those comments from the human resources department," said Midge. "They are complaining because I won't buy into some of their programs. I'm not saying their programs are not worthwhile. It's just that I have the right to choose how to budget my time.

"I don't like the heavy-handed tactics they are using to force me to cooperate. Are the line departments here to please staff departments? Who has the right to tell whom what to do?"

1. How does this case incident illustrate line versus staff conflict?
2. How much authority should the human resources department have in influencing Baxter to view their film?
3. How else might have the human resources department have attempted to resolve the conflict with Baxter?
4. How should Gomez handle the conflict between Baxter and the personnel department?

A Human Relations Role Play

IMAGE EXCHANGING

Assume that Vince Gomez attempts to resolve this conflict by getting Midge Baxter and a representative from the human resources department to exchange images. One person plays the role of Baxter, and another the role of the human resources manager who reported her lack of cooperation to Gomez. Play out an image exchange, going through the steps outlined in Table 6–1. The four key elements are as follows: (1) Baxter's side of the story, (2) Baxter's perception of the human resource official's side of the story, (3) the human resource official's side of the story, and (4) the human resource official's perception of Baxter's side of the story.

After the two sides have exchanged images, both engage in additional dialogue about their conflict.

Notes

1. H. Kent Baker and Philip I. Morgan, "Building a Professional Image: Handling Conflict," *Supervisory Management*, February 1986, p. 25.
2. Deborah M. Kolb and Priscilla A. Glidden, "Getting to Know Your Conflict Options," *Personnel Administrator*, June 1986, p. 90.
3. James D. Thompson, *Organizations in Action* (New York: McGraw-Hill, 1967), p. 55.
4. Harry Levinson, "The Abrasive Personality at the Office," *Psychology Today*, May 1978, p. 78.
5. Charlotte Gold, "Assault on the Job," *Management Solutions*, June 1986, p. 5.
6. Marcia Ann Pulich, "Are You a Party to a Personality Conflict?" *Management Solutions*, July 1986, pp. 33–34.
7. T. Boone Pickens, Jr., "Professions of a Short-Termer," *Harvard Business Review*, May–June 1986, pp. 75–79.
8. Michel T. Halbouty, quoted in Robert Metz, "Hostile Takeovers Will Damage Corporate Health Over the Long Term," Rochester *Democrat and Chronicle*, June 26, 1985, p. 10D.
9. Pickens, "Professions of a Short-Termer," p. 75.
10. Janet P. Near and Marcia P. Miceli, "Retaliation Against Whistle Blowers: Predictors and Effects," *Journal of Applied Psychology*, February 1986, p. 137.
11. Howard J. Anderson, *Primer of Equal Employment Opportunity* (Rockville, MD: BNA Books, 1978).
12. "Twenty Questions on Comparable Worth," *Personnel Administrator*, April 1985, p. 64.
13. "Comparable Worth: It's Already Happening," *Business Week*, April 28, 1986, p. 52.
14. "Sexual Harassment: Companies Could Be Liable," *Business Week*, March 31, 1986, p. 35.

15. B. Terry Thornton, "Sexual Harassment, 1: Discouraging It in the Work Place," *Personnel*, April 1986, p. 18; William A. Nowlin and George M. Sullivan, "Sexual Harassment: Employers Beware," *Rochester Business Magazine*, July 1986, pp. 8–9.

16. Some of this information is synthesized in James L. Gibson, John M. Ivancevich, and James H. Donnelly, Jr., *Organizations: Behavior, Structure, Processes*, 5th ed. (Plano, TX: Business Publications, Inc., 1985), pp. 301–302.

17. Alan C. Filley, Robert J. House, and Steven Kerr, *Managerial Process and Organizational Behavior*, 2nd. ed. (Glenview, IL: Scott, Foresman, 1976), p. 391.

18. This point made in ibid., is still valid today.

19. Robert A. Baron, "Reducing Organizational Conflict: The Role of Attributions," *Journal of Applied Psychology*, August 1985, p. 434.

20. Baker and Morgan, "Handling Conflict," p. 25.

21. George S. Odiorne and Earl Brooks, *Managing by Negotiations* (New York: Van Nostrand Reinhold, 1984), p. 1.

22. A review of many negotiating strategies is found in James A. Wall, Jr., *Negotiation: Theory and Practice* (Glenview, IL: Scott, Foresman, 1985).

23. Evidence about the value of granting concessions is found in Mark S. Plovnick and Gary N. Chaison, "Relationships Between Concession Bargaining and Labor-Management Cooperation," *Academy of Management Journal*, September 1985, pp. 697–704.

24. Robert R. Blake and Jane S. Mouton, *The Managerial Grid III* (Houston, TX: Gulf Publishing, 1985), p. 101.

25. Quoted in Priscilla Petty, "In an Argument, Winning May Not Be Your Most Productive Priority," Gannett News Service article syndicated September 25, 1984.

26. "Beyond Unions: A Revolution in Employee Rights Is in the Making," *Business Week*, July 8, 1985, p. 72.

27. Alan Balfour, "Five Types of Non-Union Grievance Systems," *Personnel*, March–April 1984, pp. 67–76.

28. Don Hellriegel, John W. Slocum, and Richard W. Woodman, *Organizational Behavior*, 4th ed. (St. Paul. MN: West Publishing, 1986), p. 286.

29. Thomas J. Condon, "Use Union Methods in Handling Grievances," *Personnel Journal*, January 1985, p. 72.

Suggested Reading

BIERMAN, LEONARD, ULLMAN, JOSEPH C., and YOUNGBLOOD, STUART A. "Making Disputes Over Dismissals 'Win-Win' Situations." *Harvard Business Review*, January–February 1985, pp. 160–162.

CLARKE, LILLIAN WILSON. "Women Supervisors Experience Sexual Harassment, Too." *Supervisory Management*, April 1986, pp. 35–36.

DALTON, DAN R., and TODOR, WILLIAM D. "Gender and Workplace Justice: A Field Assessment." *Personnel Psychology*, Spring 1985, pp. 133–151.

GREENHAUS, JEFFREY H., and BEUTELL, NICHOLAS. "Sources of Conflict Between Work and Family Roles." *Academy of Management Review*, January 1985, pp. 76–88.

GUTEK, BARBARA. *Sex and the Workplace: The Impact of Sexual Behavior and Harassment on Women, Men, and Organizations*. San Francisco: Jossey-Bass, 1985.

HARTMANN, HEIDI I., ed. *Comparable Worth: New Directions for Research*. Washington, DC: National Academy Press, 1985.

McPHERSON, DONALD S., GATES, CONRAD J., and ROGERS, KEVIN N. *Resolving Grievances: A Practical Approach*. Englewood Cliffs, NJ: Prentice Hall, 1983.

NEALE, MARGARET A., and BAZERMAN, MAX H. "The Effects of Framing and Negotiator Overconfidence on Bargaining Behaviors and Outcomes." *Academy of Management Journal*, March 1985, pp. 34–49.

POWELL, JON T. "Stress Listening: Coping with Angry Confrontations." *Personnel Journal*, May 1986, pp. 27–30.

RAIFFA, HOWARD. *The Art and Science of Negotiation*. Cambridge, MA: Harvard University Press, 1983.

Working
Within
a Group

LEARNING OBJECTIVES
After reading and studying this chapter and doing the exercises, you should be able to

1. Appreciate why it is important to understand group behavior.

2. Develop a tentative strategy for improving your team play.

3. Describe the mechanics of brainstorming and the nominal group technique.

4. Pinpoint how quality circles operate and the conditions under which they are likely to be successful.

5. Identify several potential hazards of group effort, including groupthink.

WHY STUDY GROUPS?

Groups are vital to the understanding of human relations because they are the basic building blocks of the larger organization. The department you are assigned to, the division your department belongs to, the people you share a work break with, and the special committee you are assigned to are among the many groups found within an organization. A group has an identity of its own that transcends that of its members. For instance, a group of people may laugh at a comment that its members individually would not find humorous. And a group can accomplish a task that could not be accomplished by combining the contributions of its individual members. In recent years much attention has been paid to the ability of groups to achieve such ends as improving the quality of products and services and increasing productivity.

A **group** is two or more people who interact with each other, are aware of each other, are working toward some common purpose, and perceive themselves to be a group. Two police workers making their rounds in a squad car would constitute a group. So would the executive committee of an energy corporation. In contrast, 10 people waiting for a bus would not be a real group. Although they might converse, their interaction would not be on a planned or recurring basis. Nor would they be engaged in collective effort—a fundamental justification for forming a group.

The study of groups is justified only if people behave differently in groups than they do individually. A grisly example can be used to illustrate the point that group and individual behavior are not the same. Ten times during the last 25 years, riots among fans at soccer games have resulted in multiple deaths. Most of these deaths resulted from trampling. Yet almost none of the tramplers would individually stomp to death another soccer fan. Only a group can incite such violence.

Groups are also responsible for positive accomplishments, such as increased creativity and problem solving. The thrust of this chapter deals with the positive side of group effort, such as group decision making, quality circles, and effective meetings.

FORMAL VERSUS INFORMAL GROUPS

Since groups are such an important part of the workplace, they have been classified and described in many ways. The two major types of groups of most importance to the study of human behavior in organizations are formal and informal groups.

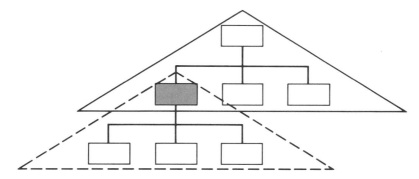

Figure 7–1 The linking-pin concept whereby the manager represents the group in the next level of management.

SOURCE: Rensis Likert, *New Patterns of Management* (New York: McGraw-Hill, 1961), p. 14.

Much of this book is concerned with the behavior of people in formal and informal groups.

Formal Groups

A **formal group** is one deliberately formed by the organization to accomplish specific tasks and achieve objectives. Formal groups are designated by the organization chart, with each group having its own box. At times formal groups are indicated on the bulletin board or through office memos (for example, "The undernamed people are hereby assigned to the safety committee"). Formal groups of a relatively permanent nature are called command groups, while those of a more temporary nature are called committees and task forces.

Command groups are the most prevalent clustering of people in almost any work organization. They consist of a manager and his or her subordinates. The formal organization is composed of a group of interconnected command groups. According to the linking-pin concept, managers are the linking pins between the many formal groups in the organization. As such each manager is a member of at least two command groups (see Figure 7–1).[1]

Command groups are easy to identify. Usually they have names that bring attention to their identity, such as information systems department, marketing division, public safety department, and department of radiology. Typically a person is assigned to only one command group at a time. Yet that same person may be assigned simultaneously to one or more special purpose temporary groups.

A **committee** is a group of people brought together to help solve a problem, usually by studying the problem and then offering advice to some higher authority. Standing committees are permanent, as illustrated by a planning committee that helps the firm cope with the future. The majority of committees are temporary. The committee is assigned a problem to study such as establishing better relations with citizens groups. Once the committee has finished its work, its recommendations are given to a high-ranking official. It is not unusual for the same committee to be reinstated next year, but this time new members are chosen. Governments and educational institutions rely heavily on the committee system to bring about important changes.

A **task force** is composed of a group of employees assigned to carry out a specialized activity, often with a time deadline. The task force usually has more formal authority to implement its recommendations than a committee. In getting the task accomplished, it is necessary for group members to coordinate their efforts. Often members of the task force are from different departments. In some instances, members of a command group have a minimum of interaction. For instance, two accountants working in the same payroll department might be handling different projects and therefore work independently of each other. By definition, then, members of a task group must work cooperatively.

Informal Groups

An organization cannot be understood by studying its formal groups alone. Informal groups are also important. An **informal group** is one that arises out of individual needs and the attraction of workers to one another.[2] These groups evolve naturally to take care of people's desire for friendship and companionship. Informal groups appear at all levels in the organization. Three examples of informal groups are as follows:

1. Five secretaries from the marketing department meet once a month for lunch to discuss mutual concerns and to seek relief from the tedious aspects of their jobs.
2. Four computer operators form a jogging club that meets three days per week at lunch to run 2 miles.
3. Three managers from different parts of the company commute to work together every business day when they are all in town. Often they discuss current events and the stock market, but they also discuss company business while commuting to work.

As examples 1 and 3 suggest, informal groups are often work related. One function of the informal organization is to fill in the gaps left by the formal organization. Few organizations have a written job description for the "coffee pot tender," yet such a person arises on a rotating basis in a good many offices. Similarly, when somebody in your department is absent for legitimate reasons, you might take care of his or her emergency work, even though it is not a formal part of your job.

Another potential advantage of the informal group is that the members may develop a mutual friendship off the job that carries over to the job. The result is that ties to the formal group become stronger, as exemplified by people becoming more loyal to the company as a consequence of bowling together.

HOW TO BE A TEAM PLAYER

In order to function effectively as a member of a formal or informal group, it is necessary to be a team player. The same principle applies to both managers and individual contributors. As the linking-pin concept indicates, each manager is a member of both his or her own work group consisting of other managers. Six suggestions are offered here which get at the essence of being a team player within a work group: be cooperative, promote the team concept, share information and opinions, be open with others, inform others of your plans, and provide emotional support to co-workers.

Be cooperative. If you display a willingness to help others and work cooperatively with them, you will be regarded as a good team player. Organizations cannot function without cooperative effort. If people do not cooperate with each other, the system breaks down. Not all employees are concerned about the smooth functioning of the total organization, but they do value cooperation from their co-workers.

Promote the team concept. A critical part of promoting the team concept is to emphasize "we" rather than "I" when talking about work accomplishments. The rationale here is that almost all accomplishments in an organization are really group accomplishments. A convenient way of emphasizing the "we" concept is to share credit with co-workers for your good ideas and accomplishments. To wit, "Here is the report I synthesized based on important input from Sally, Tom, and Rick."

Share information and opinions. Sharing of this nature helps foster a spirit of teamwork because sharing leads to closeness both on and off the job. Tamara, a public relations specialist, illustrates how information and opinions may be shared in a work setting:

> At a typical staff meeting Tamara makes comments such as "Let me share with you some important information I've picked up on that topic," "I have some scuttlebutt that might be worth something," or "Let me give you my candid, but very personal reaction to your proposal."

Be open and honest with other team members. Similar to the suggestion above is the idea of being open with co-workers in order to encourage mutual trust. Trust, in turn, leads to teamwork and group effectiveness. A good starting point in gaining the trust of other team members is to be as open and honest as the situation will allow. One sales representative does this with her co-workers by revealing any unusual behavior she engaged in to clinch a sale. A particularly effective trust builder was her casual comment, "I wish I could take full credit for having beat out the competition on that giant order you all heard about.

But it sure helped having my father's best friend as the president of the company I placed the order with."

Inform others of your plans. Another teamwork builder is to inform co-workers about your plans, in order to minimize the feeling that you tried to surprise them on purpose. An example would be to inform others in advance that you will be making a suggestion for reorganizing the department at the next staff meeting. A variation of this tactic is to gather suggestions from co-workers before finalizing your plan.

Provide emotional support to co-workers. An effective team player as well as an effective leader provides emotional support to members. Support of this nature can take the form of verbal encouragement for ideas expressed, listening to a co-worker's problems, or even providing help with a knotty technical problem. A direct approach would be to say to a co-worker who looked to be in a sullen mood, "It looks like this isn't the best day in your life. Is there anything I can do to help?"

Our attention turns next to another important part of being a group member, making decisions collectively rather than individually.

GROUP DECISION MAKING AND PROBLEM SOLVING

In organizations most complex problems are solved, and therefore most nonprogrammed decisions are made, by groups. All of the information presented in Chapter 4 about decision making and creativity also applies to group decision making because groups still rely on individuals for ideas. However, a substantial amount of information about decision making and problem solving in groups deserves separate treatment. To explain the process, we will look at three approaches to group decision making and problem solving: brainstorming, the nominal group technique, and quality circles. The latter are of such current interest that they will be described in a separate section of the chapter.

Group Brainstorming

Brainstorming is a conference technique of solving specific problems, amassing information, and stimulating creative thinking. The basic technique is to encourage unrestrained and spontaneous participation by group members. The term *brainstorm* has become so widely known that it is often used as a synonym for a clever idea. Developed by advertising executive Alex Osburn over 45 years ago, brainstorming really means to use the *brain* to *storm* a problem.[3]

Today brainstorming is used both as a method of finding alternatives to real-life problems and as a creativity training program. In the usual form of brainstorming, group members spontaneously call out alternative solutions to a problem facing them. Any member is free to enhance or "hitchhike" upon the contribution of another person. At the end of the session, somebody sorts out the ideas and edits the more unrefined ones.

Brainstorming is widely used to develop new ideas for products, find names for products, develop advertising slogans, and solve customer problems. For instance, the idea for pet seatbelts emerged from a brainstorming session. Brainstorming has also been used to develop a new organization structure in a government agency.

Rules for brainstorming. Adhering to a few simple rules or guidelines helps ensure that creative alternative solutions to problems will be forthcoming from the procedure. The brainstorming process usually falls into place without frequent reminders about guidelines. Nevertheless, here are eight rules to improve the chances of having a good session:

1. *Group size should be about five to seven people.* Too few people and not enough suggestions are generated; too many people and the session becomes uncontrolled. However, brainstorming can be conducted with as few as three people.
2. *Everybody is given the chance to suggest alternative solutions.* Members spontaneously call out alternatives to the problem facing the group. (Another approach is for people to speak in sequence.)
3. *No criticism is allowed.* All suggestions should be welcome; it is particularly important not to use derisive laughter.
4. *Freewheeling is encouraged.* Outlandish ideas often prove quite useful. It's easier to tame a wild idea than to originate one.[4]
5. *Quantity and variety are very important.* The greater the number of ideas put forth, the greater the likelihood of a breakthrough idea.
6. *Combinations and improvements are encouraged.* Building upon the ideas of others, including combining them, is very productive. "Hitchhiking" or "piggybacking" is an essential part of brainstorming.
7. *Notes must be taken during the session by a person who serves as the recording secretary.* The session can also be taped, but this requires substantial time to retrieve ideas.
8. *Do not overstructure by following any of the seven ideas too rigidly.* Brainstorming is a spontaneous group process.

Brainwriting. Debate continues as to whether individual or group brainstorming produces the best results. Individual (or private) brainstorming is also called **brainwriting,** the generation of creative alternatives by writing them down for about 15 minutes. An illustrative comparison between brainstorming and brainwriting was made at a creativity-training center.[5]

> At one brainwriting session at the Center for Creative Leadership in Greensboro, N.C., participants were asked to imagine what can be made with leftover felt from the manufacture of tennis balls. On this occasion, brainwriting produced

predictable suggestions on uses for surplus felt—furniture stuffing, novelty toys, and pads to place under lamps. The group brainstorming ideas were more imaginative—a two-sided adhesive, filters for sound boxes, wicks, felt tips for markers, and material for absorbing oil spills.

Assumptional analysis: A refinement of brainstorming. Ralph H. Kilmann has developed a refinement of brainstorming called **assumptional analysis,** a method of analyzing the assumptions used to support conclusions. According to Kilmann, conventional brainstorming falls short because the discussion never gets beyond its conclusions. With assumptional analysis, you use brainstorming to focus on the assumptions underlying the conclusions, as in this example.[6]

> An automobile company developing long-range plans for the 21st century may consider these conclusions:
>
>> The company will manufacture economy cars that compete with overseas models.
>> Return to producing, large, luxury autos.
>> Diversify into markets not currently served.

Once conclusions such as these are stated, brainstorming should focus on the assumptions on which they rest. You want to know if the assumptions are valid and if they support the conclusions. In the example at hand, here are three assumptions to investigate:

1. The price of gasoline will be relatively stable in the future.
2. The government will not restrict foreign imports.
3. Most customers will care more about styling than economy in the future.

The brainstorming groups are then selected on the basis of their expertise in investigating the validity of these assumptions. For example, marketing specialists will be asked to investigate the assumption that styling will be more important than economy in the future.

The Nominal Group Technique

At times a leader is faced with a major problem that would benefit from the input of group members. Because of the magnitude of the problem, it would be helpful to know what each member thought of the others' positions on the problem. Brainstorming is not advisable because the problem is still in the exploration phase, and requires more than a list of alternative solutions. A problem-solving technique has been developed to fit this situation. The **nominal group technique (NGT)** is a group problem-solving technique that calls people together in a structured meeting with limited interaction. The group is called "nominal" because people present their ideas without interacting with each other, as they would in a "real" group.

General description of the NGT. George P. Huber provides a general description of the NGT that will help you gain insight into the process.[7]

> Imagine a meeting room in which seven to ten individuals are sitting around a table in full view of each other. At the beginning of the meeting they are not speaking to one another. Instead, each individual is writing ideas on their pads of paper. At the end of five to ten minutes, a structured sharing of ideas takes place. Each individual, in round-robin fashion, presents one idea from his or her private list. A recorder or leader writes that idea on a flip chart in full view of other members. There is still no discussion at this point of the meeting—only the recording. Round-robin listing continues until all members indicate they have no further ideas to share.

The output from this phase is a list of ideas, such as "Why not sell three small schools and replace them with one large, central building?" or "I wonder if we should be talking about consolidation until we first obtain more information about population trends in this district." Next, discussion of a very structured nature takes place; this is called the interactive phase of the meeting. Questions and comments are solicited for each idea posted on the flip chart. ("What do you folks think about this idea of selling the smaller school buildings and constructing one new, large building?")

When this process of asking for reactions to the ideas is complete, independent evaluation of the ideas takes place. Each group member, acting alone, indicates his or her preferences by ranking the various ideas proposed. Again, these ideas may be alternative solutions to the problem or factors the group should take into consideration in trying to solve the problem. At this stage, we know the average rank the group has attached to each idea.

The seven summary steps. A good way of understanding how the NGT operates is to present a seven-step summary, as prepared by the originators of the technique:[8]

1. Group members (called the "target group") are selected and assembled.
2. Should the group be excessive in size, it is broken down into subgroups of about eight members.
3. The group leader presents a specific question (e.g., "What should we do about matching the physical facilities of our school district with the predicted enrollment for the next 10 years?")
4. Individual members write down their ideas independently and without speaking to other members.
5. Each participant (one at a time, in turn, around the table) presents one idea to the group without discussion. The ideas are summarized and written on a chalkboard, flip chart, or sheet of paper on the wall.
6. After each group member has presented his or her ideas, a discussion is held of the recorded ideas for purposes of clarification and evaluation.
7. The meeting terminates with a silent independent voting on priorities by individuals by a rank ordering or rating procedure. The final group decision is the pooled outcome of the individual votes.

Evaluation of the NGT. Since its development over two decades ago, the nominal group technique has gained considerable acceptance and recognition. It has been widely applied in business, industry, health, education, social service, and government. The process does the job of generating alternatives, keeping "bloopers" to a minimum, and satisfying group members. Much of the success of the NGT can be attributed to the fact that it follows the logic of the problem-solving method and allows for group participation. It is also somewhat more disciplined than conventional brainstorming.

QUALITY CIRCLES

A **quality circle** is a small group of employees from the same department who voluntarily and regularly meet in order to identify, analyze, and solve problems related to the work group.[9] During the last decade this group problem-solving technique has seen rapid growth, and is considered a major form of participative management. The wide-scale adoption of QCs stems from the perception that they were a major contributor to Japan's high annual rate of productivity growth.

Usually about six to twelve volunteers from the same department constitute the circle. Group members receive training in problem solving, statistical quality control, and the functioning of work groups. QCs typically recommend solutions for productivity and quality problems which are then passed along to management for approval and implementation. A facilitator who is a consultant or a staff specialist helps train circle members and keeps the group running smoothly.

Goals and objectives of QC programs include (a) quality improvement, (b) productivity improvement, and (c) improved quality of work life through employee involvement. The group usually meets 4 hours a month on company time. Members get recognition, and in rare instances, financial rewards for their suggestions.[10]

The balance of our discussion of quality circles centers around the details of the process, and the factors associated with its success.

The QC Process: Group Problem Solving in Action

All quality circles are designed to gather employee suggestions about work-related topics. Quality circle meetings are well-structured group problem-solving sessions. As such, they are far removed from employee gripe sessions or "free-for-alls." Meetings take place in a conference room or other suitable space furnished with the necessary supplies and equipment needed to discuss topics and perform analyses. Organizations fine-tune the QC approach to fit their needs. Nevertheless, six major steps in the process can be identified, as shown in Figure 7–2.[11]

Step 1: Problem identification. The circle members develop a list of problems tied directly to their jobs. The quality circles are not established with the intention of solving all the company's ills. Because circle members are regarded as experts

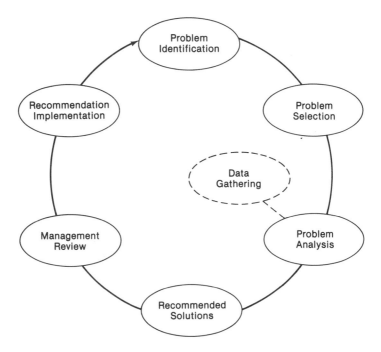

Figure 7–2 The quality circle operating process.

SOURCE: Robert J. Shaw, "Tapping the Riches of Creativity among Working People," Peat, Marwick, *Management Focus* (September–October 1981), p. 28. Copyright 1981 by Peat, Marwick, Mitchell & Co. Reprinted with permission.

in their own jobs, it is important that the problems be associated directly with the work.

Step 2: Problem selection. The QC members select from the total group of problems those they choose to tackle. A QC expert suggests: "It is advisable to address simple problems initially so that the circle develops confidence in the techniques that its members have been trained to use, in themselves operating as a group, and in management's endorsement of the program." One problem tackled by a QC in a hospital was, "How can we cut down on the amount of time required to process the discharge papers for patients?" (Many relatives of patients had complained about the long wait in line to sign release papers.)

Step 3: Problem analysis. In this step of the process, QC members apply analytical techniques to identify the cause of the problem, to gather information, and to sort out possible remedies. The QC may need to use company data that bears directly on the problem. It may also be necessary to call on experts from different departments to avoid duplication of effort. For example, in the hospital problem just cited, a systems group had also been studying the problem.

One of the analytical techniques often used in the problem analysis stage is the **80–20 principle.** It states that 80 percent of the results or problems are usually caused by 20 percent of the activities. For instance, 80 percent of the sales volume is often contributed by 20 percent of the customers. In a QC, an 80–20 analysis might reveal that 80 percent of customer complaints can be attributed to 20 percent of the features of a product. By identifying the 20 percent problem area, QC members can then make suggestions for improvement.

Step 4: Recommended solutions. In most instances the QC will arrive at a firm recommendation or a few alternative solutions. QCs have developed a good reputation for arriving at cost-effective solutions to tangible work problems.

Step 5: Management review. The output of the circle is a formal presentation to the QCs' department manager regarding the statement of the problem, the analysis, and recommendations. For many QC members, this represents the first time they have ever made a presentation to management. Management retains the prerogative of implementing or not implementing the QC recommendations.

Step 6: Implementing the recommendation. Once a recommendation has been approved by management, its implementation usually does not meet with much resistance. Employees outside the QC generally accept its value and appreciate the fact that the opinions of operating personnel have been incorporated into the suggestions.

Conditions Favoring a Successful Quality Circle

A successful quality circle is one in which (a) a high number of improvements is suggested, (b) a high number of suggestions is adopted, and (c) there is a high level of member satisfaction with the circle.[12] On balance, quality circles have been successful. Considerable cost savings and improvements in quality of work life have been achieved by using quality circles. Notable QC successes include the following:[13]

- Westinghouse's Defense and Electronic Systems Corporation attributes annual savings of $636,000 to the suggestions from one QC.
- A QC at General Electric's Room and Air Conditioner plant achieved annual savings of $150,000.
- Quality circles at Blue Cross of Washington and Alaska produced suggestions for more efficient employee procedures that have saved $430,000 in less than three years, improved customer service, and increased interdepartmental communication.

Despite these impressive results, there are many instances of failure. Tai K. Oh, a consultant on Japanese management techniques, reports that QC programs have failed in more than 60 percent of the American organizations in which they have been tried.[14]

Whether a QC succeeds or fails depends heavily upon the conditions under which it is implemented, and on certain characteristics of the circle. These conditions and characteristics are described below and listed in Figure 7–3. About half the list is based upon a study by Wayne, Griffin, and Bateman conducted with about 50 QCs in nine manufacturing plants of one company.[15]

Member cohesiveness. An effective QC, as with any other effective workgroup, is highly **cohesive;** the members stick together and work as a unit. As the group becomes effective, cohesiveness increases.

High performance norms. Effective QCs set realistically high goals, as would be predicted from goal-setting theory (refer back to Chapter 2).

High levels of member satisfaction. High levels of satisfaction with co-workers and the work itself are characteristic of effective QCs. (Here we see an example of high satisfaction being associated with high productivity.)

Organization commitment to the QC. A successful QC receives physical and psychological support from management. Indicators of support include emphasizing the importance of the program, presenting recognition awards to successful QCs, and providing payments to QC members.

Self-esteem of members. Effective quality circles are typically composed of members with high self-esteem. These people feel good about themselves and enjoy working with others.

Voluntary membership. Voluntarism facilitates bringing people into the program who are eager to contribute. However, some volunteers prove to be employees simply looking for time off from regular duties.

Competitive threat. QCs work best when the workforce believes that improvements in product quality and productivity are necessary to secure its future and/or stave off the competition. When Japan began its extensive use of QCs, many of its companies felt like underdogs in world competition.

Decentralized company philosophy. The QC should operate under a decentralized philosophy in which top management grants latitude to plant management for developing and initiating new programs.[16]

Figure 7–3 Characteristics and conditions associated with effective quality circles.

Member cohesiveness	
High performance norms	
High levels of member satisfaction	
Organization commitment to the QC	
Self-esteem of members	EFFECTIVE
Voluntary membership	QUALITY CIRCLE
Competitive threat	
Decentralized company philosophy	
Mixture of internal and external rewards	
Patience for long-term results	

Mixture of internal and external rewards. Employees should receive both internal and external rewards based upon the success of the QC program. The satisfactions derived from making creative suggestions are not sufficient to sustain worker motivation. In Japan, financial rewards are less important because of a cultural ethic that regards loyalty to co-workers and the firm as more important than financial incentives for good deeds.

Patience for long-term results. In successful QC programs, management views the QC as a long-term investment and does not push for short-term results. Since the QC method involves careful analysis and study of the problems it tackles, quick fixes are not in order. QCs are not designed to operate in a crisis mode.

CONDUCTING OR PARTICIPATING IN AN EFFECTIVE MEETING

A substantial portion of working within groups takes place within the context of a meeting, including committee meetings, staff meetings, and group brainstorming sessions. It is fashionable to decry meetings with statements such as "Ugh, not another meeting." Negative jokes about committee meetings circulate freely, such as: "A committee is a place where minutes are taken and hours are lost," or "The primary purpose of a committee is to avoid action." Despite these criticisms, collective effort would be very difficult without formal meetings.

A constructive viewpoint about meetings is not to eliminate them, but to follow guidelines for improving their effectiveness. Both leaders and participants share responsibility for attaining effectiveness. In this context, *effectiveness* refers to goal attainment and member satisfaction.

Suggestions for the Meeting Leader

Select qualified members and rely upon their expertise. Members of effective meetings are qualified for their assignments from the standpoint of knowledge and interest. For instance, if a person is planning to quit a company in six months, he or she would have little interest in serving on a profit sharing committee and therefore would make a meager contribution. During the meetings, it is important for the leader to rely on the expertise of members.[17] An obvious but often overlooked point is that a meeting cannot achieve its full purpose unless members help solve the problems.

Have a specific agenda. Efficient and effective meetings typically have a planned agenda that is given to participants in advance of the meeting. Simultaneously, it is important that the head of the meeting steer the group toward staying with the agenda. When members ask "What are we supposed to talk about today?" or take off on tangents during the meeting, time wasting is the most probable result.

Strive for balanced contributions by members. A skillful leader often has to curtail the contribution of verbose and domineering members. Equally important, the chairperson has to coax more reticent members to contribute their ideas. Without a balanced contribution, a committee fails to achieve its fundamental purpose of being a democratic process.

The leader should share power. A vital attribute of an effective problem-solving meeting is power sharing by the chairperson.[18] Unless power is shared, the members believe that the hidden agenda of the meeting is to seek approval for the chairperson's ideas. Ideally, the head of the meeting should not have preconceived ideas about the ultimate recommendation of the committee.

Effort should be directed toward surmountable problems. Many problem-solving groups make the mistake of spending time discussing "who is to blame for the problem," or "what should have been done to avoid the problem."[19] Rather than try to change the past—an impossible task—it is better to focus on how things can be improved in the future.

The meeting should start and stop on time. Meetings that start on time create a stronger sense of urgency and purpose than do meetings that begin late. If the leader guarantees that the meeting will end on time, much fidgeting and looking at watches is eliminated. Also, members will work harder at covering the planned agenda if a time limit is imposed. An agenda should be planned to fit comfortably into the allotted time.

Group members should delay the expression of affect. Recent experiments suggest that the expression of feeling and emotion about decision problems should be delayed until after alternatives to the problems have been generated. Two dysfunctional consequences are associated with the early expression of affect: a reduction in group energy and a narrowing of the range of accepted ideas. It seems that high levels of emotion hinder the capacity of the group to think clearly about the task at hand, and also foster misunderstanding and poor communication within the group.[20] An example of such early affect would be cheering when the first decent tentative solution to the problem at hand arises. The leader should help restrain emotion until additional alternatives have been explored.

Recommendations should be taken seriously. After a committee has reached its recommendations, or a task force has reached its proposed solution, these outputs should be taken seriously by the organization. People come to believe that committees and task forces are futile and powerless if they are bodies for discussion only and no action.

Suggestions for the Meeting Participant

Most of the suggestions mentioned above for the meeting leader can also be transposed to the participant's perspective. For instance, while leaders should rely on member expertise, members should contribute their expertise. The following suggestions will help you avoid frequent errors committed by meeting participants.

Make the right amount of contribution. The person who dominates a meeting is perceived just as negatively as the noncontributor. Give other people a chance to contribute, but do not be so polite that you become passive.

Be punctual and stay for the entire meeting. If you will be late or have to leave early, let the leader know in advance.

Keep your comments brief and pointed. One of the major problems facing the meeting leader is to keep conversations on track. Help the leader by setting a good example for the other participants.

Be supportive toward other members. If another participant says something of value, give that person your approval by such means as nodding your head or smiling. Support of this type encourages the free flow of ideas. Being supportive includes being tolerant of viewpoints considerably different from yours.

Listen carefully to the leader and other participants. Show by your nonverbal behavior that you are concerned about what they are saying. For example, look attentive.

Take your turn at being the leader during the meeting. To accomplish this you might volunteer to make a report during the meeting or head a subcommittee that will report back to the group later.

Avoid disruptive behavior, such as belittling another participant, frequent laughter, nail clipping, wallet cleaning, newspaper reading, napping, or yawning. Many a career has been set back because of poor etiquette displayed in a meeting.

POTENTIAL HAZARDS OF GROUP EFFORT

Working within a group has many advantages including that of **synergy**—a condition in which the total output of the group is greater than the sum of the contribution of individual members. Despite such virtues, work groups sometimes have some serious disadvantages for management and members of the group. Four notable ones are: shirking of individual responsibility, conformity to mediocre performance, stifling of creativity, and groupthink.

Shirking of Individual Responsibility

For those people not strongly work oriented, group assignments are sometimes an invitation to shirk responsibility. Unless assignments are carefully drawn and both group and individual objectives exist, an undermotivated member can often squeeze by without contributing his or her fair share. The shirker risks being ostracized by the group, but may be willing to pay this price rather than work hard. Shirking of individual responsibility is commonly found in groups such as committees, task forces, and group project teams. A professor conducting a business research seminar met one day with a class member who had a few candid comments to make:

> I've waited as long as I could before coming to you. It's about Jack. The guy is doing nothing for the group. In fact, he's messing up our whole project. He was supposed to interview ten people, and so far he has only turned in two

questionnaires. I suspect he faked the questionnaire answers. His answers came out too perfect. We're afraid of not making our deadline because of him. Can you help us out?

In this situation, the professor confronted the student with the perceptions of his work held by the other members. The student admitted that he had fallen behind schedule and expressed a willingness to be transferred to another group. Instead, he was assigned an individual research project. All situations dealing with shirking of responsibility are not so readily detected or remedied.

Conformity to Mediocre Performance

Group membership exerts pressures on individuals to conform to group standards in such ways as thinking like the average member and producing at approximately the same level as co-workers. These group standards are referred to as **norms,** the unwritten expectations for members that tell them what they ought to do. Norms become a standard of what each person should or should not do within the group.

Conformity in thinking can sometimes be detrimental. For instance, one design engineer in a group of five may believe that a car-braking mechanism is unsafe. After learning that the co-workers think the braking mechanism is safe, the engineer may reflect, "If the other members of the group disagree with me, I'm probably wrong. Why be an oddball? I'll call the braking mechanism safe." Such an act of conformity has two negative consequences. First, the engineer may be right. A pronouncement about the unsafe features of the braking mechanism could save lives (or at least a later recall) if brought to the attention of management. Second, by not casting an opinion and going along with the group, the engineer's contribution is almost zero. As one manager said about his subordinates, "If they all agree with me, why do I need all of them?"

Conformity in actions can lead to lowered performance and career retardation. A potential hazard of being accepted by your work group and identifying with its members is that you will go along with mediocre performance standards. To the extent that you try to remain "one of the gang," you will not be able to distinguish yourself from others. Your allegiance to the group may make it difficult for you to advance into management or to perform your job in a superior manner. Groups sometimes foster mediocre performance.

Nancy took the best job she could find for the summer, a chambermaid position at a resort hotel. As she perceived the situation, the pay was good, the hours delightful, and the beach superb. However, Nancy was subject to some uncomfortable group pressures. She explains what happened: "I felt some kind of obligation to do my best for the hotel owners. They were treating me fine, and I wanted to reciprocate. I charged into my jobs, literally singing as I went about my chores. Within a week I found that the other chambermaids were almost forcing me to take a coffee or soft drink break with them. They told me I was cleaning too many rooms an hour. They wanted me to slow down so they wouldn't look bad. My decision was to tell them to do what they wanted, and I would do what I wanted. My decision was the right one. I was invited back the next year as a supervising chambermaid."

Stifling of Creativity

Closely related to the problem of conformity to mediocre performance is the fact that group norms can stifle creativity. The group may foster the attitude that innovative thinking disturbs that status quo and is therefore undesirable. One manifestation of norms stifling creativity is when the person who initiates an original idea is given no recognition by the group. Unless the person is a strong individualist, he or she will probably not pursue the idea. Blake and Mouton furnish an example of how one company coped with the problem of creativity-stifling norms:[21]

> A large utilities company was able to solve problems arising from the norms that were hampering a project team's progress in making key decisions. Pressures were mounting after unexpected fuel cost increases and new technological developments triggered huge first-quarter losses.
>
> The engineering division manager faced a number of tough decisions concerning the newest plant. His project team began to flounder, even though he had handpicked the members who seemed to be best available. After he and another manager discussed the problem, and examined the norms and culture of their company, they realized that operations were conducted primarily on a "compromise" basis. Few people wished to "rock the boat" by suggesting plans or programs that departed from past precedents. To solve the problem, they developed a norm-shifting action plan that zeroed in on the major problems. For instance, they openly discussed their drift toward mediocrity and then wrote a short description of the problems as they perceived them.

Groupthink

A potential disadvantage of group decision making is **groupthink,** a deterioration of mental efficiency, reality testing, and moral judgment in the interest of group solidarity. Simply put, groupthink is an extreme form of consensus. The group thinks as a unit, believes it is impervious to outside criticism, and begins to have illusions about its own invincibility. As a consequence, the group loses its powers of critical analysis. More information about the causes and symptoms of groupthink is presented in Figure 7–4.

Examples of groupthink. Groupthink was first observed by Irving L. Janis in his research on governmental policy groups faced with difficult problems in a complex and changing environment. A widely cited example of groupthink relates to the United States invasion of Cuba in 1961. President John F. Kennedy and his staff decided to invade Cuba at the Bay of Pigs, despite information that the

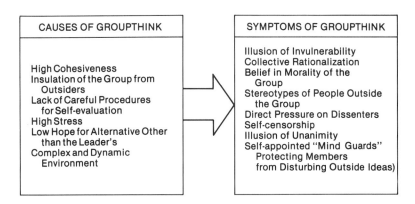

Figure 7–4 Causes and symptoms of groupthink.

SOURCE: Adapted from Irving L. Janis and Leon Mann, *Decision Making: A Psychological Analysis of Conflict, Choice, and Commitment* (New York: Free Press, 1977).

invasion would fail and damage our relations with other countries. Arthur Schlesinger, Jr., one of Kennedy's closest advisors, stated that he had strong reservations about the invasion proposal, yet he failed to present his opposing views. He felt his dissenting opinions were unlikely to sway the group away from the invasion plan and would probably have made him appear to be a "nuisance."[22]

The field of management information systems (MIS) provides a current example of the hazards of groupthink. The project involved was a complex decision support system for corporate planners. Far into the project, the systems vice-president admitted: "We had gotten sucked into something that was doomed to fail from the start." The excitement about the project camouflaged obstacles that should have forced a serious rethinking of the decision.

Unfortunately, the obstacles to the project's success were the same as its reputed benefits. The system would be powerful and flexible enough to help planners anticipate future corporate needs more accurately than in the past. However, the system was so sophisticated that it was too complicated for the planners to use. The systems vice-president analyzed why this possibility was not foreseen.

"It sounded so good," said the vice president. "Planning is such a tedious process, and with this system we were going to make users a lot more powerful. We felt we were really accomplishing something." Eventually the system was phased out in favor of a simple system that programmers can change as conditions dictate. "I guess," said the vice-president, "that when you sense something is too good to be true, it probably is."[23]

Groupthink was responsible for the construction of an unusable system because no group member was willing to challenge the value of the system. The intelligent and well-trained people assigned to the project insulated themselves from the real world in which the system would be used.

How to prevent groupthink. If you are a group leader, consider taking the following steps to guard against the potential dangers of groupthink:[24]

- Encourage all members of the group to express doubts and criticisms of proposed solutions to problems.
- Show by example that you are willing to accept criticism.
- Divide the group into subgroups to develop ideas. Then have the subgroups confront one another to examine why they differ.
- Periodically invite qualified outsiders to meet with the group and provide suggestions.
- If groupthink seems to be emerging, bring it to the attention of the group. For instance, you might say, "I get the impression we are too eager to think as one. What is your reaction to the problem?"

Summary of Key Points

☐ Groups are the building blocks of the larger organization. A group is defined as a collection of people who interact with each other, are aware of each other, are working toward some common purpose, and perceive themselves to be a group.

☐ Many different types of groups exist in an organization. A major classification of groups is formal versus informal. A formal group is one deliberately formed by the organization to accomplish specific tasks. Command groups, committees, and task forces are the main types of formal groups. An informal group is one that evolves naturally to take care of people's desire for companionship; however, it may also serve organizational purposes.

☐ Being a team player is an important part of working within a group. Strategies for achieving this end include: be cooperative, promote the team concept, share information and opinions, be open and honest, inform others of your plans, and provide emotional support to co-workers.

☐ Group decision making and problem solving are frequently practiced in organizations. Among the specialized techniques of group decision making and problem solving are group brainstorming, the nominal group technique, and quality circles.

☐ In brainstorming, a group of people spontaneously call out alternatives to a problem facing them. Any group member is free to enhance or piggyback upon the idea of another member. Notes are taken during the sessions. In brainwriting, people write down alternative solutions to the problem at hand individually. Assumptional analysis is another refinement of group brainstorming. The process involves analyzing the assumptions used to support conclusions.

☐ The nominal group technique (NGT) is a method of exploring the nature of a problem and generating alternative solutions. It involves a group of seven to ten individuals contributing their written thoughts about the problem, and then all other members responding to their ideas. Members rank or rate the ideas, and the final group decision is the pooled outcome of the individual votes.

☐ A quality circle is a small group of employees from the same department who voluntarily and regularly meet in order to identify, analyze, and solve problems related to the workgroup. Organizations usually adapt the QC format to their particular circumstances. However, the typical steps are as follows: problem identification, problem selection, problem analysis (including data gathering), recommended solutions, management review, and implementing the recommendation.

☐ The characteristics and conditions associated with effective quality circles include: group cohesiveness, high performance norms, high levels of member satisfaction, organization commitment to the QC, self-esteem of members, voluntary membership, competitive threat from the outside, decentralized company philosophy, internal and external rewards to members, and patience for long-term results.

☐ Both the meeting leader and members contribute to an effective meeting. Points for the leader to keep in mind include these: rely on the expertise of qualified members, have a specific agenda, balance the contributions of members, share power, direct effort toward surmountable problems, start and stop on time, delay expression of affect, and urge the organization to take the recommendations seriously.

☐ Points for participants include these: make the optimal contribution, be punctual and stay for the entire time, make brief, pointed comments, support other members, listen to others, take your turn at leading the meeting, and avoid disruptive behavior.

☐ Group effort has some potential hazards. Key ones include shirking individual responsibility, conformity to mediocre performance, stifling of creativity, and groupthink (an extreme form of consensus in which the group loses its powers of critical analysis).

Questions and Activities

1. Does a committee qualify as a group according to the definition of a group given in this chapter?

2. Is an employee health and fitness club a formal group or an informal one? Justify your answer.

3. To what extent do you think being a good team player is really a form of organizational politics?

4. What behaviors can you recommend for letting your co-workers know that you are more interested in "we" than "I"?

5. It has been said that for a person to become an effective executive, the person should engage in team sports during school. What do you think of this opinion?

6. How might being a superstar in any field hamper group effectiveness?

7. What similarity do you see between brainwriting and the nominal group technique?

8. How might a quality circle be used to improve patient service in a hospital?

9. Some companies have found that quality circles generate a higher number of useful ideas when there is frequent rotation of members. Why do you think this might be true?

10. What do you think is the justification for selecting QC members only from among employees who work with the problem at hand as part of their regular job?

11. Obtain one valid example of groupthink by speaking to people with experience working in groups. Be prepared to discuss your findings in class.

A Human Relations Case

THE UNBALANCED TEAM[25]

Rob called his task force together for their first meeting. Cheerfully, he said to the group, "I hope the rest of you are as excited as I am about having been chosen to work on one of the Pure Waters Agency's most pressing problems. As explained to me by the director, the Pure Waters Agency has an image problem. People resent paying money for water pollution services. Part of their resistance is because they don't know what we do. They don't understand how important we are to their health. Our job is to develop some guidelines for informing the public. But first we have to learn how big a problem we really have. What are your thoughts, Ginger, Derek, Gil, and Willie?"

Ginger spoke first: "So long as you mentioned my name first, I thought I would contribute before the good ideas were used up. It seems like a marketing research assignment to me. We have to go out into the field and find out how we are perceived by the public. After we get a clear picture of our strengths and weaknesses as the public sees us, we can plan some remedial action."

Willie commented, "I couldn't have said it better myself. But first we'll have to design a questionnaire and figure out whom we are going to interview. We have some experts in the department of statistics who can help us select the right kind of sample."

"I have a question, Rob," said Gil. "It sounds as if this task force will be pretty time consuming. Will we be getting enough time off from our regular jobs to do justice to this assignment?"

"The ground rules state that each member of this task force will be excused from twenty hours of regular work per week for up to three months," replied Rob. "I don't think we have to put that in writing."

Derek commented, "We haven't even begun and there goes Gil, trying to ensure that he's not overworked. For me, I couldn't be more pleased to be assigned to this project. I've done some depth interviewing for a course I took in consumer psychology."

"Good enough, team, let's make up a tentative list of questions right now. We still have a couple of hours till quitting time."

"Hey, I've got an idea," said Gil. "While you four are working on the questionnaire, I'll run over to the statistical department and see if they can help us draw up a sample."

Two weeks later the Public Relations Task Force was ready to begin field interviewing. Each member was assigned twenty-five interviews to be conducted in a ten-day period. After the interviewing project was one week old, Derek received a phone call from Willie:

"Derek, I've got something confidential to tell you."

"What is it? You're not in any trouble, are you?"

"Not me exactly, Derek," said Willie. "But I think our team is headed for some trouble. I've just spoken to Ginger and she agrees. Gil has been goofing off since the start of the project. He finds the cutest ways to avoid work. He was supposed to meet me one day to do a group interview. Instead he left a message in my department that he was tied up with some urgent business matters."

"That's right, Willie, I remember the first day of our meeting, he took two hours to ask the statistical department a few questions. Have you noticed any other problem?"

"For sure. Not only is Gil behind in his interviews but I think he made up most of the ones that he plans to turn in. I think he is going to single-handedly ruin the output of the group."

"Okay, Willie, what are you telling me? What should we do about the problem?"

"That's why I've called you. Ginger doesn't have any good suggestions either. She thinks we should just let the issue ride. But if we turn in a mediocre or incomplete report, everybody on the task force will look bad. This is supposed to be a team effort. I'm afraid we're stuck with a team member who won't carry his weight."

1. What alternatives do you see for Willie, Ginger, and Derek?
2. What would the advisability be of Ginger, Willie, and Derek calling a private meeting with Rob to discuss the situation?
3. What should Rob's role be in making sure that the team members make an equal contribution?
4. What does this case incident tell us about the functioning of task forces?
5. Is Gil being given a fair chance? Explain.

A Human Relations Incident

THE QC COMPLAINERS[26]

Kerry Industries formed a quality circle in its automatic bagging manufacturing operations. The QC was formed because the level of machine bag failures was unacceptably high. Rebags and equipment failures were running at 20 percent and 10 percent, respectively. The goal set for the QC improvements were rebags at a 5 percent level in six months, and equipment failures at 2 percent in three months.

Plant management moved quickly to give the QC the support it needed, including ample budgeting and hiring an outside consultant. The QC met 10 hours the first month, and 5 hours per month thereafter. After six months, the goal of 5 percent rebags was met. Equipment failures were reduced to 3 percent. Circle members believed they could achieve the goal of 2 percent improvement within another month.

As the circle completed its first six months of operation, Diane Gonzalez, the circle leader, asked to speak with Chris Kantor, the plant manager. Four minutes into their meeting, Gonzalez said to Kantor: "Let me be candid. Our group has met with excellent success. We've made tremendous strides in overcoming the two key problems in the bagging operations. But I don't think the members are going to bring forth any more money-saving suggestions."

"Why not?" asked Kantor, "You've been doing so beautifully so far."

"Because we're tired of being ripped off by management," said Gonzalez. "If one of us had submitted those great ideas to a suggestion system, he or she would have received about $4,000 in suggestion money. Since the suggestions have come out of the circle, all we will get is a recognition plaque to hang on the wall. None of us thinks that's very fair."

"Diane, I don't think you are taking this in the right spirit," said Kantor. "I will discuss your concerns with my staff and then get back to you soon."

1. What should Kantor do about the demands of the QC members for financial rewards for their efforts?

2. What should the company policy be about paying for suggestions made through the suggestion system but not the QC?

3. What is your opinion of the ethics of how circle members are behaving?

A Human Relations Exercise

A QUALITY CIRCLE SIMULATION

The purpose of this exercise is to simulate the workings of a QC. The class is divided into QCs of five to seven members, with each group appointing one person as supervisor. Next, each group has the task of improving upon the quality of a product or service familiar to most people. Potential products and services to choose from include a ten-speed bicycle, the student chair found in most classrooms, a backpack, the ballpoint pen, and student recreational facilities on campus.

Before proceeding with the exercise, it is important to review the workings of a QC described in this chapter and/or the suggested readings. The output of the group should be some tangible, potentially cost-effective, and feasible suggestions. It may be necessary to consult some people outside the circle to obtain some technical ideas. Excluding outside consultation, about 25 minutes is required to conduct this simulation.

Notes

1. Rensis Likert, *New Patterns of Management* (New York: McGraw-Hill, 1961), p. 113.
2. Henry L. Tosi, John R. Rizzo, and Stephen J. Carroll, *Managing Organizational Behavior* (Marshfield, MA: Pitman Publishing, 1986), p. 684.
3. Jack Halloran, *Applied Human Relations: An Organizational Approach* (Englewood Cliffs, NJ: Prentice Hall, 1978), p. 214.
4. Ibid., p. 216.
5. "Companies Spend Billions to Teach Execs to Be Creative," Associated Press story, February 9, 1986.
6. "Problem Solving by Assumptional Analysis," *Research Institute Personal Report for the Executive*, January 7, 1986, pp. 2–3.
7. George P. Huber, *Managerial Decision Making* (Glenview, IL: Scott, Foresman, 1980), p. 199.
8. Andrew H. Van de Ven and Andre L. Delbecq, "The Effectiveness of Nominal, Delphi, and Interacting Group Decision Making Processes," *Academy of Management Journal*, December 1974, p. 606.

9. Joel Brockner and Ted Hess, "Self-Esteem and Task Performance in Quality Circles," *Academy of Management Journal*, September 1986, p. 617.

10. Edward E. Lawler III and Susan A. Mohrman, "Quality Circles after the Fad," *Harvard Business Review*, January–February 1985, p. 66.

11. This section follows closely from Robert J. Shaw, "Tapping the Riches of Creativity among Working People," *Management Focus* (Peat, Marwick, Mitchell & Co.), September–October 1981, pp. 27–29.

12. Sandy J. Wayne, Ricky W. Griffin, and Thomas S. Bateman, "Improving the Effectiveness of Quality Circles," *Personnel Administrator*, March 1986, p. 81.

13. Ibid., p. 80; Mitchell Lee Marks, "The Question of Quality Circles," *Psychology Today*, March 1986, p. 36.

14. "The Question of Quality Circles," *Psychology Today*, p. 38.

15. Wayne, Griffin, and Bateman, "Improving the Effectiveness of Quality Circles," pp. 79–88.

16. Gerald D. Klein, "Implementing Quality Circles: A Hard Look at Some of the Realities," *Personnel*, November–December 1981, p. 4.

17. Preston C. Bottger, "Expertise and Air Time as Bases of Actual and Perceived Influence in Problem-Solving Groups," *Journal of Applied Psychology*, May 1984, p. 220.

18. George M. Prince, "Creative Meetings through Power Sharing," *Harvard Business Review*, July–August 1971, p. 52.

19. Gary Dessler, *Human Behavior: Improving Performance at Work* (Reston, VA: Reston Publishing, 1980), p. 277.

20. Richard A. Guzzo and James A. Waters, "The Expression of Affect and the Performance of Decision-Making Groups," *Journal of Applied Psychology*, February 1982, pp. 67–74.

21. Robert R. Blake and Jane Srygley Mouton, "Don't Let Group Norms Stifle Creativity," *Personnel*, August 1985, pp. 31–32.

22. Irving L. Janis, *Victims of Groupthink: A Psychological Study of Foreign Policy Decisions and Fiascos* (Boston: Houghton Mifflin, 1972), pp. 39–40.

23. Martin Lasden, "Facing Down Groupthink," *Computer Decisions*, June 1986, pp. 52–53.

24. David R. Hamptom, *Contemporary Management* (New York: McGraw-Hill, 1977), pp. 184–185.

25. Reprinted from Andrew J. DuBrin, *Foundations of Organizational Behavior: An Applied Perspective* (Englewood Cliffs, NJ: Prentice Hall, 1984), pp. 252–253.

26. The statistics in this case were researched by Roger H. Hinds.

Suggested Reading

ADIZES, ICHAK, and TURBAN, EFRAIM. "An Innovative Approach to Group Decision Making." *Personnel*, April 1985, pp. 45–49.

BERRY, WALDRON. "Group Problem Solving and How to Be an Effective Participant." *Supervisory Management*, June 1983, pp. 13–19.

BOWMAN, JAMES S. "Why Japanese Companies in the U.S. Don't Need Quality Circles." *Personnel Administrator*, October 1985, pp. 111–117.

GLADSTEIN, DEBORAH, and REILLY, NORA P. "Group Decision Making Under Threat: The Tycoon Game." *Academy of Management Journal*, September 1985, pp. 613–627.

GOODMAN, PAUL S., and associates. *Designing Effective Work Groups*. San Francisco: Jossey-Bass, 1986.

MARKS, MITCHELL LEE, and associates. "Employee Participation in a Quality Circle Program: Impact of Quality of Work Life, Productivity, and Absenteeism." *Journal of Applied Psychology*, February 1986, pp. 61–69.

SIMS, HENRY P., JR., and DEAN, JAMES W., JR. "Beyond Quality Circles: Self-Managing Teams." *Personnel*, January 1985, pp. 25–32.

SWAP, WALTER C., and associates, eds. *Group Decision Making*. Beverly Hills, CA: Sage Publications, 1984.

Leadership
and Influence

LEARNING OBJECTIVES
*After reading and studying this chapter
and doing the exercises, you should be
able to*

1. Specify how leaders go about influencing
organization members.

2. Summarize key leadership traits and behaviors
that are related to successful managerial leadership.

3. Describe several approaches to classifying leadership
styles.

4. Describe the two major contingency theories of leadership.

5. Understand the role of entrepreneurs and intrapreneurs as
leaders.

6. Develop a strategy for realizing your leadership potential.

WHAT IS LEADERSHIP?

Leadership is the process of influencing employees to attain organizations' goals,[1] excluding illegal and immoral methods of persuasion. For instance, influencing employees to kick back part of their pay by threatening them with loss of their jobs is not considered to be leadership. If influence is not necessary, leadership has not been exerted. Employees will often perform their jobs adequately without the benefit of coaching, prompting, cajoling, or being inspired by the boss. In these situations, leadership is not necessary to achieve good job performance. However, if a manager helps employees achieve performance they would not have achieved without his or her influence, leadership has been exercised.

The importance of organizational leadership has been described in these terms: "Leadership is the glue which holds organizations together, and thus is a central topic of interest to professionals, and managers or leaders alike."[2] One problem in understanding leadership is that the term must be differentiated from both management and supervision. You can exert leadership whether or not you hold the job title of manager or supervisor. Your knowledge and personal charm may influence others. Or, because co-workers trust you, you may become their informal leader or spokesperson.

Management is working with and through people to accomplish organizational goals. It involves the coordination of human, material, and financial resources to accomplish something of value. **Supervision** is essentially first-level management, or the art and practice of achieving results through people. It involves overseeing the work of others, with a particular emphasis upon leadership. Supervisors spend a higher proportion of their time interacting directly with subordinates than do higher-level managers.

The concepts of leadership, management, and supervision are thus not identical. Management and supervision involve a wide variety of activities, such as planning, controlling, organizing, scheduling, negotiating, and leading (or directing). Many people are effective with the administrative aspects of a supervisory or managerial job, but few people are effective leaders.

INFLUENCE TACTICS USED BY LEADERS

Since leadership is an influence process, it is important to be aware of some of the tactics leaders use. Much of the discussion about power and politics in Chapter 10 is relevant to understanding how leaders influence people. Here we summarize research findings, and some opinion, about influence tactics used by leaders. Most of these tactics can also be used by managers and nonmanagers.

Charisma refers to leading others based on personal charm and magnetism. Recently this type of influence has been referred to as transformational leadership. **A transformational leader** is one who helps organizations and people make positive changes in the way they do things.[3] The impact of this type of personal influence is illustrated by this anecdote:

> A production superintendent was asked by a senior vice-president why factory output was lower than in previous years. The superintendent replied, "When you folks bought us out, you made one drastic mistake. You forced Charlie Maxwell to retire. He didn't fit your image of a modern corporate executive. What you didn't realize is that the reason we worked so hard in the past is that we all loved old Charlie. He knew everybody in the factory by their first name. The new president hardly knows any of our employees."

Leading by example is a simple but effective way of influencing group members. The ideal approach to leading by example is to be a "Do As I Say and Do" manager. R. Bruce McAfee and Betty J. Ricks note that this type of manager shows consistency between actions and words. Also, actions and words confirm, support, and often clarify each other. For example, if the firm has a dress code and the supervisor explains the code and dresses accordingly, a role model has been provided that is consistent in words and actions. The action of following the dress code provides an example that supports and clarifies the words used to describe the dress code.[4]

Here are some other influence tactics:

Assertiveness refers to being forthright with your demands, expressing both the specifics of what you want done and the feelings surrounding the demands.[5] A leader might say, for example, "I'm very upset about the number of errors in your report. I want it cleaned up by tomorrow at 4:30." A leader might also be assertive by checking frequently on a subordinate.

Ingratiation refers to getting somebody else to like you, often using political behaviors. Two specific ingratiating behaviors noted in the study were, "Acted in a friendly manner prior to asking for what I wanted" and "Praised the subordinate just before asking for what I wanted." Strong leaders tend not to rely heavily on ingratiating tactics.

Rationality is simply appealing to reason and logic, and is used frequently by strong leaders. Pointing out the facts of a situation to a subordinate in order to get him or her to act is an example of rationality. One manager convinced an employee to take on a field assignment by informing her that every member of top management in the firm had spent some time in the field. The subordinate in question was ambitious, which made her receptive to a course of action that could help her achieve her goals.

Sanctions refers to using threats of punishment or actual punishments. Influence tactics of this nature include (a) giving the person no salary increase or preventing that person from getting a pay raise, and (b) threatening the subordinate with loss of promotion. Sanctions remain a frequently used downward influence tactic in organizations, yet their use is not without controversy. Do you think an effective leader needs to rely on sanctions?

Exchange is the use of reciprocal favors in order to influence others. Leaders with limited personal and position power tend to emphasize exchanging favors with subordinates. An example of exchange would be promising to endorse an employee's request for transfer providing he or she takes on an arduous and unpleasant short-term assignment.

Upward appeal means asking for help from a higher authority. Here the leader exerts influence by getting a more powerful person to carry out the influence act. A specific example is, "I sent the guy to my superior when he wouldn't listen to me. That fixed him." More than occasional use of upward appeal weakens the manager's stature in the eyes of subordinates and superiors, thus eroding effectiveness as a leader.

Blocking refers to work slowdowns or the threat thereof, thus being used primarily to exert upward rather than downward influence. However, a leader will sometimes use blocking in such ways as these: "I ignored him until he came around to my way of thinking," or "I stopped being friendly until she started listening to me."

The next major issue about leaders to address here is what traits and behaviors are often associated with success as a leader.

LEADERSHIP TRAITS AND BEHAVIORS

During the last two decades there has been a declining interest in understanding the traits, characteristics, and behaviors of leaders themselves. Substantial research has shown that leadership is best understood when the leader, the followers, and the situation in which they are placed are analyzed. Nevertheless, the leader remains an important consideration in understanding leadership. Without effective leaders, most organizations cannot prosper. Another practical reason for studying the traits and behaviors of leaders is that without such knowledge, leadership selection is left to chance.

A realistic view is that certain traits and behaviors contribute to effective leadership in a wide variety of situations. Correspondingly, similar situations require similar leadership traits and behaviors. To illustrate, a person who was effective in running a production operation in a newspaper could probably run a production operation in a book bindery. There would be enough similarity among the type of subordinates and machinery to make the situations comparable. In contrast, a high school football coach might fail dismally as the managing editor of a fashion magazine. The two situations would call for dramatically different kinds of leadership.

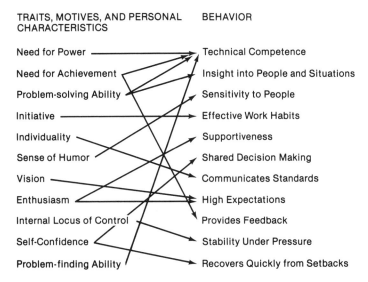

TRAITS, MOTIVES, AND PERSONAL CHARACTERISTICS · BEHAVIOR

Need for Power · Technical Competence
Need for Achievement · Insight into People and Situations
Problem-solving Ability · Sensitivity to People
Initiative · Effective Work Habits
Individuality · Supportiveness
Sense of Humor · Shared Decision Making
Vision · Communicates Standards
Enthusiasm · High Expectations
Internal Locus of Control · Provides Feedback
Self-Confidence · Stability Under Pressure
Problem-finding Ability · Recovers Quickly from Setbacks

Figure 8–1 The relationship between traits and behaviors.

Note: The arrows suggest that one trait, characteristic, or motive may lead to one or more behaviors; and that sometimes more than one trait leads to a particular leadership behavior. Also, some traits are associated with behaviors not directly mentioned in this figure, and some behaviors are associated with traits not mentioned.

The Relationship between Traits and Behavior

Contemporary writers usually draw a sharp distinction between the traits of people (including their motives, characteristics, and attitudes) and their behavior (what they actually do). Leadership theorists are the most adamant about this point, contending that it is much more profitable to study what leaders actually do than to focus on their traits. It is important to recognize, however, that behavior is attributable to both traits and the situation. Assume that an emotionally warm person occupies a leadership position. The trait of warmth will lead the person to the desirable leadership behavior of being supportive of group members. A sampling of the possible relationships between leadership traits and behaviors is illustrated in Figure 8–1.

Extensive research continues to be conducted about which traits, motives, characteristics, and behavior contribute to effective managerial leadership. The discussion in the following two sections is based on research and opinion about leadership effectiveness.[6] The distinction between traits, motives, and personal characteristics versus behavior is not always clear-cut. For example, enthusiasm can be regarded as both a trait and a behavior.

Traits, Motives, and Personal Characteristics

The traits, motives, and characteristics mentioned below are a sampling of traditional and current thinking about contributors to leadership effectiveness. Our choice of these eleven traits does not imply that traits not on the list are unimportant.

Power motive. Effective executives have a strong need to control resources. Leaders with high power drives have three dominant characteristics: (1) They act with vigor and determination to exert their power; (2) they invest much time in thinking about ways to alter the behavior and thinking of others; and (3) they care about their personal standing with those around them.[7] The high need for power is important because it means the leader is interested in influencing others.

Achievement motive. As described in our discussion of motivation, managerial leaders find joy in accomplishment for its own sake. Achievement motivation contributes to the leadership effectiveness of both entrepreneurial leaders and hired managers.

Problem-solving ability. Measures of intelligence are used extensively in the selection of people for leadership positions. The evidence suggests that effective leaders are bright, but not necessarily brilliant. They are intelligent enough to be good problem solvers, but not so intelligent that their interests lie primarily in solving abstract problems and puzzles. John D. Geary, the president of a barge company, makes this comment about intelligence and leadership success:[8]

> Sometime a less than top IQ is an advantage because that person doesn't see all the problems. He or she sees the big problem and gets on and gets it solved. But the extremely bright person can see so many problems that he or she never gets around to solving any of them.

Problem-finding ability. An effective leader looks for things that need doing. An ineffective leader might spend the workweek cleaning and rearranging files. A more effective leader in the same situation might try to determine how his or her department could make a bigger contribution to the company.

Initiative. Exercising initiative, or being a self-starter, refers to taking action without support and stimulation from others. A person aspiring toward leadership assignments should recognize that initiative is a characteristic looked for in potential leaders. Initiative is also related to problem-finding ability—you need to exercise initiative to search for worthwhile problems.

Individuality. Effective leaders tend to have a unique style, particularly at high levels of responsibility. Individuality can express itself both in the unique pattern of traits possessed by the person and in work habits. Edwin E. Ghiselli's research indicated that managers who displayed the greatest individuality in the way they did their work were also judged to be the best managers.[9] Individuality is important in understanding leaders because it contributes to charisma.

Sense of humor. Tracy, a quality-control supervisor in an electronics company, opened a department meeting with these words: "Good morning, Gang. I have some good news and some bad news. The good news is that you will all be getting an extra week of vacation next month. (Cheers from the group.) And, the bad news is that it will be without pay." (Sighs and laughter from the group.) Whether or not you laugh at Tracy's remarks, she is exhibiting a trait that is considered important for a leader. Humor serves such functions in the workplace as relieving tension, relieving boredom, and defusing hostility.[10]

The reason that humor from a leader helps to reduce hostility stems from the logic of the conflict-resolution strategy—disarm the opposition. Assume that Tracy senses the group is angry about the one-week furlough without pay. She might say to her subordinates, "Before you get too upset over this extra week of vacation, look at the good the company is doing. We're doing our share to prevent the economy from overheating and prevent you from becoming a bunch of workaholics. Enjoy your break." Humor further contributes to leadership effectiveness by helping the leader appear to be warm and human.

Vision. Top-level managerial leaders need a visual image of where they see the organization headed and how it can get there. Organizational progress is dependent upon the top executive having this sense of vision. "Furthermore," Richard I. Lester reports, "effective leaders project ideas and images that excite people, and they develop choices that are timely and appropriate for the situation at hand. Therefore, leaders with vision inspire their employees to do their best.[11]

Enthusiasm. In almost all leadership situations it is desirable for the leader to be enthusiastic. The same model applies: a trait (enthusiastic) leads to behavior (enthusiasm). Subordinates tend to respond positively to enthusiasm, partially because enthusiasm may be perceived as a reward for constructive behavior. Enthusiasm is also a desirable leadership trait because it helps build good relationships with subordinates. The trait can be expressed both verbally ("Fabulous job" or "I love it") and nonverbally through gestures, touching, and so forth.

Internal locus of control. As described in Chapter 5, people with an internal locus of control believe they are the primary cause of events happening to them. Current research indicates that supervisory leaders with an internal locus of control are favored by group members.[12] Part of the reason is that an "internal" person is perceived as more powerful than an "external," because he or she takes responsibility for things happening.

Self-confidence. In virtually every leadership setting it is important for the leader to be realistically self-confident. A leader who is self-assured without being bombastic or overbearing instills confidence in subordinates. Aside from being a psychological trait, self-confidence or self-assurance refers to the behavior exhibited by a person in a number of situations. It is akin to being cool under pressure. We can conclude that a given person is a confident supervisor if he or she displays such behavior as retaining composure when an employee threatens to file a grievance or calmly helping an employee fix a jammed machine when the department is behind schedule.

Leadership Behaviors

Listed below are behaviors or actions associated with effective managerial leadership. Figure 8–2 also sheds insight into successful leadership behavior in a variety of situations. As with the discussion of traits, the list is comprehensive but not exhaustive.

Technical competence. An effective leader has to be technically or professionally competent in some discipline, particularly when leading a group of specialists. It is difficult to establish rapport with group members when you do not understand what they are doing and they do not respect your technical skills. At a minimum, the manager of specialists has to be *snow proof* (not readily bluffed about technical matters by subordinates). Thomas R. Horton, president of the American Management Association, made these comments about technical competence and leadership:[13]

> It is a fantasy that a really good manager can manage anything. The best managers have always been those who really know their business, and know it inside out. Bill Marriott, Jr., of the Marriott Corporation, has built that organization into the fastest growing hotel chain in the world. Marriott attributes his success to the fact that he thoroughly knows the hotel and restaurant business. He spends about half his time outside the office visiting Marriott properties.

Insight into people and situations. **Insight** is a depth of understanding that requires considerable intuition and common sense. Insight into people and situations involving people is an essential characteristic of managerial leaders. A manager with good insight is able to make better work assignments and do a better job of training and developing subordinates. The reason is that such a manager makes a careful assessment of the strengths and weaknesses of subordinates. Another major advantage of being insightful is that the leader can size up the situation and adapt his or her leadership approach accordingly. For instance, in a crisis situation, group members would welcome a directive and decisive style of leadership.

Burt K. Scanlon has prepared a leadership checklist that specifies a number of important behaviors for leaders. If you have worked as a supervisor, go through this eighteen-point list as a method of evaluating your leadership behavior. The more frequently you answer "Yes" to these questions, the more effective your leadership behavior. If you prefer, use this list to evaluate a past or present boss. If you have no work experience, use this checklist to evaluate a past or present instructor. Simply substitute the word *student* for *employee*.

LEADERSHIP CHECKLIST

1. Have I made it clear what is expected in terms of results? Do I discuss these results with employees?
2. Have I let the employees know where they stand?
3. Do the employees know how to do the work?
4. Have I done a good job of training and development?
5. Do I give employees all the support I can?
6. What have I done or not done to cultivate positive personal relationships?
7. Do the employees know why their jobs are important, how they fit into the overall company structure, and the ramifications of poor performance?
8. Are employees kept informed on what is going on in the department and the company? Not just "need to know" items, but "nice to know"?
9. Do employees have adequate freedom in which to work?
10. Are employees too often put in a defensive position regarding performance?
11. What have I done to get employees mentally and emotionally involved in their jobs?
12. Have employees been allowed to participate in setting goals and deciding means of achieving them?
13. Have good aspects of performance received adequate and periodic recognition?
14. Do I accentuate the positive instead of the negative?
15. Have I shown adequate concern for employees as individuals? For their personal goals?
16. Am I flexible about listening to employees and giving them a chance to implement ideas and suggestions?
17. Have I ever consciously assessed employees' strengths and weaknesses with the idea of structuring the work to capitalize on the former?
18. Are employees adequate and reasonably challenged?

Figure 8–2 Important behaviors for leaders.

SOURCE: "Managerial Leadership in Perspective: Getting Back to Basics," by Burt K. Scanlon, copyright March 1979. Reprinted with the permission of *Personnel Journal*, Costa Mesa, California; all rights reserved.

Sensitivity to people. It has long been recognized that being sensitive to the needs of people is an important leadership behavior. Recent research documents the fact that insensitivity prevents many up-and-coming managers from reaching the top. In a study of top executives, psychologists compared "derailed" executives with those who had progressed to senior management positions. The leading category of fatal flaws was insensitivity to others, characterized by an abrasive, intimidating, bullying style.[14] Abrasive and intimidating behavior is most likely to show up when the manager is placed under stress.

Effective work habits. In today's information-based world of work, it is important for organizational leaders to possess effective work habits. (Chapter 18 deals exclusively with this topic.) Even if directing the activities of artistic, free-spirited individuals, the leader contributes to organizational effectiveness if he or she is well organized. For example, in an advertising agency somebody needs to keep track of contracts, budgets, and expense accounts.

Supportiveness. Supportive behavior toward subordinates is frequently associated with leadership effectiveness. A supportive leader (one who gives encouragement and praise to subordinates) usually increases morale and often increases productivity. Supportive behavior stems from personal characteristics such as empathy, warmth, and flexibility.

Shared decision making. Effective leaders encourage subordinates to share in making decisions that affect them. Shared decision making is the key component to participative leadership. Much attention has recently been paid to worker participation as it relates to the quality of work life and the success of Japanese-style management (see Chapter 16).

Communicating work standards. Letting subordinates know what to expect and what is expected of them is characteristic of effective leaders. A review of 3,500 leadership studies concluded that this was the *only* leadership quality that encourages both productivity and satisfaction.[15]

Maintaining high expectations. Burt K. Scanlon says: "Low expectations breed low performance and apathy, while high expectations lead to high performance and a more demanding performance tone."[16] As described in our discussion of motivation, this phenomenon has been called the Pygmalion effect in leadership.

Providing feedback. Letting subordinates know where they stand is another vital leadership behavior. Feedback of this nature has two aspects. First, employees must know where they stand with respect to performance goals. In this way, if they are falling short, they can take corrective action. Second, employees must be informed when a job is being done well. Such information is a crucial ingredient of positive reinforcement.

Stability under pressure. Effective leaders are steady performers, even under heavy workloads and uncertain conditions. Remaining steady under conditions of uncertainty contributes to effectiveness because it helps subordinates cope with the situation. When the leader remains calm, group members are reassured that things will work out satisfactorily. Stability is helpful for another reason. It helps the managerial leader appear professional and cool under pressure.

Recover quickly from setbacks. Effective managerial leaders are resilient—they bounce back quickly from setbacks such as budget cuts, demotions, and being fired. An intensive study of executives revealed that they don't even think about failure, and don't even use the word. Instead, they rely on synonyms such as "mistake," "glitch," "bungle," and "setback."[17] In practice, this means that the leader sets an example to subordinates by not crumbling when something big goes wrong. Instead, the leader tries to conduct business as usual.

LEADERSHIP STYLES

The study of leadership behaviors progressed naturally to the study of **leadership styles,** the typical pattern of behaviors engaged in by the leader when dealing with employees. Styles can also be considered stereotypes of how leaders behave in most situations. It is well recognized that effective leaders try to match their style to the situation at hand—they use insight. Here we describe three of the most enduring methods of categorizing leadership styles:

1. The leadership continuum, based on the amount of authority retained by the leader.
2. Theory X and Theory Y, based on the assumptions the leader makes about group members.
3. The Managerial Grid®, based on the leader's relative concern for people and task accomplishment.

The Leadership Continuum

The leadership continuum, or classical approach, classifies leaders according to how much authority they retain for themselves versus how much is turned over to the group. Three key points on the continuum are autocratic, participative, and free-rein leaders (see Figure 8–3).

Autocratic style. An **autocratic leader** attempts to retain most of the authority granted the group. Autocratic leaders make all the major decisions and assume subordinates will comply without question. Leaders who use this style give minimum consideration to what group members are likely to think about an order or decision. An autocrat is sometimes seen as rigid and demanding by subordinates.

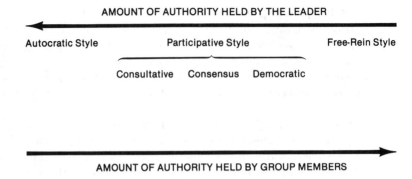

Figure 8–3   The leadership continuum.

Although the authoritarian (a synomym for autocratic) leadership style is not in vogue, many successful leaders are autocrats. One example is Jack Tramiel, the controversial executive who has occupied key positions at both Commodore and Atari. A co-worker of Tramiel's said: "Commodore was the house that Jack built, and when he left the company, so did the spirit, the aggressiveness, the drive. Decision making also went by the wayside."[18]

The autocratic style generally works best in situations where decisions have to be made rapidly, or when group opinion is not needed. One situation calling for autocratic leadership would be extinguishing a forest fire. Another would be when a company is undergoing liquidation.

Participative style.   A **participative leader** is one who shares decision-making authority with the group. The participative style encompasses so much of the leadership continuum that it is useful to divide it into three subtypes: consultative, consensual, and democratic.

Consultative leaders solicit opinions from the group before making a decision, yet they do not feel obliged to accept the group's thinking. Leaders of this type make it clear that they alone have authority to make the final decisions. A standard way to practice consultative leadership would be to call a group meeting and discuss an issue before making a decision.

Consensual leaders encourage group discussion about an issue and then make a decision that reflects the consensus (general agreement) of group members. Japanese managers typically use a consensus style of decision making. Consensus style leaders thus turn over more authority to the group than do consultative leaders. The consensus leadership style results in long delays in decision making because every party involved has to agree.

Democratic leaders confer final authority on the group. They function as collectors of opinion and take a vote before making a decision. Democratic leaders turn over so much authority to the group that they are sometimes classified as free-rein leaders. The group usually achieves its goals when working under a democratic leader. Democratic leadership has more relevance for community activities than for most work settings.

Evaluation of the participative style. The three participative styles are suited to managing competent and well-motivated people who want to get involved in making decisions and giving feedback to the leader. A participative style is also useful when the manager wants employees to commit to a course of action. A supervisor might ask the group, "What should we do with group members who smoke in nonsmoking areas?" If the group agreed on a fitting punishment, they would tend to accept the punishment if it were administered.

If procedures or alternative solutions to a problem have already been agreed upon, participative management is superfluous. For instance, in highly repetitive, machine-paced operations, little room is left for employee problem solving. Another example is that the vast majority of bank employees are not asked to participate in making decisions about setting interest rates on loans. Such decisions are made in the executive suite.

Another problem is that participative decision making is often resisted by first-level managers and middle managers because they worry about losing power and having to do extra work. Since participative management is on the upswing, supervisors and middle managers must learn to adapt to the system. The participative style works best when there is regular communication between managers and employees. Regular communication makes it easier to obtain employee suggestions.[19]

Free-rein style. A **free-rein leader** is one who turns over virtually all the authority to the group. This person issues general goals and guidelines to the group and then does not get involved again unless requested. The only limits imposed on the group are those specified by the leader's boss. Such an extreme degree of freedom is rarely encountered in a work setting. One exception would be a pure research laboratory where scientists and engineers are granted freedom to tackle whatever problems they find interesting.

Styles Based on Assumptions Made about People (Theory X and Theory Y)

A widely quoted and historically important method of classifying leadership styles is based on differences in assumptions made about people. Douglas McGregor, a social psychologist, developed this explanation of leadership because he wanted managers to challenge their own assumptions.[20] McGregor believed that these traditional assumptions were often false, leading to the demotivation of subordinates. He divided assumptions into two extremes, Theory X and Theory Y.

Theory X managers take the traditional, distrustful view of people, and therefore behave autocratically. Consequently, Theory X managers supervise quite closely. The Theory X style is based upon these assumptions:

1. People dislike work and therefore try to avoid it.
2. People dislike work, so managers are forced to control, direct, coerce, and threaten subordinates to get them to work toward organizational goals.
3. People prefer to be directed, to avoid responsibility, to seek security. In general, they are unambitious.

Theory Y managers are trustful of subordinates, and therefore allow them to participate in decision making. The Theory Y style is based on these assumptions:

1. Physical and mental work is a natural part of life, and thus not disliked by people.
2. People are self-motivated to reach goals to which they feel committed.
3. People are committed to goals providing they attain rewards when the goals are reached.
4. Under favorable conditions, people will seek and accept responsibility.
5. People have the capacity to be innovative in solving job-related problems.
6. People are basically bright, but in most job settings their potentials are underutilized.

The Managerial Grid Styles

The Managerial Grid®, developed by Blake and Mouton, is a widely used method of classifying leadership styles. The grid is also a comprehensive system of leadership training and organization development. Grid leadership styles are based on the extent of a person's concern for production and people (see Figure 8–4).[21] Concern for production includes such matters as reaults, the bottom line, performance, profits, and mission. It is rated on a 1 to 9 scale on the horizontal axis. Concern for people is reflected in such matters as showing support for subordinates, getting results based on trust and respect, and worrying about employees' job security. Concern for people is rated on a 1 to 9 scale on the vertical axis.

Key grid positions. The benchmark styles on the Managerial Grid are described below, and are also explained in Figure 8–4.

9,1 In the lower right-hand corner is a maximum concern for production combined with a minimum concern for people. A leader with this orientation concentrates on maximizing production by exercising power and authority, and dictating what people should do.
1,9 In the top left corner is the manager with a minimum concern for production and a maximum concern for people. Primary attention is placed on good feelings among subordinates and co-workers, even at the expense of achieving results.
1,1 In the lower left corner is the manager with a minimum concern for both production and people. The 1,1-oriented manager does only the minimum required to remain a member of the firm.

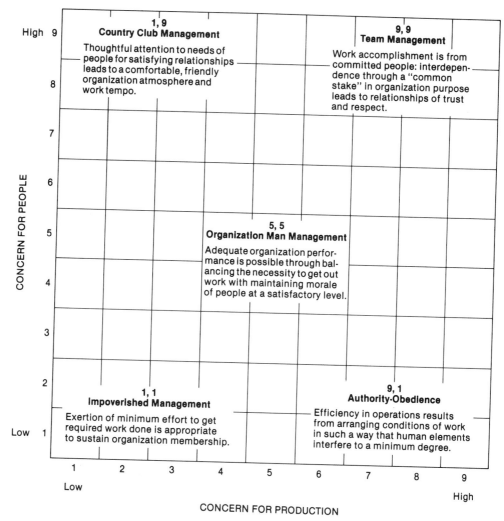

Figure 8–4 The Managerial Grid leadership styles.

SOURCE: Robert R. Blake and Jane S. Mouton, *The Managerial Grid III: The Key to Leadership Excellence* (Houston: Gulf Publishing, Copyright © 1985), p. 12. Reproduced by permission.

5,5 In the center is the 5,5 orientation. Managers with this style are "middle-of-the-roaders" who do their job but avoid making waves, and conform to the status quo.

9,9 In the upper right-hand corner is the 9,9 orientation, which integrates concerns for production and people. It is a goal-directed team approach that seeks to gain optimum results through participation, involvement, and commitment.

Managers generally have one dominant style, such as 9,1. In addition, they have a backup style. The latter tends to be used when the dominant style does not achieve the desired results. For instance, you might attempt a 9,9 approach, only to find that most of the members are not so enthusiastic about their work. It might then be necessary to shift to a 9,1 approach.

Which style is best? Blake and Mouton argue strongly for the value of team management (9,9). The team management approach usually results in improved performance, low absenteeism and turnover, and high employee satisfaction. "Nine-nine" management relies on trust and respect, which helps bring good results. Nevertheless, the Managerial Grid is not dictating that the manager mechanically use one style in trying to lead such different groups as an oil-rigging crew and a department of information systems specialists. The philosophy suggests that the leader use principles of human behavior to size up the situation at hand.

FIEDLER'S CONTINGENCY THEORY OF LEADERSHIP EFFECTIVENESS

A contingency theory of leadership specifies the conditions under which a particular leadership style will be effective. Fred E. Fiedler developed the most widely researched and quoted contingency model.[22] However, the path-goal contingency theory described later is gaining in acceptance.

Fiedler's Model

A manager's leadership style can be classified as relationship-motivated or task-motivated, similar to the concern for production versus the concern for people. The intermediate style is labeled socio-independent. By rating one's least preferred co-worker (LPC) on each of 18 dimensions (such as pleasant versus unpleasant), you derive a total score indicating your style.[23]

Next, the leadership situation is identified according to three basic classifications: high control, moderate control, and low control. A high control situation is considered favorable for the leader, while a low control situation is considered unfavorable. The control classifications are accomplished by rating the leadership situation in its three dimensions, based on straightforward questionnaires:

1. Leader-member relations measure how well the group and the leader get along.
2. Task structure measures how clearly the procedures, goals, and evaluation of the job are defined.
3. Position power measures how much authority the leader possesses to hire, fire, discipline, and grant salary increases to group members.

The three dimensions are listed in decreasing order of importance. Leader-member relations contribute as much to situation favorability as task structure and position power combined. The leader therefore has the most control in situations where relationships with members are the best.

The Leader-Match Concept. The major proposition in Fiedler's theory is the **leader-match concept:** Leadership effectiveness depends on matching leaders to situations where they can exercise the most control. It states specifically:

1. Task-motivated leaders perform the best in situations of high control and low control.
2. Relationship-motivated leaders perform the best in situations of moderate control.
3. Socio-independent leaders tend to perform the best in situations in which their control is high.

Why do task-motivated leaders perform the best in high control and low control situations? One explanation is that task-motivated leaders prefer the clear guidelines and procedures found in a high-control situation. In a low-control situation these are missing, so the leader will take charge and try to develop them. In moderate control situations, these leaders are less effective. They concentrate so heavily on the task that they ignore interpersonal problems, which leads to conflicts and poor performance.

Another explanation is that when conditions are favorable, the group is willing to accept a task-motivated leader because members do not require much emotional support. However, when the situation is unfavorable (low control), the leader needs to be task-motivated to maintain control.[24]

Why is a relationship-motivated style the most effective in a situation of moderate control or favorability? Relationship-motivated leaders are at their best when working closely with people through such means as giving them emotional support. When conditions are moderately favorable, a good deal of uncertainty and tension exist. The leader therefore has to spend time giving people emotional support. Another possible explanation is that in low control situations, relationship-motivated leaders intensify their efforts at working with people and neglect the task to be performed.

Why do socio-dependent leaders perform best in high control situations? Since these leaders strike a balance between concern for people and production, their "balancing act" works best when a situation is under high control. (We admit this is a speculative observation, awaiting further research.)

The Least-Preferred Co-Worker Scale (LPC)

Fiedler says that a leadership style is a relatively permanent aspect of behavior, thus making it difficult to modify. He reasons that once you understand your leadership style, you should work in situations that match your style. Similarly, the organization should help managers match leadership styles and situations.

The LPC scale measures the degree to which a leader describes favorably or unfavorably his or her least-preferred co-worker. The latter is an employee with whom you could work the least well. A leader who describes the least preferred co-worker in relatively favorable terms tends to be relationship-motivated. In contrast, a person who describes his or her least preferred co-worker in an unfavorable manner tends to be task-motivated, or less concerned with human relations. In short, if you can tolerate your enemies, you are relations-motivated. The LPC asks the leader to describe the person with whom he or she can work least well by making such ratings as:

Friendly	__	__	__	__	__	__	__	__	Unfriendly
	8	7	6	5	4	3	2	1	
Tense	__	__	__	__	__	__	__	__	Relaxed
	1	2	3	4	5	6	7	8	

A major problem with the LPC scale is that many people who take it, and researchers who study it, question its validity. The exercise at the end of the chapter presents a much simpler approach to measuring your leadership style.

Overall Findings: Matching the Leader to the Situation

A summary of findings with the leader-match concept is presented in Figure 8–5. To interpret the model, look first at the situational factors at the bottom of the figure. There are eight possible combinations of leader-member relations, task structure, and leader position power. This is true because all three variables are divided into two categories. Leader-member relations can be good or poor; tasks can be structured or unstructured; and position power may be strong or weak. The result is eight possible situations, shown as cells I through VIII. Cells I, II, and III are very favorable for exercising control, while cell VIII is very unfavorable for the leader to exercise control.

Leadership style is also represented in Figure 8–5. The two categories for which the most research has been conducted are the relationship-motivated and the task-motivated (or high LPC and low LPC). Findings for the socio-independent (mixed style) are more tentative. Below each situation is shown the leadership style found to be most strongly associated with effective group performance in that situation. Task-motivated leaders perform the best in situations of high control and low control. These extreme situations are represented by cells I, II, III, and VIII. Note that cell III is classified as favorable despite the leader having to deal with an unstructured task. The other major conclusion is that relations-motivated leaders are most effective when the situation is moderately favorable.

A major contribution of Fiedler's work is that it has prompted others to conduct studies about the contingency nature of leadership. It has also alerted leaders to the importance of sizing up the situation in order to gain more control.

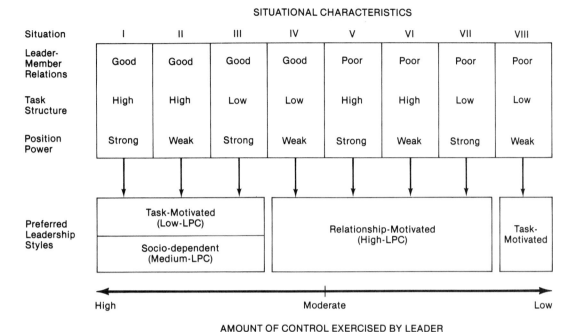

SITUATIONAL CHARACTERISTICS

Figure 8–5 Fiedler's findings on leadership performance and favorability of the situation.

For instance, if a situation was unfavorable, it could be made more favorable by granting the leader more position power.

A major problem with Fiedler's model centers around matching the situation to the leader. In most situations, the amount of control the leader exercises varies from time to time. For instance, a relations-motivated leader might ask for a transfer if the situation became too favorable for exercising control.

THE PATH-GOAL THEORY OF LEADERSHIP EFFECTIVENESS

The **path-goal theory of leadership effectiveness** is a contingency theory that specifies what the leader must do to achieve high productivity and morale in a given situation. In general, the effective leader clarifies the paths to attaining goals, helps group members progress along these paths, and removes barriers that may block goal attainment.[25] The path-goal theory, similar to the expectancy theory of motivation on which it is based, is complex and has several versions. Its key features are summarized in Figure 8–6.

The major proposition to path-goal theory is that the manager should choose a leadership style which takes into account the characteristics of the group members

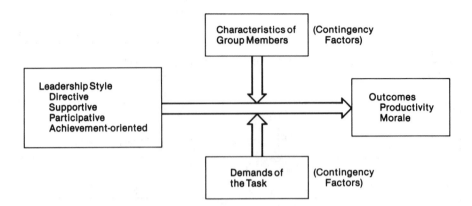

Figure 8–6 The path-goal contingency theory of leadership.

and the demands of the task. Two major aspects of this theory will be discussed: matching the leadership style to the situation, and steps the leader can take to increase productivity and morale.

Matching the Leadership Style to the Situation

A key premise of path-goal theory is that the leader should choose among four different leadership styles to achieve optimum results in a given situation. Two important sets of contingency factors are the type of subordinates and the type of work they perform. For instance, if the manager is leading capable people performing a creative task, the manager should choose a participative style. The four styles and their appropriate circumstances are as follows:

Directive. The directive leader emphasizes formal activities such as planning, organizing, and controlling. (The directive style is about the same as task-motivated.) Group members are carefully told what is expected of them. They are given specific guidelines on rules and regulations. The directive style improves morale when the task is unclear.

Supportive. The supportive (similar to relationship-motivated) leader displays concern for the well-being of group members and creates an emotionally supportive climate. The leader also emphasizes developing mutually satisfying relationships among group members. The supportive leader enhances morale when group members work on dissatisfying, stressful, or frustrating tasks. Employees who are unsure of themselves prefer the supportive leadership style.

Participative. The participative leader consults with group members to gather their suggestions, and then takes these suggestions seriously when making a decision. The participative style is best suited for improving the morale of well-motivated employees who perform nonrepetitive tasks.

Achievement-Oriented. The achievement-oriented leader sets challenging goals, pushes for work improvement, and sets high expectations for subordinates. Group members are also expected to assume responsibility. The achievement-oriented leadership style works well with achievement-oriented subordinates, and with those working on ambiguous and nonrepetitive tasks.

How the Leader Influences Performance

In addition to recommending leadership styles to fit the situation, path-goal theory offers many other suggestions to leaders. Most of these relate to motivation and satisfaction, and include the following:[26]

1. Recognize or activate group members' needs for rewards over which the leader has control.
2. Increase the personal payoffs to subordinates for attaining work goals. The leader might give high-performing employees additional recognition.
3. Make the paths to payoffs (rewards) easier by coaching and providing direction. For instance, a manager might help an employee get chosen for a high-level project.
4. Help group members clarify their expectations of how effort will lead to good performance, and how good performance will lead to a reward. The leader might say, "Anybody who has gone through this training in the past came away knowing how to do a spreadsheet analysis. And most people who learn how to run an electronic spreadsheet wind up getting a good raise."
5. Reduce frustrating barriers to reaching goals. For example, the leader might hire a temporary worker to help a subordinate catch up on paperwork.
6. Increase opportunities for personal satisfaction if the group member performs effectively. The "if" is important because it reflects contingent behavior on the leader's part.
7. Be careful not to irritate people by giving them instructions on things they already can do well.

ENTREPRENEURS AND INTRAPRENEURS AS LEADERS

What is an entrepreneurial or intrapreneurial leadership style? Many entrepreneurs and intrapreneurs use a similar leadership style that stems from their key personality characteristics and circumstances. The notable aspects of this style are described below;[27] see the accompanying box for additional insight into the entrepreneurial leader.

CASE STUDY OF AN ENTREPRENEURIAL LEADER: E. PHILIP SAUNDERS, FOUNDER OF TRUCKSTOPS CORPORATION

Once, E. Philip Saunders was a 20-year-old dreamer, trying to support a wife and two children with a failing business he'd taken over from his father. Now he is a wealthy entrepreneur who's looking for profitable things to do with his money.

Saunders is the founder of Truckstops Corporation of America. He sold the company to Ryder Systems for several million dollars. Now he is involved in running a fuel-oil distributorship, a trucking company, a dairy farm, a company that makes soda fountain products, and, since the truck stop business "is still very dear to my heart," a Truckstops of America franchise in a small town.

"I enjoy the challenge of trying to make a profit," he said. "At 43, I can't see myself retiring and becoming a golf bum." After the sale of Truckstops to Ryder, Saunders became an executive vice president and director of Ryder. He worked in "an ivory tower in Miami," he said. He never got a chance to talk to customers or employees. He just worked in an office. Four years later he decided to return to "the entrepreneurial life I enjoy." He and a business associate bought Econo-car International from Westinghouse Electric Corporation at a distress price. They restored the company to profitability and sold it to a leasing company.

Source: Phil Ebersole, "Entrepreneurship," *Rochester Democrat and Chronicle*, July 19, 1981; updated by interview conducted August 15, 1986.

- A heavy task motivation, combined with a direct approach to giving instructions to employees.
- An intense sense of urgency that motivates many people and discourages some. Many entrepreneurs have such an intense sense of urgency themselves that they expect others to feel the same way about work.
- Impatience and brusqueness toward employees because entrepreneurs and intrapreneurs are always in a hurry. Since entrepreneurs operate more on hunches than careful planning, they become discouraged with employees who insist on studying problems for a prolonged period.
- A charismatic personality that inspires others to want to do business with him or her despite their impatience.
- A much stronger interest in dealing with customers than employees.
- A strong dislike for bureaucratic rules and regulations, which makes the entrepreneur impatient during meetings. A typical example is the entrepreneur who sells his or her business to a larger firm, thus becoming a division president. Within two years, the entrepreneur leaves the firm because of frustration with rules and regulations imposed from above.

DEVELOPING YOUR LEADERSHIP POTENTIAL

Much of this book deals directly or indirectly with information that could improve your leadership effectiveness. The following chapter on communication is a case in point. Improving your communications effectiveness would be one way to enhance your ability to lead people. And Chapter 12, "Improving Interpersonal Skills," describes programs used to improve managerial skills. Formal education and management development programs also make an important contribution to enhancing one's leadership potential. Here we mention three strategies for developing your leadership potential in addition to studying and attending formal programs.

1. Acquire broad experience. Because leadership is situational, a sound approach to improving leadership effectiveness is to attempt to gain supervisory experience in different settings. A person who wants to become an executive is well advised to gain supervisory experience in at least two different organizational functions, such as marketing and operations.

First-level supervisory jobs are an invaluable starting point for developing your leadership potential. It takes considerable skill to manage a fast-food restaurant or direct a public playground during the summer. A first-level supervisor frequently faces a situation where subordinates are poorly trained, poorly paid, and not well motivated to achieve company objectives.

2. Modeling effective leaders. Another strategy for leadership development is to observe capable leaders in action and then model some of their approaches. You may not want to copy a particular leader entirely, but you can incorporate a few of the behavior patterns into your own leadership style. For instance, most inexperienced leaders have difficulty confronting others. Observe a skilled confronter handle the situation, and try that person's approach the next time you have unfavorable news to communicate to another person.

3. Self-development of leadership traits and behaviors. Our final recommendation for enhancing your leadership potential is to study the leadership traits, characteristics, and behaviors described earlier in this chapter. As a starting point, identify several you think that you could strengthen within yourself given some determination and perhaps combined with the right training program. For example, you might decide that with effort you could improve your self-starting ability and enthusiasm. You might also believe that you could remember to be more supportive of co-workers and subordinates. It is also helpful to obtain feedback from valid sources about which traits and behaviors you particularly need to develop.

Summary of Key Points

☐ Leadership is the process of influencing employees to achieve organizational goals, excluding illegal and immoral methods of persuasion. Leading, or directing, is one function of management or supervision. Among the tactics used by leaders to influence others are charisma, leading by example, assertiveness, ingratiation, rationality, sanctions, exchange, upward appeal, and blocking.

☐ Leadership is situational, yet some traits, motives, and personal characteristics contribute to effectiveness in many situations. Among them are the needs for power and achievement, problem-solving ability, initiative, individuality, sense of humor, vision, enthusiasm, internal locus of control, and self-confidence.

☐ Behaviors related to leadership effectiveness include technical competence, insight into people and situations, sensitivity to people, effective work habits, supportiveness, shared decision making, communicating work standards, maintaining high expectations, providing feedback, stability under pressure, and recovering quickly from setbacks.

☐ A leadership style is the typical pattern of behavior engaged in by the leader when dealing with employees. The leadership continuum classifies leaders according to how much authority they retain for themselves. Styles are autocratic, participative (including consultative, consensual, and democratic), and free rein. The participative style works best with people who are competent and well motivated.

☐ The Managerial Grid styles classify leaders according to how much concern they have for both production (task accomplishment) and people. Team management, with its high emphasis on production and people, is considered the ideal. The Theory X and Theory Y styles are based on the assumptions a manager makes about people. Theory X assumptions lead to an autocratic style, while Theory Y assumptions lead to a participative style.

☐ The most widely quoted and researched contingency model of leadership is that developed by Fiedler. Its key proposition is that in situations of high control or low control, the leader should use a task-motivated style. In a situation of moderate control, a relationship-motivated style is recommended. In high control situations, a socio-independent (intermediate) style can also be used.

☐ Style, in Fiedler's model, is measured by the least-preferred co-worker scale (LPC). You are relationship-motivated if you have a reasonably positive attitude toward your least-preferred co-worker. You are task-motivated if your attitude is negative, and you are socio-independent if your attitude is neutral. Situational control or favorability is measured by a combination of three factors: the quality of leader-member relations, the degree of task structure, and the leader's position power.

☐ The path-goal theory of leadership explains how leaders can bring about high productivity and morale. Effective leaders clarify the paths to attaining goals, help subordinates progress along these paths, and remove barriers to attaining goals. Leaders must choose a style that best fits the two sets of contingency factors—the characteristics of the subordinates and the task.

☐ An important style of leader is the entrepreneur or intrapreneur (an entrepreneur within a large firm). The entrepreneurial style stems from the person's personal characteristics and the circumstances of self-employment. The entrepreneurial style includes these elements: a heavy task orientation, charismatic personality, preference for dealing with customers rather than employees, and dislike for bureaucracy.

☐   A recommended approach to developing your leadership potential is to acquire supervisory experience in several different situations. Also, it is helpful to model effective leaders and to develop those traits and characteristics associated with effective leadership.

Questions and Activities

1. How does knowledge of the basic organization functions such as accounting, production, and marketing contribute to leadership effectiveness?

2. Now that you have studied this chapter, what do you think of the once-popular statement, "Leaders are born, not made"?

3. Which influence tactics would you use if you were supervising a group of people with more experience and job knowledge than you? Why?

4. In summarizing leadership traits, no mention was made of physical appearance. How does this fit with commonsense beliefs about the characteristics of leaders?

5. Identify several leadership traits that you think would be very difficult to develop. Explain your reasoning.

6. Which leadership style do you think would work the most effectively in leading the crew of a jumbo jet airliner? Why?

7. Place the president or prime minister of your country on the Managerial Grid and justify your placement.

8. Identify the leadership style of the instructor for this course and justify your reasoning. Use any method of classifying leadership style.

9. How can a leader modify a situation in order to gain more control? Use Fiedler's theory in preparing your answer.

10. According to Fiedler's theory, which leadership style is best to manage a chaotic situation such as a government agency facing extinction?

11. Make up a headline to summarize what message the path-goal theory has for leaders.

12. Compare the leadership style of any entrepreneur you know personally with the description provided in this text.

A Human Relations Case

THE OVERWHELMING LEADER

Sam Giovanni founded his chain of hardware stores about forty years ago by opening a small retail outlet in a residential neighborhood. Giovanni's prices were competitive with other retail outlets, and his physical layout was modest. Nevertheless, Giovanni Hardware was an immediate success. The competitive edge his store offered was a personalized approach to customer service.

Giovanni's approach to personalized service had a distinct meaning. Each associate was given four months of intensive training about the store's merchandise and how to advise customers on do-it-yourself projects. If an associate did not know the answer to a customer problem, he or she was instructed to ask Sam or his brother or sister, who also worked at the store.

Two years after founding the company, Sam opened another store. Over a period of twenty years, Sam opened 10 more stores. Twelve Giovanni Hardware stores are now in operation. Several of these stores evolved into huge warehouse-style home centers that sell lumber and plumbing supplies as well as a full range of hardware items. After the twelfth store was open, Sam was working 75 hours a week taking care of such major business problems as merchandising, employee selection, and bank negotiations. Also, he regularly walked through the aisles of his stores greeting customers and sometimes helping them make purchase decisions.

To ease the workload on himself and his siblings, Sam hired an operations manager, Joe Danville, and a merchandise manager, Peggy Seacrest. Danville's main job was to oversee the store operations. All 12 store managers reported to him. Seacrest's job was to help Giovanni and his two relatives with purchasing, and to make decisions about new types of merchandise for the stores. Both Danville and Seacrest were required to clear any major decision with Giovanni or his two siblings.

Three months after being hired, Danville faced a major operating decision. A hurricane hit the area and knocked out power lines, hampered telephone service, and created floods leading to stalled traffic. After studying the situation for an hour, Danville rushed into the office of Katrina Giovanni, Sam's sister. "Katrina," he said, "my decision is to close all the stores for the day. Conditions are getting out of hand, and I don't want any storm-related accidents to happen to our employees or customers."

Katrina responded, "Joe, you and I don't have the authority to make such a big decision. Sam is off the coast of Florida this week on a fishing trip. He can't be reached. We'll have to stay open until our normal operating hours. Sam is still our leader."

"Then why did you hire me as an operations manager if I don't have the authority to close the stores in a hurricane? Giovanni Hardware can no longer afford to operate as a one-person band."

"I sympathize with you," said Katrina, "but Sam is still the boss."

Discouraged by his conversation with Katrina, Joe decided to drop the issue. He thought to himself, "I'll speak to Sam about this problem a few days after he gets back from Florida. I just can't get through to Katrina."

The next day was a hectic one for Joe, the store managers, and other employees. The hurricane did considerable damage to several storefronts. Debris had to be cleaned up, broken windows had to be replaced with plywood, and insurance claims had to be filed. To ease some of the tension, Joe asked Peggy Seacrest if she could meet with him for breakfast the following day. Peggy obliged.

"Peggy," said Joe, "I'm wondering if you're experiencing the same kind of problem as I am. I was hired here as a professional manager, but I'm not being treated like a professional. This place is still clearly Sam Giovanni's operation. He's still the big decision maker."

Seacrest laughed and said, "Joe, I know what you're saying. I was hired to help the chain adopt some innovative merchandising policies. I agreed to touch base with Sam or his brother or sister on major decisions. Checking with them is a waste of time. They always tell me that they will have to speak to Sam first before giving me approval.

"Sam's a great guy and a smart businessperson. Yet he really doesn't listen to my merchandising ideas. He only approves of those ideas he would have thought of without my input. He sees himself as the only person capable of making major merchandising decisions for Giovanni Hardware. Sam just won't let go. He may be an inspired leader to the old-time employees, but he has a small-business mentality. I think his attitude is going to stifle our growth."

"I agree," said Joe Danville, "yet I don't know how to change things for the better."

1. How would you describe Sam Giovanni's leadership style?
2. What do you think of Seacrest's assessment that Giovanni has a small-business mentality?
3. What changes in Giovanni's leadership style would you recommend?
4. Assuming that Danville and Seacrest want to stay with Giovanni Hardware, what should they do about their working relationship with Giovanni?

A Human Relations Incident

WHAT KIND OF A LEADER IS DON RUMSFELD?

When Donald H. Rumsfeld took over as president and chief executive officer of G. D. Searle & Company, the big pharmaceutical manufacturer, he had absolutely no experience in business. However, he had a record of distinguished accomplishment in government, including service as a Congressman, Ambassador to NATO, White House Chief of Staff, and Secretary of Defense. In a short time Rumsfeld acted decisively to engineer what has been one of the most remarkable turnarounds in business history.

Rumsfeld says he was ready for a new challenge when he left the Pentagon. In fact, the challenge was perfect for his personal approach to achievement, which is to place himself in a difficult situation and work his way out of it, to attain the goal through sheer intelligence and unremitting drive.

The specific skill Rumsfeld applied in shaping up Searle was assessing the few key people who would be his links to the rest of the organization. "Very few people are able to do it all by themselves," he says. "Therefore, in order to attain that which is ultimately achievable by an organization, the single most important thing you can do in approaching your assignment is to address the important matter of the key people."

Asked about how he motivates his top people, Rumsfeld says, "What you have to do is be careful you don't surround yourself with people you need to energize. You can energize some, but not all. By the same token, you can't have a whole team of self-starters or your task will be one of constantly holding in the reins and cleaning up the mistakes.

"There's a certain balance to maintain. The length of the leash varies with different people, depending on your knowledge of them, your own comfort in dealing with the subject matter they are dealing in, or your assessment of them. The leashes may vary with the same person with respect to different subjects."

1. What leadership traits, motives, personal characteristics, and behaviors of Rumsfeld are revealed in the above excerpt?
2. How would you describe his leadership style?
3. How does the excerpt relate to contingency management?

Source: Excerpted and adapted from Robert C. Anderson, "Man in Charge," *Success!* December 1982, pp, 14, 16, 50.

A Human Relations Exercise

WHAT IS YOUR LEADERSHIP STYLE?

The following quiz will help you assess your leadership style whether you are currently a boss or might be in the future. Answer "agree" or "disagree" to the left of each item.

_____ 1. Ambition is essential in leadership.

_____ 2. Outdated methods in industry must be eliminated in spite of people's feelings.

_____ 3. Knowhow and initiative are two of the most important qualities a person can have.

_____ 4. What gets done is more important than how pleasant it is to perform the task.

_____ 5. A supervisor's job is more important than that of a social worker.

_____ 6. Newspapers don't give enough space to people who complete worthwhile projects.

_____ 7. My primary goal in life is to reach the top of the heap.

_____ 8. The greatest satisfaction for me is the feeling of a job well done.

_____ 9. Friends are more important than career ambition.

_____ 10. Schools should put less emphasis on competition and more on getting along with others.

Scoring and Interpretation. Task-motivated bosses would answer "agree" to items 1 through 8, and "disagree" to items 9 and 10. Relationship-motivated bosses would answer "disagree" to items 1 through 8, and "agree" to items 9 and 10. Give yourself 1 point for each answer that follows these patterns, and consider a score of 3 to 5 in either category as average. Any score above 6 is high and indicates that you would be (or are) either strongly task-motivated or relationship-motivated as a boss.

Source: Excerpted and adapted with permission from Salvatore Didato, "Do Your Employees Like You or Respect You? It's Hard to Have Both," *Rochester Democrat and Chronicle*, January 19, 1985, p. 14B.

Notes

1. R. Bruce McAfee and Betty J. Ricks, "Leadership by Example: 'Do as I Do!'" *Management Solutions*, August 1986, p. 10.

2. Adapted from John R. Hinrichs, Review of *Leadership Dynamics* in *Personnel Psychology*, Summer 1979, p. 454.

3. Bernard M. Bass, *Leadership and Performance Beyond Expectations* (New York: Free Press, 1985); Noel M. Tichy and Mary Anne DeVanna, "The Transformational Leader," *Training and Development Journal*, July 1986, pp. 27–32.

4. McAfee and Ricks, "Leadership by Example," p. 15.

5. This point forward on the list is from David Kipnis, Stuart M. Schmidt, and Ian Wilkinson, "Intraorganizational Influence Tactics: Explorations in Getting One's Way," *Journal of Applied Psychology*, August 1980, pp. 440–452.

6. General references here are Bass, *Leadership and Performance*, Burt K. Scanlon, "Managerial Leadership in Perspective: Getting Back to Basics," *Personnel Journal*, March 1979, pp. 168–171, 183; Edwin E. Ghiselli, *Explorations in Managerial Talent* (Santa Monica, CA: Goodyear, 1971).

7. David C. McClelland and Richard Boyatzis, "Leadership Motive Pattern and Long-Term Success in Management," *Journal of Applied Psychology*, December 1982, p. 737.

8. Quoted in Priscilla Petty, "If You've Been in Your Job Long, You Need to Freshen Up on Ambition," Gannett News Service column, September 30, 1986.

9. Edwin E. Ghiselli, "Managerial Talent," *American Psychologist*, October 1963, p. 640.

10. W. Jack Duncan, "Humor in Management: Prospects for Administrative Practice and Research," *Academy of Management Review*, January 1982, pp. 136–140.

11. Richard I. Lester, "Leadership: Some Principles and Concepts," *Personnel Journal*, November 1981, p. 870.

12. Avis L. Johnson, Fred Luthans, and Harry W. Hennessey, "The Role of Locus of Control in Leader Influence Behavior," *Personnel Psychology*, Spring 1984, p. 70.

13. Thomas R. Horton, "American Management: Myths and Realities," address at Rochester Institute of Technology, April 17, 1986.

14. Morgan W. McCall, Jr., and Michael M. Lombardo, "What Makes a Top Executive?" *Psychology Today*, February 1983, p. 28.

15. Bernard M. Bass, *Stogdill's Handbook of Leadership* (New York: Free Press, 1981).

16. Scanlon, "Managerial Leadership," p. 169.

17. Warren Bennis and Burt Nanus, "The Leadership Tightrope," *Success!* March 1985, p. 62.

18. Dennis Kneale, "Commodore, Readying New Computers, Reels from Its Past Errors," *The Wall Street Journal*, July 19, 1985, p. 8.

19. Leonard M. Apcar, "Middle Managers and Supervisors Resist Moves to More Participatory Management," *The Wall Street Journal*, September 16, 1985, p. 1.

20. Douglas McGregor, *The Human Side of Enterprise* (New York: McGraw-Hill, 1960), pp. 33–57.

21. Robert R. Blake and Jane S. Mouton, *The Managerial Grid III: The Key to Leadership Excellence* (Houston: Gulf Publishing, 1985), pp. 10–16.

22. Fred E. Fiedler, Martin M. Chemers, and Linda Mahar, *Improving Leadership Effectiveness: The Leader Match Concept*, 2nd ed. (New York: Wiley, 1984).

23. The outline is based partially upon Charles Boswell, "Review of *Improving Leadership Effectiveness: The Leader Match concept*, 2nd ed.," *Personnel Psychology*, Spring 1985, pp. 220–222.

24. John R. Schermerhorn, Jr., James G. Hunt, and Richard N. Osburn, *Managing Organizational Behavior*, 2nd ed. (New York: Wiley, 1985), p. 592.

25. Robert J. House, "A Path-Goal Theory of Leadership Effectiveness," *Administrative Science Quarterly*, September 1971, pp. 321–339; Robert J. House and Terence R. Mitchell, "Path-Goal Theory of Leadership," *Journal of Contemporary Business*, Autumn 1974, pp. 81–98.

26. House and Mitchell, "Path-Goal Theory of Leadership," p. 84.

27. Found at various places in Part One of Donald L. Sexton and Raymond W. Smilors, eds., *The Art and Science of Entrepreneurship* (New York: Ballinger, 1985); Daniel Goleman, "The Psyche of the Entrepreneur," *New York Times Magazine*, February 2, 1986, pp. 30–32, 59, 68; Franck A. deChambeau and Fredericka Mackenzie, "Intrapreneurship," *Personnel Journal*, July 1986, p. 40.

Suggested Reading

BLANCHARD, KENNETH, ZIGARMI, PATRICIA, and ZIGARMI, DREA. *Leadership and the One Minute Manager: Increasing Effectiveness Through Situational Leadership.* New York: William Morrow, 1985.

COHEN, MICHAEL D., and MARCH, JAMES G. *Leadership and Ambiguity*, 2nd ed. Cambridge, MA: Harvard Business School Press, 1987.

DEETS, NORMAN, and MORANO, RICHARD. "Xerox's Strategy for Changing Management Styles." *Management Review*, March 1986, pp. 32–36.

DIENSCH, RICHARD M., and LIDEN, ROBERT C. "Leader-Member Exchange Model of Leadership: A Critique and Further Development." *Academy of Management Review*, July 1986, pp. 618–634.

DRUCKER, PETER F. *Innovation and Entrepreneurship: Practices and Principles.* New York: Harper & Row, 1984.

HISRICH, ROBERT D., and BRUSH, CANDIDA G. *The Woman Entrepreneur: Starting, Financing, and Managing a Successful Business.* Lexington, MA: D.C. Heath/Lexington Books, 1985.

PORTNOY, ROBERT A. *Leadership: What Every Leader Should Know about People.* Englewood Cliffs, NJ: Prentice Hall, 1986.

RONSTADT, ROBERT. *Entrepreneurship: Text, Cases, and Notes.* Dover, MA: Lord Publishing Company, 1985.

SCHEIN, EDGAR H. *Organizational Culture and Leadership.* San Francisco: Jossey-Bass, 1985.

WALL, JIM. *Leading.* Lexington, MA: D.C. Heath/Lexington Books, 1986.

Communicating With People

LEARNING OBJECTIVES

After reading and studying this chapter and doing the exercises, you should be able to

1. Explain the basic steps in the communication process.

2. Describe the major communication pathways in organizations.

3. Understand the importance of nonverbal communication in organizations.

4. Pinpoint techniques and strategies for overcoming communication problems in organizations.

5. Develop a plan for improving your communication effectiveness.

THE IMPORTANCE OF COMMUNICATION
IN ORGANIZATIONS

Communication is the sending, receiving, and understanding of messages. It is also the basic process by which managers and staff specialists accomplish their work. A manager can coordinate the work of others only if he or she receives information from some people and transmits it to others. And staff specialists can have their recommendations implemented only if they are communicated to management in a useful manner. Even those whose work does not primarily involve people must communicate with others to ask questions or explain their work. Communication is also important because effective communication skills have always been considered a success factor for managerial workers.

The information in this chapter is aimed toward reducing communication problems among people. We approach this end in two ways: First, we explain the nature of many facets of interpersonal communication. Second, we describe methods of overcoming communication problems in organizations and methods of improving your communication skills.

STEPS IN THE COMMUNICATION PROCESS

One way to understand how people communicate is to examine the steps involved in transmitting and receiving a message (see Figure 9–1). The process involves the following sequence of events: ideation, encoding, transmission over a medium, receiving, decoding, understanding, and taking action. The clouds above and below the diagram in Figure 9–1 symbolize barriers that can arise at any step in communication.

The process is cyclical. Upon decoding a message, understanding it, and then taking action, the receiver sends out his or her own message. The cycle is therefore repeated at least once. Assume Conrad wishes to communicate to his boss, Barbara, that he wants a salary increase.

Step one is *ideation* by Conrad. He organizes his thoughts about this sensitive problem. This stage is both the origin and the framing of the idea or message in the sender's mind. Conrad says to himself, "I think I'll ask for a raise."

Step two is *encoding*. Here the ideas are organized into a series of symbols (words, hand gestures, body movements, drawings) designed to communicate

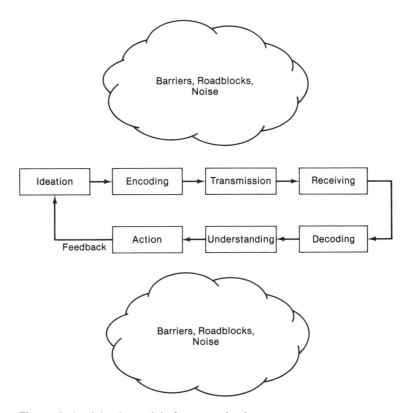

Figure 9–1 A basic model of communication process.

to the intended receiver. Conrad says, "Barbara, there is something I would like to talk to you about if you have the time. . . ."

Step three is *transmission* of the message orally or in writing. In this situation the sender chose the oral mode.

Step four is *receiving* of the message by the other party. Barbara can only receive the message if she is attentive to Conrad.

Step five is *decoding* the symbols sent by the sender to the receiver. In this case decoding is not complete until Barbara hears the whole message. The opening comment, "Barbara, there is something I would like to talk about. . . . ," is the type of statement often used by employees to broach a sensitive topic such as discussing a resignation or salary increase. Barbara therefore listens attentively for more information.

Step six, *understanding*, follows upon the decoding process. Barbara has no trouble understanding that Conrad wants a salary increase. When communication barriers exist (as described in the next section of this chapter), understanding may be limited.

Step seven is *action*. Barbara understands Conrad's request, but does not agree. She acts by telling Conrad that he will have to wait three more months until his salary will be reviewed. Action is also a form of feedback, because it results in a message being sent back to the original sender from the receiver.

COMMUNICATION DIRECTIONS

Messages in organizations flow in three primary directions—downward, sideways, and upward. It is also possible, but not easy, to communicate in a diagonal direction. People who are adept at sending messages in one direction are not necessarily adept at communicating in other directions. For example, some people are politically motivated to become good upward communicators, but they fail to communicate in a meaningful way to their peers or to lower-ranking employees.

The problems encountered in communicating messages in these three directions include the general communication problems discussed later in the section titled "Overcoming Communication Problems in Organizations." Here we will mention one or two unique problems of downward, sideways, and upward communication.

Downward Communication

The purpose of downward communication is to send information from higher levels of the organization to lower levels. Through downward communication management is able to carry out its basic functions of planning, organizing, controlling, and directing. When you receive an evaluation of your performance, you are the recipient of downward communication.

A unique problem with downward communication is that too many managers overemphasize it at the expense of inviting upward communication. Messages are sent to employees, but not enough effort and time is devoted to learning if the message has been properly received. One manager was concerned that an order of his had not been implemented by a department clerk. Exasperated, the manager said to the subordinate, "I'm still waiting for you to send that inquiry to the vendor. What happened, didn't you receive my memo?" The clerk replied, "Sure I received your memo. I read it carefully. I know what it said, but I still don't know what it means."

Another problem with some forms of downward communication is that subordinates tend to regard communications from above as indicators of dissatisfaction. The underlying sentiment is, "If management wrote a memo about the topic, it must be that we're doing something wrong."

Sideways Communication

Communication among employees at the same level is crucial for the accomplishment of work. Good coordination is the product of good communication. For instance, an employee who hears a customer complaint directly should communicate that information to a co-worker who can correct the problem. A study of problems encountered in different communication directions found that horizontal communication is the most effective process. One specific finding was that horizontal messages arrive on time about 75 percent of the time. The researcher noted that some of this communication efficiency can be attributed to formal structures, such as quality circles and project teams.[1]

Horizontal communication is less efficient when workers are isolated from each other by being grouped into different departments. The isolation leads to limited understanding, which in turn leads to rivalry and friction. One way of overcoming this type of conflict is to give people the opportunity to talk to one another in interdepartmental meetings.

Upward Communication

Upward communication is the flow of information from lower levels to higher levels, or from employees to management. Without upward communication, management works in a vacuum, not knowing if messages have been received properly, or if other problems exist in the organization. One computer company faced bankruptcy because of limited upward communication. Middle managers were aware that computers were beginning to pile up on dealer shelves. However, they failed to communicate this information until the company had a severe problem of excess inventory.

Despite the importance of upward communication, it is usually limited. Table 9–1 summarizes findings from Allan D. Frank's study of organizational communication in over 100 firms.[2] The people answering the questionnaire were human resource professionals. One interpretation of the data is that upward communication is not responded to enthusiastically, nor is it very welcome.

One barrier to upward communication is that many employees see manage-

Table 9–1 How effective is upward communication?

Question	Percent	Response Categories
"When messages are sent	0.7%	Almost never/very little
upward through formal	20.7	Sometimes/little
channels, how frequently	30.0	Often
does the receiver respond	32.0	Very often/great
to the message?"	16.7	Almost always/very great
"To what extent are	10.0	Almost never/very little
employees encouraged by	32.7	Sometimes/little
management to send	—	Often
messages upward in the	39.3	Very often/great
organization?"	18.0	Almost always/very great

SOURCE: Adapted from Allan D. Frank, "Trends in Communication: Who Talks to Whom," *Personnel*, December 1985, p. 42. Reprinted with permission from the American Management Association.

ment as being both inaccessible and unresponsive. Workers often feel that their bosses are too busy to be disturbed, or they simply cannot find their bosses when they are wanted.

FORMAL AND INFORMAL COMMUNICATION PATHWAYS

In addition to traveling in more than one direction, messages are sent over more than one pathway. Organizational communication takes place over both formal and informal channels or pathways.

Formal Communication Pathways

Formal communication pathways are the official, sanctioned paths over which messages are supposed to travel. As such, they are easy for most employees to understand and accept. Two key determinants of formal communication pathways are the organization structure and the flow of work.

Organization structure. The organization structure, as revealed by the organization chart, describes who reports to whom. It simultaneously dictates communication pathways. In large organizations, these pathways can be complex. Twelve levels of management are often found in large corporations and government agencies. Assume that a chairman of the board decides that helping to find jobs for the spouses of transferred employees is a corporate responsibility. A policy statement is then made that managers should make an effort to help the spouse of a transferred employee find a job in the new location.

Figure 9–2 shows the formal communication pathway for this message. The formal pathway indicates the least complicated route over which the message will be transmitted. In practice, the route may be much more circuitous. One side route would be managers talking to other managers at the same level about this new corporate responsibility.

Work flow. Formal communication pathways are also heavily influenced by the **work flow,** the routing of work from one person or department to another. If you are a quality specialist, you might be expected to communicate your observations directly to a supervisor. A sales representative might initiate work for a credit analyst. The "rep" makes a tentative sale on a big piece of equipment. Before the customer is approved for receiving the equipment prior to paying for it in full, the credit analyst must approve the customer's credit rating.

Informal Communication Pathways

Organizations could not get their work accomplished by means of formal communication channels alone. A supplementary system of communication, called informal communication pathways, is also needed. An **informal communication pathway**

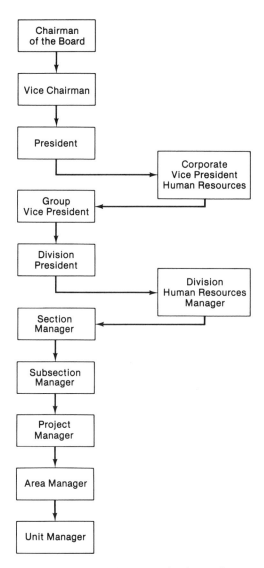

Figure 9–2 Formal communication pathway
for message from top to bottom
of a large business organization.

is an unofficial network of communications used to supplement a formal pathway
or channel. Many of these pathways arise out of necessity. For example, employees
may consult with someone outside their department to solve a technical problem.
Three key aspects of informal communication pathways are the grapevine, the
rumors it carries, and gossip.

The grapevine. The **grapevine** is the major informal communication channel in an organization. The term refers to tangled wires or branches that can distort information. Yet there are times when information transmitted along the grapevine is undistorted and accurate. For example, valid news about a pending company merger often passes along the grapevine before it is officially announced.

The grapevine is sometimes used deliberately by management to transmit information it may not want to transmit formally. One example would be to feed the grapevine with news that salary increases will be below average this year.[3] When the salary increases turn out to be average, most employees will be relieved and therefore satisfied.

A related use of the grapevine is to measure the reaction of employees to an announcement before it is transmitted through formal channels.[4] If the reaction is bad, management can sometimes modify its plans. One company wanted to test employee reaction to a productivity improvement plan to shorten lunch breaks by 10 minutes. An administrative assistant made casual mention of the plan in the cafeteria, and news about the plan spread rapidly. Reaction to the shortened lunchbreak was so negative that the company abandoned the plan.

Rumors. "Did you hear what management is up to now? They are starting a factory in Iceland. Many of us will be given the choice of being laid off or transferred to Iceland. I hear that the cost of living up there is murderous. Also, it's going to be very difficult to leave our families, friends, and neighbors behind."

Within a few days after this rumor started, about 100 concerned employees had started to look for new employment—just in case they would be asked to relocate to Iceland. As implied by this anecdote, a **rumor** is a message transmitted through the organization, although not based on any official word. Usually rumors travel along the grapevine, sometimes with the assistance of a communications hub (a person who transmits information regularly).[5] The biggest problem with rumors is that they are capable of disrupting work and lowering morale. If you are ruminating over a rumor, you are likely to divert effort away from your job. As the rumor travels along the grapevine, it will cause some people to do foolish things—like begin to look for a new job when it is not necessary.

Rumors are based on the worries, concerns, fears, anxieties and wishful dreams of people. People start rumors about topics of importance to them. The rumor about Iceland took place at a time when employees were worried about job security. Another cause of rumors is malice. One employee in a pharmaceutical firm started a rumor about impurities in a vitamin product because he had been bypassed for promotion.

Communication specialists have formulated suggestions for dealing with rumors that plague organizations both internally and externally.[6] The same principles can sometimes be used to combat rumors circulated about an individual.

- First, try to wait it out. The rumor may run its course before doing too much damage.

- If the rumor persists, make it news. If you talk about the rumor and deny it, then nobody has an exclusive. Everybody has heard about it.
- Act promptly to determine how far a rumor has spread by contacting customers, vendors, and the public.
- To cut the rumor short, communicate the information that people want. Do so promptly, clearly, accurately, and factually. At the same time, keep open formal communication channels and shorten them whenever possible to encourage more direct interaction.
- Ridicule a rumor that is absolutely untrue. Call it preposterous, stupid, crazy. People may then ridicule those who repeat it.
- As a countermeasure, feed the grapevine with actual information to get the facts through informal communication channels. If the rumor is of grave enough consequences, have members of top management meet with small groups of employees to place matters in proper persepctive.

Walter St. John suggests that preventive measures are perhaps the most effective strategy for managing rumors. He advises management to be alert to situations that promote rumors. Among them are when employees are confused about what is happening and information is unclear, incomplete or lacking; when people feel powerless to attain their desires on the job; and when there is excessive anxiety and conflict present in the workplace.[7]

Gossip. A special form of rumor is **gossip**—the idle talk or tidbits of information about people that are passed along informal communication channels. We all know that gossip can hurt reputations and wastes time. Yet gossip also serves a number of useful organizational purposes. Among them are that gossip can be a morale booster, a socializing force, and a guidebook to group norms.

Gossip can improve morale by adding spice and variety to the job. It may even make some highly repetitive jobs bearable. Robert Wieder notes that in an increasingly technological and depersonalized workplace, gossip may be an important humanizing factor. At the same time, it is a source of employee team spirit.[8]

Gossip serves as a socializing force because it is a mode of intimate relationship for many employees. People get close to each other through the vehicle of gossip. It also serves as the lifeblood of personal relationships on the job. Gossip acts as a guidebook because it informs employees of the real customs, values, and ethics of the work environment. For instance, a company might state formally that no employee can accept a gift of over $10 from a supplier. Gossip may reveal, however, that some employees are receiving expensive gifts from suppliers. Furthermore, the company makes no serious attempt to stop the practice.

NONVERBAL COMMUNICATION IN ORGANIZATIONS

Most of our discussion so far has emphasized the use of words, or verbal communication. However, a substantial amount of communication between people occurs at the nonverbal level. **Nonverbal communication (NVC)** refers to the transmission of messages through means other than words. The general purpose of NVC is to communicate the feeling behind a message. For instance, you can say "no" with a clenched fist or with a smile to communicate the firmness of your position. The terms *body language* and *silent messages* mean about the same thing as nonverbal communication.

Nonverbal communication is as broad a topic as the study of language itself. The various aspects of NVC have been classified into six categories: the environment, body placement, posture, gestures, facial expression and movements, and voice tone.[9]

The *environment* in which you send a message can influence the receiving of that message. Assume that your boss invites you out to lunch to discuss a problem with you. You will think it is a more important topic under these circumstances than if he or she met you for lunch in the company cafeteria. Other important environmental clues include room color, temperature, lighting, and furniture arrangement. A person who sits behind an uncluttered large desk, for example, appears more powerful than a person who sits behind a small, cluttered desk. This power illusion may hold even if the two people express the same message, such as "We think you have a future with us."

Body placement refers to the placement of one's body relative to someone else's body. In general, if you want to convey positive attitudes toward another person, get physically closer to that person. Putting your arm around someone is generally interpreted as a friendly act. Kenneth Blanchard observes that if an employee feels at ease with a manager's style, the employee will face the manager in a casual, relaxed manner. If the employee turns away, he or she is giving the manager the cold shoulder.[10]

Cultural differences must be kept in mind in interpreting NVC, including body placement. For example, a Frenchman is likely to stand closer to you than an Englishman if they have equally positive attitudes toward you.

Posture also communicates a message. Leaning toward another individual suggests that you are favorably disposed toward his or her messages; leaning backwards communicates the opposite message. Openness of the arms or legs serves as an indicator of liking or caring. In general, people establish closed postures (arms folded and legs crossed) when speaking to people they dislike.

Hand gestures convey specific information to others. Positive attitudes toward another person are shown by frequent hand movements. In contrast, dislike or disinterest usually produce few gestures. An important exception here is that some people wave their hands furiously while arguing. Gestures are also said to provide clues to a person's levels of dominance and submission. Research by two anthropologists indicated that the gestures of dominant people are typically directed outward toward the other person. Examples include the steady, unwavering gaze and the touching of one's partner. Submissive gestures are usually protective, such as touching oneself or shrugging one's shoulder.[11]

Facial expressions and movements, when used in combination, provide the clearest indications of messages. Lowering your head and peering over your glasses, for example, is the nonverbal equivalent of the expression, "You're putting me on." As is well known, maintaining eye contact with another person improves communication with that person. In order to maintain eye contact it is usually necessary to move your head and face. Moving your head, face, and eyes away from another individual is often interpreted as defensiveness or a lack of self-confidence.

Voice tone deals with aspects of the voice such as pitch, volume, quality, and rate which accompanies the spoken words. As with most nonverbal cues, there is a danger in overinterpreting a single voice quality. A subordinate of yours might speak to you about the status of a project in a high pitched voice not out of fear, but because of laryngitis. Anger, boredom, and joy, three emotions frequently experienced on the job, can often be interpreted from voice quality. Two communication theorists summarize these nonverbal cues in this manner:

> Anger is best perceived when the source speaks loudly, at a fast rate, in a high pitch, with irregular inflection and clipped enunciation. Boredom is indicated by moderate volume, pitch, and rate, and a monotone inflection; joy by loud volume, high pitch, fast rate, upward inflection, and regular rhythm.[12]

OVERCOMING COMMUNICATION PROBLEMS AND BARRIERS

As implied so far, communication problems in organizations are ever-present. Some interference usually takes place between ideation and action, as suggested by the "clouds" in Figure 9–1. The type of message influences the amount of interference. Routine or neutral messages are the easiest to communicate. Interference is most likely to occur when a message is complex, emotionally arousing, or clashes with a receiver's mental set.

An emotionally arousing message deals with such topics as a relationship between two people or money. A message that clashes with a receiver's mental set requires the person to change his or her typical pattern of receiving messages. The reader is invited to try this experiment. The next time you visit a restaurant, order dessert first and the entree second. The waiter or waitress will probably not receive your dessert order because it deviates from the normal sequence.

Here we will describe strategies and tactics for overcoming some of the more frequently observed communication problems in organizations, as outlined in Table 9–2. The following section deals with another major strategy for overcoming communication barriers—improving your communication skills.

Appeal to the Receiver's Needs, Motives, and Interests

A close relationship exists between communication and motivation. People tend to listen attentively to those messages that show promise of satisfying their needs, motives, or interests. The hungry person who ordinarily does not hear low tones

Table 9–2 Overcoming barriers to communication

1. Appeal to the receiver's needs, motives, and interests.
2. Reinforce words with action.
3. Use multiple channels.
4. Use verbal and nonverbal feedback.
5. Use bias-free language.
6. Avoid information overload.
7. Engage in feeling-level communication.
8. Improve the communication climate.

readily hears a whispered message, "Let's go eat." Similarly, a standard way of selling a new program to management is to emphasize how much the program will save or earn.

Reinforce Words with Action

A concrete way of demonstrating that you are honest in what you say is to back up your verbal behavior with action.[13] Stated in another way, keep your promises and you will eliminate one more barrier to communication. Reinforcing your words with action is a *proactive* process. You enhance your communication ability as your reputation develops in a positive manner. John, a vice-president in charge of mergers and acquisitions, became an effective communicator following this principle:

> Shortly after John joined the company, he made a presentation to the management group describing what he would be doing for the company. He told people that his job was to help the company find small businesses to purchase. John claimed that, by acquiring companies, new opportunities would be created for middle management. He also contended that nobody in the parent company would be replaced with a manager from an acquired company.
>
> At the end of two years many people from the company were promoted to attractive positions in several acquired companies. Furthermore, nobody was replaced by a newly acquired manager. John's reputation as a reliable person was now among the highest in the executive ranks. Whatever message John presented in speech or writing, people took seriously.

Use Multiple Channels

Repetition enhances communication, particularly when different channels are used to convey the same message. Effective communicators at many job levels follow up spoken agreements with written documentation. Since most communication is subject to at least some distortion, the chances of a message being received as intended increase when two or more channels are used. It has become standard practice in many firms for managers to use a multiple-channel approach to communicate the results of a performance appraisal. The subordinate receives a verbal explanation from his or her superior of the results of the review. He or she is also required to read the form and indicate by signature that he or she has read and understands the meaning of the review.

Use Verbal and Nonverbal Feedback

Ask for feedback to determine if your message has been received as intended. A frequent managerial practice is to conclude a meeting with a question such as, "Okay, what have we agreed upon?" Unless feedback of this nature is obtained, you will not know if your message has been received until the receiver later carries out your request. If the request is carried out improperly, or if no action is taken, you will know that the message was received poorly.

Nonverbal feedback is also important. Following are two examples of nonverbal behavior that could help you interpret whether your message is being received as intended.

- You are making a sales pitch about encyclopedias to a family. Both the husband and the wife move forward in their chairs toward you, while the two adolescent children lean back on their chairs. You probably have the parents about sold on the proposition, but need to work more with the children.
- You ask your boss when you will be eligible for a promotion and he looks out the window, cups his mouth to cover a yawn, and says, "Probably not too far away. I would say your chances aren't too bad." Keep trying. He is not yet sold on the idea of promoting you in the near future.

Receiving feedback enables you to engage in two-way communication, which is usually superior to one-way communication. One reason written messages fail to achieve their purpose is that the sender of the message cannot be sure what meanings are attached to its content. Electronic mail creates a similar barrier. Instead of interacting directly with another person in the office, a message is sent to the other person's VDT. In the process the human touch (specifically, the feeling behind the message) is often lost.[14] The antidote is to communicate in person those messages that are likely to have an emotional meaning.

Use Bias-Free Language

An important implication of semantics is that certain words are interpreted by some people as a sign of bias. When people perceive a statement to be biased, or discriminatory, an emotional barrier may be erected against the message being sent. The use of bias-free language therefore avoids one type of discrimination and helps to overcome one more communication barrier. An example of a biased statement would be for a supervisor to say, "I need a real man for this job." The bias-free expression would be, "I need a courageous person for this job."

Table 9–3 presents a list of biased words and terms, along with their bias-

Table 9–3 Biased terms and their bias-free substitutes

	Biased	*Bias-Free*
Gender-related	Girl	Woman
	Boy	Man
	Salesman, saleswoman	Sales representative
	Woman crane operator	Crane operator
	Hotel maid	Housekeeper
	Cleaning man	Custodian, cleaner
	Flag man, flag woman	Flagger
	Chairman, chairwoman	Chairperson, chair
Disabilities	Handicapped	Physically challenged
	Deaf	Hearing impaired
	Blind	Visually impaired
	Confined to a wheelchair	Uses a wheelchair
Race	Nonwhite	Black, Afro-American, Oriental, Indian
	Whitey	White, white person, Caucasian
Nationality, ethnic background	Jewish person	Jew
	"Scottish in me"	"My frugality"
	Ethnic jokes	Jokes with nationality unspecified

SOURCE: Several of the pairs of terms are from information in Judy E. Pickens, "Terms of Equality: A Guide to Bias-Free Language," *Personnel Journal*, August 1985, pp. 24–28.

free equivalent. Recognize, however, that your choice of words can never please everybody. For instance, many women prefer to be addressed as "Miss" or "Mrs." rather than "Ms."

Avoid Information Overload

A major communication barrier facing today's manager or professional is **information overload,** the state of receiving more information than one can handle. So much information comes across one's desk that it is often difficult to figure out which information should receive one's attention and which should be discarded. If all office communications were attended to, the actual work of the firm would go unattended.[15] Photocopying machines and computer printers have been a major contributor to information overload.

A flood of information reaching a person is a communication barrier because people have a tendency to stop receiving when their capacity to process information becomes taxed. Literally, their "circuits become overloaded" and they no longer respond to messages.

Steps are already being taken to deal with the problem of information (or communication) overload. It is becoming common practice for managers to be sent only summaries of general information, while critical information is sent in fuller form. You can decrease the chances of succumbing to information overload by organizing and sorting through information before plunging ahead with reading. Do you think students suffer from information overload?

Engage in Feeling-Level Communication

When a person speaks, we too often listen to the facts and ignore the feelings. If feelings are ignored, the true meaning and intent of the message is likely to be missed, thus creating a communication barrier. **Feeling-level communication** emphasizes the feelings, emotions, and attitudes that are exchanged when people communicate. Baker and Morgan recommend that whenever you are faced with emotionally charged statements, you should use the following steps to improve the communication flow:[16]

1. Identify the feelings. Try to determine if the sender's message involves primarily a feeling statement or a factual statement. Identifying the feelings helps you obtain a clear interpretation of the message.
2. Encourage the sender to express his or her feelings. Allow for a reasonable expression of feelings. Communication is incomplete when feelings are suppressed.
3. Check the correctness of your perceptions. State how you think the other person feels and ask for feedback. For instance, "I think you are upset because your budget was rejected. Am I correct?"
4. Verbalize your own feelings. Share your feelings with the sender about how he or she makes you feel. For instance, "I am concerned that you are so upset about the rejection of your first draft of your budget."

Improve the Communication Climate

An organizationwide strategy for improving interpersonal communication is to establish a positive communication climate or atmosphere. A **communication climate** is the degree to which an organization permits or promotes a free and open exchange of ideas and information among its members.[17] Since the communication climate is part of the organization culture, it develops over a long period of time. One way of promoting such a climate is for organization members to strive to share useful information. Another way is for managers to be receptive to employee suggestions for improvement.

IMPROVING YOUR COMMUNICATION SKILLS

Aside from helping you to overcome communication barriers, effective communication skills are a success factor in organizational life. Unless you own a business or receive a political appointment, it is difficult to occupy a managerial or professional position without having adequate communication skills. A person intent upon improving his or her communication effectiveness should take a course, attend a workshop, or read books and articles geared toward that purpose.[18] Here we suggest a few methods to serve as a reminder for improving your communication effectiveness in four modes: face-to-face speaking, listening, writing, and nonverbal communcation.

Face-to-Face Speaking

Most people could use improvement in public speaking, but only high-level executive positions require that the incumbent give speeches. What most people do need is improved ability to express their ideas in face-to-face encounters, such as conferences and two-way discussions. Any course in conference leadership would help you achieve this end. Implementing these experience-based suggestions should help you improve your face-to-face speaking skills.

1. Take the opportunity to speak in a meeting whenever it arises. Volunteer comments in class and committee meetings, and capitalize on any chance to be a spokesman for a group.
2. Obtain feedback by listening to tape recordings or dictating equipment renditions of your voice. Attempt to eliminate vocalized pauses and repetitious phrases (such as "Okay" or "you know") that detract from your communication effectiveness. Ask a knowledgeable friend for his or her opinion on your voice and speech.
3. Use appropriate models to help you to develop your speech. A television talk show host or commercial announcer may have the type of voice and speech behavior that fits your personality. The goal is not to imitate that person, but to use him or her as a guide to generally acceptable speech.
4. Practice interviewing and being interviewed. Take turns with a friend conducting a simulated job interview. Interview each other about a controversial current topic or each other's hobby.
5. Practice expressing the feelings behind your factual statements. For example, you might rehearse an imaginary situation in which your boss has bypassed you for a special assignment several times. A factual statement might be, "How does one get chosen for a special assignment?" A statement that combines facts with feelings is, "So far I have not been chosen for a special assignment. I'm worried that I'm doing something wrong, and I would like to discuss the situation with you."

Listening

Listening is a basic part of the communication process. Unless you receive messages as they were intended, you cannot perform your job properly or be a good companion. John W. Richter describes listening as our primary communication activity. Studies demonstrate that we spend about 80 percent of our waking hours communicating; 45 percent of that time is spent in listening.[19] Listening is a particularly important skill for managers because so much of their work involves eliciting information from others. For example, in order for a manager to resolve conflict between two subordinates, the manager must listen to each side carefully.

Another key reason for improving the listening ability of employees is that insufficient listening is extraordinarily costly. Listening mistakes lead to retyping of letters, rescheduling of appointments, and reshipping of orders. Also of note, ideas get distorted by up to 80 percent as they travel up the chain of command of a large organization.[20]

Improving your listening skills begins with an appreciation of the difference between listening and hearing. **Hearing** is the physical reception of sound, while **listening** is the mental translation of sound into meaningful communications. Oliver L. Niehouse explains this distinction:[21]

> Skill in listening takes the transmission of sound into meaningful communications one step further. It fine tunes through the senses what has been communicated, giving consideration to all of the nuances and implications based on the context within which the communications were made.

Specific suggestions for improving listening skills are summarized in Figure 9–3. As with any other suggestions for developing a new skill, considerable practice (with some supervision) is needed to bring about actual changes in behavior. One of the problems a poor listener would encounter is the difficulty of breaking old habits in order to acquire these new habits.

Writing

Every reader of this book has probably already taken one or two courses designed to improve writing skills. Nevertheless, five brief suggestions are in order to serve as a refresher.

1. *Read a book or article about effective business report writing, or letter writing, and attempt to implement the suggestions it offers.* One such set of tips is provided in the box. You are advised, however, that you may not want to follow the advice of one expert. Some people, for example, might think that the advice given by Mr. Forbes in the box leads to writing that is too choppy and "cutesy." What constitutes good writing is based to some extent on subjective opinion.

2. *Read material regularly that is written in the style and format that would be useful to you in your career.* The Wall Street Journal and Business Week are useful models for most forms of job-related writing. Managerial and staff jobs require you to be able to write brief, readily understandable memos and reports. If your goal is to become a good technical report writer, read technical reports in your field or specialty.

3. *Practice writing at every opportunity.* As a starting point, you might want to write letters to friends and relatives or memos to be placed in the file. Successful writers constantly practice writing. Stephen King, the popular mystery writer, says that writing is a matter of exercise: "If you work out with weights for 15 minutes a day over a course of ten years, you will get muscles. If you write for an hour and a half a day for ten years, you will turn into a good writer."[22]

4. *Get feedback on your writing.* Ask a co-worker to critique a rough draft of your reports and memos. Offer to reciprocate; editing other people's writing is a

These keys are a positive guideline to better listening. In fact, they're at the heart of developing better listening habits that could last a lifetime.

Ten Keys to Effective Listening	The Bad Listener	The Good Listener
1. Find areas of interest	Tunes out dry subjects	Seeks opportunities; asks, "What's in it for me?"
2. Judge content, not delivery	Tunes out if delivery is poor	Judges content, skips over delivery errors
3. Hold your fire	Tends to enter into argument	Doesn't judge until comprehension complete
4. Listen for ideas	Listens for facts	Listens for central themes
5. Be flexible	Takes intensive notes using only one system	Takes fewer notes; uses four or five different systems, depending on speaker
6. Work at listening	Shows no energy output; attention is faked	Works hard, exhibits active body state
7. Resist distractions	Is distracted easily	Fights or avoids distractions, tolerates bad habits, knows how to concentrate
8. Exercise your mind	Resists difficult expository material; seeks light, recreational material	Uses heavier material as exercise for the mind
9. Keep your mind open	Reacts to emotional words	Interprets color words; does not get hung up on them
10. Capitalize on fact *thought* is *faster* than speech	Tends to daydream with slow speakers	Challenges, anticipates, mentally summarizes, weighs the evidence, listens between the lines to tone of voice

Figure 9–3   Ten keys to effective listening.

SOURCE: John W. Richter, "Listening: An Art Essential to Success," *Success* (September 1980), p. 26.

valuable way of improving your own. Feedback from a person with more writing experience and knowledge than you is particularly valuable. For instance, comments made by an instructor about a paper would be highly valued.

5. *Learn to use a word processor.* Writing will always be tedious unless you mechanize the process. Typing in place of writing by hand is a moderate step forward; learning to use a word processor is a giant step forward. My observation is that the true payoff from word processing is in writing quality, although the gains in speed may also be impressive. Writing quality improves because it is so easy to correct mistakes and edit as you go along. You can also rearrange your paragraphs. And when it comes time to do a second draft of your paper, you simply recall the original document from the computer memory and re-edit.

HOW TO WRITE A BUSINESS LETTER

Some thoughts from Malcom Forbes, president and editor-in-chief of *Forbes magazine*

A good business letter can get you a job interview. Get you off the hook. Or get you money. It's totally asinine to blow your chances of getting whatever you want with a business letter that turns people off. Business letters that come across my desk seem to fall into three categories: stultifying if not stupid, mundane (most of them), and first-rate (rare). Here's the approach I've found that separates the winners from the losers—it starts *before* you write your letter.

KNOW WHAT YOU WANT

If you don't, write it down—in one sentence. "I want to get an interview within the next two weeks." List the major points you want to get across—it'll keep you on course. If you're *answering* a letter, check the points that need answering and keep the letter in front of you while you write. This way you won't forget anything.

PLUNGE RIGHT IN

Call the person by name and be sure to get it right. That'll get the person (thus, you) off to a good start. (Usually, you can get his or her name just by phoning the company—or from a business directory.) *Tell what your letter is about in the first paragraph.* One or two sentences. Don't keep your reader guessing.

WRITE SO THE READER WILL ENJOY IT

Write the letter from the reader's point of view. What's in it for him or her? Surprise the reader by answering questions and objections he or she might have.
Be positive. The reader will be more receptive to what you have to say. *Be nice.* I admit it's not easy when you've got a gripe. To be agreeable while disagreeing—that's an art. *Be natural—write the way you talk.* Business jargon too often is cold, stiff, unnatural. The acid test is to read your letter *out loud* when you're done. You might get a shock—but you'll know for sure if it sounds natural.
Don't be cute or flippant. The reader won't take you seriously. This doesn't mean you've got to be dull. Remember these three points: First, have a sense of humor—a nice surprise in a business letter. Second, be specific. If I tell you there's a new fuel that could save gasoline, you might not believe me. But suppose I tell you this:

> "Gasohol"—10% alcohol, 90% gasoline—works as well as straight gasoline. Since you can make alcohol from grain or corn stalks, wood or wood waste, coal—even garbage—it's worth some real follow-through.

Now you've got something to sink your teeth into.
Three, lean heavier on nouns and verbs, lighter on adjectives. Use the active voice instead of the passive. Your writing will have more guts. Which of these is stronger? Active voice: "I kicked out my money manager." Or, passive voice: "My money manager was kicked out by me."

GIVE IT THE BEST YOU'VE GOT

Make your letter look appetizing. Or you'll strike out before you even get to bat. Type it on good quality 8½″ ×11″ stationery. Keep it neat. And use paragraphing that makes it easier to read. Keep your letter short—to one page if possible. Keep your paragraphs short. For emphasis *underline* important words. And sometimes indent sentences as well as paragraphs.

Make it perfect. No typos, no misspellings, no factual errors.

Use good English. Take all the English and writing courses you can. Also get the 71-page gem by Strunk & White, *Elements of Style.* It's fun to read and it's loaded with tips on good English and good writing.

Distinguish opinions from facts. Your opinions may be the best in the world. But they're not gospel. You owe it to the reader to let him or her know which is which. The reader will appreciate it and admire you.

Edit ruthlessly. Words are like inflated money—the more you use the less each one is worth.

SUM IT UP AND GET OUT

The last paragraph should tell the reader exactly what you want him or her to do— or what *you're* going to do. Short and sweet. "May I have an appointment? Next Monday, the 16th, I'll call your secretary to see when it'll be most convenient for you."

Close with something simple like, "Sincerely." And for heaven's sake sign legibly. The biggest ego trip I know is a completely illegible signature.

SOURCE: Excerpted and adapted with permission from an International Paper Company advertisement. Copyright 1982, International Paper Company.

Word processors can also improve your motivation to write. They eliminate the problem of staring at a blank sheet of paper. Filling a small screen with words is less burdensome than trying to fill a sheet of paper. Word processing can also help overcome writer's block. If you are blocked on one section of the report, you can move to another section in which words flow more readily. Later, the more difficult parts can be inserted.[23] Remember to copy all important work on a second disk, and to command the computer to print after every two pages. Many valuable documents are lost because of computer or disk failure.

Nonverbal Communication

Nonverbal communication can also be improved. Published information related directly to improving NVC is difficult to find. Here are five suggestions to consider.

1. *Obtain feedback on your body language by asking others to comment upon the gestures and facial expressions that you use in conversations.* Have a videotape prepared of you conferring with another individual. After studying your body language, attempt to eliminate those mannerisms and gestures that you think detract from your effectiveness (such as moving your knee from side-to-side when being interviewed).

2. *Learn to relax when communicating with others.* Take a deep breath and consciously allow your body muscles to loosen. The tension-reducing techniques discussed in Chapter 5 should be helpful here. A relaxed person makes it easier for other people to relax. You are likely to elicit more useful information from other people when you are relaxed.

3. *Use facial, hand, and body gestures to supplement your speech. But do not overdo it.* A good starting point is to use hand gestures to express enthusiasm. You can increase the potency of enthusiastic comments by shaking the other person's hand, nodding approval, smiling, or patting him or her on the shoulder.

4. *Avoid using the same nonverbal gesture indiscriminately.* To illustrate, if you want to use nodding to convey approval, do not nod with approval even when you dislike what somebody else is saying. Also, do not pat everybody on the back. Nonverbal gestures used indiscriminately lose their communications effectiveness.

5. *Use role playing to practice various forms of nonverbal communication.* A good starting point would be to practice selling your ideas about an important project or concept to another person. During your interchange, supplement your spoken messages with appropriate nonverbal cues such as posture, voice intonation, gestures, and so forth. Later, obtain the other person's perception of the effectiveness of your nonverbal behavior.

Summary of Key Points

☐ Communication is the basic process by which managers and staff specialists accomplish their work, yet many communications problems exist in organizations. Communication among people is a complex process that can be divided into seven stages: ideation, encoding, transmission, receiving, decoding, understanding, and action.

☐ Communication in organizations flows in three primary directions: downward, sideways, and upward. Downward communication is used to send information from higher to lower levels; sideways communication is used to send messages to co-workers; and upward communication is used for sending messages up the organization.

☐ Formal communication pathways are determined to a large extent by the organization structure and the technological requirements of the situation. Three major manifestations of informal communication pathways in organizations are the grapevine, rumors, and gossip. False rumors can be disruptive to morale and productivity, and therefore should be dealt with quickly and openly.

☐ Nonverbal communication also plays an important part in sending and receiving messages. It includes such diverse behaviors and things as the environment in which the message is sent, body placement in relation to others, hand gestures, facial expressions and movements, and voice tone.

☐ Among the methods of overcoming communication problems in organizations are (a) appeal to the receiver's needs, motives, and interests, (b) reinforce words with action; (c) use multiple channels; (d) use verbal and nonverbal feedback; (e) use bias-free language; (f) avoid communication overload; (g) engage in feeling-level communication; and (h) improve the communication climate. You need effective communication skills in order to succeed in managerial, staff, and sales positions. Four different modes of communication require attention: face-to-face speaking, listening, writing, and nonverbal communication.

Questions and Activities _____

1. Since communication skills are so important for management, would several years of acting experience help prepare you for a managerial position?

2. How fair is it to evaluate communication skills as part of an employee's performance appraisal?

3. Give two examples of sideways communication that take place on the job.

4. Give two examples of upward communication that take place on the job.

5. Is there a grapevine in your school? If your answer is "yes," give an example of information heard over this grapevine.

6. In what ways might gossip be disruptive to the organization?

7. Give three examples of nonverbal communication used by players during an athletic contest. Do not include straightforward hand signals such as that used for "timeout."

8. Describe any differences in body language you have observed between men and women.

9. Visualize the last time you made a large purchase, such as a stereo, automobile, or life insurance policy. Describe some of the nonverbal communication used by the salesperson.

10. What objections do you have to any of the "bias-free" terms listed in Table 9–3? To what extent do you think some biased and bias-free terms change over time?

11. Identify a high-paying job for which communication skills are relatively unimportant. Explain why this is true.

A Human Relations Case

BIG BASH AT GULF STREAM

The employees of Gulf Stream Mobile Homes streamed into the posh Blue Gardenia party house. A sense of excitement filled the air as they began to circulate around the bar to get started celebrating the holiday party. Thanks to a well-designed product and a hard-hitting marketing team, Gulf Stream had enjoyed another notable year of sales and profits. Top management hoped this big party would help express their appreciation for the year of hard work turned in by Gulf Stream employees.

After about thirty minutes into the party, people had begun to cluster into small groups of two or more people. Nearby the entrance to the party area, Scott from research and development was talking to Bill, the controller. "Bill," he asked, "Are you aware of some of the great deeds research and development is trying to accomplish? We are poised to come up with some breakthroughs in the mobile home industry."

"Sounds good," replied Bill, "Gulf Stream is always looking for profitable breakthroughs."

"I'm glad you think that way," responded Scott. "All we need now is for the company to increase our budget by about twenty-five percent, and we'll be on our way. I hope we can get together next week on this topic."

At the other end of the main room, nearby the bay window, Barry from the quality-control department was talking intently to Brenda from purchasing. Gesturing with a can of beer in his right hand, Barry whispered to Brenda, "You know Brenda, I've always admired you. I've always wanted to be your friend. Now that my marriage is just about officially on the rocks, I have a little more freedom than I did in the past. I've always wondered if perhaps we could get to know each other a little better."

"Sorry to disappoint you," replied Brenda, "But my marriage is not officially on the rocks. See you later, I have to go find my husband."

Close to the entrance to the dining room, Andrea, from the purchasing department, was conversing with Stephanie, a clerk within her department. With an appreciative smile on her face, Andrea told Stephanie, "I'm glad I've got you cornered. It's about time I told you what a superperson you are. You're the glue that holds our department together. I never met anybody before who took such personal pride in keeping records straight. I hope the company is doing enough for you in return."

"It's so nice to get a warm fuzzy like that," said Stephanie. "You've made my evening."

Near these two women, Gary, from manufacturing engineering, was conversing with Betty Lou, one of the technicians reporting to him. "Betty Lou, things have been so hectic back at the shop, I haven't had the time to talk to you in a week. But how are things with your mother? I heard she had a brain tumor operation last month."

"She died two weeks ago. This is my first night out since then, and I prefer not to talk about the situation. You'll have to excuse me now."

As the crowd sat down to dinner, Irene, an accounting supervisor, said to Ralph, her husband and guest, "Well look at old Mr. Schaefer. Who would have thought he would ever be smiling and laughing. I've never seen the president act like this before. I do believe that he's actually had a few too many to drink. I bet the office will be buzzing Monday morning."

At 2 A.M., as the last straggler left the party, Quincy, the head of human resources, said to himself: "What a bash. I hope it served some useful purpose."

1. What do you see as some of the advantages of this office party from the standpoint of organizational communications?
2. What do you see as some of the disadvantages of this office party from the standpoint of organizational communications?
3. How does this case relate to the topic of informal communication channels in organizations?

A Human Relations Incident

MEMO WARFARE

OFFICE MEMO

To: Office staff of Pleasure Time Travel Agency
From: Jerry Prince, Owner and President
Subject: Budget overrun on photocopying

It has been brought to my attention that we are now 24 percent over budget on photocopying expenses, with a full one-third of the year remaining. Somehow this abuse of photocopy privileges must stop. This is certainly no way to run a travel agency. I see three alternatives facing us. Number one, we can close down the agency for the year, thus avoiding any more copying expenses (an alternative *most* of you would not desire). Number two, we can stop making photocopies for the rest of the year. Number three, we can all develop a responsible and mature approach to budget management by making more prudent use of the photocopier.

OFFICE MEMO

To: Jerry Prince
From: Sheila LaVal
Re: Your memo about photocopying

I read your recent memo with dismay, since it is my department that makes extensive use of the photocopying machine. We use copies mostly for very important purposes like getting trip information to clients in a hurry. Are we in the business of taking care of the travel needs of clients or in the business of pinching pennies on photocopy costs?

OFFICE MEMO

To: Sheila LaVal
From: Jerry Prince, President
Subject: Your response to my memo about photocopying

It is obvious to me Sheila that you are resisting the philosophy of budgeting. In today's business world, both the IBMs and the Pleasure Time Travel Agencies must learn to respect the limits imposed by budgets. Perhaps it is time you and I had a serious discussion about this matter. Please make an appointment to see me at your earliest convenience.

1. What communication problems are illustrated by this incident?
2. Rewrite Jerry Prince's first memo in such a way that it will be less likely to make Sheila LaVal defensive.
3. Rewrite Sheila LaVal's memo in such a way that it will be less likely to make Jerry Prince counter-defensive.

A Human Relations Exercise

OVERCOMING MEMO WARFARE

Use the Memo Warfare incident as background information for this role-play. One person plays Sheila LaVal, who takes the initiative to make an appointment with Jerry Prince. The other person plays Jerry Prince, who agrees to make the appointment at his earliest convenience. Jerry Prince is still angry, but Sheila LaVal wants to overcome the communication barriers erected by the exchange of memos. Run the scenario for about 10 minutes.

Notes

1. Allan D. Frank, "Trends in Communication: Who Talks to Whom?" *Personnel*, December 1985, p. 42.
2. Ibid., p. 44.
3. Walter St. John, "In-House Communication Guidelines," *Personnel Journal*, November 1981, p. 877.
4. Ibid.
5. Stephen P. Robbins, *Organizational Behavior: Concepts, Controversies, and Applications*, 2nd ed. (Englewood Cliffs, NJ: Prentice Hall, 1983), pp. 274–275.
6. Donald B. Simmons, "The Nature of the Organizational Grapevine," *Supervisory Management*, November 1985, p. 42.
7. St. John, "In-House Communication Guidelines," p. 877.
8. Robert S. Wieder, "Psst! Here's the Latest on Office Gossip," *Success!* January 1984, pp. 22–25.
9. Walter D. St. John, "You Are What You Communicate," *Personnel Journal*, October 1985, pp. 40–43; John Baird, Jr., and Gretchen Wieting, "Nonverbal Communication Can Be a Motivational Tool," *Personnel Journal*, September 1979, pp. 607–610.
10. Kenneth Blanchard, "Translating Body Talk," *Success!* April 1986, p. 10.
11. Salvatore Didato, "Our Body Movements Reveal Whether We're Dominant or Submissive," Gannett News Service Article, December 20, 1983.
12. Baird and Wieting, "Nonverbal Communication," p. 610.
13. James L. Gibson, John M. Ivancevich, and James H. Donnelly, Jr., *Organizations: Behavior, Structure, Processes*, 4th ed. (Plano, TX: Business Publications, 1982), p. 405.
14. Daniel Goleman, "The Electronic Rorschach," *Psychology Today*, February 1983, p. 42.
15. Charles A. O'Reilly III, "Individuals and Information Overload in Organizations: Is More Necessarily Better?" *Academy of Management Journal*, December 1980, pp. 684–696.
16. H. Kent Baker and Philip Morgan, "Building a Professional Image: Using 'Feeling-Level' Communication," *Supervisory Management*," January 1986, pp. 21–25.
17. Cowin P. King, "Crummy Communication Climate (and How to Create It)," *Management Solutions*, July 1986, p. 30.
18. See the Suggested Reading section of this chapter. The business or communication skills section of most libraries and bookstores have ample information on this topic.
19. John W. Richter, "Listening: An Art Essential to Success," *Success!* September 1980, p. 26.
20. Ibid.
21. Oliver L. Niehouse, "Listening: The Other Half of Effective Communications," *Management Solutions*, August 1986, p. 27.
22. "The Novelist Sounds Off," *Time*, October 6, 1986, p. 80.
23. Robert Sekuler, "From Quill to Computer," *Psychology Today*, February 1985, p. 38.

Suggested Reading

AULT, ROBERT E. "Draw on New Lines of Communication." *Personnel Journal*, September 1986, pp. 72–77.

BASTA, NICHOLAS. "Corporate Communications." *Business Week's Guide to Careers*, March–April 1985, p. 49.

CORBETT, WILLIAM J. "The Communication Tools Inherent in Corporate Culture." *Personnel Journal*, April 1986, pp. 71–74.

DRAKE, BRUCE H., and MOBERG, DENNIS J. "Communicating Influence Attempts in Dyads: Linguistic Sedatives and Palliatives." *Academy of Management Review*, July 1986, pp. 567–584.

ELSEA, JANET G. "Strategies for Effective Presentations." *Personnel Journal*, September 1985, pp. 31–34.

PENLEY, LARRY E., and HAWKINS, BRIAN. "Studying Interpersonal Communication in Organizations: A Leadership Application." *Academy of Management Journal*, June 1985, pp. 309–326.

REPP, WILLIAM. *Complete Handbook of Business English*. Englewood Cliffs, NJ: Prentice Hall, 1983.

SMITH, FRANK EDMUND. "Does Your Writing Send the Wrong Signals?" *Personnel Journal*, December 1985, pp. 28–30.

SPROULL, LEE S. "Using Electronic Mail for Data Collection in Organizational Research." *Academy of Management Journal*, March 1986, pp. 159–169.

SWEETNAM, SHERRY. "How to Organize Your Thoughts for Better Communication." *Personnel*, March 1986, pp. 38–40.

Power
and Politics

LEARNING OBJECTIVES
After reading and studying this chapter and doing the exercises, you should be able to

1. Differentiate between power and politics.
2. Pinpoint several reasons for the prevalence of organizational politics.
3. Identify the major sources and types of power in organizations.
4. Describe a number of political tactics used to acquire power directly.
5. Identify devious and unethical political tactics.
6. Understand how to control excessive amounts of political behavior.

THE MEANING OF POLITICS AND POWER

Being competent in your job is still the most effective method of achieving career success. After skill comes hard work and luck as important success factors. A fourth ingredient is also important for success—political awareness and skill. Few people can achieve success for themselves or their group without having some awareness of the political forces around them and how to use them to advantage. It may be necessary for the career-minded person to take the offensive in using ethical political tactics. It may also be necessary to defend yourself against the maneuvers of people trying to discredit you or weaken your position.

What Is Organizational Politics?

As used here, **organizational politics** refers to gaining advantage through any means other than merit or luck. Politics are played to reach such diverse ends as power, getting promoted, receiving a good performance appraisal, obtaining a bigger budget, or receiving a favorable transfer. Organizational politics is also referred to as OP, office politics, job politics, or politically oriented behavior.

Our definition of OP is nonevaluative. Many other writers on the topic regard organizational politics as emphasizing self-interest at the expense of others. For instance: "Organizational politics consist of intentional acts of influence undertaken by individuals or groups to enhance or protect their self-interest when conflicting courses of action are possible."[1] We nevertheless draw a clear distinction between ethical and unethical political behavior.

The career advancement tactics described in Chapter 17 can also be considered part of organizational politics. In this chapter we concentrate upon political behavior geared toward gaining other types of advantage.

What Is Power?

Power and politics are closely interrelated. In general, **power** refers to the ability to control anything of value, while **politics** refers to methods of acquiring power.[2] The primary reason for behaving politically is to acquire power. More specifically, power has been defined as "The ability to mobilize resources, energy, and information on behalf of a preferred goal or strategy."[3] The concept of power is readily understood by anybody who has worked in a large organization or dreamed of becoming an influential person.

FACTORS CONTRIBUTING TO ORGANIZATIONAL POLITICS

Organizational politics is all around us. People jockey for position and try a variety of subtle maneuvers to impress the boss in most places. To understand OP, it is important to understand why such actions are omnipresent. These reasons include, but extend beyond, the use of politics to acquire power. The reasons underlying organizational politics are summarized in Table 10–1.

Table 10–1 Factors contributing to organizational politics

1. Pyramid-shaped organizations
2. Competitiveness within the firm
3. Subjective standards of performance
4. Environmental uncertainty
5. Need for acceptance
6. A desire to avoid work
7. Machiavellian tendencies of people

Pyramid-Shaped Organizations

The very shape of large organizations is the most fundamental reason organizational members are motivated toward political action. Only so much power is available to distribute among the many people who would like more of it. As you move down the organization chart, each successive layer has less power than the layer above. At the very bottom of the organization, people have virtually no power. Furthermore, organizations have been described as political structures that operate by distributing authority and setting the stage for the exercise of power.[4]

Competitiveness within the Firm

A pyramid-shaped organization creates competition among employees seeking advancement. Other factors that breed competitiveness also foster politicking. For instance, when a firm hires a large number of ambitious people, competitiveness increases. When a firm is being trimmed down in size, employees compete for the remaining positions. Whatever reason people feel compelled to compete with one another, they often resort to office politics to improve their competitive edge.

Subjective Standards of Performance

People often resort to job politics because they do not believe that the organization has an objective (fair) way of judging their suitability for promotion. Similarly, when management has no objective way of differentiating effective from less effective people, they will resort to favoritism. The adage, "It's not what you know but who you know," does apply to organizations that lack clear-cut standards of performance.

Environmental Uncertainty

Environmental uncertainty contributes to OP in a way similar to subjective performance standards. When people, or the organizational subunits they represent, operate in an unstable and unpredictable environment, they tend to behave politically.[5] The reason could be that OP is used to create a favorable impression because it is difficult to specify what a person really should be accomplishing in an uncertain situation. Since top management may not understand themselves how you should respond to the unstable environment, you resort to political approaches to win favorable evaluation from them.

An analysis of electronic firms in Southern California revealed a pattern of high political activity on the part of those business functions dealing with the most uncertainty. The electronics business is characterized by custom orders, relatively short-term contracts, "pirating" technical employees from one another, and subcontracting work when internal costs get too high. Marketing and sales divisions are the most directly involved in dealing with customer uncertainties. It was found that these two groups engaged heavily in political behavior. In contrast, the accounting and production function of these firms engaged in much less political activity. The reason offered by the researchers is that these functions engage in more clearly defined (less uncertain) tasks.[6]

Emotional Insecurity

Some people resort to political maneuvers to ingratiate themselves with superiors because they lack confidence in their talents and skills. As an extreme example, a Nobel prize winning scientist does not have to curry favor with the administration of his or her university. The distinguished scientist's work speaks for itself. Winning a Nobel prize has given this scientist additional self-confidence; he or she is therefore emotionally secure. A person's choice of political strategy may indicate that he or she is emotionally insecure. For instance, an insecure person might laugh loudly at every humorous comment made by his or her boss.

Need for Acceptance

Many employees who practice politics in the office are not particularly intent upon climbing the organizational ladder. They simply want to be accepted and liked by others. To accomplish this end they do favors for others and carry out other relatively harmless ploys. Tom, a first-level supervisor, earned the nickname "Candy Man" based on one of his strategies for gaining acceptance from others.

Tom kept an amply supplied candy dish on his desk, which helped maintain a steady stream of visitors to his desk.

A Desire to Avoid Work

Some employees use various forms of office politics to avoid hard work. By performing favors for the boss, or showing the boss approval in a variety of ways, the poorly motivated employee escapes undesirable assignments. For example, a warehouse employee told a researcher he was allowed to take naps in the storeroom because he ran personal errands for the boss.

Machiavellian Tendencies of People

A fundamental reason people engage in political behavior is because they possess **Machiavellian tendencies,** a desire to manipulate other people. It also relates to an ability to shape the attitudes and desires of others so that it turns out for personal advantage. Research conducted by Gerald Biberman provided the evidence for the relationship between Machiavellianism and political behavior. He found a high correlation between scores on a test of Machiavellian attitudes and DuBrin's organizational politics scale.[7] An abbreviated version of this scale is presented in Figure 10–1.

Figure 10–1   How political are you?

> To gain some tentative insight into the extent of your tendency toward engaging in political behavior, answer the following questionnaire.
>
> THE ORGANIZATIONAL POLITICS QUESTIONNAIRE
>
> **Directions:** Answer each question "mostly agree" or "mostly disagree," even if it is difficult for you to decide which alternative best describes your opinion.
>
> | | Mostly Agree | Mostly Disagree |
> |---|---|---|
> | 1. Only a fool would correct a boss's mistakes. | ___ | ___ |
> | 2. If you have certain confidential information, release it to your advantage. | ___ | ___ |
> | 3. I would be careful not to hire a subordinate with more formal education than myself. | ___ | ___ |
> | 4. If you do somebody a favor, remember to cash in on it. | ___ | ___ |
> | 5. Given the opportunity, I would cultivate friendships with power people. | ___ | ___ |

Figure 10–1 (*continued*)

	Mostly Agree	*Mostly Disagree*
6. I like the idea of saying nice things about a rival in order to get that person transferred from my department.	_____	_____
7. Why not take credit for someone else's work? They would do the same to you.	_____	_____
8. Given the chance, I would offer to help my boss build some shelves for his or her den.	_____	_____
9. I laugh heartily at my boss's jokes, even when they are not funny.	_____	_____
10. I would be sure to attend a company picnic even if I had the chance to do something I enjoyed more that day.	_____	_____
11. If I knew an executive in my company was stealing money, I would use that against him or her in asking for favors.	_____	_____
12. I would first find out my boss's political preferences before discussing politics with him or her.	_____	_____
13. I think using memos to zap somebody for his or her mistakes is a good idea (especially when you want to show that person up).	_____	_____
14. If I wanted something done by a co-worker, I would be willing to say "If you don't get this done, our boss might be very unhappy."	_____	_____
15. I would invite my boss to a party at my house, even if I didn't like him or her.	_____	_____
16. When I'm in a position to, I would have lunch with the "right people" at least twice a week.	_____	_____
17. Richard M. Nixon's bugging the Democratic Headquarters would have been a clever idea if he wasn't caught.	_____	_____
18. Power for its own sake is one of life's most precious commodities.	_____	_____
19. Having a high school named after you would be an incredible thrill.	_____	_____
20. Reading about job politics is as much fun as reading an adventure story.	_____	_____

Interpretation of Scores. Each statement you check "mostly agree" is worth one point toward your political orientation score. If you score 16 or over, it suggests that you have a strong inclination toward playing politics. A high score of this nature would also suggest that you have strong needs for power. Scores of 5 or less would suggest that you are not inclined toward political maneuvering and that you are not strongly power driven.

SOURCES AND TYPES OF POWER

Organizational power can be derived from many sources. How you obtain power depends to a large extent upon the type of power you are seeking. Therefore, to understand the mechanics of acquiring power, you also have to understand what types of power exist and the sources and origins of these types of power. Here we examine four sources, or types, of power:

1. Power granted by the organization
2. Power stemming from the characteristics of the person
3. The power of subordinates
4. The power derived from capitalizing upon opportunity

Power Granted by the Organization

A standard method of classifying power is based upon whether the power stems from the organization or the individual. Three of these bases of power stem from the organization, and three from the individual, as described by French and Raven.[8]

Legitimate power. Power granted by the organization is referred to as **legitimate power.** People at higher levels in the organization have more power than people below them. However, the culture of an organization helps establish the limits to anybody's power. A company president who suggests donating most of the company profits to a political party may find his or her decision overruled by the board of directors. A supervisor who tells employees what hairstyle to wear may find such orders ignored. Employees disregard orders they perceive as being illegitimate.

Reward power. The authority to give employees rewards for compliance is referred to as **reward power.** If a sales manager can directly reward sales representatives with cash bonuses for good performance, this manager will exert considerable power. Leaders can use reward power effectively only when they have meaningful rewards at their disposal.

Coercive power. The power to punish for noncompliance is referred to as **coercive power.** It is based upon fear. As noted in Chapter 2, punishment and fear achieve mixed results as motivators. The leader who relies heavily upon coercive power runs the constant threat of being ousted from power.

Power Stemming from Characteristics of the Person

The fourth and fifth sources of power described by French and Raven stem from characteristics or behaviors of the power actor: expert power and referent power.[9] Both are classified as **personal power,** because they are derived from the person rather than the organization.

Expert power. Highly knowledgeable people have power even when their organizational rank is low or they are self-employed. They possess **expert power,** the power stemming from specialized knowledge. A representative example would be a product development specialist who had good intuition about what makes a winning product. The specialist might be highly valued by the firm, although his or her organizational rank is relatively low.

Referent power. Power stemming from one's ability to influence others because of personal characteristics is labeled **referent power.** Also referred to as **charisma** or **transformational leadership,** this type of power is helpful in influencing people over whom the leader has no direct control. Entrepreneurial leaders typically have high referent power. A leader's charisma, however, is based upon a subjective reaction to his or her personal characteristics. Even highly popular leaders are not appreciated by all organization members.

Subordinate Power

Subordinate power is any type of power organization members can exert upward in the organization. When subordinates perceive orders as nonlegitimate, they will rebel. Legitimate orders lie within a range of behaviors that the employee regards as acceptable—they fall within the zone of indifference. The **zone of indifference** encompasses those behaviors toward which the employee feels indifferent (does not mind). If the manager pushes beyond that zone, the leader loses power. For example, an administrative assistant will sometimes refuse to run personal errands for the boss, and a computer specialist may refuse to debug nonworking software on New Year's Eve. Do you think the two people just cited are being fair to their employers?

Expert power is an important source of subordinate power. A relatively low-ranking employee with unusual talent can sometimes force his or her demands upon management, as happened in one firm.

> A research laboratory tolerated the frequent rule-breaking of an eccentric scientist for many years. Although his attendance was shoddy and he was late with many reports, he had a remarkable talent for writing grant proposals that led to research contracts. A special demand he placed on management was the half-time use of a personal assistant, a privilege no other scientist was granted.

Power Stemming from Capitalizing upon Opportunity

Power can be derived from being at the right place at the right time and taking the appropriate action.[10] You also have to have the right resources to capitalize upon the opportunity. Capitalizing upon opportunity has four components, as shown in Figure 10–2.

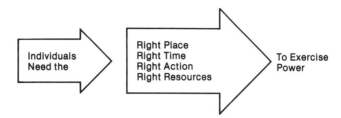

Figure 10–2 Power based on capitalizing upon opportunity.

Being in the right place. It pays to be "where the action is" if you want to gain power through capitalizing upon opportunity. For example, if you work in a multidivision company, the best opportunities lie in the growth division of a company. One woman who went to work for a public utility did not receive a promotion during her first three years and therefore had acquired very little power. Yet her former roommate who entered the utility at the same time had received two promotions. The former woman had been assigned to the steam-generating division (a declining business), while the latter was assigned to the nuclear-plant division (a growth area).

The right time. The time has to be right to work on an organizatonal problem that will bring you power. For example, introducing a new program in government during a period of budget tightening might bring you into disfavor. During more prosperous times, introducing that same program might lead you to a department-head position, and therefore increase your power base.

The right action. If you take the right action at a critical time, you are likely to acquire more power. During a recession in the auto business, a dealer launched a program of offering customers a loan rate of 5.9 percent. The typical bank interest loan for cars at the time was 17 percent. The dealer sold a record-breaking 600 cars in one week. Within one year the auto company he represented authorized him to acquire two more dealerships. Note the circular reasoning in this kind of power acquisition. Because the auto dealer had the power to take the right action of decreasing interest rates, he acquired more power. Or, "People have power if they get things done; if they have the power they can get things done."[11]

The right resources. If you are in control of people, money, material, or ideas, by definition you have power. Control over these resources is related to your rank: Higher-ranking officials have more say in the commitment of resources. Also, a person's location in the firm can facilitate his or her controlling the vital resource of information. A low-ranking organization member who has "the ear of the president" achieves some power and status because of this fact. Some go out of their way to be nice to the person who can get their demands brought to the attention of top management.

In the next three sections of this chapter we describe a variety of political tactics and strategies designed to acquire the sources and types of power described above. Most of these tactics and strategies are familiar to experienced managers, as indicated in Figure 10–3.

Figure 10–3 How much do managers know about organizational politics?

To answer this question, a team of five researchers interviewed 87 managerial personnel (30 chief executive officers, 28 high-level staff managers, 29 supervisors). One question asked the managers was "Organizational politics takes many forms. What are the tactics of organizational politics of which you are aware?"

The managers supplied their own definitions of *organizational politics* (another term for job or office politics). They were told not to restrict their observations to their present places of employment. The eight categories of political tactics most frequently mentioned are presented next, along with the percent of respondents who mentioned the tactic.

- Attacking or blaming others—such as making the rival look bad in the eyes of influential organization members. As the saying goes, "When something goes wrong the first thing to be fixed is the blame." (54.0%)
- Use of information (such as withholding or distorting information or using it to overwhelm another person). (54.0%)
- Image building/impression management—includes general appearance, dress and hair style, drawing attention to successes, and creating the appearance of being on the inside of important activities. (52.9%)
- Support building for ideas—including getting others to understand one's ideas before a decision is made and setting up the decision before the meeting is called. (36.8%)
- Praising others, ingratiation—supervisors used expressions such as "buttering up the boss," "apple polishing," and other more colorful, but less printable remarks. (25.3%)
- Power coalitions, strong allies—getting key people on your side. (25.3%)
- Association with influential people—both business and social situations are considered important. (24.1%)
- Creating obligations/reciprocity—the norm of reciprocity is invoked when assistance is required; "You scratch my back and I'll scratch yours." (12.6%)

SOURCE: Excerpted from Robert W. Allen and others, "Organizational Politics: Tactics and Characteristics of Its Actors," *California Management Review*, Fall 1979, 77–83.

STRATEGIES AIMED DIRECTLY AT GAINING POWER

All political tactics are aimed at acquiring and maintaining power. In this section we describe eight tactics aimed directly at power acquisition (see Table 10–2). In the next two sections we describe indirect power-acquisition tactics, those

Table 10–2 Strategies and tactics aimed directly at gaining power

1. Identify powerful people.
2. Maintain alliances with powerful people.
3. Control vital information.
4. Keep informed.
5. Plant an ally.
6. Acquire seniority.
7. Play "camel's head in the tent."
8. Make a quick showing.

designed to develop good relationships with superiors and co-workers. Power accrues as a by-product of developing these relationships.

Identify powerful people. A key strategy for gaining power is to identify the people behind major decisions. [12] Usually these are people who have considerable position power, such as a president or vice-president. It is also necessary to identify those individuals who influence the key decision makers. These less obvious powerful people might include employees who are major stockholders in the firm, close associates of executives, influential staff assistants, and executive secretaries. One office politician put it this way: "I finally started getting support for my programs after I figured out who the president went to for advice—a forty-year veteran with the company who held an inconspicuous job in the purchasing department."

Maintain alliances with powerful people. After you have identified the powerful people, alliances with them must be established and maintained. An executive newsletter observes, "Cultivating friendly, cooperative relationships with those who have organizational clout can make your cause that much easier to advance." [13] One method of doing this is to extend yourself socially, such as throwing a party and inviting powerful people and their spouses or guests. A frequent practice is for the power-seeker periodically to invite power-holders to lunch or breakfast.

Control of vital information. Power accrues to those who control vital information, as indicated in the discussion of expert power. Many former government or military officials have found convenient power niches for themselves in industry after leaving the public payroll. Frequently such individuals are hired as the Washington representative of a firm that does business with the government. The vital information they control is knowledge of whom to contact to shorten some of the complicated procedures in getting government contracts approved. The esoteric knowledge of how to write a proposal to suit the government's requirements gives that individual power.

Controlling vital information becomes a devious and unethical strategy when the person controls information that is stolen or should be shared with others.

An example would be when an executive switches firms and takes information about customers to a competitive firm.

Keep informed. In addition to controlling vital information, it is politically important to be kept informed. Management consultant Eugene Schmuckler aptly describes the situation in these terms:[14]

> We are all aware of the significance of having one's name removed from the distribution list of internal memos. Although the information is not always accurate we recognize the value of being able to tap into the corporate grapevine. Successful managers attempt to develop a "pipeline" or information source so that they can stay abreast and, in some cases, ahead, of what is happening in their organization. For the same reason, it is a wise individual who befriends the president's secretary. No other source offers the potential of information as does the executive secretary.

Plant an ally. If you want your cause championed, it helps to have an insider talk about the advantages of your cause. Your ally thus functions as a third party endorsement of the idea or program that you want sponsored. A human resource manager believed strongly that the company should embark upon an employee-assistance program. To help create a favorable climate for her proposal, she asked two of her friends to begin discussing the merits of an EAP while having casual discussions with their managers. By the time she made her formal proposal to management, key people in the organization were already talking about the merits of such a program. The program was approved with little resistance from top management. Planting an ally *may* have helped.

Acquire seniority. Longevity in an organization still garners some respect and privilege. Although seniority alone will not prevent you from being ousted from the organization or guarantee you more power, it helps. The compulsive job hopper is forever working against the implicit threat of the last in, first out personnel policy, even at the managerial level:

> One manager in the food business accepted a position with a Boston company as the manager of new product development. Three months after he arrived he was informed that the company had no funds left to invest in new product development. He was given one month's severance pay and faced with the embarrassment and awkwardness of finding a comparable level position. Eight months later, he found a job as a food-processing engineer at a substantially lower level of pay than his previous two positions.

Play "camel's head in the tent." A gradual approach is sometimes the most effective means of acquiring power. Just as the camel works his way into the tent inch by inch, you might acquire power in a step-by-step manner until you emerge victorious. An administrative assistant in a furniture company took care, one by one, of all the details relating to a line of office furniture. Finally her boss said, "Rosalin, why don't we make you the product manager for office furniture? At this stage you know more about the product line than I do." Rosalin achieved just the position she wanted. If she had suggested at the outset that she be made product manager, her proposal might have been refused.

Make a quick showing. A display of dramatic results can be useful in gaining acceptance for your efforts or those of your group.[15] Once you have impressed management with your ability to work on that first problem, you can look forward to working on the problems that will bring you greater power. An information systems specialist provides this example of "make a quick showing":

> Our group agreed to set up a database of credit ratings on customers. This was a bread-and-butter item but we were willing to take on any assignment to show our skills. The database was a winner. We then suggested a program for tutoring executives on the use of personal computers. Based on our past success, our ideas were accepted. Our acceptance in the firm has gone way up now that we are working closely with key executives throughout the firm.

BUILDING RELATIONSHIPS WITH SUPERIORS

In this section we describe tactics and strategies aimed at cultivating good relationships with one's immediate superior and other managers (see Table 10–3). The political purpose of building good relationships with superiors is to gain power through such means as being recommended for promotion and rewarding assignments. Good relationships can also be established with one's superiors simply for the nonpolitical purpose of trying to get one's job accomplished. A given tactic is political only if it is intended to be political. If you dress stylishly because you want to be stylish, you are not behaving politically. If you dress stylishly just to please your superiors, you are acting politically.

Help your boss succeed. The primary reasons you are hired is to help your superior achieve the results necessary to succeed.[16] Avoid an adversarial

Table 10–3 Techniques and strategies for building relationships with superiors

1. Help your boss succeed.
2. Become a crucial subordinate.
3. Display loyalty.
4. Volunteer for assignments.
5. Manage your impression.
6. Laugh at your boss's jokes.
7. Use discretion in socializing with your boss.
8. Offer assistance to a poorly performing superior.

relationship with your boss. Also figure out both obvious and subtle ways of ensuring the boss's chances for success. One subtle way of increasing your boss's chances for success is to help that person out when he or she is under attack. One example would be to supply data to support your boss's position on a controversial issue.

Become a crucial subordinate. A variation of "help your boss succeed," this strategy means that you help your superior with a task upon which his or her performance depends. You are crucial because you help your superior with crucial assignments. Unless a superior is fearful of capable subordinates this tactic helps you gain favor in the organization. Your task in becoming a crucial subordinate is to identify crucial tasks facing your superior and then to demonstrate your interest in helping.

> Cal worked as a registrar's assistant in a private university. His superior, the associate registrar, had overall responsibility for the registration system at the university. Cal soon learned that the registration system in current use was perceived as disastrous by students and faculty. Students were frequently billed for courses they had never taken. Many class sections were overcrowded, while others meeting at equally desirable times were so small that they were eligible for cancellation.
>
> Assuming that his boss must be under pressure to improve the registration system, Cal volunteered to head up a task force to develop a new system. His boss happily gave Cal the opportunity to help him out with this vexing problem. Cal's task force produced a system that was a vast improvement over the current one. When his boss became the registrar in an organizational shuffle, Cal was selected over two other candidates for promotion to associate registrar. His boss had given Cal outstanding praise for the system he developed and helped implement.

Display loyalty. A loyal worker is a valued worker because organizations prosper more with loyal than disloyal employees. Blind loyalty, in which you believe your organization cannot make a mistake, is not called for. You may recall that such loyalty contributes to groupthink. An obvious form of loyalty to the organization is longevity. A study by an executive recruiting firm supports the value of this type of loyalty. The average chief executive of 1,300 of the nation's largest firms has spent 22.5 years with the firm. In some companies, 90 percent of the senior staff is promoted from within.[17]

Loyalty can also take other forms, such as defending your company when it is under attack, avoiding making negative statements about superiors, and using company products and services. For instance, if you work for an automobile manufacturer, owning a car made by a competitor is strongly frowned upon by management.

Volunteer for assignments. An easily implemented method of winning the approval of your superiors is to become a "handraiser." By volunteering to take on assignments that do not fit neatly into your job description, you display the kind of initiative valued by employers. Among the many possible activities to volunteer for are fund-raising campaigns assigned to your company, membership in a committee, and working overtime when most people prefer not to work overtime (for example, on a Saturday in July).

Manage your impression. As noted in Figure 10–3, this strategy includes behaviors directed at enhancing your image by drawing attention to yourself. Often the attention of others is directed toward superficial aspects of the self, such as clothing and appearance. Other variations of this strategy include telling people about your successes or implying that you are on the inside of activities. Displaying good manners has received renewed attention as a key part of impression management. Here is a sampling of the many suggestions for proper business etiquette offered by Letitia Baldrige:[18]

- When you meet strangers at a business function, include the name of your firm with your name.
- In making introductions, remember that a young person should be introduced to an older one, that the person of no rank should be introduced to a person of high rank.
- Do not argue over who is going to pay when you are in a restaurant. Decide beforehand on who is going to be the host.
- As a host at the restaurant, remember to have the server take your guest's order before your own.
- Wait until your boss or other superior invites you to lunch. Do not be pushy and invite them first.
- Remember, the secret of good manners is to make other people feel comfortable.

Laugh at your boss's jokes. When you indicate by your laughter than you appreciate your boss's sense of humor, it helps establish rapport between the two of you. An indicator of good two-way communication between people is when the two parties comprehend each other's subtle points. Most humor in the workplace deals with subtle meanings about work-related topics. To implement the tactic of laughing at your boss's jokes, you therefore do not have to worry excessively about having heard the joke before.

Use discretion in socializing with your boss. A constant dilemma facing employees is how much and what type of socializing with the boss is appropriate. Advocates of socializing contend that off-the-job friendships with the boss lead to harmonious work relationships. Opponents say that socializing leads to **role confusion,** being uncertain what role you are occupying. One guideline is to have cordial social relationships with the boss of the same kind shared by most employees, such as group luncheons. Another guideline is to strive to be regarded as an employee rather than a member of the boss's family. By so doing, you will not fall into the trap of getting emotionally involved in the boss's personal problems.[19]

Deal compassionately with a poorly performing boss. At some points in their careers, most people work for a poorly performing immediate superior. Political advantage can be gained from such a situation by acting meritoriously. Instead of finding subtle ways of exposing the poorly performing boss, it is preferable to offer him or her professional and emotional support. Although the boss may not admit to others that you bailed him or her out, your contribution will probably be recognized. If your boss's poor performance persists to the point that it is damaging your performance, a job switch may be in order.

The recommended strategy for getting away from your boss is to market yourself to key managers in the organization.[20] Tactics here include making other managers aware of your accomplishments through volunteering for committee work, or getting your name in the organization newsletter.

BUILDING RELATIONSHIPS WITH CO-WORKERS AND LOWER-RANKING EMPLOYEES

Another general strategy for increasing your power base is to form alliances with co-workers and employees of lesser rank. You need the support of these people to get your work accomplished. Also, when you are being considered for promotion, co-workers and lower-ranking employees may be asked their opinion of you. Here we describe eight representative techniques for cultivating employees at or below your level (see Table 10–4).

Develop allies. A general strategy for cultivating co-workers and lower-ranking employees is to create allies rather than enemies. Your allies can support you when you need help. It has been noted, for example, that "the elevator starter in the lobby may alert you to the arrival of a VIP whom you might have missed." Equally important, a network of allies establishes you as a leader, which increases your chances for promotion.[21] Most of the remaining tactics in this section are specific ways of developing allies.

Table 10–4 Techniques and strategies for developing relationships with co-workers and lower-ranking employees

1. Develop allies.
2. Be a team player.
3. Express an interest in their work.
4. Make effective use of praise.
5. Exchange favors.
6. Ask advice.
7. Avoid being abrasive.
8. Follow group standards of conduct.

Be a team player. As described in Chapter 7, being a team player helps you work effectively as a group member. The same tactic is essential for developing allies among team workers. The group member who is not perceived as a team player will be hard pressed to gain the cooperation of co-workers and employees at lower levels.

Express an interest in their work. A simple yet valuable technique for cultivating lateral and downward relationships is to express genuine interest in the work of others. A basic way to accomplish this end is to ask other employees such questions as:

> How is your work going?
> How does the firm use the output from your department?
> How did you master the software you use on the job?

Make effective use of praise. Knowing how and when to praise people is a valuable skill when trying to build your reputation in an organization. Those people whom you praise sincerely will find your very presence reinforcing, thus giving you a small degree of reward power.

Two suggestions about the dispensing of praise should be kept in mind. First, it is generally more effective to praise a person's actions than him or her as an individual. Following this logic, it would be better to tell your boss, "You really got your points across to the people," than, "You really are a good speaker." When you point to something specific that a person has done well, it appears more sincere than generalized praise. Second, do not use praise indiscriminately. If you are seen praising your superiors for a wide range of their activities, your praise loses its reward value.

Exchange favors. Many of the informal agreements that take place on the job are based on exchanging favors with other employees. In legislative circles, the term for the same behavior is *log rolling*. The tactic of exchanging favors is also referred to as *collect and use IOUs*. The adept political player performs a favor for another employee without asking a favor in return. The IOU is then cashed in when a favor is especially needed.

> Phil, a junior faculty member, agreed to cover a Saturday morning class for a senior faculty member, Alice, because she wanted to take a getaway weekend. Later that year Phil needed a letter of recommendation from two other faculty members in order to apply for tenure. He turned first to a close friend, and then turned to Alice, who was willing to help out such a cooperative colleague.

Ask advice. Asking advice on technical and professional topics is a good way of building relationships with other employees. Asking another person for advice—whose job does not require giving advice—will usually be perceived as a compliment. Asking advice transmits the message, "I trust your judgment enough to ask your opinion on something important to me." You are also saying, "I trust you enough to think that the advice you give me will be in my best interest."

To avoid hard feelings, inform the person whose advice you are seeking that his or her opinion will not necessarily be binding. A request for advice might be prefaced with a comment such as, "I would like your opinion on a problem facing me. But I can't guarantee that I'll be in a position to act on it."

Avoid being abrasive. An abrasive person is someone who "rubs people the wrong way." The primary characteristics of the abrasive personality are self-centeredness, isolation from others, perfectionism, contempt for others, and a tendency to attack people.[22] Being abrasive toward co-workers and lower-ranking employees tends to erode one's power base. Abrasiveness may create enemies who will seize the opportunity to retaliate. One way would be to mention to higher management that the abrasive individual "cannot get along with people." Such a reputation can disqualify a person for promotion.

Follow group standards of conduct. A summary principle to follow in getting along with other employees is to heed **group norms,** the unwritten set of expectations for group members. If you do not deviate too far from these norms, much of your behavior will be accepted by the group. If you deviate too far, you will be subject to much rejection and therefore lose some of your power base. Yet if you conform too closely to group norms, higher management may perceive you as unable to identify with management. Employees are sometimes blocked from moving up the ladder because they are regarded as "one of the gang."

UNETHICAL AND DEVIOUS POLITICAL BEHAVIOR

Any technique of gaining power or favor can be devious if practiced in extreme. A person who supports a boss by helping him or her carry company property out the door for personal use is being devious. Some approaches are unequivocally devious, such as those described next. Each one of them is *precisely what we are recommending not to be followed.*

Blackmail. Extortion has been a long-standing criminal activity. It has also been used by company politicians to gain power and/or favor. A curious aspect of company blackmail is that one deviant person threatens to make public the deviant behavior of another, unless the former makes certain concessions to the latter. Blackmailers, however, lead a hazardous existence—they are liable to exposure at any time by the "blackmailee."

Character assassination. According to Ed Roseman, character assassins are as skillful and lethal as underworld "hit men." Rarely are they openly critical of their victims. Instead they drop innuendoes:

> The salesman I worked with in the field used the visual aid as instructed, but I had the definite impression that he didn't completely understand what we were trying to accomplish. I wonder if the sales manager is failing to explain this to him properly?[23]

In this situation, the product manager making these derogatory hints about the sales manager has some particular reason to have the latter removed from the scene. Perhaps he believes that the sales manager in question is not giving him enough support.

Remove the opposition. The ultimate weapon in outdistancing a rival for promotion, or ridding the company of a key person who has a negative opinion of you, is to have that person physically removed. Precipitating a rival's dismissal by making negative comments about another individual rarely leads to a person's dismissal. Unless there is other supporting evidence, most rational managers will not fire one person upon the word of another. Anybody who tries to remove another physically by resorting to "framing" risks being faced with a libel suit.

A still devious, but less criminal-like approach, to removing others is attempting to have a rival transferred or promoted out of your area. At high levels this tactic can take the form of bringing your rival's name and credentials to the attention of an executive employment agency or search firm. Or the manager from another department, division, or firm can be told about the virtues of the "really promising person who is being underutilized where he (or she) is now."

Divide and rule. An ancient military and governmental strategy, this tactic is sometimes used in business. The object is to have subordinates fight among themselves, therefore giving you the balance of power. If subordinates are not aligned with each other, there is an improved chance that they will align with a common superior. One company general manager used this technique to short-range advantage by dropping innuendoes during staff meetings.

> Once in a meeting called to discuss the production schedule on a new product, Vic, the general manager, said to Don, the head of manufacturing, "They tell me engineering isn't holding up its end of getting things ready for production." Two weeks later Vic dropped another conflict-arousing comment, this time to the head of engineering. "It's too bad you're having so many problems with manufacturing trying to figure out how to build the product you've designed."
>
> Vic's techniques did create rivalry and hard feelings between engineering and manufacturing. Ultimately, his top staff saw through his divide and conquer tactics and his effectiveness as a leader diminished. Realizing he was no longer effective as a leader, higher executives in the company asked him to resign.

The setup. The object of a setup is to place a person in a position where he or she will look ineffective. A young man considered by the company to have high potential was assigned to a manager's department. Suspecting that this new arrival might be intended as his replacement, the manager set up the young man to fail. He placed him in charge of an operation he knew nothing about. In a short period of time the acclaimed individual was in trouble on the job. Believing that they perhaps had overrated this man's potential, management transferred him to another department. He was also relegated to lesser tasks.

Receive undue credit. A devious approach widely practiced by managers is to take credit for work performed by subordinates and not allow them to share in the recognition. A typical example would be when you submit a useful idea to your boss. Your boss then proposes the idea to his or her boss without mentioning that it was your idea. One suggestion for dealing with this problem is *discreetly* to confront your boss about not receiving recognition for your ideas. Another approach is to present a valid reason for seeking recognition. For instance, you might point out that you want to earn recognition so you can advance in the organization.[24]

STEMMING THE TIDE OF ORGANIZATIONAL POLITICS

Carried to excess, job politics can hurt an organization and its members. Too much politicking can result in wasted time and effort, therefore lowering productivity. Human consequences can also be substantial, including lowered morale and the turnover of people who intensely dislike playing office politics. Three particularly helpful approaches to combating job politics will be mentioned here.

Provide objective measurements of performance. A primary reason we have so much politicking in some organizations is that those organizations do not provide objective methods of measuring performance. When a person knows exactly what it is he or she has to do in order to qualify for promotion, there is less need for political maneuvering. Even more fundamental, you tend to curry favor with a superior when there seems to be no other way to determine if you are competent in your job.

Provide an atmosphere of trust. Several management observers have noted that this is the best overall antidote to excessive playing of politics. If people trust each other in a company, they are less likely to use devious tactics against each other. People often resort to cover-up behavior because they fear the consequences of telling the truth about themselves.

Set good examples at the top. When people in key positions are highly political, they set the tone for job politicking at lower levels. When people at the top of the organization are nonpolitical in their actions, they demonstrate in a subtle way that political behavior is not desired. A new vice-president squelched job politicking in a hurry through an unusual confrontation:

Brad called his first official staff meeting as vice president of finance. After a few brief comments about his pleasure in joining the company, he said bluntly: "I've been here only two weeks, yet I've noticed some strange actions that I want stopped right now. I know it's part of the American culture to please the boss, but don't be so naive about it. I'm not pointing the finger at any one person in particular, but you people have been milling around my office like birds waiting for crumbs. If you have some official business and you want to make an appointment with my secretary, Betty, fine. But if you don't have a legitimate business purpose in seeing me, don't drop by my office. We've got too many things to accomplish to spend time in coffee klatches."

ORGANIZATIONAL POLITICS AND CAREER SETBACKS

People who do not achieve their career goals frequently attribute their lack of success to office politics. They believe that favoritism has worked against them— that a less deserving person has been promoted instead. At other times, people contend that office politics cost them their job. One way this can happen is to form alliances with those the boss perceives to be enemies.[25] Nevertheless, organizational politics should not be blamed for long-term career problems. Marilyn Moats Kennedy makes this analysis:[26]

"It is the commonest thing in the world to say that you were a political victim. But maybe you victimized yourself. The number of people who are actually the victims of any concerted office plot or plan is pretty small.

"For instance, the most common way to victimize yourself is to say: 'I don't want to do it that way. I want to do it my way.' O.K., you've made a choice, and it's the wrong one. To me, politics is a process of choices. You get to choose the work environment. You even get to choose the boss you'll work for if you do your homework."

We believe that Kennedy is essentially correct. However, contentions about having been cast aside by political forces are not necessarily the product of paranoid thinking. If you are politically naive, you probably will not achieve the success you desire. The antidote is to practice ethical and sensible organizational politics. One strategy would be for you to become recognized by upper management for your willingness to volunteer for assignments and your participation in company and social functions. Under such circumstances, politics might work in your favor. Another antidote is to leave an organization when you are convinced that you are no longer aligned with powerful people. In this way you cannot permanently blame organizational politics for retarding your career.

Summary of Key Points

☐ Organizational politics (OP) refers to gaining advantage through any means others than merit or luck. Power is the ability to mobilize resources, energy, and information on behalf of a preferred goal or strategy. Politics is thus used to attain power. Some political strategies are generally ethical, while others are clearly unethical.

☐   Contributing factors to organizational politics include (a) pyramid-shaped organizations, (b) competitiveness within the firm, (c) subjective standards of performance, (d) environmental uncertainty, (e) need for acceptance, (f) a desire to avoid work, and (g) Machiavellian tendencies of people.

☐   Organizational power stems from four general sources: power granted by the organization, power stemming from characteristics of the person, the power of subordinates to refuse orders, and power stemming from capitalizing upon opportunity. The last source of power stems from being in the right place at the right time, taking the right action, and having the right resources.

☐   Strategies and tactics aimed directly at gaining power include: (a) identify powerful people, (b) maintain alliances with them, (c) control vital information, (d) keep informed, (e) plant an ally, (f) acquire seniority, (g) play "camel's head in the tent," and (h) make a quick showing.

☐   Strategies and tactics aimed at building relationships with superiors include: (a) help your boss succeed, (b) become a crucial subordinate, (c) display loyalty, (d) volunteer for assignments, (e) manage your impression, (f) laugh at your boss's jokes, (g) use discretion in socializing with your boss, and (h) offer assistance to a poorly performing superior.

☐   Strategies and tactics aimed at building relationships with co-workers and lower-ranking employees include: (a) develop allies, (b) be a team player, (c) express an interest in their work, (d) exchange favors, (e) ask advice, and (f) avoid being abrasive.

☐   Unethical and devious tactics of organizational politics sometimes found in organizations include: blackmail, character assassination, remove the opposition, divide and rule, set people up to fail, and receive undue credit.

☐   Three ways of decreasing excessive politics are (a) provide objective measurements of performance, (b) establish an atmosphere of openness and trust, and (c) set good examples in top management.

☐   If political forces have worked against you and you are no longer in power, it may be necessary to start fresh in another department or organization. In this way, organizational politics cannot be held responsible for a permanent career setback.

Questions and Activities

1. Estimate the approximate score of the following people on the OP questionnaire in Figure 10–1: (a) the head of your country, (b) Lee Iacocca, and (c) your instructor in this course.

2. Which tactic of organizational politics have you observed most frequently on the job? For what purposes is it (or was it) used?

3. Is there such a thing as "classroom politics"? If this phenomenon does exist, give two examples of it in practice.

4. What similarity do you see between governmental politics and organizational politics?

5. It has been observed that workers tend to engage in more office politics during the middle than early or late in their careers. Why do you think this might be true?

6. If a friend said to you, "I want to be a big success in my career, but I refuse to play office politics," what advice would you offer your friend?

7. Should organizations have policies about the use of office politics? Explain your answer.

8. October 16 is Boss's Day in the United States. What should an astute office politician do to observe boss's day?

9. A large communications firm has identified a group of managers from whom the company's future executives will be selected. All these managers are encouraged to read the same book about office politics. What do you think of this practice?

10. One experienced industrial psychologist contends that ethical office politics is simply good human relations. What do you think?

A Human Relations Case Problem

NEGATIVE CHEMISTRY

Gunther Wortman looked forward to a career as a quality specialist. He began working for Micro Tech as a quality control inspector. As a result of hard work and additional study, he was promoted to quality control technician, and then to quality control supervisor. As a supervisor he now reported to Alan Tombak, manager of quality assurance. Four other supervisors also reported to Tombak.

Gunther approached his new job with his usual enthusiasm. He was proud to be a supervisor, and believed that his big career break had finally arrived. Gradually Gunther began to sense that things were not going so well for him in his new position. One day he felt particularly despondent. Ten days previously he had sent Tombak a detailed proposal for the use of a new inspection machine. So far Tombak had not even acknowledged his proposal.

Concerned about his feeling that things were not going so well between himself and his boss, Gunther decided to call Diane Garcia, a personnel specialist. He asked Diane if she would join him for lunch to discuss a career problem he was facing. Gunther and Diane agreed to meet for lunch the following Friday at a nearby sushi restaurant.

As the two dug into their fish, Gunther began to talk about his concern. "Diane, maybe you can help me," he said. "I just don't seem to be hitting it off with my boss, Alan Tombak. He hardly acknowledges my presence. He usually ignores my suggestions. He doesn't even laugh at my jokes. When I'm at a staff meeting with the other supervisors, he acts as if I don't even exist. Do you have any suggestions for handling this situation?"

Diane said, "Gunther, it sounds like you do have a problem. Either you're paranoid, or you have failed to impress Tombak. I know you well enough to be sure that you're not paranoid. So there must be a real problem between you and Tombak. What have you done about the problem so far?"

"I've put my nose to the grindstone like I have in every other assignment with Micro Tech. Nothing about me seems to impress Tombak. That's why I've asked for your help."

After thinking for a moment, Diane responded, "I have a plan. This month I'm supposed to help the managers in your area with their human resource planning. This usually involves a discussion of key employees. I'll see what Tombak has to say about you. I'll then get back to you with my findings."

Ten days later, Diane did help Alan with human resource planning. The conversation led naturally to a discussion of the strengths and weaknesses of the supervisors reporting to Tombak. "What is your evaluation of Gunther Wortman, your newest supervisor?" asked Diane coyly. "Good question," said Alan. "I don't really know what to make out of him. He does seem to try hard. But there's negative chemistry between us. The guy just doesn't turn me on as an employee. I think he's overrated. Maybe I'm missing something, but he's just a neutral entity to me. Yet, I'm certainly not trying to get rid of him. That's all I can say."

Diane thought to herself, "Tombak has been brutally honest. Gunther and he just don't hit it off. I guess it's my duty as a friend to tell Gunther about this problem. But I wouldn't want him to leave Micro Tech over it."

1. Should Diane give Gunther a full report of her feelings?
2. What should Gunther do about this problem of negative chemistry between himself and his boss?
3. Is Diane acting ethically in her method of helping Gunther?
4. Should Gunther confront Alan directly about his problem?

A Human Relations Incident

THE SQUEEZED OUT DIRECTOR[27]

Lee, 61, has been director of engineering for American Semiconductor for 14 years. He is very bright and a fine manager but has not kept abreast of new developments in technology.

American Semiconductor's manufacturing process creates substantial quantities of toxic materials. Lee's casual attitude toward the disposal of these chemicals has resulted in a number of environmental citations. The firm is now tied up in court on two cases and will probably be forced to pay a considerable amount in damages. Yet Lee still does not perceive the disposal problem as urgent. For three years, Charlie, the executive vice-president, has tried to persuade Lee to make this a priority issue but has failed. Charlie has reluctantly concluded that Lee must be taken out of his position as director of engineering.

Charlie recognizes that it would demoralize the other managers if he were to fire Lee outright. So Charlie decides that he will begin to tell selected individuals that he is dissatisfied with Lee's work. When there is open support for Lee, Charlie quietly sides with Lee's opposition. He casually lets Lee's peers know that he thinks Lee may have outlived his usefulness to the firm. He even exaggerates Lee's deficiencies and failures when speaking to Lee's co-workers. Discouraged by the waning support from his colleagues, Lee decides to take an early retirement.

1. What tactics of organizational politics are illustrated in this incident?
2. What do you think of the ethics of Charlie's behavior?

A Human Relations Role Play

THE NEGATIVE CHEMISTRY CONFRONTATION

Refer back to the case about negative chemistry. Assume that after hearing from Diane, Gunther decides to confront his boss about the problem of negative chemistry. Gunther makes an appointment to discuss the problem with Tombak. He wants to improve—not worsen—his relationship with his boss. Tombak is upset by this confrontation, yet he wants to keep things on a level footing and not prompt Gunther to quit. Tombak sees no grounds for dismissing Gunther, yet he does not see him as a star on his team. The roles to be played, of course, are Gunther Wortman and Alan Tombak.

Notes

1. Barbara Gray and Sonny R. Ariss, "Politics and Strategic Change Across Organizational Life Cycles," *Academy of Management Review*, October 1985, p. 707.
2. R. Wayne Mondy and Shane R. Premeaux, "Power, Politics, and the First-Line Supervisor," *Supervisory Management*, January 1986, p. 30.
3. Gerald P. Cavanagh, Dennis J. Moberg, and Manuel Velasquez, "The Ethics of Organizational Politics," *Academy of Management Review*, July 1981, p. 363.
4. Abraham Zaleznik, "Power and Politics in Organizational Life," *Harvard Business Review*, May–June 1970, p. 47.
5. Dan L. Madison et al., "Organizational Politics: An Exploration of Managers' Perceptions," *Human Relations*, February 1980, p. 95.
6. Ibid.
7. Gerald Biberman, "Personality and Characteristic Work Attitudes of Persons with High, Moderate, and Low Political Tendencies," *Psychological Reports*, 1985, 57, p. 1309.
8. John R. P. French and Bertram Raven, "The Basis of Social Power," in *Studies in Social Power*, ed. Dorwin Cartwright (Ann Arbor, MI: Institute for Social Research, 1959), p. 150; Hugh R. Taylor, "Power at Work," *Personnel Journal*, April 1986, pp. 42–48.
9. Ibid.
10. Morgan McCall, Jr., *Power, Influence, and Authority: The Hazards of Carrying a Sword* (Greensboro, NC: Center for Creative Leadership, 1978), p. 5.
11. Cited in ibid., p. 12.
12. "Building the Power Base to Sway a Decision Your Way," *Supervisory Management*, May 1986, p. 16.
13. "How to Win at Organizational Politics—Without Being Unethical or Sacrificing Your Self-Respect," *Research Institute Personal Report for the Executive*, 1985, p. 13.
14. Eugene Schmuckler, book review in *Personnel Psychology*, Summer 1982, p. 497.
15. William H. Newman, *Administrative Action: The Techniques of Organization and Management* (Englewood Cliffs, NJ: Prentice-Hall, 1963), p. 90.

16. Eugene E. Jennings, *The Mobile Manager: A Study of the New Generation of Top Executives* (Ann Arbor: The University of Michigan Press, 1967). Several other tactics of boss relationships on our list are based on the work of Jennings.

17. Study cited in David Greising, "Company Loyalty Lifts Aggressive Executives Up the Corporate Ladder," *Chicago Sun Times*, November 29, 1983.

18. Letitia Baldrige, "A Guide to Executive Etiquette," *Business Week Careers*, October 1986, pp. 60–63; see also *Letitia Baldrige's Complete Guide to Executive Manners*, ed. Sandi Gelles-Cole (New York: Rawson Associates, 1985).

19. "Beware Your Boss's Tender Trap," *Research Institute Personal Report for the Executive*, May 28, 1985, p. 6.

20. "How to Win at Organizational Politics," p. 15.

21. "Power Comes to Those Who Plan for It," *Research Institute Personal Report for the Executive*, July 9, 1985, p. 5. The preceding quote is also from this source.

22. Harry Levinson, "The Abrasive Personality at the Office," *Psychology Today*, May 1978, p. 79.

23. Ed Roseman, "How to Play Clean Office Politics," *Product Marketing*, May 1976, p. 33.

24. "How to Win at Organizational Politics," p. 15.

25. Marilyn Moats Kennedy, "10 Reasons People Get Fired," *Business Week Careers*, October 1986, p. 40.

26. "Playing 'Office Politics'—How Necessary?" (Interview with Marilyn Moats Kennedy), *U.S. News & World Report*, January 1981, p. 36.

27. Cavanagh, Moberg, and Velasquez, "The Ethics of Organizational Politics," p. 369. Reprinted with permission.

Suggested Reading

CULBERT, SAMUEL A., and McDONOUGH, JOHN J. *Radical Management: Power Politics and the Pursuit of Trust.* New York: Free Press, 1985.

GINSBERG, SIGMUND G. "How to Protect Your Rear and Sharpen Your Elbows." *Supervisory Management*, June 1985, pp. 42–43.

KAKABADSE, ANDREW. *The Politics of Management.* New York: Nichols Publishing Company, 1984.

LOMBARDO, MICHAEL M., and McCALL, MORGAN W., JR. *Coping With an Intolerable Boss.* Greensboro, NC: Center for Creative Leadership, Special Report, 1984.

MACHER, KEN. "The Politics of Organizations." *Personnel Journal*, February 1986, pp. 81–84.

MINTZBERG, HENRY. "Power and Organization Life Cycles." *Academy of Management Review*, April 1984, pp. 207–224.

PAYNE, STEPHEN L., and PETTINGILL, BERNARD F. "Coping with Organizational Politics." *Supervisory Management*, April 1986, pp. 28–31.

PINSEL, E. MELVIN, and DIENHART, LIGITA. *Power Lunching.* New York: Turnbull and Willoughby, 1984.

SRIVASTA, SURESH. *Executive Power: How Executives Influence People and Organizations.* San Francisco: Jossey-Bass, 1986.

YATES, DOUGLAS, JR. *The Politics of Management: Exploring the Inner Workings of Public and Private Organizations.* San Francisco: Jossey-Bass, 1985.

Employee Coaching and Counseling

LEARNING OBJECTIVES

After reading and studying this chapter and doing the exercises, you should be able to

1. Understand how to use the control model to improve employee performance.

2. Explain how to criticize an employee constructively.

3. Develop a good understanding of guidelines for employee coaching and counseling.

4. Pinpoint how a manager should handle the problem of alcohol and drug addiction on the job.

5. Describe outplacement in organizations.

THE MEANING OF COACHING AND COUNSELING

"Debbie, the way you handle your job is really getting to be a problem," said her boss Charlie. "If I tell you to do some routine thing, it does get done. But you never anticipate anything important. And what I need is someone who can anticipate."

"Charlie, I wish you would be more specific," said Debbie. "Tell me what you mean about my never anticipating anything important."

"I'm getting at things like this. You knew that I had a big meeting with my boss on Wednesday about the budget. Why did I have to ask you to gather up the budget information? You should have had that information on my desk by at least Friday."

This exchange between Charlie and Debbie represents a brief sample of a vital part of managerial leadership. Effective managers spend considerable time coaching and counseling employees toward improved performance. Few managers face a situation in which all of their employees are so competent that no assistance is required. One major use of coaching and counseling is to assist an effective employee reach even higher levels of performance. Another is to assist an employee overcome maladaptive behavior that results in substandard performance.

Coaching versus Counseling

Coaching and counseling are similar but not identical processes. **Coaching** is a method of helping employees grow and improve their job competence by providing suggestions and encouragement.[1] **Counseling** is a formal discussion method for helping another individual overcome a problem or improve his or her potential. A counselor listens more than a coach does and is more concerned with feelings than with action. A coach might give you a tip on how to prepare tax depreciation schedules properly. A counselor might listen to you complain how preparing depreciation schedules does not exactly fit your career objectives.

Counseling, in general, involves the long-term development of an employee, whereas coaching deals with present job performance. In practice, the terms counseling and coaching are often used synonymously, and no great confusion is caused in doing so. Both techniques are primary methods for improving employee performance.

Purposes of Coaching

According to Richard V. Concillio, coaching has three purposes. The first is to close a gap between the actual and desired level of performance. Thus a manager might coach a sales representative on how to close more sales. The second purpose of coaching is to foster employee growth on the job in order to prepare the employee for additional responsibility. For instance, a manager might coach an assistant on how to prepare budgets. The third purpose of coaching is to prepare the employee for promotion.[2] It is common practice, for example, for a manager to prepare an employee to take over his or her job.

In this chapter we study coaching and counseling by examining a control model for their application, their relationship to performance appraisal, and suggestions for being a better coach or counselor. We also describe two important aspects of dealing with substandard performers: discipline and the handling of substandard performance. We also describe how organizations help surplus employees find new jobs and careers.

A CONTROL MODEL FOR COACHING AND COUNSELING

A recommended approach for coaching, counseling, and disciplining employees is the control model shown in Figure 11–1. It provides a systematic approach to improving performance. The model is most often used with substandard performers, but can also be used to assist good performers to do even better. The control model is divided into six steps that should be followed in sequence.

Establish Performance Standards

As with any other control technique, performance standards must be defined before an employee can be informed that improvement is necessary. It is equally important to communicate these standards clearly to all employees. Defining acceptable performance also helps the manager spur employees on toward higher levels of performance. For instance, a manager might say to a packaging design specialist: "Your package designs are acceptable because our clients aren't complaining. Yet I think you can lend more creativity to your designs and get our clients excited about your work."

Detect Need for Coaching or Counseling

Detection is the process of noting when an employee's performance could stand improvement. To make such detections, the manager has to stay in contact with the activities of the department. Another approach to detection is for the manager to have frequent discussions with group members about their job performance.

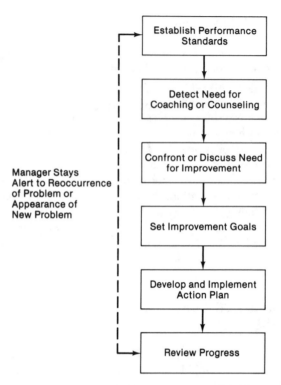

Figure 11–1 The control model for coaching, counseling, and disciplining employees.

Straightforward questioning may uncover areas for improvement. One such question is, "How close are you to meeting the deadline on Project 37?"

When a worker displays a consistent pattern, rather than a one-time deviation from standard performance, coaching is usually required. Note one important exception to the "consistent pattern" principle: Some departures from acceptable performance or behavior are so significant they must be brought to the immediate attention of the employee. These departures relate to violations of company policy or the law.

Confront or Discuss Need for Improvement

After detecting the problem, the manager must bring it to the attention of the employee. Supervisors have a general tendency to dislike confronting subordinates because of the defensive or hostile reaction confrontation may elicit. A general principle here is for the manager to focus on the substandard behavior itself, and not upon the individual. People usually become defensive and uncooperative when they believe their traits or personal characteristics are under attack. According to this principle, a teller who borrowed money informally from the bank teller might be approached in this manner:

> We have something serious to talk about. A routine audit showed that you borrowed one hundred dollars from your cash drawer before leaving for lunch. Apparently it was returned by the end of the day. Borrowing money from the bank without making formal application for the loan is absolutely forbidden. It could lead to a person's immediate dismissal.

A less effective approach would be to confront the teller about his or her "loan," and simultaneously insult the teller's character. To illustrate:

> I caught your little act of petty thievery. You were very sneaky about it. Don't use any lies to cover up for your dishonesty. You've been caught.

Confrontation is unpopular. Direct confrontation of the ineffective subordinate problem occurs infrequently in large corporations. More reliance is placed on the strategies of transferring and "working around" problem employees.[3] A basic reason for this situation is that many managers both feel uncomfortable about and have limited skill in criticizing employees. To deal with this problem, training programs have been developed to help managers learn the art of constructive criticism. The box summarizes the content of a successful program along these lines. Similarly, the suggestions for coaching and counseling presented later in this chapter can help you develop confrontation skills.

Set Improvement Goals

To bring about change, it is helpful to set specific improvement goals that specify what kind of behaviors are required. Improvement goals that are vague, such as "Become a more productive employee," do not give the person a specific improvement target. More helpful would be an improvement goal such as, "Do not leave a customer inquiry unprocessed for more than 24 hours." It is also helpful to set short-range rather than long-range goals in most disciplinary situations. By setting short-range goals, the subordinate can readily see if he or she is making progress. Assume that a manager is reviewing the work performance of a budget analyst whose reports are invariably late. The improvement goal for the next month might be for her to turn in three out of five reports on time. If this target is reached, she and her boss might make the goal four out of five on-time reports for the following month. For the third month, the goal might be five out of five timely reports.

Jointly set goals. By collaborating with the boss in setting improvement goals, the employee feels emotionally involved in the counseling process. It is also another way of the superior and subordinate sharing in the discipline situation. Nevertheless, at times the principle of mutual goal setting must be preempted by organizational realities. Assume that in the above instance, management needs all five reports on time before the third month. The manager would then be forced to impose goals upon the subordinate with an explanation of why these goals are necessary.

TRAINING FIRST-LINE SUPERVISORS TO CRITICIZE CONSTRUCTIVELY

Two-hundred and forty first-line supervisors from six different organizations were given the opportunity to improve their skills in evaluating performance and making constructive use of criticism. The skill-development sessions were of six weeks duration, meeting once a week for two and one-half hours. Measures were taken both before and then ten weeks after training on how comfortable the supervisors felt with three aspects of their jobs: evaluating employee performance, communicating negative performance evaluation results, and handling discipline problems. The program resulted in supervisors feeling more comfortable in handling these problems. According to Guvenc G. Alpander, the training program director, "The average change in feelings for the 200 supervisors who took the posttest was from being uncomfortable to being rather comfortable, or at least indifferent."

One session of the supervisory development workshop was devoted to how to criticize constructively. The subjects covered during the two and one-half hour session were drawn from the following material (presented here in condensed form):

TECHNIQUES FOR CRITICIZING INADEQUATE PERFORMANCE

1. **Differentiate between Two Basic Causes of Inadequate Performance.**
   Identify whether ineffective performance is caused by deep-seated personal problems, such as alcohol, drugs, or family life. The supervisor needs professional assistance here. If the reduced performance is not due to these special problems, then proceed to Step two.
2. **Analyze the Reasons for Inadequate Performance.**
   Possible reasons may be: a) circumstances beyond employee's control, b) improper guidance, c) employee lacks needed skill and training, d) low effort, and e) good performance not rewarded.
   After effectively analyzing the possible reasons behind poor evaluations, the next step is a corrective conference with the subordinate.
3. **Prepare for the Appraisal Interview.**
   a. *Don't waste your time*—If the employee is already performing to the best of his or her ability, no improvement will take place.
   b. *Establish policies and guidelines*—Subordinates will test a supervisor to see what his or her limits are. If strong, but just, the supervisor will be respected and admired.
   c. *Pick the time carefully*—If possible, tell the employee what is wrong immediately after poor performance. The best time would probably be in the morning, at the beginning of the week. Be sure to time the reprimand so that you have an opportunity to talk to the employee again before the day is over.
   d. *Know the target*—Is the person you are criticizing looking for ways to improve, or is he or she defensive? If you aren't certain, the safest way is to be gentle

and reassuring. Suggestions and maintaining an attitude of counseling and understanding work best. However, be consistent; charges of favoritism will result if one subordinate is reprimanded and another is not.

    e. *Know the facts*—If you have all the facts, and the employee knows you have them, there will seldom be a dispute regarding any discipline administered.

4. Conduct the Interview with Care.

    a. *Keep it private*—Public criticism is more often than not disastrous. It burns itself into the mind and can never be erased.

    b. *Criticize selectively*—An emphasis on important, job-related performance causes attention to be focused on the job's crucial aspects.

    c. *Take one point at a time*—Too much criticism can be very harmful. Also, subordinates may become confused about where to begin making improvements.

    d. *Criticize constructively*—Constructive criticism is specific and must equip employee with all the information needed for good performance.

    e. *Be consistent over time*—Never ignore a violation of the rules. To overlook first-time offenses is to condone them and encourage repeat performances.

    f. *Face facts squarely*—The "sandwich" technique has often been mistakenly advocated. This is when you start with a compliment to create a glow, then throw in a criticism and end with more compliments. A better sequence would be: first, weaknesses; second, strengths; and third, the future.

    g. *Don't make a joke of it*—A light touch often seems pretty heavy when handed to the victim. Very few people have the gift of conveying criticism through kindly humor.

    h. *Attack the act*—Tell subordinates what is wrong with their work, not themselves. By attacking a person's self-image you only succeed in producing hostility and damaged feelings.

    i. *Criticize without comparison*—Unfavorable comparisons produce hostility within the work group.

    j. *Recognize your own power*—To your subordinates, you may be the most influential person in the company—particularly at those moments which call for criticism.

    k. *Don't expect popularity as an umpire*—Your job is not to make friends; your job is to be respected and to get the work done. So, state your criticisms clearly and in absolute terms with the knowledge that you are in the right.

SOURCE: Reprinted with permission from Guvenc G. Alpander, "Training First-Line Supervisors to Criticize Constructively," *Personnel Journal*, March 1980, pp. 218–221.

Sample goals. Following are five improvement goals which specify the type of behavior that constitutes improved performance. As such, they can serve as a guide to action. Although these goals may appear to be set from the perspective of the organization, we can assume that achieving them is also in the best interest of the employee. Therefore, they may have been set jointly.

    1. *Retail clerk*: Decrease the number of bogus checks you accept by insisting upon proper identification before accepting a check.

    2. *Human resources specialist*: Volunteer only for those projects that you have the time to take care of properly.

3. *Computer programmer*: Consider no programming assignment complete until you have run the program twice without error.

4. *Newspaper reporter*: Include no "facts" in your stories that cannot be authenticated by a second party.

5. *Truck driver*: No hitchhikers allowed unless the person given the ride is an accident victim.

Develop and Implement an Action Plan

An **action plan** is a description of what steps will be taken to improve performance. In some instances the action plan might be as simple as this: "Make a mental and written note to engage the security system when you leave the store at closing." At other times the action plan might be more complex because new skills are required in order to improve performance. A group member might be preparing disorganized, clumsily written reports. Part of the action plan in this situation would be for the person to take a course in report writing.

The specific nature of the action plan is tied to the cause of the problem that is creating substandard performance, or blocking top-level performance. Marcia Ann Pulich has outlined some of the possible action plans for improving substandard performance:[4]

1. *Change the work environment.* Redesigning a job would be one way of implementing this action plan. In one firm a sales order specialist would regularly express irritation toward customers when he had to handle more than one phone call simultaneously. The company solved the problem by installing a phone answering system that automatically placed customers on hold when the specialist was handling another call.

2. *Improve the selection process.* Poor performance can sometimes be attributed to selecting the wrong person for the job. Future problems can be minimized by improving selection procedures.

3. *Improve training.* Performance can often be improved with adequate training, including the manager coaching the employee on a new work method or technique. For example, a manager might give an assistant more training in preparing a travel expense report.

4. *Improve communications.* Substandard performance, or less than peak performance, sometimes stems from poor communication between the manager and the employee. A frequent problem here is that the employee has not clearly understood instructions.

5. *Transfer.* If a mismatch exists between the employee and the job, a transfer to a job better fitting the employee's capabilities would be warranted. One difficulty in implementing this action plan is that other managers are often reluctant to accept an employee who is being transferred because of performance problems.

6. *Demote.* If an employee is demoted to a less demanding job, he or she may perform better. A successful demotion makes it possible for the employee to remain with the firm. Pulich notes: "Some employees actually welcome demotion because it places them in a position where they can again be successful and feel in control of their job performance."[5] Nevertheless, the majority of employees will resent a demotion.

7. *Termination.* When all other attempts at improving performance fail, including appropriate discipline, termination may necessary. Current employment practice dictates that employees be given ample opportunity to improve before being terminated.

Implementation stems logically from establishing the action plan. There are times, however, when action plans are drawn but never implemented. As inferred from the above action plans, they must be implemented with sensitivity and tact.

Review Progress

After a subordinate is coached or counseled about improvement, some form of systematic follow-up is required. At an elementary level, the follow-up could consist of the supervisor checking to see that the desired actions have been taken. If the employee were coached not to wear jeans to staff meetings, his or her compliance with the request could readily be detected.

When the new behavior is more complex, formal review sessions are in order. For example, Phil, a drafting technician, might be coached about his relationships with engineers. An improvement goal set is, "Decrease incidences of conflict with engineers over technical matters." After three months, the technician and his manager might discuss progress toward this goal. The manager might have inquired in the engineering department about incidences of conflict, while Phil might have reached his own conclusion about his relationship with the engineers. When both agree that substantial progress has been made, the manager might conclude: "It looks like we have this problem licked. We can touch base on the problem six months from now. In the interim, proceed as you have been doing. It's working."

Use of positive reinforcement. The comments made by the drafting manager above illustrate the use of positive reinforcement. Giving employees encouragement, or other forms of PR, is one of the most effective tools for coaching and counseling at the disposal of the manager. Making rewards contingent upon good performance increases the probability that the improvements will be lasting. A major purpose, then, of the review sessions is for the manager to dispense rewards for tangible progress toward the improvement goals.

Use of discipline. Positive reinforcement usually works more effectively than punishment and other negative motivators in bringing about performance improvements. It is better to reward people for the improvement they have made than to punish them for the improvement they have not made. However, some employees respond better to punishment or the threat of punishment than rewards. If progress has not been made, the control model suggests that it may be necessary to administer discipline. More will be said about discipline later in this chapter.

Repeating the Cycle

The coaching and counseling process is rarely completed. After progress is made in overcoming one aspect of deficient performance, channels of communication must remain open. One reason is that improvements are rarely permanent. A person whose performance improves may slip back to his or her previous level of performance, particularly under heavy job pressure.

> An automobile service manager was criticized by his boss for telling customers who brought their cars for servicing at close to quitting time to return the next day. He agreed to mellow in his approach. However, when the season for change-over to snow tires came back, so did the service manager's abruptness. Three customers complained to the dealership owner that they were treated rudely by the service manager. Additional counseling was necessary to correct an old problem.

COACHING AND COUNSELING LINKED TO PERFORMANCE APPRAISAL

A **performance appraisal** is a formal system of evaluating employee performance and conveying this evaluation to the employee. Performance appraisals meet two general purposes. First, they serve administrative purposes because they provide a basis for determining salary increases, promotions, terminations, and other personnel decisions. Second, performance appraisals serve developmental purposes to the extent that employees are provided with specific job feedback, assistance, and coaching and counseling to improve future job performance.[6] It should be noted that not every manager capitalizes upon the opportunity to coach and counsel that the performance appraisal session provides.

Dozens of methods have been developed for appraising employee performance.[7] A comprehensive study of these methods is better suited for a course in personnel and human resource management than human relations or organizational behavior. Our purposes will be served here by describing the method called *behaviorally anchored rating scales (BARS)*. Although not widely used, the BARS is well suited for coaching because it points to specific behaviors that might need improvement. Managers using the BARS do not have to imagine what is unacceptable, satisfactory, or outstanding performance. Instead, they can see an actual example in the behavioral anchor.[8] In contrast, many conventional performance appraisal instruments rely on adjectives such as "energetic," "productive," or "ambitious."

To illustrate the process, the rating scale shown in Figure 11–2 would be helpful in coaching a tax advisor (or "income tax preparer"). The evaluator would be able to pinpoint specifically *why* the evaluee is being given a particular rating. It could be said, "You are being rated as 'ineffective' largely because you have difficulty with all but the most routine tax forms."

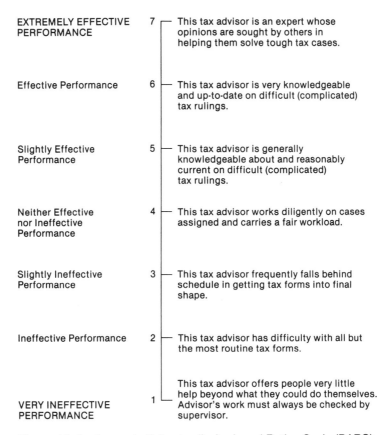

Figure 11–2   A sample Behaviorally Anchored Rating Scale (BARS).

A BARS is scientifically developed. Each statement on the scale has been assigned a weight on the basis of the average importance assigned that behavior by a group of knowledgeable judges. About five to ten rating scales are needed to evaluate each job, because a separate scale is developed for each job dimension. In Figure 11–2, the rating scale has been developed for the dimension of "technical competence." Another important dimension for the job of tax advisor might be "relationships with clients." Still another might be "relationships with co-workers."

The scientific nature of a BARS is both a strength and a weakness. Behavioral anchors are useful in coaching, but they require considerable time and money to develop. The task cannot be accomplished without the participation of the high-performing job incumbents and their superiors. In addition, since the job analysis performed for one job is not valid for another, the entire process must be repeated for each job.[9]

SUGGESTIONS FOR COACHING
AND COUNSELING

Coaching and counseling employees requires skill. One way of acquiring this skill is to study basic principles, and then practice them on the job. Another way is to attend a training program for coaching and counseling that involves modeling (learning by imitation) and role playing. Here we describe 13 suggestions for effective coaching and counseling, as outlined in Figure 11–3. These suggestions supplement the information about constructive criticism presented in the box on pp. 300–1. If implemented with skill, the suggestions from both sources will improve the chances that coaching and counseling will lead to improved performance.

1. Provide specific feedback. Instead of making generalities about the employee's substandard performance or unacceptable behavior, pinpoint areas of concern. A generality might be, "You just don't seem like you're into this job." A specific in regards to the same problem might be, "You neglect to call in on days that you are going to be out ill." Sometimes, it can be effective to make a generalization (such as not being "into the job") after you first provide several concrete examples.

2. Be honest about the source of your evaluation. Human resource management specialists N. B. Winstanley and Rosemarie Winstanley tell us that the manager should respond to a subordinate's query about how an appraisal conclusion was reached: "State exactly how you did do it. If there is a subjective element in your judgment, don't be defensive about it. Be open, frank, and self-confident enough to say so. If you had to make a comparative judgment, say so. Do not, however, use names. And above all, don't argue, or worse, get personal."[10]

3. Listen actively. Listening is an essential ingredient to any counseling, coaching, or disciplinary session. An active listener tries to grasp both the facts

Figure 11–3 Suggestions for employee coaching and counseling.

---

1. Provide specific feedback.
2. Be honest about the source of your evaluation.
3. Listen actively.
4. Encourage the employee to talk.
5. Give emotional support.
6. Help solve barriers to good performance.
7. Help establish realistic goals.
8. Reflect feelings.
9. Reflect content or meaning.
10. Interpret what is happening.
11. Give some constructive advice.
12. Gain a commitment to change.
13. Allow for modeling of desired performance and behavior.

---

and feelings of what is being said.[11] Observing the employee's nonverbal messages is another part of active listening. It also requires that the manager be patient and not poised for a rebuttal to any difference of opinion between him or her and the subordinate.

Listening is also valuable because it may lead to uncovering outside factors that may be hampering job performance. In one situation a quality-control inspector persisted in allowing too many electronic circuit boards to pass inspection that were in fact defective. Rather than chastising the inspector for persisting in his errors, the manager asked, "Why is it that you cannot make the agreed-upon improvements?" The inspector replied, "My problems with my wife are still making it difficult for me to concentrate." Working through the employee assistance program, a family service agency was identified that proved helpful to the inspector in resolving his marital problems. He was then able to overcome much of his distractibility, thus improving his job performance.

4. *Encourage the employee to talk.* As implied in the above example, part of being an good listener is encouraging the person being counseled, coached, or disciplined to talk. Counseling, in particular, is more effective when the person being counseled does most of the talking. A standard tactic of encouraging conversation is to ask *open-ended questions.* Closed questions do not provide the same opportunity for self-expression and they often elicit short, uninformative answers.

An example of a closed question is, "Was it your fault that our personal computer was stolen?" An open-ended question such as, "What were the circumstances surrounding the loss of the computer?" will encourage the employee to talk more expansively.

5. *Give emotional support.* By being helpful and constructive, the superior provides much needed emotional support to the subordinate whose performance requires improvement. A counseling or coaching session should not be an interrogation. An effective way of providing emotional support is to use positive rather than negative motivators.

6. *Help solve barriers to good performance.* Many problems of poor work performance are caused by factors beyond the employee's control. By showing a willingness to intervene in such problems, the boss displays a helpful and constructive attitude and gives emotional support. One boss helped his advertising and sales promotion manager improve performance through a simple remedy:

> **Marketing manager:** The main job objective that you missed this review period was having the flyers sent out on time to introduce our new line of personal computers. What happened?
>
> **Advertising and sales promotion manager:** As I've hinted at several times in the past, our budget for support help is too tight. It was virtually impossible to have those flyers out on time without more help.
>
> **Marketing manager:** Then I'll get you more help if I have to lend you my own assistant one day per week.

7. *Help establish realistic goals.* An improvement goal that a person cannot reach because of insufficient education, training, or native ability is unrealistic

and usually leads to frustration stemming from failure. A sales manager leaned heavily upon one of his best sales reps to produce almost flawless reports that would be sent to the market research department. After failing to make the improvement desired by the manager for two consecutive review periods, the sales representative commented:

> Sorry, there is just nothing I can do to make my reports any better. One of the reasons I went into sales 20 years ago is that I hate paperwork. I want to cooperate with the market researchers. Let them interview me instead of my doing their work for them. I'm at my best dealing with customers, not doing staff work.

8. *Reflect feelings.* The counseling professional is adept at reflecting feelings. Some reflection of feelings is recommended in a job situation, but too much is inappropriate.[12] Reflection-of-feeling responses typically begin with, "You feel. . ." Suppose you ask the shipping supervisor why a shipment was late. She answers, "Those jerks in manufacturing held me up again." You respond, "You are angry with manufacturing?" The head of shipping, now feeling encouraged, might vent her anger about manufacturing. Your reflection of feelings communicates the fact that you understand the real problem. Because the employee feels understood, she *might* be better motivated to improve.

9. *Reflect content or meaning.* Reflecting feelings deals with the emotional aspects of a person. Reflecting content or meaning deals with the intellectual or cognitive aspects of a person. A good way of reflecting meaning is to rephrase and summarize concisely what the employee is saying. A substandard performer might say, "The reason I've fallen so far behind is that our department has turned into a snakepit. We're being hit right and left with impossible demands. My in-basket is stuffed a foot high." You might respond, "You are falling behind because the workload is so heavy." The employee might then respond something like, "That's exactly what I mean. I'm glad you understand my problem."

10. *Interpret what is happening.* An interpretation given by a manager in a counseling, coaching, or disciplinary session is an explanation of why the employee is acting in a particular manner. It is designed to give the employee insight into the true nature of the problem. For instance, a food service manager might be listening to the problems of a cafeteria manager with regard to cafeteria cleanliness. After a while the food service manager might say, "You're angry and upset with your employees because they don't keep a careful eye on cleanliness. So you avoid dealing with them, and it only makes problems worse." If the manager's diagnosis is correct, an interpretation can be very helpful.

11. *Give some advice.* Too much advice-giving interferes with two-way communication, yet some advice can lead to improved performance. Richard J. Walsh suggests that the manager should assist the subordinate in answering the question, "What can I do about this problem?"[13] Advice in the form of a question or suppositional statement is often effective. One example is, "Could the root of your problem be insufficient planning?"

12. *Gain a commitment to change.* Unless the manager receives a commitment from the subordinate to carry through with the proposed solution to the problem, he or she may tend to continue aimlessly as before. An experienced counselor-manager develops an intuitive feel for when employees are serious about turning around ineffective performance. Two clues that commitment to change is lacking are (a) overagreeing about the need for change, and (b) agreeing to change without display of emotion.

13. *Allow for modeling of desired performance and behavior.* An effective coaching technique is to show the employee by example what constitutes the desired behavior. The service manager alluded to earlier was harsh with customers when under heavy pressure. One way the boss coached the service manager was for the boss to take over the manager's desk during a busy period. The service manager then observed the boss deal tactfully with demanding customers.

DISCIPLINE AND PERFORMANCE IMPROVEMENT

The underlying assumption in counseling and coaching is that the organization is willing to provide assistance to an employee who wants to remain a member of the firm. Counseling and coaching are thus adjuncts to **corrective discipline,** any type of discipline that emphasizes improving employee behavior. In corrective discipline, employees are informed that their behavior is unacceptable and that corrections must be made if they want to stay with the firm. Offenses such as below-standard job performance, excessive absenteeism, tardiness, and gambling on company premises usually call for this type of discipline. We describe two types of corrective discipline, progressive discipline and positive discipline. We then describe **summary discipline,** an approach used for major violations of company policy or the law.

Progressive Discipline (The Traditional Approach)

Progressive discipline is the administering of punishments in increasing order of severity until the person being disciplined improves or is terminated. Many labor-management agreements call for progressive discipline, and most other organizations also practice this commonsense approach to improving substandard performance. Progressive discipline proceeds in five steps:

Step 1: Counsel the employee about the problem.

Step 2: Oral warning—the employee is told that if the problem continues more severe penalties will be in order.

Step 3: Written warning—if a second violation occurs, the manager again counsels the employee but notes that a written violation will be entered in his or her file. Written notice may also be given of future sanctions (organizational punishments).

Step 4: Suspension or disciplinary layoff—if another violation occurs, or substandard performance persists, the employee is suspended without pay or given a disciplinary layoff.

Step 5: Discharge—since the employee has been fairly warned, but still does not improve, the employee is terminated.

Although progressive discipline seems fair, its effectiveness in improving performance has been seriously questioned. A representative indictment of progressive discipline appeared in *Harvard Business Review.* The report concluded that few organizational systems are more accepted yet less productive than the traditional progressive discipline. A major problem is that progressive discipline prevents self-discipline. Consider this case history of progressive discipline:[14]

> In a plant of a major food-processing company, disciplinary problems became so severe that in a space of nine months, managers fired 58 of the 210 employees. Supervisors eagerly wrote up infractions with the intent of running off "troublemakers." The atmosphere turned poisonous; obscene messages began appearing in the plant's products.

Positive Discipline (Motivating Employees to Improve Performance)

Positive discipline is an approach to improving substandard performance and behavior that emphasizes coaching, individual responsibility, and a mature problem-solving method.[15] Progressive discipline, in contrast, places more emphasis on punishment. The control model for coaching, counseling, and disciplining incorporates positive discipline.

Positive discipline focuses on motivating employees to improve performance, rather than punishing them for poor performance. Written and verbal warnings are replaced with:[16]

> Discussions and written reminders of employee responsibility. The term *reminder* is used in preference to *warning.*
> The employee's agreement to maintain certain standards of performance and behavior.
> A paid day off as the final step in the disciplinary process.

The cornerstone of positive discipline is the **decision-making leave,** a paid one-day suspension to help the employee think through the disciplinary problem. If preliminary measures fail, the employee is given one day off with full pay. During the time off the employee is supposed to decide to remain on the job and meet performance standards, or resign. If the employee decides to remain with the firm, the supervisor helps that person develop improvement goals and action plans. The supervisor encourages the employee, but makes it clear that failure to reach goals will result in termination.

Many managers are naturally skeptical about the merits of a paid suspension for ineffective performance, yet the system appears to be working. A study conducted in the Tampa Electric Company found that decision-making leaves reduce the need for employees to get even with the organization. Also, employees did not abuse the system in an attempt to gain a "free day off." (One explanation here is that a one-day suspension, even with pay, would still be perceived as a punishment by most employees.) Tangible results of the positive discipline program included fewer terminations, less absenteeism, and virtually no formal employee complaints.[17]

Summary Discipline

Summary discipline is not as humanitarian as either progressive or positive discipline. It involves the immediate discharge of an employee for having committed a major offense. A labor relations official at Detroit Edison observes: "Offenses such as theft, physically assaulting a supervisor, and gross insubordination usually warrant immediate discharge regardless of the employee's previous work record."[18] In many companies, receiving kickbacks from suppliers is grounds for summary discipline.

Summary discipline can be used only when the violation is clear-cut, and ample evidence exists that the violation took place. If this is not the case, the employee can sue for **wrongful discharge,** the firing of an employee for arbitrary or unfair reasons. In recent years, many employers have been sued for wrongfully discharging employees. Many employees—acting alone, or assisted by their unions—have been awarded damages in these cases.[19]

COACHING AND COUNSELING SUBSTANCE ABUSERS

Alcoholism and drug abuse among employees and managers constitute a significant management problem. At least 10 percent of the workforce at any given time experiences lowered job performance because of **substance abuse,** the overuse of any substance that enters the bloodstream.[20] Substance abuse is usually associated with alcohol, prescription drugs, and illegal drugs. Yet it can also include the abuse of tobacco, coffee, soft drinks, nonnutritional food substances, and vaporous fluids. The manager plays an active role in controlling substance abuse when he or she follows the control model described in this chapter.

Using the Control Model with Substance Abusers

Our recommended procedure for turning around the employee substance abuser stems directly from the guidelines contained in the control model in Figure 11–1. To use the control model, it is necessary for the manager to recognize common symptoms of substance abuse. These symptoms are summarized in Figure 11–4.

Figure 11–4 Symptoms of alcohol and drug abuse.

Alcohol Abuse	Drug Abuse
Sudden decrease in performance	Sudden decrease in performance
Decreased mental alertness	Decreased mental alertness
Long lunch hours, tardiness	Employee hiding out on premises
Unexplained absences from work	Unexplained absences from work
Altered gait	Dilated pupils
Slurred speech	Unusual bursts of energy and excitement
Frequent use of breath freshener	Prolonged and serious lethargy
Depressed mood	Unexplainable states of apathy or elation
Trembling of hands and body	Errors in judgment and concentration
Errors in judgment and concentration	Urgent financial problems
Financial problems	Sleepy appearance to eyes
Sleepy appearance to eyes	Frequent sniffing
Denial of drinking problem	Appearance of being detached from reality
Lost time due to physical illness	Elaborate alibis for work deficiencies
Elaborate alibis for work deficiencies	

Assume that Ralph, an advertising account executive, uses cocaine off the job, and sometimes during working hours. Janet, his immediate superior, observes that Ralph's performance is suffering. He is often late with work for clients, and he sometimes appears to be in a frenzied, hyperactive state. Janet thus *detects* the need for counseling. Janet *confronts* Ralph about the problem: "The way you've been acting lately, I can't trust you with important work for clients. When you are in a frenzied state, you make serious errors, such as calling a client product by the wrong name. Go get help from the employee assistance program, or I will have to recommend severe disciplinary procedures."

Janet and Ralph then jointly *set the goal* of Ralph improving his concentration on work within 15 days. The two then develop an *action plan* whereby Ralph gets help with his drug abuse problem through an EAP the agency uses. (The agency is not big enough to have its own EAP, so it uses an EAP shared by many firms in the area.) The action plan is *implemented* by Ralph working closely with a drug counselor.

A *review of progress* is made weekly. Ralph has controlled his cocaine habit to the point that he does not display drug-related symptoms on the job, and his performance improves. Janet therefore gives Ralph encouragement and support for his progress. If at any point Ralph again shows signs of drug abuse on the job, Janet will *repeat the cycle*.

Drug and Alcohol Testing of Present Employees

Assume that the advertising agency described above had a policy of terminating any employee known to use illegal drugs. Janet would then have been justified in referring Ralph for drug testing. His job performance was suffering, and she suspected cocaine use. However, referring an employee for drug testing is fraught with difficulty. Some people regard the testing of employees as a legitimate employment practice. Others regard such testing as a violation of civil liberties and an indignity. Another part of the controversy is that drug testing is not 100 percent reliable. Also, the amount of drugs in the bloodstream required to impair job performance is not known precisely.

The legally soundest policy about alcohol and drug abuse is to focus on job performance, not the use of alcohol or drugs themselves. A labor-relations attorney notes that the precise legal status of drug and alcohol testing remains undefined. An employer's use of testing has many potential liabilities. Random drug or alcohol testing invades personal privacy too far to be condoned. Yet drug testing of employees in occupations with high potential for serious accidents, such as pilots, bus drivers, and window washers, is defensible. Also, few legal objections have been voiced against the drug testing of job applicants.[21]

OUTPLACEMENT: COUNSELING AND COACHING SURPLUS EMPLOYEES

Another important form of job counseling and coaching is used when employees are considered surplus for any reason but summary discipline. About two-thirds of large firms offer some form of **outplacement,** company-sponsored programs to minimize the personal and organizational trauma associated with job loss.[22] The large number of mergers and acquisitions in recent years has spurred a rapid growth in outplacement services. These programs are administered by in-company specialists and by outside consultants.

Key Elements in an Outplacement Program

Programs vary from one firm to another, but usually have three components. First is personal evaluation, whereby outplaced employees obtain a clear evaluation of themselves. Using tests, interviews, and other diagnostic procedures, outplacement counselors identify the counselee's strengths and weaknesses. Former employees are also taught to identify their transferable skills and professional goals, so they can seek positions that will further their careers.

Second is counseling and coaching about such topics as resume writing, job search techniques, using contacts to advantage, and interview techniques (see Chapter 17). When the job search lingers on, counselees are provided with additional help, including gentle prodding to persist in the job search.

Third is institutional support in the form of a base of operations for conducting the job search. Included here are office space, telephones, clerical support, and photocopying privileges. Fourth is emotional support, in the form of job seekers working together to help each other find a job. These employees form their own support groups, discuss the job market, share tips, and bolster each others' egos.[23]

Evaluation of Outplacement

On balance, outplacement services are well received by employees and regarded as worthwhile by employers. One study showed that relatively new executives were much more likely to value the help of outplacement services than were long-term executives.[24] Outplacement services can be cost-effective because they often cut the time required for a successful job search in half. As a result, less money is required for unemployment compensation and separation payments. Outplacement also improves morale and is better for the company image than laying off large numbers of people without offering them help.

A notable criticism of outplacement services is that they place too much emphasis on the marketing of employees. Using highly polished techniques, substandard employees are marketed into positions they are not qualified to fill. (Remember, however, that not all outplaced employees are poor performers. They may be declared surplus because of a merger or for political reasons.) Also, employers may be deceived into believing that certain applicants are more qualified than they are. Often this process leads to putting the same employees in a situation where they will once again be forced to look for new employment.[25] And who wants to be outplaced more than once in a career?

Summary of Key Points

☐ Coaching and counseling are used to improve the performance of both good performers and substandard performers. Coaching helps employees grow and improve by providing suggestions and encouragement. Counseling serves a similar purpose but is more concerned with feelings than action, and focuses more on the long range.

☐ A recommended approach for coaching, counseling, and disciplining employees is a control model, consisting of seven steps: (1) establish performance standards, (2) detect need for coaching or counseling, (3) confront or discuss need for improvement, (4) set improvement goals, (5) develop and implement action plan, (6) review progress, and (7) repeat the cycle if necessary.

☐ Constructively criticizing subordinates is a complex skill that may require an understanding of the principles involved and sometimes special training. The manager needs special assistance if inadequate performance is caused by deep-seated personal problems such as alcohol, drugs, and family life.

☐ A substantial portion of counseling and coaching takes place in the context of performance appraisal—a formal system of both evaluating employee performance and conveying this evaluation to the employee. Behaviorally Anchored Rating Scales (BARS) are well suited for coaching employees because they pinpoint work activities that need improvement.

☐ Coaching and counseling can be improved by following these suggestions:

1. Provide specific feedback.
2. Be honest about the source of your evaluation.
3. Listen actively.
4. Encourage the employee to talk.
5. Give emotional support.

6. Help solve barriers to good performance.
7. Help establish realistic goals.
8. Reflect feelings.
9. Reflect content or meaning.

10. Interpret what is happening.
11. Give some constructive advice.
12. Gain a commitment to change.
13. Allow for modeling of desired performance and behavior.

☐ Counseling and coaching are also used in corrective discipline. One form of corrective discipline is progressive discipline, administering punishments in increasing order of severity until the person being disciplined improves or is terminated. Positive discipline, a newer form, emphasizes coaching and individual responsibility. It features a decision-making leave—a paid one-day suspension to help the employee decide about his or her future performance. Summary discipline is the immediate discharge of an employee for a major offense, and does not involve coaching and counseling.

☐ Coaching and counseling substance abusers is also part of a manager's job. A recommended approach is to follow the control model, with an emphasis on using an employee assistance program as an action plan. Current legal opinion is to regard substance abuse as a management concern primarily when the abuse lowers job performance. Drug testing of current employees must therefore be limited to exceptional situations, such as those employees whose jobs can potentially endanger the lives of others.

☐ Outplacement services are company-sponsored programs to minimize the personal and organizational trauma associated with job loss. "Outplaced" employees can be substandard performers or those who are declared surplus for other reasons. Outplacement programs usually involve four types of activities: personal evaluation, counseling and coaching about job finding, institutional support such as office space, and emotional support.

Questions and Activities

1. In what way does the perspective of this chapter differ from the perspective of all previous chapters?

2. What kind of evidence should a manager have before confronting an employee about poor performance?

3. Which leadership style described in Chapter 8 do you think would include ample coaching and counseling? Explain your answer.

4. It has been said that an effective supervisor is a "coach," not a "player." What do you think this statement means?

5. Show how you would use the control model to improve the job performance of a sales representative who disliked making cold (unsolicited) sales calls.

6. Why is it important to include coaching and counseling in a performance appraisal?

7. Identify five offenses by a worker at any level that you think require summary discipline.

8. What is your opinion about the risk that employees might take advantage of a decision-making leave just to get a day off with pay?

9. What traits and characteristics described in the leadership chapter do you think would tend to help a manager be a good coach?

10. Ask any experienced manager his or her opinion about the importance of coaching and counseling in a manager's job. Be prepared to discuss your findings in class.

A Human Relations Case

THE HOSTILE LOSS-PREVENTION MANAGER

Mark Gulden, the zone loss-prevention manager (LPM) at Keystone Stores, prided himself on his managerial skill. As he explained to the case researcher, "I'm in complete control all the time. And control is the name of the game in the loss-prevention field. Inventory shrinkage is a big problem with us. We therefore have to keep an accurate account of our inventory. If a piece of merchandise has not been sold, and it is not on the shelf or in the storeroom, we can assume that it's been stolen."

"If I find an audit coming back from one of my stores, I demand an answer right away. And I don't pussyfoot. I let the local LPM know right away that a mistake has been made that must be corrected. My LPMS respect me for my toughness as a manager."

Later, the case researcher spoke to several of the loss-prevention managers to learn of their perspective on the working relationship between the LPMs and their zone manager. Bud, a 24-year-old man in charge of security at the highest volume store in his zone, offered these observations:

"I'm afraid for Mark Gulden. No doubt in my mind he's a Type A personality who is headed for an early heart attack. He takes his job too seriously. If Gulden finds one little error, he goes bananas. Sometimes he swears at me as if I have stolen some missing merchandise. I don't take it personally. I guess it's just his way. But overall I think Gulden gets the job done. No big complaint on my part."

Melissa, an LPM at another store in the zone, had this view of her boss, Mark Gulden:

"So long as this is confidential, I can tell you with a straight face that the man is a lunatic. When things are going fine, he's fine. But when he sees a problem, he flies off the handle. He's a fire-spitting dragon who spits too much fire at the wrong people. Some days he swears at me over the phone. It ruins my whole day. In fact, I've got to do something about the problem soon. But I wouldn't want to lose my job over complaining to my boss."

1. How should Melissa deal with this problem?
2. Should Bud speak to Mark about Mark's method of criticizing him?
3. What type of coaching should Mark Gulden be receiving from his boss?
4. Which principles of constructive criticism is Mark violating?

A Human Relations Incident

WHO ARE YOU TO COACH ME?

Mindi Gomez, a claims examiner for Century Insurance Corporation, was at her office one Friday afternoon, taking care of paperwork. Her paperwork load had increased substantially in recent weeks because of a sudden surge in the claims workload. While she was preparing a claims report on her most recent investigation, Jim Barone, her claims manager, walked over to her desk.

"Busy week, Mindi?" he asked rhetorically. "I notice you've been churning out a lot of claims reports lately. I must say the volume of your work is certainly above average."

"I take it then that you are pleased with my output?" asked Mindi. "I certainly have been putting in long work weeks lately."

"I can't say that I am entirely pleased with your work, Mindi," said Jim. "Your work is getting a little sloppy. You are missing out on so many important details that I think the Century is giving away too much money to policyholders. In fact, I don't think that your recent work has been very professional."

With an angered expression, Mindi commented: "No offense, Jim. But are you really in a position to coach me on how to do a good job on preparing a claims report? I have a specialized degree in insurance. And I know that you don't even have much experience as a claims examiner."

"What you say is irrelevant to the fact that I'm the boss, and that gives me the right to coach you. If you can't accept this basic fact of business life, I may have to initiate disciplinary proceedings."

Mindi thought to herself, "Oops, I may have put my foot in a bucket."

1. Does Jim have a right to coach Mindi?
2. How would you evaluate Jim's approach to coaching Mindi?
3. What do you think of Mindi's response to Jim?

A Human Relations Exercise

THE COUNSELING AND COACHING ACCEPTABILITY CHECKLIST

Employees vary considerably in what they consider to be acceptable areas for counseling and coaching on the job. Complete the following brief questionnaire, indicating whether you consider each statement to be a warranted topic for counseling and coaching by a boss. Later, results for the entire class can be tabulated. Conclusions can then be drawn about definite trends revealed by the data.

Behavior	Okay for boss to counsel or coach employee about this matter	Not okay for boss to counsel or coach about this matter
1. Employee consistently arrives at work two minutes late.	———	———
2. Employee chews garlic on the job.	———	———
3. Male employee wears dress to work.	———	———
4. Female employee wears man's suit to work.	———	———
5. Employee takes home about two ball point pens per week.	———	———
6. Employee works on own income tax return during slow period at work.	———	———
7. Stockbroker reads *Wall Street Journal* during office hours.	———	———
8. High-performing employee stays home from work on birthday and offers no other excuse for absence.	———	———
9. Employee falls asleep once during staff meeting.	———	———
10. Employee joins Communist Party.	———	———
11. While in the office, employee brags about the use of competitive product.	———	———
12. Employee has strong body odor.	———	———

Notes

1. Lynn McFarlane Shore and Arvid J. Bloom, "Developing Employees Through Coaching and Career Management," *Personnel*, August 1986, p. 34.
2. Richard V. Concillo, "Will Coaching Pay Off?" *Management Solutions*, September 1986, pp. 20–21.
3. Richard G. Martin, "Five Principles of Corrective Disciplinary Action," *Supervisory Management*, January 1978, p. 24.
4. Marcia Ann Pulich, "What to Do with Incompetent Employees," *Supervisory Management*, March 1986, pp. 14–16.
5. Ibid., p. 15.
6. Peter W. Dorfman, Walter G. Stephan, and John Loveland, "Performance Appraisal Behaviors: Supervisor Perceptions and Subordinate Reactions," *Personnel Psychology*, Autumn, 1986, pp. 579–580.
7. A survey of performance appraisal techniques is found in Hermine Zagat Levine, "Performance Appraisals at Work," *Personnel*, June 1986, pp. 63–71.

8. Uco Wiersma and Gary P. Latham, "The Practicality of Behavioral Observation Scales, Behavioral Expectation Scales, and Trait Scales," *Personnel Psychology*, Autumn 1986, pp. 619–628; Craig Eric Schneier and Richard W. Beatty, "Developing Behaviorally Anchored Rating Scales (BARS)," *Personnel Administrator*, August 1979, pp. 59–68.

9. J. Peter Graves, "Let's Put Appraisal Back in Performance Appraisal: Part I," *Personnel Journal*, November 1982, p. 848.

10. N. B. Winstanley and Rosemarie Winstanley, "Feedback: Discussing the Appraisal and Merit Increase," unpublished brochure, Rochester Institute of Technology, revised 1987, p. 5.

11. Gary Dessler, *Personnel Management: Modern Concepts and Techniques* (Reston, VA: Reston Publishing, 1978), p. 327.

12. Suggestions 8 and 9 are based on Richard J. Walsh, "Ten Basic Counseling Skills," *Supervisory Management*, July 1977, pp. 2–9.

13. Ibid., p. 9.

14. David N. Campbell, R. L. Fleming, and Richard C. Grote, "Discipline without Punishment—At Last," *Harvard Business Review*, July–August 1985, p. 163.

15. Alan W. Bryant Jr., "Replacing Punitive Discipline with a Positive Approach," *Personnel Administrator*, February 1984, p. 79.

16. "Positive Discipline: Motivating Employees to Improve Performance," *Business Update*, vol. 1, Issue 9, 1985, p. 15.

17. Campbell, Fleming, and Grote, "Discipline without Punishment," pp. 163, 170.

18. Martin, "Five Principles of Corrective Disciplinary Action," p. 24.

19. David A. Bradshaw and Linda Van Winkle Deacon, "Wrongful Discharge: The Tip of the Iceberg?" *Personnel Administrator*, November 1985, pp. 74–76.

20. Roger K. Good, "A Critique of Three Corporate Drug Abuse Policies," *Personnel Journal*, February 1986, p. 96.

21. Rusch O. Dees, "Testing for Drugs and Alcohol: Proceed with Caution," *Personnel*, September 1986, p. 54.

22. Hermine Zagat Levine, "Outplacement and Severance Pay Practices," *Personnel*, September 1985, p. 13.

23. "Outplacement Counseling Services," *Research Institute Personal Report for the Executive*, January 21, 1986, p. 5.

24. William E. Fulmer, "Outplacement Services: A View from the Top," *Personnel*, September 1985, p. 19.

25. Joel A. Bearak, "Termination Made Easier: Is Outplacement Really the Answer?" *Personnel Administrator*, April 1982, p. 71.

Suggested Reading

ANGAROLA, ROBERT J. "Drug Testing in the Workplace: Is It Legal?" *Personnel Administrator*, September 1985, pp. 79–89.

ARGYRIS, CHRIS. "Skilled Incompetence." *Harvard Business Review*, September–October 1986, pp. 74–79.

BENSINGER, ANN, and PILKINGTON, CHARLES F. "Treating Chemically Dependent Employees in a Non-Hospital Setting." *Personnel Administrator*, August 1985, pp. 45–52.

BRAMMER, LAWRENCE M., and HUMBERGER, FRANK E. *Outplacement and Inplacement Counseling*. Englewood Cliffs, NJ: Prentice Hall, 1984.

DEETS, NORMAN R., and TYLER, D. TIMOTHY. "How Xerox Improved Its Performance Appraisals." *Personnel Journal*, April 1986, pp. 50–52.

FRIEDMAN, MARTIN G. "10 Steps to Objective Appraisals." *Personnel Journal*, June 1986, pp. 66–71.

KLEIN, ALFRED. "Employees Under the Influence—Outside the Law?" *Personnel Journal*, September 1986, pp. 56–63.

LOWE, TERRY R. "8 Ways to Ruin a Performance Review," *Personnel Journal*, January 1986, pp. 60–62.

MATEJKA, J. KENNETH, ASHWORTH, D. NEIL, and DODD-MCCUE, DIANE. "Managing Difficult Employees: Challenge or Curse?" *Personnel*, July 1986, pp. 43–46.

MCCONNELL, PATRICK L. "Is Your Discipline Process the Victim of RED Tape?" *Personnel Journal*, March 1986, pp. 64–71.

SHAIN, MARTIN, SUURVALI, HELEN, and BOUTILIER, MARIE. *Healthier Workers: The Role of Health Promotion and Employee Assistance Programs.* Lexington, MA: D.C. Heath/Lexington Books, 1986.

Interpersonal Skill Training

LEARNING OBJECTIVES
*After reading and studying this chapter
and doing the exercises, you should be
able to*

1. Pinpoint the conditions under which interpersonal skill training will be effective in
   organizations.

2. Understand how interactive video is used for interpersonal skill training.

3. Explain how assertiveness training (AT) can improve
   your interpersonal effectiveness.

4. Identify and explain the key concepts in transactional analysis (TA).

5. Describe how the assessment center method can be used to
   improve interpersonal skills.

6. Present an overview of the nature of encounter groups.

Karl, a paramedic, was being considered for promotion to supervisor. So far, Karl had not been informed of this development. Roger, Karl's supervisor, was discussing his pending promotion with his boss and the personnel director. Roger spoke first: "I am very much in Karl's corner. But the guy is just not ready for supervisory responsibility. He's a fine paramedic, and he's saved many lives. But he gets under people's skin. Time and time again, he rubs people the wrong way."

"I wonder if there's a training program we can send Karl to that would help smooth out his rough edges?"

Scenarios similar to the one above take place so often that many training programs have been developed to help workers improve their effectiveness in dealing with people. Often these activities are referred to as human relations training. Our concern in this chapter is with training programs designed specifically to improve effectiveness in dealing with others. We therefore refer to them as **interpersonal skill training,** the teaching of skills in dealing with others so the skills can be put into practice.

Other chapters in this book describe activities that can enhance interpersonal skills, such as resolving conflict and listening. Here we describe several formal training programs to achieve interpersonal effectiveness. Such programs are more likely to be successful when they are carefully planned and designed.

FRAMEWORK FOR INTERPERSONAL SKILL TRAINING

Interpersonal skill training should proceed in a systematic manner that allows for correction and renewal. A model to achieve these ends is presented in Figure 12–1. The model states that you first identify what conditions need improvement, select an appropriate training program, allow for practice, and then apply the skill.

Identification of Individual and Organizational Needs

Before embarking upon any training program, it is important to identify what kinds of training are needed. Training of individuals should be based upon their **developmental needs,** the specific areas in which a person needs improvement.

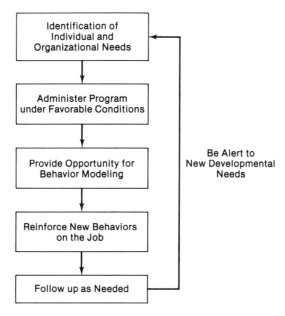

Figure 12–1   Framework for interpersonal skill training.

For instance, some people may be too shy, some too abrasive, and some may not give others the encouragement they need. Ideally, a person's developmental needs should influence what particular interpersonal skill training program he or she attends.

Organizational requirements also weigh heavily in the choice of a program for improving relations effectiveness. In one firm, middle managers might be practicing discrimination against women. To help remedy this situation, a program of management awareness training about sexism might be selected. Another firm might conclude from a human resources forecast that much of its future workforce will be under age 30. Encounter group meetings might be used to help managers become more sensitive to the demands of younger workers.

Administer Program under Favorable Conditions

Under the appropriate conditions, most human relations training programs can contribute to individual and organizational effectiveness. Under the wrong conditions, the program might even be harmful. In general, the program must be technically sound, the participants must have the capacity and willingness to change, and the organization must welcome the changes.

To determine whether a given program of interpersonal skills will be effective, answers should be sought to questions such as these:

1. Does the participant have the motivation and problem-solving ability to benefit from the program?
2. Is the participant involved sufficiently in the job to benefit from training?[1]
3. Is the program tied to the development needs of the participant?
4. Is the program tied to the objectives of the organization?
5. Will the organization provide the participant the opportunity to practice the new skills learned in the program?

Allow for Behavior Modeling

A standard way of learning interpersonal skills is to first observe somebody practicing them correctly and then to imitate or *model* that person. The process is similar to learning an athletic move or dance step by observing a competent performer. Modeling has been used effectively to train sales representatives in how to handle customer complaints. First, they observe an effective model handle such as problem situation in a film. Next, they role-play the constructive behavior shown by the model. For instance, one person would role-play the irate customer, while the other assumes the role of the sales rep handling the complaint.

Although behavior modeling usually leads to learning, it less frequently leads to improvement in actual job performance.[2] A challenge to the trainer and the manager, therefore, is to identify skills that are truly associated with good performance. For instance, teaching a sales rep to smile will not improve job performance unless smiling at customers actually leads to more sales.

Reinforce New Behaviors

If new learning is not practiced and reinforced, it will be forgotten. A case in point would be the situation of Derek, a chemist who attends an assertiveness training workshop. By the end of the workshop, Derek says to himself, "I agree with everything I've heard. I should learn to express my feelings in a positive, forthright manner. That way people won't take such advantage of me."

Back on the job, he receives no encouragement for attempting to be more assertive. He says to his boss, "My opinion as a chemist is that we cannot properly perform these experiments unless we purchase the equipment I recommended." His boss replies, "Accept the working conditions as they are or we will find somebody else to do your job. There are loads of good chemists out looking for work these days." After one or two more episodes like this, Derek decides to discontinue his attempts at being more assertive on the job.

Follow Up as Needed

A common failing of most interpersonal skill training programs is that they are "one-shot affairs." A person attends the program, perhaps tries out the new skills, and after a while returns to his or her former ways of doing things. A convenient way of circumventing this problem is for the organization to sponsor periodic "refresher" or "reminder" courses.

Be Alert to New Developmental Needs

As new skills are developed, they often create the need for the development of additional skills. Irma, a first-level supervisor, might attend a transactional analysis workshop. She becomes more proficient at complimenting others and making them feel good. Because of this skill her subordinates now feel more comfortable in coming to her for help with work problems. Irma decides that she could benefit from a developmental program that would enhance her skills in coaching and counseling subordinates. As people improve their interpersonal skills, they often begin to identify areas for growth.

INTERACTIVE VIDEO FOR INTERPERSONAL SKILL TRAINING

A new technique for interpersonal skill training is the **interactive video,** a computer-assisted video system in which the trainee interacts with the training material. Interactive video is an extension of computer-based training that has been widely used to teach factual material. Interactive video appears to have promise for teaching interpersonal skills because the behavior of the actors on the screen is contingent upon the trainee's responses. To appreciate the possibilities of interactive video, it is necessary to visualize its hardware and software.

Interactive Video Hardware

The hardware for interactive video includes five elements, as illustrated in Figure 12–2: (1) TV monitor; (2) laser videodisc player, similar to the ones available for home stereos; (3) laser disc interface—the central component in an interactive video system (The interface fits into a slot of the microcomputer. It provides total user control of the videodisc player through a computer program executed on the computer.); (4) a computer—mainframe, mini, or micro; (5) an input-output device such as a touch screen, mouse, or keyboard (voice commands may be forthcoming).[3]

Interactive Video Software

The software for interactive video includes filming the training scenarios, and is thus complex and imaginative. Assume that an interactive video system were developed to help people deal effectively with threats of sexual harassment. The trainee observes the screen. One person says to another across the desk, "I think you are dressed very sexy today. You also look very sexy."

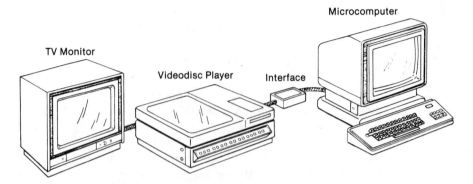

Figure 12–2 Hardware required for interactive video.

SOURCE: Mary Jane Ruhl and Keith Atkinson, "Interactive Video Training: One Step Beyond," *Personnel Administrator*, October 1986, p. 70. Used with permission.

The following question flashes on the screen: Which of the two following statements should the woman make?

"Well thank you, that is a nice compliment."

"That's strange. I don't feel sexy today, and I have no intention of dressing sexy. I'm here to conduct business."

If the trainee selects the second alternative, the man responds, "Okay, here are the figures I want you to review for me." If the trainee selects the first response, the man in the film responds, "I'm glad you took it as a compliment. Why don't we have dinner together after work?"

The effectiveness of an interactive video system depends upon creating plausible scenarios to illustrate what happens when the trainee makes a particular response. The different scenarios that surface on the screen when different responses are made are the *branches*, as illustrated above. The cycle for creating an interactive video beings with organizing a *storyboard*. Then the developer films the video and constructs the videodisc. Finally, the software is developed for graphics overlay and program control.[4]

The software or "courseware" often has to be tailor-made for a particular organization, and may take six months to develop. An interactive video training program is costly. Yet, the developers of these systems contend that the cost is less than that required for hiring classroom trainers. Do you think interacting with a videodisc is as effective as interacting with a live instructor?

ASSERTIVENESS TRAINING

A widely used method of improving interpersonal skills is **assertiveness training (AT).** AT is a self-improvement training program that teaches people to express their feelings and act with an appropriate degree of openness and candor. The method is derived from a technique of psychotherapy, and is a by-product of the human potential movement. The goals of assertiveness training include (1) know how you feel, (2) say what you want, (3) get what you want, and (4) overcome anxiety about confronting others.

Passive, Aggressive, and Assertive Behaviors

The true goal of assertiveness is to help an individual make a clear statement of what he or she wants, or how he or she feels in a given situation, without being abusive or obnoxious. It is also implied that the individual will learn to avoid the passive mode of suppressing feelings and actions. From another perspective, the nonassertive (passive) individual is stepped on and the aggressive person steps on others, whereas the assertive person deals with a problem in a mature and explicit manner. A frequent situation in organizational life—that of being appointed to a committee—can be used to illustrate these differences.

> Opening his morning mail, project manager Lloyd notices a letter from another project manager, which says in part: "Congratulations, you have been appointed area captain to collect money for the Veterans of Foreign Wars. You will find it both an honor and a privilege to serve your country in this manner."

Lloyd is already heavily committed to community activities, including serving as a precinct worker in upcoming elections. He can respond in three different ways:

> *Passive behavior:* Lloyd does nothing and awaits further instructions. He is sim-mering with anger, but grits his teeth and hopes that the assignment will not be as time-consuming as he now estimates.
>
> *Aggressive behavior:* Lloyd grabs the phone, calls the other project manager, and says, "Who do you think you are assigning me to your cockamamie committee? When I want to be on a committee, I'll volunteer."
>
> *Assertive behavior:* Lloyd calls the other project manager and says, "I appreciate your thinking of me in connection with your committee. But I choose not to serve. Good luck in finding another captain."

General Methods of Assertiveness Training

Although the specific content and format of assertiveness training programs differ, they concentrate on the development of the following kinds of skills.[5]

- The ability to cope with manipulation and criticism without responding in a like manner or withdrawing in fright with hurt feelings, guilt or shame, or the intention of later counterattack.
- The ability to make requests and state points of view in a confident, straightforward manner, without becoming pushy, annoyed, or angry.
- The ability to cooperate with others in solving problems in an adult manner, so that both parties are satisfied.

- How to manage others without being aggressive or manipulative.
- Resolving conflict through assertive behavior.

In order to acquire these skills, AT makes extensive use of role plays, role reversal, and modeling—much like many other interpersonal skill training programs. *Role plays* are used to create a situation in which the participants act out an assertive behavior they think would make them effective in a similar real-life situation. One example would be role playing being interviewed for a job. You want the job, but you don't want to appear too desperate or too laid back. Role playing is helpful because it give participants new experiences to add to their repertoire that can be drawn upon later.

Role reversal is a process whereby one person pretends he or she is the adversary of the person who is acting assertively. (It is therefore a special type of role playing.) In this way the first person experiences what it is like to have to deal with an assertive person. Later, the two people reverse roles: The adversary becomes the assertive person and the assertive person becomes the adversary.

Modeling is an essential part of AT. Participants in the training program are given the opportunity to observe a person who displays assertive behavior. The model may be physically present or observed on a videotape.

Three Exercises for Developing Assertion Skills

So far we have described the general concepts underlying AT and the general exercises used in most AT programs. Here we look at three specific exercises designed to improve your assertion skills. You are encouraged to try them to develop a better understanding of how AT can lead to constructive change.

Exercise A: Learning the steps to assertion. Some AT workshops begin by asking participants to engage in self-examination about their current level of assertiveness. The self-examination raises your level of awareness about your specific developmental needs. Here is one such AT self-examination exercise:[6]

Steps to Assertion: A Checklist

1. Clarify the situation and focus on the issue. What is my goal? What exactly do I want to accomplish?
2. How will assertive behavior on my part help me accomplish my goal?
3. What would I usually do to avoid asserting myself in this situation?
4. Why would I want to give that up and assert myself instead?
5. What might be stopping me from asserting myself?
   a. Am I holding on to irrational beliefs? If so, what are they?
   b. How can I replace these irrational beliefs with rational ones?
   c. (For women only) Have I, as a woman, been taught to behave in ways that make it difficult for me to act assertively in the present situation? What ways? How can I overcome this?

   d. What are my rights in this situation? (State them clearly.) Do these rights justify turning my back on my conditioning?
6. Am I anxious about asserting myself? What techniques can I use to reduce my anxiety?
7. Have I done my homework? Do I have the information I need to go ahead and act?
8. Can I
   a. Let the other person know I hear and understand him/her?
   b. Let the other person know how I feel?
   c. Tell him/her what I want?

Exercise B: Fogging. This subtle technique provides insight into the nature of assertiveness training. In **fogging, you respond to manipulative criticism as if you were a fog bank.** The criticism just passes through like a punch into a fog. You are thus virtually unaffected by the criticism, and you will be able to get across your point. The learner is instructed to offer no resistance to the criticism.[7] Fogging is usually learned through the standard techniques of role playing, role reversal, and modeling. Here are three samples of fogging dialogue used in an AT program:

Critic: I see that you are as sloppy looking as usual.

Learner: That's right. I look the same today as I usually do.

Critic: How atrocious! You made five errors in preparing that corporate tax return.

Learner: That's true. I counted the errors you red circled. There were exactly five.

Critic: Have you ever thought of giving up your career and dropping out of college to become a beachcomber?

Learner: I could see some merit in dropping out of college and becoming a beachcomber.

Exercise C: Rehearsal. Another popular training exercise to improve your assertion skills is to rehearse an assertive response to an anxiety-provoking situation. By imagining how you would handle them, you should increase your skill in handling similar situations in real life. This time, imagine you are in the AT program, and rehearse your response to these two scenarios:

1. You are waiting in line at a bank to cash a check, and you are getting close to being late for an important appointment. An angry looking man, weighing about 250 pounds, steps in ahead of you.
2. You diligently prepare a term paper. With considerable pride, you submit your report. It is returned one week later with a grade of "D," and the comments, "Incoherent piece of trash, shows almost no effort."

On balance, AT has proved to be a sensible and effective way of improving an important aspect of interpersonal relations—getting what you want without being too pushy, or failing to get what you want because you are too passive.

Part of AT's popularity can be attributed to its simplicity. Criticisms of AT center around two points. First, many graduates of AT programs become "pains in the neck" who push for demands deemed inappropriate by the organization. A case in point is that of a middle manager who hounded his company to reimburse him for a suit he lost on a business trip. Second, many graduates wind up being assertive about trivial things while remaining unchanged in more important areas.

TRANSACTIONAL ANALYSIS TRAINING

Another notable interpersonal skill training program is **transactional analysis (TA),** a technique for improving interpersonal relationships that focuses on the transactions between people. A general goal of transactional analysis is to help people relate to each other in a mature, adult manner, thus easing tension and getting important things accomplished. An overview of key TA concepts is necessary to understand how TA can be applied to making you more effective on the job.[8]

Ego States

According to transactional analysis, the human personality is composed of three parts, called **ego states.** The three ego states are parent, adult, and child. A healthy person moves from one ego state to another depending upon the demands of the situation. Most work situations demand that the person behave in an adult manner.

The parent. The *parent* ego state dictates that we act as our parents once did. It is a body of recordings in the brain that reflects the unquestioned events perceived by a person during his or her childhood. According to TA, the parent is highly judgmental and moralistic. A person acting in the parent state will display such characteristics as being overprotective, distant, dogmatic, indispensable, and self-righteous. Clues that someone is acting in the parent state include wagging the finger to show displeasure, reference to laws and rules, and reliance on ways and values that were successful in the past.[9] ("I told you never to take an auto trip without first checking your oil and tires.")

The adult. When people are acting and thinking rationally, when they are gathering facts and making judgments based upon these facts, they are in the *adult* ego state. The adult is an information seeker and processor who basically follows the decision-making model described in Chapter 4.

You can tell a person is in the adult ego state when he or she concentrates and engages in factual discussion.

The child. When people act and feel as they did in childhood, or when they behave immaturely, they are in their *child* ego state. It is the data recorded in the brain as a result of experiences taking place during ages one to five. Characteristics of the child include temper tantrums, creativity, conformity, depression, anxiety, dependence, fear, and hate. Because childhood experiences are so varied, people show varied behavior when in their child state. Despite this variation, a clue that a person is being a child is when he or she is nonlogical and demands immediate gratification of impulses. ("I want what I want when I want it.") Other clues are temper tantrums, giggling, coyness, attention seeking, and stony-faced silence.

The key to successful performance on and off the job is for the adult ego state to act as an executor and determine the appropriate expression of all three ego states during a specific situation. At a farewell party for a retiring executive, it would be helpful for middle managers to display a good deal of their child state. However, the adult should rescue the child before the middle managers exhibit such childlike behavior as rowdyism or drunkenness.

Analysis of Transactions

To apply TA, it is necessary to identify the transactions taking place between the ego states of people who are dealing with each other. In TA training, much time is devoted to analyzing transactions. Recognizing the ego states of the two people involved in the transaction can help the people communicate more effectively. Transactions are classified into *complementary* and *crossed*, or noncomplementary. Complementary transactions lead to effective interaction and *positive strokes* or ego-building compliments. Crossed transactions lead to ineffective interaction and *negative strokes*, or ego-tearing insults.

Complementary transactions are shown in Figure 12–3. All are effective

Figure 12–3   Complementary transactions.

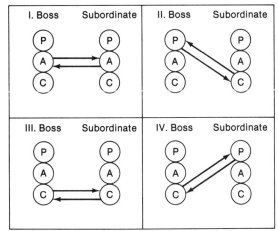

P is Parent; A is Adult; C is Child

transactions because both people receive the positive stroking they want. In cell I, a boss acting in an adult ego state might say to an employee, "When will I get my report?" The employee replies, "It will be ready tomorrow at three o'clock."

In cell II, the boss, in a parent state, says, "Be here early tomorrow; it's an important day." To which the subordinate replies, "Don't worry, I'll be here."

In cell III, the child-acting boss says, "Let's have a few drinks at lunch." The subordinate replies, "Maybe we can even drink right up to quitting time."

In cell IV, the child-acting boss says, "We're so overwhelmed with work in this department, I don't think we'll ever catch up." In a parentlike fashion, the subordinate responds, "I'll get things under control."

Crossed transactions, shown in Figure 12–4, result in negative strokes and ineffective transactions between people.

In cell I, the boss, in a child state, says, "I desperately need your cooperation," hoping for a parent response. Instead, the boss hears, "I'm doing all I can right now. What more do you expect?"

In cell II, the parent boss, hoping for a child response from his subordinates, says, "Your work is sloppy and needs immediate correction." Instead a parentlike subordinate says, "I'll be the judge of the neatness of my work."

In cell III, an adult boss, hoping for an adult response, says: "Have you ever thought of getting help from the EAP?" Acting as a parent, the subordinate says, "That sir, constitutes an invasion of privacy."

In cell IV, a parent-acting boss says: "You are totally without self-discipline." Instead of acting as a whipped or obedient child, the subordinate responds in an adult manner, "In what way am I lacking in self-discipline?"

Figure 12–4   Crossed transactions.

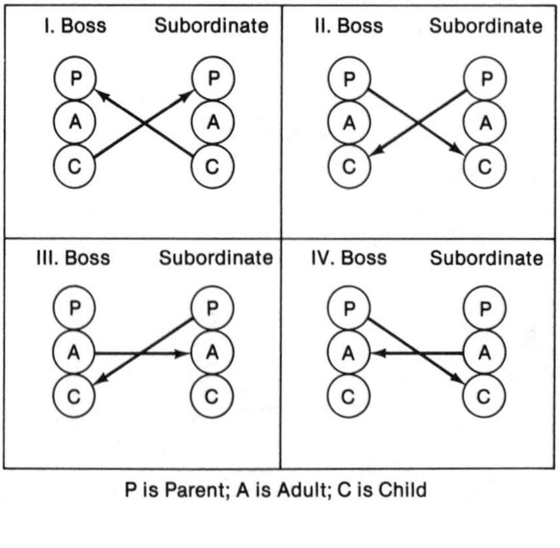

P is Parent; A is Adult; C is Child

Figure 12–5 An ulterior transaction.

Ulterior transactions occur when communications break down because the real meaning of the message is disguised. The sender of the message says one thing but means another. In an ulterior transaction, the receiver of the message is usually unsure whether to respond to the surface message or its hidden meaning. When a person initiates an ulterior transaction, the person's body language is usually inconsistent with the spoken message. For example, a boss may say to an employee: "I'm happy that you're not working so hard that you experience job stress." However, the boss speaks in a sarcastic tone, and shows a frown of disappointment. An ulterior transaction often leaves the receiver of the message confused about its true meaning.

As illustrated in Figure 12–5, the words of the boss appear to be coming from the boss's adult ego state. In reality, the message is coming from his child to the employee's parent. The boss wants the employee to see the need for working harder. The boss would have a better chance of achieving his or her goal by saying, "I would like you to work harder. Your current level of effort does not bring you up to company standard."

Life Scripts and Life Positions

Another key concept in TA is that the individual develops a **life script**—a plan or drama acted out during a person's life. It is as if people have a compulsion to live a preprogrammed life. Some people are forever manipulating others; some are losers; some are winners; some are chronic procrastinators. If a manager understands the script being followed by a subordinate, co-worker, or superior, it might make it easier to deal with that person. For example, if Michelle is a "winner," all things being equal her boss will send her out on a difficult mission.

In early childhood, the person develops a life script by being submerged in a culture, interacting with the family unit, viewing television, and being exposed to printed information. Part of developing a life script is finding answers to questions such as: Who am I? What am I doing here? Who are these people around me? What are these people doing here?

A script leads to the development of a life position, as diagrammed in Figure 12–6. Once these life positions have been established, they become a set of expectations that the individual uses to guide his or her behavior. The four life positions, to be described next, may also be considered sets of assumptions about one's self in relation to others.

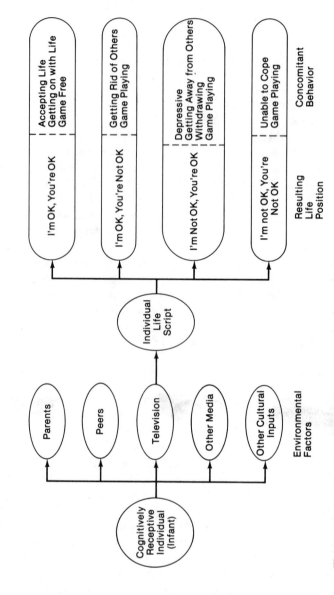

Figure 12-6 Development of life positions and resulting behavior.

SOURCE: Reprinted, by permission of the publisher, from "The TA Approach to Employee Development" by Laird W. Mealiea, p. 14, SUPERVISORY MANAGEMENT, August 1977. ©1977 by AMACOM, a division of American Management Associations, New York. All rights reserved.

I'm Not OK—You're OK is the life position in which the child predominates because the child frequently feels inadequate in comparison to the more confident and powerful adult. A person who follows this script is subject to frequent depression. An employee who assumes "I'm not OK—You're OK" may need reassurance and affection from the boss.

I'm OK—You're Not OK is the life position of the parent ego state—experienced, all-knowing, guiding, correcting, and controlling. In extreme, this life position leads to paranoid-like (very suspicious) thinking. Employees whose script have led to this life position frequently blame others when things go wrong on the job.

I'm Not OK—You're Not OK is a pathological life position, usually stemming from prolonged mental illness. Few people maintaining this position prosper on the job. When they are able to stay employed, their jobs are unskilled, involving minimum contact with people.

I'm OK—You're OK is the ideal life position on which authentic, game-free relations are based. The mature adult ("healthy, well-rounded employee") has developed a script that leads him or her to believe "I'm OK—You're OK."

How to Use TA in Your Own Life

Transactional analysis is supposed to be of major benefit to its followers. Yet there is a big gap between reading about TA or attending TA training, and applying it to your own life. The comments made about TA in this chapter point you toward an understanding of several of its major concepts. Three examples will help you understand how TA might improve your communications—and therefore your relationships—with people.

Removing communication blocks. A direct application of TA is to overcome communication blocks between you and another person. The key here is to decide which ego state the other person is using: parent, adult, or child. You strive for a complementary transaction. If someone is acting as an adult, the best way to "get through" to that person is to act as an adult yourself. Child-to-child, parent-to-child, and child-to-parent transactions all help you communicate better with another individual. The interchanges between people presented earlier to explain Figure 12–3 are all examples of using TA to remove communication blocks.

Another important way of using TA to enhance communication is to follow its communication rules. Abe Wagner, the developer of these rules, believes that changing your words can change your personality. It also invites others to change their personalities. His rules relate directly to the idea of owning your own feelings, thoughts, and behavior, and no one else's. Six of his suggestions are as follows:[10]

1. *Use the word I.* Speak in the first person when you want to express your own point of view and feelings, instead of using "one," "people," or "they." The word "I" personalizes your comments and indicates that you take responsibility for your own ideas.

2. *Say "I won't" instead of "I can't."* To say "I can't" implies that you have no control over your action, and this is rarely the case. To say "I won't" implies that this is your decision not to do something.

3. *Avoid saying "I don't know" when you do know.* Save "I don't know" for occasions when you are asked for information you really do not have. If you do know something but are not willing to share your answer, "I'd rather not say" is an OK response.

4. *Avoid hedging.* When you have a definite point of view, avoid words like "perhaps," "probably," and "maybe," or "I'm not sure." Definite points of view encourage others to be open with you in return.

5. *Don't try, do.* You communicate much stronger conviction to another person when you say you will do something, rather than you will try to do something. Which sounds more effective, "I will try to get back to you next week," or "I will get back to you next week"?

6. *Use eye contact.* Eye contact is an important aspect of nonverbal communication, and it is a good indicator of which ego state is operating. The child breaks eye contact; the parent looks down from above; the adult uses a comfortable, level gaze.

Improving your leadership style. TA has much to say about leadership styles. If you want to be an autocratic boss, it is usually necessary to maintain parent-to-child transactions with people. In some situations, this helps you to overcome communication barriers. However, in the long run it is more beneficial to the organization to have more people relating to one another in an adult-to-adult manner. Such transactions require a participative style of management. Using this approach, the leader is able to achieve a climate of mutual trust and respect for each other's competence. A follower of TA will thus strive to be a participative leader in most situations.

The free-rein style is sometimes a child-to-child relationship. A leader of this type leaves subordinates to their own devices and provides no leadership. In the long range, the organization suffers and the individuals are left with a feeling of frustration because they have not accomplished much.[11]

Giving positive strokes to folks. An important message of TA is similar to that derived from reinforcement theory: You can enhance your relationships with others by dispensing positive reinforcement. Transactional analysis has a set of catchy terms of its own for the same approach to handling people. Perhaps you have met a person who attended a weekend workshop in TA or read a book on the subject. Often he or she will make statements such as, "Wow, that was a warm fuzzy," or "I guess you need some stroking." If TA makes you more sensitive to the importance of positive reinforcement in daily relationships, that alone is an important contribution.

How Good Is TA?

Transactional analysis training for improving interpersonal skills on the job has shown some decline in popularity in recent years. TA does seem to lead to gains in human relations skills, but it does so in a cumbersome manner. Many of the standard TA ideas can be explained in much less complex, and more practical terms. As one critic notes, the distinction between "I'm OK" thought patterns and "I'm not OK" thought patterns may be just a matter of self-confidence or self-esteem.[12] Another criticism of TA is that its results are much more difficult to evaluate than those of other human relations training programs. For example, how do you measure whether or not a supervisor has begun to engage in a greater number of complementary transactions with subordinates?

ASSESSMENT CENTERS FOR INTERPERSONAL SKILL TRAINING

Another method of acquiring improvement in interpersonal skills is to participate in the activities of an assessment center. In recent years assessment centers have been widely used by large and small organizations to help select candidates for management and sales positions. However, another important use of assessment centers is to develop the interpersonal and problem-solving skills of employees.[13]

Assessment center programs do not follow a standardized format. Whatever common elements there are to these programs include assessment in groups, assessment by groups, and the use of multiple assessment techniques with emphasis on situational exercises that simulate job conditions. Assessment centers also make use of psychological tests and selection interviews. A typical program lasts a few days. When the assessment center method is used in selecting present employees for possible future promotion, prospects are sent by nomination from their superiors. Sometimes job candidates from the organization are sent to an assessment center conducted by a consulting firm. The assessors used include personnel specialists, psychologists, and managers and staff specialists from departments other than personnel.

How do you improve your interpersonal skills? There are two general ways of attaining personal development by way of the assessment center method. One way is that the participant typically receives a professionally prepared report with suggestions for personal improvement. The report is given to the individual within the context of a counseling session. Suppose a person is judged to behave abrasively toward other people when under pressure. For example, the individual might have become very hostile when his or her suggestion was rejected by the group. Here is how a portion of the individual's report might look:

> You might do well to attend an assertiveness training workshop. It looks to us that you need to learn how to express your differences of opinion with people without making them feel uncomfortable. You could also profitably supplement this activity with some appropriate reading about getting along effectively with others. Have you seen *The Art of Managing People?*[*] It might provide you some useful tips on the subject of interacting smoothly with others.

[*] Philip Hunsaker and Anthony Alessandra, *The Art of Managing People* (Englewood Cliffs, NJ: Prentice Hall, 1980).

Another way of improving human relations skills is through the process of participating in an assessment center exercise. As you try to deal with others in group exercises, you improve your ability to handle people. Practice, of course, does not automatically guarantee improvement, but it can lead to improvement in many situations.

Leaderless group discussion (LDG). Every assessment center puts candidates through some type of group discussion or situational exercise. Following the usual format, five or six people are placed together to solve a work problem; no leader is appointed. As the team works on its problem, a group of outside observers rate their performance on a variety of factors. These could include important aspects of behavior such as "leadership," "organizing ability," and "interpersonal skills." The raters are given complete definitions of the evaluation factors. In one assessment center exercise, candidates are asked to handle this problem:

> You people are office supervisors. All members of upper management are away at a management conference. Your responsibility is to make a tight deadline on a shipment. If you are late on this order, your firm will lose $2,000,000 in penalties. You are a nonunion shop. An employee who claims he is the spokesperson for all the factory employees comes to you with an urgent message: "Either we all get a $100 bonus, or we all walk off the job this evening." You have 45 minutes to decide on what appropriate action to take.

Part of the underlying rationale for such an exercise is that it gives the assessors an opportunity to observe the candidate's performance under stress. The exercises themselves place the candidate under pressure. Also, candidates perceive the simulation exercise to be stressful because they believe their performance could have a big impact on their careers. This tends to be true even when the stated purpose is training, not selection.

A sample rating sheet is shown in Figure 12–7. The comments and observations are often as helpful as the ratings. Raters often provide such candid comments as, "I wouldn't want that guy working with me even if he were my brother-in-law. Strictly a hot head"; "That's the kind of woman we need around here. She gets things done through people without kicking sand." In some approaches to assessment center development, the participants are provided such feedback once the sessions are completed. The feedback sometimes provides clues for personal change.

ENCOUNTER GROUPS

An established method of improving interpersonal effectiveness both in work and personal life is the **encounter group.** The term refers to a variety of small-group experiences in which the members encounter each other with an open

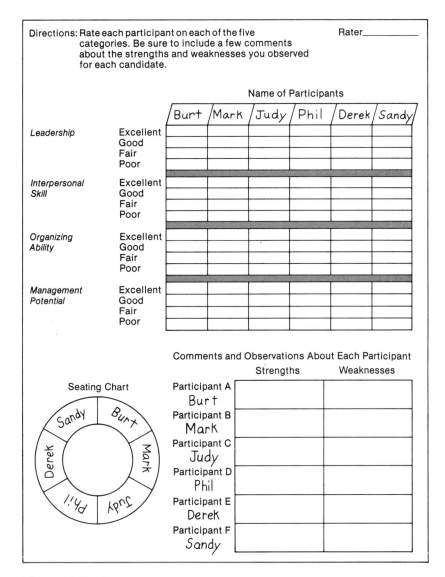

Directions: Rate each participant on each of the five categories. Be sure to include a few comments about the strengths and weaknesses you observed for each candidate.

Rater_____

Figure 12-7 An assessment center rating sheet.

expression of feelings.[14] Whether these groups are used in mental health settings or in work organizations, they attempt to help people become more sensitive to people. In the process, encounter group participants often experience a boost in self-esteem because they typically receive emotional support from other group members. A good deal of negative feedback also takes place, which can lead to a lowering of self-esteem for some people.

Goals and Purposes

People vary in what they expect to derive from an encounter group experience, and encounter group leaders vary in what they hope the group members will achieve. Despite this diversity, a few consistent purposes emerge. These include the following:

- Make participants more sensitive to how they are perceived by others and how their behavior affects others.
- Acquire knowledge about the processes that help and hinder group functioning.
- Help participants become more aware of their own feelings and how these feelings influence behavior.
- Help participants, in general, achieve greater self-understanding, including insight into their conflicts, feelings, defenses, and impact on others.
- Develop specific behavioral skills such as improved listening ability, praising and criticizing others, and communicating with body language.

What Actually Happens during an Encounter Group?

In a pure form of encounter group the leader provides no direction at the start of the session. It is hoped that by providing no rules or agenda people will begin to talk about the here and now. Such groups often begin as generalized bull sessions until people get the point that the encounter group is a unique experience. The group then begins to focus on each other and what is happening to them. Because a completely unstructured group takes so long to "get moving" and so many people find it frustrating (including some group leaders), a variety of semi-structured exercises are now used in encounter groups. A sampling of an encounter group exercise is presented next.

> *Group Leader* (beginning of third hour):   I get the impression we are becoming more candid with each other. Everybody has received some feedback on how he or she is perceived by everybody else. Now I would like everybody to share with the group the most pressing problem you are facing. But it must be a problem you don't feel uncomfortable telling others about. Let's begin with Alison. It's Jack's turn to be last.
>
> *Alison:*   My biggest problem is that I love so many people and I like to do so many things. Sometimes it's difficult to make choices. I hope to be a magazine editor in a large city, but that would mean leaving behind my parents and friends.
>
> *Chuck:*   Money is my big hassle. I have two dollars in my pocket right now to last me until Friday. I need more money.
>
> *Aaron:*   I have a real hang-up with my parents. They want me to pursue a career in religion, and I'm not into that in a big way. My dad's a rabbi. I love him and wouldn't want to disappoint him, but I'm just not cut out of that cloth.
>
> *June:*   My future in-laws are driving me crazy. My fiancé is Italian, and they want a tremendous Old World wedding. When I tell them I'm not interested

in such a big wedding, they tell Mario he should have never become engaged to a girl who wasn't Italian.

Steve: My biggest problem is my height. I'm afraid I'm being discriminated against because I'm five feet four. Every executive in my company is six feet or over. I feel I'm being held back because of my height. But nobody will level with me.

Bob: My bowling score is five points below where it should be. That's a real problem.

Group Leader: Bob, I think you mean that right now you are not willing to share anything personal about yourself with the group.

Bob (blushing): You're right. I don't feel too comfortable telling other people my feelings. Okay, here's a problem. I hate my job, yet I can't get up enough courage to quit.

Gil: I'm very much in love with a wonderful woman whom I've been dating for three months. Yet she doesn't want an exclusive relationship with me, and she doesn't want to marry me.

Peggy: I'm a very aggressive person. I'm also very ambitious. Because of it people may think I'm a strong feminist. I wish people would realize I'm just being me.

Rolf: I've been out working for awhile and I'm getting discouraged. There are so many talented people out there that I wonder if I can hack it.

Jack: I'm 25, and I've never really had a long-term job. I just don't know where I'm headed. I wish I were one of these kids whose parents decided for him at age 12 that he should be an engineer or a doctor. I'm aware of a lot of things I don't want to do, but I have no good fix on what it is I want to do.

How might a session like this have benefitted the participants? One potential benefit derives from sharing problems with other people. Talking about the problem may lead to clarification. Although it is not revealed in the portion of the session presented, the group members give each other emotional support. Such support often helps make it easier to face their problems. The previous session alluded to benefitted the participants by giving them candid feedback about their traits and behaviors. For instance, one person was told that she did not maintain eye contact with others when speaking to them. Improving her eye contact would help her become a more effective communicator.

Evaluation of Encounter Groups

Encounter groups have always been controversial, and they are used less frequently today than during the last two decades. However, they have led to the still widely used team-building groups described in Chapter 16. Encounter group proponents believe that they are highly effective in helping people become more sensitive to the needs of other people and in elevating one's feeling of self-worth. Opponents of encounter groups believe that the benefits some people receive are far outweighed by the damages done to others.[15] A key issue about the merits of encounter groups is that they encourage people to be candid. Unfortunately candor in both work and personal settings can be helpful or detrimental.

Many modern human relations techniques encourage people to be open and forthright with criticism. In many situations, this proves to be a worthwhile strategy. Constructive feedback about mistakes can lead to positive change. Nevertheless, tact, diplomacy, and kindness continue to be important leadership traits.[16] Total candor in work settings is often interpreted as rudeness and insensitivity. In personal life, also, candor may backfire. Imagine saying to your spouse on the first day of your marriage, "I must be honest. You were really my second choice as a mate. I have always had fantasies about marrying your best friend." It has been said that there is a bit of sadism in absolute truthfulness.[17]

Summary of Key Points

☐ An interpersonal skill training program should first determine what kind of improvement is necessary, taking into account individual and organizational needs. The program should be administered under favorable conditions, it should provide for modeling or other active practice, and new learning should be reinforced by the organization. A follow-up refresher experience may be needed.

☐ A new technique for interpersonal skill training is interactive video, a computer-assisted video system in which the trainee interacts with the training material. A key feature of interactive video is that a different branch of the story develops contingent upon the trainee's response to a situation.

☐ Assertiveness training (AT) helps you to learn how to recognize and constructively state your true feelings in both work and social situations. An assertive person is forthright, rather than abusively aggressive or passive. Three important methods of AT are role playing, role reversal, and modeling. Specific training exercises include learning the steps to assertion, fogging, and rehearsal.

☐ Transactional analysis (TA) training has been widely applied to improving communication among people in work settings. Applying TA to the job requires that you learn its jargon and be able to analyze the transactions that take place between yourself and others. Most work situations demand that you behave in an adult manner to be truly effective. TA helps you recognize your "script" (roughly, a programmed pattern of behaving) and change it to your advantage. Life scripts lead to life positions. The healthy adult life position is "I'm OK—You're OK."

☐ TA can be applied to your own life in ways such as removing communication blocks with others, improving your leadership style (relate to subordinates in an adult-to-adult manner), and giving positive strokes to people.

☐ Aside from their basic use in the selection of employees, assessment centers can also be used for interpersonal skills training. Improvement in dealing with others takes place through (a) the feedback a participant receives and (b) the practice involved in carrying out the assessment center exercises.

☐ Encounter groups are useful for developing better insight into yourself and others and improving interpersonal effectiveness. One problem with encounter groups, however, is that they encourage candor. If overdone, candor can lead to problems in work and personal life.

Questions and Activities

1. How could you diagnose accurately what kind of interpersonal skill training you need?

2. How could you diagnose accurately what kind of interpersonal skill training is needed by the organization?

3. Assertiveness training has probably become the most widely used method of interpersonal skill training. What do you think accounts for its popularity?

4. In what way might TA be used to improve face-to-face communication skills?

5. Some highly successful people in all fields are abrasive, rude, and pushy. How would you therefore defend the value of AT?

6. Describe a potential application of transactional analysis for handling delicate situations with customers (such as an airplane passenger demanding an extra alcoholic beverage).

7. What would give you a clue to another person's life script?

8. What is your life script? Should it be changed?

9. The assessment center method has been criticized for placing too much emphasis on verbal skills and social smoothness. What do you think about the validity of this criticism?

10. Encounter groups were originally developed to help managers be more candid and open with people. To what extent do you think this need still exists?

A Human Relations Case

WHAT WE NEED AROUND HERE IS BETTER HUMAN RELATIONS

Hank called his three highest-ranking managers together for a surprise luncheon meeting. "Have a drink on United Mutual," said Hank, "You may need it to loosen up your thinking about an important topic I want to bring to your attention."

After Madeline, Raymond, and Allen ordered their drinks, Hank launched into the agenda:

"As office manager, I think we have to move into a rigorous human relations training program for our front-line supervisors. It's no longer a question of whether we should have a program, it's now a question of what kind and when."

Allen spoke out, "Okay, Hank, don't keep us in suspense any longer. What makes you think we need a human relations training program?"

"Look at the problems we are facing. Twenty-five percent turnover among the clerical and secretarial staffs; productivity lower than the casualty insurance industry national standards. What better reasons could anybody have for properly training our supervisory staff?"

Madeline commented, "Hold on Hank. Training may not be the answer. I think our high turnover and low productivity are caused by reasons beyond the control of supervision. Our wages are low, and we expect our people to work in cramped, rather dismal office space."

Hank retorted, "Nonsense. A good supervisor can get workers to accept almost any working conditions. Training will fix that."

"Hank, I see another problem," said Allen." "Our supervisors are so overworked already that they will balk at training. If you hold the training on company time, they will say that they are falling behind in their work. If the training takes place after hours or on weekends, our supervisors will say that they are being taken advantage of."

"Nonsense," replied Hank. "Every supervisor realizes the importance of good human relations. Besides that, they will see it as a form of job enrichment."

"So long as we're having an open meeting, let me have my input," volunteered Raymond. "We are starting from the wrong end by having our first-line supervisors go through human relations training. It's our top management who needs the training the most. Unless they practice better human relations, you can't expect such behavior from our supervisors. How can you have a top management that is insensitive to people and a bottom management that is sensitive? The system just won't work."

"What you say makes some sense," said Hank, "but I wouldn't go so far as to say top management is insensitive to people. Maybe we can talk some about the human relations program after lunch."

1. Should Hank go ahead with his plans for the human relations training program? Why or why not?
2. What do you think of Raymond's comment that top management should participate in human relations training first?
3. What is your opinion of Hank's statement that good leadership can compensate for poor working conditions?
4. If you were in Hank's situation, would you try to get top management to participate in a human relations training program?
5. What type of human relations training program would you recommend for first-level supervision at United Mutual?

A Human Relations Incident

THE PATERNALISTIC BOSS

Arthur Bennington, a department store manager, was receiving his annual performance appraisal from his boss, Shelly Wolf, the regional manager. Wolf began her evaluation with these comments:

"No doubt Art, you have turned in another six months of sterling performance. Your sales volume is up 27 percent and your profits have increased 12 percent. I'm happy with your performance, but I do notice that your personnel costs are running high. Your profits might have increased more if your turnover were lower."

"Thank you for the compliment about a good year. I do think though that the high personnel costs are beyond my control. My sales help keep leaving because they dislike being supervised conscientiously."

"Art, I think your definition of conscientious might differ from the usual meaning of the word. In your attempts to be conscientious you may be trying to exert too much control over the lives of your store personnel."

"Shelly, what do you mean that I exert too much control?" asked Arthur Bennington.

"Here is the nature of the complaints we've been receiving through the personnel department and unsolicited letters: A number of your employees think that you confuse your role as a store manager with that of an overpowering parent or relative. You told one of the women who quit that she would never amount to anything unless she finished business school. You told one of the men who quit that his punk hair style makes him unfit to associate with people from decent backgrounds.

"It could be that your preaching to your employees is driving them out the door."

"Shelly," replied Arthur, "You may be overreacting. What the young generation needs from management is guidance that will help them in life, not just the job."

1. Do you think Shelly is justified in criticizing Arthur for his approach to supervision?

2. What type of interpersonal skill training do you think would be the most helpful to Arthur Bennington?

A Human Relations Exercise

WHAT ARE YOUR DEVELOPMENTAL NEEDS?

The following exercise is designed to heighten your self-awareness of areas in which you could profit from personal improvement. It is not a test, and there is no scoring, yet your answers to the checklist may prove helpful in mapping out a program of interpersonal skills training.

THE INTERPERSONAL SKILLS CHECKLIST

Directions: Below are a number of specific aspects of behavior that suggest a person needs improvement in his or her interpersonal skills. Check each statement that is generally true for you. You can add to the validity of this exercise by having one or two other people who know you well answer this form as they think it describes you. Then compare your self-analysis with their analysis of you.

Place check in this column

1. I'm too shy. _____

2. I'm too mean. _____

3. I'm too much of a bully. _____

4. I have trouble expressing my feelings. _____

5. I make negative comments about people too readily. _____

Place check in this column

6. Very few people listen to me.   _____
7. My personality isn't colorful enough.   _____
8. People say that I'm a clown.   _____
9. I don't handle myself in a very mature way.   _____
10. People find me boring.   _____
11. It is very difficult for me to criticize others.   _____
12. I'm too serious most of the time.   _____
13. I avoid controversy in dealing with others.   _____
14. It is difficult for me to find things to talk about with others.   _____
15. I don't get my point across very well.   _____
16. _____   _____

Now that you (and perhaps another person) have identified specific behaviors that may require change, action plans should be drawn. Describe briefly a plan of attack for bringing about the change you hope to achieve for each statement that is checked. Ideas for your action plan might come from information presented in this chapter or elsewhere in the text. Also investigate the suggested readings at the end of this and the previous chapter. A basic example would be to participate in an AT workshop if you checked "I'm too shy."

Notes

1. Raymond A. Noe and Neal Schmitt, "The Influence of Trainee Attitudes on Training Effectiveness: The Test of a Model," *Personnel Psychology*, Autumn 1986, pp. 497–523.
2. James S. Russell, Kenneth H. Wexley, and John E. Hunter, "Questioning the Effectiveness of Behavior Modeling in an Industrial Setting," *Personnel Psychology*, Autumn 1984, p. 479.
3. Mary Jane Ruhl and Keith Atkinson, "Interactive Video Training: One Step Beyond," *Personnel Administrator*, October 1986, p. 70.
4. Ibid.
5. *American Management Association Course Catalog*, August 1986–April 1987, p. 30.
6. Lynn Z. Bloom, Karen Coburn, and Joan Pearlman, *The New Assertive Woman* (New York: Dell, 1976), pp. 175–176.
7. Manuel J. Smith, *When I Say No I Feel Guilty* (New York: Bantam Books, 1975), pp. 104–115.
8. Two job-related explanations of TA are Muriel James and John James, *The OK Boss* (Reading, MA: Addison-Wesley, 1975); Dorothy Jongeward and Philip Seyer, *Choosing Success—Transactional Analysis on the Job* (New York: Wiley, 1978).

9. James and James, *The OK Boss*, p. 32.

10. Abe Wagner, *The Transactional Manager: How to Solve People Problems with Transactional Analysis* (Englewood Cliffs, NJ: Prentice Hall, 1981), p. 7.

11. Donald D. Bowen and Raghu Nath, "Transactions in Management," *California Management Review*, Winter 1975, pp. 82–83.

12. Comment by Philip G. Benson in book review, *Personnel Psychology*, Autumn 1981, p. 875.

13. Andrew J. DuBrin, *Contemporary Applied Management: Behavioral Science Techniques for Managers and Professionals*, 2nd ed. (Plano, TX: Business Publications, 1985), pp. 265–282; Virginia R. Boehm, "Assessment Centers and Management Development," in Kendrith M. Rowland and Gerald R. Ferris, *Personnel Management* (Boston: Allyn and Bacon, 1982), pp. 346–352.

14. Morton Lieberman, Irvin Yalom, and Matthew Miles, *Encounter Groups: First Facts* (New York: Basic Books, 1973).

15. Gerald Biberman, "Trainer Behavior in a T-Group Setting," *Small Group Behavior*, November 1979, pp. 501–522.

16. W. H. Weiss, "Tact and Diplomacy: Two Skills Worth Developing," *The Effective Executive*, Bulletin of the Dartnell Corporation, 1983.

17. Quoted in Maya Pines, "To Tell the Truth . . . Hurts," *The New York Times*, May 29, 1982.

Suggested Reading

BURLEY-ALLEN, MADELYN. *Managing Assertively: How to Improve Your People Skills.* New York: Wiley, 1983.

DECKER, PHILIP J., and NATHAN, BARRY R. *Behavior Modeling Training: Principles and Applications.* New York: Praeger, 1985.

ELGOOD, CHRIS. "Games Managers Play." *Supervisory Management*, April 1986, pp. 2–7.

FRIEDMAN, PAUL G., and YARBROUGH, ELAINE A. *Training Strategies from Start to Finish.* Englewood Cliffs, NJ: Prentice Hall, 1985.

GOLDSTEIN, IRWIN L. *Training in Organizations: Needs Assessment, Development and Evaluation*, 2nd ed. Monterey, CA: Brooks/Cole, 1986.

HARRIS, THOMAS A., and HARRIS, AMY BJORK. *Staying OK.* New York: Harper & Row, 1985.

HASSETT, JAMES, and DUKES, SHEREE. "The New Employee Trainer: A Floppy Disk." *Psychology Today*, September 1986, pp. 30–36.

LAMBERT, LARRY L. "Nine Reasons That Most Training Programs Fail." *Personnel Journal*, January 1985, pp. 62–67.

MEININGER, JUT. *Success Through Transactional Analysis.* New York: Grosset and Dunlop, 1983.

RUSS-EFT, DARLENE F., and ZENGER, JOHN H. "Common Mistakes in Evaluating Training Effectiveness." *Personnel Administrator*, April 1985, pp. 57–62.

WASHING, HARRY A., and BOVEINGTON, KURT W. "How Useful Are Skills Inventories?" *Personnel*, June 1986, pp. 13–19.

PART FOUR
Working with
and
Understanding
the
Organization

The Effective Organization

LEARNING OBJECTIVES
After studying this chapter and doing the exercises, you should be able to

1. Describe several external measures of an effective organization.

2. Describe several internal measures of an effective organization.

3. Summarize the systems view of organizational effectiveness.

4. Explain how productivity and quality are linked to organizational effectiveness.

5. Pinpoint the principles of organizational excellence as defined by Peters and Waterman.

WHAT IS ORGANIZATIONAL EFFECTIVENESS?

Your reaction to many places of work you know about has probably been, "I wonder how they continue to operate." About other places you may have commented, "What a smooth-running outfit. No wonder they are tops in their field." This chapter examines the issue of what and who determines organizational effectiveness. A major justification for including this chapter is that so many organizations today are striving for effectiveness, if not excellence.

There are many different opinions of what constitutes an effective organization. Organizational effectiveness is therefore measured in different ways. Despite this diversity of opinion, we need a central definition of organizational effectiveness. As defined here, **organizational effectiveness** is the extent to which an organization is productive and satisfies the demands of its interested parties. **Productivity** is the ratio of output to input, taking into account both quality and quantity. Among the interested parties that need to be satisfied are employees, customers, clients, the general public, labor unions, and the governments.

Another complexity in evaluating organizational effectiveness is the time dimension. Some measures of organizational effectiveness deal with the long range, while others deal with the intermediate or short range.[1] For instance, a company that loses money in one year may be temporarily ineffective. If the same company continues to earn a profit after the first five years, it might be considered effective in the intermediate and long range.

A SYSTEMS VIEW OF ORGANIZATIONAL EFFECTIVENESS

Systems theory has contributed to the understanding of organizational effectiveness. As diagrammed in Figure 13–1, an organization is part of a larger system—society itself. An effective organization makes wise use of natural resources (inputs), by processing them (process or throughput) into something useful for society (outputs). The effective organization is thus productive. As these outputs are placed in the environment, the effective organization changes in response to new demands from the environment. Often this means using different inputs.

Another important aspect of systems theory is that organizations are open systems. They interact with the outside world, as noted by two elements of

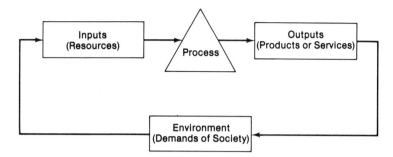

Figure 13–1 A systems view of organization.

Figure 13–1: Outputs are fed into the environment, and the environment furnishes the inputs necessary to keep the organization functioning.

A business analogy will help explain these relationships further. An automobile dealership uses the *inputs* of (1) new and used cars, and (2) people in the form of sales, shop, and office personnel in order to provide a service to the public. The cars taken into the dealership are *processed* to the extent that they are prepared for sale and displayed on a lot or in a showroom. Offering financing and insurance programs to the public is part of the process that takes place in the dealership.

The *output* is private transportation for the public. As tastes and requirements change (for example, a demand for more luxurious automobiles), the dealership receives *feedback*. Such feedback helps inform the dealer and manufacturer what types of inputs (new cars) the dealer should be offering next. As long as the dealership responds to the tastes of the public, while at least breaking even, it will be able to meet its objective of delivering cars to the public. If these objectives are met, the organization is considered to be effective.

PRODUCTIVITY, QUALITY, AND ORGANIZATIONAL EFFECTIVENESS

Private and public organizations alike strive to be productive and offer high-quality goods and services to the public. As mentioned above, quality should be considered part of productivity. Nevertheless, since productivity and quality are related but not synonyms, each topic requires separate attention. After describing productivity and quality, we will examine how employee factors can affect them adversely.

Productivity

Later in this chapter we present numerous criteria of organizational effectiveness. None of these criteria, or determinants of effectiveness, are so important that they override the importance of productivity. A modern definition of productivity

$$\text{Productivity} = \frac{\text{Output (quantity and quality of goods and services produced)}}{\text{Input (amount of human, material, and financial resources consumed)}}$$

Figure 13–2   The meaning of productivity.

is shown in Figure 13–2, and also described in Chapter 2. The productive organization makes efficient use of resources. Low productivity has serious negative consequences. Among them are a business failing to make a profit, a health maintenance organization showing an operating loss, and a government agency losing its funding. High productivity has serious positive consequences of the opposite kind—profits, staying within budget, and retaining funding.

Productivity also has behavioral consequences. Morale tends to be high when people perceive themselves to be productive but not subject to exorbitant work demands. And morale tends to erode when an organization achieves low productivity. As described in Chapter 3, job satisfaction and morale can also influence productivity.

Quality

According a leader in the quality movement, Philip B. Crosby, **quality** is conformance to requirements.[2] If the public and company officials require a watch battery to last 500 days, and it does, the battery has acceptable quality. Have you ever dialed 800-424-1040 to receive answers to a question about your federal income tax? If the service conformed to your requirements, you would conclude that the IRS is offering a high-quality service. If you spent 4 hours trying to get through and then were put on hold for 35 minutes, you would conclude the service was of low quality.

Providing high-quality goods and services has become a widely accepted measure of organizational effectiveness. An advertising strategy for some firms is to mention the quality of both their products and services, and the people making or providing them. Observe the mention of product and people quality in the box.

THE EMPHASIS PLACED ON QUALITY IN AN AUTOMOTIVE ADVERTISEMENT

AT CHRYSLER MOTORS, "QUALITY" HAS NEW MEANING

At Chrysler Motors, "quality" has taken on new meaning through our companywide emphasis on a broad, step-by-step quality improvement process. The new process will deliver quantum-leap improvements in quality and will have a direct effect on the products that customers get from Chrysler Motors and its dealers.

QUALITY WILL HELP SLASH COSTS

Better quality will also help on costs; to remain competitive, we're out to slash our costs by a full 30 percent by 1990. That's a big task, and we're not going to get there just by trying harder. We're making fundamental changes in the way we do business and going after every inefficiency in our system.

To accomplish this, we're sending every Chrysler Corporation employee—including myself (Lee Iacocca) back to school.

Source: *Chrysler/Plymouth Spectator*, Spring 1986, p. 5. Reprinted with permission of Chrysler Corporation.

Employee Factors Contributing to Productivity and Quality Problems

Poor management practices, poor equipment, and inadequate technology are important contributors to productivity and quality problems. Employees also contribute to low productivity and quality. One major factor is poor motivation. Some employees are much more interested in leisure and personal life than in work. They regard productivity and quality improvement as somebody else's responsibility. When threatened with being fired, some of these employees may show a temporary spurt in productivity. After the threat wears off, they once again decrease their work effort.

Another important employee factor leading to work errors is poor attention. Even well-motivated workers sometimes have problems concentrating on their work because they are preoccupied with personal problems. A data entry specialist in a bank made a large number of errors in transferring information from canceled checks to monthly statement sheets. Customer complaints about mistakes not in their favor, along with an audit, brought the problems to management's attention. The data entry specialist blamed her errors on her concerns about personal finances.

Poor ability can also contribute to low productivity and quality. The employee may simply not be able to perform at the required level. Similarly, insufficient training and education can lower productivity and quality. A planning specialist in a government agency persisted in making forecasts that were out of line with past experience and common sense. When confronted about these unusual forecasts, the specialist said: "I apologize. I really don't understand how to use the right forecasting statistics. So I was probably way off in my calculations."

SELECTED MEASURES OF ORGANIZATIONAL EFFECTIVENESS

As mentioned above, no single measure determines whether an organization is effective. For example, the criterion of profitability does not tell the whole story of an organization's effectiveness. A profitable firm may be creating undue stress for employees, leading to an exodus of people from the firm once they can find new jobs. Ultimately, what constitutes an effective organization depends upon a person's values—what he or she thinks is important.

A realistic view is that organizational effectiveness is usually measured by multiple criteria. To illustrate, an effective hospital would have to accomplish such ends as taking care of sick and injured people, staying within budget, providing employment to the disabled, contributing to an esthetic environment, and conducting research. A substantial number of measures of organizational effectiveness are described next to help you appreciate the complexity of specifying what constitutes organizational effectiveness.[3]

To help clarify these many measures of effectiveness, they are sorted into two different types of measures. *External measures* refer to output variables such as the production of goods and services. *Internal measures* refer to processes such as maintaining good morale and a high quality of work life.

As you read through these various measures of organizational effectiveness, it will become obvious that they are not all uniquely different from one another. For example, there is a high correlation between "profit making" and the "efficient use of resources." If resources are squandered, it will be difficult to make a profit.

External Measures of Organizational Effectiveness

External measures of organizational effectiveness center around the interaction of the organization with the outside world. As such, they are logical and fit into a systems view of organizations.

Overall effectiveness is a composite measure taking into account many factors such as those mentioned below. Overall effectiveness can be measured by combining performance records or obtaining the judgment of people who are familiar with the organization, such as customers, clients, or stockholders.

Goal attainment is a general measure of how well the organization accomplishes what it set out to accomplish. Assuming that an organization's goals are not destructive or harmful to others, there is much to be said for this criterion. A subset of this criterion is *achieving new goals*. A successful organization emphasizes the attainment of new and important goals. An important new goal for a business firm, for example, might be to ward off a hostile takeover from a group of investment bankers.

Profit making, or a favorable "bottom line," is often considered the most important measure of effectiveness for a business. Unless a firm makes a profit, it cannot afford to accomplish other objectives such as making charitable contributions or providing job training to culturally disadvantaged people. Yet an overemphasis on profit can result in such practices as firing people indiscriminately or imposing exorbitant work demands on employees.

Staying within budget is a nonprofit firm's equivalent of making a profit. Unless an organization stays within budget, it risks losing much of its public support. Managers of nonprofit organizations are as budget conscious as those employed by businesses. Nonprofit firms that overspend risk extinction.

Productivity is providing goods and services in a cost-effective manner (or the ratio of output to input, taking into account quality and quantity). For an organization to be considered productive, it must generate goods and services that are in demand, yet of acceptable cost. A confusing point here is the unpredictability of acceptable cost. One company manufactures fountain pens that are in high demand despite an average retail price of $125. Since these pens are in demand and the company is profitable, the organization is considered effective.

Quality is the fact that an effective organization produces goods or services with a reputation for utility and dependability. To achieve this end, some firms hold every employee responsible for quality—not just the quality control department.[4]

Social responsibility is the extent to which the organization attempts to solve social problems that it contributes to or causes.[5] A case in point would be a distillery that chooses to conduct a campaign against drunk driving.

Practicing good ecology is the satisfaction of a number of groups in the organization's environment.[6] Practicing good ecology is thus a more general case of being socially responsible. When certain key groups in society are satisfied, we can say that the organization is effective or successful.

In a study of 97 small businesses, the researchers identified seven different groups (constituencies) who have a vested interest in the welfare of the company. To the extent that these parties are satisfied, the organization can be classified as effective or successful. The seven groups are customers, creditors, suppliers, employees, owners, the community, and government. Many of the expectations these groups have of a small business are similar. For example, all groups want the company to stay in operation. Other concerns are more meaningful to one group than another. The government is strongly interested in a given company obeying safety regulations, whereas a creditor would be more concerned about prompt payment of bills.[7]

The different criteria of organizational effectiveness used by the seven groups are shown in Figure 13–3. The same figure also illustrates an important theme of this chapter—that organizational effectiveness is multidimensional.

Growth is an increase in such factors as total workforce, plant capacity, assets, sales, profit, market share, and number of new products or services. To many observers, the absence of growth is the equivalent of organizational ineffectiveness. In the current era, however, the relevance of growth as a measure of effectiveness is diminishing. The reason is that many organizations are trimming down in size, including business corporations selling large units to other companies.

Voluntarism is the extent to which people want to continue as members of the organization. An organization that many people are eager to join, and few want to leave, might be considered effective. Hewlett-Packard Corporation and the Boston Celtics are two organizations that score high on voluntarism. In contrast, when most of the members want to leave at the earliest opportunity,

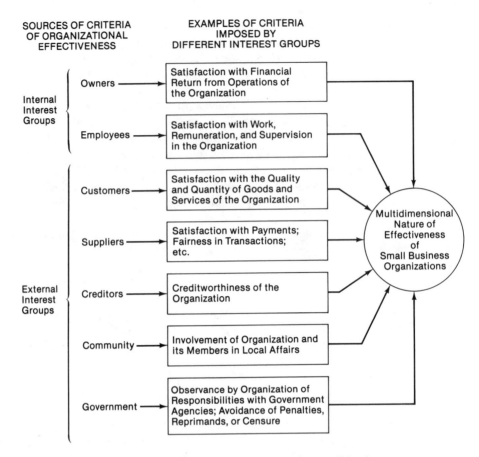

Figure 13–3 Criteria of organizational effectiveness for small businesses.

SOURCE: Hal Pickel and Frank Friedlander, "Seven Societal Criteria of Organizational Success," *Personnel Psychology*, Summer 1967, pp. 165–178. The synthesis of this material is prepared by Robert H. Miles, *Macro Organizational Behavior* (Santa Monica, CA: Goodyear Publishing, 1980), p. 365.

it could mean the organization is ineffective. Among the exceptions are hospitals and prisons, where most of the employees want to remain, but the patients and prisoners, respectively, want an early exit.

Readiness to perform means carrying out the organization's purpose as required by its constituents. An organization that can successfully perform on short notice can be considered effective. A fire department that gets its firefighters out on time to minimize physical and human loss is an effective department. On the other hand, an orthopedic medical practice that requires people with backaches to wait three months for an appointment is not totally effective.

Survival means staying in existence over time by being able to cope with a changing environment. An organization that survives in the long range is probably meeting the demands of some section of society. A 100-year-old college is undoubtedly performing a legitimate service. A construction company that has been in business in the same community for 40 years has undoubtedly earned the right to survive.

A major contributor to survival is the organization's capacity to adapt to change. An adaptable organization has good problem-solving ability, combined with the capacity to react with flexibility toward changing environmental demands. Organizations with the ability to adapt to necessary changes have been labeled **organic.** In order to be adaptive or organic, the firm would have to receive valid information and then communicate it internally. Specialists such as strategic planners and market researchers play an important role in gathering and interpreting valid information from the environment.

Sears, the largest retailer, can be considered an adaptive organization because it is generally able to shift with the changing tastes of the public. From time to time, however, even Sears has suffered a sales slump because it misjudged the retail preferences of customers. (See the exercise at the end of this chapter to gather facts about the incidence of nonsurviving organizations.)

Internal Measures of Organizational Effectiveness

An internal measure of organizational effectiveness relates to processes and techniques similar to those described throughout this text. For example, a successful organization would use effective methods of motivating and communicating with people, and would resolve disputes and grievances promptly and fairly. In our opinion, internal measures are less meaningful than external measures in determining organizational effectiveness. For instance, good motivational systems are relevant only if the people are motivated to engage in work that society thinks is valuable (an external measure of effectiveness). Following is a sampling of internal criteria of organizational effectiveness.[8]

Organizational mental health is a measure of the organization's sense of identity, integration of the subparts, and adaptability. An organization has a **sense of identity** when it is aware of what it is and what it is trying to accomplish. When people in the organization see it as seen by others, a sense of identity is fostered.[9] Apple Computer and Harvard University represent organizations with a strong sense of identity—both have a purpose seen by insiders and outsiders.

Integration is achieved when the subparts of the organization fit together and therefore are not in severe conflict or working at cross purposes. When employees believe that they can prosper in an organization only by lying and stealing, the opposite of integration has occurred. When the various departments of a company realize that only through teamwork will they all succeed, integration occurs.

Adaptability has already been mentioned as an external measure or organizational effectiveness. It also classifies as an internal measure because it is an inner quality that leads to effective coping with the environment.

Managerial skills is the ability of managers to accomplish tasks by working with and through people. Few people would argue that an organization can become or remain effective without managers who possess both task and interpersonal skills. Task skills refer to those skills related directly to work accomplishment. Interpersonal skills include the extent to which managers give support, facilitate constructive interaction, and generate enthusiasm for meeting goals and achieving superior performance.

Planning and goal setting means figuring out what needs to be done and how to accomplish it. Successful organizations are typically committed to goal setting and action planning at all levels. Long-range goals are set at the top, while shorter-range goals are set at lower levels. The importance of goal setting has been described in Chapter 2 on motivation, and in Chapter 11 on coaching and counseling.

Goal agreement is the extent to which organization members achieve consensus on what the organization should be trying to achieve. An organization increases its chances for success when the vast majority of members perceive the same goals for the organization. This situation would take place only when top management clearly articulates the goals, or when the goal is obvious. A strike team attempting to free a group of hostages would probably experience goal agreement.

Control is how well management measures performance and corrects deviations from desired performance. The control model described in Chapter 11 explains the nature of control of human performance. Controls are also important in areas such as finance, operations, inventory shrinkage, and safety and health.

Participative decision making is the extent to which people throughout the organization contribute to important decisions and make suggestions. An organization is likely to increase its effectiveness when it solicits expertise from a wide range of members. The higher the quality of the workforce, the higher the yield from participative decision making.

Morale is a predisposition in organization members to put forth extra effort in achieving organizational goals and objectives. As implied in Chapter 3, it includes feelings of commitment and extra effort on the part of the group. High morale contributes to effectiveness in such ways as retention of organization members, lower accident rates, less waste, and "good-mouthing" the organization in the community.

Turnover and absenteeism is an index of the rate of attraction of the organization to its members. The extent of avoidable turnover and absenteeism serve as a rough index of organizational effectiveness. Involuntary turnover as well as voluntary turnover detracts from organizational effectiveness. A firm that is forced to terminate or lay off employees may have made errors in selection or in satisfying consumer demands. Turnover and absenteeism are significant indexes of organizational effectiveness because they are often caused by low morale.

Accident frequency and severity is the rate and intensity of job-related physical injuries to employees. Accident control is important for both humanitarian and economic reasons. An effective organization does not waste human life or incur needless fines. Nor does it pay excessive insurance premiums because of poor safety practices.

Human resources of high value means valuing employees. An effective organization has talented and motivated people whose value is recognized by the firm. Most organizations claim that human resources are their most valuable asset; successful firms believe it. An organization with talented people is usually in a better position to recover from adversity than a firm with less valuable human resources. Human resources of high value therefore contribute directly to organizational survival. Placing a value on human resources is so important that it has led to an activity called *human resource accounting*. One of its applications is to assess the true cost of losing a valuable employee.[10]

Courage in the face of adversity means coping effectively with hard times. Recent research has shown that most managers become cautious and embrace the status quo just when new ideas are the most needed.[11] This holding back can be attributed to a concern that one will be criticized or fired if the risky idea fails. A more effective organization is more willing to take a risk when it is most needed. One such legendary act of organizational courage was Chrysler's introduction of the mini-van at a time when the firm was close to defaulting on loans. The gamble paid off handsomely.

Trust between management and employees is a belief that the other side is acting in your best interest, combined with a mutual concern for each other. Trust contributes to organizational effectiveness because it builds employee loyalty and sometimes enhances motivation. Also, employees who trust management are willing to identify organizational problems because they do not fear being blamed for causing the problems. Consultant Gordon Shea observes that the actions of supervisors communicate how much they trust employees: "Tight control and heaviness of management—looking down people's throats—reveals low trust."[12]

PRINCIPLES OF ORGANIZATIONAL EXCELLENCE

Another way of understanding organizational effectiveness is to study the principles that guide successful organizations. Such an approach was undertaken by two best-selling books about management, *In Search of Excellence* and *Passion for Excellence*.[13] Peters and Waterman, the authors of the first book, selected their sample on the basis of opinions and facts about organizational performance. First, they interviewed executives who were known for their skill, experience, and wisdom. Next, they talked to a number of faculty members from a dozen business schools in the United States and Europe. Based on these discussions, and their own experience as management consultants, Peters and Waterman identified a number of excellent companies. They also discovered the principles underlying their excellence.

Two more steps were involved in choosing the final sample. The authors used six measures of long-term productivity (such as average return on capital). To qualify for the sample, a company had to be in the top half of its industry on at least four of the six measures for 25 years. Finally, industry experts were selected to rate the companies' history of innovativeness. Sixty-two companies were included in the final sample.[14]

Eight Principles for Excellence

The findings are described in the eight principles listed in Table 13–1. Several of these principles emphasize organization structure, such as principle 3 about breaking the organization into small companies. Several principles emphasize behavioral tactics—for example, principle 1, a bias for action instead of overanalyzing problems. The remaining principles deal with organizational values and climate, such as fostering dedication to the values of the company.

Criticism of the Principles for Excellence

The approach under study to identify guiding principles of organizational success has met with considerable criticism from researchers. A recent critical analysis of the principles of excellence builds upon past criticism and offers new quantitative

Table 13–1   Eight principles for excellence

1. *Bias for action*: A preference for doing something—anything—rather than sending a question through many cycles of analyses and committee reports.
2. *Staying close to the customer*: Learning the customer's preferences and catering to them.
3. *Autonomy and entrepreneurship*: Breaking the corporation into small companies and encouraging them to think independently and creatively.
4. *Productivity through people*: Creating in *all* employees the awareness that their best efforts are essential and that they will share in the rewards of the company's success.
5. *Hands-on, value driven*: Insisting that executives keep in touch with the firm's essential business.
6. *Stick to the knitting*: Remaining with the business the company knows best.
7. *Simple form, lean staff*: Few administrative layers, few people at upper administrative levels.
8. *Simultaneous loose-tight properties*: Fostering a climate where there is dedication to the central values of the company, combined with tolerance for all employees who accept those values.

SOURCE: From Thomas J. Peters and Robert J. Waterman, Jr., *In Search of Excellence: Lessons from America's Best Run Companies* (New York: Harper & Row, 1982).

data. Michael A. Hitt and R. Duane Ireland compared 14 of the excellent firms to a larger sample from *Fortune's* 1000 industrial firms on indicators of stock market performance. They also evaluated how well these firms fared on the four principles of excellence included in *Passion for Excellence* (leadership; close to the customer; innovation, autonomy and entrepreneurship; and productivity through people).

Hitt and Ireland concluded that several of the firms included in the original list may not have been excellent, and other firms may have been erroneously excluded. Additionally, the results showed that three of the four excellence principles described in *Passion for Excellence* were unrelated to performance. However, the principle of innovation, autonomy, and entrepreneurship was significantly related to performance. It was therefore concluded that managers should be cautious about uncritically accepting these principles of excellence.[15]

Despite these well-founded criticisms, Peters and his associates have made a notable contribution to organizational effectiveness. They have reinforced a growing awareness that small units within larger bureaucratic structures tend to foster innovation.

CHARACTERISTICS OF THE 100 BEST-RUN COMPANIES

The two books just mentioned emphasized business success as the key measure of organizational effectiveness. Another book about organizational effectiveness, *The 100 Best Companies to Work for in America*, focused on job satisfaction instead of business success.[16] The authors of *100 Best Companies* interviewed hundreds of people about what they thought were the best places to work. Among the people interviewed were consultants, recruiters, friends, relatives, business school professors, reporters, media personnel, advertising people, and physicians. The top 10 of the 100 were Bell Labs, Trammell Crow, Delta Airlines, Goldman Sachs, Hallmark Cards, Hewlett-Packard, IBM, Pitney Bowes, Northwestern Mutual Life, and Time Inc. Twenty-one of companies on this list of 100 were also included in the list of excellent firms cited by Peters and associates.

Once 100 fine employers were identified, the authors interviewed from 6 to 30 people in each company. The interviews were analyzed to arrive at a list of characteristics typical of a good employer, as shown in Table 13–2. A comparison of Tables 13–1 and 13–2 suggests that managers and employees do not agree strongly on what makes for an excellent company. The principles Table 13–1 are derived mostly from managers' perceptions, while those in Table 13–2 are derived mostly from employee perceptions. However, both groups do mention such factors as autonomy, quality, values, and decentralization.[17]

Table 13–2 Characteristics of 100 best companies

---

1. Employees are made to feel that they are part of a team, or in some cases, a family.

2. Open communication is encouraged; people are informed of new developments, and are encouraged to offer suggestions and complaints.

3. Promotions are from within; employees are allowed to bid on jobs before outsiders are hired.

4. Quality is emphasized, enabling people to feel pride in the products or services they are providing.

5. Employees are allowed to share in profits through profit sharing or stock ownership or both.

6. Distinctions in rank between top management and employees in entry-level jobs are reduced. Everyone is addressed by his or her first name; executive dining rooms and exclusive perks for executives are barred.

7. Attention and resources are devoted to creating as pleasant a work environment as possible, and good architects are hired.

8. Employee activity in community service is encouraged by giving money to organizations in which employees participate.

9. Employee savings are assisted by matching the funds they save.

10. Employees are not laid off without management first making an effort to place them in other jobs within the company or elsewhere.

11. Physical fitness centers and regular exercise and medical programs are provided, indicating concern about employee health.

12. Employee skills are expanded through training programs and reimbursement of tuition for outside courses.

SOURCE: From Robert Levering, Milton Moskowitz, and Michael Katz, *The 100 Best Companies to Work for in America* (Reading, MA: Addison-Wesley, 1984).

Summary of Key Points

☐ There are many different opinions of what constitutes an effective organization, and effectiveness can be measured for different time periods. A working definition used here is that organizational effectiveness is the extent to which an organization is productive and satisfies the demands of its interested parties.

☐ Systems theory helps us understand the nature of organizational effectiveness. An effective organization makes wise use of natural resources (inputs) by processing them into something useful for society (outputs). As these outputs are placed in the environment, the effective organization changes in response to the new demands from the environment.

☐ Productivity and quality are important aspects of organizational effectiveness. Productivity is the ratio of output to input, taking into account both quality and quantity. Quality is conformance to requirements. Organizations today are particularly concerned about offering high-quality goods and services. Many productivity and quality problems are created by employees. Among the contributing factors are poor motivation, attention, and ability.

☐   Organizational effectiveness is usually measured by multiple criteria. External criteria of effectiveness include: overall effectiveness, goal attainment, profit making, staying within budget, productivity, quality, social responsibility, practicing good ecology, growth, voluntarism, readiness to perform, and survival.

☐   Internal measures of organizational effectiveness include: organizational mental health (sense of identity, integration, and adaptability), managerial skills, planning and goal setting, goal agreement, control, participative decision making, morale, turnover and absenteeism, accident frequency and severity, human resources of high value, courage, and trust between management and employees.

☐   Another approach to understanding organizational effectiveness is to identify the principles and characteristics that make organizations successful. The principles of organizational excellence identified by Tom Peters and his associates are (1) bias for action, (2) staying close to customers, (3) autonomy and entrepreneurship, (4) productivity through people, (5) hands-on, value driven, (6) stick to the knitting, (7) simple form, lean staff, and (8) simultaneous loose-tight properties. The accuracy of these principles has been questioned by researchers.

☐   Characteristics typical of a good employer, as perceived by employees, include such factors as making employees feel they are part of a team, open communications, promotion from within, a pleasant work environment, and minimizing layoffs.

Questions and Activities _____

1. Provide an example of an organization you classify as being effective, and explain the reason for your choice.

2. Provide an example of an organization you classify as being ineffective, and explain the reason for your choice.

3. How does the systems view of organizational effectiveness coincide with the philosophy of "survival of the fittest"?

4. What is your reaction to the argument that high-quality goods often cost so much to make that they would have to be priced noncompetitively?

5. Which attributes of a product or service lead you to conclude that it is of high quality?

6. Since few organizations are probably ineffective by choice, why don't ineffective organizations become effective?

7. Which characteristics of an organization are the most influential in determining whether it will be effective? (Feel free to identify factors not mentioned in this book.)

8. Identify the key groups that a postsecondary educational institution must satisfy in order to be successful.

9. *In Search of Excellence* became the best-selling management book of all time. What do you think accounts for its popularity?

10. Identify two characteristics of a well-run company you think are quite important that are not included in Table 13–2.

A Human Relations Case

BIG BLUE'S QUEST FOR EXCELLENCE

Several years ago, the world's largest maker of office equipment and computers, International Business Machines Corporation, decided to strengthen itself internally and in the marketplace. A major reason IBM decided to embark upon far-reaching changes was that earnings had dipped, and competitiors were gaining ground.

Top management candidly admitted that some of its own practices, as well as a business downturn, were responsible for the company's slump. Task forces were assigned to answer such questions as: "Has IBM become so bureaucratic that some decisions are made too slowly?" "Has the company not paid enough attention to the needs of its customers?" The strategies enacted by IBM to improve its situation are summarized in the next several paragraphs.

IBM's top priority is cost-cutting. The company planned to reduce its costs 7 percent in a twelve-month period. Reduced costs include: $1 billion in capital spending; $500 million through attrition of employees (voluntary quits and retirements) and other personnel programs; and $500 million in discretionary spending for travel, consultants, expense accounts, and other miscellaneous costs.

A major thrust toward reducing costs and decreasing delays in decision making will be to reduce the force of 40,000 managers worldwide. At some IBM manufacturing facilities there are five or six layers of management. As each layer of management passes judgment on the merits of a decision, it can take a long time to make a needed change. A top IBM official noted that in many areas of the company, planning is so complex that making an important change takes a year. The company, however, is not talking about laying off managers. Instead, many managers who leave voluntarily will not be replaced, and many other managers will be reassigned to sales, professional, and technical positions.

IBM will strengthen its marketing force, which is already the biggest in the industry. The company decided to create 5,000 new sales and marketing jobs by transferring headquarters and manufacturing employees into customer-contact assignments. These moves were planned to increase the sales staff by 22 percent to 28,000 people. Another change planned was for marketing personnel to listen even more carefully to customers, so it can match their requirements. IBM also planned to install systems that incorporated equipment from competitors, a maneuver prohibited in the past.

Another improvement planned by IBM is to accelerate its strategy to diversify its product line. The company plans to offer more software and services (such as equipment maintenance) because this business is more profitable than selling hardware.

Another area of potential change was to examine IBM's strategy of relying so heavily on company insiders for innovative ideas. Many competitive companies hire people from other companies in order to bring new perspectives into the firm.

1. Relate the above changes proposed by IBM to the criteria of organizational effectiveness presented in this chapter.
2. Relate the above changes to the principles of excellence expounded by Peters and Waterman.
3. Relate the above changes to the characteristics of the 100 best companies.
4. What is your evaluation of the soundness of IBMs plan for strengthening itself? Offer at least one constructive criticism or caution.

THE FUEL-HUNGRY FURNACES

You are working as an administrative assistant to the manufacturing vice-president at Allied Heating Equipment Company. After eight months on the job, you have learned to admire the manufacturing efficiency of the company and its impressive earnings records. One day you ask your boss why Allied has become so successful in a field you think is competitive. He answers:

"No mystery there. Through certain economies in manufacturing we are able to price our furnaces about 25 percent below the competition. This way we are the favorites of the large home developers who are trying to cut corners."

Still curious about the reasons for the success of your company, you decide to conduct some informal market research. After speaking to about ten homeowners who have Allied furnaces, one consistent complaint is sounded: The furnaces consume much more fuel than the owners believed they would. You inform your boss of your findings. He now comments:

"Why should we care at Allied? It's hard to please both the builder and the homeowner. It's the builders we are trying to impress. They want to save dollars and don't care too much about their customers' fuel bills. When we get complaints from the builders, I'll start worrying."

You begin to wonder if you are really working for an effective organization. What should you do about your concerns?

ORGANIZATIONAL SURVIVAL

One criterion of organizational effectiveness is survival. Its rationale is that since so many organizations of all types do not survive, being able to survive deserves some credit. The purpose of this exercise is for you to estimate the "organizational survival rate" in your area. Proceed as follows:

1. Each member of the class telephone 12 organizations of any kind listed in the Yellow Pages or the white pages of your local telephone directory. Make the sample somewhat random by such methods as calling every ninth (or any number you choose) firm listed.
2. If the phone is disconnected, assume the firm has not survived, or at least the local branch of the firm has not survived.
3. If somebody answers, politely state: "Thank you for answering. We are doing a brief survey of organizational survival rates. You have answered our question. We appreciate your cooperation, and thank you for your time."
4. Combine data to arrive at the rate of organizational survival from one year to the next in your area. (Telephone directories are reprinted each year.)

Before implementing your part of the assignment, write down your prediction of what percentage of organizations listed in the telephone directory are still in business.

Notes

1. Stanley E. Seashore, "Criteria of Organizational Effectiveness," *Michigan Business Review*, July 1965.
2. Philip B. Crosby, *Quality without Tears: The Art of Hassle-Free Management* (New York: McGraw-Hill, 1984), p. 59.
3. Based on a synthesis of the literature in Robert B. Miles, *Macro Organizational Behavior* (Santa Monica, CA: Goodyear Publishing, 1980), pp. 356–359.
4. Tom Peters, *A World Turned Upside Down* (Palo Alto, CA: The Tom Peters Group, 1986), p. 14.
5. H. Gordon Fitch, "Achieving Corporate Social Responsibility," *Academy of Management Review*, January 1976, p. 38.
6. Miles, *Macro Organization Behavior*, p. 377.
7. Hal Pickle and Frank Friedlander, "Seven Societal Criteria of Organizational Success," *Personnel Psychology*, Summer 1967, pp. 165–178.
8. Based in part on the synthesis in Miles, *Macro Organizational Behavior*, pp. 356–359.
9. Patrick E. Connor, *Organizations: Theory and Design* (Chicago: Science Research Associates, 1980), p. 440.
10. Eric G. Flamholtz, *Human Resource Accounting: Advances in Concepts, Methods and Applications*, 2nd ed. (San Francisco: Jossey-Bass, 1985).
11. Harvey A. Hornstein, "When Corporate Courage Counts," *Psychology Today*, September 1986, p. 58.
12. Priscilla Petty, "Companies Must Cultivate an Atmosphere of Trust Among Employees," Gannett News Service syndicated column, August 27, 1985.
13. Thomas J. Peters and Robert H. Waterman, Jr., *In Search of Excellence: Lessons from America's Best Run Companies* (New York: Harper & Row, 1982); Thomas J. Peters and Nancy Austin, *A Passion for Excellence* (New York: Harper & Row, 1985).
14. Summary of research procedures based on book review by Terence R. Mitchell in *Academy of Management Review*, April 1985, pp. 350–355.
15. Michael A. Hitt and R. Duane Ireland, "The Quest for Excellence," *The Academy of Management Executive*, May 1987, pp. 91–98.
16. Robert Levering, Milton Moskowitz, and Michael Katz, *The 100 Best Companies to Work For in America* (Reading, MA: Addison-Wesley, 1984).
17. Mitchell book review, p. 352.
18. Facts based on "How IBM Is Fighting Back," *Business Week*, November 17, 1986, pp. 152–157.

Suggested Reading

CAMPBELL, JOHN P. "On the Nature of Organizational Effectiveness," in Paul S. Goodman and Johannes Pennings, eds., *New Perspectives in Organizational Effectiveness*. San Francisco: Jossey-Bass, 1977, pp. 13–55.

KENDRICK, JOHN W. *Improving Company Productivity: Handbook with Case Studies*. Baltimore: Johns Hopkins University Press, 1984.

KETS, DE VRIES, MANFRED, F. R., and MILLER, DANNY. "Unstable at the Top." *Psychology Today*, October 1984, pp. 26–34.

KETS, DE VRIES, MANFRED, F. R., and MILLER, DANNY. *The Neurotic Organization.* San Francisco: Jossey-Bass, 1984.

MILLER, DANNY, and FRIESEN, PETER H., in collaboration with Mintzberg, Henry. *Organizations: A Quantum View.* Englewood Cliffs, NJ: Prentice Hall, 1984.

SAYLES, LEONARD R. *The Complete Book of Practical Productivity.* New York: Boardroom Books, 1984.

SINHA, MADHAV, and WILBORN, WALTER O. *The Management of Quality Assurance.* New York: Wiley, 1985.

TOWSEND, PATRICK. *Commit To Quality.* New York: Wiley, 1986.

ULRICH, DAVID, and BARNEY, JAY B. "Perspectives in Organizations: Resource Dependence, Efficiency, and Population." *Academy of Management Review,* July 1984, pp. 471–481.

PART FOUR
Working with
and
Understanding
the
Organization

Getting Along in a Bureaucracy

LEARNING OBJECTIVES

After reading and studying this chapter and doing the exercises, you should be able to

1. Describe the difference between the popular and technical meanings of the term *bureaucracy*.

2. Specify key advantages and disadvantages of a bureaucracy.

3. Give your own example of an "inversion of means and ends."

4. Pinpoint several methods organizations can use to prevent or overcome problems sometimes created by a bureaucracy.

5. Pinpoint several methods individuals can use to cope with the problems sometimes created by a bureaucracy.

THE MEANING OF BUREAUCRACY

In its popular meaning, the term *bureaucracy* is associated with a number of negative attributes. Most people think a bureaucracy is an organization rampant with the rigid application of rules and procedures, slowness of operation, buck-passing, repetition of effort, empire building, exaggerated secrecy, and frustrated employees. Yet to a social or behavioral scientist, a **bureaucracy** refers to a form of organization in which division of effort, rank, rules, and regulations are carefully defined. It is a rational, systematic, precise form of organization. The following description of a bureaucracy gives a clue to its true nature:[1]

> The classical bureaucratic model is characterized by a pyramid consisting of positions which are ordered into a hierarchical system of super- and subordination. Each position has well-defined activities and responsibilities, demanding specialized competence, and with authority delimited to that necessary for the discharge of its duties. Employees function as representatives of particular positions, which define the degree of formality and the nature of the relationships to be observed.
>
> Ultimate control of the organization rests at the top of the hierarchy. Reliability of behavior is maintained by directives, by rules and regulations, and by standard operating procedures which prescribe the exact manner in which duties are to be performed.

Most readers of this book have dealt or will deal with a bureaucracy as an employee, customer, client, or citizen. It is thus worthwhile to examine the nature of bureaucracies and suggest strategies and tactics for overcoming their potential problems.

CHARACTERISTICS OF A BUREAUCRACY

Max Weber, a German sociologist, believed that bureaucracy was the pure form of organization, designed to achieve efficiency and effectiveness. He also reasoned that a state bureaucracy was the most expedient method of dominating and controlling people.[2] A bureaucracy has certain identifying characteristics.[3]

- *A division of labor based on functional specialization.* Thus companies have departments such as engineering, manufacturing, marketing, data processing, accounting, and personnel. People in these departments possess specialized information that contributes to the overall welfare of the firm.

- *A well-defined hierarchy of authority.* The person granted the most power sits at the top of the hierarchy (chairman of the board or president). As you move down the organization chart, people at each level have less power than those people at the levels above them, as shown in Figure 14–1.
- *A system of rules covering the rights and duties of employees.* In a truly bureaucratic organization each person has a precise job description and knows what he or she can expect from the company. In a few large corporations, for example, you are entitled to an extra day's vacation should you get sick one day during your vacation.
- *A system of procedures for dealing with work situations.* In a bank, for example, each teller knows exactly what to do when a customer wishes to deposit money in his or her account. No deviation from bank policy is encouraged or allowed.
- *Impersonality of interpersonal relations.* Even when you smile sweetly at the civil servant in the motor vehicle department, he or she will not renew your registration until you meet specified requirements.
- *Promotion and selection based on technical competence.* To make this characteristic of a bureaucracy true to life, technical competence must also include managerial or administrative competence. Thus in a bureaucracy laughing at your boss's jokes can never be an official reason for your receiving a promotion.

ADVANTAGES OF A BUREAUCRACY

The world could probably not function without bureaucracy.[4] Imagine the chaos in the United States if state and regional telephone companies did not have elaborate procedures for cooperating about interstate phone calls. When you call from a phone booth in Wisconsin, the operator might tell you, "I'm sorry you cannot call Georgia. The Georgia phone company will not cooperate with

Figure 14–1 The bureaucratic form of organization.

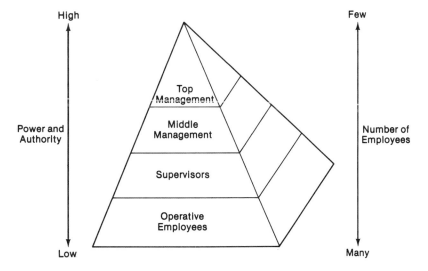

us." Imagine also the chaos if each middle manager at General Motors established his or her own pay scale and retirement policies for supervisors.

Machinelike efficiency. As its best, a bureaucracy is a highly efficient form of organization. Max Weber believed that "the fully developed bureaucratic mechanism compares with other organizations exactly as does the machine with the nonmechanical modes of production . . . precision, speed, unambiguity, continuity, discretion, unity . . . These are raised to the optimum point in a strictly bureaucratic adminsitration."[5]

IBM represents a modern example of what Weber envisioned when he spoke of a methodically efficient organization. A purchasing agent in one company had this comment to make about IBM's penchant for thoroughness: "When we don't know where something is in our company, we call our IBM account representatives. The people from IBM seem to know more about our company than we do."

Personally given orders become unnecessary. A bureaucratic manager can smugly point to the rule book and say, "Any employee who is late five consecutive days will be docked one day's pay." He or she thus cannot be accused of discriminating against you personally, nor can you legitimately feel that you were unjustly treated. At its best, a bureaucracy prevents people from being treated arbitrarily or unfairly.

Repetition of orders is unnecessary. A bureaucratic manager can tell you that each day at closing time the money in your cash register must be balanced. In the future, this order does not have to be repeated. Somewhere in the back of the store a rulebook exists that tells you this must be done every day. Theoretically, given a carefully designed rulebook, employees would need a minimum of supervision (which, of course, works best with competent and well-motivated employees).

Remote control of people. Top management can control people from a distance when those individuals are governed by a rational set of rules and regulations. When first-line supervisors are given a thorough grounding in machine safety including rules in writing, frequent on-the-spot checks should not be necessary. At the other extreme, when management has not established a clear set of rules, there is need for extensive visitation to remote areas of the organization. An effective set of rules allows people to be managed properly without constant supervision.

Punishment becomes legitimate. In some instances, reprimands or punishments are necessary in a complex organization. Since most people resent punishment, they tend to question its legitimacy. A college policy may state that any individual who fails to attain a C average will not graduate. A person with a 1.8

average cannot cry "unjust punishment" when he or she does not graduate. A supervisor has every right to dismiss a forklift truck operator who drives his or her truck while drunk. The rules make such punishment legitimate.

Equitable division or resources. In a bureaucracy, the job each manager is supposed to perform is well defined. Each manager would prefer that he or she have substantial resources to carry out his or her mission. Most managers, if given a choice, would perfer that another staff member be added to the department. A bureaucracy usually prevents people overallocating resources for their own purposes. Managers at the top of the hierarchy try to divide up resources in an equitable fashion. Unfortunately, this advantage of a bureaucracy is sometimes subverted through the practice of **empire building**—adding people to your organizational unit more to acquire power than to serve the good of the firm.

Promotion of democracy in the workplace. In its ideal form, a bureaucracy fosters democracy in the workplace. Weber developed his bureaucratic model to help overcome the arbitrary treatment of employees.[6] In a bureaucracy personal favoritism is supposed to be minimized. Furthermore, the bureaucratic form of organization has had a significant democratizing effect in advancing certain minority interests and in implementing certain democratic principles. These principles include representation, democratic decision making, and equality.

The heavy reliance on group decision making and committees found in a bureaucracy also contributes to the democratic process. Each committee member, for example, has the opportunity to express his or her opinion on the issue under consideration. Although this contributes to the slowness in decision making characteristic of a bureaucracy, it does allow the democratic process to take place.

PROBLEMS CREATED BY A BUREAUCRACY

Despite these potential advantages of the bureaucratic form of organization, bureaucracies are better known for their disadvantages. Bureaucracies are currently under attack because they are frequently perceived as cumbersome and inefficient. The problems sometimes created by a bureaucracy are described below and summarized in Table 14–1.

Delays in Decision Making

Bureaucracies move painfully slowly on complex decisions. Recognition of this problem has led many large organizations to eliminate one or two layers of management in order to hasten decision making.[7] The delay occurs because so many people have to concur before a final decision is made on important issues. In some bureaucracies, minor as well as major decisions are made slowly, as illustrated by this incident.[8]

Table 14–1   Disadvantages of a bureaucracy

1. Delays in decision making
2. Confusion and inefficiency
3. High frustration and low job satisfaction
4. An inversion of means and ends
5. Insensitivity to individual problems
6. Rigidity in behavior
7. Adverse changes in personality
8. Avoiding responsibility
9. Weakening of the connection between hard work and rewards
10. Placing incompetent people into key positions

> A manager sought authorization to subscribe to a trade newsletter that cost $35 per year (current price). After four weeks of memos and countermemos, the final decision was, "No, there are four months left on your present subscription." About fifteen people were involved in making the decision. At one point a telephone call was made from California to New York about the subscription.

Confusion and Inefficiency

When bureaucracies become large, they often breed confusion and inefficiency. Large firms are needed to carry out large-scale tasks. Nevertheless, there is a growing recognition that a small organization, or small subunit within a larger organization, is more efficient than a large, complex organization. It is common practice for large firms to subcontract some tasks to smaller firms because the smaller firms can perform the work more inexpensively. Also, many large firms are discovering that increasing their size decreases their effectiveness. The box describes the problem of bigness in the advertising business.

WHY MANY CLIENTS ARE LEAVING MEGA-AGENCIES

In recent years, many large advertising agencies have merged with each other creating mega-agencies with unprecedented total billings. One example was the merger of three major agencies (BBDO International, Doyle Dane Bernbach Group, and Needham Harper) to form the Omnicom Group. Another was the acquisition of Ted Bates Worldwide by the British firm of Saatchi & Saatchi, to create an ad group with annual billings of $7.5 billion.

The judgments of the clients of these huge agencies is that bigger is not necessarily better. A large number of important clients have quit the two supergroups mentioned above. One such advertiser took away $32 million in accounts from Omnicom and $96 million from Saatchi & Saatchi/Ted Bates. The chairman of the advertiser observed that the mergers may help the shareholders and managements of the agencies, but service to the client may not have been improved.

At the time of the mergers, the supergroups boasted that their worldwide scope would help clients reach international markets. However, some clients believe that the increased size of the agencies will create as many drawbacks as benefits. One concern is that creativity will be stifled in such large organizations. Another problem is that different ad agencies in the same group represent competitive companies. Morale can also suffer because of the layoffs that are needed to eliminate redundant jobs resulting from a merger. Another concern is that such a powerful ad agency will change the usual relationship in which the agency is subservient to the client.

As a result of the concerns about the size of the mega-agencies, a number of smaller ad agencies have picked up clients who are shopping for an agency of more traditional size.

Source: Facts derived from Stephen Koepp, "The Not-So-Jolly Advertising Giants," *Time*, November 17, 1986.

High Frustration and Low Job Satisfaction

Untold numbers of people find life in a bureaucracy frustrating and dissatisfying. Among the sources of frustration and dissatisfaction are "red tape," loss of individuality, and inability to make an impact on the organization.

Research evidence has been collected providing additional support to the belief that working in a bureaucracy creates some job dissatisfaction.[9] The subjects were 78 staff employees drawn from six large manufacturing organizations in the Midwest. They represented the areas of accounting, personnel, engineering, architecture, and market research. Among the information collected were measures of the style of organization (bureaucratic, collaborative, coordinative) and job satisfaction. A major finding was that job satisfaction decreased as the bureaucratic properties of the organization increased. According to the authors of the study, "This can be explained by the lack of individual responsibility and control characterizing bureaucratic structures."

Inversion of Means and Ends

A major problem associated with bureaucracy is the **inversion of means and ends,** a situation in which the methods for attaining a goal become more important than the goal itself. The inversion typically occurs when rigid adherence to rules or following procedures becomes an end in itself. Under these circumstances, the people involved become more concerned about following or carrying out procedures than accomplishing organizational objectives. Understanding the nature of a means-end inversion will help you develop insight into the potential pitfalls of a bureaucracy. Cost control sometimes results in an inversion of means and ends, as observed in the following case history:

> Top management in one company decided to exert tight controls over the use of photocopying in a effort to save money and therefore increase profits. In

order to stay in the good graces of top management, many middle managers went out of their way to minimize their use of photocopying machines. Soon there was an increase in the number of mistakes made in handling customer requests because employees were quite often not sent copies of important information. Also, it was observed that many secretaries were being asked to print several originals of documents on word processors—a much more costly procedure than photocopying. Following the rules of limiting photocopies was the means by which the end of improved profits was supposed to take place. But rigidly following these rules was actually interfering with achieving the objectives of the organization.

Another variation of a means-end inversion occurs when tools become more important than the problems they were intended to solve. Equipping managers with personal computers sometimes results in a peculiar inversion of means and ends. The purpose of managers using personal computers is to improve productivity. However, some managers have become so enamored of the computers that they neglect dealing with their people. As a result, their true productivity as a manager declines.

Insensitivity to Individual Problems

Since rules in a bureaucracy are applied uniformly, individual circumstances are sometimes ignored. The person whose situation deserves an exception to the rule does not receive a waiver, particularly from lower-level organization officials. Here is an example.

> A woman attempted to purchase two stereo speakers with her consumer credit card. Because of the size of the purchase, a check was made of her available line of credit. The sales associate reported back to the woman, "I'm sorry, our records show that you are not allowed to charge any more merchandise until you pay the amount you have past due." The woman protested that a serious error had been made by the computer. Somehow a charge of $556 was entered for a purchase she had never made. She had already spent one hour on the phone trying to resolve this mistake. The associate said that she knew nothing about the phone conversation; therefore, the woman could not use her credit card to purchase the stereo equipment. Only by demanding to see the store manager did the woman resolve her problem. The store manager checked with the central credit department to finally iron out the problem.

Rigidity in Behavior

Literal compliance with rules and regulations results in a rigidity in interpreting policy and carrying out procedures. The sales associate would not listen to the customer's explanation, or even bother to check. Robert Merton offers an explanation of why some bureaucrats are so rigid. The clients the bureaucrat serves become disenchanted because the impersonal treatment given by the bureaucrat doesn't take into account individual problems. Faced with this dissatisfaction, the bureaucrat relies increasingly on rules, routines, and impersonality as defense mechanisms.[10]

Adverse Changes in Personality

Besides being rigid, the person who works for a long time in a bureaucracy may show **bureaupathic behavior,** a strong need to control others based on insecurity. The need to control leads to an increasing number of rules and a decreased tolerance for deviation from them.

Bureaupathic behavior becomes more pronounced when managers have administrative responsibility over specialists whose work they do not understand. The performance of these specialists directly influences the performance of the manager, intensifying the problem of insecurity. The bureaupathic personality responds to this insecurity by issuing more rules, regulations, and procedures. As the result, organizational effectiveness may not improve, but the manager feels more in control.

As the superior exerts more and more control, conflict between the manager and the employee increases. An unfortunate amount of modeling may also take place. As the employee is controlled from above, he or she becomes more formal in relating to subordinates. Attempts at formalizing the organization eventually reach pathological proportions.[11]

Avoiding Responsibility

A bureaucracy is designed to pinpoint responsibility, yet in practice many people use bureaucratic rules to avoid responsibility.[12] Faced with a decision that he or she does not want to make, the buck-passing official will say, "That's not my job," or "That decision lies outside my sphere of influence," or "I'm afraid you will have to speak to my boss about that problem."

Closely related to avoiding responsibility is the avoidance of innovation so frequently found in a bureaucracy. Rather than risk trying a new procedure, the bureaucratic boss may say, "What you are suggesting violates tradition. Around here we don't do things that way." This was the response a marketing-oriented banker received from his boss when he suggested that the bank hold a "money sale." (It consisted of an advertising campaign offering loan rates lower than the competition.) The young banker whose suggestion was denied became doubly irritated when three months later a competitive bank held a successful money sale.

Weakening of the Connection between Hard Work and Rewards

Based on interviews with over 100 managers, Robert Jackall has published a scathing indictment of bureaucracy. One of his major conclusions is that bureaucracy betrays the belief that the way to get ahead is to work hard and make sound decisions. Instead, the bureaucrat must concentrate on impressing others, making contacts, and avoiding blame. Also, bureaucracy creates a confusion about moral values in this manner:[13]

> In the bureaucratic world, one's success, one's sign of election, no longer depends on one's own efforts and on an inscrutable God but on the capriciousness of one's superiors and the market; and one achieves economic salvation to the extent that one pleases and submits to one's employer and meets the exigencies of an impersonal market.

Placing Incompetent People into Key Positions

Two decades ago, a whimsical explanation was proposed of why so many incompetent people are allegedly found in bureaucracies. The now famous Peter Principle states: "In a hierarchy every employee tends to rise to his or her level of incompetence."[14] In other words, many people get promoted once too often. The Peter principle is satirical, but it does contain an element of truth, although many organizations use personal selection techniques that minimize the promotion of people into position for which they are unqualified.

An example of the principle in action is when a competent baseball coach is promoted to a front-office position and becomes an incompetent administrator. Similarly, many competent technical or sales personnel are promoted into management jobs or administrative assignments for which they are ill suited by temperament.

ORGANIZATIONAL COPING STRATEGIES

Although bureaucracies often create problems for their own members and outsiders to the organization, it is unreasonable to suggest that bureaucracy does not serve a useful purpose in society. A more promising approach to dealing with the problems of a bureaucracy is to make the bureaucracy more adaptable to the demands of a given situation. Three approaches toward this end are (1) use bureaucracy for recurring tasks, (2) use flexible organizational units within the bureaucracy, and (3) select and promote people more carefully.

Use Bureaucracy for Recurring Tasks

It is generally agreed that the bureaucratic form of organization is the best structure for organizations dealing with a stable, predictable, relatively homogeneous environment. One such environment would be the processing of social security payments by the federal government. Bureaucracy is noted for its efficiency in handling recurring problems. Rather than create a new policy or rule for each situation, the manager applies a previously prepared rule or policy, and the problem is solved.

Use Flexible Organizational Units

Although a bureaucracy is geared to dealing with a large-scale, repetitive operation, it must also deal with some small-scale, unique problems. Thus if a bureaucracy is to be totally effective, parts of the organization must be more loosely structured. For example, temporary task forces and project teams may be embedded within the larger organization structure. According to the concept of **contingency organization design**, you choose the structure best suited to deal with the problem at hand.

The appropriate organizational structure depends to a large extent on the production technology and the external environment. When the environment and technology are stable and predictable, the traditional pyramidal organization appears to work best. Thus, if you are a production supervisor in a mass production assembly operation, accept the fact that a bureaucracy is best suited to accomplishing the task at hand.

In contrast, where the product is customized and the environment is unpredictable, a loose, nonhierarchical structure appears more appropriate. Should you be assigned to an intelligence operation within the Central Intelligence Agency, your mission would probably be best accomplished by a project or task force organization structure. The ombudsman described in Chapter 6 is another valid example of how a bureaucracy can be made more responsive to the problems of its members.

The skunk works organizational unit described in Chapter 4 is another example of the value of creating small, semi-autonomous units within the larger organization. You may recall that these small units offer two important advantages—they encourage innovation, and they can accomplish results quickly.

Use Flat Structures

A logical alternative to the multilevel bureaucracy is to use flat organization structures, as diagrammed in Figure 14–2. Eliminating several layers of management serves two important ends. First, there is a substantial cost savings in running an organization with fewer managers. Second, decisions can be made more quickly because fewer people pass judgment on a given decision. Major corporations that have flattened their organization structure in recent years include AT&T, Ford, CBS, Unisys (the combination of Burroughs and Sperry), and Johnson & Johnson. Small business have traditionally used flat structures because they "run lean."

Consultant Tom Peters reports that many firms today have moved toward an organization structure in which the ratio of managers to nonmanagers is 1 to 100 at the bottom of the firm, and 1 to 20 at the top. The traditional number of employees supervised by one manager is about 1 to 15 at the bottom at 1 to 5 at the top of the organization.[15]

The flattening of organization structures does not necessarily mean that

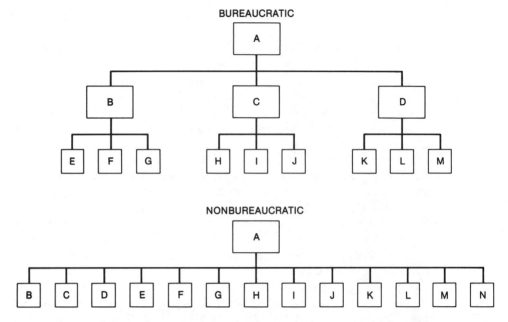

Figure 14–2 The contrast between a bureaucratic (tall) and a nonbureaucratic (flat) organization structure.

Note: This figure represents the contrast between two organizational subunits. A comparison between two total organizations would depict several more layers of management.

most middle managers will be terminated or that fewer business graduates will be hired. Instead of working as middle managers, many of these people will contribute directly to the enterprise through sales, product development, research, and manufacturing. Also, many people who would have worked as middle managers will now work as first-level superiors. One reason is that the position of first-level manager has grown in stature and responsibility in recent years. Many supervisors now perform some of the work performed by middle managers in the past.[16]

Improved Methods of Selection and Promotion

Several of the problems of a bureaucracy can be overcome by using valid methods of selecting and promoting employees. The Peter Principle, for instance, is not nearly so inevitable in organizations where people are carefully screened before being promoted. If it appears that an individual is unsuited to administrative work, that person should not be promoted into management. Such evidence could be obtained because of his or her performance on temporary assignments or on the administrative portions of his or her current responsibilities.

Another problem of misplacement in a bureaucracy is the "bureaucratic personality" who hides behind rules and regulations in order to avoid responsibility or conflict. If management detects these characteristics early in an individual's career, he or she can be appropriately counseled. Without improvement, that person is ineligible for promotion.

Sophisticated methods of personnel selection and promotion do exist. Much of the field of human resource management and personnel psychology is concerned with this matter. A number of large organizations, and some smaller ones, make effective use of assessment centers. Aside from using psychological tests and interviews, the assessment center method measures the performance of people on simulated work tasks. Before a person is promoted to a leadership position, his or her performance as a temporary leader has been carefully observed by several people (see Chapter 12).

INDIVIDUAL COPING STRATEGIES

Individuals too play an important role in coping with the problems sometimes created by a bureaucracy. The most general strategy is for you as a person embedded within a large bureaucracy to understand why the problem exists. For example, many people complain bitterly about the amount of "red tape" in government without recognizing why the problem came into being. Recognition, in turn, often leads to tolerance. A serious study of red tape offers an explanation of its origins in big government: "There are watchdogs who watch watchdogs watching watchdogs. . . . Much of the often-satirized clumsiness, slowness, and complexity of government procedures is merely the consequence of all these precautions."[17]

Here we will offer a number of tactical (and perhaps political) approaches to coping with problems often created by a bureaucracy. The reader is cautioned to select that strategy or strategies that best fits his or her personality and circumstance.

The competent person trick. However disorganized and ineffective a large bureaucracy may appear, there is usually a cadre of people at the lower levels who process the work. It is these people who keep track of the important transactions of the firm and who can furnish the information you might need to get your job accomplished. Once you discover this type of competent individual, write down his or her name and telephone extension.

Exchange favors. Reciprocity is another method commonly used by people who successfully cut their way through red tape. Usually this technique is a follow-up step to having identified a competent person. After he or she provides you the information you need to get your job accomplished, you reciprocate at some later date.

Do not put everything in writing. In a bureaucracy, once something goes into writing, it becomes a permanent record and could be subject to misinterpretation by any one of several people who receive the original or a copy. The person who did you a favor that required bending of a policy is therefore liable for reprimand.

Explain your problem to the right person. A curious aspect about most bureaucratic organizations is that many of the people who listen to your complaints are not empowered to do anything about them. Even if these *organizational buffers* are sympathetic to your problem, the best they can do is represent your point of view to a higher-ranking official. Taking your story to the right person eliminates the frustration of having to repeat your complaint several times.

Explain how your proposition fits into the system. If your demand or proposition can be tucked under an existing regulation or policy, it has a reasonable chance to being approved. If new policy is necessary in order to accept your proposition, its chances for acceptance are lowered. A case in point was the situation of a plant superintendent who wanted the plant repainted during a period of limited expenditures for refurbishing. He was able to acquire funds for repainting by tying the request into a proposal for reducing energy costs. The white paint he requested would pay for itself in the decreased amount of illumination required in the plant because of the painting.

Explain the problems created by a particular regulation. One logical approach to overcoming red tape is to confront the responsible official with the problems created by an unreasonable rule or regulation. The responsible official may be lacking a first-hand report of the way in which a particular directive is creating a dysfunction. One national field service manager was faced with the problem of high turnover among field engineers. Basically the job of field engineer consisted of repairing broken equipment under tight time constraints. An informal survey by the manager revealed that the field engineers were quitting because they were looking for promotion to managerial positions. The national service manager then requested that the "college graduate only" regulation be removed from the hiring standards.

The manager reasoned that field engineers who graduated from technical institutes would be less concerned about promotion to managerial positions. They would therefore remain longer in field engineering assignments. Confronted with the negative implications of the regulation about hiring only college graduates, the president said to the national service manager:

> It looks like we goofed on that one. You're the national service manager. Make up your own qualification list for field engineers. But don't overcompensate in the process by giving anybody who likes to tinker with mechanical equipment a job as a field engineer in our company.

Summary of Key Points

☐ In its technical meaning, bureaucracy refers to a form of organization in which the division of effort, rank, and rules and regulations are carefully defined. Ultimate control of the organization rests at the top of the organization. At its best, a bureaucracy is a rational, systematic, and precise form of organization.

☐ A bureaucracy is designed for maximum efficiency. Among its characteristics are (a) a division of labor based on functional specialization, a well-defined hierarchy of authority, (b) a system of rules covering the rights and duties of employees, (c) procedures for dealing with work situations, (d) impersonality in handling people, (e) promotion and selection based on technical competence.

☐ A bureaucracy offers some potential advantages: (a) personally given orders are unnecessary, (b) orders do not have to be repeated, (c) people can be controlled from a distance, (d) punishment for rule violation is legitimate, (e) an equitable division of resources, (f) machinelike efficiency, (g) promotion of democracy in the workplace.

☐ A bureaucracy also has some potential disadvantages: (a) delays in decision making, (b) confusion and inefficiency, (c) high frustration and low job satisfaction, (d) inversion of means and ends, (e) insensitivity to individual problems, (f) rigidity in behavior, (g) adverse changes in personality, (h) avoiding responsibility, (i) weakening of the connection between hard work and rewards, and (j) placing incompetent people into key positions.

☐ Four broad organizational strategies for coping with problems created by a bureaucracy are these: (a) use bureaucracy for recurring tasks, (b) use flexible organizational units, (c) use flat structures, and (d) use improved methods of selecting and promoting people.

☐ You can better cope with a bureaucracy if you understand why certain forms of red tape exist. In addition, (a) use the competent person trick, (b) exchange favors, (c) do not put everything in writing, (d) explain your problem to the right person, (e) explain how your proposition fits into the system, (f) explain the problems created by a particular regulation.

Questions and Activities

1. What connotations does the term "bureaucrat" have for most people?

2. Why are many people quite content to work in a bureaucracy?

3. Many small business owners contend they dislike bureaucracy. Nevertheless, these same people prefer large bureaucratic firms as customers. How do you reconcile these two points of view?

4. What is "red tape," and why is it often found in a bureaucracy?

5. What style of leadership do you suspect would probably be appropriate in most bureaucratic firms?

6. Bureaucracies are characterized by frequent staff meetings and committee meetings. What factors do you think lead to this preference for so many meetings?

7. Is your local Kentucky Fried Chicken a bureaucracy? Use the characteristics of a bureaucracy developed in this chapter to help develop your answer.

8. Some observers contend that once an organization prospers and then stabilizes in growth, it inevitably becomes a bureaucracy. Why might this be true?

9. A federal government executive told me: "Make sure your readers realize how flexible and responsive a bureaucracy like the government can be." Provide an example to support this position.

10. What problem might arise if large numbers of workers used the individual strategies for coping with a bureaucracy described in this chapter?

A Human Relations Case

I WISH YOU WOULD STOP FIGHTING THE SYSTEM

Fred Reed entered the world of big business at age 22 as a loss-prevention technician in Trans National Insurance Company. His major job responsibility was to work as part of a team effort in providing advice to insureds (customers) about how to prevent losses. Potential losses include fire, theft, water damage, and job-related accidents. Fred's role on the team effort was to collect information and feed that information to a team leader. Within a month or two, a report would be sent to the insured firm about potential trouble spots. For example, on one field visit Fred discovered that an innocent-looking water stain on an office ceiling was a symptom of a leaking water pipe. If the pipe were not repaired, the leak could enlarge thus causing substantial water damage.

Between field trips, Fred's job duties included such items as checking the arithmetic and looking for typographical and factual errors in reports, studying company manuals, and studying insurance claims reports filed in the past. Fred much preferred being in the field to working in the office. Poring over old reports at his work station one day, Fred thought to himself: "I need some action. Sitting here studying insurance history is for the birds." He then proceeded to request a conference with his boss, Barbara.

"What can I do for you today, Fred?" said Barbara.

"Really I just wanted to rap about company policies and procedures. I know Trans National is a giant in its field. And maybe that is part of the problem."

"Part of what problem?" asked Barbara with a puzzled look.

"Trans National could be suffering from company arteriosclerosis. You know, hardening of the arteries from being so big. A friend of mine joined the army after graduation. I think he has more freedom on the job than I do.

"Freedom?" asked Barbara, "You have plenty of freedom. You're out in the field about two-thirds of the time."

"I mean the freedom to be more of my own man. I would like to have the authority to tell the insureds directly what steps I think they should take to prevent losses. Like that water spot on the ceiling. I don't see why we had to spend two weeks writing a report. I could have just marched into the maintenance supervisor's office and told him to fix or replace the leaking pipe."

"I can see your point of view, Fred. But an insurance company the size of ours just doesn't operate off the cuff. We are a tightly regulated industry. We therefore have to follow carefully hundreds of rules and regulations.

"Fred, so long as we're on this topic, there is something else I should bring to your attention. Mr. Gantt, our marketing vice president for personal lines of insurance, sent a memo to me about you. It said that you stopped him in the halls to suggest that Trans National set up insurance booths in department stores, the way Allstate does in Sears stores. Maybe that is a good idea, but you have to go through channels.

You should bring your suggestions to me. I would then send them along through appropriate channels."

"I guess it's these appropriate channels that bugs me," said Fred. "I like the insurance field, but I do have some problems with doing everything the company way."

"Fred, I'm glad you like the insurance field. We are pleased with your enthusiasm and imagination. But I wish you would stop fighting the system."

1. Why is this case included in a chapter about bureaucracy?
2. How can Fred learn to stop fighting the system? Or should he be required to stop fighting the system?
3. What criticisms would you make of Barbara's approach to dealing with the complaint by the marketing vice-president?

A Human Relations Incident

THE INTRACTABLE SAVINGS BANK

Carla Gonzalez, the owner of budget printing center, began to earn a profit two years after setting up shop. She then took the initiative to establish a Keogh Plan (a retirement plan for the self-employed). Carla's plan was established at a local savings bank. The Keogh Plan she chose allowed the investor to make deposits of any size, and at any time during the year.

Each month Carla would make deposits into her plan of anywhere from $50 to $275. Once her taxes were filed, Carla would know precisely how much she could pay into her plan, since a Keogh Plan owner can contribute up to 15 percent of net profits to the plan annually. Each time a Keogh Plan owner makes a deposit into his or her account, the contributor is assigned a new account number. Over the first five years of the plan, Carla made 51 deposits and received 51 account numbers.

Carla then relocated to new headquarters a few blocks away from her original location. She filed all the necessary address changes, including notifying the savings bank. Mysteriously, the bank continued to send most—but not all—of its correspondence to Carla's old address. Carla filed another address change with the bank, but the problem persisted. Irritated, Carla called the savings bank and was given this explanation of what happened:

"According to our regulations, each account requires a separate change of address. We send out correspondence based on individual account numbers. So far you have only notified us of an address change for one account number. If you want all your mail going to your new address, you will have to file 51 change of address notices— one for each account. I'm sorry, but these are our regulations."

1. In what way is the bank behaving bureaucratically?
2. How could one defend the bank's position?
3. How should Carla handle this situation?
4. If you were Carla, would you file 51 change of address notices?

A Human Relations Exercise

DO YOU HAVE A BUREAUCRATIC ORIENTATION?

A person with a bureaucratic orientation is one who fits comfortably into the role of working in a bureaucracy. Unless the world were populated with people who adjust readily to working for a bureaucracy, organizations such as AT&T or the Ford Motor Company could not function. Other people—those with a low bureaucratic orientation—experience feelings of discomfort working for a bureaucracy. The bureaucratic orientation scale presented next gives you a chance to acquire tentative (not scientifically proved) information about your position on this important aspect of work life.[18]

Directions: Answer each question "mostly agree" or "mostly disagree." Assume that you are trying to learn something about yourself. Do not assume that your answer will be shown to a prospective employer.

	Mostly Agree	Mostly Disagree
1. I value stability in my job.	___	___
2. I like a predictable organization.	___	___
3. The best job for me would be one in which the future is uncertain.	___	___
4. The military would be a nice place to work.	___	___
5. Rules, policies, and procedures tend to frustrate me.	___	___
6. I would enjoy working for a company that employed 85,000 people worldwide.	___	___
7. Being self-employed would involve more risk than I'm willing to take.	___	___
8. Before accepting a job, I would like to see an exact job description.	___	___
9. I would prefer a job as a freelance house painter to one as a clerk for the Department of Motor Vehicles.	___	___
10. Seniority should be as important as performance in determining pay increases and promotion.	___	___
11. It would give me a feeling of pride to work for the largest and most successful company in its field.	___	___
12. Given a choice, I would prefer to make $50,000 per year as a vice-president in a small company to $60,000 as a staff specialist in a large company.	___	___
13. I would regard wearing an employee badge with a number on it as a degrading experience.	___	___
14. Parking spaces in a company lot should be assigned on the basis of job level.	___	___
15. If an accountant works for a large organization, he or she cannot be a true professional.	___	___

16. Before accepting a job (given a choice), I would want to make sure that the company had a very fine program of employee benefits. _____ _____

17. A company will probably not be successful unless it establishes a clear set of rules and procedures. _____ _____

18. Regular working hours and vacations are more important to me than finding thrills on the job. _____ _____

19. You should respect people according to their rank. _____ _____

20. Rules are meant to be broken. _____ _____

Scoring and Interpretation. Give yourself a plus one for each question that you answered in the bureaucratic direction:

1. Mostly agree	8. Mostly agree	15. Mostly disagree
2. Mostly agree	9. Mostly disagree	16. Mostly agree
3. Mostly disagree	10. Mostly agree	17. Mostly agree
4. Mostly agree	11. Mostly agree	18. Mostly agree
5. Mostly disagree	12. Mostly disagree	19. Mostly agree
6. Mostly agree	13. Mostly disagree	20. Mostly disagree
7. Mostly agree	14. Mostly agree	

Although the bureaucratic orientation scale is currently a self-examination and research tool, a very high score (15 or over) would suggest that you would enjoy working in a bureaucracy. A very low score (5 or lower) would suggest that you would be frustrated by working in a bureaucracy, especially a large one.

Notes

1. Leonard V. Gordon, "Measurement of Bureaucratic Orientation," *Personal Psychology*, Spring 1970, p. 3.

2. Richard W. Weiss, "Weber on Bureaucracy: Management Consultant or Political Theorist?" *Academy of Management Review*, April 1983, p. 243.

3. Max Weber, *Economy and Society: An Outline of Interpretative Sociology* (New York: Bedminster Press, 1968; originally published in 1925), pp. 956–958; Michael J. Wriston, "In Defense of Bureaucracy," *Public Administration Review*, March–April 1980, p. 179.

4. The first four advantages described here are an extension of the reasoning in Alvin W. Gouldner, *Patterns of Industrial Bureaucracy* (New York: Free Press, 1954).

5. Max Weber, *Essays in Sociology*, quoted in Gary Dessler, *Organization and Management* (Englewood Cliffs, NJ: Prentice Hall, 1976), p. 31.

6. Wriston, "In Defense of Bureaucracy," p. 180.

7. "Cost-Conscious Firms Trim their Middle Management," *Washington Post* story syndicated October 27, 1985.

8. J. D. Donavid (pen name), "The Bureaucracy Lives," *Dun's Review*, April 1972, pp. 93–96.

9. Nicholas Dimarco and Steven Norton, "Life Style, Organization Structure, Congruity, and Job Satisfaction," *Personnel Psychology*, Winter 1974, pp. 581–591.

10. Robert K. Merton, "Bureaucratic Structure and Personality," *Social Forces*, vol. 18, 1940.

11. Victor Thompson, "Bureaucracy and Innovation," *Administrative Science Quarterly*, June 1965, pp. 1–20; Christopher W. Allinson, *Bureaucratic Personality and Organisation Structure* (Brookfield, VT: Gower Publishing Company, 1984).

12. B. J. Hodge and William P. Anthony, *Organization Theory: An Environmental Approach* (Boston: Allyn and Bacon, 1979), p. 435.

13. Robert Jackall, "Moral Mazes: Bureaucracy and Managerial Work," *Harvard Business Review*, September–October 1983, p. 130.

14. Laurence J. Peter and Raymond Hull, *The Peter Principle* (New York: William Morrow, 1969), p. 26.

15. The Tom Peters Group, *A World Turned Upside Down* (Palo Alto, CA: Excel, 1986), p. 16.

16. "The Old Foreman Is on the Way Out, and the New One Will Be More Important," *Business Week*, April 25, 1983, p. 75; Andrew J. DuBrin, *The Practice of Supervision: Achieving Results through People*, 2nd ed. (Plano, TX: Business Publications, 1987), p. 5.

17. Herbert Kaufman, *Red Tape: Its Origins, Uses, and Abuses* (Washington, DC: The Brookings Institution, 1977).

18. The idea for this scale stems from the research of Leonard V. Gordon (see note 1).

Suggested Reading

BESS, JAMES L., ed. *College and University Organization: Insights from the Behavioral Sciences.* New York: New York University Press, 1984.

FISCH, FRANK, and SIRIANNI, CARMEN, eds. *Critical Studies in Organization and Bureaucracy.* Philadelphia: Temple University Press, 1984.

HAGE, JERALD, ed. *Futures of Organizations.* Lexington, MA: Lexington Books, 1986.

HALL, CHARLES. "The Informal Organization Chart." *Supervisory Management.* January 1986, pp. 40–42.

HUMMEL, RALPH P. *The Bureaucratic Experience*, 2nd ed. New York: St. Martin's Press, 1982.

MEYER, MARSHALL W., STEVENSON, WILLIAM, and WEBSTER, STEPHEN. *Limits to Bureaucratic Growth.* Hawthorne, NY: Walter de Gruyter, Inc., 1984.

TOWNSEND, ROBERT. *Further Up the Organization.* New York: Knopf, 1984.

WERHANE, PATRICIA. *Persons, Rights, and Corporations.* Englewood Cliffs, NJ: Prentice Hall, 1985.

Organizational Culture and Quality of Work Life

In this chapter we study two aspects of organizations that are related to effectiveness, organizational culture and quality of work life. Culture, as described in Chapter 2, deals with the norms and beliefs that govern the behavior of organizational members. Quality of work life focuses on how well the needs of organization members are being met on the job, as described in Chapter 13. Culture and QWL are closely related. As Figure 15–1 shows, the organizational culture directly influences quality of work life. From this perspective, organizational culture is considered to be a major component of quality of work life.[1]

In addition to providing insight into the nature and meaning of organizational culture and quality of work life, we will also describe formal attempts to improve organizational culture and QWL.

DEFINITIONS AND DIMENSIONS OF ORGANIZATIONAL CULTURE

In recent years, the idea of organizational culture has gained in stature and importance. Many observers have noted that the organizational culture influences performance both positively and negatively. If the culture encourages good performance, the organization will generally prosper. If the culture discourages good performance, improved work systems and motivational methods are unlikely to enhance productivity. A good starting point in understanding organizational culture is to review its many definitions and dimensions.

Figure 15–1   The link between organizational culture and QWL.

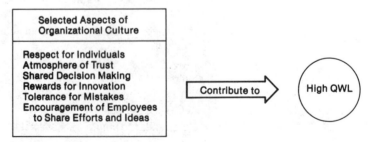

Figure 15–2　Representative definitions of organizational culture.

1. Unspoken rules and assumptions that determine how the organization operates and what it is like.
2. Norms by which the organization operates.
3. The soul of the organization.
4. The invisible force behind the organization.
5. An individual's theory of what co-workers know, believe, and mean, of the code they are following, and the game they are playing.
6. The sum total of an organization's beliefs, values, philosophies, traditions, and sacred cows.
7. A subtle and complex set of unwritten rules and matter-of-fact prejudices; a value system.
8. Deeper level of basic assumptions and beliefs that are shared by members of an organization, that operate subconsciously, and that define in a basic "taken-for-granted" fashion an organization's view of itself and its environment.
9. A system of shared values and beliefs that actively shape the firm's management style and employee's day-to-day behaviors.

SOURCE: Definitions (1), (3), and (4) are from Ralph H. Kilmann, "Corporate Culture," *Psychology Today*, pp. 62–68; definition (5) is from Roger Keesing, "Theories of Culture," in *Annual Review of Anthropology*, no. 3, 1974, p. 73; definition (6) is from Robert Desatnick, "Management Climate Surveys: A Way to Uncover an Organization's Culture," *Personnel*, May 1986, p. 49; definition (7) is from Jane C. Linder, "Computers, Corporate Culture and Change," *Personnel Journal*, September 1985, p. 49; definition (8) is from Edgar H. Schein, "Are You Corporate Cultured?" *Personnel Journal*, November 1986, p. 84; definitions (2) and (9) are general information.

Definitions of Culture

Since culture has become so important, it has been defined in many ways, as shown in Figure 15–2. Despite this diversity of opinion, the definition of culture presented in relation to work motivation encompasses most meanings of the term: **Organizational culture** is a system of shared values and beliefs that actively influence the behavior of organizational members.

Dimensions of Culture

Stemming from the definition of organizational culture are its dimensions (components, ingredients, or important aspects). Research about the dimensions of culture began when culture was described as **climate,** an organization's personality as seen by its members. Culture now refers to shared assumptions, while climate refers to shared perceptions.[2] Pinpointing the dimensions of culture is important because it helps one understand the nature of the subtle forces that influence every employee's actions. For instance, the dimension of "risk taking" will encourage employees to try new procedures without undue concern that they will be punished for failed ideas.

An important fact about the dimensions of culture is that many of them overlap (are intercorrelated or interrelated). To illustrate, a firm with a steep hierarchy is also likely to have many rites and rituals, such as formal management meetings. The dimensions of culture described below are associated with culture in more recent studies.[3] Insight into dimensions of organizational climate can be obtained from the questionnaire on measuring organizational climate presented later in the chapter.

Values. Values are the foundation of any organizational or corporate culture. The organization's philosophy is expressed through values, and values guide behavior on a day-to-day basis. Representative values include concern for employee welfare, a belief that the customer is always right, a commitment to quality, and an enduring desire to please stockholders. A manager whose firm's strongest value was to please stockholders would be willing to lay off employees in order to increase short-range profits.

Heroes and heroines. Corporate heroes and heroines are the people who introduce innovations, who "make waves," inspire others, and have a vision of the future of the firm. Terrence Deal and Allan Kennedy draw a contrast between heroes and heroines and the managers who are more disciplined and take care of the status quo.[4] Among the terms used to identify heroes and heroines are "crown princes and princesses," "comers," and "fast trackers." In some firms these people are given special opportunities for good assignments and special training. At AT&T Communications, for example, heroes and heroines make up the Manager Succession Group.

Rites and rituals. Part of an organization's culture is its traditions, its rites and rituals. Few organizations think they have rites and rituals, yet an astute observer can always identify them. Examples include regular staff meetings, retirement banquets (even for fired executives), and receptions for visiting executives. More details about organizational rites are presented in Figure 15–3. Do you see most of these rites as serving a useful purpose?

Cultural networks. Cultural networks function as grapevines for telling stories that communicate organizational norms. The networks are indispensable for maintaining a culture, because cultural values, beliefs, and practices, are unwritten. A story that circulates throughout Domino's Pizza concerns how pizza dough was flown into a branch location that was running short. The message is that customer satisfaction is so important the company will spend huge sums of money to avert dissatisfaction, even for one night. (Note that stories told through the cultural networks can be real or imagined. The Domino story is true.)

Relative diversity. The existence of an organizational culture assumes some degree of homogeneity. Nevertheless, organizations differ on how much deviation

Figure 15–3 Organizational rites.

Type of Rites	Examples
Rites of passage	Induction and basic training in army
Rite of degradation	Firing and replacing top executive
Rites of enhancement	Mary Kay seminars (for sales reps of beauty products)
Rites of renewal	Organizational development activities (see Chapter 16)
Rites of conflict reduction	Collective bargaining
Rites of integration	Office holiday party

SOURCE: Adapted with permission from Harrison M. Trice and Janice M. Beyer, "Studying Organizational Cultures Through Rules and Ceremonials," *The Academy of Management Review*, October 1984, p. 657.

from conformity they tolerate. Many firms are highly homogeneous: Executives talk in a similar manner and even look alike; people from similar educational backgrounds and fields of specialty are promoted into key jobs. Many conglomerates, for example, promote only managers with financial backgrounds into key positions. Here is a representative example of a cultural value against diversity:[5]

> After moving into several floors of a New York City office building, the chief executive officer (CEO) had an assistant make regular tours of all offices. There had been a corporate "decorating" plan dictating number and style of wall decorations, placement as well as style of furniture, and a clear rule that nothing was to be left out on horizontal surfaces at the end of the work day. Violators spotted by the presidential assistant received sharply worded reprimands from the president.

Resource allocation and rewards. How money and other resources are allocated has a critical influence on culture. The investment of resources sends a message to people about what is valued in the firm. Assume the head of a government agency contends that client service must be improved. If new budget allocations are made to support programs for improved service, employees will believe that client service is important. Conversely, if no new resources are allocated, employees will believe that talk about improved client services is only rhetoric.

The status system of the organization is also shaped by decisions about resource allocation. Increasing an organizational unit's budget and providing it with new office space increases the unit's status. Conversely, receiving a substantial budget cut results in a loss in status. Being moved to a lesser office has a similar effect.

Steepness of the hierarchy. The culture of some organizations is very hierarchical (bureaucratic). Such a culture is maintained by heavy emphasis on formal, written memos; going through channels; and the discouragement of informal contacts. Bypassing a layer of management is taboo, and few people have contact with the CEO except for immediate subordinates. Another cultural feature of a steep hierarchy is that senior managers rarely visit the work sites. In a flatter organization, top managers regularly visit the offices, factories, and stores (operations).

Firms with steep hierarchies are more concerned with controls and securities than firms with flatter hierarchies. In steep firms there are many procedures for multiple approvals and signoffs. Even top managers must receive approval for minor expenditures. Some of the slowness in decision making observed in a bureaucracy is attributed to this penchant for security.

Degree of stability. A fast-paced, dynamic organization has a different culture and climate from a slow-paced, stable one. Top management sends out signals, by its own energetic or lethargic stance, about how much it welcomes innovation. "Change-oriented organizations have a distinctive tempo; everything moves faster and more deliberately, in contrast to the slow-paced beat to which stability-oriented organizations march."[6]

Administrative practices. A final dimension of culture to be considered here are the various administrative practices of key functional groups such as finance, accounting, or production. One example is how much emphasis the firm has traditionally placed on reaching financial targets. For instance, if the firm values ever-increasing yearly profits, it may be difficult to invest heavily in modernization of equipment and facilities. Administrative practices that emphasize financial performance may also discourage managers from investing too much time and money in the development of personnel. This situation is similar to a basketball coach not giving lesser players much playing time in order to maximize winning margins.

The dimensions described here can lead to an understanding of the culture of a given organization. Simultaneously, they hint at how organizational cultures are formed.

HOW ORGANIZATIONAL CULTURES
ARE FORMED AND MEASURED

Another approach to understanding organizational cultures is to examine how they are formed, and how researchers have attempted to measure them.

The Formation of Organizational Cultures

An organization's culture typically has its origins in the values, administrative practices, and personality of the founding executives. In many practices, a charismatic founder shapes the culture of the organization. A prime example is Thomas

Watson of IBM, who originated the values of going to great lengths to please customers, and insisted that employees observe rules carefully. Leonard R. Sayles and Robert V. L. Wright observe that culture responds to and mirrors the conscious and unconscious choices, behavior patterns, and prejudices of top management. Furthermore, top managers are not the victims, but the architects of the organizational climate.[7]

Another major way in which cultures are established is through **socialization,** how employees come to understand the values, norms, and customs essential for adapting to the organization.[8] Socialization is therefore a method of indoctrinating employees into the organization in such a way that they perpetuate the culture. If new employees were not socialized, the culture would lose its distinctiveness. Socialization continues throughout an employee's stay with the firm, for there are constant subtle reminders of which behaviors and values are appropriate.

The socialization process is carried out formally and informally. Larger firms are more likely to have a formal socialization process that includes training and orientation programs. A well-known investment firm, for example, sends its new financial consultants to a six-week training program in New York City. Aside from intensive training to prepare for a broker's license, the recruits are familiarized with the beliefs and values of the firm. Trainees are given tips on dress codes, professional appearance and behavior, and ethical client behavior. Directors of the program are encouraged to help weed out those men and women who show resistance to these norms.

Informal socialization take such forms as listening to more experienced workers, and observing what others are doing and saying. New employees are often not consciously aware that they are being socialized. Yet they gradually incorporate key aspects of the culture into their behavior and speech. One example is the new employees hired by a U.S. Navy support group. Several months after joining, the employees will pepper their speech with the question, "How does this support the fleet?" The value they are expressing is that everything one does in this organization should ultimately help the sailors at sea.

Stephen P. Robbins notes that a formal socialization process is more controllable; there is a higher probability that the culture will be perpetuated in the desired way. The informal socialization process is dependent upon whom the new employee uses as a socializing agent.[9] Some employees subscribe more to the culture than do others.

The Measurement of Organization Culture

Managers, staff specialists, and researchers alike are concerned about measuring organizational culture. One reason is that culture has important consequences, as we will see. Another reason is that culture is difficult to change if it cannot be measured. The typical way of measuring culture is simply to observe what organization members do and say, and then make inferences. For instance, if employees are demoted for disagreeing with their bosses at meetings, we can conclude that one dimension of culture is "extreme loyalty" or "rigid conformity."

Another way of measuring organizational culture is to use a written questionnaire. One such questionnaire is the Organizational Climate Index Survey (OCIS) shown in Figure 15–4. The questionnaire measures four components of climate (or culture): job, communication, management, and motivation/morale. James L. Nave, developer of the OCIS, says that evalaution of survey results offers a variety of information. In addition to measuring attitudes toward the climate, the scores identify areas for improvement.[10] The questionnaire method of measuring organizational climate is a version of the survey feedback approach to organization development described in Chapter 16.

Figure 15–4 A questionnaire for measuring organizational climate.

Organizational Climate Index

The following survey will be used to determine the state of our organizational climate. Rate each item on the basis of the following:

90–100	Excellent
80–89	Good
70–79	Fair
60–69	Poor
0–59	Very Poor

Your thoughtful, accurate responses will help make our organization stronger and a better place to work. If you have questions about the survey, please ask your supervisor. If you do not have sufficient information to answer a question or have no opinion on a topic, do not answer that question. Place your complete unsigned survey in the box

located at _____ by _____ _____
                    (location)   (date)   (time)

SECTION I: JOB

1. Our organization provides adequate training for new employees.   _____
2. Our organization provides adequate training for new employees to develop new skills.   _____
3. Job expectations are realistic and clearly stated.   _____
4. Our facilities are clean, safe, and functional.   _____
5. Information, materials, and equipment necessary to do my job are provided.   _____
6. My job is challenging and contains enough variety to be interesting.   _____
7. The quantity of work associated with my job is not too much or too little.   _____

                                                          Subtotal   _____

SECTION II: COMMUNICATION

1. Our organization has clear, well-written policies, procedures, and guidelines. _____
2. There is an adequate amount of communication within our organization. _____
3. Methods of communication within our organization are varied (individual contact, group meetings, memos/letters, newsletters, etc.). _____
4. Communication within our organization is timely, accurate, and complete. _____
5. Two-way communication is encouraged and present in our organization. _____
6. There is regular direct person to person contact and opportunity for communication between supervisiors and staff. _____

Subtotal _____

SECTION III: MANAGEMENT

1. Effective planning is a characteristic of our organization. _____
2. Decision making is timely and effective. _____
3. People are given an opportunity to participate in decisions that affect them. _____
4. Evaluations are handled in a fair and professional manner. _____
5. Disciplinary action is taken only when justified and actions taken are appropriate. _____
6. Grievance situations are handled in a fair and unbiased manner. _____
7. Authority is adequately delegated in our organization. _____
8. Our organization is receptive to innovation and change. _____

Subtotal _____

SECTION IV: MOTIVATION AND MORALE

1. Salaries are fair in relation to job requirements, experience, and quality of work. _____
2. Benefits are adequate. _____
3. Working relationships with co-workers are positive and enjoyable. _____
4. Working relationships with supervisors are positive and enjoyable. _____
5. There is tolerance for individual differences and dissent within our organization. _____
6. Good work brings appreciation and recognition. _____
7. A spirit of cooperation and respect for others exists in our organization. _____
8. Employees take pride in their work and our organization. _____

Subtotal _____
Organizational Climate Index _____

SOURCE: James L. Nave, "Gauging Organizational Climate," *Management Solutions*, June 1986, pp. 16–17. Reprinted with permission of the American Management Association, copyright © 1986.

CONSEQUENCES AND IMPLICATIONS
OF ORGANIZATIONAL CULTURE

Organizational culture has received much attention in this text and elsewhere because it has a pervasive impact on organizational effectiveness. The major consequences and implications of organization culture are outlined in Figure 15–5, and summarized below.

Productivity and Morale

A major justification for studying, or trying to change, an organization's culture is that it influences the level of productivity and morale.[11] A culture that emphasizes productivity encourages workers to be productive. And a culture that values the dignity of human beings tends to foster high morale and job satisfaction. Conversely, a culture that encourages mediocre performance leads to low productivity. And a culture that has no real commitment to the welfare of employees is beset with problems of low morale and low job satisfaction.

Implementation of Organizational Goals

Edgar H. Schein reports that many firms have found they can devise new strategies that make sense from a marketing or financial viewpoint. Yet often they cannot implement those strategies because they require changes in values and beliefs that differ from the culture. One company could not implement the goal of selling to a less sophisticated market because the salespeople unconsciously looked down upon these new potential customers.[12]

Competitive Advantage

An example of a valuable culture is one that contains the eight characteristics of a successful organization cited by Peters and Waterman (see Chapter 13). A rare culture is one that is statistically infrequent, such as a firm in which employees

Figure 15–5 Consequences and implications of organizational culture.

- Productivity and Morale
- Goal Implementation
- Competitive Advantage
- Compatibility of Mergers and Acquisitions
- Recruitment and Retention of Creative Employees
- Directs Activities of Leaders

volunteer to take a pay cut when business is poor. A unique or special culture is important, because it prevents other firms from becoming directly competitive. One of the many reasons such a culture may be difficult to imitate is that it has developed over a long period of time.[13]

Compatibility in Mergers and Acquisitions

Evidence is mounting that a substantial numbers of mergers and acquisitions lead to poor results—the performance of the combined partners often decreases. A major reason for these failed mergers is incompatibility between the cultures of the merged firms.[14]

General Motors decided not to risk a clash of cultures when it acquired Hughes Aircraft Company. The high-tech, risk-taking culture of Hughes was thought to be incompatible with the more conservative GM. A GM executive said: "Hughes has a culture we don't want to disturb and a technology we want to tap." The aircraft company was therefore turned into an independent subsidiary.[15]

Directing Leaders' Activities

Yet another important consequence of culture is that it directs the activities of organizational leaders. Much of a leader's time is spent working with the subtle forces that shape the attitudes and values of organization members. Schein states that leadership is the ability to manage culture. However, this is a complex and confusing role, because culture determines such things as how the internal system of authority and work is organized.[16]

CHANGING THE ORGANIZATIONAL CULTURE

Given the importance of organizational culture to the success of the firm, there are many times when it would be advisable to change it in a positive direction. A firm might want to encourage innovation and risk taking at all levels in order to be more competitive. An organization's culture is difficult and time-consuming to change, and is much like a human changing his or her personality. Two general strategies for changing organizational culture are (1) deliberate effort by top management, and (2) formal change programs.

Managerial Strategies for Changing the Culture

Top management can sometimes bring about a change in culture because most of the dimensions of culture mentioned above are mutable. Culture responds to and reflects the conscious and unconscious choices, behavior patterns, and biases of top management. To bring about change, top management would have to deal with the organization's total internal structure, with relationships among people, and with work systems. Sayles and Wright recommend that the chief executive officer (CEO) take these specific steps to reshape his or her organizational culture:[17]

> First, accept culture as an instrument of leadership, not as a deterrent to leadership.
>
> Second, using trusted assistants, obtain feedback on current action, and on the stated or unstated signals being communicated.
>
> Third, compare current actions within the firm with actions that would be desirable to support and sustain new directions for the organization. (To stimulate a critical assessment, it is advisable to ask what type of culture would be ideal if one were to start from scratch.)

These statements may sound abstract. To better understand what a CEO must do to change a culture, visualize a situation in which you are trying to make an entire firm more conscious of giving high-quality service to its clientele. Just imagine how many practices would have to be changed, from employees being more prompt in gathering information to fixing broken pedals on water fountains.

Formal Programs for Changing the Culture

A more concrete approach to changing the culture is to conduct organization development programs geared toward this purpose. A comprehensive program of this kind was developed by William Ouchi. The major purpose of his program was to help American firms develop a Japanese-style climate that encourages widespread employee participation. His program included getting top management to develop a philosophy of heavy commitment to employees. Ouchi labeled the Japanese-style firm Type Z, while the typical American firm is Type A (autocratic).[18]

One formal program for improving the organizational culture has been developed by Larry B. Meares. It begins with a careful assessment of the current culture, using interviews with managers to gather such information as:

- How organizational decisions are made
- How employees react, verbally and nonverbally, to strangers
- What people think, know, and repeat about the organization's origins
- How hierarchical levels are structured

After analyzing the information from the interviews, the human resource professional prepares a workshop for management aimed at bringing about necessary changes in culture. Members of management then meet many times with the workshop leader to discuss strategy for making the improvements. The ideal is to create a work environment "in which employees are treated as adults, and participation and the open exchange of ideas is encouraged."[19] The change process is so comprehensive that it even involves reviewing the compensation system and issuing new policy manuals.

One concern we have about this type of change effort is that it is too comprehensive. It is like asking management to correct everything that is wrong with the organization. Usually it is more fruitful to tackle one problem at a time.

QUALITY OF WORK LIFE TODAY

Quality of work life, as shown in Figure 15–1, is now linked to certain aspects of organizational culture. However, quality of life on the job has been of interest to human relations specialists for over 50 years. Today such interest is part of the quality of work life (QWL) movement. It is based on the premise that people need quality work experiences in order to function properly. Workers who perceive themselves as having a high QWL also enjoy better physical and mental health.[20] Many years of studying the relationship between work and health led Robert L. Kahn to conclude:[21]

> Providing work is paramount for individual and social well-being; for this reason jobs should be created as necessary. The adequacy of jobs is almost as important as their availability; the quality of work experience should therefore become a matter of national priority.

Although the vast majority of company, government, and union officials do not think that quality of work life programs should be mandated by law, thousands of such programs have emerged in recent years. Before describing some of these programs, it is important to pin down the meaning of quality of work life. One approach to defining quality of work life equates a high QWL with the existence of a certain set of working conditions and management practices. To illustrate, it is argued that a high QWL exists when jobs are enriched, participative management is practiced, employees are involved in their work, and safe working conditions exist.

The second major approach to defining quality of work life equates a good quality of work life with the impact working conditions have on the well-being of individual workers. A good QWL would therefore be a workplace in which individuals are safe, experience job satisfaction, and are able to grow and develop as human beings. Thus QWL is equivalent to the degree to which the full range of human needs is met.[22]

The reason we have presented two approaches to defining QWL is that the concept is so broad. To simplify matters, the following definition of QWL is recommended: **Quality of work life** is the extent to which employees are able to satisfy important needs through their work experiences, with particular emphasis on participating in important decisions about their work.

HOW EMPLOYEES PERCEIVE QUALITY OF WORK LIFE

Quality of work life, like organizational climate and work stress, is based on employees' perceptions. If they perceive work as satisfying the needs they want satisfied on the job, their QWL will be high. Conversely, unmet needs lead to a low quality of work life. It is generally assumed that participation in decision making is the major contributor to a positive QWL. Mark E. Levine took a more scientific approach by surveying worker perceptions of the components of quality of work life.[23]

The population for his study was the entire workforce employed by a small microchip manufacturer in Idaho. The sample consisted of 126 employees engaged in all production, staff, and managerial functions. Levine began by interviewing employees about quality of work life, using group decision-making techniques. Interview responses were later converted into a written questionnaire to allow for quantitative analysis.

The Six QWL Criteria

Analysis of the interview responses resulted in a list of 68 QWL concepts. These were later reduced by statistical methods to a final 6 criteria of quality of work life, as perceived by the workforce. The final criteria are known to be relatively independent (minimum amount of overlap), as determined by a technique called *regression analysis*:[24]

1. *Relationship between home life and working life.* When the two operate in harmony, QWL tends to be high. An example of harmony would be when your work does not interfere with family obligations.
2. *Basic individual needs.* Unless a person's basic needs (such as remuneration and job security) are met on the job, work life cannot be of high quality.
3. *Open area.* People in this sample felt they needed ample physical space in order to enjoy life on the job. In general, workers do not like to feel physically constrained and cramped.
4. *Committee representation.* Workers believed that being part of a labor-management committee improved their work life. (This is in line with the current meaning of QWL.)
5. *Growth potential of work-related activities.* As described in the two-factor theory of job satisfaction and motivation, the opportunity for growth leads to worker satisfaction (see Chapter 3).
6. *Identification with product quantity.* In the microchip manufacturing industry, the counting of wafer chips is the lifeline to survival. For this reason, identification with product quantity is an important criterion of QWL among these employees.

Research Conclusion

Levine concluded that aspects of the industry, the design of the organization, and the external environment affect the definition of QWL. For instance, in an era of high unemployment and competitive pressures in the microchip business, it is not surprising that "basic individual needs" surfaced in importance. It was also concluded that the components of QWL are not universal: Different employee groups tend to have their own perceptions of what constitutes a good quality of work life.

LABOR-MANAGEMENT COMMITTEES AND QWL

Although these research findings have merit, most QWL programs center around **labor-management committees,** joint problem-solving groups composed of members of labor and management. Labor-management committees (LMCs) are also referred to as labor-management participation teams or worker-participation teams. Here we will describe one historically important QWL program and the conditions associated with successful QWL programs.

The Jamestown Area Labor–Management Committee[25]

Jamestown, New York, is the site of one of the best known and most successful communitywide joint labor-management committees in North America. The Jamestown Area Labor-Management Committee (JALMC) reversed the long decline of this heavily unionized industrial community of 75,000 people in the northeastern United States. In doing so, it has received prominent media attention. Jamestown has become a haven for students of quality of work life and industrial vitalization. Our interest here focuses on the use of worker-participation teams to make revitalization possible and in the process to enhance the quality of work life.

Why the program began. The origins of JALMC go back to the late 1960s. Jamestown had a reputation for having poor labor-management relations, characterized by eager-to-strike unions. Although the city's overall work stoppage record was in line with many other localities with a similar industrial base, its poor reputation helped speed the exodus of manufacturing jobs to the southern United States, and made industrial recruitment efforts difficult. A large proportion of the area's jobs were in wood furniture manufacturing and metal fabrication—industries deeply affected by the southern job migration.

The event that triggered the formation of the labor-management committee was the closing of Art Metal, a Jamestown firm employing 700 that had been in operation for 70 years. Art Metal's demise was especially disturbing because it was one of the area's largest employers and had recently built a large plant in a nearby suburb. In addition, several other plant closings were imminent, and over 2,000 workers feared they would lose their jobs. The impending crisis led Jamestown's mayor to bring together union and company officials to form the Jamestown Area Labor-Management Committee.

The mission of the joint committee was to save Jamestown's faltering industrial base. A committee structure was set up with union and management co-chairpersons. The governing body of JALMC included the two co-chairpersons, the mayor, the coordinator of the committee, and an equal number of labor and management representatives. A strategy was formulated to attempt to renew existing manufacturing firms. It was intended to increase union-management cooperation, develop the area's human resources, and provide technical and financial assistance to individual companies. It emphasized self-reliance rather than externally developed economic development. The labor committee facilitated the formation of worker-management participation teams (referred to here as labor-management committees) that helped the company solve a variety of technical, production, and personnel problems. A flavor of the contribution made by production workers under these arrangements can be obtained by reading the case illustration presented next.

Redesigning an old foundry. Visitors to Jamestown are often told the story of the redesign of the local Carborundum ceramic mold foundry. The plant was deemed to be a woefully inefficient and expensive operation. At one point the board of directors of the parent corporation weighed two alternatives. One, they could close the plant and relocate in a more favorable region. Two, they could make a substantial investment to bring the Jamestown facility up to modern standards.

The corporation hired an industrial engineering consulting firm to prepare cost estimates and a renovation plan. Almost concurrently, the plant's labor-management committee formed a working group on plant layout. Astounded by the consulting firm's $10.5 million renovation estimate (which many thought would force a corporation decision to shut down the plant), the layout subcommittee and plant engineers began to create an alternative set of plans. The plans incorporated over 100 suggestions from employees themselves.

Two years after the board of directors faced its decision, the twelve-member labor-management committee presented its design package to Carborundum's president. Four months later, the corporation approved a $5.5 million renovation plan that was largely based on the working group's recommendations. Note that its projected cost was about half that proposed by the consulting firm. However, the final outcome was not a total victory for the labor-management committee.

The newly rebuilt foundry was indeed much more efficient than before. As a result, a small number of production jobs were cut. One local union official interpreted the job cutting as a double-cross and pulled the union out of the plant committee. Two years later the official did rejoin the committee, but he became more cautious in dealing with management. "It taught us how important it is to keep a permanent record of who said what," he noted.

Where does QWL fit in? Membership in the joint committee contributes to quality of work life because many workers enjoy getting involved in decision making. The quality of work life is enhanced for other reasons too. Another union official noted that because of the joint committee, plant management is much more open, flexible, and willing to tailor production demands to the needs of employees. When layoffs become necessary, they are now scheduled in advance and timed in order to minimize the disruption of employees' lives. Management also presents the economic justification for layoffs to the union.

Shop-floor democracy. Another contribution of the LMCs at Jamestown is that they brought shop-floor democracy to several plants. **Shop-floor democracy** is the granting of decision-making authority to production workers. Production (or shop) workers have participated in several key management areas: plant rede-sign, bidding for jobs, purchasing new equipment, identifying training needs, and implementing new training programs. Jamestown's uniqueness lies in the sheer number of innovative practices among member firms.

The Jamestown Area Labor-Management Committee operated under the assumption that involving production workers in managerial decisions makes good sense and benefits both labor and management. Labor participation is motivated by knowledge that improving the production efficiency of a plant means greater job security. Participation also leads to greater commitment to the firm's well-being. The comments of one union leader illustrate this point:

> The company wanted to buy new spraying equipment for the paint shop. The employees who work there are highly skilled; it takes them seven or eight years to learn some of these jobs, and they knew that the new stuff would be a waste of money. So they told the company about it before it was too late. In the old days, it would have been bought, it would have broken down, and would never have been used again.

How QWL Ties in with Job Satisfaction and Productivity

At their best, quality of work life programs increase job satisfaction and productivity. When QWL programs do improve productivity, the improvement often comes about because of improved satisfaction. Edward M. Glaser explains this indirect relationship in terms of a labor union's perspective. As the union sees it, the major aspect of developing a QWL program is to create a climate that promotes employee job satisfaction. The key focus is not on improved productivity or reduced labor costs, but creating an atmosphere in which workers can participate in decisions that affect them.[26] By so doing, their job satisfaction is increased. Productivity improvement is a likely fallout from such worker involvement (as illustrated at Jamestown). Many managers believe that productivity gains should be a primary objective of quality of work life programs.

Some QWL programs have failed to achieve improvements in satisfaction and productivity while others have succeeded. A practical lesson to be learned from these successes and failures is that certain conditions are associated with successful programs. When these conditions are met, both job satisfaction and productivity are likely to increase. Nine of these conditions are as follows:[27]

- *QWL must be defined.* An organization's definition of QWL will shape the effort and eventual outcomes of its quality of work life program. If the definition is broad, for example, the program will lead to greater change.
- *Labor and management must be committed.* If top management and union officials involved in the QWL program are unwilling to accept changes in their own organization's function, the QWL effort will not lead to significant improvements.
- *Involve subordinate levels in QWL activities.* Employees at all levels should be involved in the planning of the QWL program. A negative example of this principle took place in a large consumer products organization. Both senior management and senior union officials in effect killed QWL efforts in one plant by mandating the adoption of these programs in their organization.
- *Learn from mistakes.* If an error is made in implementing a QWL program in one division of a company, that mistake should serve as a lesson for implementation in other divisions. You may recall the Jamestown incident in which a union official was miffed about layoff of production workers due to improved efficiency. From that point on, such contingencies were put in writing.
- *Do not bypass middle management.* Once top management agrees to installing a QWL program, it often pushes ahead to create a joint union-management committee. This approach bypasses the involvement of middle management in learning about, defining, and commiting themselves to the QWL program. Middle layers of union management should also be involved to prevent later heel dragging.
- *Beware of personalities.* The people placed in leadership positions in the QWL program should have a leadership style appropriate to the situation. Errors have been made by appointing authoritarian-style managers in these positions. The result is that the spirit of workplace democracy is lost, dooming the QWL effort.
- *Identify goals.* Lee Ozley and Judith Ball recommended that organization members describe in some detail what they want their organization to be like over the long haul. "This description should address interpersonal processes such as how decisions get made and how people feel about the organization and each other."[28]
- *Use outside consulting help as needed.* The process of management and labor jointly developing a QWL program is a delicate one, often including a good deal of conflict resolution. Outside consultation is therefore often helpful. The external quality of work life facilitator (or consultant) should work with internal people in launching the program.
- *Personnel should be selected who can be motivated to strive for excellence in job performance.*[29] Amen!

Summary of Key Points

☐ Organizational culture refers to the norms and beliefs that govern the behavior of organizational members. Quality of work life refers to how well people's needs are being met on the job. The various dimensions of organizational culture include: values, heroes and heroines, rites and rituals, cultural networks, relative diversity of members, resource allocation and rewards, steepness of the hierarchy, degree of stability, and administrative practices.

☐ An organization's culture typically has its origins in the values, administrative practices, and personalities of the founding executives. Cultures are also formed and perpetuated through socialization, the process of understanding the values, norms, and customs essential for adapting to the organization.

☐ Organizational culture can be measured by observing what organizations do and say, and then making inferences about the culture. Another way of measuring organizational culture is by a written questionnaire such as that shown in Figure 15–4.

☐ The major consequences and implications of organizational culture are: (a) productivity and morale, (b) goal implementation, (c) competitive advantage for the firm, (d) compatibility of mergers and acquisitions, (e) recruitment and retention of creative employees, (f) directing the activities of leaders.

☐ Organizational cultures can sometimes be changed through managerial action, including providing new directions for the firm. Another approach to changing the culture is through formal programs designed for this purpose which involve diagnosing the culture and then making comprehensive changes in areas needing improvement. Despite these two methods, organizational culture is resistant to change.

☐ QWL is defined here as the extent to which employees are able to satisfy important work needs through their work experience, with particular emphasis on participating in important decisions about their work. Employee perceptions heavily influence whether their work life is of high quality. One study revealed that six criteria of QWL were particularly relevant for one group of employees. The same six criteria might be less relevant for another group of employees in another work setting.

☐ A well-known QWL program was initiated by the Jamestown Area Labor-Management Committee (JALMC). The latter was formed to cope with a declining industrial environment. The JALMC also facilitated the formation of labor-management committees that helped companies solve a variety of technical, production, and personnel problems. Workers participated in key management areas such as plant redesign, bidding for jobs, purchasing new equipment, identifying training needs, and implementing new training programs.

☐ The QWL programs typically increase job satisfaction, but less frequently lead to productivity gains. Nine conditions have been identified which, if present, foster positive outcomes from QWL programs:

1. Clear definition of the QWL program
2. Commitment from both labor and management
3. Involvement of employees from many levels in the program
4. Learning from mistakes made early in the program
5. Not bypassing middle management in planning the program
6. Choosing leaders for the program with the appropriate leadership style
7. Identifying program goals
8. Using outside consulting help as needed
9. Selecting workers who can be motivated to achieve excellent performance

Questions and Activities _____

1. What similarity do you perceive between the usual meaning of "culture" and "organizational culture"?

2. Consultant and author Tom Peters contends that his rumpled clothing made him a poor fit at his former employer, the consulting firm of McKinsey and Company. What does Peters' statement tell you about the culture at McKinsey?

3. Visualize a McDonald's restaurant (or visit one soon). What conclusions about its culture can you make?

4. It has been said that U.S. manufacturing firms must change their cultures to compete effectively with industries in countries such as Japan, Taiwan, and South Korea. What aspects of culture might these critics be referring to?

5. Describe any organizational norm you have heard communicated over a cultural network.

6. Describe the relationship between QWL and work stress.

7. What is the underlying reason that worker participation leads to an improved quality of work life?

8. Labor-management committees often work better in small rather than in large communities. Why do you think this might be true?

9. In what ways might a bureaucracy actually enhance QWL?

10. How can you explain the fact that many QWL programs emerged during a period of poor economic conditions?

A Human Relations Case

WHAT DO WE DO WITH THE BAD IDEAS?

"Is Smokestack America dead? Not by a long shot!" shouted Barney Nevins, president of Toledo Stampings, as he moved toward the conclusion of his speech to the management group. "And we at Toledo Stampings are very much part of this revitalization process that is taking place in factories, mills, and foundries from Florida to British Columbia.

"Tonight I am announcing a plan of action what will help us enjoy new heights of productivity and morale. Many of you have heard about labor-management participation teams being used by other companies who are bounding back from the inroads made by foreign competition. Now it's our turn at Toledo Stampings. Our industrial engineering department will fill you in on the details of the program. For now, I'll present you the big picture.

"We want to create a cooperative climate in our factories by tapping employees' knowledge and giving them a voice in production-related decisions on the plant floor. These labor-management participation teams [LMPTs] will consist of ten to fifteen workers and supervisors. They will be formed at the department level within our company. Workers and supervisors will be given a chance to deal with problems such as production snags, safety and health issues, the efficient use of tools, absenteeism, incentive pay, product quality, and other matters.

"Weekly meetings will be held. And they will have top priority. Toledo Stampings is going to be revitalized from the production worker and production supervisor level. Let's all think positive and let's all think LMPT.

"Are there any questions?"

Within four months the Toledo Stamping LMPT program was in operation. Labor-management participation teams had been formed at all the designated locations. The one important detail to be worked out was to decide which ideas generated by the teams should be implemented, which ones should be returned to the teams for further refinement, and which should be discarded. Pedro Garcia, chief of industrial engineering at the Toledo factory, was responsible for collecting and editing the suggestions. During his first report to top management, Pedro made these observations:

"Look guys, we're supposed to play hardball around here. You pay me a fabulous salary to put my professional knowhow on the line. We're faced with heavy competition so you decided to have a bunch of amateurs solve any problem they can get their hands on. That's okay with me, if it's okay with you. I understand that QWL is hot these days.

"I'm flexible, but I can't stand by and watch the LMPT drive us over a cliff."

"What are you really telling us?" asked Barney Nevins.

"I'll be very candid. Some of the first group of suggestions generated by the LMPT are of negative value. If we use them, we keep people happy, but they could cost us a lot of wasted time and money. Look at some of these losers, I'll read them to you as they were presented to my department:

> 'Those of us who so choose should be able to work twenty consecutive days, followed by six days off. This would give us time to really enjoy life.'

> 'We could save a lot of fuel costs and clean up the place by a giant throwout day once a month. For two different thirty-minute blocks, employees from the office and factory would gather up all the junk that has collected during the last month. All of that debris would be placed on a pallet and rolled on over to the blast furnace. Old furniture, newspapers, files, discarded ballpoint pens and pencils would go. Employees could even be encouraged to bring some garbage from home.'

> 'Let's find a way to make our auto chassis out of polyurethane instead of steel. It would help make cars lights, and we wouldn't have to worry so much about lower-priced Japanese steel.'

"Get my point?" said Pedro. "As chief industrial engineer, am I supposed to let any off-the-wall suggestions go through?"

1. What mechanism would you suggest the company use to deal with the problem of LMPT ideas that may be of limited value?
2. How should the company deal with the potential conflict between the LMPT and the industrial engineering department?
3. What parallels do you see between implementing quality circles and labor-management participation teams?
4. Do you think Barney Nevins is expecting too much from the LMPT program?
5. Do you think Pedro Garcia is suffering from the NIH syndrome (discounting ideas that were "not invented here")?

A Human Relations Incident

"GET ME A NEW CULTURE"

Sunny Chai, human resource specialist at the Security Oceanic Trust Company, was working with a team of outside consultants to diagnose problems the company might be facing. As Chai pored over the results of the survey, he thought to himself: "The data are as clear as any I've seen in any survey. The reason our bank is not performing as well as management would like is that our culture doesn't fit the times. Loads of our employees see each other as being too conservative, too unwilling to take risks.

"It's too bad they don't see themselves as part of the problem. If they did, maybe we could move faster as a company and increase our profits."

Two weeks later, Chai, along with two members of the outside consulting firm, presented their findings to top management. Chai and the consultants went into detail about how the culture of "not making waves" and "protecting your hide at all costs" was slowing the progress of Security Oceanic.

After hearing the complete presentation, the president said: "I'm convinced what you say is right. I've noticed some of those problems myself. I agree that things have got to change. Sunny, I would like you and the two consultants to give us a new culture within 45 days."

1. How should Chai respond to the president's request?
2. How realistic is the president's request?

A Human Relations Exercise

DESCRIBING THE ORGANIZATIONAL CULTURE

The class will form teams of four or five people who will attempt to measure and describe the culture of the organization in which you are taking this course (college, school, institute, company, and so forth). Before venturing out on the task, the group will agree on what questions should be asked of organization members in order to measure culture. Figures 15–1 and 15–2 may provide some clues. Clues can also be obtained from the section called "Dimensions of Culture." A sample question to ask people would be, "What are some of the most important values held by people around here?"

After the teams have completed their investigation, discuss the results and draw a composite picture of the culture of the organization in which you are taking this course.

Notes _____

1. Phillip L. Hunsaker and Curtis W. Cook, *Managing Organizational Behavior* (Reading, MA: Addison-Wesley, 1986), p. 551.

2. Blake E. Ashforth, "Climate Formulation: Issues and Extensions," *Academy of Management Review*, October 1985, p. 841.

3. Dimension 1 through 4 are from Terrence Deal and Allan Kennedy, *Corporate Cultures: The Rites and Rituals of Corporate Life* (Reading, MA: Addison-Wesley, 1982), pp. 13–14; dimensions 5 through 9 are from Leonard R. Sayles and Robert V. L. Wright, "The Use of Culture in Strategic Management," *Issues & Observations*, November 1985, pp. 1–9.

4. Deal and Kennedy, *Corporate Cultures*, p. 14.

5. Sayles and Wright, "The Use of Culture," p. 2.

6. Ibid., p. 2.

7. Ibid., p. 8.

8. Stephen P. Robbins, *Organizational Behavior: Concepts, Controversies, and Applications*, 2nd ed. (Englewood Cliffs, NJ: Prentice Hall, 1983), p. 455.

9. Ibid., p. 458.

10. James L. Nave, "Gauging Organizational Climate," *Supervisory Management*, June 1986, pp. 14–18.

11. Jay B. Barney, "Organizational Culture: Can It Be a Source of Sustained Competitive Advantage?" *Academy of Management Review*, July 1986, p. 659.

12. Edgar H. Schein, "Are You Corporate Cultured?" *Personnel Journal*, November 1986, p. 84.

13. Barney, "Organizational Culture," p. 662.

14. Mitchell Lee Marks and Philip Harold Mirvis, "The Merger Syndrome," *Psychology Today*, October 1986, pp. 36–42.

15. David E. Whiteside, "Roger Smith's Campaign to Change the GM Culture," *Business Week*, April 7, 1986, p. 84.

16. Schein, "Are You Corporate Cultured?" p. 96.

17. Sayles and Wright, "The Use of Culture," p. 8.

18. William G. Ouchi, *Theory Z: How American Business Can Meet the Japanese Challenge* (Reading, MA: Addison-Wesley, 1981).

19. Larry B. Meares, "A Model for Changing Organizational Culture," *Personnel*, July 1986, p. 42.

20. Robert W. Rice and associates, "Organizational Work and the Perceived Quality of Work Life: Toward a Conceptual Model," *Academy of Management Review*, April 1985, p. 308.

21. Robert L. Kahn, *Work and Health* (New York: Wiley, 1981), p. 2.

22. Both approaches described in Edward E. Lawler III, "Strategies for Improving the Quality of Work Life," *American Psychologist*, May 1982, p. 27.

23. The criteria, but not the explanations of them, are from Mark E. Levine, "Self-Developed Quality of Working Life Measures," *Academy of Management Proceedings '83*, p. 220.

24. Ibid.

25. This section is excerpted and paraphrased with permission from Martin D. Hanlon and John C. Williams, "Labor-Management Committee at Work," *QWL Review*, Sum-

mer 1982, pp. 2–8. (Publication of Civil Service Employees Association, New York State.)

26. Edward M. Glaser, "Productivity Gains through Worklife Improvement," *Personnel*, January–February 1980, p. 73.

27. The first eight suggestions are from Lee M. Ozley and Judith S. Ball, "Quality of Work Life: Initiating Successful Efforts in Labor-Management Organizations." *Personnel Administrator*, May 1982, p. 27.

28. Ibid., p. 30.

29. Glaser, "Productivity Gains," p. 73.

Suggested Reading

DAVIS, STANLEY M. *Managing Corporate Culture*. New York: Ballinger, 1984.

HOFSTEDE, GEERT. "The Cultural Relativity of Quality of Life Concept." *The Academy of Management Review*, July 1984, pp. 389–398.

KOLODNY, HARVEY F., and VAN BEINUM, HANS, eds. *Quality of Working in the 1980s*. New York: Praeger, 1984.

KETS, DEVRIES, MANFRED, F. R., and MILLER, DANNY. "Personality, Culture, and Organization." *The Academy of Management Review*, April 1986, pp. 266–279.

KILMANN, RALPH H., SAXTON, MARY, and SERPA, ROY. *Gaining Control of the Corporate Culture*, San Francisco: Jossey-Bass, 1985.

MICELI, MARCIA P., and NEAR, JANET P. "Characteristics of Organizational Climate and Perceived Wrongdoing Associated with Whistle-Blowing Decisions." *Personnel Psychology*, Autumn 1985, pp. 525–544.

MILLER, LAWRENCE M. "Creating the New High-Commitment Culture." *Supervisory Management*, August 1985, pp. 21–28.

SCHLESINGER, LEONARD A., and BALZER, RICHARD J. "An Alternative to Buzzword Management: The Culture-Performance Link." *Personnel*, September 1985, pp. 45–51.

SHAMIR, BOAS, and SALOMON, ILAN. "Work-at-Home and the Quality of Working Life." *Academy of Management Review*, July 1985, pp. 455–464.

SOLOMON, ESTHER E. "Private and Public Sector Managers: An Empirical Investigation of Job Characteristics and Organizational Climate." *Journal of Applied Psychology*, May 1986, pp. 247–259.

PART FOUR
Working with
and
Understanding
the
Organization

Organization
Change
and Development

LEARNING OBJECTIVES

LEARNING OBJECTIVES

After reading and studying this chapter and doing the exercises, you should be able to

1. Understand why some workers resist change and how to overcome some of this resistance.

2. Explain how organization development (OD) contributes to constructive change in organizations.

3. Describe a form of OD at the individual, small group, and organization level.

4. Summarize the key features of Japanese management and explain how it can be used as a form of organization change.

5. Pinpoint a few of the potential limitations of Japanese management.

THE RELEVANCE OF ORGANIZATION CHANGE
AND DEVELOPMENT

In several business firms today, a standard question asked of other employees by top management is "What have you changed today?" One key implication of this question is that in order to survive and prosper, an organization must constantly change its work methods, procedures, and attitudes. In this final chapter about macro organizational behavior, we describe formal methods of bringing about constructive changes in the workplace. The three general methods chosen for discussion are (a) managing resistance to change, (b) organization development, and (c) adopting Japanese-style management.

Our discussion of organization change and development is a logical conclusion to the three previous chapters. Organization change and development can be perceived as systematic methods of (a) improving organizational effectiveness, (b) decreasing problems associated with a bureaucracy, (c) revamping the organization culture, and (d) improving the quality of work life. As shown by the dotted line in Figure 16–1, QWL programs can also be regarded as a method of organization development.

MANAGING RESISTANCE TO CHANGE

When significant change is brought into the organization, employees react in various ways (as would be predicted from the model of human behavior described in Chapter 1). Some employees perceive major change so negatively that they experience job stress. Many cases have been reported of job stress experienced by employees when word is released that the company is purchasing robots. At the other extreme, some employees are predisposed to react positively to change. They welcome the excitement and challenge of a major disruption. Many employees, for example, jump at the chance to be relocated, take on a new job, or learn a new skill.

A more typical reaction to change than negative shock or joy is some form of resistance. The resistance can be *direct*, in the form of outright refusal to do something, such as the employee who said: "Sorry, I refuse to work a four-day week, ten hours per day." The solution was to transfer him to another division of the company with a conventional work schedule. Another form of resistance is *passive-aggressive behavior* or heel-dragging, such as the employee who conven-

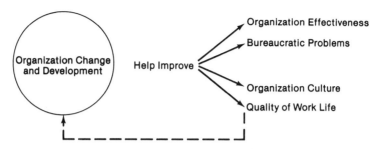

Figure 16–1 Broad purposes of organization change and development.

iently neglected to report when a robot was malfunctioning. To understand resistance to change, it is helpful to understand why it comes about.

Why Workers Often Resist Change

When people resist change, it is usually because they think the particular change will do them more harm than good. Expectancy theory (refer back to Chapter 2) has been used as a general model to predict whether people will resist or welcome change. People formulate subjective hunches about the effects of a particular change. If their subjective probability is high that the change will be beneficial, they are positively inclined toward the change. Conversely, if they calculate that the odds of the change helping them are not in their favor, they resist change.[1]

Six more specific factors will be reviewed here that seem to account for most of the reasons employees sometimes resist (or even obstruct) change: financial reasons, fear of the unknown, disruptions in personal relationships, personal inconveniences, difficulty in breaking a habit, and a previous experience with change.[2]

Financial reasons. Money enters into the decision-making process of most workers. If the organization introduces a change that employees think will provide them more money, they will be positively disposed toward that change. If employees think that a work-related change will cost them money, they will most probably resist that change. For example, sales representatives often resist new compensation plans because they question whether it will be to their economic advantage. The antidote is for management to explain carefully the anticipated financial impact of any change (as would be suggested from expectancy theory).

Fear of the unknown. An exception to the idea that people accept change they think is potentially beneficial relates to fear of the unknown. People sometimes resist change simply because the outcome of the change is not entirely predictable.

The situation of a supervisor in Buffalo, New York, who developed sinusitis, illustrates this principle:

> A physician told the supervisor that the only permanent cure would be to live in a warm, dry climate. The supervisor succeeded in obtaining a transfer to a distribution center the company operated in Phoenix, Arizona. At the point of making final arrangements, the supervisor declined the transfer. His explanation to both the company and his wife was, "I guess I'll suffer along with a pain in the head a little longer. At least I know what I'm dealing with here in Buffalo. Who really knows what's going to happen to us in Phoenix?"

Disruptions in personal relationships. A classic discussion about overcoming resistance to change contends that employees rarely resist technical changes.[3] What they do resist is changes in personal relationships associated with technical changes. One sales company came close to going out of business because it overlooked the importance of changes in personal relationships. Management decided to hire its own commission sales representatives to replace the manufacturer's sales representatives it had been using for ten years.[4] Shortly after making these changes, the business suffered a 40 percent decrease in sales. The old customers resented losing long-established contacts with the manufacturer's representatives.

Instead of continuing to order from the same company, thus dealing with new people, they continued their association with the manufacturer's reps. The difference was that the reps now represented another company. Most of the customers had formed allegiances to the manufacturer's reps, not the company. Differences in product were not a factor, because the company sold novelty items of very low technology.

Personal inconvenience. Most changes encountered by employees result in personal inconvenience of some kind. Relocation of an office, even within the same city, is a prime example. Because of the move some employees will have to get up earlier and return home later; others will be forced to change their bank; and virtually everybody will face the problems of clearing out files, packing, and unpacking. Inevitably some important items will be temporarily misplaced.

Difficulty in breaking a habit. Closely related to some of the problems involved in relocation is the problem of breaking an established habit. Stan Kossen notes that it is difficult to implement some changes because the old one has become a habit.[5] Each major habit is usually associated with a series of minor habits that people also resist breaking. If a new layer of management is introduced into a firm, many employees will have to learn new habits of bringing information to new managers. Simultaneously they will have to break old habits of going directly with problems to certain other managers.

Employee habits retard change, but most employees eventually do acquire new habits that are important to their work. Many employees first forced to work with computers were worried that "An entire day's work can be wiped out with one press of the wrong button." After a while this resistance was overcome to a large extent because the one-button disaster is relatively rare. (Or has it happened to you?)

Previous experiences with change. A person who had bad experiences with change in the past will resist change in the future. The relevant previous experiences can trace back into childhood. One pertinent example has to do with the prospects of moving. Adult attitudes toward relocation vary dramatically. Among the many contributing factors (including how much family inconvenience is anticipated) is how well relocation has worked out for the person in the past.

> An executive interviewed about the relocation problem responded, "You've asked the wrong person. Several years ago when I relocated, my new job lasted less than one year, and I had to move again. A new management team took over the company, and I was squeezed out in a power play. Now I will only accept employment in a large city. If my job sours, there's a good chance I won't have to move to find another job.
> "To top that off, I had horrible experiences as a child when my Dad was forced to move. I lost many good friends and had a hard time making friends in the new community."

Reducing Employee Resistance to Change

Since changes are inevitable and many employees resist change, a manager often faces the task of reducing or overcoming such resistance. A general strategy for introducing change effectively is to take into account the reasons people will probably resist the particular change. A change strategy can then be formulated. If time-recording devices are to be introduced as part of flexible working hours, the manager can predict some resistance due to fear of the unknown. Employees from other parts of the firm who have lived with the system might be invited to discuss the issue. (We assume flexible, positive employees are chosen as discussion leaders.)

Eight tactics are described next for reducing or overcoming resistance to change that take into account most of the reasons for resistance described in the previous section.[6]

Understand the process of change. The famous psychologist Kurt Lewin presented a three-step analysis of the change process. First, unfreeze the status quo. Second, move to the desired change. Third, refreeze the new level, which becomes the new status quo.[7] The balance of the techniques described here incorporate this basic model of the change process. In brief, it works this way:

1. *Unfreezing* involves reducing or eliminating resistance to change. As long as employees are dragging their heels about a change, it will never be implemented

effectively. Many a management consultant has seen a technically sound system torpedoed by an employee group that distrusts the system.

2. *Moving to a new level or changing* usually involves considerable two-way communication, including group discussion. According to Lewin, "Rather than a one-way flow of commands or recommendations, the person implementing the change should make suggestions, and the changees should be encouraged to contribute and participate."[8]

3. *Refreezing the status quo* involves such factors as pointing out the successes of the change and looking for ways to reward the people involved in implementing the change. Here is an example of using a reward to bring about change.

> Management in one bank thought productivity would improve if customers visited a branch office for a preliminary screening of mortgage applications. In the past, branch personnel would refer these customers to the central office. Yet customers who insisted on first visiting the central office would not be refused. The branch with the highest number of mortgage applications processed was rewarded with another full-time mortgage specialist. As word of this reward spread, other branches soon processed a higher number of applications. (Branch managers welcomed an additional staff member.)

Discuss the changes. A straightforward technique for reducing resistance to change is to discuss the changes with the employees affected. A written document explaining the changes might be a masterpiece of communication. Yet unlike a manager, a written document cannot answer questions. Two-way communication helps reduce some of the concerns employees might have about pending work changes. Often they are really asking, "How is this change really going to affect me personally?" Self-interest is a strong motivator.

Allow for participation. The best-documented way of overcoming resistance to change is to allow people to participate in the changes that will affect them. Much of the success of Japanese management is said to be attributed to the fact that there is wide-scale participation in decisions of any consequence. Thus, people affected by a change automatically participate in planning the change. Each person who approves the change puts a personal seal of approval on the change.[9]

Avoid change overload. Too much change in too short a period of time leads to stress for many people. It is therefore often helpful to avoid overloading employees with too many sweeping changes over a short time period. This suggestion would appear to run counter to the sentiment sometimes expressed as "Let's make all our layoffs at once. This way we won't have people sitting around wondering who is next." In this case, however, the stress from ambiguity is greater than the stress from the change of having co-workers laid off. Therefore, the sentiment is probably correct, and so is the suggestion.

Allow for negotiation. Resistance to change can be reduced by negotiating some of the more sensitive aspects of the change.[10] In exchange for employees (including a labor union) accepting automated equipment, it is not uncommon for management to grant some concessions. One example would be to limit the number of layoffs of employees because of new labor-saving machinery. One firm that ended the practice of providing certain personnel company cars negotiated the issues of mileage allowance on personal cars and a new cost-of-living adjustment. At 30 cents per mile and a $3,000 per year adjustment, most complaints about eliminating company cars subsided.

Point out the financial benefits. Since so many employees are concerned about the financial consequences of work changes, it is helpful to discuss these matters openly. (The example above is germane here too.) If employees will earn more money as a result of the change, this fact can be used as a selling point. An unwritten rule seems to exist in work organizations that a change toward a more hazardous (or more inconvenient) assignment carries with it a boost in pay. At one community college, for example, instructors who teach a course in a nearby state prison receive bonus pay. And, North American employees who relocate to the Middle East are compensated far beyond the differences in cost of living between the two areas.

Avoid social upheavals. One way to reduce resistance to change is to minimize changes in personal relationships stemming from the change. Some types of change, such as geographic relocation, inevitably result in social changes unless an entire organization is relocated. Under those extreme circumstances, there are still major changes in social contacts outside of work.

It is a difficult task for a manager to control most social changes when a major modification takes place, such as the formation of work teams instead of departmental structures. Nevertheless, sometimes employees can be asked to nominate individuals with whom they would like to work. Where feasible, teams could be formed of people who wanted to work together, thus minimizing social upheavals. Two precautions are in order. One, employees may nominate people with whom they socialize too much, with lowered productivity as the result. Two, some employees might not be nominated by anybody!

Place adaptable people in key spots. An important strategy for the effective introduction of change is to place the right people into jobs most directly associated with the change. The "right people" in this instance are those with a reputation for being adaptable and flexible. When a new machine is introduced into the workplace, there are usually grumbles to the effect that the new machine is inferior. If an adaptable, flexible, and optimistic person is the key operator of the new machine, this person will help bring about acceptance.

We have examined managerial strategies for the successful introduction of change (including overcoming its resistance). Our attention turns next to formal programs of bringing about change in organizations.

ORGANIZATION DEVELOPMENT AS A METHOD OF CREATING CHANGE

When it is necessary to bring about long-term, significant changes in the organization, a formal method of creating change—organization development—is often used. **Organization development (OD)** is any strategy, method, or technique for making organizations more effective by bringing about constructive, planned change. OD usually relies upon behavioral science techniques. In its pure form, organization development attempts to change the culture of the firm. At other times, OD is aimed at bringing about changes in the organizational system, as well as the culture. OD is less concerned with bringing about changes in the technical or operational and administrative systems.[11]

The *social system* is made up of people in different positions interacting to achieve organizational and individual goals. The *technical or operational system* refers to the method for getting work done, including the arrangement of people, equipment, and processes. Between the social and technical or operational systems is the *administrative system*, formalized procedures for setting down the standards, rules, and regulations for getting work accomplished. The relationship of OD to organization change is shown in Figure 16–2.

A major point of confusion over OD is that it sometimes refers to only long-term, large-scale attempts to make major changes in an organization. At other times, OD is more limited in scope. One problem is that some organization development specialists include as part of OD virtually every human relations technique designed to improve work behavior. Thus techniques such as those described in the chapters on improving interpersonal skills and resolving conflict are considered part of OD.

To help you appreciate the potential contribution of OD and how it leads to useful change in organizations, we will describe three standard OD techniques:

Figure 16–2 The impact of organization development on systems within the organization.

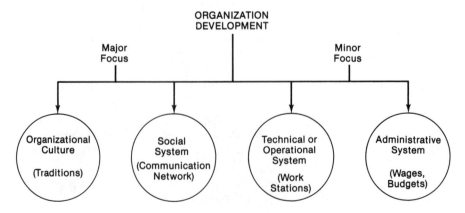

job enrichment, team building, and the survey feedback method. Job enrichment represents an organization development at the level of the individual employee; team building is OD at the small group level; and the survey feedback method is OD at the level of the total organization.

Job Enrichment

A direct application of the two-factor theory of job motivation discussed in Chapter 2 is **job enrichment** (JE). Its basic thrust is to increase the satisfaction and productivity of workers by giving them the opportunity to perform more interesting and responsible tasks. By increasing the attractiveness of the *intrinsic* aspects of a job, less reliance need be placed on *extrinsic* factors (such as praise and financial rewards). However, the ideal combination is to increase both the extrinsic and intrinsic rewards associated with a job. An enriched job will not be looked upon with favor if the individual whose job is enriched perceives it as a substitute for a salary increase. Nor does an enriched job mean that people will no longer care about hygiene and safety factors such as having properly ventilated work areas or clean washrooms.

Job enrichment can be considered an OD method because the organization is gradually strengthened as the individual employee becomes more productive and satisfied. Job enrichment can take a variety of forms, limited only by those designing the jobs, financial constraints, and the willingness of workers to have enriched jobs. The box on custodial workers describes a novel approach to enriching the jobs of first-level workers.

CAN THE JOBS OF CUSTODIAL WORKERS BE ENRICHED?

A large retail store was faced with the problem of low productivity among its custodial workers. The director of operations proposed that the store attempt to enrich the jobs of the custodial workers in order to improve their job performance. Highlights from this program, as adapted from a full report by William A. Nowlin (a key figure in bringing about the reported changes), follow:

> It was agreed that the term *custodial assistant* would replace the sexist terms *porter* and *maid*. Also, the name of the department was changed from "Housekeeping" to "Environmental Services." Another problem tackled was the limited amount of supervision given the custodial assistants. One manager was supervising the work of 40 employees cleaning 600,000 square feet of store spread out over eight floors. Two positions, labeled *work leaders*, were created. Each work leader was responsible for supervising a designated group of floors, as well as carrying out a specific cleaning responsibility. One work leader was promoted from within, and a retired custodian from a local school was hired to fill the other position.

Bill Nowlin explains, "We wanted some expertise from the outside, but we also wanted other employees to see growth opportunities."

Some enrichment had already existed in the job of custodial assistant. Those workers who ran machines were perceived by other assistants as the elite. It was therefore deemed advisable to train more custodial assistants to use the floor scrubbers, the buffers, and other machinery. Aside from giving more assistants an enriched experienced, the store would benefit from having more coverage in case of absenteeism and turnover.

The main thrust of enrichment was to allow each custodial assistant to do all the work in his or her assigned area. Cleaning territories were therefore reassigned. The assistants were given sections for which they were completely responsible. Previously three to five custodial assistants might have been assigned a piece of the job, such as sweeping, mopping, or waxing the floor, or cleaning the walls. Under this system, no one employee had total responsibility for the cleanliness of the area.

The job of custodial assistant was also enriched in two other ways. One way was to allow them to participate in purchasing decisions. Custodial assistants were given the opportunity to suggest purchases for supplies, material, and equipment. Another way was to engage them in a repair referral program. Custodial assistants were now encouraged to report orally or in writing: (a) any repair work necessary for equipment or fixtures, and (b) any problems with the buildings.

The biggest payoff to management and customers from the job enrichment program has been an improvement in store cleanliness. Custodial assistants have benefited in terms of the feelings of pride now associated with their work. Fewer complaints about dirty facilities filter back to the assistants, and, above all, "They are now perceived as more professional, and capable of contributing to the organization."

Source: Adapted from William A. Nowlin, "Improving Productivity through Job Enrichment," *Cleaning Management*, August 1982, pp. 45–48.

Characteristics of an enriched job. A good way to understand the general concept of JE is to summarize the eight characteristics of an enriched job as described by Fred Herzberg, the person who developed the concept (also see Figure 16–3).[12]

1. *Direct feedback.* A worker should get immediate knowledge of the results he or she is achieving. This evaluation of performance can be built into the job (such as a highway patrol person catching a speeder) or provided by a supervisor.

2. *Client relationships.* An employee with an enriched job has a client or customer to serve, whether that client is inside or outside the organization. In this regard both a hair stylist and a staff photographer have enriched jobs.

3. *New learning.* An enriched job allows its incumbent to feel that he or she is psychologically growing. In contrast, an impoverished job allows for no new learning.

4. *Scheduling of own work.* Employees should have the freedom to schedule some part of their own work, such as deciding when to tackle which assignment.

5. *Unique experience.* An enriched job has some unique qualities or features, such as the custodial assistants having the opportunity to report on building damage to management.

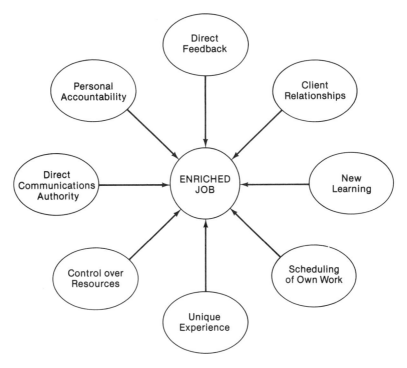

Figure 16–3   Characteristics of an enriched job.

6. *Control over resources.* Herzberg suggests that groups of workers should have their own minibudgets and be responsible for their own costs. Or the individual workers might be authorized to order as many supplies as needed to get the job done (such as the purchase of diskettes for a microcomputer).

7. *Direct communication authority.* An enriched job allows the worker to communicate directly with other people who use his or her output, such as a quality control technician handling customer complaints about quality.

8. *Personal accountability.* A good job makes workers accountable for their results. In this way they can accept congratulations for a job well done and blame for a job done poorly.

A superenriched job would have all eight of these characteristics, while an impoverished job would have none. The more of these characteristics present, the more enriched the job. Most employees would welcome an enriched job, while others would prefer an unenriched job.

The importance of the desire for job enrichment. Job enrichment can lead to increases in performance and satisfaction in situations where employees *want* more interesting, exciting, or challenging work assignments. As a starting point, job enrichment should be voluntary. Those people who are motivated by extrinsic factors should be left to perform routinized, repetitive work. Support for this generalization was obtained through a survey of 3,053 employees in 53 manufacturing companies. Within each company the sample was stratified to obtain approximately 50 percent employees in production or assembly-line jobs, 20 percent first-level supervisors, and 30 percent middle management, clerical, or staff positions.

Employees with more enriched jobs generally reported greater job satisfaction and received higher performance ratings from superiors. The most influential factor in determining whether or not job enrichment was associated with higher performance and satisfaction was the desire for enrichment.[13] If you want to know whether job enrichment will motivate or satisfy a given employee, ask: "Do you want an enriched job, and if so, what would you like to see changed?"

Desire for an enriched job is influenced by a host of personal and situational considerations. This complexity is illustrated by the comments of two employees. One 35-year-old woman with three children told the researchers: "I've got too many things to worry about at home. I just don't need any more responsibility here." She was content to perform a routine job since it seemed to add an element of stability and tranquility to her life. On the other hand, a 40-year-old man commented: "My job will probably be phased out five years from now. If I don't learn how to do other things I probably won't have a job before too long." His desire for job enrichment was motivated by economic security. He perceived job enrichment as a method of securing further employment.[14]

Team Building

The most popular form of OD is **team building,** a systematic method of improving the interpersonal and task aspects of regular work groups. Top management readily sees the relevance of a program that promises to help people work more effectively together and solve problems better. Team effectiveness is improved by ironing out interpersonal problems, and by developing action plans to achieve work goals.

Two assumptions about group behavior underlie team building. First, in order for groups to work productively, they must cooperate and coordinate their work. Second, the personal welfare and emotional needs of the group must be met. Most forms of team building work on both these aspects simultaneously. The usual strategy is for the team builder to help the group confront underlying issues that members find frustrating. Once these are uncovered, task accomplishment is usually facilitated.

Team building takes many different forms, all centering around the idea of improving teamwork and solving work problems. A representative team-building program is described by Jeffrey P. Davidson. Its purpose is to accomplish work goals and generate team spirit along the way. The team-building activity consists of seven weekly 2-hour sessions involving a work unit of between four and seven people. The sessions proceed as follows:[15]

> *Session 1:* The team assembles, and begins to identify general areas in which the group's work problems lie. Group members discuss the importance of assuming

responsibility and minimizing the blaming of others. A questionnaire asking for information about goals and methods of resolving conflict is administered.

Session 2: The group brainstorms to develop a consensus on team problems and agree on group goals, such as "We will develop a new marketing plan for microwave ovens by March 31 of this year."

Session 3: The team considers potential obstacles it may create to prevent itself from accomplishing its mission (overall goal). Members are instructed to ask themselves: "How can I communicate with others to obtain results that contribute to the team's mission?" Team members write problem statements in the form of how-can-I questions, such as "How can I get the marketing information on other brands of microwave ovens that I need?"

Session 4: After completing the problem statements, the group divides into three- or four-person subgroups to help one another solve problems. Action plans are drawn based on both brainstorming and fact finding. Each subgroup member has the opportunity to examine others' problem statements and action plans. In this way, additional input into problem solving is obtained.

Session 5: Participants negotiate with one another to overcome work problems. The problems may be technical, administrative, or interpersonal. For instance, Pete might say to Janis: "I could accomplish my data analysis sooner if you would stop looking over my shoulder while I'm working." Or Cora might say to Hector: "I could get my monthly sales figures on microwave ovens sooner if you needed less help with your forecasts."

Session 6: Team members assemble in three-person subgroups, each consisting of two individuals who bargain and one third party who observes to help resolve conflicts. Members often report that as a result of this process: "They have subdued their egos for the good of the team; individual assignments have not changed, but are now pursued with a new perspective and vigor; for possibly the first time, the whole unit is seeking the same bottom line."[16]

The session ends after team members write out agreements they have made, such as "I will get the data analysis on time, if you give the figures on time and in usable form."

Session 7: Here the members develop unit (group) goals based on the individual performance goals they have developed in the previous sessions. Representative unit goals include simplifying the financial reporting system, obtaining more consumer reaction to the microwave oven, or developing a simplified form for data collection. During this session, members also share thoughts about the team-building process. For instance, they may notice that they have developed feelings of harmony and cooperation.

An eighth session is sometimes held to evaluate progress since the first meeting. The questionnaire administered in the first session is done again. Participants compare how much progress they have made in clarifying goals and resolving conflict. Davidson reports that results almost always reflect progress over the 7-week period. His observations are in line with the majority of published reports about the effectiveness of team building.[17]

Survey Feedback

The **survey feedback** is an OD method that involves taking a survey of organizational problems and feeding this information back to management and survey participants.[18] It is a well-structured, well-organized method that has a long history of good performance. In essence, the survey feedback involves (1) taking a survey of organizational problems through questionnaires and interviews; (2) reporting these results back to the organization; (3) developing action plans to overcome the problems uncovered; and (4) follow-up.

Administering the survey. A survey designed by a specialist in attitude measurement is administered to a total organization, an organizational unit, or a representative sample of either. Both multiple-choice and write-in items (questions) are found in the questionnaire, as illustrated in Figure 16–4.

Figure 16–4 Sample questions for an attitude survey.

Objective Questions

	Strongly Disagree	Disagree	Neutral	Agree	Strongly Agree
1. We have a major communications problem here.	_____	_____	_____	_____	_____
2. Our management makes all the decisions.	_____	_____	_____	_____	_____
3. Most people are proud to work for our company.	_____	_____	_____	_____	_____
4. Our employees are treated with dignity and respect.	_____	_____	_____	_____	_____

Sample Write-in Question:
    In your opinion, what are the three biggest problems facing our company? Write your answer in the space provided below. Use the back of this page if necessary.

_____

_____

_____

_____

_____

_____

_____

An employee attitude survey (another name for the survey feedback method) typically asks the following types of questions:[19]

> *Goals.* Do you have clear and reasonable goals? Does your department have clear and reasonable goals? Does your organization have clear and reasonable goals?
>
> *Managerial leadership.* Are your managers and supervisors supportive and friendly? Do they encourage you and help you with work problems?
>
> *Co-worker relationships.* Are your co-workers friendly? Do they listen to your problems and help you attain job standards?
>
> *Job satisfaction.* Are you happy with your job, your salary, your opportunities for advancement, and your boss?
>
> *Organizational climate.* Is your company interested in your welfare? Does the company try to improve working conditions?
>
> *Role conflict.* Do you have enough authority to carry out your job? Do you have a clear statement of what is expected of you on the job? Do you report to two or more bosses?

Feedback sessions. After an analysis of the survey results has been conducted, the information is fed back to survey participants. Both items of relevance to most organizations and a few company-specific items are included. For example, if the human relations specialist developing the questionnaire knew that tight budgets were recently imposed in the company, a question like this might appear:

> Our budgets are realistic and fair.
> Strongly disagree _____   Disagree _____   Neutral _____
> Agree _____   Strongly agree _____

Develop action plans. A major difference between OD and merely "conducting a survey" is contained in this step. Participants are asked for recommendations about how some of the problems uncovered in the survey should be resolved. A final report of the survey is not released until the action plans developed by people at several levels in the organization have been incorporated. At the University of Michigan Survey Research Center, the following rule has been formulated:[20]

> No report containing recommendations based solely on their own analysis of data will be given to the client. Instead, they present data in preliminary form and involve members of the client organization in interpreting the data and deciding on specific courses of action.

A dominant theme uncovered in one OD survey was that employees were unsure of the future of their company. Many people wrote in comments such as these: "Rumors have it that our plant will be closed within six months. That's no way to live when you have a daughter ready for college." The action plan developed by middle management was straightforward and workable. They suggested an open meeting with top management to discuss the future of the company at that location. Top management complied. In the meeting it was explained that the rumors had a grain of truth, but were essentially incorrect. The company would not close the plant, but all expansion would take place in states with lower tax and utility rates.

Follow-up. Without continuous feedback and correction, OD fails, or at best is a short-lived, interesting experience. Several months after the survey is conducted, a check should be made to determine if the action plans developed in the earlier stages are being implemented. In one company an action plan was developed to realign the wage scale of first-line supervision. A three-month checkup revealed that nothing had been done. Prodding by the OD consultant and a representative from first-line supervision helped management begin some long-needed changes.

Evaluation of OD

Organization development programs have frequently been evaluated by researchers. In recent years, many of these studies have been characterized by careful attention to the requirements of scientific research.[21] Frequently evaluations of OD programs show good results in terms of such objective criteria as turnover, profits, quantity, and quality. However, many OD programs show neutral or negative results (conditions actually worsen).

Despite positive as well as negative results, OD programs have been criticized by both managers and management researchers. One division president passed an edict that no more OD programs would be conducted in his division. His objection was that group discussions about problems were stirring up discontent in his company. (Few managers, however, object to OD methods targeted specifically at work improvement programs such as job enrichment.)

Researchers often criticize OD because they believe not enough solid evidence supports its widespread application. The same criticism, however, is made by scholars about virtually every approach to improving human relations effectiveness. In defense of the OD practitioner, it is difficult to develop accurate measures of the kinds of changes brought about by some OD programs. Many an employee has said: "My boss is sure a changed person since attending those team-development meetings. He (or she) is much easier to work for." Such anecdotal evidence may reflect worthwhile changes, but is not easily translated into objective measures of improvement, such as increased profits or decreased costs. Nevertheless, worker perceptions of the boss may influence their job satisfaction and their personal lives for the better (see Chapter 3).

JAPANESE-STYLE MANAGEMENT AND ORGANIZATION CHANGE

In recent years a number of North American firms have purposely shifted to style of management characteristic of large, successful Japanese firms. Many American organizations—those referred to as Theory Z firms—have been practicing this highly participative and humanistic style of management for years. Hewlett-Packard, IBM, and Eastman Kodak are three prominent examples.[22] A curious feature of this shift to Japanese-style management is that the Japanese first heard of companywide employee participation from American managers. As far back as the early 1950s, human relations and applied psychology texts had information about the potential value of participative management.

Why the Current Interest in Japanese Management?

Productivity increases in Japan have been two or three times the American rate during the past three decades. Absenteeism and turnover rates in most Japanese firms are lower than in American firms, and employee commitment to the firm is high. And many consumers believe that the quality of Japanese automobiles and electronic equipment (radios and TVs in particular) is higher than those manufactured by American manufacturers. So Americans have become interested in learning how the Japanese do it.

American executives recognize that not all the productivity increase in Japan can be attributed directly to management practices. Other influential factors include heavy investments in capital equipment and research, a cultural ethic that values harmony on the job, and a highly cooperative relationship between government and industry. Nevertheless, the fact that Japanese companies have developed management practices tied in with high productivity and employee commitment led to an explosive interest in Japanese practices during the early 1980s. By the mid-1980s a more balanced perspective emerged about the contribution of Japanese management itself, and its applicability to North American companies.

Here we describe a general model of Japanese management that is being adopted both in part and in total by many American firms trying to emulate the Japanese success. The model incorporates the key ideas found in the highly publicized Theory Z. Note that we are not talking about directly transposing Japanese management practices to North American firms. Instead, organization change would be achieved by adapting those aspects of Japanese management most suited to the American culture. For instance, it would be illegal for a North American firm to imitate the Japanese style of management by offering permanent, full-time employment only to men.

A Model of Japanese Management

The essence of Japanese management is a focus on human resources. It has been said that people are Japan's only natural resource, since it is poor in natural resources and small in area. The focus on human resources is expressed in three interrelated strategies, as summarized in Figure 16–5. Substantial organizational change will usually result if a firm not already operating under such a management

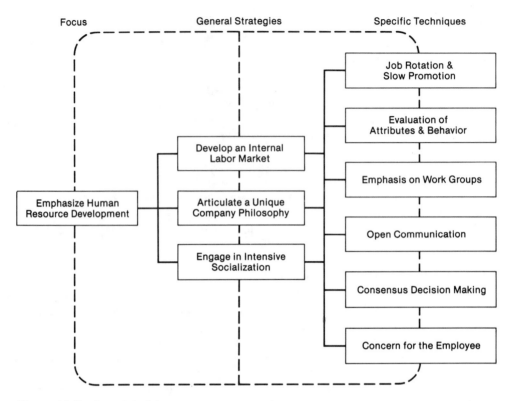

Figure 16–5 A model of Japanese management.

SOURCE: Adapted from Nina Hatvany and Vladimir Pucik, "An Integrated Management System: Lessons from the Japanese Experience," *Academy of Management Review*, July 1981, p. 470.

philosophy adopts this model. Partial adoption of the model (such as simply shifting to consultative decision making) will also result in change. The discussion that follows describes the components of the model of Japanese management.

Focus

Emphasize human resource development. If a firm truly focuses on the development of its human resources, the other components of the model fall into place. Unless this emphasis exists, change in the direction of Japanese-style management is unlikely. A recent study revealed that 57.9 percent of executives familiar with Japanese-controlled American companies believe that "the core of Japanese management is the deliberate attention to the humanistic aspects of work."[23]

General Strategies

Develop an internal labor market. A policy in large Japanese companies is that when a male employee is hired after graduation from high school or college, an effort should be made to retain him for his entire working career. In contrast, the female workforce is temporary. Using women part-time workers and subcontractors helps Japanese firms adjust to changing business conditions while at the same time claiming to have a full-employment policy. As the reader would suspect, this full-employment policy for males only has been the subject of much criticism.

Another method Japanese firms use to minimize job hopping is to underpay workers at early stages of their career relative to what they contribute. Later on in their career they are somewhat overpaid: The wages of high-seniority employees may exceed the pay of new employees by 200 to 400 percent. Highly paid senior workers are rarely hired by other firms.

Articulate a unique company philosophy. Many chief executives of large Japanese firms have written manuals and books expressing their philosophy of work and management. (And so have the chief executives of Theory Z American firms.) The firm is often depicted as a family with a unique character. *Wa* (harmony) is the norm of family life most frequently articulated, to the point that some observers believe that *wa* is the distinguishing characteristic of Japanese firms.

The commitment of the corporate family to the employee is expresed in policies of avoiding layoffs and providing ample employee benefits. Without this reasonable employment security, it would be almost impossible to foster the spirit of cooperation and teamwork known as *wa*. As Japanese firms have faced formidable competition from companies in Taiwan and South Korea, they have begun to offer less job security. Consequently, they are beginning to encounter less loyalty to the group and more self-interest among employees.

Engage in intensive socialization. Japanese personnel policies are geared toward developing a cohesive workforce. A major reason for bringing recent graduates into the firm is that they can be readily assimilated into the firm's unique environment—they can be more readily socialized the way the company prefers. To be hired, the young person must display moderate views and a harmonious personality. Job competence is obviously important, "but applicants may be eliminated during the selection process if they arouse suspicion that they cannot get along with people, possess radical views, or come from an unfavorable home environment." After a while each employee is expected to assume the identity of a "company man." The employee's occupational specialty or professional identification is much less important.

Do you think you would enjoy the socialization process used by large Japanese firms?

Techniques

The authors of the model note at this point that the strategies which focus on human resources are interrelated and so are the specific techniques through which the strategies are achieved.

Job rotation and slow promotion. Under a strategy of lifetime employment, employees must learn to accept relatively slow promotion unless an organization is expanding dramatically. Since unplanned job vacancies occur rarely, job rotation plays a major role in career development. Carefully planned lateral transfers also add substantial flexibility to job reward and recognition.

Flexibility in promotion is also enhanced by a dual promotion ladder. Promotion in status is based on past performance appraisals and seniority within the firm. Promotion in position depends on past appraisals and vacancies in the level above. A person can be given a status promotion and receive a salary increase, along with more respect.

Evaluation of attributes and behavior. Departing somewhat from current American practice, the employee is not made to feel that productivity is the main factor in evaluating performance. Japanese management reasons that such outputs may be beyond the control of the worker. Instead, the evaluation criteria include not only hard performance measures, but also desirable personality traits and behaviors, such as creativity, loyalty, emotional maturity, and cooperation with others. Many firms place more emphasis on personality and behavior than outputs, reasoning that personality and behavior lead to outputs. For example, if the employee is very cooperative, it will enhance teamwork, which in turn will lead to higher-quality goods.

Although work-group harmony is valued, employees are appraised in comparison to each other. A somewhat counteracting force is that group performance is used as a criterion of individual performance. Peer pressure is therefore exerted on the individual to contribute to group performance. It might help your performance appraisal if somebody performs more poorly than yourself, but you still need that employee's help to achieve decent group performance.

Emphasis on work groups. Harmonious work groups are critical to the success of a Japanese firm, as they are to firms almost anywhere. Japanese companies create policies that foster strong work groups. The quality circles described in Chapter 7 are a prime example of this emphasis. Typically, tasks are assigned to groups rather than to individuals. This, along with job rotation and feedback on group performance, encourages group cohesion.

Open communication. Extensive face-to-face communication takes place in Japanese companies. It is encouraged by the emphasis on team spirit in work groups and the friendships that employees develop during their long stay with the firm. Open communication is also built into the physical setup of the Japanese firm. Work spaces are open and crowded with employees at different levels in the hierarchy. Workers at all levels are aware of what others are doing, and even executives rarely have private offices.

A well-publicized feature of the open communication in Japanese firms is "management by walking around." Japanese executives regularly circulate among and converse with employees on the shop floor and in the production yard. Middle managers are also expected to interact with employees and help out with the manufacturing process.[24]

Consensus decision making. In Japanese firms, subordinates participate in all decisions they will be responsible for implementing. The extent of participation varies somewhat, as it does in American firms. More firms appear to use consensus decision making in which everybody involved in a decision places a personal stamp of approval (*hanko*) on the decision. In other firms, management consults with employees before making a final decision, but personal approvals are not necessarily sought.

An important point is that ratification of the decision does not indicate unanimous approval, but it does imply a willingness to implement the decision. Thus, whether a specific Japanese firm uses a participative or consultative decision-making style, the result is a decision that subordinates stand willing to implement.

Concern for the employee. The Japanese firm expresses concern for the employee in a number of formal and informal ways. Formal expressions of concern include the sponsoring of various cultural, athletic, and other recreational activities, resulting in a busy schedule of company social affairs. Among the formal benefits are family allowances, employee housing (dormitories), and company scholarships for employees' children. One informal expression of concern for employees is the great deal of time spent talking to them about everyday matters. Another expression of concern is an attempt to build a good relationship with each subordinate.

Some Cautions in Shifting to the Japanese Model

The Japanese model of management has achieved an enviable track record. Japanese firms have met with considerable success in worldwide competition, and Japanese takeovers of American firms have generally been quite successful. For example, two plants once owned by Firestone Tire & Rubber are being run by Japanese companies (ATR Wire & Cable Co. and Bridgestone). Both companies have dramatically improved productivity and labor relations.[25] In a few instances, Japanese takeovers have led to poor productivity and labor problems. One surprising example is Sanyo's Arkansas plant, which prospered originally by Japanese takeover. The harmony that had been achieved proved to be a false harmony, and bitter labor-management disputes erupted several years later.

The Japanese approach to management is not for everybody. Workers who value autonomy and who are impatient for progress are not content in a Japanese-style firm. Discontent has also surfaced among middle managers who are tired of working 60 to 70 hours a week for relatively low pay. After finishing work for the day, Japanese managers are often expected to entertain clients until late at night.

The potential negative aspects of the Japanese system indicate that precautions must be taken before a firm decides to convert. Some of the precautions described below point to the conditions under which Japanese management is most likely to lead to constructive change in other cultures. They are contingency factors for applying Japanese management.

First, firms in relatively stable and dominant industrial positions are better able to adopt the Japanese managerial model than those in weak and unstable positions. The main reason is that they can provide their employees with lifetime (or at least long-term) employment and make substantial investments in employee training. Since they do not have to worry about short-term survival, they can take a long-range perspective.[26]

Second, if the selection is made carefully, many Japanese managerial practices can be transferred—not all of them are culture-bound. Quality circles and attention to plant maintenance are two key examples. An example of a relatively nontransferable program would be slow promotion with an emphasis on seniority. Americans, Canadians, and West Germans, for example, believe strongly in promotion based on merit and talent.

Third, the Japanese managerial practices that emphasize consensual decision making and group harmony are not suited to firms pursuing aggressive and risky ventures. Chung and Gray make this analysis:

> The Japanese systems are good at managing the nuts and bolts of manufacturing activities, but the emphasis on group harmony and consensus can easily smother creative thinking and innovative behavior. When technological innovation is the key to organizational survival, the American way of managing people, stressing creative ideas and individualistic performance, can be more advantageous than the Japanese approach.[27]

Fourth, to change successfully to a Japanese-style managerial system, a company has to prepare the foundation on which the newly adopted system can stand. The new foundation includes selecting the right people, investing in employee training on a continuous basis, and moving decision-making authority far down the organization. In a unionized firm, a partnership relationship with the union would have to be developed (similar to the labor-management committees described in the previous chapter). Shifting to Japanese-style management thus requires a change in a firm's whole philosophy of managing people. Firms already operating under a philosophy of management similar to the Japanese model are undoubtedly already carrying out many of the practices that characterize Japanese management.

A fifth precaution in shifting to a Japanese style of management is that considerable false information is circulating about Japanese management practices. Andrew Weiss compared the practices of five Japanese electronics companies with those of Western Electric Company. He found simple explanations for Japan's outstanding productivity—personnel and investment practices designed to encourage high performance. Weiss translated his findings into some myths and realities about management practices in the firms he studied.[28]

> *Myth 1: Lower absenteeism.* Western Electric companies have a lower rate of absenteeism than their Japanese counterparts.
>
> *Myth 2: Greater corporate loyalty.* The quit rate for the Japanese companies is actually higher than for the Western Electric employees. Women in Japanese companies quit more frequently than Western Electric women, while men in the Japanese companies have a slightly higher quit rate than Western Electric men.
>
> *Myth 3: Harder-working employees.* The Japanese firms studied run their assembly lines at a slower pace than does Western Electric. Similar conclusions were reached by Weiss about other Japanese manufacturing companies.

After citing these myths, Weiss concluded that superior productivity in Japan is not attributable to an "Oriental" style of management or to Japanese corporate culture. Instead, it hinges on straightforward decisions made by Japanese managers.

> *Reality 1: More engineering support for production workers.* In the Japanese companies, one engineer was present for about every four workers. In Western Electric, the ratio is one to eight. The high level of engineering support usually increases productivity.
>
> *Reality 2: Selective hiring.* The Japanese firms studied hire quite selectively and recruit the elite of the Japanese labor force. Job applicants are thoroughly tested for intelligence, skill, and motivation. References are also carefully checked. Successful American companies in the electronics field, such as Hewlett Packard, also screen production workers carefully.
>
> *Reality 3: Considerably higher pay to experienced workers.* Experienced workers stay with the firm because they are paid so highly. And since newer workers are paid much less, they make a substantial contribution to profitability. The wage differentials are less in American companies.
>
> *Reality 4: Substantially higher pay for top employees over the lifetime of their employment.* Despite the emphasis on seniority, high-performing employees are amply rewarded. For example, a 50-year-old employee in the top tenth of the pay scale would earn twice as much as a 50-year-old in the bottom tenth.
>
> *Reality 5: Healthy investment practices.* One of many examples is that Japanese companies invest more extensively in equipment than do American companies. Although the Japanese equipment may not be more advanced, the fact that more of it exists boosts productivity.

Summary of Key Points

☐ Although the general topic of this chapter is organizational change and development, change must first be understood as it affects individuals. Among the responses to change or perceived change are enthusiasm and aggressive behavior. A more common response is some form of resistance. The general reason people resist change is that they think it will do them more harm than good. Specific reasons for resistance include (a) financial reasons, (b) concerns about disruptions in personal relationships, (c) personal inconvenience, (d) difficulty in breaking a habit, (e) adverse experience with change in the past.

☐ Strategies for reducing employee resistance to change include (a) understanding the basic process of change (unfreezing, changing, and refreezing), (b) discussing the changes, (c) avoiding change overload, (d) allowing for negotiation, (e) pointing out the financial benefits, (f) avoiding social upheavals, (g) placing adaptable people in key spots.

☐ Organization development (OD) is a general strategy for making organizations more effective by bringing about some kind of constructive, planned change. Job enrichment (JE) is an example of OD at the individual level. Its basic thrust is to increase the satisfaction and productivity of workers by giving them the opportunity to perform more interesting and responsible tasks. The characteristics of an enriched job include direct feedback, client relationships, new learning, scheduling, unique experience, control over resources, direct communication authority, and personal accountability. JE works best when employees want an enriched job.

☐ Team building is a popular form of OD aimed at improving the interpersonal and task aspects of regular work groups. Team effectiveness is improved by ironing out interpersonal problems and developing action plans to achieve work goals. Team building takes many different forms, all centering around the idea of improving teamwork and solving work problems.

☐ Survey feedback is a well-structured form of OD at the organizational level. Its key components are (a) take a survey of organizational problems through questionnaires and interviews; (b) report these results back to the organization; (c) develop action plans to overcome the problems; and (d) follow up to see if the action plans are implemented.

☐ A comprehensive method of organization change is to shift to a Japanese model of management. The focus of the model is to emphasize human resources development. Three general strategies are used to achieve this focus: develop an internal labor market; articulate a unique company philosophy; and engage in intensive socialization of employees. Six related techniques stem from the focus and general strategies: (a) job rotation and slow promotion, (b) evaluation of attributes and behavior, (c) emphasis on work groups, (d) open communication, (e) consultative decision making, and (f) concern for the employee.

☐ In order for a shift to Japanese managerial practices to work in the North American culture, several conditions should be met. First, stable and strong firms are in the best position to adopt the model. Second, those practices that are not culture bound (such as quality circles) are best suited to adoption. Third, Japanese managerial practices are not well suited to firms pursuing aggressive and risky ventures where innovation is required. Fourth, the company may have to shift its philosophy of managing people to a heavy concern for their welfare. Fifth, there are myths as well as realities about Japanese management. For instance, much of Japan's high productivity can be attributed to personnel and investment practices designed to encourage high performance.

Questions and Activities _____

1. If people are so resistant to change, why has computerization spread so widely throughout places of work?

2. College graduates who take a full-time, professional job frequently complain that senior employees in the firm are resistant to change. How do you think this perception comes about?

3. It was predicted about twenty years ago that the United States would have shifted almost entirely to the metric system by 1980. Why do you think this large-scale change was never implemented?

4. What objections to job enrichment do you think many labor unions have?

5. How would you go about enriching the jobs of retail salespersons and restaurant managers? If you do not think that one or both of these jobs require(s) enrichment, indicate why.

6. If you were attending a team-building session with your boss, how candid would you be in criticizing him or her?

7. A study reported in the June 1986 issue of the *Academy of Management Journal* found that team building did not improve the productivity of hard-rock miners. How would you explain this finding?

8. What factors do you think influence how honest people are in answering employee attitude surveys?

9. In what way might student evaluations of instructors be considered an example of the survey-feedback approach?

10. An American manager working in a Japanese-owned American company said he was at a disadvantage when attending meetings with executives present. He claimed they spoke Japanese as soon as discussion became heated. What advice can you give this manager?

A Human Relations Case
THE SENSITIVE TEAM-BUILDING MEETING

Organization development consultant Margot entered the motel conference room after the other members of the team-building group had arrived. Looking around the room, she commented: "It's good to see everybody here on time. It shows you aren't resisting the heavy stuff. As we agreed upon in our previous session, this morning we look at some of the roadblocks facing us. I want you to explain candidly to each other anything you see that one team member is doing to another that detracts from rather than enhances productivity.

"A convenient way to begin is for each of you in turn to describe how another team member might be making it difficult for you to accomplish your job. We'll begin with Peggy, seated here to my left."

Peggy: (*Laughs nervously*) You really sprung that one on me, Margot. I wasn't prepared. But let me give it a try. I want to say something to you, Conrad. You're a fine fellow and all that, but you are very slow in getting answers back to me. You're supposed to be our resident management information systems specialist, but it takes forever to get information back from you. I feel better now that I said it. (*Conrad squirms and the other members laugh.*)

Gary: Margot, have you ever thought about the problems you're creating? This soft stuff is driving me up the wall. I should be back in my office working on my budget rather than shooting the bull about teamwork. I'm wondering if these sessions are cost-effective.

Paul: Gary, I think your comments about Margot tell us more about you than about her. It's your insensitivity to people problems that creates a lot of difficulty. If you can't attach a number to something, you dismiss its relevance. The last time I tried to get you to deal with a serious morale problem, your only concern was how the situation affected the bottom line. If you would become a little more sensitive to people, I think you would be a better controller.

Greg: Peggy, let me have a crack at you. Everybody around here says what a fabulous human resource specialist you are. I don't deny that you're a good personnel professional. Yet I have this vague feeling that you're a phony. There seems to be a big gap between what you say and what you are really thinking. The upshot is that if you say you agree with me on an issue, I'm not sure that you really do agree. It shows up when you don't follow through on something we agreed on.

Laura: Okay, Paul, it's your turn to get a little well-intended feedback. (*The group laughs.*) No doubt, you're a marketing pro, and it's often fun to work with you. But you're so impatient, it serves as a communication block. You come across to me and others as if you would rather be doing something else. On your worst days, it seems as if you resent the time you have to spend in meetings with us. Other than that, it's a pleasure working with you.

Conrad: There's an issue with you Laura, that I want to bring up. I hope you'll take it as a constructive suggestion. You're basically the operations manager of our chain of retail stores. That means that you have to spend enormous amounts of time in the field, supervising operations. I accept that.

What I question is whether you're making a contribution to our management team. You go out on your trips, but you never come back with any suggestions for improvement. I like you, but I wonder what you are doing for the firm.

1. Give several examples of task issues being faced by the team.
2. Give several examples of interpersonal issues being faced by the team.
3. What similarities do you see between this team development meeting and an encounter group (refer back to Chapter 12)?
4. How effective do you think Margot is as an OD consultant?

A Human Relations Incident
THE COMPANY OLYMPICS[29]

Mr. Tanemichi Sohma, vice-president, administration, for Sanyo Manufacturing Corporation was responsible for his firm's takeover of a United States television manufacturing plant located in Arkansas. Sohma noted that American workers might be unwilling to sing company songs and wear company uniforms. As an alternative to these methods of building harmony, Sanyo now has a company "Olympics," which had these origins:

"The president of the corporation came after our strike and said: 'Sohma, there is something missing. Maybe the human relationship is still weak. Why don't you, like our entire company, do some sports event like a small Olympics?' I got the union people together and told them this. Not forcing, but from the heart, we want to do it together. The union officers said: 'That's the best idea we ever heard. We want to do it.'

"Next day I called all the salaried people and asked them. They said, 'No, it won't work in this country.' So I said: 'Salaried people are supposed to be with the corporation. That is why you are called white-collar workers. And what kind of attitude do you have? You better go back, cool your heads, and come back tomorrow morning.' Sure enough, next morning everything changed. They said: 'Let's do it, but we don't know how.' I offered to bring them the materials from Japan and show them how to do it. From there on we worked and set up all the different committees: food committee, game committee, ground committee, security committee, everything that we could think of. We did a beautiful organization job and had a fantastic Olympics.

"The president of the entire corporation in Japan felt so happy about this thing that he gathered all the executives and their friends to fly in to see that Olympics. I was worried because American people never had experienced that kind of sports event. I didn't know if this would work, because on a beautiful autumn day American people love to go out fishing, hunting, and golfing. Why should they come to the factory with no pay and do something like that? I never prayed so hard in my life.

"The next day was a beautiful day, and then the opening at 8:30. Many athletes were there—480, each team has 40 members, 12 different teams. They all wore different colored T-shirts. And they were lining up. Then the people started coming—2,000 people. And this has become something of a tradition with Sanyo, Arkansas.

"We worked for them: The captain of the team was a janitor, and we were vice presidents working under him. And he told us what to do: 'You're running too slowly.' This thing not only really amazed the people, but the people liked it. Then they came to us and said: 'Let's do it again next year.' The second time we did a much better one—and 4,000 people showed up.

"This is the way Sanyo wants to work with people. No matter how old our company is, our equipment is old compared with some new companies that are coming in from Japan with automation and robots and so forth. We don't have any. But we have a good human resource in Arkansas. So as long as we work with it, I think we can make the operation successful."

1. How useful as a morale builder do you think a company-wide Olympics would be in most United States and Canadian firms?

2. And what kind of impact do you think the Olympics would have on productivity?

A Human Relations Exercise

THE PROSPECTIVE TEAMMATES

We assume that at this stage in the course many of the class members are familiar with each other. Perhaps you have worked together in a discussion group or observed each other make comments in class. At an absolute minimum, you may have observed a few of your classmates in the halls or during class break. If none of the preceding statements apply to you, simply observe other classmates participating in the following exercise.

The class is organized into teams of about seven people. The first volunteer introduces himself or herself to the other six group members and makes a few comments about personal experiences in working as part of a team effort. Proceeding in clockwise fashion, the other members of the group then share the following perception with the first volunteer: "So far from what I know about you, this is the kind of teamworker I think you would make: . . . ." After the first person has heard all six perceptions, he or she should express his or her feelings about these perceptions. Each group member receives a turn at being "sized up."

When everybody has had a turn, a general discussion will follow focusing on which characteristics seem to be desirable or undesirable for teamwork.

Notes

1. Joseph Tiffin and Ernest J. McCormick, *Industrial Psychology*, 5th ed. (Englewood Cliffs, NJ: Prentice Hall, 1965), p. 425.

2. Stan Kossen, *The Human Side of Organizations*, 3rd ed. (New York: Harper & Row, 1983), pp. 292–297; Donald L. Kirkpatrick, *How to Manage Change Effectively: Approaches, Methods, and Case Examples*. San Francisco: Jossey-Bass, 1985.

3. Paul R. Lawrence, "How to Deal with Resistance to Change," *Harvard Business Review*, May–June 1954, p. 54.

4. Howard Klein, *Stop! You're Killing the Business* (New York: Mason & Lipscomb, 1974), Chap. 7.

5. Kossen, *The Human Side*, pp. 294–295.

6. Kossen, *The Human Side*, pp. 294–295; R. Wayne Mondy, Robert E. Holmes, and Edwin B. Flippo, *Management: Concepts and Practices*, 2nd ed. (Boston: Allyn and Bacon, 1983), pp. 430–433.

7. Kurt Lewin, *Field Theory and Social Science* (New York: Harper & Row, 1964), Chaps. 9, 10.

8. As interpreted by Mondy, Holmes, and Flippo, *Management*, p. 427.

9. Charles Y. Yang, "Demystifying Japanese Management Practices," *Harvard Business Review*, November–December 1984, p. 173.

10. Mondy, Holmes, and Flippo, *Management*, p. 433.

11. William G. Dyer and W. Gibb Dyer, Jr., "Organization Development: System Change or Culture Change?" *Personnel*, February 1986, p. 14.

12. Frederick Herzberg, "The Wise Old Turk," *Harvard Business Review*, September–October 1974, pp. 70–80.

13. David J. Cherrington and J. Lynn England, "The Desire for an Enriched Job as a Moderator of the Enrichment-Satisfaction Relationship," *Organizational Behavior and Human Performance*, February 1980, pp. 139–159.

14. Ibid., pp. 155–156.

15. Jeffrey P. Davidson, "A Task-Focused Approach to Team Building," *Personnel*, March 1985, pp. 17–18.

16. Ibid., p. 16.

17. Paul F. Buller and Cecil H. Bell, Jr., "Effects of Team Building and Goal Setting on Productivity: A Field Experiment," *Academy of Management Journal*, June 1986, pp. 305–307.

18. Current information about survey feedback is found in James Gavin and Joseph C. Montgomery, "Field Study and Replication of the Survey Feedback Method," *Academy of Management Proceedings '83*, pp. 230–234.

19. Gene Milbourn and Richard Cuba, "OD Techniques and the Bottom Line," *Personnel*, May–June 1981, p. 39.

20. George F. Wieland and Robert A. Ullrich, *Organizations: Behavior, Design, and Change* (Homewood, IL: Richard D. Irwin, 1976), p. 504.

21. John M. Nicholas and Marsha Katz, "Research Methods and Reporting Practices in Organization Development: A Review and Some Guidelines," *Academy of Management Review*, October 1985, p. 37.

22. William G. Ouchi, *Theory Z: How American Business Can Meet the Japanese Challenge* (Reading, MA: Addison-Wesley, 1981), appendix.

23. James S. Bowman, "The Rising Sun in America (Part Two)," *Personnel Administrator*, October 1986, p. 83.

24. Ibid., p. 84.

25. "The Difference Japanese Management Makes," *Business Week*, July 14, 1986, p. 48.

26. Kae H. Chung and Margaret Ann Gray, "Can We Adopt the Japanese Methods of Human Resource Management?" *Personnel Administrator*, May 1982, p. 41.

27. Ibid., p. 46.

28. Andrew Weiss, "Simple Truths of Japanese Manufacturing," *Harvard Business Review*, July–August 1984, pp. 119–125.

29. Audrey Freedman, "Japanese Management of U.S. Work Forces," *The Conference Board Research Bulletin*, no. 119 (1982), p. 6. Adapted with permission.

Suggested Reading

BARNEY, JAY B., and OUCHI, WILLIAM G., eds. *Organizational Economics: Toward a New Paradigm for Understanding and Studying Organizations*. San Francisco: Jossey-Bass, 1986.

BURACK, ELMER H., and TORDA, FLORENCE. *The Manager's Guide to Change*. Lake Forest, IL: Brace-Park Press, 1985.

COBB, ANTHONY T. "Political Diagnosis: Applications in Organizational Development." *Academy of Management Review*, July 1986, pp. 482–496.

LIPPITT, GORDON L., LANGSETH, PETTER, and MOSSOP, JACK. *Implementing Organizational Change: A Practical Guide to Managing Change Efforts.* San Francisco: Jossey-Bass, 1985.

NEILSEN, ERIC H. *Becoming an OD Practitioner.* Englewood Cliffs, NJ: Prentice Hall, 1984.

NONAKA, IKUJIRO, and JOHANSSON, JOHN K. "Japanese Management: What about the 'Hard' Skills?" *Academy of Management Review,* April 1985, pp. 181–191.

REICH, ROBERT B., and MANKIN, ERIC D. "Joint Ventures with Japan Give Away the Future." *Harvard Business Review,* March–April 1986, pp. 78–86.

ROBINSON, RICHARD D. *The Japanese Syndrome: Is There One?* Atlanta: College of Business Administration, Georgia State University, 1985.

TUNG, ROSALIE L. *Key to Japan's Economic Strength: Human Power.* Lexington, MA: D. C. Heath/Lexington Books, 1984.

WARRICK, D. D. *Contemporary Organization Development: Current Thinking and Applications.* Glenview, IL: Scott, Foresman, 1985.

WOODMAN, RICHARD W., and WAYNE, SANDY J. "An Investigation of Positive Findings Bias in Evaluation of Organization Development Interventions." *Academy of Management Journal,* December 1985, pp. 889–913.

Developing Your Career

LEARNING OBJECTIVES

After reading and studying this chapter and doing the exercises, you should be able to

1. Recognize your responsibility for developing your own career.

2. Understand how people find career fields for themselves.

3. Conduct an effective job campaign.

4. Establish career goals and a tentative career path for yourself.

5. Summarize at least ten career advancement strategies and tactics.

6. Recognize how career switching and retirement planning fit into career development.

THE INDIVIDUAL AND ORGANIZATIONAL
RESPONSIBILITY FOR CAREER DEVELOPMENT

Clark Klinkenberg, while attending college, started his Dow Jones association as a part-time mail clerk in Illinois. Five months later he accepted a full-time position as a peripheral equipment operator when a position opened. He worked in that capacity for a year and a half.

Klinkenberg then evaluated his career goals and wrote a "druthers" letter indicating his interest in circulation management. His immediate goal was to work as an Assistant Circulation Service Manager. Clark's work performance and education were compatible with such a position.

When a position became available four months later in Pennsylvania, he was selected and transferred there. Since then he worked for two years in Massachusetts, and was recently promoted to Circulation Manager and transferred to Georgia.

His career planning and the Druthers Program (a company program allowing for individual preferences) allowed him to meet his goal.[1]

The example presented here illustrates how organizations today are helping individuals plan and develop their careers. **Career development** is a planned approach to achieving growth and satisfaction in work experiences. Today there is a growing recognition that career development benefits employers and employees alike.[2] Despite this current awareness of the value of career development, you must still assume the major responsibility for developing your career. One fundamental reason is that you might change employers, voluntarily or involuntarily. Another is that you and your employer might have a different perception of what constitutes a satisfying and rewarding career.

This chapter presents key information about career development from the perspective of the individual taking the initiative to plan his or her own career. The other perspective would be that of the organization providing career development programs for individuals.[3] The information in this chapter is organized according to the logical flow of events a person generally experiences in developing a career:

Finding a field $\longrightarrow$ finding a job $\longrightarrow$ establishing career goals and a career path $\longrightarrow$ selecting relevant career advancement strategies $\longrightarrow$ switching careers if the need arises $\longrightarrow$ retirement planning

FINDING A SUITABLE FIELD

Finding a field that holds the promise of bringing you personal satisfaction and material rewards is a critical early step in developing your career. We say "early" because it is difficult to establish a zero point in career development. As soon as you begin to even think about making an occupational choice, you have begun to develop your career. Despite the importance of choosing a career, the process is usually done unsystematically. Few people are even aware that this major life choice can be done systematically. Among the more frequent ways in which people find a field—or occupation within that field—to pursue are these:

1. *Influence of parent, relative, or friend.* "My aunt owned a restaurant so I became interested in restaurant management at an early age."
2. *Reading and study.* "While in high school I read about investments so I decided to become a stock analyst."
3. *Natural opportunity.* "I was born into the business. Who would give up a chance to be a vice president by the time he was 25? Our family has always been in the retail business."
4. *Forced opportunity.* "I had never heard about electronics until I joined the army. They told me I had aptitude for the field. I enjoyed working as an electronics technician. After the army I applied for a job with IBM as a field service engineer. It has worked out well."
5. *Discovery though counseling and or testing.* "I took a computer-based guidance program after I entered business school. The program indicated I had interests similar to those of an industrial sales representative. Not knowing what else to do, I decided to become a sales rep for machine tools."
6. *Matching yourself with a compatible person.* A novel way of finding a field and occupation within that field is first to locate a person with whom you have similar interests. You then choose that person's field of work for yourself, using this reasoning, "I seem to like what that person likes in most things. All things being equal, I would probably like the kind of work he or she does."

The Use of Occupational Information

In addition to the methods just listed, it is important to seek valid information about career fields so you can find a good fit between yourself and existing opportunities. Most libraries and bookstores are well supplied with this type of information.[4]

Reference books about career information. The most comprehensive source document of occupational information is the *Occupational Outlook Handbook*, published every two years by the U.S. Department of Labor. Each occupation listed is described in terms of (1) nature of the work, (2) places of employment, (3) training, (4) other qualifications for advancement, and (5) employment outlook. Using the *Handbook*, one can find answers to such questions as, "What do city planners do and how much do they earn?" A similar source is the *Encyclopedia of Careers and Vocational Guidance*.

Computer-assisted career guidance. Several career guidance-information systems have been developed for access by computer. The information contained in these systems is designed to help users plan their careers. Guidance-information systems go beyond printed information, because you can interact with the software. For instance, when you are keyed in on a specific occupation, you can ask: "What is the promotion outlook? "What effect will technology have?"

The most widely used of these systems are *Guidance Information System*, DISCOVER, and SIGI PLUS (System for Interactive Guidance and Instruction). Many counseling centers and guidance offices use one of these software packages. Here we will describe the basic version of SIGI.[5]

The purpose of SIGI is to help people seeking career information learn three things: (1) which values are important to them, (2) factual information about various occupations, and (3) how to make better career decisions. SIGI has five subsystems, each of which contributes to learning about occupations.

You begin with the *Values* subsystem, which rates how much you like values such as independence and leadership. The second subsystem is *Locate*, which shows you the occupations listed in SIGI that match your values. The third subsystem, *Compare*, gives the user a chance to ask up to 28 questions about the listed occupations. One such question is, "What is the income potential?"

Planning is the fourth subsystem. It provides information about the type of education and the special skills and abilities required for the occupation. *Planning* takes into account both interest in a particular field and an individual's willingness to prepare for the occupation in terms of education and training.

Strategy is the fifth subsystem. It helps you evaluate the advantages and disadvantages of an occupation for you in terms of rewards, risks, and values. Ideally, *Strategy* helps you combine reward and risk to make a sound occupational choice.

Career information in newspapers and magazines. The topic of careers is of such interest today that is regularly covered in newspaper and magazine articles. The business section of most newspapers regularly runs both career columns and feature stories about people in different occupations. These articles are usually based on current industry surveys, recent government statistics, and interviews with people who are first-hand sources of information. *Business Week's Guide to Careers* features career information. Published every few months, this periodical contains current information on job opportunities in business and related fields. The Job Market section of the *Guide* describes job opportunities in specific fields.

Speaking to people. By speaking directly to informed people yourself, you can generate first-hand information about occupations. Many people have identified a field to pursue precisely in this manner. Seek out a person gainfully employed in any field or occupation in which you might be interested. Most people welcome the opportunity to talk about themselves and the type of work they do. If you do not know anyone engaged in the career field that interests you, do some digging. A few inquiries will usually lead to a person you can contact. It is preferable to interview that person in his or her actual work setting to obtain a sense of the working conditions people face in that field.

Speaking to people at different stages and levels of responsibility can be illuminating. If you ask a neophyte teller about the banking field, you will receive a very different answer from that of a 40-year-old vice-president of commercial loans.

CONDUCTING A JOB CAMPAIGN

Some people who have identified a field do not have to look for a job. Among these people are those who enter a family business, and those in an unusually high-demand field (such as air traffic controller, currently). Most other people have to conduct a job campaign upon graduation, and perhaps at various times in their career. The process usually takes about six months.[6] The three major aspects of the job campaign are job-hunting tactics, preparing a résumé, and performing well in an interview.

Job-Hunting Tactics

Some of the tactics described below and outlined in Table 17–1 will seem elementary, while others are not as well known. We recommend using this list of tactics as a checklist to ensure that you have not neglected something important. The list should be supplemented with suggestions from placement offices and from an entire book about the topic.[7]

Identify your objectives. An effective job search begins with a clear perception of what kind of job or jobs you want. Most people can more readily identify what jobs they do not want than those they do want. Your chances for finding employment increase considerably if a large number of positions will satisfy your job objective. One woman with a background in writing might be willing to accept only a job as a newspaper reporter (always a difficult position to find).

Table 17–1   Key job-hunting tactics

---

1. Identify your objectives.
2. Identify your contribution.
3. Use multiple approaches.
4. Use networking.
5. Persist.
6. Take rejection in stride.
7. Avoid common mistakes.

Another woman with the same background is seeking a job as (1) a newspaper reporter, (2) a magazine staff writer, (3) a copywriter in an advertising agency, (4) communications specialist in a company, or (5) copywriter in a public relations firm. The second woman has a better chance of finding a job.

Identify your potential contribution. A man responded by phone to a want ad with this initial comment: "Hello, this is Tom Crawford. I've just got to have a job. I've been laid off and I have a family to support. I need something right away." Poor Tom probably did need the job, but the company he was calling was more interested in *receiving* than in *giving* help. If Tom had used the following approach he might have increased his chances for being granted an interview (and getting hired): "Hello, this is Tom Crawford. I see you need somebody to help ship packages. I know how to ship packages in a fast and economical way. When could I talk to you about it in person?"

Use multiple approaches and tactics. No one job-hunting approach or tactic works best in most situations. The job seeker is therefore advised to use several of the tactics described in this section, and to explore several sources of job leads. Many an individual has claimed "I've tried everything," when he or she has pursued only a few job-finding channels. Among the possible approaches are school placement offices, employment agencies, government employment services, classified ads in local and national newspapers, ads in trade magazines, employment booths at trade associations and conventions, inquiries through friends and relatives, and cold canvassing. One recently developed approach is to have your résumé entered into a computerized database. Subscribers to the system across the country would then have access to your résumé.

Another standard approach is to place a situation wanted ad in local and national newspapers. The following ad helped one graduate find a job: "Productivity-minded problem solver wants in on your management training program. Try me. I'll give you a big return on your investment. Write Box 7943 this newspaper."

Use networking. It has been estimated that up to 95 percent of successful job campaigns stem from personal contacts.[8] **Networking** is seeking friends and acquaintances and building systematically on these relationships to create a still wider set of contacts who might lead to employment.[9] You use networking to establish contacts. Networking is particularly helpful because it taps you into the "insider system" or internal job market. The **internal job market** is the large array of jobs that have not been advertised, and that are usually filled by word of mouth or through friends and acquaintances of employees.

About 85 percent of job openings are found in the internal job market. The other 15 percent are advertised or registered with employment agencies and placement offices.[10] The best way to reach these jobs is by getting someone to recommend you for one. When looking for a job, it is important to tell every potential contact of your job search. The more influential the person, the better.

Be specific about the type of job you are seeking. A variation of this approach is to ask people how a person with qualifications such as yours might find a job. This approach does not put people on the spot as much as asking directly for a job lead.

To use networking effectively, it may be necessary to create contacts aside from those you already have. Potential sources of contacts include almost anybody you know, as summarized in Table 17–2.

Another way of reaching the internal job market is to write dozens of letters to potential employers. A surprisingly large number of people find jobs by contacting employers directly. Prepare a prospective employer list, including the names of executives to contact in each firm. The people who receive these letters become part of your network.

Persist. Finding a job is a tedious and time-consuming activity for many people. Persistence is vital in turning up good leads, and may help you find a job even after you have had some rejections. Marilyn Moats Kennedy explains that even in a recession, about 10 percent of the people who take a job fail after three months. Sometimes they are fired at the end of the probationary period, or they leave because of low interest or inability to perform on the job. It therefore pays to check back with the companies who said you were their second choice.[11]

Take rejection in stride. Finding a new job is fraught with rejection. It is not uncommon for a college graduate or an experienced career person to send out 150 letters of inquiry to find one job. When your job search is confined to places that are trying to fill a position that matches your specialty, you still may have to be interviewed many times in order to find one job. Often you will be rejected when it appears to you that your qualifications match perfectly those required for the job opening. The employment interviewer may have interviewed

Table 17–2 Potential sources of contacts for a network

Friends
Parents and other family members
Faculty and staff
Former or present employer (assuming you hold a temporary job)
Former graduates of your school
Athletic teams
Community groups, churches, temples, and mosques
Trade and professional associations
Student professional associations
Career fairs
People met in airports and on airplanes

SOURCE: Many of the items on this list are from Karen O. Dowd, "The Art of Making Contacts," *The Honda How to Get a Job Guide*, published by *Business Week's Guide to Careers*, 1985, p. 24.

another applicant that he or she thinks is even better qualified than you. In short, do not take rejection personally. It is an inevitable part of job hunting.

Avoid common mistakes. A good way of integrating information about job hunting is to be aware of mistakes to avoid in searching for a job. Several of these mistakes cover the points mentioned above. Robert B. Nelson suggests that the job seeker avoid the following:[12]

- Not knowing what type of work you want to do.
- Not taking the initiative to generate job leads.
- Going to too few prospects.
- Not viewing the job from the employer's perspective. (Employers are more interested in knowing what you can do for them, rather than vice versa.)
- Asking too directly for a job. (It is preferable to discuss job opportunities in an "informational interview.")
- Not making contact with the people with whom you would be working.
- Approaching prospects in an impersonal way. (Never address a letter "To Whom It May Concern." Instead, write to a specific person whose name can be found through a directory or phone call.)
- Overlooking your selling points. (For example, you might have exceptional computer skills or communication skills.)
- Not making follow-up contacts after you have generated a lead.
- Having a poor résumé.

The Job Résumé and Cover Letter

No matter what method of job hunting you use, inevitably somebody will ask you for a résumé. Your author is fully aware that many job-hunting books are adamant about not handing out a résumé and instead insisting on a personal interview. The reality is that virtually every company requires a résumé before seriously considering a job candidate from the outside. Résumés are also important for job hunting within your own firm. You may need one in order to be considered for a transfer within a large firm.

The purpose of a résumé is to help you obtain a job interview, not a job. Very few people are hired without a personal interview, although it can happen if the demand for your skills is strong enough. Your résumé must therefore attract enough attention to invite you for an interview. Effective résumés are straightforward, factual presentations of a person's experiences and accomplishments. They are neither overdetailed nor too sketchy. Considerable debate and subjective opinion exists about the desirable length for a résumé. Certainly less than one page would seem superficial, while a three-page or longer résumé may irritate an impatient employment specialist. Two pages is therefore recommended.

To attract attention, some job seekers print résumé on tinted paper, in a menu-like folder, or on an unusual size of paper. Still others do not print them.

Instead, they dictate the résumé onto a tape cassette. (Can you think of any swifter method of irritating a prospective employer?) If done in a way to attract positive attention to yourself, the nonconventional résumé formats have merit. The menu-like folder has worked well for a number of job seekers, but do not (as one joker did) label your job objective "the appetizer," your work experience "the entree," and your education, "the dessert." Unconventional résumés work best for jobs requiring artistic creativity, such as advertising copywriter.

Three types of résumés. The three most commonly used formats are the chronological, functional, and target.[13] You might consider using one of these types, or a blend of them, based upon what information about yourself you are trying to highlight. Whichever format you choose, you must include essential information.

The **chronological résumé** presents your work experience, education, and interests, along with your accomplishments in reverse chronological order. A chronological résumé resembles the traditional résumé, with the addition of accomplishments and skills. Some people say the chronological résumé is too bland. However, it contains precisely the information that most employers demand, and it is easy to prepare. A sample chronological résumé is presented in Figure 17–1.

The **functional résumé** organizes your skills and accomplishments into the functions or tasks that support the job you are seeking. A section of the functional résumé might read:

SUPERVISION: Organized the work activities of ten employees as a restaurant manager, resulting in two years of high profits and customer satisfaction.
Trained and supervised five data-entry technicians to produce a smooth-running data-entry operation.

The functional résumé is useful because it highlights the things you have accomplished and the skills you have developed. An ordinary work accomplishment might seem more impressive following this format. For instance, the tasks listed under "supervision" may appear more impressive than listing the jobs of "assistant restaurant manager" and "data-entry supervisor." One problem with the functional résumé is that it omits the factual information many employers demand.

The **targeted résumé** focuses on a specific job target, or position, and presents only information that supports the target. Using a targeted résumé, an applicant for a sales position would list only sales positions. Under education, the applicant would focus on sales-related courses, such as communication skills and marketing. A targeted résumé is helpful in dramatizing your suitability for the position you are seeking. Yet this type of résumé omits other relevant information about you. Also, a new résumé must be prepared for each target position.

Common mistakes in résumés. Despite the abundance of useful information available about résumé preparation, many job seekers continue to prepare résumés

JOB RÉSUMÉ

Jack Paradise   Born: August 8, 1964
210 Alabaster Road   Single, no dependents
Dallas, Texas 75243   (312) 381-8902

JOB TARGET: Industrial sales position, handling large, complex
                         machinery. Willing to work largely on commission
                         basis.

MAJOR BUSINESS ACCOMPLISHMENT:

                         In one year sold at a profit $250,000 worth of
                         excess machine inventory. Received letter of
                         commendation from company president.

WORK HISTORY:

   1988 - present   Industrial account representative, Bainbridge
                         Corporation, Dallas. Sell line of tool and die
                         equipment to companies in Southwest. Duties in-
                         clude servicing established accounts and canvas-
                         sing for new ones.

   1986 - 1988   Inside sales representative, Bainbridge Corporation.
                         Answered customer inquiries. Filled orders for re-
                         placement parts. Trained for outside sales position.

   1982 - 1986   Tool and die maker apprentice, Texas Metals, Inc.,
                         Dallas. Assisted senior tool and die makers during
                         four-year training program. Worked on milling ma-
                         chines, jigs, punch presses, numeric control devices.

FORMAL EDUCATION:

   1982 - 1984   Madagascar College, Dallas, Texas. Associate De-
                         gree in Business Administration; graduated with
                         3.16 grade point average. Courses in marketing,
                         sales techniques, consumer behavior, accounting, and
                         statistics. President of American Marketing Assoc-
                         iation, student chapter.

   1978 - 1982   Big Horn High, Dallas. Honors student; academic
                         major with vocational elective. Played varsity
                         football and basketball. Earned part of living by
                         selling magazine subscriptions.

CAPABILITIES   Competent sales representative. Able to size up
AND SKILLS: customer's manufacturing problem and make recom-
                        mendation for appropriate machinery. Precise in
                        preparing call reports and expense accounts.

PERSONAL INTERESTS AND HOBBIES:

                         Personal computer enthusiast (write programs
                         for own computer), scuba diving, recreational
                         golf player, read trade and business magazines,
                         dance competitively.

Figure 17-1 A general-purpose job résumé.

that virtually disqualify them from further consideration in the eyes of employers. Do your best to avoid most of these errors by editing your own résumé and asking at least two other people to do the same:[14]

- Too lengthy, containing much useless information.
- Disorganized, including the same type of information presented under different headings.
- Poorly typed or word processed, including narrow margins and writing in the margins.
- Skimpy or insufficient information—only dates, titles, and incomplete addresses.
- Excessive information including inconsequential information (such as facts about a company you worked for).
- No listing of accomplishments or skills.
- Misspellings, typographical errors, poor grammar, and the frequent use of the word "I."
- Overly elaborate résumé, such as fancy typesetting or plastic binder.
- So much emphasis on nontraditional résumé that basic facts are missing (for example, work experience and addresses of schools attended). Since company official cannot verify facts or assess qualifications, he or she places résumé in circular file.
- Inflating facts about yourself that prove to be untrue when references are checked. This type of résumé error usually leads to immediate disqualification. If the error is discovered after the candidate is hired, he or she is liable for dismissal.

The cover letter. A résumé should almost always be accompanied by a cover letter explaining who you are and why you are applying for this particular job. The cover letter serves to customize your approach to a particular employer, while the résumé is a more general approach. Even a targeted résumé is sent to more than one employer. Most job applicants use the conventional (and somewhat ineffective) approach of writing a letter attempting to impress the prospective employer with their background. A sounder approach is to capture the reader's attention with a punchy statement of what you might be able to do for them. Later in the letter you might present a one-paragraph summary of your education and the highlights of your job and educational experience. Here are two examples of opening lines geared to two different types of jobs:

1. Person seeking employment in credit department of garment maker: "Everybody has debt-collection problems these days. Let me help you gather in some of the past-due cash that you rightfully deserve."
2. Person looking for position as administrative assistant in hospital where vacancy may or may not exist: "Is your hospital drowning in paperwork? Let me jump in with both feet and clear up some of the confusion. Then you can go back to taking care of sick people."

Handling Yourself in a Job Interview

The job-hunting steps described so far, if successful, lead to a job interview. The one exception is that you could conceivably be hired for an out-of-town position without being interviewed. Job hunters typically look upon the employment interview as a game in which they must outguess the interviewer. A sounder approach is to present a positive but accurate picture of yourself. The suggestions presented next should help you appear to be a sincere and responsible job seeker.

1. *Rehearse being interviewed.* Being a good interviewee requires practice. Some of this practice may be acquired while going through interviews. In addition, you can rehearse simulated job interviews with friends. Practice answering the questions in Figure 17–2. Videotaping these interviews is valuable because it provides feedback on how well you handled yourself.

2. *Prepare in advance.* Be familiar with pertinent details about your background, including your social security number and names and addresses of references. It is also important to know some important facts about your prospective employer. Annual reports, brochures about the company, and newspaper and magazine articles can be helpful. Also, speak to current and past employees of the prospective employer.

3. *Dress appropriately.* So much emphasis is placed on dressing well for job interviews that some people overdress. Instead of looking businesslike, they appear to be dressed for a wedding. The safest tactic is to wear moderately conservative business attire when applying for most positions.

4. *Ask a few good questions.* The best questions to ask the interviewer are sincere ones that reflect an interest in the nature of the work itself (content factors as described in Chapter 2). Following are several questions that will usually meet with good reception in an employment interview. Ask them during a period of silence or when you are asked if you have any questions.
   a. If hired, what would I actually be doing?
   b. What kind of advancement opportunities are there in your firm for outstanding performers?
   c. Whom would I be working with aside from people in my own department?
   d. What is the company's attitude toward people who make constructive suggestions?
   e. What kind of person would you ideally like to hire for this position?
   f. What would I have to do to be considered an outstanding performer in your firm?
   g. Is there anything else I've said so far that requires elaboration?

5. *Be ready to discuss your strengths and weaknesses.* Most employment interviewers will ask you about your strengths and weaknesses. Being unable to describe personal strengths would suggest a lack of self-confidence. Being unable to identify areas for improvement would suggest a lack of insight or defensiveness. A mildly evasive approach is to emphasize weaknesses that could be interpreted as strengths. A case in point: "People say I'm too much of a perfectionist about pleasing the customer."

6. *Show how you can help the employer.* To repeat, an effective job-getting strategy is to explain to a prospective employer what you think you can do to help the company. This gains more for you than telling the prospective employer of your good qualities and characteristics.

7. *Allow the interviewer to talk.* Although a skilled interviewer lets the interviewee do most of the talking, there may be times when the interviewer wants to communicate something to you. In addition, make a few encouraging comments to the interviewer such as "That's very informative."

A useful way of preparing for job interviews is to rehearse answers to the kinds of questions you will most likely be asked by the interviewer. The following questions are of the same basic type and content encountered in most employment interviews. Rehearse answers to them prior to going out on job interviews.

1. What are your career goals?
2. What do you expect to be doing five years from now?
3. What are your present income requirements?
4. How much money do you expect to be earning ten years from now?
5. What are your strengths (or good points)?
6. What are your weaknesses (or areas for improvement)?
7. Why did you prepare for the career you did?
8. How would you describe yourself?
9. How would other people describe you?
10. Why should we hire you instead of other candidates for the same job?
11. If hired, how long would you be working for us?
12. How well do you work under pressure?
13. What makes you think you will be successful in business?

Figure 17–2 Questions frequently asked of job candidates.

Up to this point in the chapter we have described finding a field and finding a job. Before examining goal setting and career advancement, it is helpful to understand that career development does not always imply promotion and advancement.

CAREER ORIENTATIONS OF TODAY'S WORKERS

According to popular belief, everyone wants to get ahead and climb the organizational ladder. C. Brooklyn Derr contends that this widely held assumption has never been true, and is even less true in today's world of changing career values. Yet many managers still manage employees as if they had the same career goal— vertical growth. As a result, people are mismanaged and productivity and morale suffer. It is helpful for both the individual and the organization to recognize that people have different career orientations. Understanding your orientation will help you establish meaningful career goals. Derr's research points to these five orientations:[15]

> *Getting Ahead*—pursuing the traditional definition of career success involving vertical mobility in the organization. Many employees perceive themselves to be failures if they are not promoted at least once every five years.

Getting Secure—seeking job security and an identity with the firm more than advancement or challenge. The security seeker typically is a low risk taker because taking risks is often associated with low job security. If you do not take big risks, you lower the probability of failing.

Getting Free—wanting autonomy and independence, and the opportunity to choose one's own methods of solving problems. Many professional workers, such as accountants, computer scientists, and engineers, have this orientation.

Getting High—valuing excitement, challenge, and the content of the work. The orientation of getting high in a career is characteristic of those with a strong need for thrill seeking (refer back to Chapter 2).

Getting Balanced—giving equal priority to one's career, family, friends, leisure, and self-development. People with a strong "getting balanced" orientation value total life satisfaction as much as job satisfaction. Rarely do they become workaholics or career dropouts. Instead, they seek a healthy balance between work and personal life.

ESTABLISHING CAREER GOALS AND A CAREER PATH

Career planning in the form of goal setting and establishing a career path ideally precedes finding a job. This sequence, however, is not rigid. In practice, most people do not engage in serious career planning until they have some job experience in their field. Thus they establish career goals sometime after conducting a successful job campaign.

Establishing Career Goals

A person's chances for achieving career success and personal satisfaction increase if he or she establishes career goals. The opposite of goal setting is referred to as *winging it*. A fortunate few "wingers" work their way into rewarding jobs and careers. One vice-president of marketing began employment in his company as a drafting technician. A sales manager asked him to try his hand at selling because he was familiar with the technical details of the machines sold by the company. Ultimately this person rose to the rank of vice-president without any early goal that related to marketing. Nevertheless, for most people goal setting facilitates success. (Chapter 2 explains why goal setting often leads to success.)

A **realistic goal** is challenging but not set so high that frustration is the inevitable result. Most of your career goals should be realistic in terms of your capabilities and job opportunities. As you achieve each goal, you can continue to raise your sights. Nevertheless, it is good for your mental outlook to entertain some fantasies about extraordinary accomplishments for yourself. Typically, a fantasy goal is far beyond attainment at your present stage in life, but could someday become a realistic goal.

Sometimes reading or hearing about the unusual accomplishments of a person you admire can give you ideas for an exciting career fantasy. Recent corporate fast trackers include two people who held key jobs at age 35: Sharon Y. Young, corporate planning manager of Scott Paper, and Michael K. Lorelli, a senior vice-president of PepsiCo, Inc.[16]

Establishing a Career Path

Career goals become the basis for a **career path,** a series of positions in one or more organizations leading to a long-range goal. A career path laid out in one firm should be integrated with the present and future demands of the organization. For instance, if a company is decreasing the number of staff positions and increasing the number of line positions, a career path should consider this circumstance.

It is also desirable for a career path to integrate personal plans with work plans. Some lifestyles, for example, are incompatible with some career paths. It would be difficult to develop a stable community life if one aspired toward occupying field positions with the Central Intelligence Agency.

Contingency plans should also be incorporated into a well-designed career path. For instance, "If I don't become an agency supervisor by age 35, I will seek employment in the private sector." Or, "If I do not get promoted within two years, I will enroll in a business school program."

A sample career path is shown in Figure 17–3. Each rung on the ladder represents a position the person would have to attain to reach his or her long-range goal.

CAREER ADVANCEMENT STRATEGIES AND TACTICS

The strategies and tactics of organizational politics described in Chapter 10 can be interpreted as ways of advancing your career because most of them help one acquire more power. Here we describe 14 specific career advancement strategies and tactics (see Table 17–3). However, indiscriminate use of any of these approaches may backfire. For example, if you overdo the tactic of "find the right organization," you may never find an employer suited to your needs.

Make an accurate self-appraisal. An important aspect of career planning is to have an accurate picture of your strengths, areas for improvement, and preferences.[17] Feedback of this nature can be obtained from performance appraisals, opinions of peers and friends, and from career counselors. The career development inventory presented in the exercise at the end of this chapter is an example of a self-appraisal device that an individual completes without assistance from others. A novel approach to self-appraisal was obtained in this way:

> A sales representative constructed a brief form asking questions about himself, such as "What have I done that displeased you this year?" He gave this form

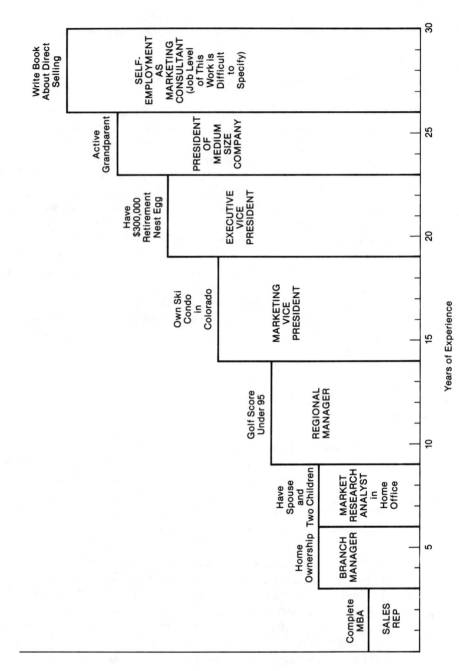

Write Book About Direct Selling

SELF-EMPLOYMENT AS MARKETING CONSULTANT (Job Level of This Work is Difficult to Specify)

Active Grandparent

PRESIDENT OF MEDIUM SIZE COMPANY

Have $300,000 Retirement Nest Egg

EXECUTIVE VICE PRESIDENT

Own Ski Condo in Colorado

MARKETING VICE PRESIDENT

Golf Score Under 95

REGIONAL MANAGER

Have Spouse and Two Children

MARKET RESEARCH ANALYST in Home Office

Home Ownership

BRANCH MANAGER

Complete MBA

SALES REP

Job Level

Years of Experience

5   10   15   20   25   30

458

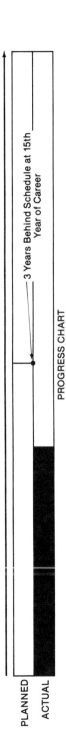

PLANNED

ACTUAL

PROGRESS CHART

3 Years Behind Schedule at 15th
Year of Career

CONTINGENCY PLANS

1. Will seek new employment by stage 3 if not promoted to home-office assignment.

2. If not promoted to marketing vice-president by stage 5, will purchase established retail business.

3. If develop stress disorder, such as cardiac disease, at any point, will seek employment as inside sales representative in well-managed (non-hectic) company.

Figure 17–3   Sample career path for a marketing professional.

Table 17–3   Career advancement strategies and tactics

---

1. Make an accurate self-appraisal.
2. Stick with what you do best.
3. Identify growth fields and growth companies.
4. Find the right organization for you.
5. Display good job performance.
6. Obtain broad experience.
7. Find a sponsor.
8. Find a mentor.
9. Document your accomplishments.
10. Rely on networking.
11. Manage your personal life carefully.
12. Make the necessary career transitions.
13. Cope with career plateaus.
14. Manage luck.

---

to customers, his boss, and the support staff in his office. The information he received helped him become more effective with others. In this regard he learned that he was standing too close to people when he talked to them.

Stick with what you do best. Any serious study of the topic leads to the conclusion that the true path to career success is to identify your best talents and build a career around them. Becoming wealthy and achieving recognition is a byproduct of making effective use of your talents. The late columnist Sydney J. Harris claims that the only advice he ever gave to young people who came to him for career counseling consisted of ten one-syllable words: "Find out what you do best and stick with it."[18]

Identify growth fields and growth companies. A sound strategy for career advancement is to seek jobs in growth situations. Generally this means seeking growth industries, but it can also mean seeking growth firms or areas of the country with plentiful job opportunities. Information about growth opportunities may be found in government reports (such as the *Occupational Outlook Handbook*), books on the topic, and the newspapers. Local banks and the chamber of commerce can be a valid source of information about growth firms in your area. A summary of good job opportunities for the next decade is shown in Table 17–4.

Find the right organization for you. Ideally, you should work for an organization in which there is a good fit between your style and its climate. For example, if you are adventuresome and aggressive, you would most likely prosper in a firm that welcomes employees with these characteristics. Although finding a fit between your personality and the personality of the organization may sound difficult to achieve, it may prove vital to your career advancement.

Information about a potential employer can be found through such means as reading annual reports (if it is a business corporation) and asking the opinion of a broker, customer, or supplier. Best of all, seek the opinion of several current or past employees. Choosing the wrong organization can be hazardous to your career. An organization that is "wrong" for you can be "right" for another person, and vice versa. You may not be able to tolerate an organization that expects its higher-level employees to work a 55-hour week under intense pressure. Another person might thrive in such an atmosphere.

Display good job performance. Good performance is the bedrock upon which you build your career. Job competence and talent are still the number one success ingredients in all but the most heavily political firms. All other talk about success strategies is fanciful without first assuming that the ambitious person turns in good job performance. Before anybody is promoted in virtually every organization, the prospective new boss asks, "How well did this person perform for you?"

Obtain broad experience. A widely accepted strategy for advancing in responsibility is to strengthen your credentials by broadening your experience.

Table 17–4   Good job opportunities for the next decade

Professional and Technical Jobs

Business Specialists

Accountant and auditor; Advertising specialist; Bank officer; Human resources (personnel) specialist; Stocks, bonds, and financial services sales representatives; Manufacturer's representative; Telemarketing specialist; Real estate agent, broker; Retail store buyer; Purchasing agent, buyer (industrial company); Logistics (distribution and transportation) specialist.

Computer Specialists

Operator; Programmer; Service and repair technician; Systems analyst; Robotics engineer, technician, service technician; Computer-aided manufacturing technician.

Engineering

Civil engineer; electronic and electrical engineer, technician; Mechanical engineer; industrial engineer; Laser engineer and technician; Hazardous waste technician.

Administrative and Support Services

Administrative assistant; Medical secretary; Legal secretary, paralegal assistant; Office automation equipment operator.

Health Care Provider

Dental assistant; Dental hygienist; Registered nurse; Practical nurse; nurse's aide; Physician's assistant; CAT scan technician; Physical therapist.

Table 17–4   (*continued*)

Managerial Jobs

Sales

National account manager; Brand manager; International sales coordinator.

Finance

Security investments manager; General accounting; Financial planning director; Bank manager; Chief internal auditor.

Personnel and Human Resources

Management training director; Personnel and human resources manager; Labor relations director; Employee training and development manager.

Manufacturing

Plant manager; Quality assurance manager; Materials handling manager; Purchasing manager.

Computer and Information Systems

Service and repair manager; Management information systems director; Computer operations supervisor; Robotics supervisor.

Engineering and Research

Research and development director; Corporate construction director; Chief industrial engineer.

Public Service

City manager; Urban planning manager.

SOURCES: Based on information in John Stodden, "Jobs With a Future," *Business Week's Guide to Careers How to Get a Job Guide,* 1986 edition, p. 40; Otis Port, "Where the Jobs Will Be," *Business Week's Guide to Careers,* Spring–Summer 1985, p. 62.

Broadening can come about by performing a variety of jobs, or sometimes by performing essentially the same job in different organizations. At one time it was believed that job hopping (moving from firm to firm) led to more rapid advancement than being loyal to one employer. Evidence collected during the last decade, however, points to the value of staying with one firm in order to advance your career.

Job hopping can help people in the early stages of their career acquire valuable experience as well as sharpen career goals. Eventually, the job hopper does pay the price in terms of income and job opportunities. Malcolm Carter contends that prospective employers may regard the overly mobile manager as an opportunist whose services are available to the highest bidder. They may also conclude that the job hopper cannot get along with co-workers or superiors.[19] And, by switching from firm to firm, you lose the power derived from acquiring seniority.

Find a sponsor. A swift route to career progress is to find somebody at a high place in the organization who is impressed with your capabilities. Such a person can even be a blood relative or one by marriage. One reason that task force and committee assignments are so helpful to career progress is that they provide you with the opportunity to be seen by a variety of key people in your organization. Many an individual who has performed well in an activity such as the United Way has found a bigger job in the process. In general, any tactic that brings favorable attention to yourself can help you find a sponsor.

Find a mentor. A **mentor** is a boss who takes a subordinate under his or her wing and teaches and coaches that person. An emotional tie exists between the protégé (or apprentice) and the mentor. A relationship with a sponsor involves much less teaching, coaching, and forming of emotional ties. Effective mentors are said to perform these functions for their protégés: providing resources, supplying information, showing an interest in the apprentice's work, being a role model, setting high standards, building the apprentice's confidence, coaching him or her, and protecting the apprentice when the latter makes poor decisions.[20]

Mentoring is typically an informal relationship. Several firms (including the Internal Revenue Service), however, are attempting to formalize mentoring by assigning a senior manager a group of junior managers to mentor. Sometimes the junior manager is given a choice of mentors. The purpose of these mentor programs is to develop managers.[21]

One criticism of the mentor system is that if your mentor leaves for some reason, or falls out of power, your career is set back. Another frequent criticism of the mentor system is expressed by Julie, a middle manager: "I've heard all the arguments about the importance of finding a key person who can pull you up the organization. But it isn't easy if you're a woman. First of all most of the people in big jobs are male. They would prefer to be a mentor to a male. Some of them are afraid that if they are a woman's mentor, somebody will think the two of them have something going between them."

As Julie indicates, it is more difficult for a woman than a man to find a mentor in most large organizations. However, the high-performing woman who practices many of the career-development strategies outlined in this chapter will increase her chances of finding a mentor. People in organizations are gradually accepting the fact that high-ranking males can take a personal interest in lower-ranking females of high capability, without romantic links.

Document your accomplishments. Keeping an accurate record of what you have accomplished in your career can be valuable when you are being considered for promotion. An astute person can point specifically to what he or she has accomplished in each position. Here are two examples from different types of jobs:

1. As ski-shop store manager, increased sales to hearing-impaired skiers by 338 percent in one year by hiring an interpreter to work in our shop on Saturday mornings.
2. As industrial engineer, saved my company $36,000 in one year by switching from steel to nylon ball bearings in our line of bicycles and baby carriages.

Rely on networking. Establishing a network of contacts is valuable for finding a job and for advancing one's career. The value of networking is so widely accepted that formal networking groups have emerged. In many cities, for example, nightclubs hold an occasional "networking night" in which businesspeople exchange information and business cards, and develop contacts. Another example of formalized networking is a national organization called "Xerox-X," consisting entirely of former Xerox Corporation employees. Members of Xerox-X share information on job opportunities, business services, and investment opportunities, and can develop sales leads.[22]

Men have always relied on networking for career advancement. During the last two decades, women have made increasing use of networking. Women who have previously relied almost exclusively on males as sponsors or mentors are now looking to influential women for support, guidance, and role modeling. The president of Take Charge Consultants says that the current literature conveys this message: "As women in the marketplace, you must work together; you must help one another and make the way smoother for those coming after. Support systems have existed for men since organizations began. You can initiate the process in a simple way by being supportive to women."[23]

The same executive cautions, however, that women who choose networking should not ignore the help of successful men or the personnel department.

The current trend in networking is for men and women to become part of the same network. The "good old boy" and "good old girl" systems have been replaced by the "good old friend" system. For example, the networking clubs mentioned attract both men and women.

Manage your personal life carefully. A well-managed personal life is enjoyable for its own sake and also makes it easier to concentrate on your career. One of the biggest challenges facing the modern couple is to meet the challenges of being a dual-career (two-income) family successfully. Dividing up household chores and money equitably is one challenge. Another is the problem of whose career receives top priority. When one partner is transferred or promoted, the impact on the other partner has to be considered. In recognition of this fact, many companies help the trailing partner find a job in the partner's new community. (A *trailing partner* is a person who uproots to follow a transferred partner.)[24]

Make the necessary career transitions. Your career development is facilitated if you make smooth transitions from one career stage to another. To accomplish this, you must understand the transitions and cope with the unique demands at each stage. Gene W. Dalton and Paul H. Thompson contend that "novations" are needed to make these transitions. A **novation** is the substitution of a new obligation for an old one by the mutual agreement of the parties concerned.[25] Your obligations change as you move from one stage to another. For instance, you are required to check less with your boss when you leave the apprentice stage. And when you arrive at your last career stage, you are expected to sponsor younger people. Dalton and Thomson divide careers into these stages:

> **Stage I.** Beginner or apprentice
> **Stage II.** Independent contributor
> **Stage III.** Providing leadership and mentorship within one's area of specialization
> **Stage IV.** Director; the professional is expected to perform key organizational functions, such as providing direction to the organization

Cope with career plateaus. A **career plateau** is the point where it becomes evident that further job advancement is permanently or temporarily blocked.[26] The vast majority of the workforce reach a career plateau at least once or twice.[27] Some people reach an early plateau and stay there until retirement. The worldwide economy has settled into a period of stability or gradual expansion. It follows logically that many more people than in the past will encounter plateaus (no vertical growth and no slippage) in their careers. The best antidote to a plateau is to control your impatience and make constructive use of the time. Specifically, you might consider these strategies:

1. Learn to appreciate growth within your job. Develop new skills on your present job that will help you when you finally do receive a promotion in the future.
2. Since the demands on your time tend not to be excessive during a career plateau, invest some of that time in self-development including reading in your field, attending workshops and seminars, and increasing your formal education.

Manage luck. Good fortune weighs heavily in most successful careers. Without one or two good breaks along the way (such as your company suddenly expanding and being in need of people for key jobs), it is difficult to go far in your career. The effective strategist to some extent *manages luck* by being prepared for the big break. Douglas T. Hall offers two suggestions about dealing with chance events:[28]

> First, you can anticipate what conditions might arise and develop *contingency plans* for them (e.g., "If we have a recession, I'll go back to graduate school"). Ask yourself, "What are all the things that could go wrong?" and "How would I respond to each course of events?" Second, you can prepare yourself to be ready to take advantage of opportunities when they come along.

CAREER SWITCHING

Career switching (changing from one career to another) has gained in popularity in recent years.[29] People switch careers for such reasons as boredom with the present career, being forced into early retirement, or being laid off and unable to find a job in one's present field. Switching careers effectively requires long-range planning. Sometimes a long-term avocation can be converted into an occupation, assuming a high level of skill has been developed. For example, an industrial engineer who collected and repaired electric trains for a hobby started a new career as an electric train repair technician.

In order to switch careers effectively, you should follow the suggestions offered for finding a field or first career. To avoid making what might turn out to be a costly and time-consuming error, you should:[30]

1. Narrow your interests to a few specific areas and job titles
2. Try part-time or evening work in your desired area
3. Get into an apprenticeship program (this usually requires completion of some specialized education)
4. Do volunteer work in your field of interest
5. Take a course or two in the potential new field
6. Determine if you should return to college full-time or part-time

RETIREMENT PLANNING

Retirement planning completes the career cycle. People who do not plan adequately for retirement, both psychologically and financially, are setting themselves up for bitter disappointment in the years after full-time work. Many ambitious, energetic, career-minded people deteriorate quickly from a mental and physical standpoint shortly after retirement. Their basic problem is that they did not plan a new lifestyle that would bring rewards similar to those they received during their working years. Comments made by the wife of a retired executive illustrate the importance of preretirement planning:

> Jake was happy at first when the company urged him to accept retirement. We had the usual dreams of wonderful trips, unlimited golf, and the time to read and dream. But it didn't work out quite that way. Jake gradually sank into a deep funk, and he looked terrible. He seemed to have aged about five years in his first three months of retirement. Jake finally came alive again when he found something useful to do. He joined a group of retired executives who give free advice to small business owners. Now I can honestly say my husband is enjoying his retirement years.

Retirement planning encompasses at least three broad areas: financial, leisure, and work continuation. Company-sponsored programs frequently provide information to retiring employees about these specific topics:[31]

Health	Company benefits
Housing	Working in retirement
Social security benefits	Money management
Legal matters	Leisure activities

USING A CAREER COUNSELOR

The vast majority of people manage their careers with no outside professional help. But what is common practice is not always the best practice. Using a career counselor may be a sound investment in time and money, but not every counselee is helped.[32] Two key advantages of career counseling are (1) it might provide you new insights into yourself, and (2) you may become aware of more alternatives. Next is a sampling of a counseling session that provided the counselee new insights and new alternatives:

> *Counselor:* You say that there is almost nothing else in life an engineering technician can do but work as an engineering technician.
>
> *Engineering Technician:* Darn right. That's my problem. As I explained last week, I'm tired of sitting at a desk or in front of a computer solving detailed problems. I need some space, some freedom.
>
> *Counselor:* Okay, so you've burnt out a little on solving technical problems. So have lots of people. Do you think if you put your technical problem-solving skills to work just part of the time you would be happy?
>
> *Engineering Technician:* You mean I should work just part-time? I can't afford it. I've got too many expenses.
>
> *Counselor:* (*Laughs good naturedly.*) What I'm talking about is putting your analytical skills to work in a job that also gives you some freedom and space. My impression is that companies that sell high-technology products are always looking to convert technical people into sales reps or sales engineers.
>
> *Engineering Technician:* Why didn't I think of that? I bet I could make it as a sales rep for our firm. I know the product. I think I would just have to brush up on my speaking skills.
>
> *Counselor:* It sounds like you're enthused about this idea. What are you going to do about it?
>
> *Engineering Technician:* I'm going to try to get an interview with the sales manager, real soon.

Summary of Key Points _____

☐ You must accept the major responsibility for developing your career despite whatever help is offered by your employer. Career development is a planned approach to achieving growth and satisfaction in work experiences. The process usually helps both employee and employer.

☐ Finding a field is a critical early step in developing your career. Systematic methods of selecting a field include making use of valid occupational information, and talking to job holders in fields of potential interest to you.

☐ Recommended job-hunting tactics include (a) identify your objectives, (b) identify your contribution, (c) use multiple approaches, (d) use networking, (e) persist, (f) take rejection in stride, and (g) avoid common mistakes.

☐ Effective résumés are straightforward, factual presentations of experiences, accomplishments, and skills. Three types of résumés are the chronological, functional (emphasizing tasks), and the target (focuses on a specific target position). A recommended résumé format, combining all three types of résumés, is presented in Figure 17–1. A résumé should be accompanied by a cover letter explaining who you are and why you are applying for a particular job.

☐ Suggestions for performing well in a job interview include (a) rehearse being interviewed, (b) prepare in advance, (c) dress appropriately, (d) ask a few good questions, (e) be ready to discuss your strengths and weaknesses, (f) show how you can help the employer, and (g) allow the interviewer to talk.

☐ A desire for advancement is only one career orientation. Others include getting secure, getting free, getting high (excitement), and getting a balanced life.

☐ An important part of career planning is to establish career goals and map out a career path. A career path is a series of positions in one or more organizations leading to a long-range goal. In laying out a career path, personal plans can be integrated with career plans. Contingency plans should also be incorporated into a well-designed career path.

☐ Career advancement strategies and tactics include (a) make an accurate self-appraisal, (b) stick with what you do best, (c) identify growth fields and growth companies, (d) find the right organization for you, (e) display good job performance, (f) obtain broad job experience, (g) find a sponsor, (h) find a mentor, (i) document your accomplishments, (j) rely on networking, (k) manage your personal life carefully, (l) make the necessary career transitions, (m) cope with career plateaus, and (n) manage luck.

☐ Career switching requires long-range planning and also involves many of the same approaches as finding an initial field. It is helpful to phase into a new career by trying it out part-time and preparing for it educationally.

☐ Retirement planning completes the career cycle. It encompasses at least three broad areas: financial, leisure, and work continuation. Many companies offer retirement counseling to their employees.

☐ Career counseling can be useful in developing your career. Ideally, it may help you acquire useful insights about yourself and an awareness of a wider range of career alternatives.

Questions and Activities _____

1. What benefits is the organization likely to derive from career development programs?

2. What steps have you already taken to develop your career?

3. If some very successful people are "wingers" rather than "planners," why should you plan your career?

4. Which of the 14 career advancement tactics mentioned in this chapter do you think are the most political?

5. What are the transitions people have to make when they move from the student stage of their career to Stage I or Stage II?

6. In your opinion, what obligations should an organization have toward the "trailing partner"?

7. Why are so many people so concerned about being on a career plateau?

8. What is the difference between changing jobs and switching careers?

9. Give two examples of career switching you have observed among people you know.

10. Ask two retired people what advice they would offer others about preretirement planning. Be ready to discuss your findings in class.

A Human Relations Case

THE YOUNG CAREER SWITCHER[33]

David Oltmann has often thought about his career switch from the priesthood to selling life insurance. He compares the emotional stress he underwent to dealing with death or divorce. "When you're in the monastery, you think about all the freedom out there," Oltmann said. "Then you leave it, and it isn't like that. My sister was going through a divorce at the same time I was leaving the priesthood. We became very close because we were going through a lot of the same things."

Oltmann kept a journal during that period and wrote in it every day. He took up running to relieve stress. But he credits his counselor at the adult counseling center of the local university with helping him cope with the decision. "I was trying to annihilate the past, to put it out of my mind. The fact is, the priesthood was a big part of my past. Now I can let it go and grow from it."

Oltmann attended a seminary for six years then took a leave. During the leave he moved into a Trappist monastery where he worked in a bakery for over two years. Then he moved to town. He volunteered as a paralegal to learn the court system because he thought he might be interested in a legal career. He supported himself by working as a waiter for more than a year and a half.

"I liked being with people, but I knew I didn't want to be a waiter all my life. I thought about going back to the monastery, but I didn't have a strong reason to return."

Oltmann, who was 28 then, said he figured most people his age were married and starting families and, as a result, was confused about what he should be doing. He said his inner time clock told him you're supposed to get married in your 20s, acquire property in your 30s, and become president of your company at age 40.

"I felt like a nothing. I felt empty. My self-image was low."

Then one evening last fall, a friend told him about the adult counseling center at the university. Oltmann made an appointment. During a free, 30-minute preliminary interview, Oltmann and counselor Bill Tammoro discussed the approach Oltmann's career counseling should take.

"I didn't want to do my own thing because I had been doing that for two years, I wanted to get some answers and I needed a time frame to work in. You can do something 'someday' or you can do it today."

Since Oltmann didn't have a specific career in mind, Tammoro gave him some tests during the initial visits to help clarify his aptitude and interests. Jointly, David

Oltmann and the counselor decided that selling life insurance and related financial services might be a field worth trying for him.

1. What factors do you think led to the successful outcome of this career counseling case?
2. Aside from the counseling center, what other sources of help in making a career switch might this man have explored?
3. What do you think would have been another realistic career switch for this counselee?
4. Do you think David Oltmann will be happy selling life insurance and related financial services? Why or why not?

A Human Relations Incident

THE FALTERING MENTOR

Alana Wong entered her company as a management trainee. One year later she was given a permanent assignment in the purchasing department as an assistant buyer. Al Bolton, the vice-president of purchasing, took a strong interest in Wong's career. He regarded her as intelligent and ambitious. After a while, Wong became Bolton's protégé, and most people in the purchasing department thought Wong was headed for a purchasing manager's position early in her career.

After several months of association, the working relationship between Bolton and Wong became closer. With the approval of her boss, Bolton gave Wong a series of special assignments. When Bolton gave a presentation to other executives, he brought along Wong who was asked to assist in the presentation.

Scarlett Overmeyer, Wong's boss, invited her to lunch one day. She said to Alana, "The news I have for you isn't very pleasant. But it's something you should know. Al Bolton has fallen out of power. He's made several really bad purchasing decisions that have cost the company close to $1,000,000. If I were you I would drop him as a mentor right away. If he goes, you are likely to go too."

"Are you sure, Scarlett?" asked Alana.

"Absolutely," replied Scarlett. "Two independent sources have told me the same story."

1. What should Wong do next?
2. How might Wong discuss this topic with Bolton?
3. Has Overmeyer overstepped her bounds?

A Human Relations Exercise

THE CAREER DEVELOPMENT INVENTORY

Career development activities inevitably include answering some penetrating questions about yourself. Following are 10 representative questions to be found on career development inventories. You may need several hours to do a competent job answering these questions. After individuals have answered these questions by themselves, it may be profitable to hold a class discussion about the relevance of the specific questions. A strongly recommended procedure is for you to date your completed inventory and put it away for safekeeping. Examine your answers in several years to see (a) how well you are doing in advancing your career, and (b) how much you have changed.

Keep the following information in mind in answering this inventory: Professor William Mihal conducted an experiment in which he documented the fact that people are generous in their self-evaluation when they answer career development inventories.[34] So you might want to discuss some of your answers with somebody else who knows you well.

1. How would you describe yourself as a person?
2. What are you best at doing? Worst?
3. What are your two biggest strengths or assets?
4. What are the two traits, characteristics, or behaviors of yours that need the most improvement?
5. What are your two biggest accomplishments?
6. Write your obituary as you would like it to appear upon the termination of your life.
7. What would be the ideal job for you?
8. Why aren't you more rich and famous?
9. What career advice can you give yourself?
10. Describe the two peak experiences in your life.
11. What are your five most important values? (The things in life most important to you.)
12. What goals in life are you trying to achieve?

Notes

1. Richard K. Brozeit, " 'If I Had My Druthers . . .' (A Career Development Program)," *Personnel Journal*, October 1986, p. 90.
2. Abby Brown, "Career Development in 1986," *Personnel Administrator*, March 1986, p. 45.
3. Zandy B. Leibowitz, Caela Farren, and Bevery L. Kaye, *Designing Career Development Systems* (San Francisco: Jossey-Bass, 1986).

4. A major reference here is John L. Holland, *Making Vocational Choices: A Theory of Vocational Personalities and Work Environments*, 2nd ed. (Englewood Cliffs, NJ: Prentice Hall, 1985).

5. *The Guidance Information System*, Time Share Corporation; *DISCOVER*, American College Testing, *System of Interactive Guidance and Career Information* (SIGI PLUS), Educational Testing Service.

6. Peggy Schmidt, "When to Start Looking for a Job," *Business Week's Guide to Careers*, February 1986, p. 7.

7. The best known of these books is Richard N. Bolles, *What Color Is Your Parachute: A Practical Guide for Job Hunters and Career Changers* (Berkeley, CA: Ten Speed Press, 1987 and revised about every year).

8. Loretta D. Foxman and Walter L. Polsky, "Career Counselor," *Personnel Journal*, April 1985, p. 18.

9. "Career Tactics," *Business Week's Guide to Careers*, September 1986, p. 150.

10. Karen O. Dowd, "The Art of Making Contacts," *The Honda How to Get a Job Guide*, published by *Business Week's Guide to Careers*), 1985, p. 24.

11. Marilyn Moats Kennedy, "How to Job Hunt," *Success!*, October 1982, p. 30.

12. Robert B. Nelson, "10 Common Mistakes Job Hunters Make," *Business Week's Guide to Careers*, November 1986, 91–93.

13. Sandra Grundfest, "A Cover Letter and Resume Guide," *The Honda How to Get A Job Guide*, (published by *Business Week's Guide to Careers*, 1986), p. 9.

14. Most of the information in this list is adapted from Tom Jackson, "Writing the Targeted Resume," *Business Week's Guide to Careers*, (Spring 1983), p. 26; Bill Repp, *Why Give It Away When You Can Sell It?* (Rochester, NY: Creative Communications, 1982), pp. 121–24.

15. C. Brooklyn Derr, *Managing the New Careerists: The Diverse Career Success Orientations of Today's Workers* (San Francisco: Jossey-Bass Inc., 1986).

16. Teresa Carson, "Fast-Track Kids," *Business Week*, November 10, 1986, p. 91.

17. Karen O. Dowd, "How to Realistically Assess Yourself," *Honda How to Get a Job Guide*, (published by *Business Week's Guide to Careers*), 1986, pp. 4–7.

18. Sydney J. Harris, "Career Advice: Stick with What You Do Best," syndicated column September 16, 1982.

19. Malcom Carter, "Job Hop," *Money Magazine*, October 1981.

20. Gene W. Dalton and Paul H. Thompson, *Novations: Strategies for Career Management* (Glenville, IL: Scott Foresman and Co., 1986). (As cited in book review appearing in *The Academy of Management Review*, October 1986, p. 873.

21. Michael G. Zey, "Mentor Programs: Making the Right Moves," *Personnel Journal*, February 1985, p. 56.

22. Ed Lopez, "Xerox-X Looking for Members in this Area," Rochester *Democrat and Chronicle*, May 4, 1986, pp. 1F, 8F.

23. Philomena D. Warichay, "The Climb to the Top,: Is the Network the Route for Women?" *Personnel Administrator*, April 1980, p. 55.

24. Irene Pave, "Move Me, Move My Spouse: Relocating the Corporate Couple," *Business Week*, December 16, 1985, p. 57.

25. Dalton and Thompson, *Novations*, p. 1.

26. James F. Kelly, Jr., "Coping with the Career Plateau," *Personnel Administrator*, October 1985, p. 65.

27. Christopher M. Dawson, "Will Career Plateauing Become a Bigger Problem?" *Personnel Journal*, January 1983, pp. 78–81.

28. Douglas T. Hall, *Careers in Organizations* (Santa Monica, CA: Goodyear Publishing, 1976), p. 188.

29. Richard C. Dolan, *Fresh Starts: Charting a New Career* (Chicago: Pluribus Press, 1985).

30. Linda Kline and Lloyd L. Feinstein, "Creative Thinking for Switching Careers," *Success!* March 1983, p. A2.

31. Patrick J. Montana, "Preretirement Planning: How Corporations Help," *Personnel Administrator*, June 1986, p. 128.

32. Vernon G. Zunker, *Career Counseling: Applied Concepts of Life Planning*, 2nd ed. (Monterey, CA: Brooks/Cole 1986).

33. Adapted from Betty Utterback, "Counseling Relieved His Stress from Career Change," Rochester *Democrat and Chronicle*, July 12, 1982, pp. 1B, 3B.

34. William L. Mihal, "An Assessment of the Accuracy of Self-Assessment for Career Decision Making," paper presented at the Academy of Management annual meeting, August 1983.

Suggested Reading

BROWN, DUANE, BROOKS, LINDA, and associates. *Career Choice and Development: Applying Contemporary Theory to Practice*. San Francisco: Jossey Bass, 1984.

CLAWSON, JAMES G., KOTTER, JOHN P., FAUX, VICTOR A., and MCARTHUR, CHARLES C. *Self-Assessment and Career Development*, 2nd ed. Englewood Cliffs, NJ: Prentice Hall, 1985.

HILL, NORMAN C. "Career Counseling: What Employees Should Do and Expect." *Personnel*, August 1985, pp. 41–46.

JONES, EDWARD W., JR. "Black Managers: The Dream Deferred." *Harvard Business Review*, May–June 1986, pp. 84–93.

NUSBAUM, H. J. "The Career Development Program at DuPont's Pioneering Research Laboratory." *Personnel*, September 1986, pp. 68–75.

ODIORNE, GEORGE S. "Mentoring—an American Management Innovation." *Personnel Administrator*, May 1986, pp. 63–70.

SEIBERT, EUGENE H., and SEIBERT, JOANNE. "Retirement: Crisis or Opportunity." *Personnel Administrator*, August 1986, pp. 42–49.

SHORE, LYNN MCFARLANE, and BLOOM, ARVID J. "Developing Employees Through Coaching and Career Management." *Personnel*, August 1986, pp. 34–41.

SORCHER, MELVIN. *Predicting Executive Success: What It Takes to Make It into Senior Management*. New York: Wiley, 1985.

STOLLMAN, RITA. "When to Switch Jobs." *Business Week's Guide to Careers*, March 1986, pp. 62–66.

Improving Your Work Habits and Time Management

LEARNING OBJECTIVES
After reading and studying this chapter and doing the exercises, you should be able to

1. Become a more productive person.
2. Develop insight into how you can decrease any personal tendencies toward procrastination.
3. Understand how attitudes and values influence work habits and time management.
4. Describe at least seven skills and practices that lead to improvements in work habits and time management.
5. Prepare an action plan for improving your work habits and management of time.

THE IMPORTANCE OF GOOD WORK HABITS
AND TIME MANAGEMENT

By improving your work habits and time management, you can improve your productivity on the job and enhance your personal life. Good work habits and proper management of time improve productivity because they result in more being accomplished in the same amount of time. Improved work habits and time management improve personal life for two main reasons. First, you have more time available for personal life. Second, since your work is under control you can concentrate better on—and therefore derive more enjoyment from—personal life.

Good work habits and time management practices are also important for defensive reasons. People are much more likely to be fired from the job or flunk out of school because of poor work habits rather than poor aptitude or insufficient basic skills.

We have organized information about developing better work habits and time management practices into three categories. One is overcoming procrastination, a problem that plagues almost everybody to some extent. The second is developing the attitudes and values that allow you to become more efficient and effective. The third category is the lengthiest—developing the proper skills and techniques that lead to personal productivity.

COPING WITH THE PROCRASTINATION PROBLEM

Procrastination is the delaying of action for no good reason. It is the major time waster for most people. Unproductive people are the biggest procrastinators, but even highly productive people have some problems with procrastination. If these people did not procrastinate, they would be even more productive. A reporter for *People* magazine had this to say about procrastinators: "Some of the most talented writers in the country are practically starving. Magazine editors respect their talents, but they know that if these writers are given an assignment, it will not be completed on time. The writers I'm talking about just can't get it together to meet deadlines."[1]

The enormity of the problem makes it worthwhile to examine the most probable underlying causes of procrastination and the tactics for minimizing procrastination. Only a charlatan would propose that procrastination can be *eliminated*.

Before reading ahead, see Figure 18–1 to obtain further insight into the signs of procrastination.

Why People Procrastinate

Procrastination has many roots. One major cause is a fear of failure, including a negative evaluation of one's work.[2] For example, if you delay preparing a report for your boss, that person cannot criticize its quality. The fear of bad news is another contributor to procrastination. If you think the monitor on your personal computer is burning out, delaying a trip to the repair shop will postpone the diagnosis: "You're right. Your monitor is on its way out. We can replace it for $375."

Fear of success is another cause of procrastination. People who fear success share the conviction that success will bring with it some disastrous effect, such as isolation or abandonment.[3] Or some may simply prefer to avoid the responsibility that success will bring. And a quick way to avoid success is to procrastinate over something important, such as completing a key assignment.

A deep-rooted reason for procrastination is **self-destructive behavior,** a conscious or unconscious attempt to bring down personal failure. For instance, a person might be recommended for an almost ideal job opportunity. Yet the person delays sending along a résumé for so long that the potential employer loses interest. Self-destructive behavior and fear of success are closely related: The person who fears success may often engage in self-destructive behavior.

Procrastination may also stem from a desire to avoid uncomfortable, overwhelming, or tedious tasks. A person who itemizes tax deductions might delay preparing his or her tax return for all these reasons.

Figure 18–1   How do you know when you are procrastinating?

When you have no valid excuse for not getting things accomplished, you are probably procrastinating. The signs of procrastination can also be much more subtle. You might be procrastinating if one or more of the following symptoms apply to you:

- You overorganize a project by such rituals as sharpening every pencil, meticulously straightening out your desk, and discarding bent paper clips.
- You keep waiting for the "right time" to do something such as getting started on an important report.
- You underestimate the time needed to do a project, and say to yourself, "This won't take much time, so I can do it next week."
- You trivialize a task by saying it's not worth doing.

SOURCE: Based on information in "Procrastination Can Get in Your Way," *Research Institute Personal Report for the Executive*, December 24, 1985, pp. 3–4.

Ways of Reducing Procrastination

A general method of coping with procrastination is to raise your level of awareness about the problem. When you are not accomplishing enough to meet your work or personal goals, ask yourself if the problem could be that you are procrastinating over some important tasks. Then try to overcome that incident of inaction. In addition, consider using one or more of the six strategies described next, and summarized in Figure 18–2.

Calculate the cost of procrastination. Alan Lakein believes that you can reduce the extent of your procrastination by calculating its cost.[4] One example is that you might lose out on obtaining a high-paying job you really want by not having your résumé and cover letter ready on time. Your cost of procrastination would include the difference in salary between the job you do find and the one you really wanted. Another cost would be the loss of potential job satisfaction.

Apply behavior modification to yourself. You can implement this strategy by reinforcing yourself with a pleasant reward soon after you accomplish an arduous task instead of procrastinating. You might, for example, go swimming with a friend after completing a research paper on time. A second part of the strategy is to penalize yourself with something you abhor immediately after you procrastinate.[5] How about cleaning out a barn floor as a punishment for mailing out bills late?

Arouse enthusiasm for performing the task. Psychiatrist Henry C. Everett notes that enthusiasm for doing a job varies inversely with the opportunity to act on it. When it is time for action, you therefore try to recapture some of that enthusiasm. Try to figure out what was so special about the occasion when your ideal motives were the strongest. "Look for ways to reproduce that atmosphere, and act on your impulses when they occur."[6]

Cut the task down into manageable chunks. To reduce procrastination, cut down a project that seems overwhelming into smaller projects that seem less formidable. If your job calls for your inspecting twenty locations within

Figure 18–2 Ways of reducing procrastination.

1. Calculate the cost of procrastination.
2. Apply behavior modification to yourself.
3. Arouse enthusiasm for performing the task.
4. Cut the task down into manageable chunks.
5. Make a public commitment.
6. Remove temptation.

thirty days, begin by making dates to inspect the two closest to home. It also helps ease the pain by planning the job before executing it. In this situation you would plan an itinerary before starting the inspections. The planning would probably be less painful than actually getting started making all the arrangements.

Make a public commitment. Here you try to make it imperative that you get something done on time by making a commitment to one or more other people. You might simply announce to co-workers that you are going to get something accomplished by a certain date. If you fail to meet this date you are likely to feel the pangs of embarrassment. One manager used this technique to help him get performance appraisals (an arduous task) done on time. He would announce in a department meeting, "Your performance reports will be done by September 30th. If I'm late with even one of them I want you to write a complaint letter to the president."

Remove temptation. One type of procrastination involves failing to set a starting point to stop a counterproductive habit, such as quitting smoking. Get rid of every cigarette in your office or living quarters. If you want to stop spending most of your lunch hour playing video games, avoid temptation by eating lunch where video games are not nearby (perhaps the company cafeteria).

Often the best approach to reducing procrastination is to combine one or more of the six methods just mentioned. A relatively limp strategy such as "arousing enthusiasm" probably will not have a big impact on procrastination. Everett concludes that if you find a few friends to join you in a task, they may serve to arouse enthusiasm, ease the pain, make the task imperative, and remove temptation.[7]

DEVELOPING THE PROPER ATTITUDES AND VALUES

Developing good work habits and time-management practices is often a matter of developing the right attitudes toward your work and toward time. If, for example, you think that your job is important and that time is a precious resource, you will be on your way toward developing good work habits. In this section we summarize a group of attitudes, values, and beliefs that can help a person make good use of time and develop productive work habits. These attitudes and values are summarized in Figure 18–3.

Try to discover what is blocking you. Some forms of poor work habits and time-management practices have deep psychological roots. If you can figure out what this problem is, you might be able to overcome problems like forgetting to do important assignments. One potential block is fear of success, described previously. It would take a shrewd bit of self-analysis to determine if you feared

Figure 18–3   Productive attitudes and values for work
habits and time management.

---

1. Try to discover what is blocking you.
2. Value your time.
3. Value good attendance and punctuality.
4. Avoid perfectionism.
5. Question the value of schmoozing.
6. Learn to say no.
7. Strive for both quantity and quality.
8. Ask "What is the best use of my time right now?"
9. Recognize the importance of rest and relaxation.

---

success. A recommended approach would be to supplement self-analysis by discussing the topic with a trusted friend and/or professional counselor.

Unresolved personal problems can also block personal efficiency and effectiveness. This is especially true because effective time utilization requires good
concentration. When you are preoccupied with a personal problem, it is difficult
to give your full attention to the task at hand. The solution is to do something
constructive about whatever problem is sapping your ability to concentrate. Sometimes a relatively minor problem, such as being out of checks in your checkbook,
can impair your work concentration. At other times, a major problem, such as a
broken romance, interferes with good work habits. In either situation, your concentration will suffer until you take appropriate action.

Value your time.   People who place a high value on their time are propelled
into making good use of time. If a person believes that his or her time is valuable,
it will be difficult to engage that person in idle conversation during working
hours. Being committed to a goal is an automatic way of making good use of
time. Imagine how efficient most employees would be if they were told, "Here
is five days of work facing you. If you get it finished in less than five days, you
can have all that saved time to yourself." One negative side effect, however, is
that many employees might sacrifice quality for speed.

Value good attendance and punctuality.   At all job levels, good attendance
and punctuality are essential for developing a good reputation. Also, you cannot
accomplish much if you are not physically present in your work area. An important
exception, however, is when a person works at home. But such arrangements
should be spelled out in advance with one's immediate superior. The "at home"
worker must also value starting work on time in order to be productive. Another
caveat is that being late for or absent from meetings sends out the silent message
to most people that you do not regard the meeting as important.

Avoid perfectionism.   Thoroughness is a virtue on most jobs until it reaches
the point of diminishing returns. If every typographical error were removed

from a newspaper, the price of the paper would have to be increased to an unrealistic level. Even worse, the paper would usually be late. Striving for excellence is certainly worthwhile, but striving for perfectionism is often self-defeating. Two work-habit consultants advise us:[8]

1. Don't run all over town looking for a particular report folder when second-best will do.
2. Don't have letters retyped to be picture perfect; the recipients will just file them or throw them away.
3. Realize that *below average to a perfectionist often is perfectly acceptable to others.*

Question the value of schmoozing. A poor work habit practiced by countless employees is **schmoozing,** socializing on the job. The schmoozer engages in such activities as telling jokes; lingering at the water cooler or copying machine; telephoning retail stores on company time; wandering around the factory, office, or store; and taking a long lunch break. Many people hold the attitude that the company owes them this opportunity to socialize on the job. Since schmoozing relieves employee monotony and boredom, and occasionally tension, it has some value.[9] But schmoozing does cut down on personal and organizational productivity. Also, the schmoozer runs the risk of being perceived as a time waster.

Learn to say no. You cannot take care of your own priorities unless you learn tactfully to decline requests from other people that interfere with your work. Your boss, of course, is more difficult to turn down than a co-worker. If your boss interrupts your work with an added assignment, point out how the new task will conflict with higher-priority ones and suggest alternatives.[10] When your boss recognizes that you are motivated to get your major tasks accomplished, and not to avoid work, you may be able to avoid getting saddled with less-important tasks.

A word of caution: Do not turn down your supervisor too often. Much discretion and tact is needed in using this approach to work efficiency.

Strive for both quantity and quality. You will recall that productivity takes into account both quantity and quality. Most employers want a great deal of work accomplished, but they also need high-quality work. Thus a commitment to both quality and quantity leads to effective work habits. As a first principle, work as rapidly as you can just before the point at which you are committing an unacceptable number of errors. Striving for perfection is not worth the price, but achieving high-quality goods and services is highly valued in most firms today.

Ask, "What is the best use of my time right now?" A key mental set for improving your efficiency and effectiveness is to ask this important question. It helps you justify your every action. Lakein notes that a particularly good time to ask this question (which he originated) is when you have been interrupted by a visitor or phone call. When it is over, he advises to check whether you should go back to what you were doing or on to something new.[11]

Recognize the importance of rest and relaxation. A valid suggestion for improving your work habits is to develop the attitude that overwork can be counterproductive, leading to negative stress and burnout. Proper physical rest contributes to mental alertness. Workaholics—people who are obsessed with work—often approach their jobs in a mechanical, unimaginative manner. (A small number of workaholics, however, are creative people at the top of their fields. But to these people, work is truly relaxing.)

Incessant attention to work is often inefficient. It is a normal human requirement to take enough rest breaks to allow oneself to approach the job with a fresh perspective. Each person has to establish for himself or herself the right balance between work and leisure, within the bounds of freedom granted by the situation. A young middle manager painted this picture of working conditions at his company: "Sure I believe in leading a balanced life. But at my company you can't if you want to climb the ladder. Management expects us to work about sixty hours per week. You dare not be caught leaving the building before 6:30 P.M. at night." Do you think this man should try to switch companies?

DEVELOPING THE PROPER SKILLS AND TECHNIQUES

In addition to minimizing procrastination and developing attitudes, values, and beliefs, you also need the right skills and techniques to become efficient and effective. Most books, articles, and workshops dealing with the topic of work habits and time management cover similar ground. Below we summarize most of the skills and techniques mentioned in these sources, along with a few original ones. The same skills and techniques are listed in Figure 18–4.

Prepare a list and set priorities. At the heart of every time-management system is list making. Almost every successful person in any field composes a list of important and less important tasks that need to be done. Some executives and professional people delegate their list making and errand running to a subordinate.

Before you can compose a useful list, you need to set aside a few minutes a day to sort out the tasks at hand. Such activity is the most basic aspect of planning. As a person's career advances, his or her list becomes longer. Many people find it helpful to set up "to do" lists for both work and personal life. The list a small-business owner brought to a time management workshop is presented in Figure 18–5.

Figure 18–4 Skills and techniques for effective work habits and time management.

1. Prepare a list and set priorities.
2. Concentrate on important tasks.
3. Concentrate on one task at a time.
4. Stay in control of paperwork.
5. Work at a steady pace.
6. Schedule similar tasks together.
7. Make use of bits of time.
8. Remember where you put things.
9. Capitalize upon your natural energy cycles.
10. Set a time limit for certain tasks.
11. Keep an orderly desk (within reason).
12. Minimize interruptions.
13. Use the telephone efficiently.
14. Be decisive and finish things.

Where do you put your lists? To prevent losing "to do" lists, or having small slips of paper containing lists scattered around, many people put these lists in a calendar. R. Alec Mackenzie says that "to do" lists on separate slips of paper have become obsolete.[12] It is preferable to put these lists in a combined

Figure 18–5 A sample "to do" list.

From the Desk of Hank Evans

JOB

Find new grill for '78 Corvette
Do estimate on '86 Toyota
Find vacation replacements for Tony and Jim
Call accountants to work on books
Pay utility bill
Have broken phone fixed
Call insurance company about payment for Caddy job
Estimate doll-up price for Buick Electra
Have outside sign fixed

HOME

Order pizza for tonight
Birthday present for Margot
Heels replaced on two pairs of shoes
Doctor's appointment for knee cartilage
Buy grass fertilizer
New pair of jeans
Keg of beer for Saturday's party

HANK'S COLLISION SERVICE
Atlanta, Georgia

daily planner and calendar such as the one illustrated in Figure 18–6. Such calendars also serve as a convenient place to log expenses.

Setting priorities. Everything on a "to do" list is not of equal importance; therefore priorities should be attached to each item on the list. A typical system is to use A to signify critical or essential items, B to signify important items, and C for the least important ones. Although an item might be regarded as a C (for example, refilling the paper clip jar), it still has a contribution to make to your management of time and well-being. Many people report that they obtain a sense of satisfaction from crossing off an item on their list, however trivial. Second, if you are at all conscientious, small, undone items will come back to interfere with your concentration. As you try to enjoy your evening that unfilled paper clip jar will be lurking in the back of your mind.

Concentrate on important tasks. To become more productive, you have to concentrate on tasks in which superior performance could have a large payoff.

Figure 18–6 A combined activity calendar and "to do" list.

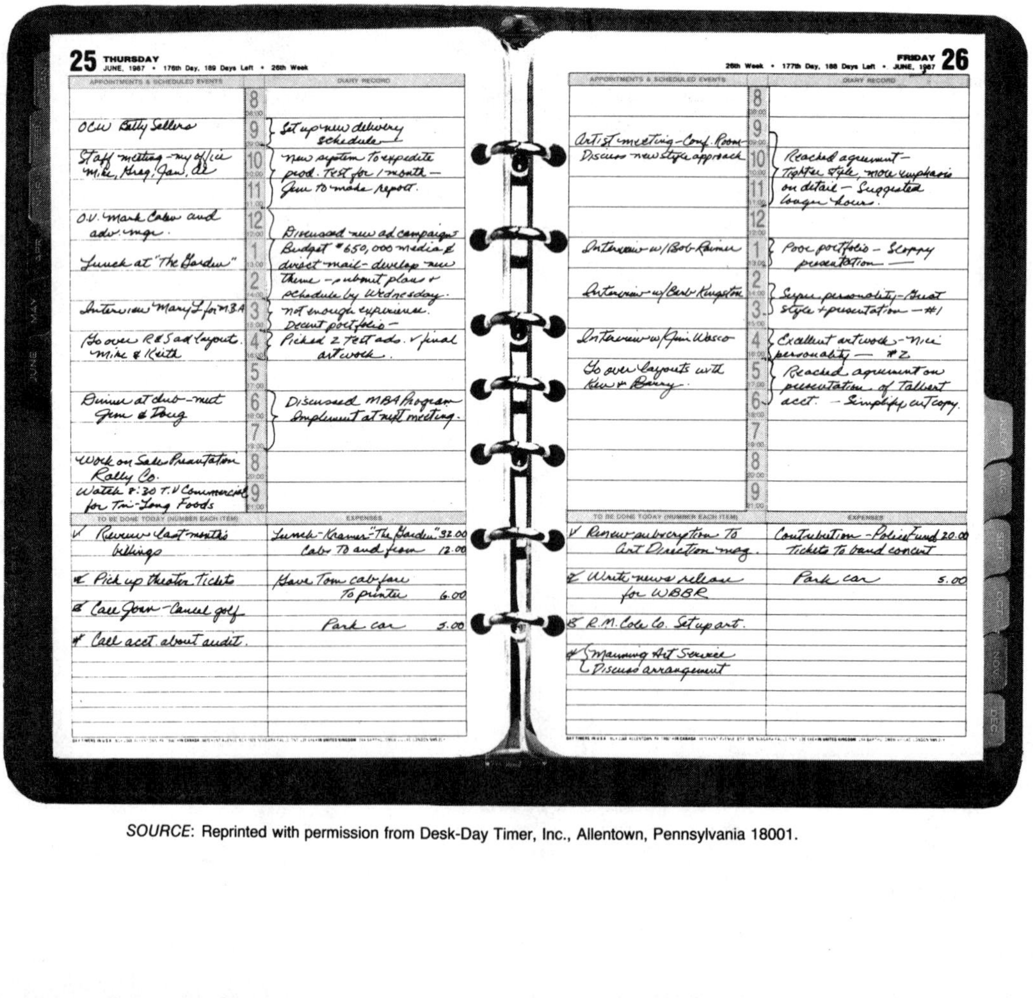

SOURCE: Reprinted with permission from Desk-Day Timer, Inc., Allentown, Pennsylvania 18001.

Concentration on these tasks facilitates achieving peak performance. Charles A. Garfield observes that an important behavior of peak performers is their goal orientation: "They do not waste time on activities that are not tied to reaching their goals."[13] No matter how quickly Hank Evans takes care of making sure that his utilities bills are paid on time, this effort will not make his collision shop a success. However, if he gets the work out on time and the quality is high, the reputation of his shop will spread.

In following the A-B-C system, you should devote ample time to the essential tasks. You should not pay more attention than absolutely necessary to the C (least important) items. Many people respond to this principle of time management by saying, "I don't think concentrating on important tasks applies to me. My job is so filled with routine that I have no chance to work on the big breakthrough ideas." True, most jobs are filled with routine requirements. The antidote is to spend some time, perhaps even one hour a week, concentrating on tasks of potentially major significance.

Another problem associated with implementing the tactic of working on important tasks is that many people work on trivial tasks to avoid the stress associated with working on major tasks. Psychologists Ronald N. Ashkenas and Robert H. Schaffer have observed that to avoid job-related anxiety, managers often spend time on unproductive work. Specifically, they have discovered that three requirements of executives' jobs—organizing day-to-day activities, improving performance under pressure, and getting subordinates to be more productive—create the most tension and anxiety. As a defense, many managers retreat to performing routine tasks that they already know how to do.[14] One such routine task would be corresponding with suppliers about new products and services. From a time-management standpoint, it would be better for these managers to delegate routine tasks and concentrate on the important tasks themselves. However, they would first have to overcome their emotional blocks.

Concentrate on one task at a time. Productive people have a well-developed capacity to concentrate on the problem or person facing them. The best results from concentration are achieved when you are so absorbed in your work that you are aware of virtually nothing else at the moment. Concentration is also useful because it reduces absentmindedness. If you concentrate intensely on what you are doing, the chances diminish that you will forget what you intended to do.

Researchers have discovered that conscious effort and self-discipline can strengthen concentration skills. "There are two types of concentration: passive and active," explains Auke Tellegen. "The former is used when you are drawn into something riveting, such as a good novel. The latter demands self-constraint." The best way to sharpen your concentration skills is to set aside 15 minutes a day and focus on something repetitive, such as your breathing or a small word. The same approach is used in meditation to relieve stress.[15]

Stay in control of paperwork. Although it is fashionable to decry the necessity of having to do paperwork in responsible jobs, the effective career person does not neglect paperwork. Paperwork includes reacting to correspondence, computer printouts, memos, and to advertisements sent through the mail. Unless paperwork is handled efficiently, a person's job may get out of control. Once a job is out of control it leads to lowered productivity and stress. Ideally, a small amount of time should be invested in paperwork every day to prevent the task from getting out of hand.

Most systems of managing paperwork are similar to making up a list of tasks and setting priorities. You sort out the papers facing you and assign them priorities. Dru Scott recommends that every day you sort all your papers into three priority piles:[16]

    I. Centrals and essentials
    II. Secondary matters
    III. Marginal matters

The ideal is to get rid of as many papers on the spot as you can. This means throwing away as many of the marginal matters as possible so you won't have to handle them again. The secondary matters should be put in a special place for later action. (An example of a secondary matter might be a request for you to participate in a company survey.) A decision must be reached about each piece of paper with a priority of I (centrals and essentials):

    1. What action should be taken?
    2. Who should take it?
    3. What should the timetable be?

One example would be a memo from your boss asking for your opinion on reorganizing the department. Your answers to the above might be: (1) I should write a report and request to discuss it with my boss; (2) I'm the one who has to take action; and (3) This is a top priority item. I'll get it done within three working days.

Work at a steady pace. In most jobs, working at a steady clip pays dividends in efficiency. The spurt worker creates many problems for management. Some employees take pride in working rapidly, even when the result is a high error rate. An important advantage of the steady-pace approach is that you accomplish much more than someone who puts out extra effort just once in a while. The completely steady worker would accomplish just as much the day before a holiday as on a given Monday. That extra hour or so of productivity adds up substantially by the end of the year. Despite the advantages of maintaining a steady pace, some peaks and valleys in your work may be inevitable. The seasonal demands placed on public accountants is a prime example.

Schedule similar tasks together. An efficient method of accomplishing small tasks is to group them together and perform them in one block of time. To illustrate, you might make most of your telephone calls in relation to your job from 11:00 to 11:30 each workday morning. Or you might reserve the last hour of each workday for correspondence and filing. It is also helpful to group your visits to people away from your work area. In this way you minimize the amount of time you are away from your own work area. Time spent "traveling" on company premises is usually not very productive. (And remember to minimize schmoozing).

By scheduling similar tasks together you develop the necessary pace and mental set to go through chores in short order. In contrast, when you jump from one type of task to another, your efficiency may suffer.

Make use of bits of time. A truly efficient person makes good use of miscellaneous bits of time, both on and off the job. While waiting in line at a bank or post office, you might update your "to do" list; while waiting for an elevator you might be able to read a 100-word report; and if you have finished your day's work ten minutes before quitting time, you can use that time to clean out a drawer in your desk. By the end of the year your productivity will have increased much more than if you had squandered these bits of time.

Remember where you put things. How much time have you wasted lately in looking for items such as an important file, your keys, or the auditron for the office copying machine? If you can remember where you put items of this nature, you can save a lot of wasted time and motion. Turla and Hawkins offer two practical suggestions for remembering where you put things:[17]

1. *Have a parking place for everything.* This would include putting your keys and pocket calculator back in the same place after each use.
2. *Make visual associations.* In order to have something register in your mind at the moment you are doing it, make up a visual association about that act. Thus if a woman named Alison parks her car in section A-6 of a giant parking lot, she might say to herself, "I parked at A-6 and it makes sense. 'A' stands for Alison, and '6' stands for the number of letters in my first name."

Capitalize upon your natural energy cycles. The old saws, "I'm a morning person" or "I'm a late afternoon person," have scientific substantiation. According to the study of biorhythms, people vary somewhat as to their hours of peak efficiency. A week or two of charting should help you discover the hours at which your mental and physical energy is apt to be highest or lowest.

After you have discovered your strong and weak energy periods, you should be able to arrange your work schedule accordingly. Tackle your intellectually most demanding assignments during your energy peaks. Avoid creative work or making major decisions when fatigue has set in. Items rated I in priority demand a fresh outlook. III items are fine to handle when you feel fatigued or discouraged.

Set a time limit for certain tasks. As a person becomes experienced with certain projects, he or she is able to make accurate estimates of how long a new project will take to complete. Thus Hank Evans might say, "I think we can fix this wreck in ten working days." A good work habit to develop is to estimate how long a job should take, then proceed with strong determination to get the job completed within the estimated period of time.

A variation of this technique is to decide that some low-priority and medium-priority items are only worth so much of your time. Invest that much time in the project, but no more. A new employee might say, for example, "Learning about the company policies and philosophy is of medium importance. Therefore, I'll study the company manuals one hour per week. But that's it. It's more important that I learn my new job well."

Keep an orderly desk (within reason). A controversy in time management is whether or not a clean, well-organized desk reflects an uncluttered, organized mind. Some people contend, "What difference does the appearance of my desk make? What counts is whether or not I know where things are." Some time-management specialists contend that an orderly desk is not linked directly to productivity.[18]

A partial resolution of the controversy is to recognize that a tidy desk is more important for some types of work than others. Executives tend to prefer a well-organized desk, whereas artists, writers, scientists, and professors tend to prefer a cluttered desk. If you work in a bureaucracy, an orderly desk is impressive. A disorderly desk gives you a negative image.

An orderly desk has two striking advantages. For one, it helps you concentrate on one piece of paper at a time—an important habit for accomplishing things. Second, it decreases drastically the amount of time you devote to searching for notes, forms, and other work-related material. Despite these two impressive arguments for an organized, tidy desk, some highly successful people have disastrous looking desks.

Minimize interruptions. The job of managers, and many individual contributors as well, is fraught with interruptions. What constitutes an "interruption" depends upon your value and priorities. A people-oriented leader might perceive an impromptu visit by a troubled subordinate as an important part of his or her role. A task-oriented leader might regard the same visit as an interruption, keeping him or her from doing much more important things. Another important consideration about interruptions is that they have political implications. If you communicate to your boss the impression that he or she is interrupting you by requesting your presence, you may fall into disfavor.

One solution to the problem of interruptions is for you to schedule a period of time during the day in which you have uninterrupted work time.[19] You give co-workers a definite time during which you want to be disturbed with emergencies only. It is also helpful to inform co-workers of the nature of the important work you ordinarily conduct during your quiet period. Figure 18–7 offers some practical tips on protecting yourself from time-wasting visitors (schmoozers). It is important to recognize the difference between a schmoozer and somebody with a legitimate reason for communicating with you. Team effort requires frequent interaction among co-workers about work-related topics.

Use the telephone efficiently. Much business today is conducted over the telephone, including both calls from outside and within the firm. Using the telephone efficiently can thus save you a substantial amount of time. One major

Figure 18–7

PROTECTING YOUR PRIVACY

What should you do when your co-workers want to socialize, but you want to work? Must you resign yourself to a 45-minute illustrated lecture on the adventures of your co-worker's grandchild when you have a difficult sales presentation to prepare? Or should you risk offending the proud grandfather by throwing him bodily out of your office? Fortunately there is some middle ground. Consider this list of suggestions for politely but firmly protecting your privacy—and your sanity—published by GF Business Equipment, Inc.:

1. A direct statement is most effective. Simply say, "I'm sorry, but I'm busy and can't be disturbed." If you are concerned that others will take this personally or consider you antisocial, compensate by going out of your way to be friendly with these people at other times.
2. Keep your responses brief and let your tone of voice convey your reluctance to engage in conversation.
3. Avert eye contact with unwelcome visitors. It's harder for people to sustain conversation with people who won't look at them.
4. If you were about to make a phone call when someone enters, do not replace the receiver. Keeping it in your hand clearly signals your intention to proceed momentarily.
5. Do not sit down if you want to keep the visit brief.
6. Stand up when you are ready for your visitor to leave. This is an unmistakable signal.
7. If you occupy a work space with relatively low partitions (five feet or less), place or attach articles such as plants, in/out trays, lamps, clocks, or vases on the partition surface or edge to prevent others from leaning into your space.
8. If possible, use task lighting to focus on your work. This emphasizes your absorption in your task and creates a bond between you and your work that others will hesitate to break.

Source: Abridged and adapted from Greg Daugherty, "Protecting Your Privacy," *Success*, April 1982, pp. 10–11. The privacy guide itself was prepared by GF Business Equipment, 229 East Dennick Avenue, Youngstown, OH 44501.

problem with telephone conversations is identical to the problem with in-person conversations. Many people are slow to come to the point. Executives tend to move quickly to the heart of the matter when engaged in phone conversation. A typical conversation might be, "Hi, how are things going? The reason I'm calling is that I need your input on this problem. (The manner in which the executive asks the question, "How are things going?" usually suggests he or she is not really looking for a response other than something like, "Fine.")

When you receive a telephone call, a time-saving approach is to say, "Hello, how may I help you?" This encourages specifics from long-winded, poorly organized callers.[20]

Be decisive and finish things. Our last specific suggestion for improving your work habits and time management is to be decisive. Move quickly, but not impulsively, through the decision-making steps outlined in Chapter 4 when you are faced with a nonprogrammed decision. Once you have evaluated the alternatives to the problem, implement one of them. Superintelligent people are sometimes poor decision makers because they keep on collecting facts. The result is that they procrastinate instead of acting. Some people of more modest intelligence waste time when faced with a decision not because they want more facts, but because they are fearful of committing themselves. In short, if you agonize too long over too many decisions, your personal productivity will suffer.

Another aspect of being decisive is to make the decision to finish tasks you have begun. Incompleted tasks lower your productivity, and rarely does one receive credit for an unfinished project.[21]

GETTING STARTED IMPROVING YOUR WORK HABITS AND TIME MANAGEMENT

Assume you were able to implement every suggestion in this chapter and you also followed carefully the decision-making steps outlined in Chapter 4. You would now be on the road toward being one of the most productive and well-organized people in your field. The flaw in this logic is that no one is equipped to implement, immediately, every suggestion. One limiting factor is that you might not be able to identify or do much about the underlying problems blocking your productivity.

The recommended way to begin improving your work habits is to start small. Select one or two strategies that seem focused on a major work-habit or time-management problem facing you. Try the strategy. Monitor your progress and move on to another strategy.

A helpful starting point for almost anyone seeking to improve work habits is to sort out the tasks facing you and make a prioritized list. An equally valid approach would be to do the human relations exercise at the conclusion of this chapter. It helps you identify areas where you might be deficient. Act first on those areas where you have a problem. For example, if you are courageous enough to admit that your biggest problem is a tendency to procrastinate, you would act first by attempting to decrease your procrastination.

How personal characteristics influence ability to improve one's work habits. Some people will find it easier than others to improve their productivity. Above all, one needs the right talent and motivation to make much improvement feasible. Another factor is that certain personality characteristics are related to work habits and time management. At the top of the list is **compulsiveness,** a tendency to pay careful attention to detail and to be meticulous. A compulsive person takes naturally to being well organized and neat. If you are less concerned about detail and meticulousness by nature, it will be more difficult for you to develop exceptional work habits. People who are spontaneous and emotional also tend to be naturally inclined toward casual work habits.

A note of caution: Compulsiveness can sometimes be detrimental to productivity. Compulsive people may have a difficult time concentrating on important tasks. They often get hung up on details and fail to see the "big picture." The truly productive person finds an optimum balance between concern for detail and being able to look at the "big picture."

Summary of Key Points

☐   By improving your work habits and time management, you can improve your job productivity and enhance your personal life. Also, improving in these areas can help prevent one from flunking out of school or being fired.

☐   Procrastination is a major problem for many people. The major causes of procrastination are fear of failure, fear of bad news, self-destructive behavior, and the desire to avoid uncomfortable, overwhelming, or tedious tasks.

☐   Awareness of the procrastination problem may lead to its control. Six other methods for reducing procrastination are (a) calculate the cost of procrastination, (b) apply behavior modification to yourself, (c) arouse enthusiasm for performing the task, (d) cut the task down into manageable chunks, (e) make a public commitment about performing the task, (f) remove the temptation to engage in a counterproductive habit.

☐   Developing good work habits and time-management practices is often a matter of developing the right attitudes toward your work and toward time. Nine such attitudes, values, and beliefs are as follows:

1. Try to discover what is blocking you.
2. Value your time.
3. Value good attendance and punctuality.
4. Avoid perfectionism.
5. Question the value of schmoozing.
6. Learn to say no.
7. Strive for both quantity and quality.

8. Ask, "What is the best use of my time right now?"
9. Recognize the importance of rest and relaxation.

☐ Fourteen skills and techniques to help you become more productive are as follows:

1. Prepare a list and set priorities.
2. Concentrate on important tasks.
3. Concentrate on one task at a time.
4. Stay in control of paperwork.
5. Work at a steady pace.
6. Schedule similar tasks together.
7. Make use of bits of time.
8. Remember where you put things.
9. Capitalize upon your natural energy cycles.
10. Set a time limit for certain tasks.
11. Keep an orderly desk (within reason).
12. Minimize interruptions.
13. Use the telephone efficiently.
14. Be decisive and finish things.

☐ The best way to begin improving your work habits and management of time is to start small. Select one or two attitudes, beliefs, strategies, or methods that appear particularly relevant to your circumstances and give them a try. Monitor your progress, and then move on to another tactic. In trying to improve, be aware that if you are not somewhat compulsive, it will require extra effort to become neat and well organized.

Questions and Activities _____

1. Why are good work habits and time management practices so essential for the self-employed person?

2. Identify two annoying habits you have observed among well-organized people.

3. When you meet a stranger, how would you diagnose if that person is well organized?

4. Give an example from your life of how striving for perfection was not worth the price.

5. If you followed all the suggestions in this chapter, do you think it would inhibit your creativity? Explain.

6. What is your reaction to this statement: "A clear and orderly desk reflects a clear and orderly mind"?

7. One time-management practice was deliberately omitted from this chapter. Called "double up on time," it deals with such behaviors as sorting through your mail while conducting a phone conversation. Should this tactic have been included? Why or why not?

8. Which of the suggestions made in this chapter are particularly applicable to becoming a more productive student?

9. What information presented in the previous chapters would also contribute to turning in peak performance?

10. Ask a successful person what he or she does to stay organized while under heavy job pressure. Be prepared to discuss your findings in class.

A Human Relations Case

THE OVERWHELMED ADMINISTRATIVE ASSISTANT

Mary looked into the storeroom mirror and thought to herself, "You're looking bad, kid. Somehow you've got to get your life straightened out. You're on a treadmill, and you don't know how to get off. But it's a bad time to be thinking about myself right now. It's time to meet with my boss, Beatrice. I wonder what she wants?"

Beatrice Reynolds began the meeting with Mary Converse in her usual open manner: "Mary, I'm concerned about you. For a long time you were one of the best administrative assistants in our firm. You received compliments from me and the other department heads who had contact with your department. Now you're hardly making it. You've become so irritable, so lacking in enthusiasm. And a lot of your work contains glaring errors and is also late. The reason I'm bringing the subject up again is that things have gotten worse. What's your problem?"

"I wish it were only one problem, Beatrice. I feel like the world is caving in on me. I work here about 40 hours a week. I'm trying to upgrade myself in life. As you know I'm taking two courses in a business program. If I can keep up the pace, I'll have my degree by next spring. But it's getting to be a grind."

"How are things at home, Mary?"

"Much worse than they are here. My husband works too, and he's getting fed up with never seeing me when he comes home. It seems that when he's home, I'm either working late at the office, in class, or studying at the library. Thursday is the one weekday night I'm home for sure. And that's Tony's bowling night."

"Our son Steve isn't too happy either. He's only 5 but the other day he asked me if Daddy and I were getting divorced. Steve doesn't see us together much. When he does see us, he can feel the tension between us."

"So, you're under pressure at the office and at home," said Beatrice.

"Add school to that list. I'm having a devil of a time getting through my business statistics course. If I flunk, my chances of getting a degree are set back considerably."

"Do the best you can, Mary. I'm sympathetic, but I need better performance from you."

As Mary left Beatrice Reynolds' office, she said: "Thanks for being candid with me. My problem is that my boss, my husband, my child, and my professors all want better performance from me. I wish I knew how to give it."

1. What suggestions can you offer Mary for working her way out of her problems?

2. Why is this case included in a chapter about improving your work habits and time management?

3. What stress symptoms is Mary experiencing?

4. How well do you think Reynolds handled the interview?

A Human Relations Incident

WHAT DO YOU DO WHEN EVERYBODY WANTS TO SEE THE BOSS?

Lloyd Bartow, a management consultant, was conducting a workshop about time management at a newspaper. Midway through the presentation, Spike Meadows, head of the machine maintenance department, said: "Oh, sure your idea about spending one hour per day on paperwork and planning sounds great in theory. But in my line of work, I don't even have five spare minutes to myself. The job of my department is to make sure that the presses keep running. We're hit with requests all day.

"When somebody has a problem, he or she insists on speaking to me. If I'm out to lunch or on vacation, the person will say, 'Well, I'll speak to Spike when he gets back. I'm in a trap and there is no way out.' "

Bartow replied, "But there must be some way that you can appoint an acting department head for the times when you are taking care of paperwork or planning."

"That's what you as an outsider might think. But everybody in this newspaper wants to see the boss when they have a machine maintenance problem."

1. What should Lloyd tell Spike?
2. What underlying problem do you think might really be blocking Spike?
3. Do you think it might be true that a "firefighter's" job such as Spike's might not leave room for planning or taking care of paperwork during normal working hours?

A Human Relations Exercise

IMPROVING YOUR WORK HABITS AND TIME MANAGEMENT

Casually reading this chapter will rarely lead to improvements in personal productivity. You need to back up these ideas with a specific action plan for improvement, as described in the section entitled "Getting Started Improving Your Work Habits and Time Management." A useful mechanical aid toward achieving this end is to scan the checklist presented below. It covers the strategies, techniques, and tactics described in this chapter. Select the six areas on this checklist in which you need the most help. For each item you select, write a one- or two-sentence action plan. Suppose you checked "Be Decisive and Finish Things." Your action plan might take this form:

> Next time I'm faced with an important decision, I'll make up my mind within two days, instead of the usual entire week. I'll make note of the date on which the problem faced me and the date on which I finally made up my mind.

The Work Habit and Time-Management Checklist

Attitude, Skill, or Technique

1. Be aware of the procrastination problem. _____
2. Calculate the cost of procrastination. _____
3. Apply behavior modification to yourself. _____
4. Arouse enthusiasm for performing the task. _____
5. Cut the task down into manageable chunks. _____
6. Make a public commitment. _____
7. Remove temptation. _____
8. Try to discover what is blocking you. _____
9. Value your time. _____
10. Value good attendance and punctuality. _____
11. Avoid perfectionism. _____
12. Question the value of schmoozing. _____
13. Learn to say no. _____
14. Strive for both quantity and quality. _____
15. Ask, "What is the best use of my time right now?" _____
16. Recognize the importance of rest and relaxation. _____
17. Prepare a list and set priorities. _____
18. Concentrate on important tasks. _____
19. Concentrate on one task at a time. _____
20. Stay in control of paperwork. _____
21. Work at a steady pace. _____
22. Schedule similar tasks together. _____
23. Make use of bits of time. _____
24. Remember where you put things. _____
25. Capitalize upon your natural energy cycles. _____
26. Set a time limit for certain tasks. _____
27. Keep an orderly desk (within reason). _____
28. Minimize interruptions. _____
29. Use the telephone efficiently. _____
30. Be decisive and finish things. _____

Notes

1. Personal communication with Cable Neuhaus.
2. Jane Burka and Lenora Yuen, *Procrastination: Why You Do It, What to Do about It* (Reading, MA: Addison Wesley, 1984).
3. Bryce Nelson, "Do You Fear Success?" *The New York Times* syndicated story, February 16, 1983.

4. Alan Lakein, *How to Gain Control of Your Time and Your Life* (New York: Peter H. Wyden, 1973), pp. 141–51.

5. Albert Ellis and William J. Knaus, *Overcoming Procrastination* (New York: New American Library, 1979), p. 111.

6. Henry C. Everett, M.D., "Conquering Procrastination," *Success*, June 1981, p. 28.

7. Ibid., p. 49.

8. Peter A. Turla and Kathleen L. Hawkins, "The Flaws of Perfectionism," *Success*, December 1982, p. 23.

9. Robert Schrank, "How to Relieve Worker Boredom," *Psychology Today*, July 1978, pp. 79–80.

10. Edwin C. Bliss, "Give Yourself the Luxury of Time," *Mainliner*, December 1976, p. 56.

11. Lakein, *How to Gain Control*, p. 99.

12. R. Alec Mackenzie, "The 'To Do' List Is Obsolete," *Supervisory Management*, September 1985, p. 42.

13. "Peak Performance—It Can Be Learned. And Taught," *Management Solutions*, June 1986, p. 26.

14. Robert N. Ashkenas and Robert H. Schaffer, "Managers Can Avoid Wasting Time," *Harvard Business Review*, May–June 1982, p. 98.

15. "Increase Your Powers of Concentration," *Research Institute Personal Report for the Executive*, January 7, 1986, p. 7.

16. Dru Scott, *How to Put More Time in Your Life* (New York: Signet Books/New American Library, 1980), p. 175.

17. Peter A. Turla and Kathleen L. Hawkins, "Remembering to Remember," *Success!*, May 1983, p. 60.

18. See, for example, Scott, *How to Put More Time in Your Life*, p. 172.

19. Peter A. Turla and Kathleen L. Hawkins, "A Personal Achievement Guide to Time Management," *Success!*, November 1982, p. A6.

20. Ibid., p. A7.

21. Beth Brophy and Diane Cole, "10 Timely Tips," *USA Weekend*, October 25–27, 1985, p. 22.

Suggested Reading

BAKER, H. KENT, and MORGAN, PHILIP I. "Building a Professional Image: Dealing with Time Problems." *Supervisory Management*, October 1985, pp. 36–42.

BERNARDO, STEPHANIE. "Time Is Money." *Success!* September 1985, pp. 50–53.

"Don't Procrastinate." *Practical Supervision*, January 1986, p. 3.

EDWARDS, PAUL AND SARAH. *Working from Home*. Los Angeles: J. P. Tarcher, 1985.

JANUZ, LAUREN R., and JONES, SUSAN K. *Time Management for Executives*. New York: Scribner's, 1981.

NIEHOUSE, OLIVER L. "Managerial Procrastination: Solving This Major Business Obstruction." *Piedmont Airlines*, November 1985, pp. 81–85.

WEBBER, ROSS. *Time Is Money: The Key to Managerial Success*. New York: Free Press, 1980.

Supplementary
Module:
Research
in Human
Relations and
Organizational
Behavior

Research in Human Relations and Organizational Behavior

LEARNING OBJECTIVES

The purpose of this supplementary learning module is to help the reader understand how the scientific method and research contribute to knowledge about human relations and organizational behavior. Four topics are chosen to achieve this purpose:

1. The contribution of theory and research.
2. Methods of data collection.
3. Research methods.
4. Sources of error in research about human behavior.

THE CONTRIBUTION OF THEORY AND RESEARCH

Many people with job experience taking their first course in human relations or organizational behavior comment, "Skip the theory and research. Let's get to practical applications. I'm taking this course so I can improve my effectiveness on the job." Although this text takes a job-oriented approach, it has not entirely skipped theory and research. Sound research, followed by sound theory, leads to generalizations that will help you function more effectively on the job.

A case in point is the accumulated wisdom about goal setting described in Chapter 2. Behavioral scientists have demonstrated through research that setting realistic goals leads to improved performance. Practicing managers can now use such knowledge as a guide to action. Thoman H. Jerdee explains how theory and research contribute to knowledge about human behavior on the job:[1]

> Theory is simply the orderly summarization of verified knowledge about phenomena and their interrelationships. As such, it is the wellspring of human progress in mastering the environment. Prescriptions for action must be derived from theory, and different people may reasonably derive varying prescriptions from the same theory, depending on their values and priorities. Here, perhaps, is where the real gap between theoretician and practitioner develops, rather than in regard to theory itself.

Despite these comments, the establishment of theory sometimes precedes data collection. A human relations specialist, for example, might develop a theory through "armchair reasoning" and then test the theory by collecting data.

An important purpose of the theories presented in this book is to help you understand human behavior in organizations. If we merely describe what happens—without providing explanation—human relations is entirely unscientific. For instance, the path-goal theory of leadership effectiveness explains why a particular leader is effective. (The leader smooths the path to attaining goals.) If we merely described an effective leader in action, we would miss out on the unifying principle that helps to explain leadership effectiveness.

METHODS OF DATA COLLECTION

The four most frequently used methods of collecting data in human relations and organizational behavior are questionnaires, interviews, direct observation of behavior, and unobtrusive measures.

Questionnaires

Questionnaires have appeared at various places in this text, and you have probably filled out dozens of research questionnaires. Before preparing a final questionnaire, a scientist collects relevant facts and generates hypotheses (educated guesses) about important issues to explore. The questionnaires are carefully designed to measure relevant issues about the topic under survey. Review the Bureaucratic Orientation questionnaire presented in Chapter 14 for a sampling of how a questionnaire touches upon relevant issues. Questionnaire construction is a complex art, despite the deceptively straightforward appearance of one that is well designed.

Interviews

The researcher about human behavior on the job relies heavily upon the interview as a method of data collection. Even when a questionnaire is the primary method of data collection, it is probable that interviews were used to obtain ideas for survey questions. Interviews are also helpful in uncovering explanations about phenomena and furnishing leads for further inquiry. For instance, a researcher conducting interviews about productivity uncovered the fact that workers "goofing off" was a major source of low productivity. Written questions would probably have missed this issue. Fill-in questions on written surveys, such as "Is there anything else you would like to add?" may also be useful in providing explanations and diagnostic information.

Another advantage of interviews is that a skilled interviewer can probe for additional information. One disadvantage of the interview method is that skilled interviewers are required. Another disadvantage is that the interviewer has to be trusted in order to obtain accurate results.

Interviews can be classified into *structured* and *unstructured*. The structured interview asks standard questions of all respondents. Highly structured interviews take on the tone of a written questionnaire, particularly when they ask two-response-category questions such as "Are you satisfied with your pay?"

Unstructured interviews encourage the free flow of conversation and appear less scientific than structured interviews. The unstructured interview is used to gather general impressions about the job, the firm, or the employee. During the unstructured interview, the interviewer shifts to whatever question seems suited to uncovering important information. By contrast, the structured interview follows a more rigid pattern.

Systematic Observation

Much information about human behavior on the job is collected by observers placing themselves in the work environment. Systematic observations are then made about the phenomena under study. One concern about this method is that the people being observed may turn in atypical performances when they know they are being observed.

A variation of systematic observation is *participant observation*. The observer becomes a member of the group about which he or she is collecting data. For instance, to study the job stress experienced by some VDT operators, a researcher might work in a word-processing department.

Unobtrusive Measures

One problem with the methods of data collection mentioned so far is that the researcher interacts with the person providing the data. To get around this problem, some researchers collect information without the awareness of the people being studied. One example would be observations about the job satisfaction of sales associates in a store made by visiting the store as a customer. If people do not know what a participant observer is doing, that person is using unobtrusive measures.

RESEARCH METHODS

The methods of data collection just described are the basic tools for conducting research about human behavior in organizations (and in business). These methods of data collection are applied to different methods or strategies for conducting an investigation. Research methods can be classified as follows: case study, correlational study, and experiment (including laboratory and field experiments).

Case Study

Cases have been presented throughout this text. Although they are a popular teaching method, cases are often looked upon critically as a method of conducting research. Case information is usually collected by an observer recording impressions in his or her mind or in a notepad. People have a natural tendency to attend to information specifically related to their own interests or needs. The following incident illustrates the problem of filtered perceptions:

> One researcher prepared a case report showing examples of how the initiative of word processing technicians was hampered by an authoritarian supervisor. Another researcher prepared a report in the same department emphasizing how much the technicians enjoyed not having to make decisions themselves.

Both researchers were correct within the limits of their selective perception. Both sets of events probably took place, but each researcher saw only a partial view of reality. Despite this subjective element in the case method, cases provide a wealth of information that can be used to explain what is happening in a given situation.

Correlational Study

A widely used research method is to correlate scores on one measure (an independent variable) with scores on some outside criterion (a dependent variable). Often the dependent variable represents "hard data" (objective information), such as salary, number of units shipped, or number of patents issued. The independent variable is typically measured by a questionnaire. An example of this type of study would be correlating a measure of leadership style with group productivity.

A major limitation of correlational studies is that they can be misinterpreted as revealing the cause of something. All that can be safely concluded from a correlational study is that the two variables measured vary in a similar fashion. In the example above, a particular leadership style might not be the true cause of group productivity. The true cause might be that one style of leader encourages more goal setting than does another.

Experiment

An experiment is the most rigorous research method. The essence of conducting an experiment is to make sure that only the variable under study is influencing the results. This procedure is referred to as *controlling* for the influence of independent variables. The two most frequently used experiments in organizational behavior and human relations are the laboratory experiment and field experiment.

Laboratory experiment. A major characteristic of the laboratory experiment is that the conditions are supposedly under the experimenter's control. A group of people might be brought into a room to study the effects of stress on problem-solving ability. The stressor the experimenter introduces is an occasional blast from a siren. In a field setting, assuming the experiment were permitted, the experimenter might be unaware of what other stressors the employees were facing. A major concern about laboratory experiments is that their results might not be generalizable to the outside world.

Field experiment. Field experiments are an attempt to apply the experimental methods to real-life situations. Variables can be controlled more readily in the laboratory than in the field, but information obtained in the field is often more relevant. The experiment about flexible working hours described in Chapter 1 illustrates a field experiment. Here we provide more details about the nature of the experimental method.

Suppose an experimenter were interested in studying the influence of assertiveness training (AT) on the career progress of women. One experimental method to investigate this matter would be to measure how AT influences the salary growth and rate of promotion of women. A conventional research design to study this problem is shown in Figure M–1.

Figure M–1   A research design based on the experimental method.

Procedures and Steps	Experimental Group	Control Group I	Control Group II
Assign women randomly to groups	Yes	Yes	Yes
Record current salary	Yes	Yes	Yes
Record current job level	Yes	Yes	Yes
Administer AT program	Yes	No	No
Conduct group discussions about careers	No	No	Yes
Allow time to pass without interacting with participants	Yes	Yes	Yes
Record salary level at one- and two-year periods	Yes	Yes	Yes
Record job level at one- and two-year periods	Yes	Yes	Yes

The experimenter would make statistical comparisons of the salary progress and job-level progress of the experimental and control groups. If the women who underwent AT scored higher in salary and job level, it would be concluded tentatively that AT helped career progress more than did (1) no such training or (2) group discussions about career progress. Using the second control group helps to rule out the possibility that talking about improving one's career is as effective as AT.

SOURCES OF ERROR IN RESEARCH ON HUMAN BEHAVIOR IN ORGANIZATIONS

Research in human relations and organizational behavior has many more problems than does research in most physical and biological sciences. Here we mention ten of the most common sources of error when conducting research on human behavior in organizations.

1. *Inaccurate information.* For example, people sometimes respond to questionnaires insincerely, and productivity figures used as dependent variables may be misleading and unreliable.

2. *Limited generalizability of results.* Research is often conducted in healthy organizational climates characterized by trust between top managers and employees. When the same techniques are applied in less trustful environments, the results might not be as good.

3. *Apathy, indifference, and anxiety of participants.* People participating in research studies may not care about the study or may be fearful of telling the truth. Consequently, the results of the study are inaccurate, leading to the experimental error listed above.

4. *The social desirability factor.* Participants often say things in response to research questions that they think will make them look good (be socially desirable). For instance, virtually all managers contend that they consult with employees before making a decision. And few people blame themselves for productivity problems.

5. *Invalid measures of experimental variables.* Many questionnaires are not a true measure of what they intend to measure, thus limiting the possibility of achieving useful results. For example, a questionnaire about leadership style might really be measuring how much the respondent enjoys working with people.

6. *Influence of the measuring instrument on the outcome (reactivity of methods).* A measurement is *reactive* when an attempt to measure something alters the state of the person being measured. For instance, if a person begins to experience stress symptoms while completing a questionnaire about job stress, the questionnaire is reactive. Asking people about job satisfaction may bring to mind issues of dissatisfaction.

7. *Extraneous influences on the dependent variable.* Sometimes an outside factor enters the experiment during the course of the study. The outside factor then changes the results. For example, a study might be conducted about the influence of flexible working hours on productivity. During the experiment, a new manager is appointed who is so effective that productivity increases because of her leadership approach. Leadership style thus becomes the extraneous influence on the outcome of this study, and the possible influence of flexible working hours is difficult to measure.

8. *Nonrandom selection.* When people are assigned to experimental and control groups on any basis other than random selection, the results could be biased. An illustrative source of bias is that volunteers for a given program or experiment are sometimes psychologically different from nonvolunteers. For instance, they might be more adventuresome and self-confident, thus tending to do well in a given training program or respond well to any treatment.

9. *Loss of subjects.* In field research, particularly, some participants may drop out of the experiment before it is completed. Randomness is thus not insured. In the AT and career development program mentioned earlier, it is conceivable that some of the subjects who responded well to AT may have become so assertive that they left the firm for better opportunities elsewhere.

10. *The influence of moderator variables.* In most research about human behavior in organizations, certain factors are present which influence the results for some groups but not for others. These factors are referred to as **moderator variables,** factors that specify the condition under which an independent variable influences a dependent variable. One factor mentioned in the text was the moderating influence of employee preference on the effectiveness of job enrichment. A study might show that job enrichment had no impact on job satisfaction. Assume that the criterion groups were categorized into those who wanted job enrichment versus those who did not want job enrichment. The outcome of the experiment would then be quite good—for the criterion group that wanted job enrichment.

Note

1. Thomas H. Jerdee, book review in *Personnel Psychology*, Winter 1976, p. 655.

Suggested Reading

CRONBACH, LEE J. *Essentials of Psychological Testing*, 4th ed. New York: Harper & Row, 1984.

DANSEREAU, FRED, ALUTTO, JOSEPH A., and YAMMARINO, FRANCIS J. *Theory Testing in Organizational Behavior: The Variant Approach*: Englewood Cliffs, NJ: Prentice Hall, 1984.

LAWLER, EDWARD E. III, and associates. *Doing Research That Is Useful for Theory and Practice*. San Francisco: Jossey-Bass, 1985.

SCHERMERHORN, JOHN R., JR., HUNT, JAMES G., and OSBURN, RICHARD N. *Managing Organizational Behavior*, 2nd ed. New York, Wiley, 1985.

Glossary

Abrasive personality   A self-centered individual who is isolated from others, perfectionist, contemptuous, and prone to attack.

Achievement need   The desire to set and accomplish goals for their own sake.

Action plan   A description of the steps that need to be taken to achieve an objective or bring performance back to an acceptable standard.

Affiliation need   A desire to seek out close relationships with others and to be a loyal employee or friend.

Aggressive personality   A person who physically or verbally attacks other people frequently.

Anger   A feeling of extreme hostility, indignation, or exasperation.

Appeals procedure   A formal method of resolving conflict by bringing the issue to a higher level of authority.

Artificial intelligence (AI)   The capability of a computer to perform functions usually considered part of human intelligence, such as learning, reasoning, and listening.

Assertiveness training (AT)   A self-improvement program that teaches people to express their feelings and act with an appropriate degree of openness and candor.

Assumptional analysis   A method of analyzing the assumptions that are used to support conclusions.

Attitude   A predisposition to respond in a particular way.

Autocratic leader   A person in charge who attempts to retain most of the authority granted to the group.

Behavior modification   An attempt to change behavior by manipulating rewards and punishments.

Behavior shaping   The rewarding of any response in the right direction and then rewarding only the closest approximation.

Biofeedback training   A relaxation technique involving an electronic machine that helps one develop an awareness of muscle sensations, pulse rate, breathing rate, and other physiological stress symptoms.

Brainstorming   A conference technique of solving specific problems, amassing information, and stimulating creative thinking.

Brainwriting   *See* **Private brainstorming.**

Bureaucracy   A form of organization in which division of effort, rank, rules, and regulations are carefully defined.

Bureaupathic behavior   A strong need to control others based on insecurity.

Career development   A planned approach to achieving growth and satisfaction in work experiences.

Career development program   A planned approach to helping employees enhance their careers while at the same time integrating individual and organizational goals.

Career path   A series of positions in one or more organizations leading to a long-range goal.

Career plateau   The point in a career where it becomes evident that further job advancement is permanently or temporarily blocked.

Charisma   Personal charm and magnetism that is used to lead others.

Chronological résumé   A job résumé that presents work experience, education, and interests along with accomplishments in reverse chronological order.

Coaching   A method of helping employees grow and improve their job competence by providing suggestions and encouragement.

Coercive power   The ability to punish for noncompliance.

Cognitive viewpoint (or model)   An explanation of human behavior that emphasizes the internal mental processes that take place whenever a person is subject to an external force.

Command group   A clustering of workers consisting of a manager and his or her subordinates.

Communication   The sending, receiving, and understanding of messages.

Communication climate   The degree to which an organization permits or promotes a free and open exchange of ideas and information among its members.

Compulsiveness   A tendency to pay careful attention to detail and to be meticulous.

Comparable worth   The doctrine that people who perform similar jobs with different titles, but of comparable value to the firm, should receive equal pay.

Compressed work week   A full-time work schedule that allows 40 hours to be accomplished in less than five days.

Compromise   Settlement of differences by mutual concession.

Computer shock   A strong negative reaction to being forced to spend many more hours working at a computer than one expected or desires.

Conflict   A situation in which two or more goals, values, or events are incompatible or mutually exclusive.

Consensual leader   A person in charge who encourages group discussion about an issue and then makes a decision that reflects the general agreement (consensus) of group members.

Consultative leader   A person in charge who solicits opinions from the group before making a decision, yet does not feel obliged to accept the group's thinking.

Contingency theory of leadership   An explanation of leadership that specifies the conditions under which a particular leadership style will be effective.

Control group   A comparison group that is similar to the experimental group except that it not exposed to the variable being studied.

Corporate culture   *See* **Organizational culture.**

Corrective discipline   Any type of discipline that emphasizes improving employee behavior.

Counseling   A formal discussion method for helping another individual overcome a problem or improve his or her potential.

Creative problem solving   The ability to overcome obstacles by approaching them in novel ways.

Creative worker   Someone who approaches problems in a new or unique way.

Creativity   The ability to develop good ideas that can be put into action.

Decision making   The process of choosing among the alternatives that exist to solve the problem.

Decision-making leave   A paid one-day suspension to help an employee think through a disciplinary problem.

Decision-making software   Any computer program that helps the decision maker work through the problem-solving and decision-making steps.

Democratic leader   A person in charge who confers final authority on the group.

Developmental need   A specific area in which a person needs improvement.

Distress   The wrong type and amount of stress, which results in negative outcomes for the individual and the organization.

Ego state   As defined in transactional analysis, the three parts of the human personality (parent, adult, child).

Eighty-twenty principle   The generalization that 80 percent of the results or problems are usually caused by 20 percent of the activities.

Employee assistance program (EAP)   A formal organization unit designed to help employees deal with personal problems adversely affecting job performance.

Encounter group   A variety of small-group experiences in which the members encounter each other with an open expression of feelings.

Eustress   A positive force that is the equivalent of finding excitement and challenge.

Entrepreneur   A person who converts an innovative idea into a business.

Environmental determinism   The doctrine of behaviorism stating that our past history of reinforcement determines, or causes, our current behavior.

Eureka factor   The sudden illuminating flash of judgment that guides many executives.

Executive rap sessions   Semi-structured or informal meetings in which top-level managers meet with a cross section of employees to discuss their concerns.

Expectancy   In expectancy theory, the probability assigned by the individual that effort will lead to performing the task correctly.

Expectancy theory (ET)   An explanation of work motivation based on the premise that how much effort people expend depends upon how much they expect to receive in return.

External locus of control   The belief that external forces controls one's fate.

Extinction   In behavior modification, decreasing the frequency of undesirable behavior by removing the consequence of such behavior.

Fear   Worry and anxiety about a punishment that might be forthcoming.

Feeling-level communication   A form of sending and receiving messages that emphasizes the feelings, emotions, and attitudes that are exchanged when people communicate.

Fight-or-flight response   The body's physiological and chemical battle against the stressor in which the person tries to cope with the adversity head-on, or tries to flee the scene.

Flextime   A method of organizing hours of work so that employees have flexibility in choosing their own hours.

Formal communication pathways   The official, sanctioned route over which messages are supposed to travel in the organization.

Formal group   A work unit deliberately formed by the organization to accomplish specific tasks and achieve objectives.

Free-rein leader   A person in charge who turns over virtually all the authority to the group.

Frustration   A blocking of need or motive satisfaction.

Functional résumé   A résumé that organizes skills and accomplishments into the functions or tasks that support the job being sought.

Grapevine   The major informal communication channel in an organization.

Grievance procedure   A formal mechanism for filing employee complaints.

Group   Two or more people who interact with each other, are aware of each other, are working toward some common purpose, and perceive themselves to be a group.

Group cohesiveness   The attractiveness of the group to its members, which leads to a feeling of unity and "togetherness."

Group norms   The unwritten set of expectations for group members.

Groupthink   A deterioration of mental efficiency, reality testing, and moral judgment in the interest of group solidarity. Also, an extreme form of group consensus.

Hawthorne effect The tendency for people to behave differently when they receive attention because they respond to the expectations of the situation.

Hearing The physical reception of sound.

Hearing officer A staff specialist who is employed by the firm to arbitrate disputes between employees and management.

Hostile takeover A corporate takeover in which one firm takes over another against its will.

Human potential movement The growth of interest in the importance of developing one's potential.

Human relations (HR) The art and practice of using systematic knowledge about human behavior to achieve organizational and/or personal objectives.

Image exchanging A method of conflict resolution in which the two antagonists make it clear that they understand each other's point of view.

Individual contributor Employees who accomplish work primarily by themselves rather than through others.

Informal communication pathway An unofficial network of communications used to supplement a formal pathway or channel.

Informal group A group that arises out of individual needs and the attraction of workers to one another.

Information overload The state of receiving more information than one can handle. As a result, the person becomes overwhelmed and does a poor job of processing information.

Instrumentality In expectancy theory, the probability assigned by the individual that performance will lead to certain outcomes or rewards.

Integration A situation that occurs when the subparts of the organization fit together and therefore are not in severe conflict or working at cross purposes.

Interactive video A computer-assisted video system in which the trainee interacts with the training material.

Internal job market The large array of jobs that have not been advertised, and that are usually filled by word of mouth or through friends and acquaintances of employees.

Internal locus of control A belief that fate is pretty much under one's control.

Interpersonal skill training The teaching of skills in dealing with others so the skills can be put into practice.

Intrapreneur A company employee who engages in entrepreneurial thinking and behavior for the good of the firm.

Inversion of means and ends A situation in which the methods for attaining a goal become more important than the goal itself. An example would be a computer programmer who cares more about writing interesting programs than solving company problems.

Jelly bean motivation The heaping of undeserved rewards upon another person.

Job burnout A state of emotional, mental, and physical exhaustion in response to prolonged job stress.

Job discrimination An unfavorable action brought against a person because of a characteristic of that person unrelated to job performance.

Job satisfaction The amount of pleasure or contentment associated with a job.

Job sharing A modified work schedule in which two people share the same job, both usually working half-time.

Job stress The body's response to any job-related factor that threatens to disturb the person's equilibrium.

Labor-management committees Joint problem-solving groups composed of members of labor and management who typically try to improve productivity and/or quality of work life.

Law of effect In behavior modification, behavior that leads to a positive consequence for the individual tends to be repeated, while behavior that leads to a negative consequence tends not to be repeated.

Leader-match concept The idea that leadership effectiveness depends on matching leaders to situations where they can exercise the most control.

Leadership The process of influencing employees to attain organizational goals, excluding illegal and immoral methods of persuasion.

Leadership style The typical pattern of behavior engaged in by the leader when dealing with employees.

Leading by example A simple way of influencing group members in which the leader acts as a positive model.

Lean organization An organization in which there is a minimum of nonessential functions and employees.

Legitimate power Power granted by the organization.

Life script In transactional analysis, a plan or drama acted out during a person's life.

Limited tolerance for ambiguity A tendency to be readily frustrated when situations and tasks are poorly defined.

Listening The mental translation of sound into meaningful communication.

Lose-lose conflict resolution Any method of resolving conflict in which neither side wins.

Machiavellian tendencies A desire to manipulate other people.

Management Working with and through people to accomplish organizational goals.

Managerial Grid A framework for simultaneously examining the concern for production and people dimensions of leadership, thus classifying a leader's style.

Manager Employee who accomplishes work through others and has the authority to use resources such as company money to get things done.

Mentor A boss who takes a subordinate under his or her wing and teaches and coaches that person.

Moderator variable A factor that specifies the condition under which an independent variable influences a dependent variable.

Modified work schedule Any formal departure from the traditional hours of work, excluding shift work and staggered work hours.

Morale A mixture of feelings, attitudes, and sentiments that contribute to a general feeling of satisfaction.

Motivation An internal state that leads to effort expended toward objectives. Also, an activity performed by managers or any other person to get others to accomplish work.

Motive A socially learned force that requires satisfaction, such as the desire to accumulate power.

Need A deficit within the individual, such as a need for recognition or accomplishment.

Negative lifestyle factor Any behavior that predisposes one to stress, such as poor eating habits, exercise habits, and heavy ingestion of caffeine, alcohol, and other drugs.

Negative reinforcement Rewarding people by taking away an uncomfortable consequence of their behavior. It is the withdrawal or termination of a disliked consequence.

Negotiating (bargaining) Conferring with another person in order to resolve a problem.

Networking Seeking out friends and acquaintances and building systematically on these relationships to create a still wider set of contacts to gain employment or advance one's career.

Nominal group technique A group problem-solving technique that calls people together in a structured meeting with limited interactions.

Noncognitive viewpoint An explanation of human behavior emphasizing that behavior is determined by the rewards and punishments an individual receives from the environment.

Nonprogrammed decision A decision for which a new solution is required because alternative solutions have not been prescribed in advance.

Novation The substitution of a new obligation for an old one by the mutual agreement of the parties concerned (in reference to career advancement).

Nonverbal communication (NVC)   The transmission of messages through means other than words.

Ombudsman   A neutral person designated by the firm to help resolve employee conflicts.

Open-door policy   A policy in which any employee can bring a gripe to higher management's attention without checking with his or her immediate manager.

Organic organization   An organization with the ability to adapt to necessary changes.

Organization development (OD)   Any strategy, method, or technique for making organizations more effective by bringing about constructive, planned change.

Organizational behavior (OB)   The study of individual and group behavior in organizations.

Organizational climate   The general atmosphere or personality of an organization.

Organizational culture   A system of shared values and beliefs that actively influence the behavior of organizational members; the organizational norms.

Organizational effectiveness   The extent to which an organization is productive and satisfies the demands of its interested parties.

Organizational politics   Gaining advantage through any means other than merit or luck.

Outplacement   Company-sponsored programs to minimize the personal and organizational trauma associated with job loss.

Participative leader   One who shares decision-making authority with the group.

Path-goal theory of leadership effectiveness   A contingency explanation of leadership that specifies what the leader must do to achieve high productivity and morale in a given situation.

Perception   The process of interpreting events in the external world.

Performance appraisal   A formal system of evaluating employee performance and conveying this evaluation to the employee.

Performance-reward-satisfaction model   An explanation of job satisfaction stating that if you perform well and receive an equitable reward, your satisfaction will increase.

Personality   The persistent and enduring behavior patterns of the individual that are expressed in a wide variety of situations.

Personality conflict   A situation in which people clash because they basically dislike each other.

Personal power   The ability to control others derived from characteristics and qualities of the controller.

Positive discipline   An approach to improving substandard performance and behavior that emphasizes coaching, individual responsibility, and a mature problem-solving method.

Positive reinforcement   Increasing the probability that behavior will be repeated by rewarding people for making the desired response.

Power   The ability to control anything of value.

Power need (or motive)   The desire to control other people and resources.

Private brainstorming   Arriving at creative ideas by jotting them down by yourself.

Problem solving   A method for closing the gap between the actual situation and the desired situation.

Procrastination   The delaying of action for no good reason.

Productivity   The ratio of output to input, taking quality of work into account.

Programmed decision   A decision in which the alternative solutions are determined by rules, procedures, or policies.

Progressive discipline   Administering punishments in increasing order of severity until the person being disciplined improves or is terminated.

Quality   Conforming to requirements.

Quality circle (QC)   A small group of employees from the same department who voluntarily and regularly meet in order to identify, analyze, and solve problems related to work groups.

Quality of work life (QWL)   The extent to which workers are able to satisfy important needs through their job and other experiences with the organization.

Realistic goal   A goal that is challenging but not set so high that frustration is the inevitable result.

Referent power   The ability to control others stemming from one's personal charactersitics.

Reinforcement model   *See* **Noncognitive viewpoint.**

Relaxation response (RP)   A bodily reaction in which the person experiences a slower perspiration rate and heart rate, lowered blood pressure, and lowered metabolism.

Reward power   The ability to control by giving employees rewards for compliance.

Role   A set of behaviors or attitudes appropriate to a particular position, regardless of who occupies that position.

Role ambiguity   A condition in which the job holder receives confusing or poorly defined expectations.

Role conflict   Having to choose between competing demands or expectations.

Role confusion   Being uncertain what role you are occupying.

Role overload   A burdensome workload.

Role underload   Having too little work to perform.

Schmoozing   Socializing on the job.

Self-destructive behavior   A conscious or unconscious attempt to bring down personal failure.

Sense of identity   For an organization, an awareness of what it is and what it is trying to accomplish.

Sexual harassment   Any unwanted advance toward another individual, including spoken comments, touching, or demands for sexual favors.

Shop-floor democracy   The granting of decision-making authority to production workers.

Skunk works   A secret place in an organization to conceive new products.

Small business owner   An individual who establishes and manages a new business for the primary purpose of furthering personal goals.

Socializing   How employees come to understand the values, norms, and customs essential for adapting to the organization.

Specialist or **individual contributor**   An employee who gets things accomplished primarily working alone rather than through others.

Strain   The adverse effects of stress on an individual's mind, body, and actions.

Stress   *See* **Job stress.**

Stressor   A force bringing about stress.

Subordinate power   Any type of power organizational members can exert upward in the organization.

Substance abuse   The overuse of any substance that enters the bloodstream.

Summary discipline   The immediate discharge of an employee for having committed a major offense.

Superordinate goals   Common ends that might be pursued by two or more groups, yet cannot be achieved through the independent efforts of each group separately.

Supervision   First-level management, or the art and practice of achieving results through people.

Survey feedback   A method of organization development that involves taking a survey of organizational problems and feeding back this information to management and survey participants.

Synergy   A combination of things with an output greater than the sum of the parts.

Targeted résumé   A resume that focuses on a specific job target, or position, and presents only information that supports the target.

Team building   A systematic method of improving the interpersonal and task aspects of regular work groups.

Telecommuting   An arrangement in which employees perform their regular work duties from home or at another location.

Theory X   Douglas McGregor's famous statement of the traditional management view that considers people as usually lazy and needing to be prodded by external rewards. A rigid and task-oriented approach to management.

Theory Y   Douglas McGregor's famous statement of an alternative to traditional management thinking. It emphasizes that people seek to fulfill higher-level needs on the job and that management must be flexible and human-relations-oriented.

Traditional mental set   A conventional way of looking at things and placing them in familiar categories.

Transactional analysis (TA)   A technique for improving interpersonal relationships that focuses on the exchanges between people.

Transformational leader   (1) A person in charge who helps organizations and people make positive changes in the way they do things. (2) A person in charge who influences people on the basis of his or her personal characteristics (charisma).

Type A behavior   Behavior that is demanding, impatient, overstriving, and hostile, therefore leading to distress.

Type T personality   An individual who is driven to a life of constant stimulation and risk taking.

Value   A strongly held belief that guides action.

Valence   In expectancy theory, the value, worth, or attractiveness of an outcome.

VDT stress   An adverse physical and psychological reaction to prolonged work at a video display terminal (VDT).

Wa   A Japanese word for harmony, unity, kinship, or love. It is said to lead to cooperative manager-employee relationships.

Wellness   A focus on good health rather than simply the absence of disorder.

Wellness programs   Formal programs to help employees stay well and avoid illness.

Whistle blowing   The disclosure of organizational wrongdoing to parties who can take action.

Win-win conflict resolution   An approach to resolving conflict in which both sides gain something of value after the conflict has been resolved.

Work flow   The routing of work from one person or department to another.

Work motivation   Effort expended toward organizational objectives.

Wrongful discharge   The firing of an employee for arbitrary or unfair reasons.

Zone of indifference   The area of behavior in which an employee is prepared to accept direction or influence. Orders that lie within the zone of indifference are seen as lawful and within the employee's value system.

Index

NAME INDEX

SUBJECT INDEX